The Physiology of Cognitive Processes

The Physiology of Cognitive Processes

Edited by

ANDREW PARKER
ANDREW DERRINGTON
AND
COLIN BLAKEMORE

Originating from the proceedings of a
Royal Society Discussion Meeting. This
book was originally published as an issue
of the Philosophical Transactions of the
Royal Society, Series B (Volume 357
Number 1424) but has been materially
changed and updated.

 THE ROYAL
SOCIETY

OXFORD
UNIVERSITY PRESS

OXFORD

UNIVERSITY PRESS

Great Clarendon Street, Oxford OX2 6DP

Oxford University Press is a department of the University of Oxford.
It furthers the University's objective of excellence in research, scholarship,
and education by publishing worldwide in

Oxford New York

Athens Auckland Bangkok Bogotá Buenos Aires Kolkata
Cape Town Chennai Dar es Salaam Delhi Florence Hong Kong Istanbul
Karachi Kuala Lumpur Madrid Melbourne Mexico City Mumbai
Nairobi Paris São Paulo Shanghai Taipei Tokyo Toronto Warsaw

Oxford is a registered trade mark of Oxford University Press
in the UK and in certain other countries

Published in the United States
by Oxford University Press Inc., New York

© Royal Society, 2003

The moral rights of the author have been asserted

Database right Oxford University Press (maker)

First published 2003

British Library Cataloguing in Publication Data

Data available

Library of Congress Cataloging in Publication Data

Data available

ISBN 0-19-852559-1 (hardback)
ISBN 0-19-852560-5 (paperback)

1 3 5 7 9 10 8 6 4 2

Typeset by
Newgen Imaging Systems (P) Ltd., Chennai, India
Printed in Italy
on acid-free paper by
LegoPrint

Contents

Introduction

About half a century ago, the first micro-electrode recordings of sensory neurons in mammalian visual cortex transformed our thinking about how vision works. Since that time, the physiology of cognitive processes has developed into a mature and complete discipline. New techniques have been developed and the old techniques are being deployed in new ways. However, the most spectacular development has been the growth in the range of topics that are now addressed by this discipline.

Recording with micro-electrodes is still at the centre of the stage, but its application is no longer restricted to anaesthetized, paralysed animals. Today neurons can be studied in awake animals that are looking, learning, remembering and making decisions. Non-invasive techniques, such as functional magnetic resonance imaging (fMRI) of the brain and measurement of scalp potentials, are constantly being developed and improved. Therefore we can now also approach the study of the physiology of cognition in the intact human brain.

Lesions are still used to study the location of function in the brain. But today they are much more subtle and selective than before. Now they may disconnect structures, so that interactions can be studied, rather than removing or destroying them. Destruction may be selective for cell bodies, or for a particular type of cell body, so that fibre tracts can be spared. Again, imaging techniques have greatly improved the precision of this approach with human subjects.

The papers in this issue form the record of a Discussion Meeting on the physiology of cognitive processes that was held in December 2001. The topics include sensation, perception, decision making, attention, memory, the application of rules to guide our behaviour and the use of sensory information to control our movement. To deepen our understanding of leading-edge technology, we also have two papers of a more technical nature dealing with operation of visual cortex: one on the nature of neural codes in visual cortex and the other on the neural correlates of the fMRI bold signal.

One of the most basic questions one can ask about a perceptual process is 'where in the brain does it take place?' Brian Wandell and his colleagues (Wade *et al.* 2002) addressed this question in the case of colour vision, using fMRI in the human brain.

Cortical colour areas in the human brain can be identified by their responses to colour stimuli in fMRI and by the characteristic form of the cortical map of the visual field. Cortical signals for colour have an expanded representation for the central zone of the retina, because this zone has a fundamental role in the generation of colour perception. The ventral surface of the occipital lobe has been identified on the basis of lesion studies as an important area for human colour vision. The paper by Wade *et al.* describes visual field mapping of the ventral surface of the occipital lobe with fMRI. One novel finding is a full map of the contralateral half of the visual field adjacent to V3, which these authors regard as the human equivalent of V4. They also identified a further partial or fragmented map, which includes substantial parts of central visual field. Both these areas give strong responses to colour signals.

Derrington *et al.* (2002) consider whether colour analysis by the visual system always operates to identify colours or whether the importance of colour may be that it supports image segmentation. They showed that, even for a primate species with relatively poor colour vision (the marmoset), colour is a fundamental attribute of visual stimuli. Male marmosets, all of which are dichromats, rapidly learn to distinguish coloured from non-coloured stimuli. A proportion of neurons in visual cortex respond in a way that distinguishes between the presence and absence of colour, regardless of which particular colour is present.

To interpret the significance of variations in the firing of visual neurons we need to know the nature of the neural code. Usually the assumption is that it is a very simple code. Oram *et al.* (2002) consider a more sophisticated range of possibilities. The paper reviews the way information is encoded by neurons in monkey visual cortex and considers whether neurons could carry multiple signals concurrently.

A more pressing issue concerning interpretation arises in the case of fMRI, which is widely used to chart the activity associated with perceptual and cognitive processes in the human brain. Critically, however, the link between neural activity and the haemodynamic responses that are monitored by fMRI has not been established. Logothetis (2002) sets this right in his paper, which is a technological *tour de force*. He describes simultaneous micro-electrode and fMRI measurements, in which he compares the fMRI signal with local field potentials, which represent the synaptic activity in a brain region, and with spiking activity, which represent the output. The better prediction of the fMRI responses is given by local field potentials, which suggests that much of the fMRI response represents the neural processing within a cortical area rather than the output from that area.

The somato sensory system is the subject of a highly sophisticated study of sensory processing in which Ranulfo Romo and his colleagues (Romo *et al.* 2002) use micro-electrode recording to track the elements of a sensory discrimination process across several cortical areas in the monkey. Their paper shows that neurons in primary somatosensory cortex (S1) generate sensory representations of vibrating tactile stimuli; neurons in two other areas, the second somatosensory area (S2) and medial premotor cortex, appear to display the memory of the stimulus and to compare it with subsequent stimuli as the monkey makes decisions about them.

Sensory decisions are also the topic of the paper by Parker *et al.* (2002), who seek to identify the neural events that underlie decisions about ambiguous visual stimuli. A monkey is faced with a task of deciding the direction of rotation of a cylindrical surface that rotates about an axis perpendicular to his line of sight. To make the judgement he needs to assign different depths to two fields of dots moving in opposite directions. Most of the stimuli he views are unambiguous because he has independent sensory information—stereopsis—to assign depths to the dots. By analysing how neurons in the cortical V5/MT area—which are selective both for stereoscopic depth and for direction of motion fire in response to ambiguous and non-ambiguous stimuli, and by analysing the correlation between neuronal firing and the monkey's decisions on ambiguous stimuli they are able to infer which neurons influence the monkey's decision.

Maunsell & Cook (2002) also describe responses to motion by neurons in the cortical V5/MT area and compare them with neurons in the VIP area. They examine how attention modulates sensory performance and neural firing in the two different areas. They track the influence of attention both on a monkey's ability to perform visual discriminations and on the responses of visual neurons. Attention generally increases neuronal responsiveness and improves behavioural performance, but to different degrees. Moreover the effect of attention on neural responsiveness is different for different areas with some brain areas showing larger neuronal effects of attention than the improvement in behavioural performance. They conclude that, in most cortical areas, links between neural activity and sensory discrimination may vary with attentional state.

In many natural situations, when we shift attention to an object we make a saccade to fixate on it. In his paper, Schall (2002) discusses the neural processes that select which targets the eyes will fixate during a search task and the processes that produce the eye movement that changes fixation. He shows that different neurons control the selection of targets to be fixated and the production of saccades to fixate those targets. He points out that only by separating target selection from saccade production can the system be flexible.

The first of three papers on memory considers the neural substrate of recognition memory. One of the important processes of recognition memory is the discrimination between what is novel and what is familiar. In their paper, Brown & Bashir (2002) discuss evidence that neurons in the perirhinal cortex of the temporal lobe respond when a stimulus is novel, but not if the monkey has seen it before. They show that selective failure to respond to familiar stimuli can be the basis of an efficient memory storage system and that long-term synaptic depression is a form of neural plasticity that might be the basis of such a system.

In the second paper on memory Rugg et al. (2002) describe their recent investigations of the encoding and retrieval of memories for events using non-invasive neuro-imaging techniques in humans. Encoding events in memory appears to involve the same brain regions that process those events online. Retrieval appears to involve lateral parietal cortex and regions of dorsolateral and anterior prefrontal cortex.

In his paper, Gaffan (2002) argues persuasively against the widely accepted idea that the temporal lobe contains specialized memory systems. This idea is based on the fact that memory deficits are often associated with damage to the temporal lobe in humans and damage to the temporal lobe in monkeys may also cause amnesia. However Gaffan points out that temporal cortex has perceptual functions and that amnesia can be produced by disconnecting the temporal lobe from the brainstem and basal forebrain. He suggests that memories are likely to be widely distributed in cortex, particularly prefrontal cortex.

The paper by Miller et al. (2002) describes recordings from single neurons in prefrontal cortex in monkeys that are classifiying stimuli according to arbitrary rules. A substantial proportion of neurons in monkey prefrontal cortex appear to represent the rules that the monkey follows for categorizing visual stimuli. When the monkey is trained to classify the same stimuli in new ways, the responses of the neurons reflect the newly learned categories, not the old ones. In a task where the monkey has to switch rules from trial to trial, individual prefrontal cortex neurons appear to fire according to which rule is in place on a particular trial.

In the final paper, Daniel Wolpert and colleagues (Van Beers et al. 2002) discuss three aspects of the way variability in neural signals limits our ability to control our movements. First, variability of sensory signals limits our knowledge of the position of the parts of our bodies. These inaccuracies may be different for different senses, such as proprioception and vision. The brain integrates signals from different senses to make the best estimate of position. Second, variability of neural signals to control the muscles produces further inaccuracies, but movements are planned so as to minimize the errors caused by these inaccuracies. Finally, motor signals have to be integrated with sensory signals to predict current disposition of the body, particularly its limbs. The paper considers theoretically how this integration should be best achieved.

The underlying theme of all the papers is to understand the neuronal events and processes that are responsible for the remarkable range of cognitive performance that can be achieved. The meeting represented some of the major components of this theme, with a particular emphasis on current advances. The next 10 years will no doubt see the transformation of this knowledge in specific areas. However, such transformations will come about chiefly through the continued application of the unified approach that is represented by this sample of work.

The editors would like to thank Froniga Lambert and her colleagues for their expert assistance during the organization of the meeting and Ruth Hinkel-Pevzner for her unswerving dedication to meeting deadlines during the editing of this set of papers. They also thank Helen Winser, Jessica Mnatzaganian and Michelle McNeely for so ably seeing the issue through to press.

A. P.   *October 2002*

A. D.

C. B.

References

Brown, M. W. & Bashir, Z. I. 2002 Evidence concerning how neurons of the perirhinal cortex may effect familiarity discrimination. *Phil. Trans. R. Soc. Lond.* **B 357**, 1083–1095. (DOI 10.1098/rstb.2002.1097.)

Derrington, A. M., Parker, A., Barraclough, N. E., Easton, A., Goodson, G. R., Parker, K., Tinsley, C. J. & Webb, B. S. 2002 The uses of colour vision: behavioural and physiological distinctiveness of colour stimuli. *Phil. Trans. R. Soc. Lond.* **B 357**, 975–985. (DOI 10.1098/rstb.2002.1116.)

Gaffan, D. 2002 Against memory systems. *Phil. Trans. R. Soc. Lond.* **B 357**, 1111–1121. (DOI 10.1098/rstb.2002.1110.)

Logothetis, N. K. 2002 The neural basis of the blood-oxygen-level-dependent functional magnetic resonance imaging signal. *Phil. Trans. R. Soc. Lond.* **B 357**, 1003–1037. (DOI 10.1098/rstb.2002.1114.)

Maunsell, J. H. R. & Cook, E. P. 2002 The role of attention in visual processing. *Phil. Trans. R. Soc. Lond.* **B 357**, 1063–1072. (DOI 10.1098/rstb.2002.1107.)

Miller, E. K., Freedman, D. J. & Wallis, J. D. 2002 The prefrontal cortex: categories, concepts and cognition. *Phil. Trans. R. Soc. Lond.* **B 357**, 1123–1136. (DOI 10.1098/rstb.2002.1099.)

Oram, M. W., Xiao, D., Dritschel, B. & Payne, K. R. 2002 The temporal resolution of neural codes: does response latency have a unique role? *Phil. Trans. R. Soc. Lond.* **B 357**, 987–1001. (DOI 10.1098/rstb.2002.1113.)

Parker, A. J., Krug, K. & Cumming, B. G. 2002 Neuronal activity and its links with the perception of multi-stable figures. *Phil. Trans. R. Soc. Lond.* **B 357**, 1053–1062. (DOI 10.1098/rstb.2002.1112.)

Romo, R., Hernández, A., Zainos, A., Brody, C. & Salinas, E. 2002 Exploring the cortical evidence of a sensory-discrimination process. *Phil. Trans. R. Soc. Lond.* **B 357**, 1039–1051. (DOI 10.1098/rstb.2002.1110.)

Rugg, M. D., Otten, L. J. & Henson, R. N. A. 2002 The neural basis of episodic memory: evidence from functional neuro-imaging. *Phil. Trans. R. Soc. Lond.* **B 357**, 1097–1110. (DOI 10.1098/rstb.2002.1102.)

Schall, J. D. 2002 The neural selection and control of saccades by the frontal eye field. *Phil. Trans. R. Soc. Lond.* **B 357**, 1073–1082. (DOI 10.1098/rstb.2002.1098.)

Van Beers, R. J., Baraduc, P. & Wolpert, D. M. 2002 Role of uncertainty in sensorimotor control. *Phil. Trans. R. Soc. Lond.* **B 357**, 1137–1145. (DOI 10.1098/rstb.2002.1101.)

Wade, A. R., Brewer, A. A., Rieger, J. W. & Wandell, B. A. 2002 Functional measurements of human ventral occipital cortex: retinotopy and colour. *Phil. Trans. R. Soc. Lond.* **B 357**, 963–973. (DOI 10.1098/rstb. 2002.1108.)

Contributors

Pierre Baradu   Sobell Department of Motor Neuroscience and Movement Disorders, Institute of Neurology, University College London, Queen Square, London WC1N 3BG, UK

Nick E. Barraclough   School of Psychology, University of Park, Nottingham NG7 2RD, UK

Z. I. Bashir   MRC Centre for Synaptic Plasticity, Department of Anatomy, School of Medical Sciences, Univresity of Bristol, Bristol BS8 1TD, UK

Robert J. van Beers   Sobell Department of Motor Neuroscience and Movement Disorders, Institute of Neurology, University College London, Queen Square, London WC1N 3BG, UK

Alyssa A. Brewer   Neuroscience Program, Stanford University, Stanford, CA 94305, USA

Carlos Brody   Instituto de Fisiología Celular, Universidad Nacional Autónoma de México, 04510 México, DF, México

M. W. Brown   MRC Centre for Synaptic Plasticity, Department of Anatomy, School of Medical Sciences, Univresity of Bristol, Bristol BS8 1TD, UK

Erik P. Cook   Howard Hughes Medical Institute and Division of Neuroscience, Baylor College of Medicine, One Baylor Plaza, S-603, Houston, TX 77030, USA

Bruce G. Cumming   University Laboratory of Physiology, Parks Road, Oxford OX1 3PT, UK

Andrew M. Derrington   School of Psychology, University Park, Nottingham NG7 2RD, UK

B. Dritschel   School of Psychology, University of St. Andrews, St. Andrews, Fife KY16 9JU, UK

Alexander Easton   School of Psychology, University Park, Nottingham NG7 2RD, UK

David J. Freedman   Center for Learning and Memory, RIKEN-MIT Neuroscience Research Center and Department of Brain and Cognitive Sciences, Massachusetts Institute of Technology, Cambridge, MA 02139, USA

David Gaffan   Department of Experimental Psychology, University of Oxford, South Parks Road, Oxford OX1 3UD, UK

G. R. Goodson   School of Psychology, University of Park, Nottingham NG7 2RD, UK

Richard N. A. Henson   Institute of Cognitive Neuroscience, University College London, 17 Queen Square, London WC1N 3AR, UK and Wellcome Research Department of Imaging Neuroscience, Institute of Neurology, University College London, 12 Queen Square, London WC1N 3BG, UK

Adrián Hernández Instituto de Fisiología Celular, Universidad Nacional Autónoma de México, 04510 México, DF, México

Kristine Krug University Laboratory of Physiology, Parks Road, Oxford OX1 3PT, UK

Nikos K. Logothetis Max Planck Institute for Biological Cybernetics, Spemannstrasse 38, 72076 Tübingen, Germany

John H. R. Maunsell Howard Hughes Medical Institute and Division of Neuroscience, Baylor College of Medicine, One Baylor Plaza, S-603, Houston, TX 77030, USA

Earl K. Miller Center for Learning and Memory, RIKEN-MIT Neuroscience Research Center and Department of Brain and Cognitive Sciences, Massachusetts Institute of Technology, Cambridge, MA 02139, USA

M. W. Oram School of Psychology, University of St. Andrews, St. Andrews, Fife KY16 9JU, UK

Leun J. Otten Institute of Cognitive Neuroscience, University College London, 17 Queen Square, London WC1N 3AR, UK and Department of Psychology, University College London, Gower Street, London WC1E 6BT, UK

Amanda Parker School of Psychology, University Park, Nottingham NG7 2RD, UK

Andrew J. Parker University Laboratory of Physiology, Parks Road, Oxford OX1 3PT, UK

Kris S. Parker School of Psychology, University Park, Nottingham NG7 2RD, UK

K. R. Payne School of Psychology, University of St. Andrews, St. Andrews, Fife KY16 9JU, UK

Jochem W. Rieger Department of Neurology II, Otto-van-Guericke-University, 39120 Magdeburg, Germany

Ranulfo Romo Instituto de Fisiología Celular, Universidad Nacional Autónoma de México, 04510 México, DF, México

Michael D. Rugg Institute of Cognitive Neuroscience, University College London, 17 Queen Square, London WC1N 3AR, UK

Emilio Salinas Instituto de Fisiología Celular, Universidad Nacional Autónoma de México, 04510 México, DF, México

Jeffrey D. Schall Center for Integrative and Cognitive Neuroscience, Vanderbilt Vision Research Center, Department of Psychology, 301 Wilson Hall, 111 21st Avenue South, Vanderbilt University, Nashville, TN 37203, USA

Chris J. Tinsley School of Psychology, University Park, Nottingham NG7 2RD, UK

Alex R. Wade Psychology Department, Stanford University, Stanford, CA 94305, USA

Jonathan D. Wallis Center for Learning and Memory, RIKEN-MIT Neuroscience Research Center and Department of Brain and Cognitive Sciences, Massachusetts Institute of Technology, Cambridge, MA 02139, USA

Brian A. Wandell   Psychology Department, and Neuroscience Program, Stanford University, Stanford, CA 94305, USA

Ben S. Webb   School of Psychology, University Park, Nottingham NG7 2RD, UK

Daniel M. Wolpert   Sobell Department of Motor Neuroscience and Movement Disorders, Institute of Neurology, University College London, Queen Square, London WC1N 3BG, UK

D. Xiao   School of Psychology, University of St. Andrews, St. Andrews, Fife KY16 9JU, UK**Antonio Zainos**   Instituto de Fisiología Celular, Universidad Nacional Autónoma de México, 04510 México, DF, México

Functional measurements of human ventral occipital cortex: retinotopy and colour

Alex R. Wade, Alyssa A. Brewer, Jochem W. Rieger, and Brian A. Wandell

Human colour vision originates in the cone photoreceptors, whose spatial density peaks in the fovea and declines rapidly into the periphery. For this reason, one expects to find a large representation of the cone-rich fovea in those cortical locations that support colour perception. Human occipital cortex contains several distinct foveal representations including at least two that extend onto the ventral surface: a region thought to be critical for colour vision. To learn more about these ventral signals, we used functional magnetic resonance imaging to identify visual field maps and colour responsivity on the ventral surface. We found a visual map of the complete contralateral hemifield in a 4 cm² region adjacent to ventral V3; the foveal representation of this map is confluent with that of areas V1/2/3. Additionally, a distinct foveal representation is present on the ventral surface situated 3–5 cm anterior from the confluent V1/2/3 foveal representations. This organization is not consistent with the definition of area V8, which assumes the presence of a quarter field representation adjacent to V3v. Comparisons of responses to luminance-matched coloured and achromatic patterns show increased activity to the coloured stimuli beginning in area V1 and extending through the new hemifield representation and further anterior in the ventral occipital lobe.

1.1. Introduction

In his insightful review of the neurological literature on cerebral achromatopsia and colour anomia, Meadows (1974) argued that several cortical regions are essential for colour vision. Figure 1.1, adapted from Meadows' paper, shows three cortical regions he identified: primary visual cortex, a region on the ventral surface and a region on the dorsal surface near the inferior parietal lobule.

Damage to primary visual cortex impairs most forms of conscious vision. For this reason it is not usually counted as a cortical colour specialization. We think, however, that Meadows was correct to list primary visual cortex as an essential component of the colour system. In fact, we think it is useful to go further and remember that colour specialization begins within the retina. The presence of three types of cones, the physiological mechanisms that regulate the gain of the cone signals and the opponent-colours transformations are important elements of colour appearance computations (e.g. Kries 1902; Hunt 1987; Wandell 1995; Fairchild 1998). The spatial structure of the photopic pathways, in which cones dominate the central two degrees of the fovea, is another important colour vision specialization that originates in the retina. This spatial distribution of the cone signals should be considered when we review the role of cortical regions in processing colour signals (Mullen 1991).

The best known portion of Meadows' review was his careful justification of the claim that damage to the ventral surface can interfere with normal colour vision. In this syndrome, called 'cerebral achromatopsia', colour judgements are impaired but other types of visual function (motion, form and depth) are spared. Aware of Semir Zeki's pioneering anatomical

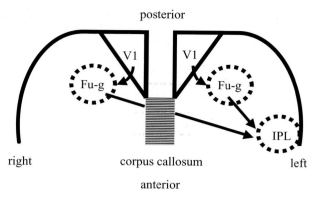

Fig. 1.1. Cortical regions identified by J. C. Meadows as important to human colour perception. The sketch shows an axial view with primary visual cortex (V1) at the occipital pole. The fusiform gyrus (Fu-g) falls on the VO surface and was shown to be associated with cerebral achromatopsia. The inferior parietal lobule (IPL) in the left hemisphere was believed to be important for the relationship between colour, language, and imagery.

and single-unit studies on colour-tuned cells in monkey dorsal V4 ('V4-complex') (Zeki 1983 *a,b*), Meadows asked whether some part of human ventral cortex might be homologous to monkey V4. Zeki subsequently reviewed the neurological literature on cerebral achromatopsia and used neuroimaging experiments to demonstrate the involvement of human VO cortex in colour perception. While the homology between monkey V4 and human VO cortex is not proved, and many other aspects of the ventral organization remain unclear, the results from many laboratories leave no doubt that Zeki and Meadows are broadly correct: the ventral surfaces of the human occipital and temporal lobes are very active during colour judgements, and damage to these regions can selectively disturb colour vision (Zeki 1990).

There are many unanswered questions about the retinotopic organization and colour signals on the ventral surface of the human brain; we address a few of these questions here. First, in contrast to the widespread assumption that there is very little retinotopy (ordered spatial mapping of the visual field) on the ventral surface, we show that much of ventral cortex is organized retinotopically. Second, we find that adjacent to ventral V3, whose spatial map spans a quarter of the visual field, there is a fourth visual area whose retinotopic map spans an entire hemifield and whose foveal representation is confluent with V1/2/3. This visual field map is not precisely analogous to macaque V4, but because of its position (adjacent to V3v) we refer to the area as 'human V4' or 'hV4'. Third, beyond hV4 there is a large ventral foveal representation that spans approximately half the area of the foveal representation found at the confluence of the early visual areas; it is one of the largest foveal representations in visual cortex. Finally, we compare the VO responses to colour and luminance-matched achromatic stimuli, and we show that responses to coloured stimuli are significantly larger in areas V1, V2, hV4, and other anterior ventral locations.

1.2. Background

Retinotopic organization can be measured in a variety of ways. One simple and useful method is to apply differential imaging (subtractive methodology) and compare responses between two stimuli at different visual field positions. For example, it is possible to identify the boundaries of visual areas V1, V2, and V3 by comparing the responses to targets along the horizontal and vertical meridia (Grill-Spector & Malach 2001). Also, it is possible to obtain a sense of the organization with respect to eccentricity by comparing the responses to foveal and peripheral targets (Levy *et al*. 2001).

If retinotopic organization is the purpose of the study, however, one may wish to extend the differential imaging measurements by studying the responses to targets at more than two positions. Rather than just comparing horizontal and vertical, for example, we might measure the responses to stimuli at a series of angles; and rather than just comparing foveal and peripheral stimuli, we might measure the responses to stimuli at a series of eccentricities. By presenting such stimuli in temporal sequence, one creates a travelling wave of activity in retinotopic cortex (Engel *et al*. 1994, 1997). The signal from each voxel modulates as the stimulus passes through the portion of the visual field that excites the neurons within that voxel; the timing of the peak response measures the visual field position that most effectively excites the neurons in that voxel. These travelling wave methods are also called phase-encoding methods because the phase of the fMRI response measures the most effective stimulus position for each voxel.

We can learn at least two things from the responses to a travelling wave stimulus. First, if the travelling wave stimulus modulates the neural response in a region, then neurons in that region must respond preferentially to stimuli in a localized part of the visual field. By contrast, if the neurons in a region respond uniformly to all spatial positions, there will be no modulation in response to the stimulus. Second, by comparing the responses in adjacent grey matter locations, we learn whether the neurons in a region of cortex form a visual field map. The presence of activity and the orderly arrangement of the visual field preferences are independent sources of information. Naturally, the response amplitudes to the travelling wave stimulus depend on various factors, such as stimulus selectivity of the neurons, spatial resolution of the measurement device and the task demands; these factors must be accounted for in interpreting the data. Still, as a first approximation, information about the size of the signal from a travelling wave stimulus measures whether the neurons in a voxel are spatially localized, while the arrangement of the responses between grey matter locations measures whether the cortical region forms a map.

Based on the first round of measurements of retinotopic organization, human visual cortex was divided into retinotopic and non-retinotopic cortex. Several retinotopically organized regions, apparently homologous to macaque areas V1, V2, V3, and V3A, were identified in the early days of fMRI imaging using 1.5 T magnetic resonance scanners and relatively simple methods. We now identify and measure these areas routinely (Wandell 1999; Koch *et al*. 2001). A common view is that anterior regions, including parietal and temporal cortex, are not activated by the simple travelling wave stimuli composed of flickering patterns. Instead, it is thought that activity in these regions is elicited only by specialized stimuli associated with the functional specialization of a cortical region; say colour, face and a specific type of object or place (Kanwisher *et al*. 1997; Epstein *et al*. 1999). These anterior regions are called non-retinotopic because in the first round of measurements no clear retinotopic responses were reported.

But the first reports of retinotopic organization are only five years old, and in our view it is too early to draw firm conclusions about the extent of retinotopic and non-retinotopic regimes. With improvements in the quality of the instruments and software tools, the extent of retinotopic cortex is increasing. We have described some advances in our understanding of the organization of dorsal visual cortex in a separate report (Press *et al*. 2001). Here, we focus on colour and the ventral pathways. In offering these results, we caution the reader that even these measurements comprise an incomplete picture of retinotopic organization and that more will be learned. By describing these results, we hope to discuss some new findings and also to forestall any hasty conclusions about the extent of retinotopic organization in human visual cortex.

1.3. Methods

The basic experimental methods have been published elsewhere, and we refer the reader to those publications for further details about the general methods (Teo *et al.* 1997; Wandell *et al.* 2000; Press *et al.* 2001). The custom software used to segment grey and white matter and to create flat maps is distributed freely on the Internet. Figure 1.2 illustrates the spatial relationships between anatomically defined regions in a three dimensional and flattened cortical view. Several major landmarks are marked in both views. We will make an effort to provide the data and additional custom analysis software upon request.

The fMRI measurements were obtained using a GE 3T scanner and a custom spiral acquisition sequence (Noll *et al.* 1995). The acquisition parameters were set to measure 128×128 sample points in a 260 mm field of view (2 mm $\times$ 2 mm resolution). The plane thickness was set to 3 mm (zero spacing). An entire set of planes was acquired, every time of repetition was 3 s, and a typical set contained 16 planes. The orientation of the planes was coronal and their position was adjusted to cover the occipital lobe and particularly the VO surface. Each stimulus condition was repeated within a scan session between two and four times and the time-series from the different repeats were averaged. There was no spatial filtering of the signals. A linear trend was removed from the time-series at each voxel and response modulations are described as per cent change about the mean signal level at that voxel.

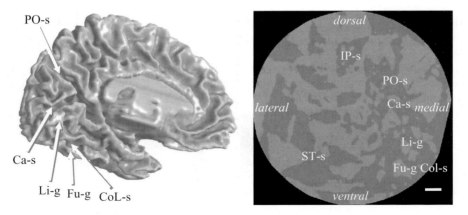

Fig. 1.2. The relationship between the flattened and folded brains. The flattened representations used in previous figures are organized so that the calcarine sulcus falls near the horizontal axis. Dark regions show sulci and light regions show gyri. Dorsal and ventral are up and down, respectively. Landmarks indicated on the flat map are as follows: IP-s, intraparietal sulcus; Ca-s, calcarine sulcus; Li-g, lingual gyrus; Fu-g, fusiform gyrus; ST-s, superior temporal sulcus; PO-s, parietal–occipital sulcus; CoL-s, collateral sulcus. Scale bar, 1 cm.

All of the responses shown in the figures are substantially above statistical threshold. This was verified by inspection of the time-series, measuring the response coherence (amplitude at the stimulus fundamental frequency divided by the summed amplitudes of all frequencies), and in some cases by converting the time-series to SPM 99 format and measuring the high statistical reliability of the indicated activations ($p < 0.001$) (Turner *et al.* 1998).

The stimuli were presented on an LCD within a shielded box placed at the foot of the scanner bed. Subjects viewed the display through binoculars so that the effective viewing distance was 0.5 m. The screen extended to 20° in the periphery. The LCD was calibrated using a spectroradiometer (PhotoResearch PR-650).

Stimuli were created and controlled using custom software based upon the Brainard–Pelli Toolbox (Brainard 1997) and running on a Apple Macintosh G4 (Apple Computers, Inc.) with a 10 bit per gun graphics card (Radius, Inc., Thunder).

The travelling wave stimuli were contrast-reversing black and white patterns that defined either an expanding ring or a rotating wedge. The patterns reversed contrast at 4 Hz and were shown at maximum contrast (*ca.* 90%). The mean screen luminance was 30 cd m^{-2}, and a fixation point was present at all times. Retinotopic organization with respect to the angular dimension was measured using a rotating wedge (angle of 90°). The retinotopic organization with respect to eccentricity was measured using a thin expanding ring (ring width of 2.5°). Both the ring and wedge stimuli had a dartboard structure (radial spatial frequency, 1 cycle deg^{-1}; angular frequency, 12 cycles per 2π). In most of the experiments, the wedges and rings passed through a full display cycle over 36 s, and six cycles were shown in each experimental scan. In some experiments the period was reduced to 24 s and eight cycles were shown.

The colour measurements were patterned after the methods developed by Zeki and his colleagues (McKeefry & Zeki 1997) though there were a few differences. The response differences between colour and achromatic stimuli were measured using a block design. A new pattern was presented every 2 s. Subjects viewed a series of patterns comprised an array of 8×8 rectangular patches spanning 24° of visual angle. During one 12 s block the subject saw a series of six random checkerboard patterns. All the patterns in each block were either pure-luminance varying or full chromatic stimuli. This stimulus is illustrated in Figure 1.3.

The colour properties of the display were specified using a simple opponent-colours scheme of luminance (L + M), S-cone, and red-green opponent signals (L − M). In one block

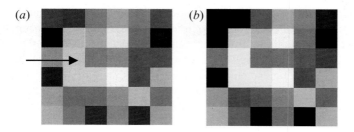

Fig. 1.3. See also Plate 1. A pair of luminance-matched stimuli used in the Mondrian colour-exchange experiments. A random draw of the pattern is shown every 2 s. For 12 s blocks the pattern is coloured (*a*) and for 12 s blocks the pattern is achromatic (*b*). To control for attention, subjects are asked to identify the orientation of the opening in the 'C' throughout the experimental scan (10 blocks). The arrow indicates the location of the C, but the arrow is not present during the experiment.

the patterns had only an achromatic (intensity scaling) contrast difference from the neutral background. In this condition, L + M and S-cone contrast were set at equal and L − M contrast was set to zero. The luminance and S-cone contrast difference between the background and each patch was randomly and uniformly selected from within the available contrast range ± 17%. In the second 12 s block the L + M contrasts matched the values in the first block; the S-cone and L − M contrasts were randomly selected from the L − M (max ± 6%) and S (max ± 17%) directions.

During the task, subjects were required to detect the orientation of a superimposed 'C' shape. The shape was created by adding a small amount of L + M signal to seven of the rectangles. The additional mean signal was very slight, and it was adjusted so that subjects scored about 80% correctly in identifying the orientation of the target. In this way, we hoped to eliminate attentional modulations that might arise because of the stimulus differences.

1.4. VO Cortex: retinotopy

(a) VO cortex responds to travelling wave stimuli

How much of visually responsive cortex is retinotopically organized? Using travelling wave stimuli, we consistently find responses that extend well onto the lateral and ventral surfaces of the occipital lobe and often into parietal and temporal cortex.

Figure 1.4 shows a region of cortex that responds reliably to a travelling wave stimulus (expanding ring). The stimulus was a flickering contrast pattern contained within an expanding ring (Figure 1.4a) or a rotating wedge (Figure 1.4b). The colour overlay indicates the principal visual field eccentricity represented at each grey matter location. The expanding ring stimulus evokes activity extending from the occipital pole far forward into parietal and temporal cortex. Note the continuous band of activity along the ventral surface of the brain in regions that have been labelled as selectively responsive to various special categories, such as faces, objects and colours.

The data shown in Figure 1.5 are a second typical example of the travelling wave measurements (expanding ring) we obtain routinely from individual observers on a 3T magnet using our current methods. In both Figures 1.4 and 1.5, the activity is plotted conservatively in that only very reliable signals (coherence greater than 0.35) are shown. The amplitudes of the harmonic components of the time-series in several cortical locations are shown in Figure 1.5b. Each of the selected regions of interest spans an area of *ca.* 6 mm × 6 mm within the grey matter. The reliability of the signal can be judged by comparing the amplitude at the fundamental frequency of the travelling wave with the amplitude at nearby frequencies. In all cases the amplitude at the fundamental frequency of the stimulus (six cycles per scan) is many standard deviations from the mean amplitude of the nearby temporal frequencies.

In measurements using the 3T system, travelling wave stimuli routinely activate regions from the occipital pole well into the VO lobe and dorsally past the parietal–occipital sulcus. We see this activation using a simple achromatic flickering contrast pattern, not an object or a face or a colourful design. As we reviewed in § 1.2, the presence of strong activity in response to a travelling wave stimulus shows that there is a preference for one portion of the visual field compared with another. Note that the responses on the ventral surface are comparable in magnitude and estimated foveal position with those in V1, further suggesting that

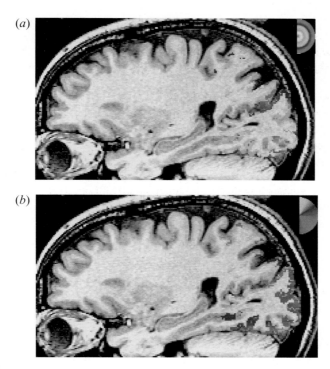

Fig. 1.4. See also Plate 2. Visual cortex activated by travelling wave stimuli. Only voxels containing neurons with a preferred retinal location will respond to the stimulus. The colour overlay in this sagittal section indicates (*a*) the preferred stimulus eccentricity or (*b*) angle at each voxel within the cortical grey matter. Only locations with a response coherence of more than 0.35 are shown.

the degree of spatial selectivity is similar. We have made additional measurements in six other individuals and found consistent results.

(b) VO cortex includes a lower visual field representation

A response to phase encoded retinotopic stimuli demonstrates a spatial preference within individual voxels but the presence of a response does not demonstrate that there is an organized map on the cortical surface. To detect the presence of a visual field map we must visualize how these spatial preferences are distributed on the grey matter surface. To visualize the spatial pattern, it is convenient to display the data either on three-dimensional renderings of the brain or on 'flat maps': computationally flattened representations of the cortical surface.

Figure 1.6 contains examples of the visual field maps of angle and eccentricity in two representative subjects. The colour overlay, which codes the visual field map, is superimposed upon a greyscale representation of the underlying anatomy. Light greyscale shading represents a gyrus and dark shading represents a sulcus (the flat map is further described in § 1.3). In Figure 1.6*a,c*, the colour overlays measure the preferred angular direction. The locations of V1, the motion complex (V5) and the ventral surface are denoted on the flat maps. There are several differences in the responses from these two subjects, but there are also several important similarities. The similarities we describe here have also been observed in four other subjects.

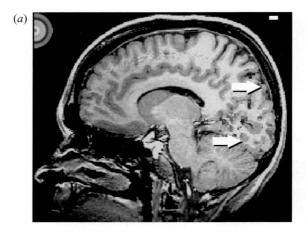

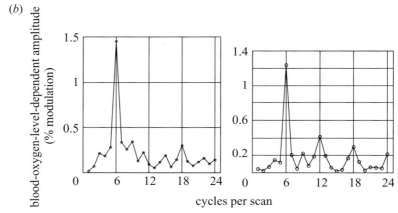

Fig. 1.5. See also Plate 3. Typical amplitude spectra of the fMRI response to an expanding ring (eccentricity) retinotopic stimulus. There were six stimulus cycles in the scan. The amplitude spectra shown in (*b*) were measured from two regions of interest that are indicated by the white arrows in (*a*). Each region occupies less than 1 cm² of cortical surface area. The signals in the anterior portions of the occipital lobe and posterior parietal and all along the ventral surface are substantially above statistical threshold. Other details as in Fig. 1.4.

First, consider the angular measurements in Figure 1.6*a,c*. Notice that the ventral surface contains a substantial lower-field representation (occupying the magenta region of the colour map). A white arrow denotes the location of one large lower-field representation in roughly corresponding locations for the two observers. At the resolution we have produced this figure, it is difficult to appreciate the precise position of this representation. In more detailed analyses of the white-circled region presented below, we find that this representation abuts the ventral V3 representation. We see this feature in all observers. Second, notice that there is an upper field (cyan) representation on the dorsal surface. A black arrow denotes the location of this representation in each of the observers. Hence, both the ventral and dorsal surfaces contain a full representation of the hemifield.

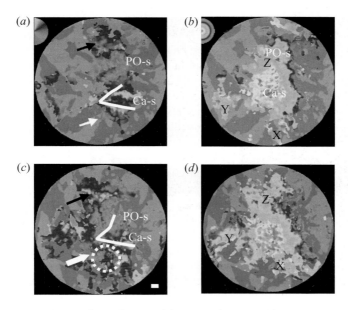

Fig. 1.6. See also Plate 4. Angular and eccentricity maps for two subjects shown on flattened representations of the left occipital lobe. The flat maps are centred near the occipital pole and have an 8 cm radius (scale bar, 1 cm). Shading indicates a sulcus (dark) or gyrus (light). Dorsal and ventral are up and down; lateral and medial are left and right. The flat maps are further described in § 1.3. (*a,c*) Measurements of angular retinotopy. The calcarine sulcus (Ca-s) and parietal–occipital sulcus (PO-s) are marked. The inset shows the preferred angular direction, ranging from cyan (upper) to blue (horizontal) to red (lower). The white line denotes the V1 hemifield representation that falls within the Ca-s. The black arrows indicate positions on the dorsal surface that respond well to the upper visual field, and the white arrows indicate positions on the ventral surface that respond well to the lower visual field. The dashed white circle indicates the region on the ventral surface that is analysed in more detail in subsequent figures. (*b,d*) Measurements of eccentric retinotopy for the same two observers. The preferred eccentricity between 0 and 20° is indic-ated by the colour overlay, with red/yellow representing the central 5°, green/cyan representing 5–10°, and blue/magenta representing 10–20°. The large red/yellow region near the occipital pole falls at the confluence of V1/2/3. The second large foveal representation (marked 'X') on the ventral surface is analysed in subsequent figures. The foveal representation on the lateral surface (marked 'Y') falls within motion-selective cortex. The foveal representations on the dorsal surface (marked 'Z') have been described elsewhere (Press *et al.* 2001). In all maps, the preferred visual field location is indicated only at cortical positions with a signal coherence of at least 0.35.

(c) VO cortex includes a very large foveal representation

The colour overlays in Figure 1.6*b,d* show those cortical regions with a preferred response within the central 20° of the visual field. The largest set of foveal representations falls at the confluence of areas V1, V2, V3, and extends from the most posterior aspect of the calcarine sulcus onto the lateral surface of the brain. The width of this set of foveal representations is close to 4.5 cm in both observers and covers a total area of between 16 and 20 cm². There is a second distinct and large foveal representation that can be plainly seen in all observers. This second foveal representation falls on the ventral surface and spans a width of *ca.* 2.5 cm and an area of *ca.* 6–10 cm². Notice that the preferred spatial location in this ventral foveal representation is very similar to the preferred locations in the large representation at the confluence of the early visual areas.

There are several other foveal representations visible in Figure 1.6. First, notice the foveal representation in the motion-selective region of cortex. This foveal representation falls within motion-selective cortex located on the lateral margin of the occipital lobe, near the temporal–parietal–occipital junction. Yet another displaced foveal representation can be seen on the dorsal surface within area V3A. We have commented on this representation and also another one that falls further anterior in area V7. We generally find that the preferred eccentricity in motion selective cortex is slightly more peripheral than the preferred eccentricities in early visual areas or on the ventral surface. This could arise for several reasons, though we suspect the difference is due to the presence of neurons with larger receptive fields in V3A/B and motion-selective cortex (Tootell *et al.* 1997; Smith *et al.* 1998; Press *et al.* 2001).

The eccentricity map on the ventral surface is shown once more in Figure 1.7. In this case, rather than using a flat map we show the preferred stimulus location on a three-dimensional rendering of the boundary between the white and grey matter of the brain.

These measurements were obtained from the posterior one-third of the brain, extending into posterior parietal and temporal cortex. The data are shown for a third subject, A. W., and also from subject B. W. whose data are shown in previous figures. Figure 1.7*a* shows a medial-ventral view of the brain. From this view, one can see the classic eccentricity map extending along the calcarine sulcus but extending well into dorsal and ventral cortex. Figure 1.5*b* shows the time-series of the fMRI responses measured from the foveal representations on the

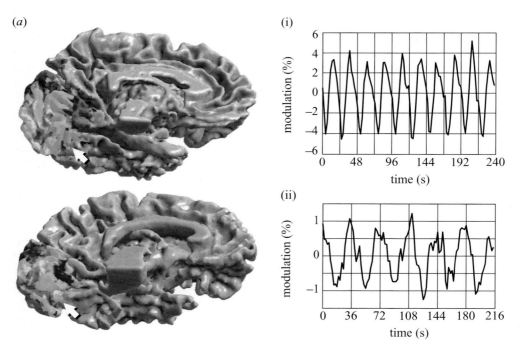

Fig. 1.7. See also Plate 5. (*a*) Three-dimensional renderings of the eccentricity map seen from a medial/ventral view. (i) Data from a third subject A. W.; (ii) data from subject B. W. (*b*) The time-series of the activity from the ventral foveal representation, indicated by the arrow. The experiments used different numbers of cycles and different duty cycles. In both cases, the time-series is well above statistical threshold. Other details as in Figure 1.4.

ventral surface. These large signals show the clear preference for foveal activation in a large ventral region. The nearby area is also organized into a map of the visual field.

(d) hV4

The importance of VO cortex for colour perception in humans was clearly established by Meadows' and Zeki's reviews of lesion data (Meadows 1974; Zeki 1990) and more recently by neuroimaging experiments using positron emission tomography and fMRI (Zeki *et al.* 1991; McKeefry & Zeki 1997; Hadjikhani *et al.* 1998; Bartels & Zeki 2000). In the neuroimaging experiments, Zeki *et al.* (1991) found a preferential response to colour compared with luminance-matched achromatic stimuli on the ventral surface and they labelled this spot hV4. McKeefry and Zeki further reported that responses to colour stimuli 2.8–10° above fixation were located adjacent to responses to stimuli placed 2.8–10° below fixation, both on the ventral surface. This showed a hemifield representation on the ventral surface: a result that is consistent with hemiachromatopsia reports in the neurological literature (McKeefry & Zeki 1997).

Hadjikhani *et al.* (1998) subsequently confirmed a VO colour responsive region with a hemifield map representation. They argued that this hemifield representation could not be V4, but rather it must be a new colour area they called V8. The new area is based upon a definition of V4v as a quarter field representation adjacent to V3v. They proposed that V8 is adjacent to V4v, contains a hemifield map, a distinct fovea, and that its angular representation is perpendicular to the V4v representation. This claim has met some resistance from Zeki and his colleagues (Bartels & Zeki 1998, 2000; Zeki 2001).

We find that the visual map adjacent to V3v represents the entire contralateral hemifield, not a quarter field as proposed by Hadjikhani *et al.* (1998). This map occupies *ca.* 4 cm² of cortex and includes a foveal representation that is confluent with that of areas V1/2/3. The homology of this area to macaque V4 is uncertain because the human map does not extend onto the dorsal surface nor does it surround V1. However, due to its location adjacent to V3v, we propose calling this hemifield representation hV4. We agree with Hadjikhani *et al.* that there is a separate and distinct foveal representation present on the ventral surface beyond hV4. This foveal representation is located 3–5 cm from the confluent V1/2/3 foveal representation and it is larger than the foveal representation in V1. In addition to this distinct fovea, there is clearly considerable retinotopic organization beyond hV4. We do not yet have adequate power in our measurements and analysis tools to confidently label these regions into functional visual areas, although this should prove possible in the future.

The justification for our proposed organization is presented in Figures 1.8 and 1.9. The coloured images in these figures show travelling wave measurements of angular and eccentric representations. The images code measurements from a 7 cm diameter region within VO cortex. The images appear blurred because these measurements are made at the current resolution limit of our instruments: there are approximately five sample points per centimetre, and the spatial blurring of the signal by the vasculature extends over several millimetres (Engel *et al.* 1997). While we use the pseudo-colour images to guide our interpretation of the spatial organization and to suggest hypotheses, our conclusions are based on the graphs and quantitative analyses presented along with these images.

The images in these figures show travelling wave measurements from two observers; the same pattern has been observed in every other observer we have measured. Angular and eccentricity measurements are shown at the top and bottom. Because no significant differences were found between the right and left hemispheres, all of the angular colour maps and

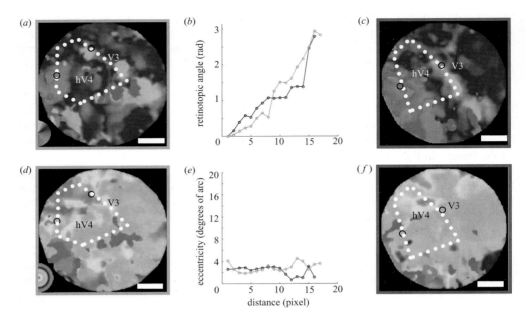

Fig. 1.8. See also Plate 6. Retinotopic organization in VO for two subjects. The images show angular (top) and eccentricity (bottom) maps; the left and right images are from two subjects (A. B. and B. W.). In the angular maps (*a,c*), cyan represents the upper vertical meridian, blue/magenta the horizontal and red the lower vertical meridian. The hemifield representation of hV4 is indicated by the dotted white polygon, and the general location of ventral V3 is shown. The eccentricity maps (*d,f*) from foveal (red/yellow) to peripheral (green and cyan) run perpendicular to the angular map. The graphs (*b,e*) show the measured angular (*b*) and eccentricity (*e*) values on a path between the black circles marked on the hV4 boundary. Data from subject A. B. are plotted in blue, data from subject B. W. are plotted in green. Along these paths the angular phase measurements span 3 rad (*b*), indicating a hemifield representation while the eccentricity measurements are approximately constant (*e*). The VO foveal representation falls at the bottoms of the maps in (*d*) and (*f*). The expanding ring stimulus extended to a 20° radius (blue/magenta), but the preferred eccentricities in hV4 were more central (cyan/blue). Scale bar, 1 cm.

positions have been adjusted to a 'left hemisphere' format where angular retinotopies are plotted in a magenta/blue/cyan pseudo-colour map and eccentricity retinotopies have a red/yellow/green map.

First, consider the angular measurements shown in Figure 1.8*a*. The large cyan colour band represents the upper visual field and defines one boundary of V3v. Beyond this boundary the preferred angular representation continues through blue (horizontal) and then onto magenta and red (lower vertical). The data indicate a continuous progression of preferred orientations that define a full hemifield representation, with the upper visual field represented medially and the lower visual field represented laterally.

We note that this arrangement is similar to that described by McKeefry & Zeki (1997). The green circles in Figure 1.8*b* measure the fMRI signal phase across this band between the two black circles in Figure 1.8*a*. The phases span 3 rad, substantially more than what would be expected if V4v were restricted to a quarter field representation.

Furthermore, by considering the image in Figure 1.8*d*, we find a consistent eccentricity map as well. There is a foveal preference (orange, yellow) that merges with the foveal representation of V3v and (not shown) V1/2. This preferred eccentricity map is orthogonal to the preferred angular map, so that this region contains a full hemifield with respect to both visual field dimensions.

The orthogonality of the two representations can be demonstrated by plotting the signal phase for the eccentricity measurements across the same path that we used to plot the angular phase. The plot marked with green circles in Figure 1.8e shows that the phases of the eccentricity measurements are close to constant, while the angular measurements shown in the upper graph span the entire hemifield with phases from ca. 0 to π rad.

The hemifield map spans ca. 2 cm on each side. This is approximately twice the width of the quarter field maps in V2 and V3. The location of this hemifield representation is indicated on the images in Figure 1.8a,c,d,f by the dashed polygon and the label 'hV4'.

The spatial organization of the eccentricity map is very systematic in four subjects (eight hemispheres) where we have focused on the ventral surface. The typical pattern is shown in more detail in Figure 1.9. Beginning in the hV4 fovea, we can trace a path to the second foveal representation. For 2 cm along this path, the eccentricity preference becomes increasingly eccentric. Then near the 10° representation (green colour code) the eccentricity map reverses and the response preference returns back towards the fovea.

This progression of preferred eccentricities can be seen in the colour images, but it is particularly clear in the measured time-series shown on the right of Figure 1.9. The graphs show the travelling wave signal measured at each of the circled grey regions of interest. In all

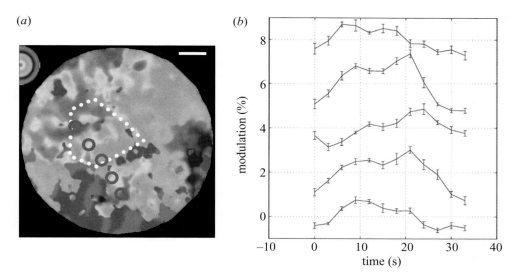

Fig. 1.9. See also Plate 7. The eccentricity map in ventral cortex near hV4. (a) The two prominent red/yellow regions represent the fovea at the confluence of V1/2/3/4 (upper left) and the displaced foveal representation on the ventral surface (bottom middle). The peripheral signals (blue) fall within areas V2/3. Area hV4 is denoted by the dashed white polygon. The grey circles indicate a series of regions of interest that fall between the two large foveal representations. (b) The average fMRI time-series during a single stimulus cycle from each region of interest on the left. The signal amplitudes are quite significant and reliable, representing about 1% modulation about the mean. The individual curves are displaced vertically for clarity; their order corresponds to the ordering of the regions of interest. The middle curve measures the time-course at the peripheral boundary of hV4. The phase of the curves varies systematically and reverses direction at this boundary. Colour overlays are included only at locations with a coherence of at least 0.35. Scale bar, 1 cm.

observers and all hemispheres, the retinotopic map varies reliably from fovea to periphery and then back. We found no way to reconcile these measurements with the proposed quarter field V4v and hemifield V8. In every case we could identify hV4 as a simple map of the entire contralateral hemifield.

A brief examination of the images shows that there are additional retinotopic maps beyond hV4. But a definitive assessment of how this region of VO is organized should await further improvements in the data and analysis tools.

(e) VO cortex: colour

Finally, we consider the relationship between the travelling wave measurements and the signals evoked by a colour experiment. We have compared the signals evoked by alternating coloured and luminance-matched achromatic patterns (see Figure 1.3), and we can confirm the general observations described in the more recent observations from Bartels & Zeki (1998, 2000) and Hadjikhani *et al.* (1998). The regions that respond preferentially to the colour stimulus begin in area V1 and continue along the ventral pathway into VO.

Figure 1.10 indicates the general position of the strongest colour activations in three observers. In all three subjects we find significant activity in V1, V2, hV4, and nearby VO regions. By comparison, there is very little preference for the coloured stimuli in dorsal regions or in ventral V3. For one of our observers (though not all) there was also a stronger response to the *achromatic* stimuli on the dorsal surface.

Figure 1.11 shows the spatial distribution of activity on the VO surface in both hemispheres of three subjects. There is very significant activation in synchrony with the colour stimulus in hV4 and the surrounding region. Only the locations with a very high activity ($p < 0.001$) are shown; if we marked every point that was active at some modest significance level (e.g. $p < 0.02$), most of this region would show activity. The most powerful responses are not constrained to the central foveal regions; though recall that the entire region appears to prefer signals within the central 10°. Hence, we do not think the punctate nature of the activation pattern is meaningful.

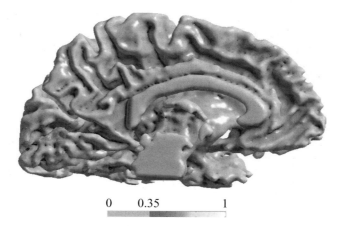

0   0.35   1

Fig. 1.10. See also Plate 8. Mid-sagittal view of colour exchange activations. Activations exceeding a coherence level of 0.4, approximately equivalent to a statistical threshold of $p < 0.001$, are shown. There is significant activation in the calcarine sulcus as well as along the ventral surface. Subject A. W.

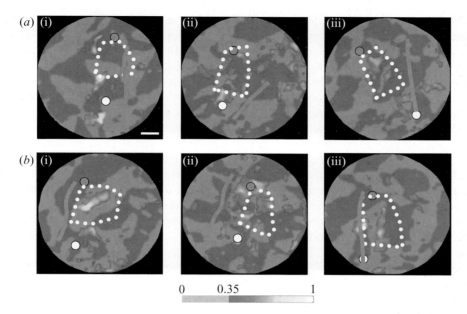

Fig. 1.11. See also Plate 9. Locations responding preferentially to chromatic compared with achromatic stimuli in three subjects. Data are shown for three subjects ((i) A. W., (ii) A. B., (iii) B. W.). (*a*) Left hemisphere; (*b*) right hemisphere. The hV4 boundary is marked by the dotted white polygon, and the collateral sulcus is marked in blue. The foveal representations in hV4 (blue dot) and VO (white dot) are marked. The unfold spans 7 cm. Only locations with response coherence greater than 0.35 are shown. Scale bar, 1 cm.

To facilitate comparisons between groups and experiments, we chose an experimental design that was similar that used by the London group (McKeefry & Zeki 1997). In this design, observers are not asked to fixate, which means that the effective stimulus visual field position is not controlled. Given that we now know that VO is retinotopically organized, we suspect that some of the differences between subjects may be caused by differences in eye movement patterns or differences in individual strategy when performing the target detection task. The experimental design choices can be modified in future studies, allowing a more precise measurement of the colour responses in VO.

1.5. Summary

We summarize our observations with three major points. First, a considerable amount of occipital cortex responds well to the travelling wave stimulus. This demonstrates that most of occipital cortex is stimulated preferentially by a restricted spatial region of the visual field. Further, these spatial preferences are generally organized into retinotopic maps. The secure identification of these maps should await additional data and improvements in the analytical tools (Koch *et al.* 2001).

Next, because of the debate in the literature, we have made a particular effort to understand the region near putative V8 (Hadjikhani *et al.* 1998; Bartels & Zeki 2000; Zeki 2001). We find a hemifield map adjacent to V3v. While we see a visual field map that is generally consistent with the reports that led to V8, we cannot reconcile the details of the angular and eccentric maps in such a way that V8 represents a hemifield adjacent to a V4v quarter field. Rather, we think that in the human, the fourth visual area represents the central 10° of the entire hemifield. We note that the presence of a ventral area adjacent to V3v that represents an entire hemifield extends a trend that can be found in macaque. In that animal, the ventral representation of V4 includes a substantial portion of the visual field that lies below the horizontal midline (Gattass *et al.*1988). We propose referring to this hemifield map as hV4.

Finally, we examined the spatial distribution of colour activations on the ventral surface. To coordinate our measurements with earlier investigators, we used a colour exchange protocol in which eye movements are uncontrolled and colour selections are randomized. Using this protocol, we do find colour activation beginning in V1 and extending onto the ventral surface. We do not find a distinctive and highly localized pattern that is consistent across observers. We expect that by using better controlled colour test stimuli (e.g., stimuli that selectively excite individual cone classes or opponent colour pathways), we will be able to learn more about the colour signals within the ventral pathways.

This work was supported by NEI RO1 EY03164. We thank Robert Dougherty for his comments.

References

Bartels, A. & Zeki, S. 1998 The theory of multistage integration in the visual brain. *Proc. R. Soc. Lond.* B **265**, 2327–2332. (DOI 10.1098/rspb.1998.0579.)

Bartels, A. & Zeki, S. 2000 The architecture of the colour centre in the human visual brain: new results and a review. *Eur. J. Neurosci.* **12**, 172–193.

Brainard, D. H. 1997 The psychophysics toolbox. *Spatial Vis.* **10**, 433–436.

Engel, S. A., Rumelhart, D. E., Wandell, B. A., Lee, A. T., Glover, G. H., Chichilnisky, E. J. & Shadlen, M. N. 1994 fMRI of human visual cortex. *Nature* **369**, 525. [Erratum in *Nature* 1994 **370**, 106.]

Engel, S. A., Glover, G. H. & Wandell, B. A. 1997 Retinotopic organization in human visual cortex and the spatial precision of functional MRI. *Cerebr. Cortex* **7**, 181–192.

Epstein, R., Harris, A., Stanley, D. & Kanwisher, N. 1999 The parahippocampal place area: recognition, navigation, or encoding? *Neurone* **23**, 115–125.

Fairchild, M. D. 1998 *Colour appearance models.* Reading, MA: Addison-Wesley.

Gattass, R., Sousa, A. P. & Gross, C. G. 1988 Visuotopic organization and extent of V3 and V4 of the macaque. *J. Neurosci.* **8**, 1831–1845.

Grill-Spector, K. & Malach, R. 2001 fMR-adaptation: a tool for studying the functional properties of human cortical neurons. *Acta Psychol. Amst.* **107**, 293–321.

Hadjikhani, N., Liu, A. K., Dale, A. M., Cavanagh, P. & Tootell, R. B. H. 1998 Retinotopy and colour sensitivity in human visual cortical area V8. *Nature Neurosci.* **1**, 235–241.

Hunt, R. W. G. 1987 *The reproduction of colour.* Tolworth, UK: Fountain Press.

Kanwisher, N., McDermott, J. & Chun, M. M. 1997 The fusiform face area: a module in human extrastriate cortex specialized for face perception. *J. Neurosci.* **17**, 4302–4311.

Koch, V., Wade, A., Dougherty, R. & Wandell, B. 2001 Automatic identification of retinotopic visual areas. *Soc. Neurosci. Abstr.* **27**, 620.14.

Kries, J. V. 1902 *Chromatic adaptation.* Cambridge, MA: MIT Press [Translation in MacAdam, D. L. 1970 *Sources of colour science.*]

Levy, I., Hasson, U., Avidan, G., Hendler, T. & Malach, R. 2001 Center-periphery organization of human object areas. *Nature Neurosci.* **4**, 533–539.

McKeefry, D. J. & Zeki, S. 1997 The position and topography of the human colour centre as revealed by functional magnetic resonance imaging. *Brain* **120**, 2229–2242.

Meadows, J. 1974 Disturbed perception of colours associated with localized cerebral lesions. *Brain* **97**, 615–632.

Mullen, K. T. 1991 Colour vision as a post-receptoral specialization of the central visual field. *Vis. Res.* **31**, 119–130.

Noll, D. C., Cohen, J. D., Meyer, C. H. & Schneider, W. 1995 Spiral K-space MR imaging of cortical activation. *J. Magn. Reson. Imaging* **5**, 49–56.

Press, W. T., Brewer, A. A., Dougherty, R. F., Wade, A. R. & Wandell, B. A. 2001 Visual areas and spatial summation in human visual cortex. *Vis. Res.* **41**, 1321–1332.

Smith, A. T., Greenlee, M. W., Singh, K. D., Kraemer, F. M. & Hennig, J. 1998 The processing of first- and second-order motion in human visual cortex assessed by functional magnetic resonance imaging (fMRI). *J. Neurosci.* **18**, 3816–3830.

Teo, P. C., Sapiro, G. & Wandell, B. A. 1997 Creating connected representations of cortical gray matter for functional MRI visualization. *IEEE Trans. Med. Imaging* **16**, 852–863.

Tootell, R. B., Mendola, J. D., Hadjikhani, N. K., Ledden, P. J., Liu, A. K., Reppas, J. B., Sereno, M. I. & Dale, A. M. 1997 Functional analysis of V3A and related areas in human visual cortex. *J. Neurosci.* **17**, 7060–7078.

Turner, R., Howseman, A., Rees, G. E., Josephs, O. & Friston, K. 1998 Functional magnetic resonance imaging of the human brain: data acquisition and analysis. *Exp. Brain Res.* **123**, 5–12.

Wandell, B. A. 1995 *Foundations of vision*. Sunderland, MA: Sinauer.

Wandell, B. A. 1999 Computational neuroimaging of human visual cortex. *A. Rev. Neurosci.* **10**, 145–173.

Wandell, B. A., Chial, S. & Backus, B. 2000 Visualization and measurement of the cortical surface. *J. Cogn. Neurosci.* **12**, 739–752.

Zeki, S. 1983*a* Colour coding in the cerebral cortex: the responses of wavelength-selective and colour-coded cells in monkey visual cortex to changes in wavelength composition. *Neuroscience* **9**, 767–781.

Zeki, S. 1983*b* The distribution of wavelength and orientation selective cells in different areas of monkey visual cortex. *Proc. R. Soc. Lond.* **217**, 449–470.

Zeki, S. 1990 A century of cerebral achromatopsia. *Brain* **113**, 1721–1777.

Zeki, S. 2001 Localization and globalization in conscious vision. *A. Rev. Neurosci.* **24**, 57–86.

Zeki, S., Watson, J. D., Lueck, C. J., Friston, K. J., Kennard, C. & Frackowiak, R. S. 1991 A direct demonstration of functional specialization in human visual cortex. *J. Neurosci.* **11**, 641–649.

Glossary

fMRI   functional magnetic resonance imaging

hV4   human V4

LCD   liquid crystal display

VO   ventral occipital

2

The uses of colour vision: behavioural and physiological distinctiveness of colour stimuli

Andrew M. Derrington, Amanda Parker, Nick E. Barraclough,
Alexander Easton, G. R. Goodson, Kris S. Parker,
Chris J. Tinsley, and Ben S. Webb

Colour and greyscale (black and white) pictures look different to us, but it is not clear whether the difference in appearance is a consequence of the way our visual system uses colour signals or a by-product of our experience. In principle, colour images are qualitatively different from greyscale images because they make it possible to use different processing strategies. Colour signals provide important cues for segmenting the image into areas that represent different objects and for linking together areas that represent the same object. If this property of colour signals is exploited in visual processing we would expect colour stimuli to look different, as a class, from greyscale stimuli. We would also expect that adding colour signals to greyscale signals should change the way that those signals are processed. We have investigated these questions in behavioural and in physiological experiments. We find that male marmosets (all of which are dichromats) rapidly learn to distinguish between colour and greyscale copies of the same images. The discrimination transfers to new image pairs, to new colours and to image pairs in which the colour and greyscale images are spatially different. We find that, in a proportion of neurons recorded in the marmoset visual cortex, colour-shifts in opposite directions produce similar enhancements of the response to a luminance stimulus. We conclude that colour is, both behaviourally and physiologically, a distinctive property of images.

2.1. Distinctiveness of colour stimuli

(a) Background

This paper is concerned with the fact that we readily distinguish between stimuli that contain colour variations and those that do not. Quite apart from any significance that we might attach to particular colours, or any use we may choose to make of colour information, we distinguish between the presence and the absence of colour in a scene, a pattern or a picture.

This distinctiveness of colour might be something that we learn from our experience of colour and greyscale images in photography, in the cinema and on television. However, this paper makes the case that the distinctiveness could arise naturally from the visual consequences of the presence of colour in an image. We shall argue in support of this latter position in three ways. First, we shall argue that the contribution of colour and, in particular, hue variations to image segmentation makes colour images qualitatively different from greyscale images. Second, we shall show behavioural evidence that a monkey, the common marmoset *Callithrix jacchus*, rapidly learns to discriminate between colour and greyscale images. Finally, we shall show physiological results indicating that the presence of colour modulates the responses of some cortical neurons to a luminance stimulus. Crucially, in this last instance, the nature of the modulation depends only on the presence of colour; it is independent of the actual colour that is present.

In the following two subsections, we consider the role of colour, and particularly of hue information, in the identification of stimuli and in the segmentation of images.

(i) Hue and stimulus identification

Specific hues, or hue combinations, may be used to detect and identify specific objects or classes of object. For example, many edible fruits may be detected against a background of foliage by the fact that they are somewhat redder than the foliage. This type of information, in which specific hues indicate specific types of object, is obviously important. Indeed, there is evidence to support the proposal that in old-world monkeys the photoreceptor pigments that support red–green colour discriminations have evolved to maximize the sensitivity of the discrimination between fruit and foliage (Osorio & Vorobyev 1996; Regan *et al.* 1998; Sumner & Mollon 2000). However, there is no reason to suppose that links between specific hues and specific objects would lead to a situation where colour images, as a class, look different from greyscale images. Each hue might have its own significance, but the importance of a coloured image would depend on which hues it contained, not on the mere presence of the variations in hue that differentiate colour from greyscale images. We consider a more general kind of information provided by hue variations that could make their mere presence in an image important.

(ii) Hue and image segmentation

One of the fundamental problems of vision is image segmentation—deciding which bits of the image should be grouped together because they represent parts of the same object. Indeed, the segregation of objects from each other and from the background is a prerequisite for most of the cognitive operations that can be performed on visual stimuli. Edge detection, the detection of lines in the image along which the luminance changes abruptly, has always been regarded as an important early computation in image segmentation (Marr 1976, 1982; Marr & Hildreth 1980). However, although edges may indicate the boundaries between objects of different reflectance, luminance edges can also be misleading because they can be caused by shadows. This problem can be confounded when objects occlude parts of each other so that a single object may be divided into several distinct areas. Hue provides two types of information that can resolve these two kinds of confusion.

First, retinal images, like most images received from the natural world are formed by light reflected from a group of objects illuminated by a single light source. It is a physical fact that, in such images hue boundaries cannot be caused by shadows. Hue boundaries must represent boundaries between differently reflecting materials, and thus potentially between different objects. Consequently, algorithms for segmenting images can be driven by searching the image for boundaries between areas of different hue (Hurlbert 1989).

Second, even when they are in different levels of shadow, if the different parts of a partially occluded object are made of the same material and lit by the same light source, they will have the same hue, though not necessarily the same lightness. Thus, in principle, the different parts of an image that represent the same object can be linked together by visual processing, which links together areas of the same hue (Mollon 1989).

Figure 2.1 shows these aspects of colour in a diagram that represents the colour information available to the animal that we used in our behavioural experiments, the male marmoset. Male marmosets are dichromats, so the information available to them about any single colour can be represented in a two-dimensional plot showing the relative extent to which it excites both photoreceptor systems (Tovée *et al.* 1992; Travis *et al.* 1988). Thus, each colour can be represented as a point in this space. We are interested in colour boundaries, such as that

A. M. Derrington *et al.*

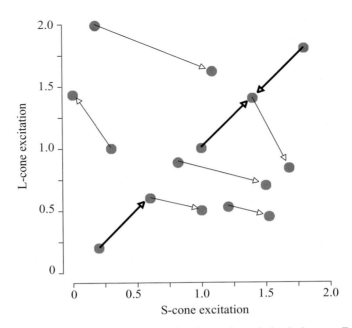

Fig. 2.1. Conventions for representing colour and luminance boundaries in images. Each point in the diagram represents the information about a hypothetical colour provided by the photoreceptors of a dichromat, such as the male marmoset: the excitations produced in the two photoreceptor systems, the L cones and the S cones. The L-cone excitation is plotted against the S-cone excitation. Borders between two areas of different colour within an image are represented as an arrow from one colour (usually the background colour) to the other (usually the foreground colour). The heavy arrows indicate boundaries that involve a change in lightness but no change of hue; they could be caused by shadows. The paler arrows indicate changes of hue (and often also lightness). In an image of reflecting objects lit by a single source, changes of hue indicate changes in the reflecting material.

between an object and its background. The convention that we adopt is to represent each boundary as an arrow with its tail on the point representing the background colour and its head on the point representing the foreground colour.

The thickly drawn arrows in Figure 2.1 all point either towards or away from the origin. They represent colour changes that do not change the ratio of excitations of the two photoreceptors. They are changes of intensity without any change in hue: each arrow represents a boundary that could be caused by a shadow. In fact, the heavy arrows in Figure 2.1 are all running along the same line pointing towards the origin, and thus all represent different intensities of the same hue. Their different start- and endpoints could all represent the same object seen in different levels of shadow. The fact that they lie on the same line radiating from the origin could be used to link together different parts of the same object.

Different hues are encoded as different ratios of photoreceptor activation and would lie on lines radiating out from the origin in different directions. Shadows on objects of each hue would be represented by arrows pointing up or down the hue line, towards the origin or away from it. The thinly drawn arrows in Figure 2.1 represent colour-shifts that could not be caused by shadows. The clue to this is that they point across the diagram along lines that do not pass through the origin. They represent boundaries in the image that are associated with changes in hue and thus necessarily correspond to changes in reflectance.

(b) Testable predictions

These two potential uses of hue in image segmentation mean that all images that contain hue variations form a distinct class for a visual system. Regardless of the actual hues involved, all images that contain more than one hue have the common property that colour algorithms can be used to segment them into patches corresponding to differently reflecting surfaces, and to link together the patches that correspond to the same surface in different levels of shadow. Thus, if colour information is used in segmentation, we can make two predictions.

First, colour and grey-scale images should naturally form different categories and it should be easy to teach animals to respond differentially to them. Specifically, once trained to respond differentially to colour and greyscale images, they should extend the differential response—without further training—to novel pairs of colour and greyscale images, including pairs in which the colour image contains only hue variations not present in the training set. In § 2.2, the behavioural section of this paper, we confirm this prediction by showing that male marmosets trained to distinguish between pairs of greyscale and colour images transfer the discrimination to novel images and to novel colours.

Our second prediction is that, at some point in the visual pathway, hue boundaries should modulate visual responses in a distinctive way. The modulation should be different from that produced in neurons whose responses are used to identify hue, in which different hues produce different responses and complementary hues usually produce opposite responses. Rather, what should happen is that the presence of a hue boundary should modulate the response of the neuron in a way that does not depend on the actual hues. The neuron should signal the presence of the hue boundary rather than either the hues that are associated with it, or its sign. In § 2.3, the physiological section of this paper, we demonstrate that a small number of neurons in the striate and prestriate cortex have their responses modulated by hue boundaries in this way.

2.2. Behavioural classification of colour and greyscale stimuli

(a) Behavioural training and testing

(i) General method

Male common marmosets (*Callithrix jacchus*) were trained to discriminate between pairs of images in a variant of the Wisconsin General Testing Apparatus (Dias *et al.* 1996a,b) that could be mounted on the side of their home cage (see Figure 2.2). One image was the positive, or rewarded stimulus, S+, and the other, the unrewarded stimulus, S−. Each image was printed on card and mounted behind a transparent cover on the front face of a backless hollow plastic cube, which measured *ca.*25 mm on each side. Each cube was mounted on a vertical spindle and could be rotated by the marmoset in order to retrieve the reward, a small piece of marshmallow, from the back of the cube containing the positive stimulus.

Before the start of each trial, the marmoset was signalled to move to the back of his cage, 0.6 m from the stimulus cubes. Two screens, one opaque and one transparent, were placed in front of the stimulus cubes, which were then loaded with the stimuli and the reward for the

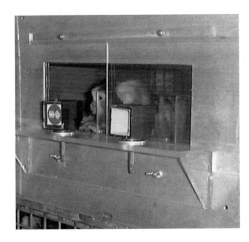

Fig. 2.2. Experimental procedure: photograph of a marmoset retrieving his reward after rotating the stimulus cube. See text for further details.

next trial. To start the trial, the opaque screen was removed, whereupon the marmoset inspected the stimuli and signalled his choice by moving towards one of the stimulus cubes. His choice was recorded and the transparent screen was removed, allowing him access to his chosen stimulus cube. If he was correct, he was able to rotate the cube, retrieve the reward and consume it, before returning to the back of the cage for the next trial.

Using this procedure, marmosets performed between 40 and 100 trials per day while being fed a normal food ration. Feeding took place after testing each day.

(ii) Stimuli
Stimuli were photographic-quality prints 23 mm square, produced by an inkjet printer (Epson Stylus Photo 750). Training stimuli were clip-art bitmaps printed in colour or greyscale. Testing stimuli were complex two-dimensional shapes drawn by doodling with a Bezier line tool in a drawing package (see Figure 2.4*a–c*) and printed as a solid shape of a single colour on a grey or coloured background.

The reflectance spectra of printed samples of the colours used in the test stimuli were measured with a Data-color SF600 reflectance spectrophotometer at 10 nm intervals between 360 and 700 nm, and interpolated at 4 nm intervals. The emission spectra of the lamps in the behavioural testing apparatus were measured at 4 nm intervals using a SpectraResearch PR650 spectroradiometer. The marmoset cone absorption spectra were calculated at 4 nm intervals using the polynomial approximation from Stavenga *et al.* (1993). Products of sets of emission, reflectance and absorption spectra were used to calculate the coordinates of the test-stimulus colours in a dichromatic cone-excitation space for the marmoset.

(iii) Pre-training and training
Pre-training was designed to teach the marmosets to select the rewarded stimulus. Once they had habituated to the apparatus, marmosets were trained to retrieve pieces of marshmallow from the stimulus cubes. Then they were trained to rotate the stimulus cubes to retrieve marshmallow. Finally, they were trained to move to the back of the cage at the start of a trial before beginning trials in which a pair of coloured clip-art pictures were used as stimuli and one of the images was consistently rewarded.

Ten pairs of pictures, chosen so that they contained a wide range of colours and image features, and so that no colour or image feature consistently predicted reward, were used as discrimination tests for pre-training. Monkeys were trained for 40 trials per day on each discrimination problem until they chose the positive stimulus on at least 36 of the 40 trials on three consecutive days. Throughout training and testing, the correct stimulus was alternated from side to side using a Gellermann sequence.

Once pre-training with mixed stimuli had been completed, the marmosets were divided into two groups and began learning to discriminate between colour and greyscale versions of the same clip-art picture. For two of them (Giles and Piers), the colour picture was rewarded and for the other two (Rupert and Hugo), the greyscale picture was rewarded. Once established for a given monkey, the association between colour and reward was retained throughout his training. At this stage, we excluded any pictures containing red, so that we could use red pictures to test whether the colour discrimination transfers to novel colours. Each colour/greyscale discrimination was learned to a criterion of 10 consecutive correct responses.

Figure 2.3a shows the numbers of errors made by four monkeys learning to distinguish between colour and greyscale versions of the same picture to a criterion of ten consecutive correct responses. Performance on the first six discriminations was extremely variable. In the

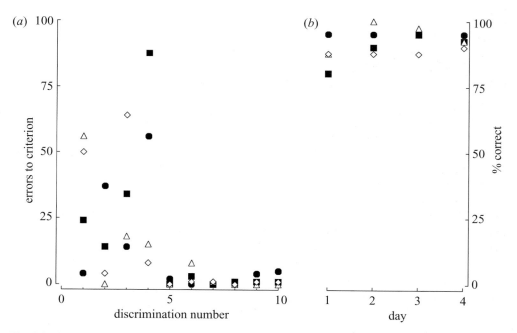

Fig. 2.3. (a) Number of errors made by four monkeys in learning a colour/greyscale image pair to a criterion of 10 consecutive correct choices, plotted against the number of discriminations learned. For Giles (squares) and Piers (circles) the colour image was rewarded; for Rupert (triangles) and Hugo (diamonds) the greyscale image was rewarded. After the sixth discrimination the monkeys were trained for 2 days on a list of the first five discriminations. (b) Performance of the same four monkeys learning a list of 10 novel colour/greyscale discriminations over four days. Each monkey was trained on the list for 40 trials per day.

best case, Rupert had an immediate preference for the second greyscale image and so learned the correct response with no errors. In the worst case, Giles made almost 90 errors while learning the fourth image pair. All four learned the fifth image with no more than one error, but the sixth image produced variable performance.

At this point, they were retrained to ensure that their performance was 90% correct over 40 trials for the first five image pairs presented as a list, that is, on each trial, any of the five image pairs could be presented with the constraint that no pair could be presented for the nth time until all had been presented $n - 1$ times. Giles, Rupert, and Piers reached 90% correct on the first day of training with the list, but Hugo took 2 days.

After this confirmation that they remembered the first five discriminations that they had learned, they resumed training with individual colour/greyscale discriminations. The last four discriminations were learned very rapidly. There were 20 errors by the four monkeys, and the modal number of errors per discrimination was zero. This suggests that, by this stage, the monkeys had learned to rely on the presence of colour to enable them to choose the correct stimulus and did not need to learn each image pair separately.

Figure 2.3*b* confirms this impression. It shows performance on a novel list of 10 colour/greyscale discriminations, which were presented in 40 trials per day over four days. Even on the first day, performance is between 80% and 95% correct. It improves slightly over the four days and is between 90% and 95% correct on day 4. This consistently high level of performance with novel stimuli indicates that, like humans, marmosets reliably distinguish images that contain colour variations from those that contain only variations in lightness: colour is a distinctive stimulus quality.

(iv) Necessary controls

In order to establish that the monkey's discrimination performance is based on the property of colour, we need to exclude two possibilities. First, we need to exclude the possibility that the marmosets are choosing between coloured and greyscale images because of luminosity differences rather than colour differences. Although we have no *a priori* reason to suppose that there are luminance differences between colour and greyscale stimuli, we do not know the marmoset's spectral luminosity function and it is possible that the colours that we used might appear to be systematically brighter (or darker) than the greys with which they are matched. Second, we need to exclude the possibility that the marmosets have simply learned a list of colours.

(v) Test procedure

In order to measure how the training transferred to specific sets of test image pairs without differentially rewarding the responses to test image pairs and without losing the effect of training, we used the following procedure.

The animal was first trained on a list of four colour/greyscale image pairs to a criterion of 90% correct in the 40 trials of a day's testing. Then, during testing sessions, 80% of the trials were 'training' trials and would use a stimulus pair from the trained list, and the reward would only be received if the correct image was chosen (colour or greyscale in accordance with the training history of the particular monkey). Twenty per cent of trials, selected at random, were 'test' trials. On test trials, a test stimulus pair was presented and both of the stimulus cubes contained a reward. Consequently, the monkey's responses on test trials are determined exclusively by his training and not by reward contingencies on previous test trials.

(b) Control for luminosity differences

To eliminate the possibility that the marmosets use luminosity differences rather than colour differences, we prepared a series of colour images that consisted of different shapes, all of the same blue on the same grey background (see Figure 2.4b). The comparison greyscale images used the same grey background but, in 50% of them, the shapes were lighter than the background and in the other 50% darker than the background. Test pairs of images drawn at random from this list were used for every fifth trial while the marmosets were performing discriminations for reward using a list of four greyscale and colour stimuli that they had previously learned (see Figure 2.3a). Whenever the luminosity test pairs were presented, both choice boxes were loaded so that whichever choice they made would be rewarded. This 'double baiting' enables us to discover how the monkey's training controls his choice from each test pair without training them on the test pair (Walsh et al. 1993).

Table 2.1 shows the performance of each monkey on the transfer tests. The overwhelming majority of their choices were consistent with the colour discrimination (Giles 97.5%, Hugo 92.5%, Piers 100%, and Rupert 97.5% on the luminance transfer test). Clearly, their colour choices are not based on luminosity differences between colours and greys because otherwise they would have made incorrect choices consistently, either on the light grey or on the dark grey images, depending on whether the blue that we had chosen appeared brighter or darker than the background.

(c) Transfer to novel colours and novel image pairs

We used a similar procedure to rule out the possibility that the marmosets are simply using a catalogue of colours, compiled during the experiment, to guide their choices. To do this, we made a set of 16 test image pairs in which the coloured images all used shapes made from a deep red on a grey background (see Figure 2.4c). None of the previously used coloured images had contained any red. As before, test image pairs selected at random were presented on every fifth trial while the marmosets were performing discriminations for reward using a pre-learned list of four greyscale and colour stimuli. Both of the images of the colour test pair were rewarded. Hugo, Piers and Rupert transferred their colour discrimination to the novel red images: they scored 95%, 98%, and 100%, respectively. Giles, however, did not transfer his colour discrimination to red images: his mean score was 41%.

One possible reason for Giles's failure is that he was unable to determine that the red test pattern was coloured because he could not distinguish between the red test colour and a dark grey. To investigate this possibility, we tried to train him to distinguish the red from dark grey by rewarding him only if he made the correct choice on trials with red test patterns. His mean performance in 160 trials over four days was 54% correct. Clearly, he was unable to make the discrimination, although his performance reached 58% on the fourth day, suggesting that he might eventually have learned to do so. However, there can be no doubt that the reason why he did not transfer the colour discriminations to red images is that, during the time he was training with these, he was unable to distinguish the red from a dark grey. It is possible that Giles's failure to make this discrimination arises because he has a different colour vision phenotype from the others, but it is equally probable that it is a difficult discrimination for all of them. We have since learned, with other stimuli, that Giles is slower than the other three to learn difficult visual discriminations.

Having established that Giles's failure to generalize the colour/greyscale discrimination to red images was caused by his difficulty in discriminating that the stimulus was coloured, we

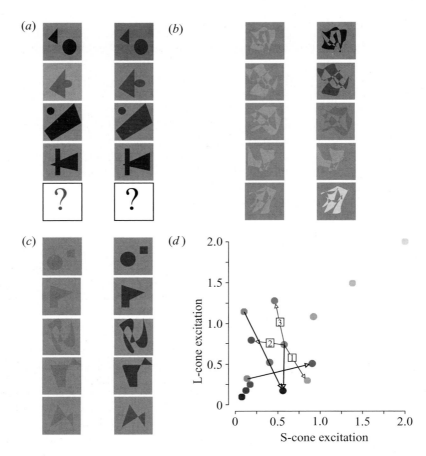

Fig. 2.4. See also Plate 10. Stimuli for colour discrimination testing. (*a*) Training stimuli and test logic for testing discriminations without differentially rewarding the discriminanda. In 80% of the trials, the monkeys were trained for reward on the list of four colour/greyscale pairs. In 20% of the trials, a pair of test stimuli was presented and both stimulus boxes contained a reward. The monkeys' performance on test trials informed us about their stimulus choices in the absence of differential reward. (*b*) Five of the 10 test stimuli used in demonstrating that the colour/greyscale discrimination is not based on an apparent luminance or contrast difference. (*c*) Five of the 16 test stimuli used in demonstrating that the colour discrimination transfers to a novel hue. (*d*) Training- and test-stimulus colours plotted in cone-excitation coordinates with arrows indic-ating the borders between background and figure colours. The three heavy arrows show the figure/ground borders of the training stimuli. The lighter, numbered arrows show the figure/ground borders of the test stimuli. No. 1 is the blue test in (*b*). No. 2 is the red 'novel hue' test from (*c*), which was successfully discriminated by Hugo, Rupert and Piers but not by Giles. No. 3 is the lighter red that was successfully discriminated by Giles. Note that the heavy arrows representing the training stimuli all run across the diagram in a direction of increasing relative S-cone excitation (down and right), whereas the arrows representing the novel hue stimuli run up and left in a direction of increasing L-cone excitation.

Table 2.1. Performance of the four monkeys on the different transfer tests

Test	Giles (%)	Hugo (%)	Rupert (%)	Piers (%)
Luminance transfer	97.5	92.5	97.5	100
Transfer to novel hue (dark red)	41	95	100	98
Transfer to novel hue (light red)	97	—	—	—
Dissimilar image pairs	80	80	92.5	85

decided to test him again using a lighter version of the same hue, which should be easier to discriminate. We changed the dark red to a lighter red (see Figure 2.4d) and repeated the transfer test. He transferred almost perfectly: his average score was 97% correct over 8 days. Thus, despite Giles's early failure, all the monkeys transferred the colour/greyscale discrimination to one or other of the novel hues.

Finally, we used the same transfer procedure to test all the monkeys to see whether the colour/greyscale discrimination would generalize to a series of 10 greyscale/colour image pairs in which the greyscale and colour images were different spatial patterns. Although the transfer was not perfect, all of the monkeys scored at substantially above chance (Giles 32 out of 40, Hugo 32 out of 40, Piers 34 out of 40, Rupert 37 out of 40). The difference between the lowest of these scores and chance performance is extremely significant ($p < 0.005$; χ^2-test).

These results show that, once they have solved a number of discriminations in which colour is the common factor, male marmosets rapidly and efficiently utilize colour to choose between new stimuli, even when those stimuli differ in other respects. They classify novel image pairs according to whether they are colour or greyscale, even when those images contain only hues that are not present in the training set. They even categorize pairs of pictures that differ in other respects, according to the colour/greyscale criterion.

The fact that an abstract image attribute, such as colour, is used in such a versatile and consistent way to guide the choice between novel stimuli is consistent with the notion that colour is a highly conspicuous stimulus property. The rapid transition from needing to learn each discrimination by reinforcement training to immediate, almost errorless performance with new discriminations (shown in Figure 2.3a) suggests that the conspicuousness of colour is not simply a consequence of the reinforcement contingencies learned in our experiments, but is innate.

The fact that the colour/greyscale discrimination transfers to novel colours on which the marmoset has not been trained (shown in Table 2.1) is consistent with the notion that, like us, the marmoset includes all colour images in a common category and it is the selection of this category that has been reinforced. The most likely reason for the perceptual salience of stimuli that contain hue variations is the usefulness of hue variations in image segmentation. This leads to the prediction that monochrome pictures, which are coloured but contain only a single hue, should be classified as 'non-coloured' images. We have not tested this prediction because it is not possible to present coloured monochrome pictures on a coloured monochrome background in our present apparatus. We are at present building apparatus that will make it possible to present such stimuli in order to test this prediction.

The next question to consider is whether the behavioural distinctiveness of colour for the marmoset is reflected in the neurophysiology of cortical visual processing.

2.3. Modulation of physiological responses by colour-shifts

In considering what kind of physiological properties might support the behavioural discrimination between the presence and absence of colour, it is, first, important to distinguish it from normal colour discriminations. In normal colour discriminations, the aim is to identify the hue rather than merely to detect the presence or absence of variations in hue. Neurons that support hue identification must respond differentially to varying hue. For example, they may only respond to a narrow range of hues (Zeki 1983*a,b*) or they may respond in an opponent fashion to complementary hues (Wiesel & Hubel 1966). Neither of these types of response will support discrimination between the presence and absence of colour. An essential requirement is a response that signals the presence of hue variations in the stimulus but that does not differentiate between hues.

A second requirement arises if we assume that the functional significance of the ability to distinguish between the presence and the absence of colour is likely to be related to the use of hue in image segmentation. Hue boundaries allow us to identify a set of edges in the image that represent reflectance changes, and hence could not be caused by shadows. In general, these hue boundaries will coincide with luminance edges. Under this assumption, the appropriate neural signal would be a change in the response to a luminance stimulus when it is associated with a hue boundary, rather than an overt response to the hue boundary.

In order to look for neural signals that fulfil both of these requirements, we have measured the responses of neurons in marmoset visual cortex to small patches of moving sinusoidal grating. The grating was of optimal spatial frequency and orientation (i.e. the spatial frequency and orientation that produced the largest response), and the patch was of optimal length and width. The grating was presented under three different conditions (see Figure 2.5). In the 'control' condition, the hue and mean luminance of the patch of grating was the same as the surrounding screen. In the two 'test' conditions, the patch was changed in hue either in a bluish or in a yellowish direction while the surrounding screen was maintained at the same hue and luminance. Thus, at the boundaries of the grating patch, the screen changed both in luminance and in hue.

(a) Physiological recording

Physiological preparation for recording from neurons with microelectrodes and for presenting visual stimuli were essentially as have been described previously (Felisberti & Derrington 2001).

(i) Visual stimulation

Visual stimuli—spots or patches of different colours and luminances—and patches of sinusoidal grating were presented on a Sony Multiscan GDM200PDST monitor at a frame rate of 120 Hz by a Macintosh computer running custom-written software. Stimuli were adjusted in position and size and, if appropriate, in orientation and spatial frequency, in order to maximize the response of the neuron. Multiple stimuli, patches of different sizes, colours and contrasts, which could be combined with sinusoidal gratings of different contrasts, were randomly interleaved so that responses to stimuli that were being compared were accumulated concurrently. Stimulus luminances were set using a lookup table to compensate for the non-linear relation between the luminance and applied voltage of the display. For coloured stimuli, cone excitations were calculated using measurements of the emission spectrum of the display screen, made at 4 nm intervals in the range 380–780 nm. Cone spectra were

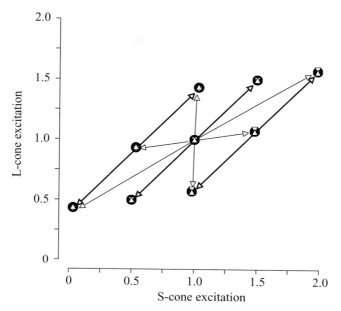

Fig. 2.5. Stimuli for the physiological experiment, plotted in cone-excitation coordinates. The point in the centre of the plot represents the baseline colour and luminance of the display monitor. To its right and left are the points representing the colour backgrounds. The heavy arrows represent the range of colours covered by each of the sinusoidal gratings. The light arrows represent, for each background, the range of colour changes between the screen surrounding the grating patch (which remained at the baseline colour and luminance of the monitor) and the different parts of the grating. The different symbols represent the same information plotted for L-cones of the three different possible peak wavelengths
Circles represent 563 nm, inverted triangles 556 nm and upright triangles 545 nm.

calculated using the approximations of Stavenga *et al.* (1993) for peak wavelengths of 423 nm for the short-wavelength-sensitive cone, and 545, 556, and 563 nm for the different possible long-wavelength-sensitive cones.

The colour changes of the grating patch are illustrated in cone-excitation coordinates in Figure 2.5. They were calculated to produce a large variation in the short-wavelength cone signal and minimal variation in the long wavelength cone signal. Such colour changes produce a strong response in colour-opponent neurons driven by blue cones. However, in this case we are not interested in direct responses to the changes in hue of the grating patch. Instead, we are interested in the possibility that the change in hue will modulate the response to luminance.

Figure 2.5 shows the hue boundaries associated with the gratings on patches of different hues. The heavy double-headed arrows connect the colours corresponding to the peaks and troughs of the sinusoidal grating. When the patch of grating is the same hue as its surround, the arrows are aligned along a line pointing to the origin. Both of the changes in hue of the grating patch change the lateral position of the arrow, without changing its orientation, so that it is no longer aligned with the origin. Thus, a mechanism designed to 'mark' spatial modulations of colour that include hue would mark the luminance changes within these gratings when they are presented on the coloured patches.

The thin arrows in Figure 2.5 show the colour changes that occur at the edge of the patch of sinusoidal grating. They connect the point that represents the luminance and colour of the unmodulated display with the points that represent the luminances and colours of the peaks, the troughs and the zero crossings of the sinusoidal gratings on coloured patches. These colour changes also include hue shifts—none of the arrows lies on a line that passes through the origin. Thus, both at their edges and within the patches of sinusoidal grating, there are strong hue shifts.

(b) Response of a single neuron to colour and luminance modulations

Figure 2.6 shows how the hue signals modulate the responses of a striate cortical neuron to a sinusoidal grating. Histograms *a–c* show the response to the moving grating presented alone (*a*) and superimposed on the two coloured patches (*b,c*). When the grating is presented on a coloured patch, the response is bigger by *ca.* 20%. The two complementary coloured patches cause approximately equal enhancements of the response magnitude. However, when the patch colours are presented in isolation (histograms *e* and *f*), they elicit no response.

The coloured patches are spatially and temporally uniform: the colour-shift is turned on at the start of the stimulus presentation and off at the end. This raises the question of whether the lack of response in histograms *e* and *f* is because the neuron is insensitive to the colours of the patches, or because it is insensitive to their spatial and temporal frequencies.

Histograms *g* and *h* answer the question. They show the responses of the same neuron to colour modulations at optimal temporal frequency of either a spatially uniform patch (*g*) or a grating of optimal spatial frequency, orientation and size (*h*). Both when it is spatially modulated at the optimal spatial frequency and when it is spatially unmodulated, the chromatic modulation (in which the colour oscillates sinusoidally between the colours of the bluish and yellowish patches) elicits no discernible response, whereas the response to a luminance modulation of the same temporal and spatial frequency is about 100 spikes per second (Figure 2.6*a*). Thus, the colour-shift enhances the response to luminance without generating an explicit response of its own.

(c) Summary of colour modulation effects

The non-selective enhancement of neuronal responses illustrated in Figure 2.6 could potentially provide a basis for the neuron to contribute to the discrimination between luminance-only edges and colour edges. In Figure 2.7, we summarize the responses of all the neurons that we have tested with the same set of stimuli by plotting the degree to which the response is enhanced by the blue hue shift, against the degree to which it is enhanced by the yellow hue shift. Neurons whose responses are enhanced by both hue shifts appear in the top right-hand quadrant and neurons whose responses are suppressed by both hue shifts plot in the lower left-hand quadrant. Colour-selective neurons, in which the hue shifts have effects of opposite sign, appear in the other two quadrants. Although the majority of the cortical neurons show no effect, a significant number—three out of the six neurons recorded in area 18 (V2) and three out of the 18 neurons recorded in striate cortex (V1)—show an enhancement of their responses by both hue shifts. One of the neurons recorded in area 18 shows a substantial suppression of its response by both hue shifts.

Also shown in Figure 2.7 are the responses of a larger sample of lateral geniculate neurons in the same experiment. None of the LGN cells shows non-selective enhancement of

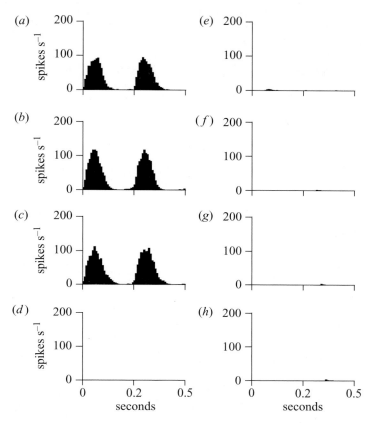

Fig. 2.6. Responses of a neuron in striate cortex to the different stimuli illustrated in Figure 2.5. (*a*) Response to a sinusoidal grating of optimal spatial frequency, length, width and orientation, moving at 4 cycles s^{-1}, presented on a background the same hue and luminance as the rest of the screen. (*b*) Response to the same sinusoidal grating as (*a*) presented on a background shifted towards the blue. The area surrounding the grating remained at constant hue and luminance. The background shift occurred abruptly and coincided with the onset of the grating. The response is bigger than in (*a*). (*c*) Response to the same grating presented on a background shifted away from the blue (towards yellow). The response is bigger than in (*a*). (*d*) Response to the blank screen. (*e*) Response to the background shift towards blue, but with no grating. (*f*) Response to the background shift away from blue, presented with no grating. (*g*) Response to the sinusoidal oscillation of the background between its two extreme colours (towards blue and away from blue) at 4 Hz. (*h*) Response to a sinusoidal grating of optimal spatial frequency, length, width and orientation, which modulates the screen between the two extreme colours of the background and moves at 4 Hz in the same direction as the grating used in Figure 2.6*a*–*c*.

responsiveness by the hue shift. Most of them lie close to the origin, showing that the response to luminance is not modulated by colour. A small number lie in the ower right quadrant, showing that the two hue shifts have opposite modulatory effects—this is the behaviour to be expected of colour-opponent neurons.

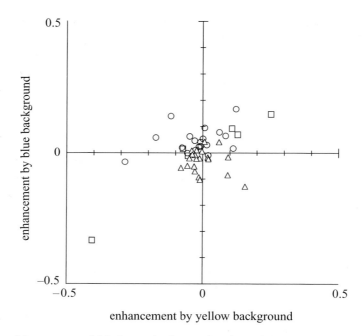

Fig. 2.7. Plots of the extent to which the two backgrounds enhanced the responses of neurons recorded in the striate cortex, area 18 and the LGN. The enhancement is measured as the log of the magnitude of the response in the presence of the background divided by the magnitude of the response in the absence of any background (i.e. the log of the ratio of the two response magnitudes). The enhancement by the blue background is plotted against the enhancement by the yellow background. Cells recorded in the striate cortex are plotted as circles, those recorded in the prestriate cortex are plotted as squares, and those recorded in the LGN are plotted as triangles. For each LGN cell the response magnitude is measured as the magnitude of the Fourier component in the discharge histogram that corresponded to the temporal frequency of the grating. For each cortical cell, the response is measured either as the mean firing rate during the presentation of the grating, or as the magnitude of the corresponding Fourier component, whichever is the larger.

2.4. Enhancement of neural responses as a basis for behavioural distinctiveness of colour

(a) Striate and prestriate cortex

Whatever the function of the perceptual salience of colour, it seems likely that its physiological basis is related to the way that it enhances the responses of neurons early in the cortical visual pathway. The increases in response magnitude caused by the hue shift are clearly detectable in the averaged responses, but modest in size, amounting to no more than about a 30% increase in firing rate in the neurons that we have studied. In the one neuron where we observed a decrease in firing rate, the effect was more dramatic: both hue shifts reduced the response by more than 50%. However, we shall focus on the functional significance of the increases in firing, since they are more common. The two questions to consider are, first, whether these physiological effects are a possible basis for the behavioural results, and second, whether they are the most likely basis for such an effect.

There can be little doubt, in principle, that the physiological response facilitation that we have observed could form the basis for the behavioural discrimination between colour and greyscale images. Although the increases in response magnitude are probably too small to be detected in a single neuron, on a single presentation of a stimulus, the fact that they can be detected in the averaged responses of individual neurons makes it extremely likely that they could be detected in a single trial by averaging across the responses of many neurons. We know that such enhancements are possible: the sensitivity of macaque monkeys in colour discriminations exceeds the sensitivity of the individual neurons that relay colour signals through the monkey LGN (Derrington *et al.* 1984; Derrington 1992). Thus, if we assume that the response enhancements occur across the neuronal population with approximately the frequency that we have observed in our sample, these increases in response magnitude should be easily detectable on a single trial by averaging across neurons.

Of course, only averaging across the population of neurons whose responses are enhanced by colour would not be enough to distinguish colour images from greyscale images. The response enhancements caused by colour could be confused with response enhancements caused by increases in contrast. The results of the luminance transfer test show that the discrimination between colour and greyscale images is independent of the contrast of the greyscale images. To resolve the confusion, the responses would have to be compared with those of similar neurons whose responses were unaffected by colour. Successful discrimination between colour and greyscale images would require a comparison between the averaged responses of the two populations of neurons.

Consequently, although the neurons that we have recorded could contribute to the discrimination, it is likely that the discrimination itself occurs at a later stage of visual processing, where the signals carried by neurons like those that we have recorded can be pooled. This, of course, raises the possibility that the response enhancements that we record could be a consequence of the colour greyscale discrimination fed back from the later stage, rather than providing the basis for the discrimination that is carried out there.

(b) Likely involvement of later stages of processing

Another reason for supposing that the discrimination between colour and greyscale occurs at a relatively late stage in visual processing is the potential role of hue boundaries in image segmentation (Hurlbert 1989). The enhancement of physiological responses associated with hue boundaries that we have observed could be a byproduct of the image segmentation process, which is likely to depend on quite late stages of visual processing. One suggestion is that visual processing in cortical area V4 is related, in a general way, to the segmentation of surfaces in the image (Lennie 1998) and that this general segmentation includes aspects of selectivity to colour that are sensitive to differences in hue between the visual stimulus and its surroundings (Zeki 1983b). Lesions in V4 appear to disrupt pattern discriminations and complex object related colour discriminations, but leave simple colour discriminations unaffected (Heywood & Cowey 1987; Heywood *et al.* 1992; Walsh *et al.* 1993). Thus, it is probable that cortical area V4 is central to the physiological and behavioural phenomena described in this paper. It is important to discover both how the responses of neurons in V4 are modulated by hue shifts such as those used in this study, and whether neurons in V1, V2, and V3 still show modulation of their responses by hue shifts when V4 is removed or inactivated.

To answer this question, we need to record from striate and early prestriate cortex in a preparation, with higher cortical areas inactivated or removed. It would also be informative to carry out the behavioural task in a preparation with higher cortical areas removed. In this respect, it is significant that macaque monkeys with inferotemporal cortex lesions show subtle deficits in colour discrimination (Huxlin *et al.* 2000), although macaques have not, to our knowledge, been tested on their ability to generalize a colour/greyscale discrimination.

2.5. The uses of colour vision

We propose that the utility of colour signals for image segmentation makes colour stimuli distinctive. If so, we should also expect that the availability of colour signals would improve our visual abilities. The evidence on this question is sparse and suggests that colour improves performance but not speed. When monkeys or humans have to classify images according to whether they contain animals or food, colour makes no difference to the speed or accuracy with which they can do the task (Fabre-Thorpe *et al.* 1998; Delorme *et al.* 1999, 2000). On the positive side, the recognition of natural scenes is improved by the availability of colour signals both during encoding and during recall. The advantage of colour during encoding is interpreted as a sensory effect, and may reflect its usefulness in image segmentation (Gegenfurtner & Rieger 2000).

(a) Different uses of L–M and short-wave systems

For convenience, we have concentrated our experiments on the short-wavelength colour-opponent channel by using male marmosets (which have only this channel) for the behavioural work and by targeting our physiological colour stimuli on the short-wavelength channel. In the following paragraphs, we consider whether our conclusions would also apply to the channel carrying signals from the long- and medium-wavelength cones, the L–M channel.

Another reason for concentrating our experiments on the short-wavelength opponent channel is that this is the primordial colour vision system possessed by most mammals that have colour vision (Jacobs 1993). Its function is therefore likely to reflect the primordial role of colour vision. It is clear that the short-wavelength sensitive opponent channel contributes to human memory because, in human X-chromosome-linked dichromats, which lack the L–M (red–green) colour-opponent channel, colour has the same enhancement of memory as it does in normal trichromats (Gegenfurtner *et al.* 1998; Gegenfurtner & Rieger 2000). However, we do not know whether the L–M colour-opponent channel makes such a contribution. This raises the question of whether we would expect the colour images that selectively stimulate the L–M colour-opponent channel of old-world primates to show the same distinctiveness that we have observed in our experiments.

One reason for supposing that the L–M colour channel might not be used in the same way as the short-wavelength channel is that its evolution is more recent (Mollon 1989) and has been linked to the specific colour discriminations associated with fruit eating (Osorio & Vorobyev 1996; Regan *et al.* 1998; Sumner & Mollon 2000). Consequently, we might expect signals in the L–M channel to be used for identifying specific classes of object but not for image segmentation. We have begun experiments with macaque monkeys to test whether the two colour-opponent channels contribute in the same way to the distinctiveness of colour images.

As in most other new-world primate species that have been studied, marmosets have a range of colour-vision phenotypes that can be accounted for by variations in the pigment sensitive to longer wavelengths, which are coded by a single gene on the X-chromosome.

There are three such pigments, with peak sensitivities at 545, 556, or 563 nm (Hunt *et al.* 1993). All marmosets share a common short-wavelength-sensitive pigment; males have a single long-wavelength-sensitive pigment and females have two, drawn at random from the three. Thus, all male marmosets and one third of female marmosets are dichromats, with only a single post-receptoral colour-opponent channel (Tovée 1994). Because of the wide variety of colour vision phenotypes and the uncertainty about the extent to which the marmoset visual system is wired to exploit the availability of trichromatic signals in the minority of marmosets that possess them, we did not attempt to investigate any contribution of a possible L–M channel either to physiological responses or to behaviour. However, care was taken to design our stimuli so that the identity of the long-wavelength cone pigment that contributes to the short-wavelength-sensitive colour-opponent channel is irrelevant. Figure 2.5 shows that the identity of the long-wavelength-sensitive cone makes only a tiny, quantitative difference to the effect of the colour modulations and so variations in cone type would not affect our results.

2.6. Conclusion

Both in their behavioural responses and in the responses of neurons in areas 17 and 18, marmosets distinguish between spatial patterns that contain only variations in luminance and those in which hue also varies. We propose that these distinctions are related to the use of colour signals for image segmentation.

This work was supported by grants from the Wellcome Trust and the BBSRC, a Wellcome Prize studentship to B. S. W. and an MRC studentship to G. R. G. The authors thank Stephen Westland and Sophie Wuerger for their help with colour calibrations, Jackie Francis and Mel Williams for their help with behavioural testing, and Peter Lennie and Anya Hurlbert for the use of their software.

References

Delorme, A., Richard, G. & Fabre-Thorpe, M. 1999 Rapid processing of complex natural scenes: a role for the magnocellular visual pathways? *Neurocomputing* **26**, 663–670.

Delorme, A., Richard, G. & Fabre-Thorpe, M. 2000 Ultra-rapid categorisation of natural scenes does not rely on colour cues: a study in monkeys and humans. *Vis. Res.* **40**, 2187–2200.

Derrington, A. M. 1992 Relative sensitivity to colour and luminance gratings in human observers and monkey parvocellular neurones. *J. Physiol.* **452**, 286.

Derrington, A. M., Krauskopf, J. & Lennie, P. 1984 Chromatic mechanisms in lateral geniculate nucleus of macaque. *J. Physiol.* **357**, 241–265.

Dias, R., Robbins, T. W. & Roberts, A. C. 1996a Dissociation in prefrontal cortex of affective and attentional shifts. *Nature* **380**, 69–72.

Dias, R., Robbins, T. W. & Roberts, A. C. 1996b Primate analogue of the Wisconsin Card Sort Test: effects of excitotoxic lesions of the prefrontal cortex in the marmoset. *Behav. Neurosci.* **110**, 872–886.

Fabre-Thorpe, M., Richard, G. & Thorpe, S. J. 1998 Rapid categorization of natural images by rhesus monkeys. *Neuro-Report* **9**, 303–308.

Felisberti, F. & Derrington, A. M. 2001 Long-range interactions in the lateral geniculate nucleus of the new-world monkey, *Callithrix jacchus*. *Vis. Neurosci.* **18**, 209–218.

Gegenfurtner, K. R. & Rieger, J. 2000 Sensory and cognitive contributions of color to the recognition of natural scenes. *Curr. Biol.* **10**, 805–808.

Gegenfurtner, K. R., Wichmann, F. A. & Sharpe, L. T. 1998 The contribution of color to visual memory in X-chromosome-linked dichromats. *Vis. Res.* **38**, 1041–1045.

Heywood, C. A. & Cowey, A. 1987 On the role of cortical area V4 in the discrimination of hue and pattern in macaque monkeys. *J. Neurosci.* **7**, 2601–2617.

Heywood, C. A., Gadotti, A. & Cowey, A. 1992 Cortical area—V4 and its role in the perception of color. *J. Neurosci.* **12**, 4056–4065.

Hunt, D. M., Williams, A. J., Bowmaker, J. K. & Mollon, J. D. 1993 Structure and evolution of the polymorphic photopigment gene of the marmoset. *Vis. Res.* **33**, 147–154.

Hurlbert, A. 1989 Colour algorithms for image segmentation. In *Models of brain function* (ed. R. M. J. Cotterill), pp. 89–113. Cambridge University Press.

Huxlin, K. R., Saunders, R. C., Marchionini, D., Pham, H. A. & Merigan, W. H. 2000 Perceptual deficits after lesions of inferotemporal cortex in macaques. *Cerebr. Cortex* **10**, 671–683.

Jacobs, G. H. 1993 The distribution and nature of colour vision among the mammals. *Biol. Rev. Camb. Phil. Soc.* **68**, 413–471.

Lennie, P. 1998 Single units and visual cortical organization. *Perception* **27**, 889–935.

Marr, D. 1976 The early processing of visual information. *Phil. Trans. R. Soc. Lond.* **B 275**, 483–524.

Marr, D. 1982 *Vision: a computational investigation into the human representation and processing of visual information.* New York: W. H. Freeman & Co.

Marr, D. & Hildreth, E. 1980 Theory of edge detection. *Proc. R. Soc. Lond.* **B 207**, 187–217.

Mollon, J. D. 1989 'Tho' she kneel'd in that place where they grew . . . , The uses and origins of primate colour vision. *J. Exp. Biol.* **146**, 21–38.

Osorio, D. & Vorobyev, M. 1996 Colour vision as an adaptation to frugivory in primates. *Proc. R. Soc. Lond.* **B 263**, 593–599.

Regan, B. C., Julliot, C., Simmen, B., Vienot, F., Charles-Dominique, P. & Mollon, J. D. 1998 Frugivory and colour vision in *Alouatta seniculus*, a trichromatic platyrrhine monkey. *Vis. Res.* **38**, 3321–3327.

Stavenga, D. G., Smits, R. P. & Hoenders, B. J. 1993 Simple exponential functions describing the absorbency bands of visual pigment spectra. *Vis. Res.* **33**, 1011–1017.

Sumner, P. & Mollon, J. D. 2000 Catarrhine photopigments are optimized for detecting targets against a foliage background. *J. Exp. Biol.* **203**, 1963–1986.

Tovée, M. J. 1994 The molecular genetics and evolution of primate colour vision. *Trends Neurosci.* **17**, 30–37.

Tovée, M. J., Bowmaker, J. K. & Mollon, J. D. 1992 The relationship between cone pigments and behavioural sensitivity in a new world monkey (*Callithrix jacchus jacchus*). *Vis. Res.* **32**, 867–878.

Travis, D. S., Bowmaker, J. K. & Mollon, J. D. 1988 Polymorphism of visual pigments in a callitrichid monkey. *Vis. Res.* **28**, 481–490.

Walsh, V., Carden, D., Butler, S. R. & Kulikowski, J. J. 1993 The effects of V4 lesions on the visual abilities of macaques—hue discrimination and color constancy. *Behav. Brain Res.* **53**, 51–62.

Wiesel, T. N. & Hubel, D. H. 1966 Spatial and chromatic interactions in the lateral geniculate body of the rhesus monkey. *J. Neurophysiol.* **29**, 1115–1156.

Zeki, S. 1983a Color coding in the cerebral-cortex—the reaction of cells in monkey visual-cortex to wavelengths and colors. *Neuroscience* **9**, 741–765.

Zeki, S. 1983b Color coding in the cerebral-cortex—the responses of wavelength-selective and color-coded cells in monkey visual-cortex to changes in wavelength composition. *Neuroscience* **9**, 767–781.

Glossary

LGN   lateral geniculate nucleus

3

The temporal resolution of neural codes: does response latency have a unique role?

M. W. Oram, D. Xiao, B. Dritschel, and K. R. Payne

This article reviews the nature of the neural code in non-human primate cortex and assesses the potential for neurons to carry two or more signals simultaneously. Neurophysiological recordings from visual and motor systems indicate that the evidence for a role for precisely timed spikes relative to other spike times (*ca.* 1–10 ms resolution) is inconclusive. This indicates that the visual system does not carry a signal that identifies whether the responses were elicited when the stimulus was attended or not. Simulations show that the absence of such a signal reduces, but does not eliminate, the increased discrimination between stimuli that are attended compared with when the stimuli are unattended. The increased accuracy asymptotes with increased gain control, indicating limited benefit from increasing attention. The absence of a signal identifying the attentional state under which stimuli were viewed can produce the greatest discrimination between attended and unattended stimuli. Furthermore, the greatest reduction in discrimination errors occurs for a limited range of gain control, again indicating that attention effects are limited. By contrast to precisely timed patterns of spikes where the timing is relative to other spikes, response latency provides a fine temporal resolution signal (*ca.* 10 ms resolution) that carries information that is unavailable from coarse temporal response measures. Changes in response latency and changes in response magnitude can give rise to different predictions for the patterns of reaction times. The predictions are verified, and it is shown that the standard method for distinguishing executive and slave processes is only valid if the representations of interest, as evidenced by the neural code, are known. Overall, the data indicate that the signalling evident in neural signals is restricted to the spike count and the precise times of spikes relative to stimulus onset (response latency). These coding issues have implications for our understanding of cognitive models of attention and the roles of executive and slave systems.

3.1. Introduction

Understanding brain function requires a precise knowledge of the information present at each stage of processing, how this information is encoded (the neural code) and how different signals associated with different processing stages are combined (integration of neural codes). While the general processing of many cortical and subcortical brain areas in both human and non-human primates is known, the way in which neurons encode inputs and process information to generate output signals is still the subject of intense debate. The neural code underlies the way in which the brain operates and therefore helps constrain the ways in which we think the brain can function by defining the mechanisms by which the brain transmits information. The processing power of the brain is restricted by the capacity of the neural responses to transmit information. If the information capacity of a single channel (neural code) is limited, then additional neural codes (signals) would increase the total information-processing potential of the brain without requiring an increase in the number of neurons.

If neural responses carry different types of information (e.g. stimulus colour and stimulus shape) using different forms of encoding (e.g. spike count and response latency), then these

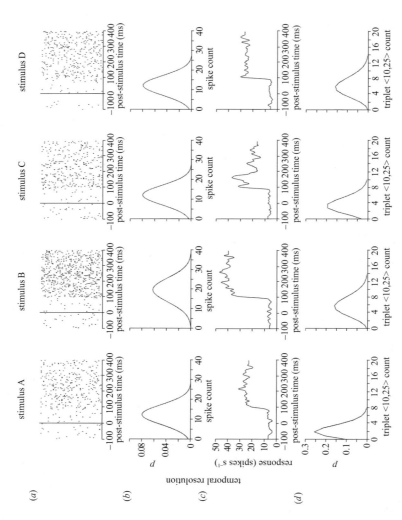

Fig. 3.1. Schematic showing the multiple neural signals. (*a*) Raw neural data. The possible responses to four stimuli (A–D) are shown in rastergram form (each row of dots is the response from a single trial with each dot representing the time when a spike occurred). (*b*) Coarse temporal resolution signals. The probability or relative frequency of each spike count (measured over the period 0–400 ms post-stimulus onset) being elicited by each stimulus (the variance of spike count is twice the mean). The spike-count distributions are identical for stimuli A, C, and D (mean of 12 spikes, variance of 24 spikes²), but the spike-count distribution elicited by presentations of stimulus B is different (mean of 21 spikes, variance of 42 spikes²). Thus, the spike count discriminates between input stimulus B and the other stimuli (i.e. carries stimulus-related information). (*c*) Medium temporal resolution signals. The spike-density function (firing rate as a function of time) for each of the stimuli (temporal resolution of 5 ms). The shape of the spike-density function of the responses to

stimulus C is different from those of the responses to stimuli A, B, and D (after adjusting for the changing spike count in the case of stimulus B). Therefore, the intermediate temporal resolution code can carry information unavailable from the spike count. (*d*) Fine temporal resolution signals (distributions of precisely timed triplets). The fine temporal measure of the probability or relative frequency of observing different numbers of triplet $\langle 10,25 \rangle$ in the response to each presentation of stimuli A–D. Triplet $\langle 10,25 \rangle$ is a triplet of spikes with intervals of 10 and 25 ms. The differences in the distributions of triplet $\langle 10,25 \rangle$ in the responses to stimuli A, B and C can be attributed to changes in the spike-count distributions (A versus B, B versus D) or the spike-density function (A versus C, C versus D). The distributions of triplet $\langle 10,25 \rangle$ differ for the responses to stimuli A and D and this difference is not a reflection of differences in either the spike count or spike-density function. Therefore, the fine (1–20 ms) temporal resolution code can carry information unavailable from either the coarse or intermediate resolution code (the spike count and spike-density function shape, respectively). Substantial evidence indicates that the mid-range temporal measures of neural responses carry information that is unavailable for coarse temporal measures. Recently it has been speculated that the fine temporal measures of responses (lower right) may carry yet more information.

types of information can be processed together ('is a red square present?') or processed separately ('is there a square present?' and 'is a red object present?'). Of current interest is the hypothesis that dynamic links between different neural populations are used to signal particular associations (Singer & Gray 1995). For example, imagine four neural populations, one of which signals the presence of the colour red, another the presence of blue, while the third and fourth populations signal squares and triangles, respectively. Simultaneous presentation of a red square and a blue triangle would activate all four neural populations. However, the decoding is not simple: does the 'red object' belong with the 'square' or the 'triangle'? If an additional code were available that linked these responses in an appropriate way, then the system would be capable of distinguishing 'red square' and 'blue triangle' from 'red triangle' and 'blue square'. Such linking or binding of features (see Singer & Gray 1995; von der Malsburg 1995; for a review) requires that there are separate codes for the attributes (red, blue, square, triangle) and the links (red square, blue triangle etc.).

The traditional method for investigating a signal that is carried by a neural response has been to count the number of spikes elicited within a relatively long time window (the spike count), typically measured in hundreds of milliseconds. As the spikes from a neuron are indistinguishable from each other, the spike-count measure captures all of the available information in the neural activity using this coarse temporal resolution measure. For the neural activity to carry more information, therefore, the encoding must utilize a different temporal resolution.

Figure 3.1 shows schematically how multiple neural codes of different temporal resolutions could be encoded in the responses of a single neuron. Responses of an imaginary neuron to four stimuli (A–D) are shown as rastergrams (*a*). Figure 3.1*b–d* depict three neural codes of different temporal resolution. The spike-count distributions (coarse temporal resolution) are identical for stimuli A, C, and D, and different from that of stimulus B. Thus, the spike count conveys stimulus related information because it distinguishes stimulus B from the other stimuli. Figure 3.1*c,d* depicts neural codes of intermediate and fine temporal resolution. The spike-density functions of stimuli A and D (firing rate as a function of time) are statistically indistinguishable. Although the spike-density functions of the responses elicited by stimuli A and B are different, the difference reflects the difference in the coarse temporal measure of spike count (i.e. one is a scaled version of the other). The spike-density function elicited by stimulus C, however, has a different shape from that of the responses to stimuli A, B, and D. Thus, the intermediate temporal resolution neural signals can carry stimulus-related information (distinguishing stimulus C from the others) that is unavailable from the coarse temporal measure of spike count. Differences in the probability or frequency distributions of the number of triplets of spikes defined by intervals of 10 and 25 ms exist in the responses elicited by each stimulus. However, only the differences between the distributions of the triplets in the responses elicited to stimulus D and the responses to the other stimuli cannot be attributed to differences in spike-count distributions or spike-density function shape. Thus, fine temporal resolution response measures have the potential to carry information unavailable from either the coarse or intermediate temporal resolution signals.

A stimulus-elicited response could convey information using the three different temporal resolutions as depicted in Figure 3.1. Information about the overall stimulus class could be carried by spike count (measured over hundreds of milliseconds; stimulus A versus stimulus B in Figure 3.1). Details of the particular stimulus could be determined from intermediate temporal resolution signals (the 'shape' of the spike-density function, stimulus A versus stimulus C in Figure 3.1, with a temporal resolution of 20–50 Hz bandwidth; Optican & Richmond 1987;

Richmond *et al.* 1987). Finally, a third type of information related to, for example, whether the stimulus was attended or not, could be encoded by the fine temporal resolution signals (stimulus A versus stimulus D in Figure 3.1; Lestienne & Strehler 1987; Abeles *et al.* 1993; Lestienne & Tuckwell 1998; Prut *et al.* 1998). We review in this article the evidence for such coding schemes and discuss the implications of the findings both for our understanding of neurophysiological encoding of information and for higher-level cognitive processes.

In visual-system neural responses, both spike count and intermediate resolution temporal variation in firing rate (20–50 ms precision) carry information that allow stimuli to be differentiated (Optican & Richmond 1987; Richmond *et al.* 1987; Tovee *et al.* 1993). Importantly, the temporal variation in firing rate carries information that is not available from spike count (Richmond *et al.* 1987; Richmond & Optican 1990; Richmond *et al.* 1990; McClurkin *et al.* 1991*a–c*; Eskandar *et al.* 1992*a,b*; Heller *et al.* 1995). Thus, different neural codes exist at coarse and intermediate temporal resolutions. It is also natural to wonder whether fine temporal characteristics (*ca.* 1–10 ms precision) carry information unavailable from either the coarse or intermediate temporal resolution signals (for reviews, see von der Malsburg & Schneider 1986; Abeles 1991; Engel *et al.* 1992; Softky & Koch 1993; Singer & Gray 1995; von der Malsburg 1995; Shadlen & Newsome 1998).

The potential for multiple neural coding to increase the processing capacity of a brain with a fixed number of neurons compared with a unitary coding scheme gives rise to the following questions.

(i) What criteria must be met to establish whether or not neural encoding utilizes more than one code?

(ii) At what temporal resolution does the brain operate and to what extent do neurons show multiple signals?

(iii) What are the implications of the neural code for higher cognitive processes (i.e. is there evidence that the brain might use neural codes of different temporal resolution)?

In the present article we review current experimental results that shed light on these issues.

3.2. Precisely timed spike patterns relative to other spikes

Precisely timed spike patterns relative to other spikes within and between neural responses have been postulated to play an important role in functions such as selection and coordination of motor output (Abeles 1991; Riehle *et al.* 1997; Villa & Bajo 1997; Prut *et al.* 1998) and linking or binding of different attributes of visual stimuli (von der Malsburg & Schneider 1986; Singer & Gray 1995; von der Malsburg 1995). Central to the proposal for a special or unique role of precisely timed spike patterns (*ca.* 1 ms precision) in brain functioning is the requirement that such patterns carry information that is unavailable from the coarse and intermediate temporal response measures. For example, if the number of synchronous spikes between the neural responses can be controlled independently of the spike count, then the number of synchronous spikes could provide information that is unavailable from the spike count. Other precisely timed spike patterns that have been investigated include oscillatory activity between pairs of neurons (for reviews, see Engel *et al.* 1992; Singer & Gray 1995) and more complex patterns of precisely timed spikes such as triplets of spikes with precisely timed intervals (the 'synfire chains' of Abeles (1991), see figure 1; Lestienne & Strehler 1987; Abeles *et al.* 1993; Prut *et al.* 1998; Lestienne & Tuckwell 1998; Oram *et al.* 1999*a,b*).

Precisely timed spike patterns can only carry information unavailable from spike count and slow variations in firing rate (coarse and intermediate temporal codes, respectively) if the precise spike patterns are controlled rather than occurring by chance. Complex relationships exist between the different temporal measures of neural responses, requiring the use of statistical models to determine the potential significance of precisely timed spikes (Dayhoff & Gerstein 1983a,b; Lestienne & Strehler 1987; Abeles & Gerstein 1988; Aertsen *et al.* 1989; Abeles 1991; Abeles *et al.* 1993; Vaadia *et al.* 1995; Lestienne & Tuckwell 1998). Several studies have indicated that the observed numbers of precisely timed spike patterns in a variety of neural systems occur more frequently than predicted from stochastic models (Lestienne & Strehler 1987; Palm *et al.* 1988; Abeles 1991; Singer & Gray 1995; Prut *et al.* 1998; Oram *et al.* 2001). However, the assumptions underlying the analysis have pronounced effects on the number and type of precisely timed spike patterns expected by chance (Figure 3.2, and see Brody 1999a–c; Oram *et al.* 1999a,b, 2001; Prut *et al.* 1998; Richmond *et al.* 1999; Treves *et al.* 1999; Baker & Lemon 2000).

The major determinants of the number of precisely timed spike patterns expected by chance are the coarse and intermediate temporal resolution aspects of the response (spike-count frequency distribution and the PSTH shape, respectively). Precisely timed patterns of spikes reflect temporal relationships or correlation within and between responses. At a sufficiently fine temporal resolution, neural responses can be described as binary events (spike or not) with a low probability of a spike occurring. Very short time bins will have a spike-count Poisson distribution. Assuming independent bins over an extended period, the distribution of spike counts of responses will also be Poisson. Whenever the observed spike-count frequency distribution over repeated trials deviates from a Poisson distribution there must be covariation between different periods of the response. The misestimation of the correlation between periods within a response (as measured by precisely timed spike patterns) due to assuming any response property is increased with measures obtained from techniques that measure the summed activity across many neurons (e.g. local field potentials and more global techniques such as electroencephalogram, functional magnetic resonance imaging and magnetoencephalogram). The accurate assessment of the statistical significance of precisely timed spike patterns is therefore restricted to data collected from multiple single neurons.

Stochastic models that assume that the spike counts follow a Poisson distribution predict fewer precisely timed spike patterns than seen in neural data (Lestienne & Strehler 1987; Abeles & Gerstein 1988; Aertsen *et al.* 1989; Abeles *et al.* 1993; Lestienne & Tuckwell 1998). As non-Poisson distributions of spike count have been reported in responses of neurons in the retina, lateral geniculate nucleus, V1, TE, parietal and frontal lobes (Tolhurst *et al.* 1983; Levine & Troy 1986; Bradley *et al.* 1987; Vogels *et al.* 1989; Snowden *et al.* 1992; Britten *et al.* 1993; Victor & Purpura 1996; Berry *et al.* 1997; Reich *et al.* 1997; Baddeley *et al.* 1997; Berry & Meister 1998; Gershon *et al.* 1998; Buracas *et al.* 1998; Lee *et al.* 1998; Oram *et al.* 1999a,b, 2001), we introduced a new stochastic model (the SCM model; Oram *et al.* 1999a,b, 2001). The SCM model extended earlier models based on non-homogenous Poisson processes by replacing the assumed Poisson distribution of spike counts with the observed frequency distribution of spike counts. Other models match the frequency distribution of spike counts but disrupt other measures that are known to influence the numbers of precisely timed spike patterns that are expected by chance. For example, randomly reordering the interspike intervals within a train maintains the interval distribution but not the PSTH; exchanging spikes between trains maintains the PSTH but not the interval distribution. Jittering the times of spikes in trains retains both the PSTH response and the interval distribution approximately but not exactly. All these model types underestimate the number of precisely timed spike

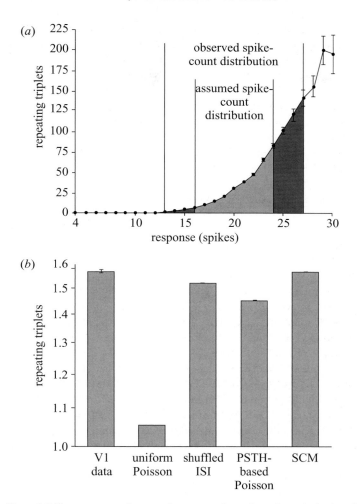

Fig. 3.2. The effect of different assumptions on the expected number of precisely timed spike patterns. (*a*) The number of precisely timed repeating triplets in a trial (mean ± s.e.m.) is a nonlinear function of the spike count. The light shaded area indicates the number of precisely timed spike patterns expected in the responses to a stimulus with the indicated assumed spike-count distribution. If the observed spike-count distribution is larger, the total shaded area (light and dark) represents the number of precisely timed spike patterns expected by chance. Thus, if the assumed distribution of spikes is smaller than the observed distribution, the chosen model will underestimate the number of precisely timed spike patterns expected by chance. (*b*) Assuming a Poisson spike-count distribution will underestimate the number of precisely timed spike patterns expected by chance (V1 data versus Poisson) as spike-count distributions of cortical neurons are super-Poisson. Correcting the coarse temporal response measure (the spike count) but ignoring the mid-range temporal measures (PSTH envelope) also underestimates the number of precisely timed spike patterns expected by chance (shuffled ISI versus V1 data). Correcting for the mid-range temporal measures but not the coarse measures also underestimates the number of precisely timed spike patterns (PSTH-based Poisson versus V1 data). When the coarse temporal response measures (spike-count distribution) and the mid-range temporal measures (PSTH envelope) are matched, the number of precisely timed spike patterns is expected by chance (SCM versus V1 data) (adapted from Oram *et al.* 1999*b*).

patterns randomly expected (Richmond *et al.* 1999). When models incorporate the observed spike-count distribution, PSTH shape and interspike intervals, the numbers and types of precisely timed patterns seen in neural data from visual and motor system responses are almost exactly predicted (Oram *et al.* 1999*b*, 2001; Richmond *et al.* 1999; Baker & Lemon 2000).

A further difficulty in assessing the potential for precisely timed spikes to carry information that is unavailable from coarse temporal response measures arises from the correlation structure of the coarse temporal response measures. The information content of populations of neural responses is dependent on the correlation between the responses of the constituent neurons (Oram *et al.* 1998; Zhang *et al.* 1998; Abbott & Dayan 1999; Panzeri *et al.* 1999; Treves *et al.* 1999). Additionally, the correlation of spike counts assessed over seconds between neurons has a substantial influence on the fine temporal structures. (*ca.* 1–5 ms precision) between responses of different neurons (Brody 1999*a–c*; Oram *et al.* 2001). For example, synchronous spikes between responses of different motor cortical neurons carry information about the timing and direction of limb movement that is unavailable from spike count if one assumes statistical independence between the engaged neurons (Abeles 1991; Vaadia *et al.* 1995; Reich *et al.* 1997; Hatsopoulos *et al.* 1998; Maynard *et al.* 1999). When the observed statistical relationships of spike counts are incorporated into the analysis, the information carried by synchronous spikes is found to be only a small fraction of that available from the coarse temporal response measures and does not therefore form a neural code that carries information that is unavailable from the spike count (Baker & Lemon 2000; Baker *et al.* 2001; Oram *et al.* 2001). Similarly, the incorporation of all the observed coarse and intermediate temporal resolution response properties reveals that the stimulus-related information carried by the precise times of spikes relative to the times of other spikes in the neural responses of the lateral geniculate nucleus and primary and inferotemporal cortices to static visual stimuli is available from the spike count assessed over hundreds of milliseconds (Oram *et al.* 1999*a,b*; Richmond *et al.* 1999).

Observing that a particular precisely timed spike pattern occurs more frequently than randomly expected does not imply that the precisely timed code conveys information that is unavailable from any other temporal measures of the neural response. For example, the mean number of synchronous spikes predicted from the SCM model underestimates the observed mean number of synchronous spikes between the responses of pairs of motor cortical neurons. Thus, there is an excess of synchrony despite the SCM model incorporating all the observed coarse and intermediate temporal characteristics both within and between the responses of the constituent neurons. Furthermore, the amount by which the observed mean number of synchronous spikes exceeded the predicted mean varied with the arm-movement direction (Figure 3.3 and Oram *et al.* 2001; see also Baker *et al.* 2001). However, when the predicted and observed mean numbers of synchronous spikes are plotted against each other, the observed mean numbers of synchronous spikes are linearly related to the numbers randomly expected (Oram *et al.* 2001). For example, if a mean of two synchronous spikes per trial was randomly expected, a mean of three was observed; whereas if a mean of six synchronous spikes was expected, a mean of nine synchronous spikes was observed. In other words, knowing the number of synchronous spikes found in the responses associated with one arm-movement direction enables the accurate prediction of the number of synchronous spikes from the spike count and the PSTH for all other conditions. Given this predictability, it is not surprising that the number of synchronous spikes carries information only available from the spike counts and the correlation of the spike counts (Oram *et al.* 2001).

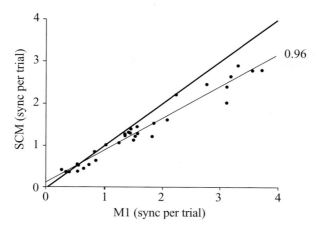

Fig. 3.3. Excess of synchrony does not imply a separable neural code. Sample plot of the number of synchronous spikes expected by chance (SCM model) and the number of synchronous spikes observed in data from simultaneously recorded pairs of neurons in motor cortex for different arm-movement directions. The SCM model underestimates the number of synchronous spikes expected by chance (dots lie to the right of the thick equality line). Regression of the model prediction on the observed number indicates that 96% ($R^2 = 0.96$) of the variability in number of synchronous spikes is explained by the stochastic SCM model. Given that virtually all the variability in numbers of synchronous spikes is explained, it is not surprising that synchronous spikes only carried information available from the coarse and mid-range temporal response measures (adapted from Oram *et al.* 2001).

(a) Interim summary: spike times relative to the times of other spikes

Precisely timed spikes have been postulated to form a neural code at fine temporal resolution that carries information that is unavailable from the coarse and intermediate temporal resolution codes. All the coarse and intermediate temporal response characteristics of the individual neurons, including the observed spike-count distribution, and the correlation between the spike count of different neurons influence the predicted relationship between the coarse and fine temporal codes. Even if the number of precisely timed spike patterns exceeds the number randomly expected, it is possible that the observed number of precisely timed spike patterns can be related to the predicted number by scale factor. When all of these criteria have been taken into account, precisely timed spike patterns can be related to and therefore predicted from the coarse and intermediate temporal resolution signals. Both this predictability and direct information measures in the data to date indicate that precisely timed spike patterns carry information that is also available from coarse temporal neural codes (Oram *et al.* 1999*a,b*, 2001).

3.3. Effects of attention on the neural code and their implications

Human psychophysical studies have shown that visual images such as shape or colour combinations are not always perceived correctly. When subjects are instructed to attend to specific feature combinations, a reduction in the number of errors (false conjunctions) is observed (Treisman 1996). As solutions to the binding problem have been explicitly linked with precisely timed spikes (von der Malsburg & Schneider 1986; Singer & Gray 1995;

von der Malsburg 1995) and because behavioural modulation of stimulus significance has been shown to influence perceptual binding (Treisman & Kanwisher 1998), it is important to assess how the behavioural significance of stimuli influences the information that is carried by the neural responses.

The effects of behavioural significance on the coarse temporal response measures (spike count over hundreds of milliseconds) in the non-human primate indicate that attention enhances responses to effective stimuli (for review, see Desimone & Duncan 1995). The DMS task manipulates the attention given to a stimulus depending on whether the stimulus is pre-sented as a sample (attended), a non-match (ignored) or a match (attended and target). It is found that the mean number of spikes elicited in response to stimuli in an attended condition is slightly higher than when ignored (e.g. Moran & Desimone 1985; Richmond & Sato 1987; Sato 1988; Fuster 1990; Desimone & Duncan 1995; Treue & Maunsell 1996; Reynolds *et al.* 2000). The information carried by precisely timed spikes within and between the responses of simultaneously recorded TE neurons of the macaque monkey during a DMS task has also been examined (Oram *et al.* 1999*a*). Concurrently with the changes in the coarse temporal measures, the numbers and types of precisely timed triplets of spikes (both within the responses of individual neurons and between responses of different neurons) changed with DMS phase. However, both the number and type of precisely timed spike patterns were predictable from the changes in the coarse and intermediate temporal response measures (spike count, spike-count variability, and temporal variations in the PSTH). Furthermore, the information available from the precisely timed spike patterns was redundant with the informa-tion available from the spike count (Oram *et al.* 1999*a,b*). Thus, the influence of behavioural significance on stimulus-elicited neural responses in the non-human primate indicates that attention acts as a 'gain control', scaling the responses to each stimulus by a constant (Motter 1994; Desimone & Duncan 1995; Treue & Maunsell 1996) but otherwise leaving the neural code unchanged (Oram *et al.* 1999*a,b*); Wiener *et al.* (2001).

The information that can be carried by a given neural code is determined by the range of possible responses and the variability of those responses. There is a strong relation-ship between the mean spike count elicited when viewing a single stimulus and the variance of the spike counts on individual trials elicited by that stimulus (e.g. Tolhurst *et al.* 1983; Vogels *et al.* 1989; Wiener *et al.* 2001). The probability of stimulus s being present given the response r, $p(s|r)$, is given by the frequency distribution of responses to stimulus s. Due to the fact that the variance is determined by the mean–variance relationship, the spike-count distribution to each stimulus is fully described by the mean response. Thus, $p(s|r)$ can be determined on a trial by trial basis for each stimulus (or more strictly the probability of each possible mean response given the response r) and hence a single rule, governed by the mean–variance relationship, can be used to decode the neural responses (Oram *et al.* 1998; Gershon *et al.* 1998; Wiener & Richmond 1999; Wiener *et al.* 2001). As the mean–variance relationship remains constant across the different conditions in a DMS task, a single rule can be used to decode the neural responses regardless of the particular DMS condition (Wiener *et al.* 2001).

As behavioural modulation of neural responses affects the mean spike count but not the mean–variance relationship or the fine temporal measures, there is an ambiguity in the signal from inferotemporal neurons during a DMS task. Imagine the responses to two stimuli, A and B. Under passive viewing conditions the mean spike count elicited by stimulus A could be higher than that elicited by stimulus B. With no signal to indicate the behavioural condition, a high spike count could be due to stimulus A being viewed under passive conditions or stimu-lus B being viewed when attended. This ambiguity could be addressed by the presence of a signal from a second source indicating whether the responses should be decoded using the mean responses associated with the attended or unattended state. The available data indicate that is unlikely to be the case. If changes in decoding are given by a concurrent signal, then the effects of attention on neural responses should be evident from the response onset. For example, responses elicited by different stimuli in the inferotemporal cortex deviate within the first few milliseconds of the response onset (Oram & Perrett 1992, 1994, 1996; Tovee *et al.* 1993). The responses to attended and unattended stimuli, however, begin to deviate from each other after a period of some 150–200 ms (e.g. Chelazzi *et al.* 1993; Lueschow *et al.* 1994). The delay from response onset to the differentiation of the neural responses due to attention modulation is consistent with top–down competitive models of attention rather than a change in the decoding of input signals (e.g. Usher & Niebur 1996; Reynolds *et al.* 1999, 2000).

The ambiguity inherent in signals modulated by behavioural context with no 'context-specific' signal can be overcome by examining the outputs from several neurons at a time—a population code. Figure 3.4*a* shows the mean spike counts of simulated neurons to different exemplars or instances of a stimulus class (e.g. 'Is this an apple or a pear?') when attended (thick lines) and when ignored (thin lines). We use the maximum-likelihood method to estimate which stimulus instance was presented. The error of the decoded estimate is taken as the difference between the estimated and actual instance averaged over 10 000 simulated trials. Under an ideal observer scheme (Foldiak 1993; Oram *et al.* 1998), the decoding of the population response utilizes the mean and variability to each stimulus–behavioural-condition combination. With the ideal observer, the accuracy of the population response to unattended stimuli remains constant across all gain-control levels (white circles in Figure 3.4*b*) while the accuracy to attended stimuli increases as the gain control increases (black circles).

If no signal is present for the behavioural condition, as with inferior temporal neural signals, decoding could occur in three ways. First, decoding may occur using a strategy that assumes the spike count on a given trial comes from the means and variances of each stimulus when the stimuli are ignored (thin lines, Figure 3.4*a*). This gives optimal decoding of unattended stimuli (white triangles, Figure 3.4*b*) but a decreased accuracy of decoding attended stimuli compared with ideal observer decoding (black triangles). With this decoding system the benefit of increased attention becomes negligible at a gain control above *ca.* 1.3–1.4. In addition, decoding could occur assuming that the incoming signal is always derived from attended stimuli (thick lines, Figure 3.4*a*). This gives rise to the optimal decoding of stimuli that are attended (black squares, Figure 3.4*b*) but decreased accuracy in determining which stimulus was present when the stimuli are unattended compared with ideal observer decoding (white squares). Finally, decoding could occur using a frequency distribution of spike counts given by a combination of the distribution associated with the unattended responses and the distribution associated with the responses from the attended state. This can be thought of as representing a decoding strategy that is learnt from repeated exposures to the stimuli in both the attended and unattended conditions. The effects of this decoding system lie between the schemes described above (unattended, white diamonds; attended, black diamonds; total distribution, 50% attended, 50% unattended; Figure 3.4*b*). Thus, attention-modulated gain control enhances the ability of a population of neurons to transmit information about which particular exemplar of the attended stimulus class is present, even when no context-specific signal is available. However, in the absence of a context-specific signal, the decrease in the size of the error with increasing attention gain control is smaller than in the presence of a context-specific signal. This indicates that there is a limited benefit in the attention-driven gain control's increasing (more than 1.3–1.4). Restriction of the attention gain-control magnitude also reduces the potential decrement in discrimination between members of a stimulus group when the group is not being attended.

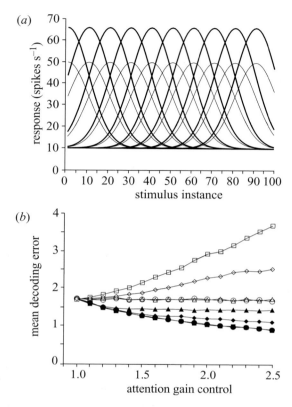

Fig. 3.4. Limitations of attention: discriminating among attended stimuli. Modelling attention as a spike-count gain control reveals the possible limitations of attention. (*a*) The mean spike counts of 10 simulated neurons are plotted for 100 different instances of stimuli (e.g. apple, pear, and orange are all instances of fruit). The variance of the responses to each instance was set as twice the mean spike count. The spike counts were either simulated as being in an unattended state (gain control = 1.0, thin lines) or in an attended state (gain control = 1.4, thick lines). (*b*) Plot of the error as a function of the multiplicative gain control due to attention. Black symbols show the error when the stimuli are presented whilst attended. White symbols show the error when the stimuli are presented but unattended. The error in estimating the most likely input stimulus from the responses of a simulated population of neurons is plotted as a function of the strength of attention gain. Mean errors from 10 000 simulated trials using four decoding strategies are plotted as follows. (1) The ideal observer who 'knows' the response distributions to each stimulus–attention condition (circles). (2) Constant decoding where the observer always assumes spike-count distributions associated with unattended stimuli (triangles). (3) Constant decoding where the observer assumes the spike-count distributions associated with attended stimuli (triangles). (4) Decoding assuming that the response distribution for each stimulus could have come from either the attended or unattended state (diamonds) (see § 3.3 for details). The method assumes an equal probability of each stimulus instance, $p(s_1) = p(s_2)...p(s_n)$; the probability of each of the possible 100 instances of the stimulus was assessed for each simulated trial for each neuron using $p(s|r) = p(r|s)/\sum_{i=1}^{100} p(r|s_i)$ where $p(s|r)$ is the probability of stimulus s being present given the trial response of r spikes, $p(r|s)$ is the probability of observing r spikes given that stimulus s was present and $\sum_{i=1}^{100} p(r|s_i)$ is the sum of the $p(r|s)$) over all n stimulus instances (for review, see Oram *et al.* 1998). The $p(r|s)$ were obtained from the truncated Gaussian distributions given by the mean and variance (Foldiak 1993; Oram *et al.* 1998; Gershon *et al.* 1998). Assuming independence, the probability of stimulus instance s being present is given by the product of the $p(s|r)$ from all neurons (for details, see Oram *et al.* 1998).

Attention not only increases the discrimination between attended stimuli but can also act as a selective filter (e.g. 'Tell me when you see a fruit' rather than 'Is the fruit an apple or pear?'). Figure 3.5 shows the effects of attention-modulated gain control on the discrimination between attended (fruit) and unattended stimuli (non-fruits). The thin lines in Figure 3.5a show the simulated mean spike counts of different neurons when stimuli of different classes are presented

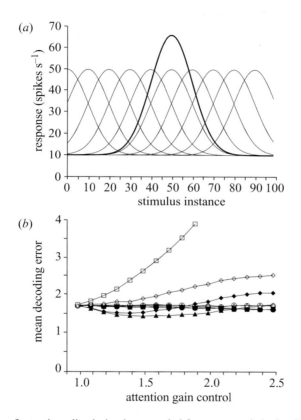

Fig. 3.5. Limitations of attention: discriminating attended from unattended stimuli. (a) The mean spike counts of 10 simulated neurons are plotted for 100 different classes of stimuli (e.g. fruit, vegetable, furniture). The variance of the responses to each instance was set as twice the mean spike count. The spike counts were either simulated as being in an unattended state (gain control = 1.0, thin lines) or in an attended state (gain control = 14, thick lines) when attention was selective towards only one stimulus class (class 50). (b) Plot of the error as a function of the multiplicative gain control due to attention. The black symbols show the error when the stimuli are presented whilst attended. The white symbols show the error when the stimuli are presented but unattended. The error in estimating the most likely input stimulus from the responses of a simulated population of neurons is plotted as a function of the strength of attention gain. Mean errors from 10 000 simulated trials using the following four decoding strategies are plotted. (1) The ideal observer who 'knows' the response distributions to each stimulus–attention condition (circles). (2) Constant decoding where the observer always assumes spike-count distributions associated with unattended stimuli (triangles). (3) Constant decoding where the observer assumes the spike-count distributions associated with attended stimuli (triangles). (4) Decoding assuming that the response distribution for each stimulus could have come from either the attended or unattended state (diamonds) (see § 3.3 for details). For a description of the method see the legend to Figure 3.4 and Oram *et al.* (1998) for details.

in the unattended state. The thick line shows the changes in mean responses during selective attention (e.g. attending stimulus class 50—fruit—selectively enhances the responses of neurons tuned to class 50 but not neurons maximally responsive to other classes). The errors of decoding such a population under different schemes (details as for Figure 3.4) are plotted in Figure 3.5*b* as a function of different levels of attention gain control.

Decoding of the population response using the mean and variability to each stimulus class–behavioural-condition combination indicates that there is only a small decrease in the error when the stimulus class is attended compared with when the stimulus class is ignored (black versus white circles). If the responses are decoded assuming all responses are derived from attended stimuli, the error for unattended stimuli rises rapidly (white squares). Decoding assuming that all responses are elicited by unattended stimuli produces a surprising result. For gain-control values from *ca.* 1.2 to 2.0, this decoding strategy shows mean errors in decoding attended stimuli that are below the error rates for all other decoding strategies. This is because the 'amplified' responses to an attended stimulus (in relation to the unattended mean and variance) are unequivocally decoded as being the attended stimulus. When the gain control becomes too large, however, stimuli that share features with the attended stimulus (i.e. are close in response space) also become so large that they are (incorrectly) decoded as being the attended stimulus.

(a) Interim summary: implications of neural coding for attention mechanisms

The effects of changing the amount of attention given to visual stimuli on neural responses are well described as a multiplicative gain control (Desimone & Duncan 1995). Changes in the fine temporal structure of the responses of individual neurons and between the responses of different neurons are predictable from the coarse and intermediate temporal resolution signals and carry only a small proportion of the information available from the spike count (Oram *et al.* 1999*a,b*). While both the mean and the variance of the spike count change with changes in attention, the mean-variance relationship remains constant, allowing for a decoding mechanism that is constant across different attentional states (Wiener *et al.* 2001). The effects of attention on neural responses are not seen for some 150–200 ms; this is consistent with a competitive mechanism of attention operating between different neurons within a given brain area (Usher & Neiber 1996; Reynolds *et al.* 1999, 2000) and inconsistent with a change in the decoding of the input signals. The absence of evidence for changes in the decoding of inputs with changes in attention and a multiplicative gain control of spike count gives rise to possible ambiguities in neural signals. Simulations of population decoding show that even without a signal of the attention state, decoding the neural spike counts elicited by attended stimuli can still give rise to improved discrimination between those stimuli compared with when the stimuli are unattended (Figure 3.4). The absence of a signal about the attentional state can provide better discrimination between attended and unattended stimuli than when the attentional state during stimuli presentation is known (Figure 3.5).

3.4. Implications of precisely timed spike patterns relative to external events

The precise times of spikes *relative to stimulus onset* (response latency) are another mechanism by which neurons could signal different stimulus attributes within a single response. Recordings from the macaque visual system show that response latency, but not response strength, is heavily influenced by stimulus contrast (Gawne *et al.* 1996; Opara and Worgotter

1996; Oram *et al.* 1997; Reich *et al.* 1997; Oram *et al.* 2002; Xiao *et al.* 2001). The temporal precision of response latency, estimated as the 'noise' required to reduce the information transmitted by latency by 50%, is *ca.* 10 ms (Reich *et al.* 1997). Conversely response strength, but not response latency, is influenced by stimulus orientation, change in perspective view, object part visibility, size or direction of motion (Oram & Perrett 1992; Oram *et al.* 1993, 2002; Oram & Perrett 1994, 1996; Gawne *et al.* 1996; Opara & Worgotter 1996; Oram *et al.* 1997; Perrett & Oram 1998; Xiao *et al.* 2001).

We have recently examined the responses of single neurons in the inferior temporal cortex and the superior temporal sulcus of the macaque monkey to stimuli of constant average luminance that varied in internal contrast (Xiao *et al.* 2001). The increase in response latency with decreasing stimulus contrast was seen for all neurons and could not be attributed to the observed changes in response magnitude (Figure 3.6). Decreasing the stimulus contrast from

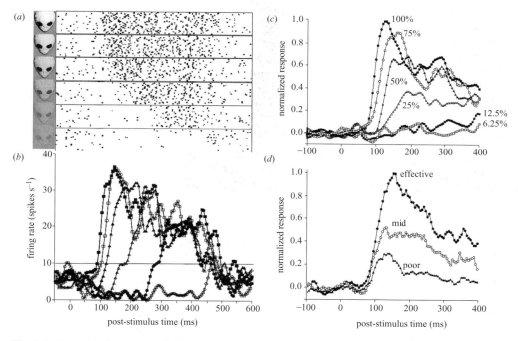

Fig. 3.6. The stimulus contrast influences the response latency. Recordings from neurons in the superior temporal cortex were made using standard techniques. (*a,b*) The effect of changing stimulus contrast on responses of a single neuron. (*a*) The rastergrams of responses to a stimulus of 100%, 75%, 50%, 25%, 12.5%, and 6.25% internal contrast (contrast = $100(L_{max} - L_{min})/(L_{max} + L_{min})$, where L_{max} is the maximum luminance and L_{min} is the minimum luminance within the image). (*b*) The spike-density functions (the sum of the individual rastergrams smoothed with a Gaussian of standard deviation of 5 ms). Black squares, 100%; white squares, 75%; black triangles, 50%; white triangles, 25%; black circles, 12.5%; white circles, 6.25%. (*c,d*) Normalized population responses across neurons. The response latency and response magnitude change with changes in the stimulus contrast (*c*); however, the response latency changes very little when the effectiveness of the stimulus is varied despite large changes in the response magnitude (*d*). Black circles, 100%; white circles, 75%; black triangles, 50%; white triangles, 25%; black squares, 12.5%; white squares, 6.25%. (Adapted from Oram & Perrett (1992) and Xiao *et al.* (2001).)

100% to 6% produced an average latency increase of over 150 ms (Xiao *et al.* 2001), some three to four times the magnitude of the effect reported in the striate cortex (Gawne *et al.* 1996). Thus, changes in stimulus contrast, but not other visual transformations, cause changes in response latency, and this relationship between stimulus contrast and response latency seems to increase as one moves through the visual system.

Changes in stimulus contrast elicit changes in response latency with little or no dependency on response magnitude, allowing for the simultaneous transmission of two neural signals. This has led to the suggestion that response latency could act as a potential signal that facilitates the binding or linking of the responses of different neurons (Gawne *et al.* 1996). For example, the stripes of a zebra close to the observer will be seen as highly contrasting. The stripes of the zebra viewed across the plain become blurred because, from the observer's point of view, the spatial frequency of a zebra's stripes increases with viewing distance. The blurring reduces the effective contrast and so will give rise to visual responses with longer response latency than the visual responses elicited by a zebra seen at close quarters. The changes in response latency, therefore, provide a cue of 'belonging-ness'. Neurons whose response onsets are close together are likely to be signalling information in their spike counts about the same object (Gawne *et al.* 1996). Computational models of object recognition that use a winner-take-all form of competition based on precise arrival times of spikes have been proposed that could utilize contrast-related signals in exactly this way (e.g. Thorpe 1990; Van Rullen *et al.* 1998).

Changes in response latency and changes in response magnitude have implications for cognitive models of brain function. We assume that behavioural decisions are only made when the relevant information has exceeded some threshold (Loftus & Ruthruff 1994; Bussey & Loftus 1994). As the neural code about stimulus identity can be summarized by spike count and response latency (see previous paragraph), we use the time for the cumulative spike count to reach a given threshold to give the predicted pattern of recognition RTs (Hanes & Schall 1996; Perrett *et al.* 1998). Figure 3.7*a* shows the responses from a population of inferotemporal neurons to stimuli of different contrast (data from Xiao *et al.* 2001). (The responses have been normalized so that the average background activity is 0 and the peak response is 1.) Figure 3.7*b* shows the cumulative response from stimulus onset (time = 0) and the cumulative response if the accumulation of the neural signal starts 200 ms after stimulus onset. Figure 3.7*c* shows the time at which the cumulative response reaches 10 spikes. The time to threshold decreases with increasing contrast when the cumulative spike count starts at stimulus onset (no delay). There is an increase in time to threshold when the cumulative count starts after 200 ms and there is no longer a dependency of time to threshold on the stimulus contrast.

Fig. 3.7*d*–*f* shows the predicted activity of temporal cortical neurons to stimuli of different orientations and the times to threshold. Figure 3.7*d* shows the spike-density functions of temporal cortical neurons to stimuli that elicited three different response strengths (data from Oram & Perrett 1992, and see Figure 3.6). As the responses of temporal cortical neurons are reduced when stimuli are rotated about 60° from upright (Ashbridge *et al.* 2000), these responses correspond to the responses to upright images, images rotated 60° from upright and inverted images (see also Perrett *et al.* 1988). The middle right panel shows the cumulative response from stimulus onset (time = 0) and the cumulative response if the accumulation of the neural signal starts 200 ms after stimulus onset. Figure 3.7*f* shows the time for the cumulative responses to reach a threshold of 10 spikes above background activity. The time to threshold depends on the stimulus orientation and, as with changes in stimulus contrast, the time to reach the threshold changes when there is a delay before the cumulative spike count starts. Critically, the response elicited by an ineffectual (inverted) stimulus takes longer

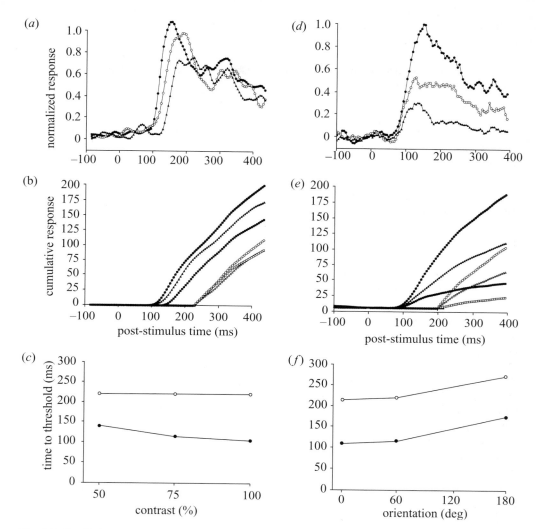

Fig. 3.7. Predicting recognition RTs from neural responses. The population responses to stimuli of different contrasts (*a–c*) and different rotations (*d–f*) are shown. The black symbols show the cumulative response when there is no delay in monitoring the population response. (*a*) The population responses to stimuli of 100% (black circles), 75% (white circles) and 50% (black triangles) contrast are shown. The response latency varies with the stimulus contrast. (*b*) The cumulative response is shown to stimuli of 100% (circles), 75% (triangles) and 50% (squares) contrast. (*c*) Time to threshold (ms) versus contrast (%): delay (white circles); no delay (black circles). (*d*) Population responses to three stimuli of different effectiveness: upright (black circles); 60° (white circles); inverted (black triangles). The responses have approximately the same latency but different magnitudes. (*e*) Cumulative response to stimuli of three different levels of effectiveness: upright (circles); 60° (triangles); inverted (squares). (*f*) Time to threshold (ms) versus orientation (°): delay (white circles); no delay (black circles).

to reach the threshold than the response to an effective (upright) stimulus regardless of the delay in monitoring the neural responses.

As a preliminary investigation into the validity of these predictions, we used human subjects in a dual-task experiment. The principle underlying dual tasks is that the decision-making processes (occurring in the 'central executive' of the working memory; Baddeley 1986) do not start on a second task until the ongoing processes associated with the first task have been completed. If one task—a counting task, for example—is being performed then no executive processing related to a second task—visual discrimination and recognition—can occur. Under this scheme, a counting task followed immediately by a visual discrimination task would involve a delay (while the first task was performed) before executive processes could monitor and process incoming visual system signals. Conversely, a long interval between the first and second tasks should result in no delay in monitoring incoming visual signals associated with the second task. We therefore predicted that recognition RTs would depend on stimulus contrast when there was no delay in monitoring but would be independent of stimulus contrast if subjects were still making decisions about another task (Figure 3.7c). Furthermore, we expected that recognition RTs would depend on stimulus orientation at both long and short intervals between a counting task and the presentation of the visual stimulus.

The preliminary results indicate that the human observers follow the pattern of results predicted in Figure 3.7. Subjects were presented with a sequence of one to four auditory 'pips' followed by the presentation of a letter (R or G) in either its normal or mirror form (reflected about the vertical). The letter (normal or mirror) was presented in different orientations ($0°, \pm 45°, \pm 90°, \pm 135°$ or $180°$ from upright) and at two contrasts (100% and 6%). The interval between the last pip and the onset of the visual stimulus was either 0 or 1000 ms. The subjects' task was first to indicate whether the letter was normal (press the Y key) or mirror (press the N key), then to indicate whether the number of pips was odd (Y) or even (N). Subjects were instructed to make their responses as fast and as accurately as they could. Recognition RTs were taken as the lag between the onset of the visual stimulus and the key press.

Figure 3.8 plots the mean recognition RTs from 11 subjects in such a task as a function of stimulus orientation. The mean RTs were longer when the interval between the last pip and the onset of the visual stimulus was 0 compared with 1000 ms. The mean RTs taken to indicate whether the letter was normal or its mirror image were longer when there was no interval between the last pip and stimulus presentation than when there was a long interval. This indicates that performing the counting task delayed the processing of the visual task (for a review, see Pashler & Johnston 1998). High-contrast images were recognized faster than low-contrast images when the interval between the two tasks was long (compare the black and white triangles in Figure 3.8). The effect of contrast on the RTs was attenuated when the visual stimulus was presented immediately after the final pip ($p < 0.005$, compare the black and white circles). The RT increased with increasing rotation from vertical across the conditions in a statistically indistinguishable way ($p > 0.3$), importantly being independent of the interval between the two tasks (compare the triangles and circles in Figure 3.8).

(a) Interim summary: latency as a precisely timed neural code

Response latency in visual-system responses forms a neural code of relatively high temporal precision (*ca.* 10 ms; Reich *et al.* 2001) where the timing is defined relative to an external event (stimulus onset). Response latency conveys information that is unavailable from the spike counts and their correlation (Gawne *et al.* 1996; Wiener *et al.* 1999; Reich *et al.* 2001)

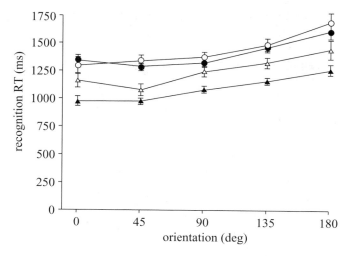

Fig. 3.8. Mean recognition RTs ($\pm$ s.e.m.) for discriminating a mirror image of a letter from a normal letter. Only data from trials where the responses to both the auditory and the visual task were correct have been included. The slope relating RT to stimulus rotation was highly significant and statistically equivalent across the four experimental conditions. The effect of decreasing the stimulus contrast was to increase the recognition RT. When there was a 1000 ms interval between the end of the counting task and the presentation of the visual stimulus an effect of stimulus contrast was seen. As predicted, the effect of stimulus contrast on the recognition RT was reduced when the visual stimulus was presented immediately after the counting task. See § 3.4 for details. Overall analysis: effect of stimulus rotation $F_{4,40} = 34.2$, $p < 0.0005$; rotation by delay $F_{4,40} = 0.27$, $p > 0.8$; rotation by contrast $F_{4,40} = 0.31$, $p > 0.8$; rotation by contrast by delay $F_{4,40} = 1.06$, $p > 0.3$. Effect of stimulus contrast $F_{1,10} = 58.1$, $p < 0.0005$; effect of delay between pips and image presentation $F_{1,10} = 36.7$, $p < 0.0005$; delay by contrast $F_{1,10} = 15.9$, $p = 0.003$. Circles, 0 ms interval; triangles, 1000 ms interval; white symbols, low contrast; black symbols, high contrast.

and therefore seems unlike other precisely timed neural codes where the spike times are defined relative to the times of other spikes. The latency of visual-system responses is influenced by changes in stimulus contrast but not other image changes such as changes in stimulus size, shape, lighting or direction of motion. Preliminary studies with human subjects indicate that changes in response latency with changes in stimulus contrast are relevant to behaviour; in particular how cognitive processes interact (Figures 3.7 and 3.8).

3.5. Discussion

The potential for neural responses to convey information using multiple codes is appealing in terms of increasing the information processing capacity without needing to increase the number of processing elements. However, we are only beginning to understand the highly complex relationship between the fine and coarse temporal codes inherent in neural activity. Even slight errors in the assumptions underlying analysis can lead to very different conclusions about the statistical significance of observed numbers of precisely timed spike patterns where the timing is defined relative to other spikes (Brody 1999a–c; Oram et al. 1999a,b; Oram et al. (2001). Furthermore, the presence of a precisely timed spike pattern, such as synchronous spikes, above chance levels does not imply that the observed spike pattern carries information unavailable from coarse temporal response measures and their correlation. This is true even if the observed number of precisely timed spike patterns exceeds the number expected by chance in responses to some experimental condition and not others (Oram *et al.* 2001). Overall, the evidence that precisely timed neural codes (where the timing is relative to other spikes) convey information unavailable from coarse temporal measures of neural activity is still inconclusive (see also Shadlen & Newsome 1994, 1995, 1998; Treves *et al.* 1999). Additionally, precisely timed spike patterns only reflect a small proportion of the information available from the spike counts (e.g. Oram *et al.* 1999*a,b*, 2001). These observations do not rule out that the *decoding* of the signals involves monitoring and processing based on precisely timed spike patterns. The data to date indicate, however, that precisely timed spike patterns do not form a code that is separable from coarser temporal neural codes in the sense of carrying information that is different from the information carried by coarse temporal neural codes (see Richmond *et al.* 1999).

Given that behavioural modulation of stimulus significance influences perceptual binding (Treisman 1996, 1998) and there is little evidence that behavioural modulation of neural responses influences the fine temporal structure, it seems unlikely that precisely timed spike patterns, such as synchrony (Singer & Gray 1995) or synfire chains (Abeles 1991), are necessarily involved in overcoming the binding problem. An alternative mechanism to precisely timed spikes to overcome the binding problem has been in the literature for many years (Wicklegren 1969; Rumelhart *et al.* 1986). This scheme differs from the precisely timed spike hypothesis in that one response parameter (e.g. spike count) codes multiple stimulus attributes (e.g. colour and form, or form and motion), with each neuron being sensitive to multiple features (Oram & Perrett 1994; Perrett & Oram 1998; Mel & Fiser 2000). Neural networks using a simple learning rule can generate output nodes that show sensitivity to combinations of stimulus attributes (Oram & Foldiak 1996; Wallis & Rolls 1997). Importantly, the feared combinatorial explosion in the number of feature conjunctions requiring coding (von der Malsburg 1995) need not arise, even when approximately two billion feature conjunctions are possible (Ullman & Soloviev 1999; Mel & Fiser 2000).

The absence of a separate neural code indicating attention modulation has implications for the processing of attention. Maximizing the discrimination between attended stimuli involves the presence of a context-specific signal (Figure 3.4). Alternatively, if the mechanisms underlying attention (the gain control) are constrained to give the maximum benefit (error reduction) in discriminating attended from unattended stimuli, then there should be no signal indic-ating whether or not a stimulus is attended. A context-specific signal indicating the state of attention is not evident in the neural codes of inferotemporal cortical neurons. Furthermore, the time delay from response onset to the effects of attention indicates that it is unlikely that such a signal is input to inferotemporal cortical neurons. Thus, the neural codes present in the ventral stream of the primate visual cortex indicate that the mechanisms of attention maximize the discrimination of attended from unattended stimuli.

Changes in response latency and response magnitude are associated with changes in stimulus contrast and changes in stimulus shape, orientation or size, respectively. These two types of coding give rise to different predictions if the evidence or information accumulation is delayed. Assuming the executive processes are simply monitoring the 'slave' visual system, the dual task paradigm achieves just this delay. The effect of changes in stimulus contrast on RTs are predicted, and shown, to decrease if subjects are actively engaged in another task when the stimuli are presented. The effects on RTs of image manipulations that change in the strength of activation of a neural representation (e.g. changes in stimulus orientation) are predicted and shown to be independent of ongoing tasks. The traditional interpretation of differences in dependency on stimulus-onset asynchrony (the delay in the onset of monitoring) has been to assume fundamentally different cognitive processes (executive and slave). The observation that the interpretation of the results from psychological experiments requires an understanding of the nature of the representations and how the underlying neural code changes with changes in the access of those representations presents a new challenge to both psychologists and cognitive neuroscientists.

References

Abbott, L. F. & Dayan, P. 1999 The effect of correlated variability on the accuracy of a population code. *Neural Comput.* **11**, 91–101.

Abeles, M. 1991 *Corticonics*. Cambridge University Press.

Abeles, M. & Gerstein, G. L. 1988 Detecting spatiotemporal firing patterns among simultaneously recorded single neurons. *J. Neurophysiol.* **60**, 909–924.

Abeles, M., Bergman, H., Margalit, E. & Vaadia, E. 1993 Spatiotemporal firing patterns in the frontal cortex of behaving monkeys. *J. Neurophysiol.* **70**, 1629–1638.

Aertsen, A. M., Gerstein, G. L., Habib, M. K. & Palm, G. 1989 Dynamics of neuronal firing correlation: modulation of 'effective connectivity'. *J. Neurophysiol.* **61**, 900–917.

Ashbridge, E., Perrett, D. I., Oram, M. W. & Jellema, T. 2000 Effect of image orientation and size on object recognition: responses of single units in the macaque monkey temporal cortex. *Cogn. Neuropsych.* **17**, 13–34.

Baddeley, A. D. 1986 *Working memory.* Oxford University Press.

Baddeley, R., Abbott, L. F., Booth, M. C., Sengpiel, F., Freeman, T., Wakeman, E. A. & Rolls, E. T. 1997 Responses of neurons in primary and inferior temporal visual cortices to natural scenes. *Proc. R. Soc. Lond.* B **264**, 1775–1783. (DOI 10.1098/rspb.1997.0246.)

Baker, S. N. & Lemon, R. N. 2000 Precise spatiotemporal repeating patterns in monkey primary and supplementary motor areas occur at chance levels. *J. Neurophysiol.* **84**, 1770–1780.

Baker, S. N., Spinks, R., Jackson, A. & Lemon, R. N. 2001 Synchronization in monkey cortex during a precision grip task: I. Task-dependent modulation in single unit synchrony. *J. Neurophysiol.* **85**, 869–885.

Berry, M. J. & Meister, M. 1998 Refractoriness and neural precision. *J. Neurosci.* **18**, 2200–2211.

Berry, M. J., Warland, D. K. & Meister, M. 1997 The structure and precision of retinal spike trains. *Proc.Natl Acad. Sci. USA* **94**, 5411–5416.

Bradley, A., Skottun, B. C., Ohzawa, I., Sclar, G. & Freeman, R. D. 1987 Visual orientation and spatial frequency discrimination: a comparison of single neurons and behavior. *J. Neurophysiol.* **57**, 755–772.

Britten, K. H., Shadlen, M. N., Newsome, W. T. & Movshon, J. A. 1993 Responses of neurons in macaque MT to stochastic motion signals. *Vis.Neurosci.* **10**, 1157–1169.

Brody, C. D. 1999*a* Disambiguating different covariation types. *Neural Comput.* **11**, 1527–1535.

Brody, C. D. 1999*b* Correlations without synchrony. *Neural Comput.* **11**, 1537–1551.

Brody, C. D. 1999*c* On artefactual spike train cross-correlations. *Neurocomputing* **26–7**, 957–962.

Buracas, G. T., Zador, A. M., DeWeese, M. R. & Albright, T. D. 1998 Efficient discrimination of temporal patterns by motion-sensitive neurons in primate visual cortex. *Neuron* **20**, 959–969.

Bussey, T. A. & Loftus, G. R. 1994 Sensory and cognitive components of visual information acquisition. *Psychol. Rev.* **101**, 446–469.

Chelazzi, L., Miller, E. K., Duncan, J. & Desimone, R. 1993 A neural basis for visual-search in inferior temporal cortex. *Nature* **363**, 345–347.

Dayhoff, J. E. & Gerstein, G. L. 1983*a* Favored patterns in spike trains. I. Detection. *J. Neurophysiol.* **49**, 1334–1348.

Dayhoff, J. E. & Gerstein, G. L. 1983*b* Favored patterns in spike trains. II. Application. *J. Neurophysiol.* **49**, 1349–1363.

Desimone, R. & Duncan, J. 1995 Neural mechanisms of selective visual attention. *A. Rev. Neurosci.* **18**, 193–222.

Engel, A. K., Konig, P., Kreiter, A. K., Schillen, T. B. & Singer, W. 1992 Temporal coding in the visual cortex: new vistas on integration in the nervous system. *Trends Neurosci.* **15**, 218–226.

Eskandar, E. N., Richmond, B. J. & Optican, L. M. 1992*a* Role of inferior temporal neurons in visual memory. I. Temporal encoding of information about visual images, recalled images, and behavioral context. *J. Neurophysiol.* **68**, 1277–1295.

Eskandar, E. N., Optican, L. M. & Richmond, B. J. 1992*b* Role of inferior temporal neurons in visual memory. II. Multiplying temporal waveforms related to vision and memory. *J. Neurophysiol.* **68**, 1296–1306.

Foldiak, P. 1993 The 'ideal homunculus': statistical inference from neural population responses. In *Computation and neural systems* (ed. F. H. Eeckman & J. M. Bower), pp. 53–60. Norwell, MA: Kluwer Academic.

Fuster, J. M. 1990 Inferotemporal units in selective visual attention and short term memory. *J. Neurophysiol.* **64**, 681–697.

Gawne, T. J., Kjaer, T. W. & Richmond, B. J. 1996 Latency: another potential code for feature binding in striate cortex. *J. Neurophysiol.* **76**, 1356–1360.

Gershon, E. D., Wiener, M. C., Latham, P. E. & Richmond, B. J. 1998 Coding strategies in monkey V1 and inferior temporal cortices. *J. Neurophysiol.* **79**, 1135–1144.

Hanes, D. P. & Schall, J. D. 1996 Neural control of voluntary movement initiation. *Science* **274**, 427–430.

Hatsopoulos, N. G., Ojakangas, C. L., Paninski, L. & Donoghue, J. P. 1998 Information about movement direction obtained from synchronous activity of motor cortical neurons. *Proc. Natl Acad. Sci. USA* **95**, 15 706–15 711.

Heller, J., Hertz, J. A., Kjaer, T. W. & Richmond, B. J. 1995 Information flow and temporal coding in primate pattern vision. *J. Comput. Neurosci.* **2**, 175–193.

Lee, D., Port, N. L., Kruse, W. & Georgopoulos, A. P. 1998 Variability and correlated noise in the discharge of neurons in motor and parietal areas of the primate cortex. *J. Neurosci.* **18**, 1161–1170.

Lestienne, R. & Strehler, B. L. 1987 Time structure and stimulus dependence of precisely replicating patterns present in monkey cortical neuronal spike trains. *Brain Res.* **437**, 214–238.

Lestienne, R. & Tuckwell, H. C. 1998 The significance of precisely replicating patterns in mammalian CNS spike trains. *Neuroscience* **82**, 315–336.

Levine, M. W. & Troy, J. B. 1986 The variability of the maintained discharge of cat dorsal lateral geniculate cells. *J. Physiol. (Lond.)* **375**, 339–359.

Loftus, G. R. & Ruthruff, E. 1994 A theory of visual information acquisition and visual memory with special application to intensity-duration trade-offs. *J. Exp. Psychol.* **20**, 33–49.

Lueschow, A., Miller, E. K. & Desimone, R. 1994 Inferior temporal mechanisms for invariant object recognition. *Cerebral Cortex* **5**, 523–531.

McClurkin, J. W., Optican, L. M., Richmond, B. J. & Gawne, T. J. 1991*a* Concurrent processing and complexity of temporally encoded neuronal messages in visual perception. *Science* **253**, 675–677.

McClurkin, J. W., Gawne, T. J., Optican, L. M. & Richmond, B. J. 1991*b* Lateral geniculate neurons in behaving primates. II. Encoding of visual information in the temporal shape of the response. *J. Neurophysiol.* **66**, 794–808.

McClurkin, J. W., Gawne, T. J., Richmond, B. J., Optican, L. M. & Robinson, D. L. 1991*c* Lateral geniculate neurons in behaving primates. I. Responses to two-dimensional stimuli. *J. Neurophysiol.* **66**, 777–793.

Maynard, E. M., Hatsopoulos, N. G., Ojakangas, C. L., Acuna, B. D., Sanes, J. N., Normann, R. A. & Donoghue, J. P. 1999 Neuronal interactions improve cortical population coding of movement direction. *J. Neurosci.* **19**, 8083–8093.

Mel, B. W. & Fiser, J. 2000 Minimizing binding errors using learned conjunctive features (vol. 12, p 247, 1999). *Neural Comput.* **12**, 731–762.

Moran, J. & Desimone, R. 1985 Selective attention gates visual processing in the extrastriate cortex. *Science* **229**, 782–784.

Motter, B. C. 1994 Neural correlates of attentive selection for color or luminance in extrastriate area V4. *J. Neurosci.* **14**, 2178–2189.

Opara, R. & Worgotter, F. 1996 Using visual latencies to improve image segmentation. *Neural Comput.* **8**, 1493–1520.

Optican, L. M. & Richmond, B. J. 1987 Temporal encoding of two-dimensional patterns by single units in primate inferior temporal cortex. III. Information theoretic analysis. *J. Neurophysiol.* **57**, 162–178.

Oram, M. W. & Foldiak, P. 1996 Learning generalisation and localisation: competition for stimulus type and receptive field. *Neurocomputing* **11**, 297–321.

Oram, M. W. & Perrett, D. I. 1992 Time course of neural responses discriminating different views of the face and head. *J. Neurophysiol.* **68**, 70–84.

Oram, M. W. & Perrett, D. I. 1994 Modeling visual recognition from neurobiological contraints. *Neural Networks* **7**, 945–972.

Oram, M. W. & Perrett, D. I. 1996 Integration of form and motion in the anterior superior temporal poly-sensory area (STPa) of the macaque monkey. *J. Neurophysiol.* **76**, 109–129.

Oram, M. W., Perrett, D. I. & Hietanen, J. K. 1993 Directional tuning of motion-sensitive cells in the anterior superior temporal polysensory area of the macaque. *Exp. Brain Res.* **97**, 274–294.

Oram, M. W., Gawne, T. J. & Richmond, B. J. 1997 Relationship of response latency and magnitude in the LGN of macaque monkey. *Soc. Neurosci. Abstr.* **23**, 450.

Oram, M. W., Foldiak, P., Perrett, D. I. & Sengpiel, F. 1998 The 'Ideal Homunculus': decoding neural population signals. *Trends Neurosci.* **21**, 259–265.

Oram, M. W., Lui, Z. & Richmond, B. J. 1999*a* Precisely timed spike patterns within the TE neuronal responses of a monkey performing a delayed match to sample task are consistent with chance. *Soc. Neurosci. Abstr.* **25**, 915.

Oram, M. W., Wiener, M. C., Lestienne, R. & Richmond, B. J. 1999*b* Stochastic nature of precisely timed spike patterns in visual system neuronal responses. *J. Neurophysiol.* **81**, 3021–3033.

Oram, M. W., Hatsopoulos, N. G., Richmond, B. J. & Donoghue, J. P. 2001 Excess synchrony in motor cortical neurons provides redundant direction information with that from coarse temporal measures. *J. Neurophysiol.* **86**, 1700–1716.

Oram, M. W., Wiener, M. C. & Richmond, B. 2002 Relationship between stimulus contrast, stimulus pattern, response magnitude and response latency in striate cortex and the lateral geniculate nucleus of the macaque monkey. (In preparation.)

Palm, G., Aertsen, A. M. & Gerstein, G. L. 1988 On the significance of correlations among neuronal spike trains. *Biol. Cybern.* **59**, 1–11.

Panzeri, S., Schultz, S. R., Treves, A. & Rolls, E. T. 1999 Correlations and the encoding of information in the nervous system. *Proc. R. Soc. Lond.* B **266**, 1001–1012. (DOI 10. 1098/rspb.1999.0736.)

Pashler, H. & Johnston, J. 1998 Attentional limitations in dual task performance. In *Attention* (ed. H. Pashler). Hove, UK: Psychology Press.

Perrett, D. I. & Oram, M. W. 1998 Visual recognition based on temporal cortex cells: viewer-centred processing of pattern configuration. *Z. Naturforsch.* C **53**, 518–541.

Perrett, D. I., Mistlin, A. J., Chitty, A. J., Smith, P. A., Potter, D. D., Broennimann, R. & Harries, M. 1988 Specialized face processing and hemispheric asymmetry in man and monkey: evidence from single unit and reaction time studies. *Behav. Brain Res.* **29**, 245–258.

Perrett, D. I., Oram, M. W. & Wachsmuth, E. 1998 Evidence accumulation in cell populations responsive to faces: an account of generalisation of recognition without mental transformations. *Cognition* **67**, 111–145.

Prut, Y., Vaadia, E., Bergman, H., Haalman, I., Slovin, H. & Abeles, M. 1998 Spatiotemporal structure of cortical activity: properties and behavioral relevance. *J. Neurophysiol.* **79**, 2857–2874.

Reich, D. S., Victor, J. D., Knight, B. W., Ozaki, T. & Kaplan, E. 1997 Response variability and timing precision of neuronal spike trains *in vivo*. *J. Neurophysiol.* **77**, 2836–2841.

Reich, D. S., Mechler, F. & Victor, J. D. 2001 Temporal coding of contrast in primary visual cortex: when, what, and why. *J. Neurophysiol.* **85**, 1039–1050.

Reynolds, J. H., Chelazzi, L. & Desimone, R. 1999 Competitive mechanisms subserve attention in macaque areas V2 and V4. *J. Neurosci.* **19**, 1736–1753.

Reynolds, J. H., Pasternak, T. & Desimone, R. 2000 Attention increases sensitivity of V4 neurons. *Neuron* **26**, 703–714.

Richmond, B. J. & Sato, T. 1987 Enhancement of inferior temporal neurons during visual-discrimination. *J. Neurophysiol.* **58**, 1292–1306.

Richmond, B. J. & Optican, L. M. 1990 Temporal encoding of two-dimensional patterns by single units in primate primary visual cortex. II. Information transmission. *J. Neurophysiol.* **64**, 370–380.

Richmond, B. J., Optican, L. M., Podell, M. & Spitzer, H. 1987 Temporal encoding of two-dimensional patterns by single units in primate inferior temporal cortex. I. Response characteristics. *J. Neurophysiol.* **57**, 132–146.

Richmond, B. J., Optican, L. M. & Spitzer, H. 1990 Temporal encoding of two-dimensional patterns by single units in primate primary visual cortex. I. Stimulus–response relations. *J. Neurophysiol.* **64**, 351–369.

Richmond, B. J., Oram, M. W. & Wiener, M. C. 1999 Response features determining spike times. *Neural Plasticity* **6**, 133–145.

Riehle, A., Grun, S., Diesmann, M. & Aertsen, A. 1997 Spike synchronization and rate modulation differentially involved in motor cortical function. *Science* **278**, 1950–1953.

Rumelhart, D. E., McClelland, J. L. & PDP Research Group 1986 *Parallel distributed processing: explorations in the microstructure of cognition.* Cambridge, MA: MIT Press.

Sato, T. 1988 Effects of attention and stimulus interaction on visual responses in inferior temporal neurones in macaque. *J. Neurophysiol.* **60**, 344–364.

Shadlen, M. N. & Newsome, W. T. 1994 Noise, neural codes and cortical organization. *Curr. Opin. Neurobiol.* **4**, 569–579.

Shadlen, M. N. & Newsome, W. T. 1995 Is there a signal in the noise? *Curr. Opin. Neurobiol.* **5**, 248–250.

Shadlen, M. N. & Newsome, W. T. 1998 The variable discharge of cortical neurons: implications for connectivity, computation, and information coding. *J. Neurosci.* **18**, 3870–3896.

Singer, W. & Gray, C. M. 1995 Visual feature integration and the temporal correlation hypothesis. *A. Rev. Neurosci.* **18**, 555–586.

Snowden, R. J., Treue, S. & Andersen, R. A. 1992 The response of neurons in areas V1 and MT of the alert rhesus monkey to moving random dot patterns. *Exp. Brain Res.* **88**, 389–400.

Softky, W. R. & Koch, C. 1993 The highly irregular firing of cortical cells is inconsistent with temporal integration of random EPSPs. *J. Neurosci.* **13**, 334–350.

Thorpe, S. J. 1990 Spike arrival times: a highly efficient coding scheme for neural networks. In *Parallel processing in neural systems and computers* (ed. R. Eckmiller, G. Hartmann & R. Hauske), pp. 91–94. Amsterdam: Elsevier.

Tolhurst, D. J., Movshon, J. A. & Dean, A. F. 1983 The statistical reliability of signals in single neurons in cat and monkey visual cortex. *Vis. Res.* **23**, 775–785.

Tovee, M. J., Rolls, E. T., Treves, A. & Bellis, R. P. 1993 Information encoding and the responses of single neurons in the primate temporal visual cortex. *J. Neurophysiol.* **70**, 640–654.

Treisman, A. 1996 The binding problem. *Curr. Opin. Neurobiol.* **6**, 171–178.

Treisman, A. 1998 Feature binding, attention and object perception. *Phil. Trans. R. Soc. Lond.* B **353**, 1295–1306. (DOI 10.1098/rstb.1998.0284.)

Treisman, A. M. & Kanwisher, N. G. 1998 Perceiving visually presented objects: recognition, awareness, and modularity. *Curr. Opin. Neurobiol.* **8**, 218–226.

Treue, S. & Maunsell, J. H. 1996 Attentional modulation of visual motion processing in cortical areas MT and MST. *Nature* **382**, 539–541.

Treves, A., Panzeri, S., Rolls, E. T., Booth, M. & Wakeman, E. A. 1999 Firing rate distributions and efficiency of information transmission of inferior temporal cortex neurons to natural visual stimuli. *Neural Comput.* **11**, 601–632.

Ullman, S. & Soloviev, S. 1999 Computation of pattern invariance in brain-like structures. *Neural Networks* **12**, 1021–1036.

Usher, M. & Neiber, E. 1996 Modeling the temporal dynamics of IT neurones in visual search: a mechanism for top-down selective attention. *J. Cogn. Neurosci.* **8**, 311–327.

Vaadia, E., Haalman, I., Abeles, M., Bergman, H., Prut, Y., Slovin, H. & Aertsen, A. 1995 Dynamics of neuronal interactions in monkey cortex in relation to behavioural events. *Nature* **373**, 515–518.

Van Rullen, R., Gautrais, J., Delorme, A. & Thorpe, S. 1998 Face processing using one spike per neurone. *Biosystems* **48**, 229–239.

Victor, J. D. & Purpura, K. P. 1996 Nature and precision of temporal coding in visual cortex: a metric-space analysis. *J. Neurophysiol.* **76**, 1310–1326.

Villa, A. E. P. & Lorenzana, V. M. B. 1997 Ketamine modulation of the temporal pattern of discharges and spike train interactions in the rat substantia nigra pars reticulata. *Brain Res. Bull.* **43**, 525–535.

Vogels, R., Spileers, W. & Orban, G. A. 1989 The response variability of striate cortical neurons in the behaving monkey. *Exp. Brain Res.* **77**, 432–436.

von Bonin, G. & Bailey, P. 1947 *The neocortex of* Macaca mulatta. Urbana, IL: University of Illinois Press.

von der Malsburg, C. 1995 Binding in models of perception and brain function. *Curr. Opin. Neurobiol.* **5**, 520–526.

von der Malsburg, C. & Schneider, W. 1986 A neural cocktail-party processor. *Biol. Cybern.* **54**, 29–40.

Wallis, G. & Rolls, E. T. 1997 Invariant face and object recognition in the visual system. *Prog. Neurobiol.* **51**, 167–194.

Wicklegren, W. A. 1969 Context-sensitive coding, associative memory and serial order in (speech) behaviour. *Psychol. Rev.* **76**, 1–15.

Wiener, M. C. & Richmond, B. J. 1999 Using response models to estimate channel capacity for neuronal classification of stationary visual stimuli using temporal coding. *J. Neurophysiol.* **82**, 2861–2875.

Wiener, M. C., Oram, M. W. & Richmond, B. J. 1999 Latency is a better temporal code than principal components in V1. *Soc. Neurosci. Abstr.* **25**, 1549.

Wiener, M. C., Oram, M. W., Liu, Z. & Richmond, B. J. 2001 Consistency of encoding in monkey visual cortex. *J. Neurosci.* **21**, 8210–8221.

Xiao, D. K., Edwards, R. H., Bowman, E. M. & Oram, M. W. 2001 The influence of stimulus contrast on response latency and response strength of neurones in the superior temporal sulcus of the macaque monkey. *Soc. Neurosci. Abstr.* **23**, 450.

Zhang, K., Ginzburg, I., McNaughton, B. L. & Sejnowski, T. J. 1998 Interpreting neuronal population activity by reconstruction: unified framework with application to hippocampal place cells. *J. Neurophysiol.* **79**, 1017–1044.

Glossary

DMS   delayed-match-to-sample
ISI   inter-spike interval
PSTH   post-stimulus time histogram
RT   reaction time
SCM   spike-count matched
TE   inferior temporal visual cortical area in the parcellation of macaque cortex by von Bonin & Bailey (1947)
V1   visual area 1, or primary visual cortex

4

The neural basis of the blood-oxygen-level-dependent functional magnetic resonance imaging signal

Nikos K. Logothetis

Magnetic resonance imaging (MRI) has rapidly become an important tool in clinical medicine and biological research. Its functional variant (functional magnetic resonance imaging; fMRI) is currently the most widely used method for brain mapping and studying the neural basis of human cognition. While the method is widespread, there is insufficient knowledge of the physiological basis of the fMRI signal to interpret the data confidently with respect to neural activity. This paper reviews the basic principles of MRI and fMRI, and subsequently discusses in some detail the relationship between the blood-oxygen-level-dependent (BOLD) fMRI signal and the neural activity elicited during sensory stimulation. To examine this relationship, we conducted the first simultaneous intracortical recordings of neural signals and BOLD responses. Depending on the temporal characteristics of the stimulus, a moderate to strong correlation was found between the neural activity measured with microelectrodes and the BOLD signal averaged over a small area around the microelectrode tips. However, the BOLD signal had significantly higher variability than the neural activity, indicating that human fMRI combined with traditional statistical methods underestimates the reliability of the neuronal activity. To understand the relative contribution of several types of neuronal signals to the haemodynamic response, we compared local field potentials (LFPs), single-and multi-unit activity (MUA) with high spatio-temporal fMRI responses recorded simultaneously in monkey visual cortex. At recording sites characterized by transient responses, only the LFP signal was significantly correlated with the haemodynamic response. Furthermore, the LFPs had the largest magnitude signal and linear systems analysis showed that the LFPs were better than the MUAs at predicting the fMRI responses. These findings, together with an analysis of the neural signals, indicate that the BOLD signal primarily measures the input and processing of neuronal information within a region and not the output signal transmitted to other brain regions.

4.1. Introduction

Modern *in vivo* imaging is one of medicine's most exciting success stories. It has optimized diagnostics and enabled us to monitor therapeutics, providing not only clinically essential information but also insight into the basic mechanisms of brain function and malfunction. Its recently developed functional variant has had an analogous impact in a number of different research disciplines ranging from developmental biology to cognitive psychology.

In the neurosciences, imaging techniques are indispensable. Understanding how the brain functions requires not only a comprehension of the physiological workings of its individual elements, that is its neurons and glia cells, but also demands a detailed map of its functional architecture and a description of the connections between populations of neurons, the networks that underlie behaviour. Furthermore, the functional plasticity of the brain, that is reflected in its capacity for anatomical reorganization, means that a mere snapshot of its architecture is not enough. Instead, we need repeated, conjoined anatomical and physiological observations of the connectivity patterns at different organizational levels. In *vivo* imaging is an ideal tool for such observations, and is currently the only tool that can link perception, cognition and action with their neural substrates in humans.

In this review, I will first very briefly describe the history and basic principles of modern imaging techniques, and then concentrate on the application of MRI to the study of the monkey brain. Emphasis will be placed on fMRI at high spatio-temporal resolution and its combination with electrophysiological measurements. Finally, the neural origin of the BOLD contrast mechanism of fMRI will be discussed.

4.2. Basic principles and history

(a) Neuronal activity, energy metabolism, and, brain imaging

Most current imaging techniques, in particular those used to assess brain function, capitalize on the interconnections among CBF, energy demand and neural activity. It is therefore worth devoting a few paragraphs to an introduction of some basic concepts. Although comprising only 2% of the total body mass, the brain receives 12–15% of the cardiac output and consumes *ca.* 20% of the oxygen entering the body (Siesjo 1978). The energy requirement of the brain, or the CMR, is usually expressed simply in terms of oxygen consumption ($CMRO_2$). This simplification is possible because *ca.* 90% of the glucose ($5\,mg\,kg^{-1}\,min^{-1}$) is aerobically metabolized, and therefore parallels oxygen consumption. $CMRO_2$ is proportional to neural activity and is four times greater in grey than in WM. At rest, the brain consumes oxygen at an average rate of *ca.* 3.5 ml of oxygen per 100 g of brain tissue per minute (Siesjo 1978; Ames 2000). Approximately 50–60% of the energy produced by this consumption supports electrophysiological function, as large amounts of energy are required for the maintenance and restoration of ionic gradients and for the synthesis, transport and reuptake of neurotransmitters (Siesjo 1978; Ames 2000). The remainder of the energy is used for cellular homeostatic activities, including the maintenance of the neuron's relatively large membrane mass.

The brain's substantial demand for substrates requires the adequate delivery of oxygen and glucose via the CBF. The space constraints imposed by the non-compliant cranium and meninges require that the blood flow be sufficient without ever being excessive. It is hardly surprising, then, that there are very elaborate mechanisms regulating the CBF and that these mechanisms are closely coupled with regional neural activity.

Angelo Mosso (1881) first demonstrated the correlation between energy demand and the CBF. He measured brain pulsations in a patient who had a permanent defect in the skull over the frontal lobes. Mosso (1881) observed a sudden increase in pulsation, presumably due to an increase in the flow, immediately after the patient was asked to perform simple arithmetic calculations. Interestingly, there was no concomitant increase in the patient's heart rate or blood pressure as commonly measured at the forearm. Some years later, the neurosurgeon John Fulton (1928) reported an increase in blood flow with increased regional neural activation in the occipital lobe of another patient with a bony defect that permitted the acoustical recording of the bruit from a vascular malformation.

Experimental evidence of the activity–flow coupling was provided by Roy & Sherrington (1890) after conducting experiments on laboratory animals. Roy & Sherrington indicated that some products of the brain's metabolism stimulated vasomotor activity that probably alters the regional vascular supply in response to local variations in the functional activity. In their seminal and remarkably insightful study, they conclude that '...the chemical products of cerebral metabolism contained in the lymph that bathes the walls of the arterioles of the brain can cause variations of the calibre of the cerebral vessels: that in this re-action the brain possesses an intrinsic mechanism by which its vascular supply can be varied locally in correspondence with local variations of functional activity' (Roy & Sherrington 1890, p. 105).

The study of Roy & Sherrington was later followed by the systematic investigations of Kety & Schmidt (1948), who introduced the nitrous oxide technique, a global flow measurement method that initially seemed to disprove the notion of a local coupling of cerebral flow and neural activity (Sokoloff 1960). Experimental verification of the regional coupling of the metabolic rate and neural activity came only from methods allowing local cerebral flow measurements. Although such methods had been used in conscious laboratory animals since the early 1960s (Sokoloff 1981), a precise quantitative assessment of the relationship between neural activity and regional blood flow was only possible after the introduction of the deoxyglucose autoradiographic technique that enabled spatially resolved measurements of glucose metabolism in laboratory animals (Sokoloff *et al.* 1977). The results of a large number of experiments with the 2DG method have indeed revealed a clear relationship between local cerebral activation and glucose consumption (Sokoloff 1977).

The first quantitative measurements of regional brain blood flow and oxygen consumption in humans were performed using the radiotracer techniques developed by Ter Pogossian *et al.* (1969, 1970) and Raichle *et al.* (1976). PET, the technology widely used today for clinical applications and research, followed (Ter Pogossian *et al.* 1975; Hoffmann *et al.* 1976) when Phelps *et al.* (1975) applied the mathematical algorithms developed by Cormack (1973) for X-ray computed tomography; for a historical review see Raichle (2000).

PET images are spatial maps of the radioactivity distribution within tissues, and are thus analogous to the autoradiograms obtained from 2DG experiments. With these PET images, it could be shown that maps of activated brain regions could be produced by detecting the indirect effects of neural activity on variables such as CBF (Fox *et al.* 1986), CBV (Fox & Raichle 1986) and blood oxygenation (Fox & Raichle 1986; Fox *et al.* 1988; Frostig *et al.* 1990).

At the same time, optical imaging using either voltage-sensitive dyes or intrinsic signals, that also relies on microvascular changes, was being developed for animal experiments and was used with great success to construct detailed maps of cortical microarchitecture in both the anaesthetized and the alert animal (Bonhoeffer & Grinvald 1996). Compared with PET, optical imaging has more limited coverage, but substantially better spatial resolution, and it can be combined easily with other physiological measurements including single-unit recordings. Finally, in recent decades another technology has emerged that could be used for conjoined anatomical and functional investigations. This new method was MRI, the technology that offers a substantially better spatio-temporal resolution than any other non-invasive method and which will be dealt with in the rest of this review.

(b) MRI

(i) Nuclear magnetism

The physical principles on which MRI is based are complex, and a thorough discussion of them is obviously beyond the scope of this article. For details, the interested reader is referred to several excellent works on this topic (Abragam 1961; Callaghan 1991; de Graaf 1998; Haacke *et al.* 1999; Stark & Bradley 1999). Here, I provide a brief description of the basic concepts to make it easier to follow the discussion of our own methodology that concludes this review.

Imaging with NMR exploits the magnetization differences that are created in a strong magnetic field. A rough description of the phenomenon can be made with a classical vector model of rotating spins, although quantum theory is needed to fully explain it. Nuclei with an odd number of protons, such as ^1H or ^{13}C, can be viewed as small magnets or magnetic dipoles, the vector representation of which is called the *magnetic dipole moment*, μ. Such dipoles are due to the fact that protons possess angular momentum or nuclear spin. When exposed to an external static magnetic field, the randomly oriented dipoles line up with and precess around the field's direction, thus creating a macroscopic magnetization. The rate of precession is given by the so-called Larmor relationship, $f = \gamma B_0/2\pi$; where f is the resonance frequency in Hz, γ is a constant called the gyromagnetic ratio, and B_0 is the magnetic field. The principal isotope ^1H of hydrogen relevant to most imaging studies has spin $I = \frac{1}{2}$. It has two permissible states with orientations parallel (lower energy) and antiparallel (higher energy) to the main magnetic field. The tissue magnetization that MRI uses is actually due to the tiny fractional excess of the population in the lower energy level (*ca.* 1/100 000 for a 1.5 T field) and varies with temperature and magnetic field strength. The lower the temperature or the stronger the field, the stronger the magnetization is. NMR refers to the frequency-specific excitation produced by transitions between these two different energy states. We are able to measure the energy emitted when the system returns to equilibrium.

Inspired by the work of Stern and Gerlach in the 1920s, Rabi *et al.* (1938, 1939) were the first to apply the method of NMR to measure magnetic moments precisely. With their landmark molecular-beam experiment, they established the fundamental principle behind the technique, the 'trick' of applying a second alternating electromagnetic field resonating with the Larmor frequency inside a constant magnetic field to cause transitions between energy states. In 1946, two groups working independently of each other, Bloch *et al.* (1946) at Stanford and Purcell *et al.* (1946) at Harvard, were able to build on this foundation to measure a precessional signal from a water and a paraffin sample, respectively. In doing so, they laid the experimental and theoretical foundation for NMR as it is used today (for a good collection of classical physics papers on NMR see Fukushima (1989)).

The experiment of Bloch *et al.* (1946) was the first to observe directly the electromotive force in a coil induced by the precession of nuclear moments around the static field, B_0, in a direction perpendicular to both B_0 and the applied RF field B_1. This is basically the way the MR signal is still acquired today. An RF coil is used to apply an RF pulse (an oscillating electromagnetic field of the order of 100 MHz) to excite the nuclear spins and cause the tissue magnetization to nutate on the transverse plane. The magnetization can be rotated by any arbitrary angle, commonly called the *flip* angle, θ. The optimum angle is known as the Ernst angle θ_E given by $\cos \theta_E = \exp(-T_R/T_1)$, where T_R is the time between successive excitations, the so-called repetition time, and T_1 is the spin-lattice relaxation time (see § 4.2b(ii)). For T_R/T_1 around 3, the relaxation between pulses is almost complete. When the pulse is off, the magnetization is subjected to the static field only, and it gradually returns to its equilibrium state emitting energy at the same radio-wave frequency. The induced voltage in a receiver RF coil has the characteristics of a damped cosine and is known as the FID. In the early days of NMR, the RF signal was a continuous wave, and only a single frequency was measured at one time. Acquisition was simplified greatly when Ernst & Anderson (1966) later introduced a technique in which a single broader-band pulse is used to excite a whole band of frequencies that can be subsequently extracted using Fourier transform analysis (Fukushima 1989, p. 84).

(ii) Relaxation processes

So far, I have described the process of obtaining an NMR signal from a tissue or sample. Two more topics need to be touched upon briefly to illustrate the principles of MRI: the process of extracting spatial information to produce an image, and that of generating contrast between the structures of that image that is, between different tissues. Image information is directly dependent on the strength of transverse magnetization; that in turn depends on the (proton) spin density, the so-called T_1 and T_2 relaxation times, and on other physical parameters of the tissue such as diffusion, perfusion or velocity (e.g. blood flow).

Proton spin density is determined by the number of spins that contribute to the transverse magnetization. In biological tissue, this corresponds roughly to the concentration of water. T_1 (longitudinal or spin-lattice) relaxation is an exponential process referring to the 'rebuilding' of the longitudinal 'z' magnetization (along the B_0 direction). Rebuilding occurs because of the Brownian motion of the surrounding molecules, called the *lattice*, that (motion) generates a fluctuating magnetic field. The closer the frequency of the fluctuation to the Larmor frequency the more efficient is the relaxation. Medium-sized molecules, such as lipids, match the Larmor frequency of most common fields more closely, and thus relax faster than water. Tissues differ in their T_1-values, thus providing contrast in T_1-weighted imaging. Figure 4.1 shows examples of relaxation curves for the grey and WM of the monkey brain. Figure 4.1a illustrates an example of a proton-density image. The image was collected with a multi-slice, multi-echo sequence using an FOV of $128 \times 128 \, \text{mm}^2$ over a matrix of 256×256 voxels. Sixteen such images are acquired using repetition time (T_R) values ranging from 50 to 8000 ms. The curves in Figure 4.1b depict the average intensity change of the voxels in cortical (blue) and WM (red) regions as a function of T_R. The spin-lattice relaxation of the WM (red curve) is faster than that of the GM (blue curve), so the former appears lighter in a typical T_1-weighted image than the latter (see Figure 4.1c). The black trace shows the differences between the two curves. The maximum contrast is obtained with a T_R close to the T_1-value of the tissue having the faster relaxation time.

T_2, also called transverse or spin-spin relaxation, however, reflects spin dephasing on the 'xy' plane as a result of mutual interactions between spins. An important mechanism at work in transverse relaxation is the energy transfer within the spin system. Any energy transition of a nucleus changes the local field at nearby nuclei. Such field variations randomly alter the frequency of the protons' precession, resulting in a loss of phase coherence and consequently of transverse magnetization. Figure 4.1d shows a spin-echo (see next paragraph) T_2-weighted image. Relaxation times for different tissues were calculated by collecting 16 such images with T_E-values ranging from 6 to 240 ms. Figure 4.1e shows the T_2-relaxation curves for cortex and WM, with the black trace denoting the difference between the two. T_2 is longer for small and shorter for large molecules, so T_2 provides a contrast with a polarity opposite to that obtained with T_1. In Figure 4.1d, for instance, the cortex (longer T_2) appears brighter than the WM (shorter T_2).

In actuality the transverse magnetization decays faster than we would expect from the spin-spin relaxation process alone. T_2 actually refers to spin-spin relaxation occurring in a perfectly homogenous magnetic field. No such field exists. Local magnetic field inhomogeneities as well as inhomogeneities caused by the application of field gradients during image acquisition (see § 4.2b(iii)), unavoidably cause an additional 'dephasing' of magnetization. For this reason the loss of transverse magnetization occurs much more rapidly, and an FID typically has a T_2^* (T_2 star), rather than T_2, time constant reflecting the *effective* transverse relaxation time. An example of a T_2^*-weighted image is shown in Figure 4.1f. To some extent the rapid signal

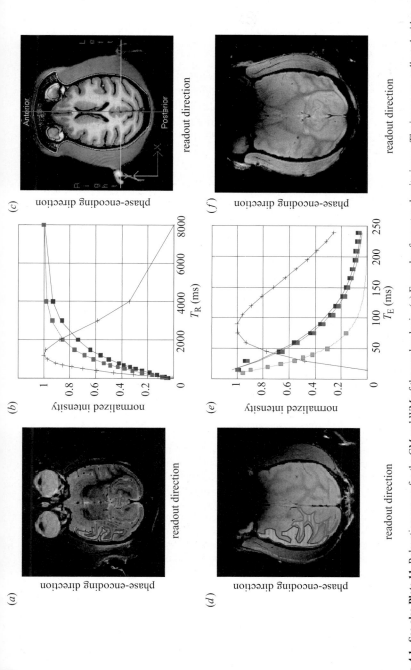

Fig. 4.1. See also Plate 11. Relaxation curves for the GM and WM of the monkey brain. (a) Example of a proton-density image. The image was collected with a multi-slice, multi-echo sequence using a FOV of 128 mm × 128 mm over a matrix of 256 × 256 voxels. Sixteen such images are acquired using T_R-values ranging from 50 to 8000 ms. (b) Average intensity change of voxels in cortical (blue) and WM (red) regions as a function of repetition time, T_R. T_1 is defined as the time required for ca. 63% of the remaining longitudinal magnetization to appear. The more 'watery' the tissue the longer its T_1 relaxation time. The WM (red curve, $T_1 = 1097$ ms) relaxes faster than the GM (blue curve, $T_1 = 1499$), so the former appears brighter in a typical T_1-weighted image than the latter (See Figure 4.1c). The black trace shows the differences between the two curves. The maximum contrast is obtained with a T_R-value close to the T_1-value of the tissue having the faster relaxation. (c) An example of a T_1-weighted image. (d) An example of a spin-echo T_2-weighted image. The relaxation times for different tissues were calculated by collecting 16 such images differing in their T_E-values. (e) The T_2-relaxation curves for the cortex and WM, with the black trace denoting the difference between the two. The T_2-values are longer for small and shorter for large molecules, and the contrast of T_2-weighted images has a polarity opposite to that obtained with T_1. The cortex (longer T_2) in (d) appears brighter than WM (shorter T_2). The green trace shows the T_2^* relaxation curve for the cortical area of (d) T_2 GM = 74 ms (blue curve); T_2 WM = 69 ms (red curve); T_2^* GM = 36 ms (green curve). (f) An example of a T_2^*-weighted image collected in a multi-shot, multi-slice with an EPI sequence. T_E: echo time; T_R: repetition time; GM, grey matter; WM, white matter.

loss can be 'recalled' by inverting the rotation direction of the spins. Indeed, the classic 'spin echo' experiment of Hahn (1950) showed that a second RF pulse (180°) applied at time τ after the initial RF excitation pulse (90°) refocuses spin coherence at 2τ ms. The measured signal is called spin echo (see Figures 4.2 and 4.3) and the time at which the echo arrives is called the echo time (T_E).

(iii) Principles of imaging

One more trick is needed to create an image with encoded spatial information. As Lauterbur (1973) showed, projections of an object can be generated and images can be reconstructed, just as in X-ray computed tomography, by superimposing linear-field gradients on the main static field. Here, the term 'gradient' designates the dynamic alternations of the magnetic field along one particular dimension (e.g. $G_x = \partial B_0/\partial x$). The Larmor relationship thus

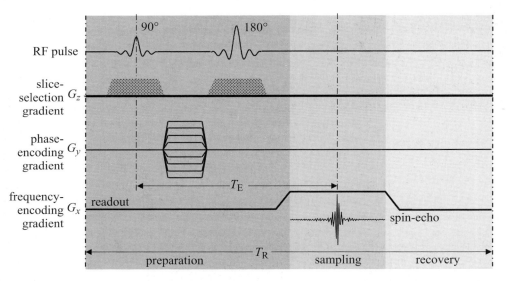

Fig. 4.2. A highly simplified pulse sequence timing diagram. The actual pulse sequences have a number of additional compensatory gradients used to negate the dephasing caused by the slice-selection and frequency-encoding gradients. For the sake of simplicity no such additional pulses are displayed here. The pulse sequence is composed of three distinct phases: (i) the preparation of transverse magnetization; (ii) the actual data collection (sampling); and (iii) sufficient recovery of the longitudinal magnetization before the next repetition starts. In the first phase, the slice-selecting gradient (G_z) is turned on during the 90° RF pulse. The phase-encoding gradient (G_y) turns on as soon as the RF activity ceases. The spatial location of the spins along this gradient is again encoded by their frequency. But when the gradient is turned off all spins return to uniform frequency, and the spatial information is only preserved in the form of their phase angles, which remain different according to their location along the y-axis (hence the phase-encoding direction). Obviously the measured phase is the vectorial sum of all phases along the y direction. Individual phases (encoding spatial location) can be only recovered by applying phase-encoding pulses of different amplitudes during each repetition, depicted here as multiple polygons. The second RF pulse (180°) combined with a second slice-selection gradient inverts the phase of the transverse magnetization and thus generates a spin echo after time $T_E/2$. Finally, a third gradient is used to create the positional dependence of frequency during the collection of the spin echo. T_E, echo time; T_R, repetition time. G_z, G_y and G_x, the slice, phase-encoding and frequency-encoding gradients, respectively.

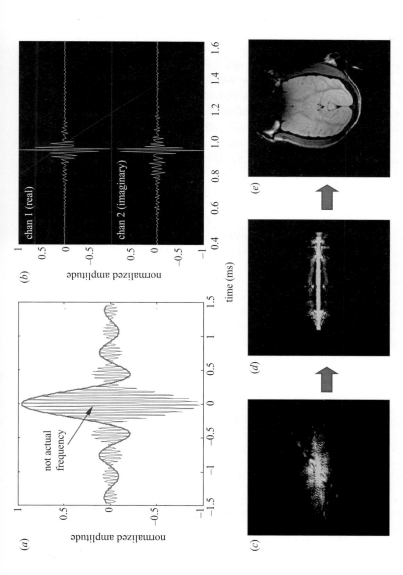

Fig. 4.3. See also Plate 12. Image formation. (*a*) A typical RF excitation pulse (here sinc(*x*) = sin(*x*)/*x*) used to nutate the net magnetization down into the *xy* plane. The RF pulse actually consists of the product of a sine wave of the Larmor frequency with the sinc function. In the 4.7 T magnet this is *ca.* 200 MHz. The blue line depicts the sine wave at much lower frequencies for illustration purposes. $\gamma = 42.57$ MHz T^{-1}; resonance frequency = 200 MHz; duration = 3 ms; BW = 1.85 kHz. (*b*) The two spin echoes produced by an inversion pulse of 180° (see also Figure 4.2). In MRI the initially very high RF signal (MHz range) is typically converted into an audio signal (kHz range) by comparing the RF signal with a reference signal (phase-sensitive detection). In fact, to improve SNR the signal is collected by two PSDs that are 90° out of phase (upper and lower panels of (*b*)). The converted signal is digitized and the two channels are represented as the real and imaginary part of complex numbers (alternatively they can be transformed into the magnitude and phase of the signal). Each row of the *k* space consists of a sequence of such numbers. $T_E = 15$ ms; duration = 3 ms. (*c*) Magnitude of the *k* space in a spin-echo experiment. Each row is an echo with the same frequency composition but different phase encoding. Top and bottom rows have the strongest phase-encoding gradient and hence the largest dephasing (weakest signal). The strongest echo is in the centre of the *k* space, where no phase-encoding occurs. (*d*) The first Fourier transformation along the phase-encoding direction resulting in the actual image. (*e*) The second Fourier transformation along the phase-encoding direction resulting in the actual image.

becomes $f = \gamma B_0 + G_x x + G_y y + G_z z$), relating spatial encoding by means of, say, a gradient G_x to the MR signal with the frequency content f. The gradient determines a range of Larmor frequencies, and those frequencies can in turn provide exact position information. This is the trick. In an actual MRI sequence there are a couple of basic elements for encoding the spatial information, that is, gradient schemes for slice selection (G_{ss}), frequency encoding (readout) (G_{ro}), and phase encoding (G_{pe}). Here, we arbitrarily assign the directions x, y and z to the readout (frequency encoding), phase encoding and slice-selection gradient directions (ro, pe, and ss, respectively).

Figure 4.2 shows a typical pulsing diagram for a spin-echo image (commonly referred to as the conventional spin-warp two-dimensional fast Fourier transform image). To select a slice, a frequency-selective RF pulse is used in combination with a field gradient perpendicular to the desired slice. Figure 4.3a shows a typical RF pulse (sinc function) used to excite the tissue and Figure 4.3b shows the spin echoes measured by two different channels (90° out of phase) combined as complex numbers. Two further orthogonal gradients are used to extract the spatial information within the slice. The 'readout' gradient is applied at the same time as the MR data are actually acquired ('read'), while the 'phase-encode' gradient encodes the second dimension in the image plane. For an image with $N_{ro}N_{pe}$ pixels, N_{ro} points are sampled with the same 'read-out' gradient G_{ro}, whereas for phase encoding the gradient G_{pe} is incremented N_{pe} times. Thus, in each readout step, the collected signal consists of the same frequencies differing only in their phases as determined by each phase-encoding step. The acquired $N_{ro}N_{pe}$ data matrix, usually termed the k space (Figure 4.3c), with $k_{ro,pe,ss} = \gamma \int G_{ro,pe,ss} dt$, represents the image in the inverse spatial domain. Performing a Fourier transform for each row extracts the amplitudes (Figure 4.3d), and performing it for each column extracts the phase angles of the frequency components (Figure 4.3e). The amplitude of the central point of the k space determines the SNR of the global image. Sampling a larger number of points farther and farther away from the k space centre encodes the image's details and increases image resolution.

In many MRI methods, the acquisition of *each row* of the k space is preceded by an RF excitation. The pulse T_R is dictated by the rate of recovery of longitudinal magnetization, and the phase-encoding steps are determined by the desired resolution. Decreasing either one will affect the image quality. This makes high-quality conventional imaging too slow for comparing the MRI signal with its underlying neural activity. EPI (Mansfield 1977) permits substantially faster data acquisition, and this is the approach currently being used in most rapid imaging experiments and the one used in the studies described here (for a comprehensive review on EPI see Schmitt *et al.* (1998)). With EPI, an entire image can be created following a single excitatory pulse because it collects the complete dataset within the short time that the FID signal is detectable, that is, within a time for most applications limited by T_2^*. Refocusing in EPI is achieved by the gradient ('gradient echo') rather than RF pulses. Along the readout direction an oscillating gradient permits the generation of a train of echoes. Along the phase-encoding direction, short blips advance the encoding to the next k space line. There are many different ways of sampling the k space corresponding to different imaging techniques (Callaghan 1991). The scheme used is very often a zigzag pattern, scanning even and odd lines from left to right and vice versa. The T_E is defined here as the time from the excitation pulse to the centre of the k space. EPI can acquire images within a very short time (less than 50 ms) and does so with a short T_R to the order of 100 ms. Its correct implementation, however, demands careful tuning of sequence parameters to minimize image artifacts.

(iv) Image quality

Image quality is determined by a number of interdependent variables, including the SNR, the CNR, and the spatial resolution. The SNR and CNR are both functions of the relaxation times, the scan properties, such as flip angle, interpulse delay times and the number of averages, the quality factor of the resonant input circuit (see § 4.4b(i)), the noise levels of the receiver, and the effective unit volume. The latter is determined by the slice thickness d, the number of phase-encoding steps N_{pe}, the number of samples in the frequency-encoding direction N_{ro} and the FOV. For an FOV of dimensions $D_{ro}D_{pe}$ the volume size is given by

$$d\frac{D_{ro}D_{pe}}{N_{ro}N_{pe}},$$

and the SNR by

$$SNR \approx \frac{dD_{ro}D_{pe}}{\sqrt{N_{ro}N_{pe}}}\sqrt{NEX},$$

where NEX is the number of excitations (or averages). SNR also depends on the sampling frequency bandwidth; reducing the bandwidth increases SNR at the cost of increased sampling time. The maximum achievable SNR is of course determined to a significant extent by the strength of the static magnetic field, B_0. Increasing the field strengthens the MR signal in an approximately linear fashion. In practice, the SNR and CNR can be estimated by measuring the signal of a tissue region or the signal difference between two different tissue regions and expressing that signal in units of the standard deviation of the background signal (noise).

Spatial resolution is the smallest resolvable distance between two different image features. In the field of optics, it is usually determined on the basis of the Rayleigh criterion, wherein objects can be distinguished when the maximal intensity of one occurs at the first diffraction minimum of the other. An analogous expression of this criterion which is directly applicable to MRI is that between two maxima the intensity must drop below 81% of its maximum value. Nominally, the spatial resolution of an MR image is determined by the size of the image elements (voxels), that in turn is defined as the volume covered (FOV) divided by the image points sampled during acquisition ($R_{nom} = $ FOV/N). In other words, voxel size is defined by the slice thickness, the number of samples in the phase and frequency-encoding directions, and the FOV. The optimal selection of voxel size is important. Large voxels will inevitably average the signal from the tissue with functional variations across space. The smearing of local information acquired with large voxels—usually termed the partial volume effect— alters both the waveform of the haemodynamic response and the fractional change in the MR signal. Reducing the voxel size, however, while reducing the partial volume effects, affects both the SNR and the CNR of the image, thus imposing strong limitations on the image quality. Such limitations can be minimized using stronger magnetic fields and smaller RF coils.

The nominal resolution of an image can be improved by Fourier interpolation (or the mathematically equivalent 'zero filling' in k space). Typically, signals acquired with a resolution of $N_{ro}N_{pe}$ can be reconstructed as $2N_{ro}2N_{pe}$ images. This improves digital resolution by making implicit information visible to the viewer, but does not change the spatial response function of the imaging method or the image resolution according to the Rayleigh criterion.

Like the SNR and CNR, the spatial resolution of an MR image depends on a number of scan factors, including gradient strength, sampling frequency bandwidth, reconstruction method and measurement sensitivity. All other factors being optimized, the last can be greatly improved by closely matching the size, shape and proximity of an RF coil to the structure of interest, a strategy that substantially improves the SNR of the image by decreasing the noise detected by the coil. A number of different coil types have been developed over the last few decades to achieve this, ranging from simple surface coils (Ackerman *et al.* 1980) to quadrature coil combinations (Hyde *et al.* 1987) and a phased array of several coil loops (Roemer *et al.* 1990). Further improvement of sensitivity can be obtained by using implantable, directly or inductively coupled RF coils (see § 4.3).

4.3. Functional MRI with bold contrast

MRI, like PET, can be used to map activated brain regions by exploiting the well-established interrelation between physiological function, energy metabolism and localized blood supply. Different techniques can be employed to measure different aspects of the haemodynamic response. For example, blood-supply changes can be used in perfusion-based fMRI, that measures blood flow quantitatively. Here, I shall concentrate on a single technique exploiting the BOLD contrast which, because of its reasonably high sensitivity and wide accessibility, is the mainstay of brain fMRI studies.

The BOLD contrast mechanism was first described by Ogawa *et al.* (1990*a,b*) and Ogawa & Lee (1990) in rat brain studies with strong magnetic fields (7 and 8.4 T). Ogawa noticed that the contrast of very high resolution images ($65 \times 65 \times 700 \, \mu m^3$) acquired with a gradient-echo-pulse sequence depicts anatomical details of the brain as numerous dark lines of varying thickness. These lines could not be seen when the usual spin-echo sequences were used, and they turned out to be image 'artefacts', signal dropouts from blood vessels (Ogawa *et al.* 1990*a*). In other words, by accentuating the susceptibility effects of dHb in the venous blood with gradient-echo techniques, Ogawa discovered a contrast mechanism reflecting the blood oxygen level, and realized the potential importance of its application by concluding that 'BOLD contrast adds an additional feature to magnetic resonance imaging and complements other techniques that are attempting to provide PET-like measurements related to regional neural activity' (Ogawa *et al.* 1990*b*). Shortly after this, the effect was nicely demonstrated in the cat brain during the course of anoxia (Turner *et al.* 1991). As is now known, the phenomenon is indeed due to the field inhomogeneities induced by the endogenous MRI contrast agent dHb.

The paramagnetic nature of dHb (Pauling & Coryell 1936) and its influence on the MR signal (Brooks *et al.* 1975) were well known before the development of MRI. Haemoglobin consists of two pairs of polypeptide chains (globin), each of which is attached to a complex of protoporphyrin and iron (haem group). In dHb the iron (Fe^{2+}) is in a paramagnetic high-spin state, as four of its six outer electrons are unpaired and act as an exogenous paramagnetic agent. When oxygenated, the haem iron changes to a low-spin state by receiving the oxygen's electrons.

The magnetic properties of dHb would be of little value if haemoglobin were evenly distributed in all the tissues. Instead, paramagnetic dHb is confined in the intracellular space of the red blood cells that in turn are restricted to the blood vessels. Magnetic susceptibility differences between the dHb-containing compartments and the surrounding space generate magnetic field gradients across and near the compartment boundaries. Pulse sequences designed to be highly sensitive to such susceptibility differences, like those used by Ogawa in his seminal studies (Ogawa & Lee 1990; Ogawa *et al.* 1990*a,b*), generate signal alterations whenever the concentration of dHb changes. The field inhomogeneities induced by dHb mean that neural activity should result in a BOLD signal reduction. However, during brain activation the BOLD signal increases rather than decreasing relative to a resting level. This is because activation within a region causes an increase in CBF and the use of glucose, but not a commensurate increase in the oxygen consumption rate (Fox & Raichle 1986; Fox *et al.* 1988). This results in a decreased oxygen extraction fraction and lower dHb content per volume unit of brain tissue.

Not surprisingly, the groundbreaking work of Ogawa excited great interest in the application of BOLD fMRI to humans. MR-based CBV imaging had already been demonstrated in humans using high-speed EPI techniques and the exogenous paramagnetic contrast agent gadolinium (Belliveau *et al.* 1991; Rosen *et al.* 1991). In 1992, however, three groups simultaneously and independently obtained results in humans with the BOLD mechanism (Bandettini *et al.* 1992; Kwong *et al.* 1992; Ogawa *et al.* 1992), starting the flood of fMRI publications that have been appearing in scientific journals ever since.

Research over the last decade has established that BOLD contrast depends not only on blood oxygenation but also on CBF and CBV, representing a complex response controlled by several parameters (Ogawa *et al.* 1993, 1998; Weisskoff *et al.* 1994; Kennan *et al.* 1994; Boxerman *et al.* 1995a,b; Buxton & Frank 1997; Van Zijl *et al.* 1998). Despite this complexity, much progress has been made toward quantitatively elucidating various aspects of the BOLD signal and the way it relates to the haemodynamic and metabolic changes occurring in response to elevated neuronal activity (Kim & Ugurbil 1997; Buxton *et al.* 1998; Van Zijl *et al.* 1998).

BOLD fMRI has also been applied successfully in anaesthetized or conscious animals, including rodents (Hsu *et al.* 1998; Lahti *et al.* 1998; Bock *et al.* 1998; Tuor *et al.* 2000; Burke *et al.* 2000; Ances *et al.* 2000; Burke *et al.* 2000; Chang & Shyu 2001), rabbits (Wyrwicz *et al.* 2000), cats (Jezzard *et al.* 1997), bats (Kamada *et al.* 1999), and recently monkeys (Nakahara *et al.* 2002; Logothetis *et al.* 1998, 1999; Disbrow *et al.* 1999; Zhang *et al.* 2000; Disbrow *et al.* 2000; Vanduffel *et al.* 2001; Dubowitz *et al.* 2001). What follows describes the use of BOLD fMRI in monkeys (*Macaca mulatta*) and its combination with electrophysiological measurements in an attempt to investigate the neural basis of the BOLD response.

4.4. MRI of the monkey brain

fMRI and microelectrode recordings are complementary techniques, providing information on two different spatio-temporal scales. The electrodes have excellent spatio-temporal resolution but very poor coverage, while fMRI has relatively poor resolution but can yield important information on a larger spatio-temporal scale. The development and application of NMR techniques (e.g. imaging, spectroscopy) for the non-human primate enables the investigation of certain levels of neural organization that cannot be studied by electrodes alone. These include the study of:

(i) long-range interactions between different brain structures;
(ii) task- and learning-related neurochemical changes by means of localized *in vivo* spectroscopy or MRS imaging; ·
(iii) dynamic changes in the magnitude and location of activated regions—over periods of minutes to days—with priming, learning and habituation;
(iv) dynamic connectivity patterns by means of labelling techniques involving MR contrast agents; and
(v) plasticity and reorganization following experimentally placed focal lesions.

In addition, the application of this technique to the behaviour of monkeys has the potential to build a bridge between human studies and the large body of animal research carried out over the last 50 years.

Monkeys are ideal experimental animals because a great deal is known about the organization of their sensory systems that are functionally very similar to those of humans. In addition, comparisons of psychophysical data from humans and the most commonly used species, the rhesus macaque, have revealed remarkable behavioural similarities between the two species. Thus, MRI in monkeys not only provides insights into the neural origin of the fMRI signals, but it can do so in the context of different types of behaviour. With this conviction, we set out to develop and apply MRI (and MRS) in monkeys, using both conventional volume coils for whole-head scanning and implanted coils allowing imaging with high spatial resolution.

Figure 4.4 shows the system used for imaging the monkey brain. It is a vertical 4.7 T scanner with a 40 cm diameter bore (Biospec 47/40v; Bruker Medical Inc., Ettlingen, Germany).

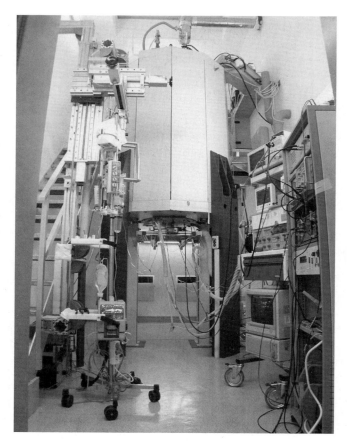

Fig. 4.4. The scanner system. A vertical 4.7 T magnet with a 40 cm diameter bore was used to image monkey brains. The magnet has local passive shielding to permit the use of neurophysiology and anaesthesia equipment. It is equipped with a $50 \, mT \, m^{-1}$ (180 μs rise time) actively shielded gradient coil (Bruker, B-GA 26) with an inner diameter of 26 cm. A primate chair and a special transport system were designed and built for positioning the monkey within the magnet.

The scanner is equipped with a $50\,mT\,m^{-1}$ (180 μs rise time) actively shielded gradient coil (Bruker, B-GA 26) of 26 cm inner diameter. A primate chair and a special transport system were designed and built to position the monkey inside the magnet (Logothetis *et al.* 1999). Whole-head scans were carried out with either linear birdcage-type coils or with custom-made linear homogeneous saddle coils. For high-resolution fMRI, we used customized small RF coils (see § 4.4*b*) which had been optimized for increased sensitivity over a given ROI (Logothetis *et al.* 2002). In the combined physiology and fMRI sessions (see § 4.5*a*), the coils were attached around the recording chamber and were used as transceivers (Logothetis *et al.* 2001).

(a) Large FOV imaging: volume coils

This section introduces a few applications with volume, whole-head coils that demonstrate the value of the technique for research involving:

  (i) the comparison of monkey and human sensory systems;
 (ii) microelectrode recordings from different sites of distributed neural networks subserving a behaviour under investigation; or
(iii) the planning of selective focal brain lesions in the context of investigations into behavioural disorders to illuminate the role of a particular brain region.

Details on these applications can be found in various recent publications (Logothetis *et al.* 1999; Rainer *et al.* 2001; Tolias *et al.* 2001; Brewer *et al.* 2002; Sereno *et al.* 2002).

(i) Activation of the thalamus and visual cortex

Figure 4.5 shows the results from a macaque monkey scanned under isoflurane (0.4%) anaesthesia (Logothetis *et al.* 1999). The left half of the figure depicts typical *z*-score maps for 12 horizontal slices. No threshold was applied to the statistical maps so that one can directly see the strength of the difference signal and its relationship to noise. On the right half, thresholded *z*-score maps showing brain activation are colour coded and superimposed on anatomical scans as slices of the computer-rendered monkey head. The activation was elicited by a polar-transformed checkerboard pattern rotating in alternating directions.

   Figure 4.5*a,b* shows a robust BOLD signal in the LGN as well as in the striate and extrastriate cortices. The anatomical scan was acquired with an FOV of 128 mm × 128 mm with a matrix of 256 × 256 and slice thickness of 0.5 mm using the three-dimensional MDEFT (Ugurbil *et al.* 1993) pulse sequence. The fMRI was carried out by multi-slice (13 slices, 2 mm thick), multi-shot (eight segments) gradient-recalled EPI, with an FOV of 128 mm × 128 mm on a 128 × 128 matrix and a voxel size of 1 mm × 1 mm × 2 mm.

(ii) Retinotopy

The robustness of activation and the spatial selectivity of the BOLD signal can be examined by exploiting the well-established retinotopic organization of the visual system. In humans, retinotopy can be reliably demonstrated in fMRI by using slowly moving, phase-encoded retinotopic stimuli (Engel *et al.* 1994, 1997; Deyoe *et al.* 1994; Sereno *et al.* 1995).

   We have used the same approach to study the retinotopical organization of the monkey visual areas. As in human studies, the stimuli consisted of a series of slowly rotating wedges or expanding rings, each wedge or ring being a collection of flickering squares (Engel *et al.* 1994, 1997; Wandell *et al.* 2000). The ring typically begins as a small spot located at the centre of the visual field and then grows until it travels beyond the edge of the stimulus display.

(a)   (b)

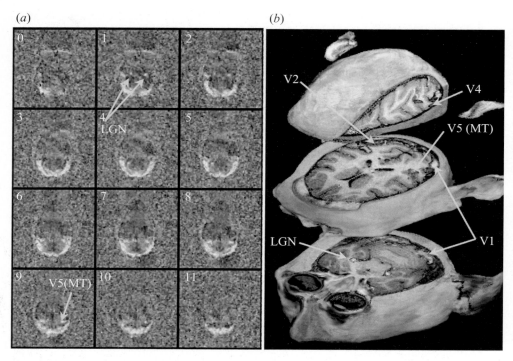

Fig. 4.5. See also Plate 13. (*a*) BOLD activation shown in terms of *z*-score maps. The specificity of the signal enables the visualization of anatomical details in the occipital lobe. (*b*) Activation maps super-imposed on anatomical three-dimensional MDEFT scans (0.125 μl voxel size). The figure shows activation of the LGN, striate and some extrastriate areas including V2, V3, V4, and V5 (MT). V1 activation covers almost the entire representation of the perifovea (the horizontal extent of the checkerboard stimulus was 30°). The V1 regions showing high activation (yellow) lie within the cortical representation of the fovea.

As it disappears from view, it is replaced by a new spot starting at the centre. Such an expanding stimulus causes a travelling wave of neural activity beginning a couple of millimetres posterior to the lunate sulcus (Figure 4.6*a,b*) and travelling in the posterior direction toward the pole of the occipital lobe. The temporal phase of the MRI signal varies as a function of eccentricity, and this phase can be used to generate the eccentricity maps shown in Figure 4.6*c* (adapted from Brewer *et al.* (2002)). This technique made it possible to identify the boundaries between visual areas V1, V2, V3, and V4, and V5 (MT) and to measure the visual-field eccentricity functions that reveal the distribution of foveal and peripheral signals within the ventral and dorsal streams, respectively (Wandell *et al.* 2000; Brewer *et al.* 2002). The maps obtained in this manner are in excellent agreement with those derived from monkeys with anatomical and physiological techniques, and they can be used to study the process of cortical reorganization after deafferentiation (e.g. Kaas *et al.* 1990; Darian-Smith & Gilbert 1995; Das & Gilbert 1995; Obata *et al.* 1999). Such applications demonstrate the quality of data that can be obtained in the monkey, and the feasibility of a direct comparison between human and non-human primate studies.

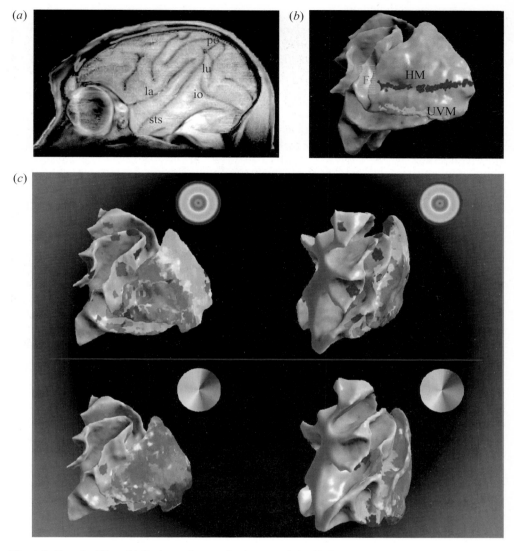

Fig. 4.6. See also Plate 14. Retinotopic organization revealed with fMRI. (*a*) Lateral view of a computer-rendered monkey brain. It shows some of the primary sulci. (*b*) Latero-caudal view of the posterior part of the brain with opened-up sulci. It shows the fovea and the horizontal and vertical meridians as determined with phase-encoding stimuli. (*c*) The upper panels show the eccentricity maps and the lower panels the orientation maps generated by using expanding-ring and rotated-wedge stimuli, respectively. Abbreviations: la, lateral; sts, superior temporal; io, inferotemporal, lu, lunate; po, parieto-occipital; HM, horizontal meridian; UVM, upper vertical meridian; F, foveal representation.

(b) High-spatial resolution imaging: surface coils

Whole-head imaging, although of great importance for the localization of activations, is of limited value when very high spatio-temporal resolution is required to study cortical micro-architecture or to compare imaging with electro-physiology. We have therefore adapted and optimized the implanted coil technique for monkeys. Very high-resolution structural and functional images of the monkey brain were obtained with small, tissue-compatible, intraosteally implantable RF coils. Voxel sizes as small as $0.012\,\mu l$ ($125 \times 125 \times 770\,\mu m^3$) were obtained with high values of the SNR and CNR, revealing both structural and functional cortical architecture in great detail.

(i) Implanted RF coils

As mentioned in § 4.2b, the RF system is a transceiver system used both to generate the alternating B_1 field and to receive the RF signal transmitted by the tissue (for a review on principles and instrumentation see Vlaardingerbroek & Den 1996; Wood & Wehrli 1999; Matwiyoff & Brooks 1999). It is typically an integral part of any imaging system, and is delivered with the magnet and all the other components of a scanner. However, coils can also be custom made in all kinds of different designs to accommodate the needs of specific experiments. They can be used as transceivers, but also as transmit- or receive-only units, the former transmitting the B_1 field and the latter receiving the FID after an adjustable delay.

Technically, RF coils are equivalent to an electrical circuit with inductance (L), capacitance (C) and resistance (R), and are tuned to a specific resonance frequency (ω) (e.g. 200 MHz at 4.7 T); for MRI this is the precessional frequency of the nuclear spin moments. Optimizing a coil commonly involves increasing its quality factor (or filling factor), Q. The latter is defined as the maximum energy stored divided by the average energy dissipated per radian, and can be improved by fine tuning the parameters L and C and minimizing R (the smaller the resistance, the sharper the resonance curve) for any given frequency. The RF coil design can be optimized (i) for signal homogeneity over the whole brain, (ii) for increased sensitivity over a given ROI, an example being the large quadrature surface coils, or (iii) for very high-resolution studies of a small area of interest (surface coils).

Small surface coils are often used in either human or animal studies to provide the highest possible SNR and to allow the use of small voxel sizes in high-resolution imaging (e.g. McArdle *et al.* 1986; Le *et al.* 1987; Rudin 1987; Garwood *et al.* 1989; Gruetter *et al.* 1990; Walker *et al.* 1991; Merkle *et al.* 1993; Hendrich *et al.* 1994; Lopez-Villegas *et al.* 1996). The SNR of such coils can be further increased by geometrically matching the coil to a specific tissue region. Finally, in animal experiments, the SNR can be substantially increased by implanting the coils in the body (Farmer *et al.* 1990; Summers *et al.* 1995; Silver *et al.* 2001). Implanted coils bring about a substantial increase in both the SNR and spatial selectivity by effectively improving the filling factor of a reception coil. The measured signal typically decreases as the distance of the coil from the ROI increases, while the noise detected by a coil increases with coil size. Thus, the smaller the coils and the closer the area of interest, the better the obtained signal.

The small RF surface coils described here were implanted intraosteally. They were made of 2 mm thick, Teflon-insulated, fine silver wire and had diameters varying from 18 to 30 mm. The implantable coils were 15 or 22 mm in diameter (see Figure 4.7). Their electronic circuitry had non-magnetic (copper-beryllium) slotted tubes to ensure a reliable electrical connection. During the surgical placement of the implanted coils, special care was taken to optimize the loaded Q of the coils. The Q factor can be directly affected by placing the coil too far from—but also too close to—the ROI. The appropriate distance of the coil from the ROI was therefore calculated based on models of the brain and skull surfaces created from anatomical scans.

(ii) High-resolution echo-planar BOLD imaging

Figure 4.8 shows anatomical and functional scans acquired with an implanted surface coil. Figure 4.8*a* is an example of a T_2^*-weighted echo planar (EP) image obtained with an actual

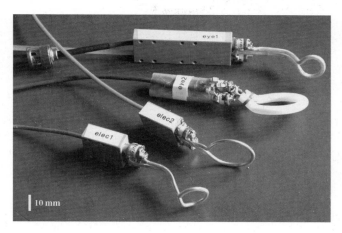

Fig. 4.7. Implantable RF coils. The coils were made of insulated silver wire and were used either as transceivers or receive-only units. All circuits were equipped with non-magnetic (copper-beryllium) slotted tubes to ensure reliable connection with the silver-wire loops.

resolution of $125 \times 125\,\mu m^2$ and a slice thickness of $720\,\mu m$. The contrast sensitivity of the image is sufficient to reveal the characteristic striation of the primary visual cortex. The dark line shown by the white arrow (Gen) is the well-known, *ca.* $200\,\mu m$ thick Gennari line between the cortical layers IVA and IVC, a result of the axonal plexus formed by the axons of pyramidal and spiny stellate cells contained in IVB. It appears dark in T_2^*-weighted images because the plexus contains a large number of horizontally arranged, myelinated (the T_2-values are shorter for fat; see § 4.2*b*(ii)) axons from collaterals, horizontal axonal branches, and ascending ramifications of spiny stellates.

Also visible in Figure 4.8*b* are the small cortical blood vessels that are known to vary in their degree of cortical penetration. Cortical vessels, that were traditionally divided into three groups (short, intermediate, and long), were further divided by Duvernoy *et al.* (1981) into six groups according to their length and termination in the various cortical layers. The green arrows show two vessels of Group 5 according to Duvernoy *et al.* (1981) consisting of arteries and veins (the MR images show the veins) that pass through the entire cortical thickness and vascularize both cortex and the adjacent WM (Figure 4.5*c,d*). Measurements after methyl methacrylate injections show that the veins of this group have an average diameter of $120\,\mu m$. The actual resolution of the presented image permits the visualization of susceptibility effects produced by such tiny vessels.

Figure 4.8*e* shows fMRI correlation coefficient maps (in colour) superimposed on the actual EPI (T_2^*-weighted) images of a monkey during visual block-design stimulation. The sections are around the lunate sulcus, and activation extends into the primary and secondary visual cortices (V1 and V2, respectively). The images have high SNR (27:1 for an ROI of 36 voxels, measured for an ROI positioned over the high-signal-intensity region in the image) and CNR (21:1 and signal modulation ranging from 2 to 7%, averaged for ROI of *ca.* 15–24 voxels). Both robust activation and good anatomical detail can be discerned.

(iii) Spatial specificity of BOLD fMRI
Gradient echo sequences like those used extensively for BOLD imaging are sensitive to both small and large vessels (Weisskoff *et al.* 1994). The significant contribution of the large vessels

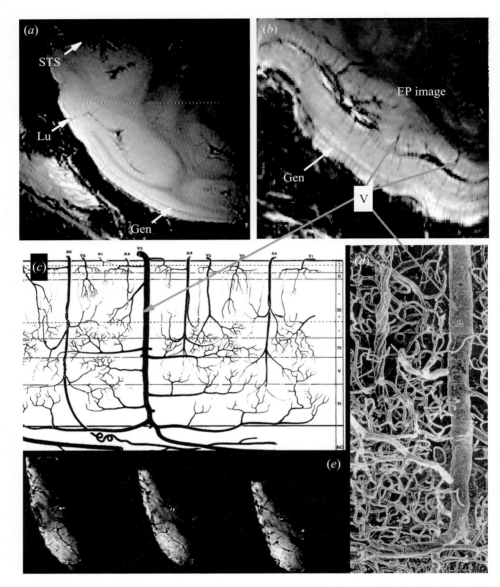

Fig. 4.8. See also Plate 15. Anatomical and functional scans acquired with an implanted surface coil. (a) T_2^*-weighted EP image obtained with an actual resolution of $125 \times 125\ \mu m^2$ and a slice thickness of $720\ \mu m$. (b) The resolution permits visualization of susceptibility effects produced by small cortical vessels with an average diameter of $120\ \mu m$. (c,d) Schematic and microphotograph of cortical vessels (see § 4.4b(ii)). (e) fMRI correlation coefficient maps (in colour) superimposed on the actual EPI (T_2^* weighted) images during visual block-design stimulation. Abbreviations: Gen, Gennari line; V, cortical vessels; Lu, Lunate sulcus; STS, superior temporal sulcus. Figure parts (c) and (d) from Duvernoy *et al.* 1981, with permission.

can lead to erroneous mapping of the activation site, as the flowing blood will generate BOLD contrast downstream of the actual tissue with increased metabolic activity. Thus, the extent of activation will appear to be larger that it really is. The contribution of large vessels depends on both field strength and the parameters of the pulse sequences (Boxerman *et al.* 1995*a*; Zhong *et al.* 1998; Hoogenraad *et al.* 2001).

Large vessels can be de-emphasized using pulse sequences designed to suppress higher flow velocities (Boxerman *et al.* 1995*a*). They are also de-emphasized in stronger magnetic fields, because the strength of extra-vascular BOLD increases more rapidly for small vessels than it does for large ones. More specifically, the transverse relaxation rate, R_2^*, increases linearly with the external magnetic field for large vessels (larger than $10\,\mu$m) but varies as the square of the field for small vessels (Ogawa *et al.* 1993; Gati *et al.* 2000). Thus, with sufficient SNR, signals originating from the capillary bed are clearly discernible in strong magnetic fields.

A loss of specificity can also result from so-called inflow effects. Both supplying pial arteries and draining vessels unavoidably bring fresh spins into the area of interest during the inter-image delay. For instance, when short repetition times are used, gradient–echo sequences yield considerable contrast between the partially saturated tissues in the imaging plane, that is, tissues whose longitudinal magnetization was not yet fully recovered, and the unsaturated blood flowing into this plane (Axel 1984, 1986). In the same vein, increased CBF in an activated tissue will lead to signal enhancement in the image of a selected slice if the time between consecutive RF excitations is insufficient for the signal within the slice to reach full relaxation. Such inflow effects can be considerably stronger than the BOLD signal itself (Segebarth *et al.* 1994; Frahm *et al.* 1994; Kim *et al.* 1994; Belle *et al.* 1995) and much less tissue specific. The shorter the repetition times, the stronger the inflow effect will be (Glover & Lee 1995; Haacke *et al.* 1995). Inflow effects can be eliminated by utilizing low flip angles and increasing the T_R time (Menon *et al.* 1993; Frahm *et al.* 1994).

Assuming the appropriate selection of pulsing parameters to minimize the above-mentioned effects, the issue of spatial specificity can be addressed by conducting specific experiments targeted at mapping functionally distinct structures with well-defined organization and topography in the brain. The activation of LGN shown in Figure 4.5 is an example of such specificity, as the structure is only *ca.* 6 mm in the rostrocaudal, and *ca.* 5 mm in the dorsoventral and mediolateral directions.

Figure 4.9 demonstrates the spatial specificity of BOLD by exploiting the non-uniform distribution of directionally selective cells across the layers of the striate cortex. About one-third of the striate cells are known to be directionally selective (Goldberg & Wurtz 1972; Schiller *et al.* 1976; De Valois *et al.* 1982; Albright 1984; Desimone & Ungerleider 1986; Colby *et al.* 1993). However, these cells do not exhibit a uniform laminar distribution. Instead, most are found in layers 4A, 4B, 4Cα and 6 (Dow 1974; Hawken *et al.* 1988). In high-field MRI such differences in neuron density can be visualized if the appropriate visual stimuli are used and the pulsing parameters are tuned to stress the extravascular BOLD signals. Figure 4.6*a,b* shows the z-score maps obtained by comparing the activation elicited by the moving checkerboard stimulus to that elicited by the blank screen and the counter-flickering checkerboard stimulus, respectively (Logothetis *et al.* 2002). The parameters used in this scan were: FOV = 32 mm × 32 mm on a matrix of 256 × 256 voxels (0.125 mm × 0.125 mm resolution), slice thickness = 1 mm, T_E/T_R = 20/750 ms, and number of segments = 8. Figure 4.9*c* illustrates the plane of the slice selected for high-resolution imaging and Figure 4.7*d* illustrates the signal modulation. For the most part, activity in V1 was found in the middle layers, usually layer IV. This activity may indeed reflect the density of active directional neurons within this

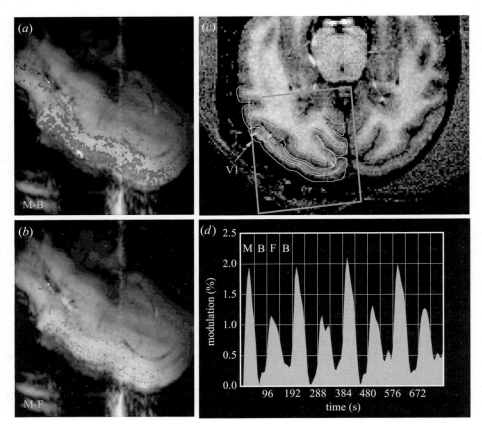

Fig. 4.9. See also Plate 16. Lamina-specific activation. (*a*) *z*-score maps obtained by comparing the activation elicited by the moving stimulus with that elicited by the blank screen. (*b*) *z*-score maps obtained in the same ROI by comparing the responses to the moving stimuli with those elicited by flickering stimuli. The green dashed line corresponds approximately to the layer 4. (*c*) Axial slice showing the ROI studied with the surface coil. The orange square is the region shown in (*a*) and (*b*). It also depicts the position of V1 and V2. (*d*) Signal modulation for all four repetitions of an observation period for all significantly activated voxels colour coded in (*b*). M-B, motion versus blank screen; M-F, motion versus counter-phase flicker; MBFB, motion, blank, flicker, blank etc.

lamina. However, it is possible that the activation in the middle layers of cortex reflects the highest capillary density that occurs at approximately layers 3C, 4 and 5 (vascular layer 3 as defined by Duvernoy *et al.* (1981)). A recent human fMRI study indicates that the origin of the BOLD signal may actually be the vascular layer 3, presumably extending into adjacent vascular layers (Hyde *et al.* 2001). Further experimentation is needed to dissect the effect of vascular density from that of neural specificity.

(c) High-temporal resolution imaging
In order to compare imaging with physiology we used a rapid scanning protocol to acquire a single slice containing the microelectrode tip (GR-EPI with four segments and $T_E/T_R = 20/250$ ms). To minimize the effects of inflow and large drainage vessels, we consistently used flip angles that were smaller than the computed Ernst angle (see § 4.4b) by 10°.

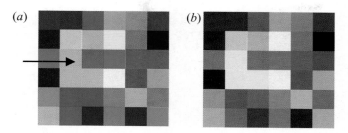

Plate 1. A pair of luminance-matched stimuli used in the Mondrian colour-exchange experiments. A random draw of the pattern is shown every 2 s. For 12 s blocks the pattern is coloured (*a*) and for 12 s blocks the pattern is achromatic (*b*). To control for attention, subjects are asked to identify the orientation of the opening in the 'C' throughout the experimental scan (10 blocks). The arrow indicates the location of the C, but the arrow is not present during the experiment. See Plate 9.

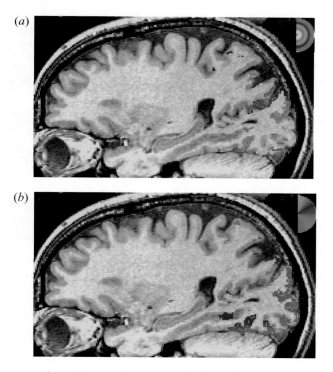

Plate 2. Visual cortex activated by travelling wave stimuli. Only voxels containing neurons with a preferred retinal location will respond to the stimulus. The colour overlay in this sagittal section indicates (*a*) the preferred stimulus eccentricity or (*b*) angle at each voxel within the cortical grey matter. Only locations with a response coherence of more than 0.35 are shown.

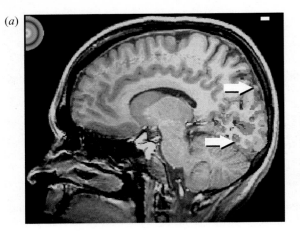

(a)

Plate 3. Typical amplitude spectra of the fMRI response to an expanding ring (eccentricity) retinotopic stimulus. There were six stimulus cycles in the scan. The amplitude spectra shown in (b) were measured from two regions of interest that are indicated by the white arrows in (a). Each region occupies less than 1 cm² of cortical surface area. The signals in the anterior portions of the occipital lobe and posterior parietal and all along the ventral surface are substantially above statistical threshold. Other details as in Fig. 1.4.

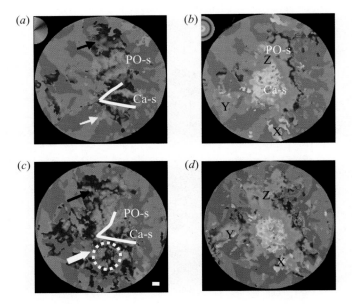

Plate 4. Angular and eccentricity maps for two subjects shown on flattened representations of the left occipital lobe. The flat maps are centred near the occipital pole and have an 8 cm radius (scale bar, 1 cm). Shading indicates a sulcus (dark) or gyrus (light). Dorsal and ventral are up and down; lateral and medial are left and right. The flat maps are further described in § 1.3. (a,c) Measurements of angular retinotopy. The calcarine sulcus (Ca-s) and parietal–occipital sulcus (PO-s) are marked. The inset shows the preferred angular direction, ranging from cyan (upper) to blue (horizontal) to red (lower). The white line denotes the V1 hemifield representation that falls within the Ca-s. The black arrows indicate positions on the dorsal surface that respond well to the upper visual field, and the white arrows indicate positions on the ventral surface that respond well to the lower visual field. The dashed white circle indicates the region on the ventral surface that is analysed in more detail in subsequent figures. (b,d) Measurements of eccentric retinotopy for the same two observers. The preferred eccentricity between 0 and 20° is indicated by the colour overlay, with red/yellow representing the central 5°, green/cyan representing 5–10°, and blue/magenta representing 10–20°. The large red/yellow region near the occipital pole falls at the confluence of V1/2/3. The second large foveal representation (marked 'X') on the ventral surface is analysed in subsequent figures. The foveal representation on the lateral surface (marked 'Y') falls within motion-selective cortex. The foveal representations on the dorsal surface (marked 'Z') have been described elsewhere (Press *et al.* 2001). In all maps, the preferred visual field location is indicated only at cortical positions with a signal coherence of at least 0.35.

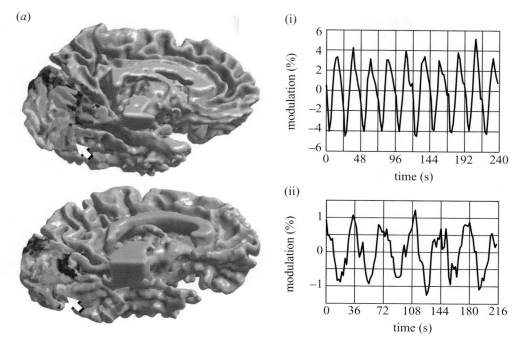

(a)

(i)

(ii)

Plate 5. (*a*) Three-dimensional renderings of the eccentricity map seen from a medial/ventral view. (i) Data from a third subject A. W.; (ii) data from subject B. W. (*b*) The time-series of the activity from the ventral foveal representation, indicated by the arrow. The experiments used different numbers of cycles and different duty cycles. In both cases, the time-series is well above statistical threshold. Other details as in Figure 1.4.

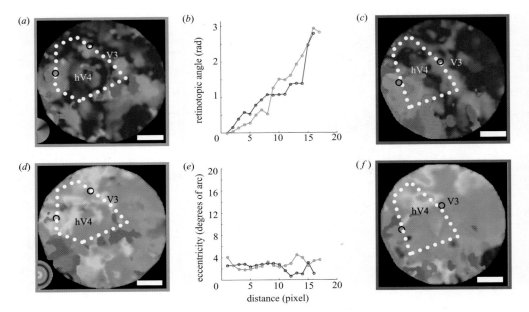

Plate 6. Retinotopic organization in VO for two subjects. The images show angular (top) and eccentricity (bottom) maps; the left and right images are from two subjects (A. B. and B. W.). In the angular maps (*a,c*), cyan represents the upper vertical meridian, blue/magenta the horizontal and red the lower vertical meridian. The hemifield representation of hV4 is indicated by the dotted white polygon, and the general location of ventral V3 is shown. The eccentricity maps (*d,f*) from foveal (red/yellow) to peripheral (green and cyan) run perpendicular to the angular map. The graphs (*b,e*) show the measured angular (*b*) and eccentricity (*e*) values on a path between the black circles marked on the hV4 boundary. Data from subject A. B. are plotted in blue, data from subject B. W. are plotted in green. Along these paths the angular phase measurements span 3 rad (*b*), indicating a hemifield representation while the eccentricity measurements are approximately constant (*e*). The VO foveal representation falls at the bottoms of the maps in (*d*) and (*f*). The expanding ring stimulus extended to a 20° radius (blue/magenta), but the preferred eccentricities in hV4 were more central (cyan/blue). Scale bar, 1 cm.

(a)

(b)

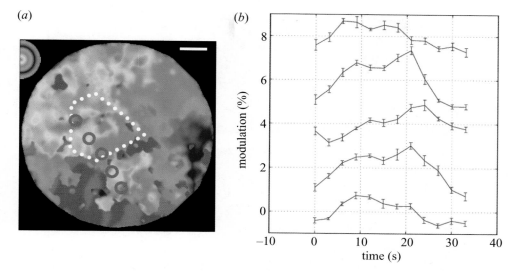

Plate 7. The eccentricity map in ventral cortex near hV4. (*a*) The two prominent red/yellow regions represent the fovea at the confluence of V1/2/3/4 (upper left) and the displaced foveal representation on the ventral surface (bottom middle). The peripheral signals (blue) fall within areas V2/3. Area hV4 is denoted by the dashed white polygon. The grey circles indicate a series of regions of interest that fall between the two large foveal representations. (*b*) The average fMRI time-series during a single stimulus cycle from each region of interest on the left. The signal amplitudes are quite significant and reliable, representing about 1% modulation about the mean. The individual curves are displaced vertically for clarity; their order corresponds to the ordering of the regions of interest. The middle curve measures the time-course at the peripheral boundary of hV4. The phase of the curves varies systematically and reverses direction at this boundary. Colour overlays are included only at locations with a coherence of at least 0.35. Scale bar, 1 cm.

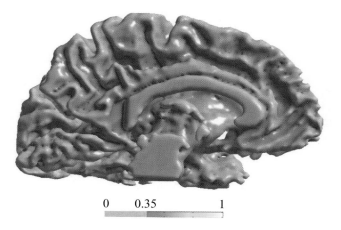

0   0.35   1

Plate 8. Mid-sagittal view of colour exchange activations. Activations exceeding a coherence level of 0.4, approximately equivalent to a statistical threshold of $p < 0.001$, are shown. There is significant activation in the calcarine sulcus as well as along the ventral surface. Subject A. W.

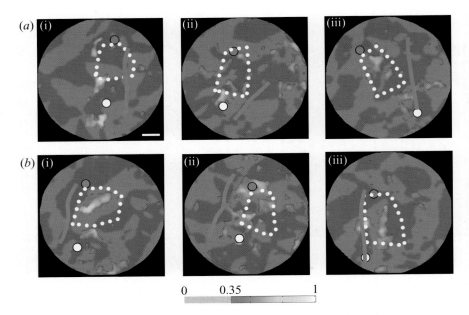

Plate 9. Locations responding preferentially to chromatic compared with achromatic stimuli in three subjects. Data are shown for three subjects ((i) A. W., (ii) A. B., (iii) B. W.). (*a*) Left hemisphere; (*b*) right hemisphere. The hV4 boundary is marked by the dotted white polygon, and the collateral sulcus is marked in blue. The foveal representations in hV4 (blue dot) and VO (white dot) are marked. The unfold spans 7 cm. Only locations with response coherence greater than 0.35 are shown. Scale bar, 1 cm.

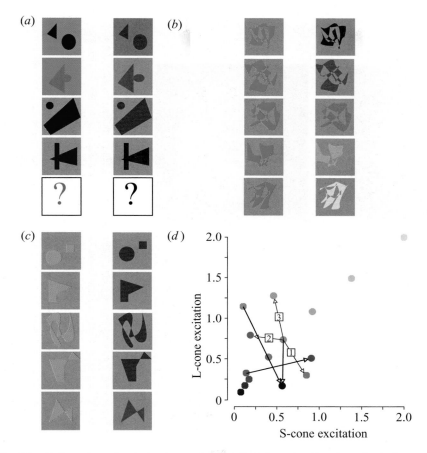

Plate 10. Stimuli for colour discrimination testing. (*a*) Training stimuli and test logic for testing discriminations without differentially rewarding the discriminanda. In 80% of the trials, the monkeys were trained for reward on the list of four colour/greyscale pairs. In 20% of the trials, a pair of test stimuli was presented and both stimulus boxes contained a reward. The monkeys' performance on test trials informed us about their stimulus choices in the absence of differential reward. (*b*) Five of the 10 test stimuli used in demonstrating that the colour/greyscale discrimination is not based on an apparent luminance or contrast difference. (*c*) Five of the 16 test stimuli used in demonstrating that the colour discrimination transfers to a novel hue. (*d*) Training- and test-stimulus colours plotted in cone-excitation coordinates with arrows indicating the borders between background and figure colours. The three heavy arrows show the figure/ground borders of the training stimuli. The lighter, numbered arrows show the figure/ground borders of the test stimuli. No. 1 is the blue test in (*b*). No. 2 is the red 'novel hue' test from (*c*), which was successfully discriminated by Hugo, Rupert and Piers but not by Giles. No. 3 is the lighter red that was successfully discriminated by Giles. Note that the heavy arrows representing the training stimuli all run across the diagram in a direction of increasing relative S-cone excitation (down and right), whereas the arrows representing the novel hue stimuli run up and left in a direction of increasing L-cone excitation.

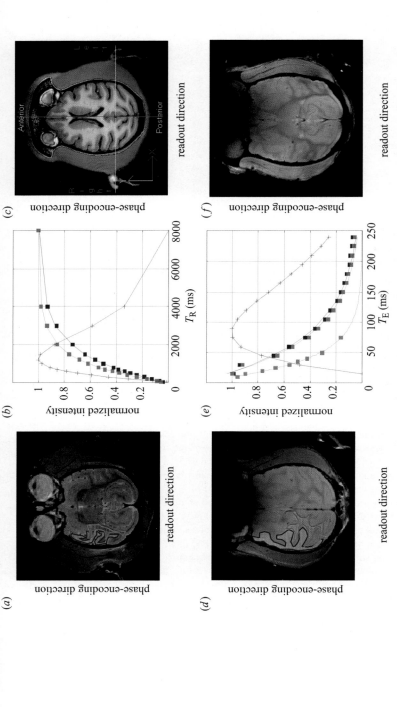

Plate 11. Relaxation curves for the GM and WM of the monkey brain. (*a*) Example of a proton-density image. The image was collected with a multi-slice, multi-echo sequence using a FOV of 128 mm × 128 mm over a matrix of 256 × 256 voxels. Sixteen such images are acquired using T_R-values ranging from 50 to 8000 ms. (*b*) Average intensity change of voxels in cortical (blue) and WM (red) regions as a function of repetition time, T_R. T_1 is defined as the time required for *ca.* 63% of the remaining longitudinal magnetization to appear. The more 'watery' the tissue the longer its T_1 relaxation time. The WM (red curve, $T_1 = 1097$ ms) relaxes faster than the GM (blue curve, $T_1 = 1499$), so the former appears brighter in a typical T_1-weighted image than the latter (See Figure 4.1*c*). The black trace shows the differences between the two curves. The maximum contrast is obtained with a T_R-value close to the T_1-value of the tissue having the faster relaxation. (*c*) An example of a T_1-weighted image. (*d*) An example of a spin-echo T_2-weighted image. The relaxation times for different tissues were calculated by collecting 16 such images differing in their T_E-values. (*e*) The T_2-relaxation curves for the cortex and WM, with the black trace denoting the difference between the two. The T_2-values are longer for small and shorter for large molecules, and the contrast of T_2-weighted images has a polarity opposite to that obtained with T_1. The cortex (longer T_2) in (*d*) appears brighter than WM (shorter T_2). The green trace shows the T_2^* relaxation curve for the cortical area of (*d*) T_2 GM = 74 ms (blue curve); T_2 WM = 69 ms (red curve); T_2^* GM = 36 ms (green curve). (*f*) An example of a T_2^*-weighted image collected in a multi-shot, multi-slice with an EPI sequence. T_E, echo time; T_R, repetition time; GM, grey matter; WM, whitematter.

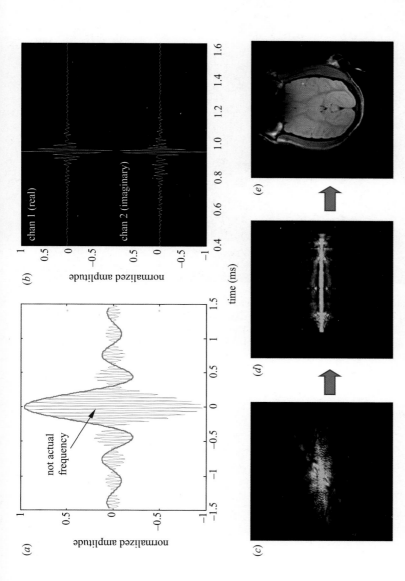

Plate 12. Image formation. (*a*) A typical RF excitation pulse (here $\text{sinc}(x) = \sin(x)/x$) used to nutate the net magnetization down into the *xy* plane. The RF pulse actually consists of the product of a sine wave of the Larmor frequency with the sinc function. In the 4.7 T magnet this is *ca.* 200 MHz. The blue line depicts the sine wave at much lower frequencies for illustration purposes. $\gamma = 42.57$ MHz T^{-1}; resonance frequency = 200 MHz; duration = 3 ms; BW = 1.85 kHz. (*b*) The two spin echoes produced by an inversion pulse of 180° (see also Figure 4.2). In MRI the initially very high RF signal (MHz range) is typically converted into an audio signal (kHz range) by comparing the RF signal with a reference signal (phase-sensitive detection). In fact, to improve SNR the signal is collected by two PSDs that are 90° out of phase (upper and lower panels of (*b*)). The converted signal is digitized and the two channels are represented as the real and imaginary part of complex numbers (alternatively they can be transformed into the magnitude and phase of the signal). Each row of the *k* space consists of a sequence of such numbers. $T_E = 15$ ms; duration = 3 ms. (*c*) Magnitude of the *k* space in a spin-echo experiment. Each row is an echo with the same frequency composition but different phase encoding. Top and bottom rows have the strongest phase-encoding gradient and hence the largest dephasing (weakest signal). The strongest echo is in the centre of the *k* space, where no phase-encoding occurs. (*d*) The first Fourier transformation along the phase-encoding direction. (*e*) The second Fourier transformation along thereadout direction, resulting in the actual image.

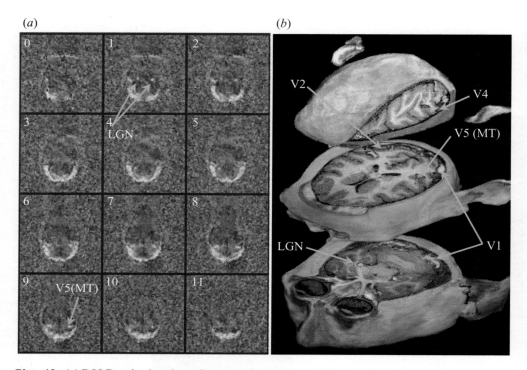

Plate 13. (*a*) BOLD activation shown in terms of *z*-score maps. The specificity of the signal enables the visualization of anatomical details in the occipital lobe. (*b*) Activation maps superimposed on anatomical three-dimensional MDEFT scans (0.125 µl voxel size). The figure shows activation of the LGN, striate and some extrastriate areas including V2, V3, V4, and V5 (MT). V1 activation covers almost the entire representation of the perifovea (the horizontal extent of the checkerboard stimulus was 30°). The V1 regions showing high activation (yellow) lie within the cortical representation of the fovea.

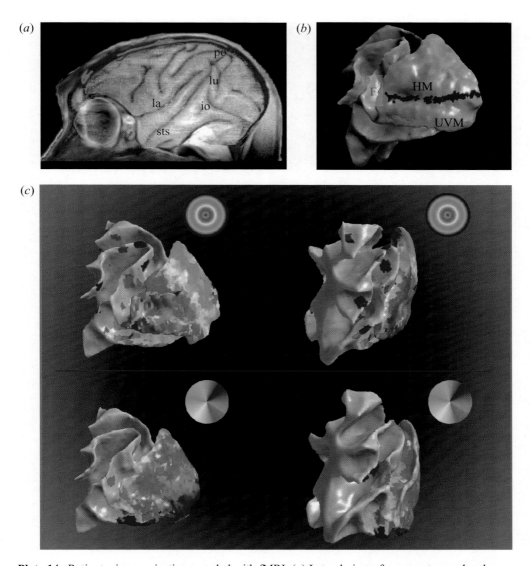

Plate 14. Retinotopic organization revealed with fMRI. (*a*) Lateral view of a computer-rendered monkey brain. It shows some of the primary sulci. (*b*) Latero-caudal view of the posterior part of the brain with opened-up sulci. It shows the fovea and the horizontal and vertical meridians as determined with phase-encoding stimuli. (*c*) The upper panels show the eccentricity maps and the lower panels the orientation maps generated by using expanding-ring and rotated-wedge stimuli, respectively. Abbreviations: la, lateral; sts, superior temporal; io, inferotemporal, lu, lunate; po, parieto-occipital; HM, horizontal meridian; UVM, upper vertical meridian; F, foveal representation.

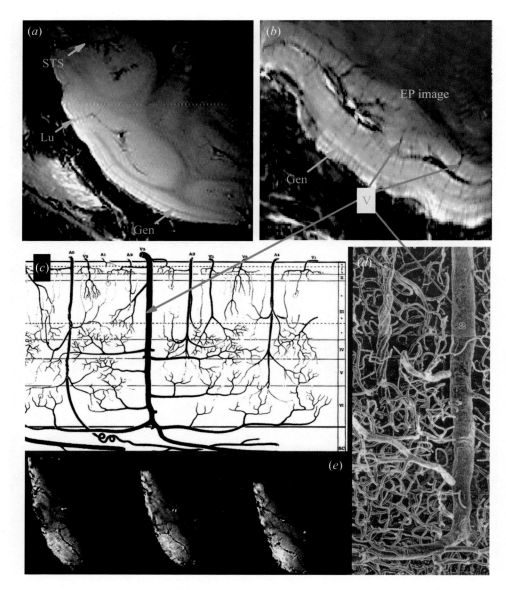

Plate 15. Anatomical and functional scans acquired with an implanted surface coil. (*a*) T_2^*-weighted EP image obtained with an actual resolution of $125 \times 125 \ \mu m^2$ and a slice thickness of $720 \ \mu m$. (*b*) The resolution permits visualization of susceptibility effects produced by small cortical vessels with an average diameter of $120 \ \mu m$. (*c,d*) Schematic and microphotograph of cortical vessels (see § 4.4*b*(ii)). (*e*) fMRI correlation coefficient maps (in colour) superimposed on the actual EPI (T_2^* weighted) images during visual block-design stimulation. Abbreviations: Gen, Gennari line; V, cortical vessels; Lu, Lunate sulcus; STS, superior temporal sulcus. Figure parts (*c*) and (*d*) from Duvernoy *et al.* 1981, with permission.

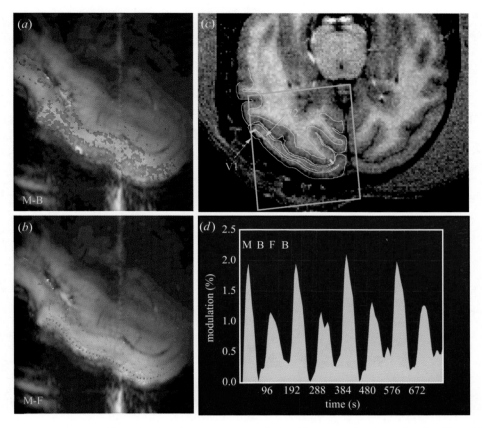

Plate 16. Lamina-specific activation. (*a*) *z*-score maps obtained by comparing the activation elicited by the moving stimulus with that elicited by the blank screen. (*b*) *z*-score maps obtained in the same ROI by comparing the responses to the moving stimuli with those elicited by flickering stimuli. The green dashed line corresponds approximately to the layer 4. (*c*) Axial slice showing the ROI studied with the surface coil. The orange square is the region shown in (*a*) and (*b*). It also depicts the position of V1 and V2. (*d*) Signal modulation for all four repetitions of an observation period for all significantly activated voxels colour coded in (*b*). M-B, motion versus blank screen; M-F, motion versus counter-phase flicker; MBFB, motion, blank, flicker, blank etc.

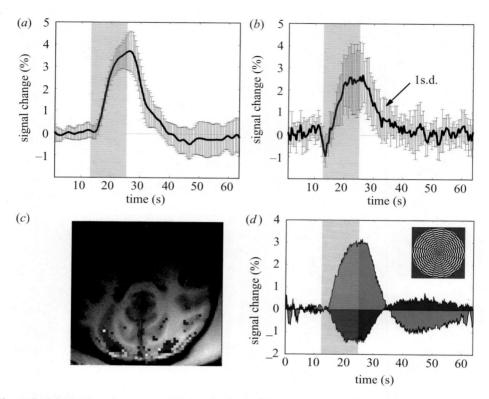

Plate 17. (*a*) Time-course of the typical 'positive' BOLD signal. Bars denote standard deviation. The trace is the average of 14 time series of the same voxel. (*b*) The initial dip (see § 4.4*c*), 14 averages of a single voxel. (*c*) *z*-score map showing areas with negative BOLD. (*d*) The time-course of the two—correlated and anticorrelated—BOLD responses.

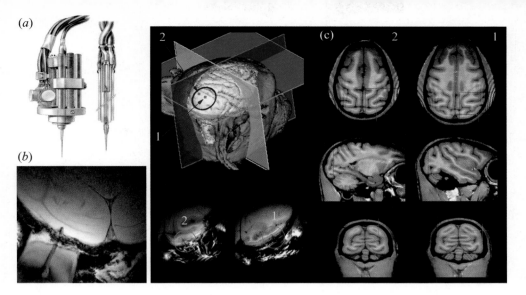

Plate 18. (*a*) The microelectrodes and their holder consisting of three concentric, metallic cylinders, the innermost serving as the contact point for the electrode, the middle as the far-interference sensor and the outermost as the ground. The three-coil magnetic-field sensor used to compensate for near interference is also shown. (*b*) FLASH scan (see § 4.5*b*(i)) showing the location of the electrode-tip in the primary visual cortex. (*c*) A reconstruction of the position of the two electrodes from the three-dimensional MDEFT scans (top left) with orthogonal views (right). At the bottom left the inversion-recovery images show the actual electrodes (double electrode recording).

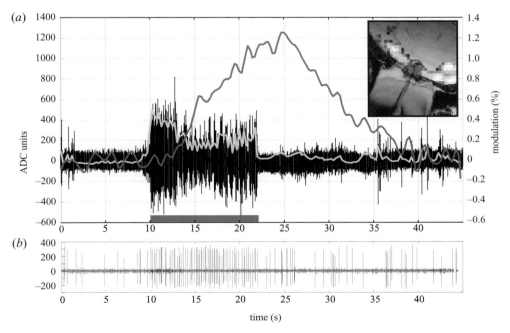

Plate 19. The neural signal. (*a*) The comprehensive signal, with its effective values in yellow and the BOLD activation in red. The BOLD response is the average time-series of the voxels within the green circle of the T_2^*-weighted image in the inset. The green horizontal bar shows the stimulus presentation period. Black trace, raw; yellow trace, root mean square. (*b*) A sequence of single action potentials included in the comprehensive signal. The spikes were isolated using statistical methods. Their rate is one of the parameters often compared with the haemodynamic response. In most extracellular recordings, in particular in those conducted with behaving animals, such isolated action potentials commonly reflect the 'output' activity of a studied area (see § 4.5*b*(v)).

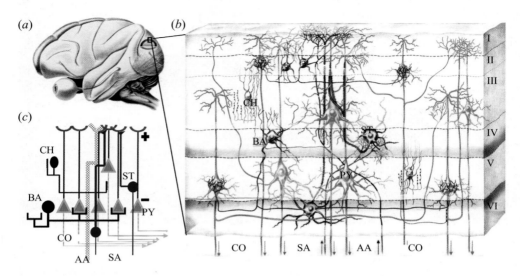

Plate 20. Cortical circuitry. (*a*) Lateral view of a monkey brain. The section is in the striate cortex. (*b*) Neuronal types and connections. (*c*) Model of basic cortical circuitry showing the 'open field' arrangement of pyramidal cells. The parallel unidirectional arrangement of apical dendrites facilitates the summation of field potentials by generating strong dipoles (see § 4.5*b*(ii)). Abbreviations: CH, chandelier; BA, basket; PY, pyramidal; ST, stellate cells; SA, specific afferents; AA, association afferents; CO, pyramidal cell axons representing cortical output.

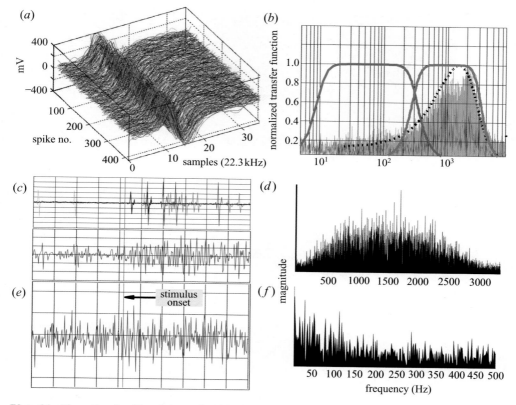

Plate 21. The rationale of band separation in extracellular recordings. (*a*) Isolated action potentials. (*b*) The average spectrum of these potentials is shown with the blue surface plot. The red and green traces represent the transfer functions of the chosen filters. They correspond to the LFPs and MUA, respectively. Red trace, LFP transfer function; green trace, MUA transfer function; dotted black trace, average spike-spectrum. (*c*) Top, using the isolated spikes, spike trains were simulated by using the interspike probability distributions measured in the actual experiment. Bottom, the simulated spikes are summed up to obtain artificial MUA. (*d*) The spectrum of such activity. (*e*,*f*) Simulations for pEPSPs.

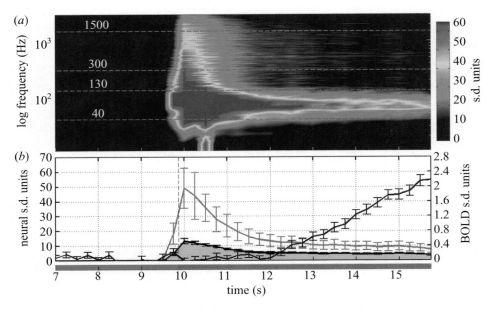

Plate 22. Time-dependent frequency analysis for the population data. (*a*) Spectrogram of the first 6 s of the neural response averaged over all data. Each time-course is expressed in units of the standard deviation of the prestimulus period. Colour coding indicates the reliability of the signal change for each frequency (SNR). Red and green dashed lines show the LFP and MUA frequency bands, respectively. Mean = 72.96; s.d. = 21.04. (*b*) Mean LFP (red), MUA (black) and total (light green surface) neural response averaged across all frequencies, together with the BOLD signal (blue). Note that the 'activity increase' seemingly occurring before the stimulus presentation is due solely to the windows used to create the spectrograms. The two vertical axes show the difference in the SNR of the neural and BOLD signals. Across all the data a difference of approximately one order of magnitude was found in the reliability of the two signals. From Logothetis *et al.* (2001), with permission.

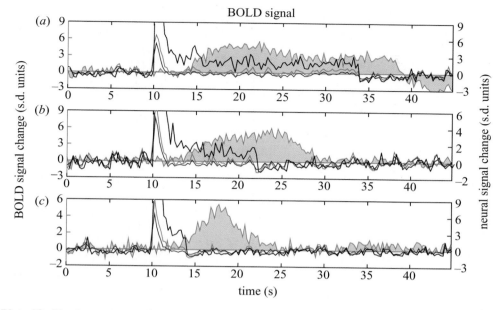

Plate 23. Simultaneous neural and haemodynamic recordings from a cortical site showing a transient neural response. (*a–c*) Responses to pulse stimuli of 24, 12, and 4 s. Pink tint, BOLD; black trace, LFP; green trace, MUA; blue trace, SDF. Note that both single- and multiple-unit responses adapt a couple of seconds after stimulus onset, with LFP remaining the only signal correlated with the BOLD response. The SDF (see § 4.6*b*) reflects the instantaneous firing rate of a small population of neurons whose action potential could be identified and isolated during the analysis using standard mathematical methods. Note the covariation of the rate of such isolated spikes with the filtered MUA. From Logothetis *et al.* (2001), with permission.

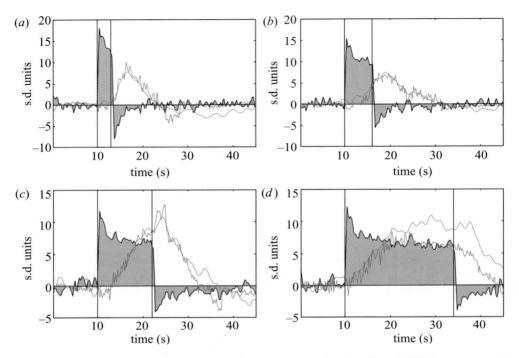

Plate 24. The measured LFP response as well as the measured and estimated BOLD response. (*a*) Pulse = 3 s; contrast = 100%; (*b*) pulse = 6 s; contrast = 6 100%; (*c*) pulse = 12 s; contrast = 100%; (*d*) pulse = 24 s; contrast = 100%. The grey trace is the measured LFP signal; the blue trace is the measured BOLD and the red trace is the estimated BOLD. Residual analysis showed an increased error for a longer pulse duration. Visual inspection of the data from a 24 s long stimulus presentation revealed greatly increased residuals after the initial ramp of the BOLD response, suggesting the existence of nonlinearities not captured by the Wiener–Kernel analysis applied here to the data.

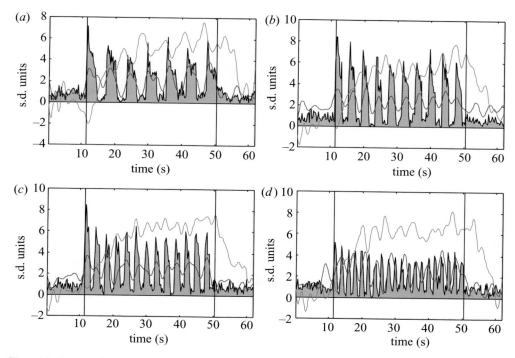

Plate 25. Deconvolution of the BOLD response. Estimation of the neural response was relatively accurate for low-temporal frequencies (0.16 Hz). Increasing the temporal frequency strongly increased the residuals; with frequencies higher than 0.21 Hz reconstruction of the neural response no longer being possible. Area plots show measured neural responses. The grey trace is the measured LFP signal, the blue trace is the measured BOLD and the red trace the estimated neural response. (*a*) Flicker rate = 0.16 Hz, contrast = 100%; (*b*) flicker rate = 0.21 Hz, contrast = 100%; (*c*) flicker rate = 0.25 Hz,contrast = 100%; (*d*) flicker rate = 0.4 Hz, contrast = 100%.

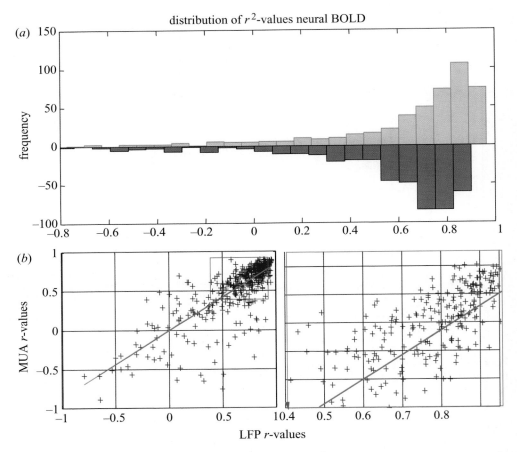

Plate 26. (*a*) Distribution of the coefficient of determination (r^2) of LFP (pink) and MUA (grey). The r^2-values for LFP were significantly higher than for MUA. The plot includes data collected with pulse stimuli of 24, 12, 6, and 4 s, with $N = 460$, LFP mean = 0.521, LFP mode = 0.672, MUA mean = 0.410 and MUA mode = 0.457. (*b*) Covariation of the estimation error. The right plot is a magnified section of the left scatter plot.

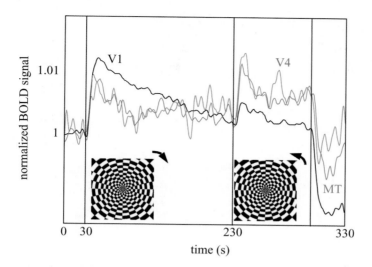

Plate 27. A visual adaptation paradigm was used to localize visual areas that process information about the direction of motion (modified from Tolias *et al*. (2001)). The BOLD signal in area V5 (MT) adapted more quickly than in V1, reflecting the difference in motion processing between these areas. Surprisingly, area V4 showed adaptation as strong and as fast as area V5, which is characterized by a much larger number of directional neurons.

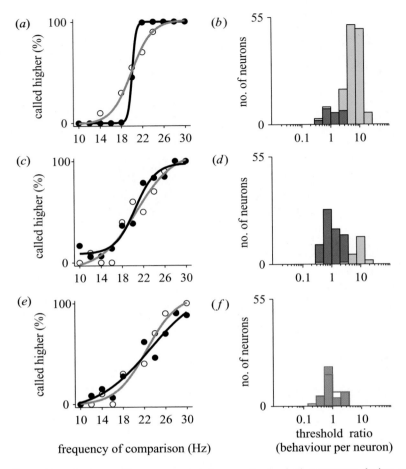

Plate 28. Comparison between S1 neurons and the psychophysical responses during vibrotactile discrimination (illustrated in Figure 5.1c). (*a,c,e*) Percentage of trials in which the comparison was higher or lower than the base. The solid lines are sigmoidal fits to the data; for each curve, the threshold is proportional to its maximum steepness. White circles and grey lines indicate the monkey's performance during one discrimination run. The black circles and black curves indicate the performance of an ideal observer that based his decision on the periodicity (*a*) or mean firing rate (*c*) of evoked spike trains of single neurons recorded while the monkey discriminated. (*b*) Numbers of S1 neurons with the indicated threshold ratios. The yellow bars correspond to neurometric thresholds based on the periodicity of evoked spike trains; the red bars correspond to neurometric thresholds based on the evoked firing rate. The data are from all neurons with significant periodic spike entrainment. (*d*) As in (*b*), but data are from all neurons with significant rate modulation. (*e*) As in (*a*) but aperiodic stimuli were applied. (*f*) Threshold ratios from all neurons tested with both periodic and aperiodic stimuli. Neurometric thresholds were computed from firing rates in periodic (red thick lines) and aperiodic (cyan bars) conditions. (Modified from Hernández *et al.* 2000.)

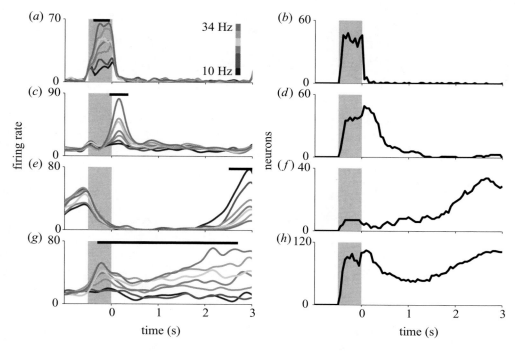

Plate 29. Neuronal response types during the delay period. (*a,c,e,g*) Single-neuron spike-density function from four different neurons. The dark bars above each plot indicate the times during which the neuron's firing rate carried a significant (*p* < 0.01) monotonic signal about the base stimulus (Romo *et al.* 1999). (*c,g*) Positive monotonic encoding neurons about the base stimulus. (*e*) Negative monotonic encoding neuron about the base stimulus. (*b,d,f,h*) Total number of recorded neurons (during fixed 3 s delay period runs) carrying a significant signal about the base stimulus, as a function of time relative to the beginning of the delay period. The base stimulus period is shaded grey; colour gradient from 10 to 34 Hz. (*a,b*) S1, (*c,d*) S2, (*e,f*) MPC and (*g,h*). PFC (Modified from Salinas *et al.* 2000; Romo *et al.* 1999; Hernández *et al.* 2002.)

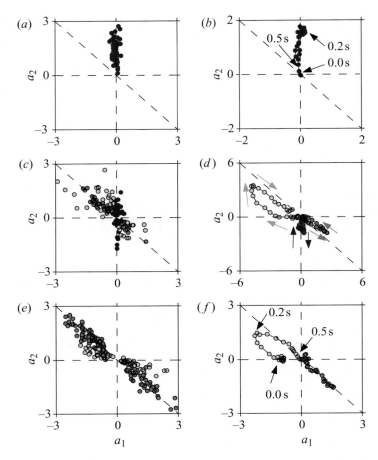

Plate 30. Responses during the second stimulus. (*a,c,e*) Coefficients resulting from fitting firing rates from S1, S2, and MPC neurons, during the second stimulus, as linear functions of both f_2 (a_2) and f_1 (a_1). Each dot represents coefficients for one neuron; only neurons with fits significantly different from (0,0) are shown. (*b,d,f*) Dynamics of individual responses for S1, S2, and MPC neurons. Each row shows data from one neuron. In all panels, time = 0 corresponds to the start of the second stimulus. Each symbol in (*b*), (*d*) and (*f*) corresponds to fits of 100 ms, separated from its neighbours in steps of 25 ms. Blue dots represent neurons that responded as a function of f_2 (sensory response); yellow dots represent neurons that carried the first information of f_1 (the memory trace) then f_1 interacted with f_2 (differential response); red dots represent neurons that indicated the difference between f_1 and f_2. (*a,b*) S1, (*c,d*) S2 and (*e,f*) MPC (Hernández *et al.* 2002; R. Romo, A. Hernández, C. Brody, A. Zainos and L. Lemus, unpublished data).

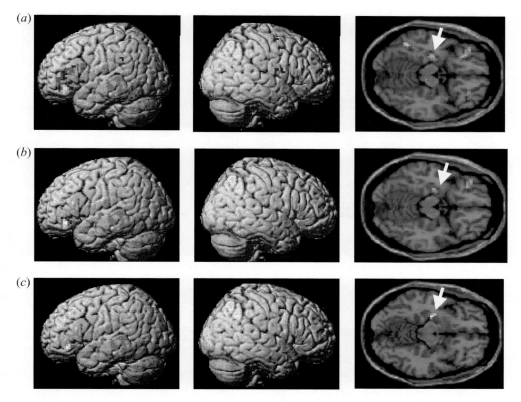

Plate 31. Data from Otten *et al.* (2001). (*a*) Regions showing significant ($p < 0.001$) fMRI signal increases for subsequently remembered versus subsequently forgotten words from the animacy task. Subsequent memory effects can be seen in the prefrontal cortex bilaterally and in two regions of the left hippocampal formation. (*b*) Subsequent memory effects in the animacy task, masked by the regions that showed significant signal increases for the animacy versus alphabetical contrast (both contrasts thresholded at $p < 0.001$). Overlap between subsequent memory and task effects was found in the left ventral prefrontal cortex and the left anterior hippocampus. (*c*) Regions showing subsequent memory effects for words studied in the alphabetical task. The effects are evident in the left ventral prefrontal cortex and the left anterior hippocampus. All results in this and subsequent figures are rendered onto the Montreal Neurological Institute reference brain. The arrows denote the left anterior hippocampus. The colour of activated voxels (red→yellow) indicates the level of statistical significance beyond the threshold.

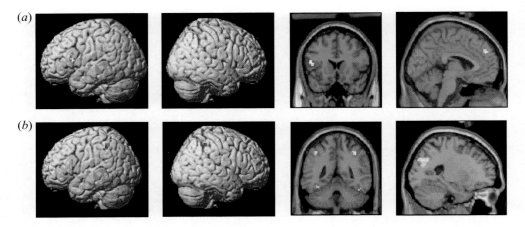

Plate 32. Regions showing significant ($p < 0.001$) subsequent memory effects in Otten & Rugg (2001a). (a) Subsequent memory effects in the animacy task were found in the left inferior and medial frontal regions. (b) Subsequent memory effects in the syllable task were found in the bilateral intraparietal sulcus, the bilateral fusiform gyrus and the left superior occipital gyrus.

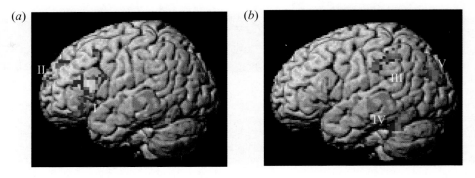

Plate 33. Comparison of the subsequent memory effects in the (a) animacy and (b) syllable study tasks of Otten & Rugg (2001a). The effects are illustrated at a significance threshold of $p < 0.01$.

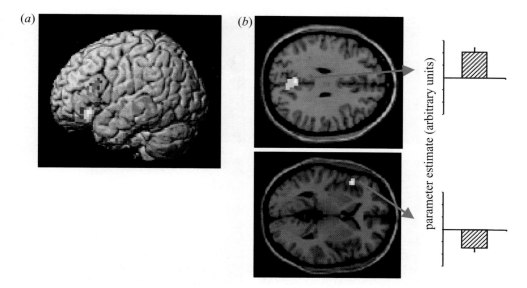

Plate 34. (*a*) Subsequent memory effects for items studied in the animacy task of Otten *et al.* (2002). Effects can be seen in the ventral and dorsal inferior frontal gyrus, and anterior ventral temporal cortex. Results are illustrated at a threshold of $p < 0.001$. (*b*) Regions where state-related activity during the animacy task blocks covaried ($p < 0.001$) with the number of subsequently recognized items. Greater activity was associated with better memory performance in the medial parietal cortex, and with worse performance in the left inferior prefrontal cortex. The bars show the mean parameter estimates and standard errors for the voxels showing the peak effect in each region.

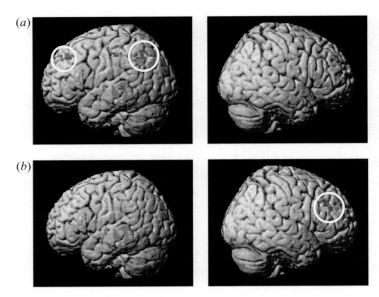

Plate 35. Data from Henson *et al.* (1999*a*). (*a*) Regions demonstrating greater activity for recognized items receiving Remember rather than Know judgements. These regions include the left anterior prefrontal and left lateral parietal cortex (indicated with white circles). (*b*) Right dorsolateral prefrontal region where the activity was greater for items receiving Know rather than Remember judgements. Images thresholded at $p < 0.01$.

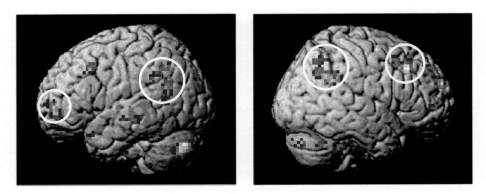

Plate 36. Data from Rugg *et al.* (2002) illustrating regions where activity was greater for correctly classified non-target items than for correctly classified new words in their recognition exclusion task. The regions include left anterior prefrontal, bilateral parietal and right dorsolateral prefrontal cortex (indicated by circles). Images thresholded at $p < 0.01$.

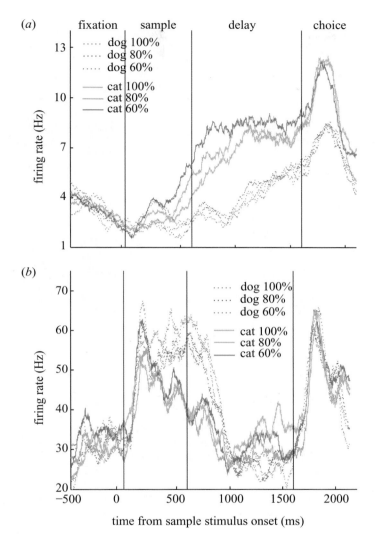

Plate 37. The average activity of two single neurons to stimuli at the six morph blends. The vertical lines correspond (from left to right) to sample onset, offset and test stimulus onset. Activity is pooled over match and non-match trials.

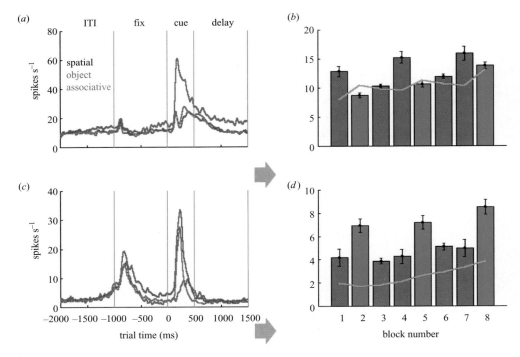

Plate 38. Spike rate versus time histograms for two neurons, each sorted by task. The final second of the three-second ITI is represented by the first 1000 ms (-2000 to -1000 ms). Fixation occurs soon after (*ca.* -1000 to -800 ms). Cue presentation occurs at the time-point marked 0 ms. Task-related differences in baseline firing rate were generally observed to begin in the fixation period. While the activity of some neurons diverged almost coincident with initial fixation (c), the activity of others diverged progressively as the appearance of the cue became more imminent (*a*). The bar graphs (*b,d*) demonstrate the reproducibility of these small task-specific changes in activity across multiple repetitions of the same task. The mean fixation-period firing rate (with standard errors) for each block of trials is shown for the two neurons in (*a*) and (*c*). The bars are colour-coded to reflect the task being performed in each block, and the colours match those in the histograms to the left. The light grey line superimposed over these bars shows the activity of these neurons during the second immediately preceding the ITI.

Modelling the haemodynamic response requires an understanding of the role of noise and its sources.

In imaging, different types of disturbances can interfere with the time-course of the haemodynamic response. In fact, EPI is one of the sequences most sensitive to disturbance, and various artefacts easily degrade EP images. Signal fluctuations are often related to physiological motion or general physiological state changes. They can also be of subtle origin, including minute fluctuations within the environment such as small changes in air pressure or temperature that by themselves are already sufficient to slightly alter the resonance frequency, phase or magnitude of the signal and prevent reproducible results in high resolution, time-resolved functional imaging. One way to reduce such artefacts is to use a technique based on 'navigator' echoes. This approach was initially used in conventional spin-echo imaging of moving structures (Ehman & Felmlee 1989) to reduce motion artefacts, and was subsequently adopted by a number of investigators (Hu & Kim 1994; Kim *et al.* 1996; Glover & Lai 1998; Pfeuffer *et al.* 2002*a*) employing susceptibility-weighted fMRI.

'Navigator' FIDs or echoes can be acquired to obtain information on a number of parameters (e.g. resonance frequency, global amplitude or phase). In our implementation with the Bruker Biospec system, for instance, the navigator echoes were two gradient echoes that were sampled with a positive and a negative readout gradient at the beginning of each acquisition. They were immediately followed by the acquisition of the phase-encoded gradient-echo train (i.e. a set of k space lines). The navigator FID was used for amplitude and frequency correction and the two navigator echoes were used for image de-ghosting (i.e. removing distortions in the phase-encoding direction). Additional ways to improve the image include corrections of direct current offset and equidistant sampling during the gradient-switch (transient) periods. The latter source of distortion originates in the way echoes are acquired in gradient-recalled MRI. More specifically, the digitization of the EPI gradient-echo sequence is done at equidistant time intervals, even while the read gradient is ramping to the desired strength. The data points acquired during ramping do not span a constant area, and therefore some correction is usually needed to achieve equidistant sampling in the k space. Finally, an important source of variability in EP imaging comes from physiologically induced global off-resonance effects. Typically, respiratory and cardiac pulsations—just like instrument instabilities—may introduce NMR phase shifts that may cause variation in the signal's amplitude as well as shifts (ghosting) between segments; such artefacts can be detected and also corrected with navigator echoes either directly in the k space (Pfeuffer *et al.* 2002*a*) or in the spatial domain.

The effects of all these corrections on the time-course of the BOLD signal are presented in Figure 4.10*a*, that shows the average of haemodynamic responses from a single voxel ($0.5\,mm \times 0.5\,mm \times 2\,mm$) to 14 stimulus (rotating checkerboards) presentations. The variability of the response can be seen in the standard deviation bars plotted for every other image.

The onset of the stimulus-induced haemodynamic response plotted in Figure 4.10*a* was delayed by about 2 s, which is consistent with previous studies (Kwong *et al.* 1992). This is the time that it takes blood to travel from arteries to capillaries and draining veins. The haemodynamic response reached a plateau in 6–12 s and returned to the baseline with a similar ramp, although often a prolonged poststimulus undershoot was evident (Frahm *et al.* 1996; Kruger *et al.* 1996; Buxton *et al.* 1998; Logothetis *et al.* 1999). It is thought that the time-course of the haemodynamic response is determined by an initial increase in oxygen consumption that alters the dHb-to-oxyhaemoglobin ratio (Malonek & Grinvald 1996), followed by an increase in CBF that overcompensates for the oxygen extraction, so that an oversupply

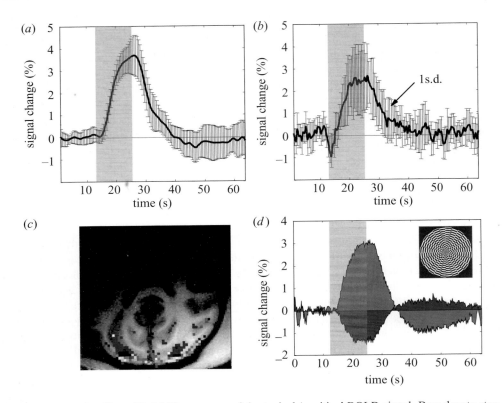

Fig. 4.10. See also Plate 17. (*a*) Time-course of the typical 'positive' BOLD signal. Bars denote standard deviation. The trace is the average of 14 time series of the same voxel. (*b*) The initial dip (see § 4.4*c*), 14 averages of a single voxel. (*c*) *z*-score map showing areas with negative BOLD. (*d*) The time-course of the two—correlated and anticorrelated—BOLD responses.

of oxygenated blood is delivered (Fox & Raichle 1986; Fox *et al*. 1988). This oversupply underlies the signal increase typically observed in BOLD fMRI (positive BOLD). Figure 4.10*a* shows an example of positive BOLD for the time-series of a single voxel, averaged over 14 repetitions. Small changes in metabolism require a disproportionately large oversupply because the passive diffusion-driven oxygen extraction from the blood is less efficient at higher flow rates (Buxton & Frank 1997; Hyder *et al*. 1998). The increased flow causes vasodilation because of the balloon-like elasticity of the venules and veins, resulting in an increase in venous blood volume (Buxton *et al*. 1998; Mandeville *et al*. 1999*a,b*). This volume increase is thought to lie at the root of the poststimulus undershoot described in § 4.4*c*.

Occasionally, a small decrease in image intensity below the baseline was observed immediately after the stimulus onset. Figure 4.10*b* illustrates this initial 'dip' for the time-series of a voxel (14 repetitions). This kind of dip has been reported in MRS experiments (Ernst & Hennig 1994) and in BOLD fMRI in humans, rats, cats and monkeys (Menon *et al*. 1995; Jezzard *et al*. 1997; Hu *et al*. 1997; Yacoub & Hu 1999; Logothetis *et al*. 1999). Optical imaging studies indicate that the initial dip reflects the early oxygen consumption, so it should be closely correlated with the metabolic demand in the parenchyma, and hence more closely related to the neuronal activity than the other components of the haemodynamic response (Malonek & Grinvald 1996; Malonek *et al*. 1997; Vanzetta & Grinvald 1999; Jones *et al*. 2001).

In a series of experiments conducted in my laboratory, we have investigated the time-course of the BOLD signal using a fast scanning protocol ($T_R/T_E = 250/20$ ms). The probability of seeing the initial dip in a single voxel at least once in 50 repetitions was found to be approximately 0.3. This variability is probably due to physiological noise. Haemodynamic responses depend not only on magnetic susceptibility but also on blood volume and flow, each of which can be selectively evaluated by various methods (Frahm et al. 1996; Kruger et al. 1996; Kim & Ugurbil 1997; Kennan et al. 1997; Bandettini et al. 1997; Davis et al. 1998; Mandeville et al. 1999b; Marota et al. 1999; Lee et al. 2001; Mandeville et al. 2001). All in all, with such sensitivity, the initial dip seems to be an extremely unreliable BOLD component for use in studies of cortical microarchitecture, a fact that explains the controversy between different investigators (Marota et al. 1999; Logothetis 2000; Kim et al. 2000; Buxton 2001; Vanzetta & Grinvald 2001; Mayhew et al. 2001; Lindauer et al. 2001; Cannestra et al. 2001).

The BOLD response is not always 'positively correlated' to the stimulus time-course the way it has been described so far. Negative signals (anti-correlations) like those shown in Figure 4.10c have also been observed and were reported in previous studies (Kennan et al. 1998; Martin et al. 1999). In our studies, we often found a negative BOLD response that was perfectly anti-correlated with the positive BOLD response, all the way to the undershoot component (see Figure 4.10c). A negative BOLD signal was seen exclusively in cortical regions that were not stimulated by the visual stimulus (e.g. a peripheral visual field beyond the extent of the stimulus). Retinotopy experiments in humans also systematically demonstrate the existence of negative BOLD (B. Wandell, personal communication), the origin of which is currently under extensive physiological investigation.

As a final point, temporally resolved fMRI is only useful for physiological studies if the images also have a high spatial resolution. In EPI, for a given spatial resolution, the acquisition time is proportional to the FOV in the phase-encoding direction, that is, to the number of k space lines. Multi-shot or *segmented* acquisition that affords better SNR and thus promises higher spatial resolution, decreases the temporal resolution by increasing the image acquisition time. It is therefore important to apply methods that use an FOV as small as the potential volume of interest. Reducing the FOV, on the other hand, causes signals outside the FOV to fold back into the image in the phase-encoding direction. Recently, a special outer-volume suppression technique was successfully employed to achieve B_1-insensitive suppression in the inhomogeneous RF field of a surface coil (Luo et al. 2001). This technique, combined with zoomed imaging that minimizes imaging time by reducing the FOV (Pfeuffer et al. 2002b), promises to be of great value in combined physiology and imaging experiments.

4.5. Combined fMRI and microelectrode recording

The success of fMRI ultimately depends on a comprehensive understanding of the relationship between the fMRI signal and the underlying neuronal activity. A number of studies in humans and animals have already combined fMRI with EEG (Menon et al. 1997; Krakow et al. 1999; Bonmassar et al. 1999; Krakow et al. 2000) or optical imaging recordings of intrinsic signals (Hess et al. 2000). But optical imaging also measures haemodynamic responses (Bonhoeffer & Grinvald 1996) and thus can offer very little direct evidence of the underlying neural activity, while EEG studies typically suffer from poor spatial resolution and relatively imprecise localization of the electromagnetic field patterns associated with neural current flow. Microelectrode recordings, however, can directly measure the activity of small neural populations, and have been used extensively to obtain data about the central nervous system in both anaesthetized and alert, behaving animals. Simultaneous electrophysiological and imaging experiments are a promising method that should reveal a great deal about the nature of the fMRI BOLD signal.

(a) Microelectrode recording in the presence of strong magnetic fields

Certain hardware, including novel electrode types and signal conditioning equipment, had to be developed before it was possible to conduct electrophysiological measurements during the MR image acquisition. Details have been given elsewhere (Logothetis *et al.* 2001). Briefly, the generation of an MR image involves a strong alternation of field gradients (see § 4.2b(iii)). Such alternations induce voltages in any existing loop in the circuit of electro-physiology equipment placed within the magnet. Conventional shielding reduces electrical interference but is ineffective against magnetic interference, while materials like μ-metals that attenuate magnetic interference contain iron, affecting the field homogeneity. Further-more, the low-noise, low-frequency voltage amplifiers typically used in neurophysiology rectify high-frequency voltage signals coupled with the input signal, an effect that occurs at all stages of their integrated circuits. In a 4.7 T magnet, for instance, amplifiers rectify the 200 MHz RF excitation pulses, resulting in a substantial disturbance of the output that only recovers several tens of milliseconds after the RF signal has subsided. Alternatively, simply placing the preamplifiers outside the gradient tube is not a solution, because the elec-trode impedance and the capacitance of the long (more than 2 m) cable necessary to connect the electrode to that preamplifier would act as a voltage divider and compromise the signal.

To avoid signal loss due to increased cable length, we developed a method of measuring cur-rent instead of voltage that is insensitive to the cable length. Current flow from the electrode tip was measured over a cable long enough to permit the placement of preamplifiers outside the gradient coil, and was then converted into voltage at the input stage of the amplifier. In addition, we identified and compensated for the interference introduced by the gradient alter-nation. Interference during imaging originated from sources located at a distance greater than that from the electrode tip to the electrode ground (far interference) and from the immediate vicinity of the electrode tip (near interference). The first is due to the metal-to-electrolyte inter-face present whenever the animal is capacitively connected to any metal contact, including connections to the ground and electrode; the latter originates and acts in the vicinity of the elec-trode tip or within the electrode holder and the cables primarily because of eddy currents. Near interference required the measurement of local magnetic field changes by means of three small, identical, orthogonally oriented coils positioned near the electrode. The two types of interference compensations ultimately permitted the collection of denoised neural data.

The denoising procedures described in the previous paragraph ensure a non-saturated, meas-urable signal which, however, may be still contaminated with a certain amount of gradient interference. By using the principal component analysis technique and by reconstructing the signal after excluding those components that best correlated with the directly recorded inter-ference, we were able to isolate the neural signal. Figure 4.11 illustrates the procedure of inter-ference removal. Figure 4.11*a* shows the recorded gradient currents of the three gradients, and Figure 4.11*b*, upper trace shows the summed signal that induced the voltages depicted by the middle trace of Figure 4.11*b*. The pattern of interference shown in the middle trace was approx-imately the same for each acquired image segment. The data were therefore initially realigned to the slice-selection pulse (signifying the beginning of collection of an image of a single *k* space segment for single- or multi-shot acquisitions, respectively), and subsequently reshaped into an $N \times M$ matrix, where N was the number of segments and M was the number of data

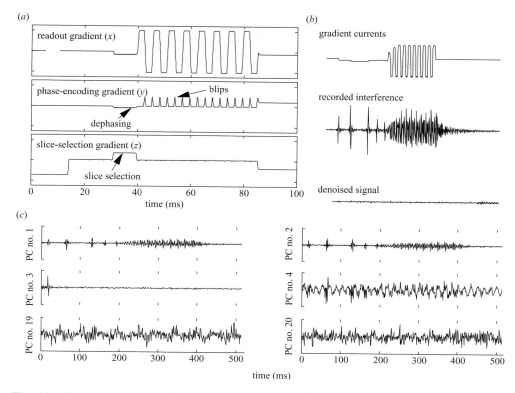

Fig. 4.11. Electromagnetic interference. (*a*) The recorded gradient currents from the slice-selection, phase-encoding and readout gradient for an EP imaging sequence. (*b*) Elimination of residual interference by applying principal component analysis. The top trace is the summation of the three gradient currents, and the middle the induced voltage at the tip of the electrode. PC analysis isolates the residual interference left after online compensation. The denoised signal is depicted by the lower trace. (*c*) Examples of principal components. PCs nos 1 and 2 capture most interference. Setting their eigenvectors to zero and reconstructing the signal with the remaining PCs eliminates any interference.

points acquired while digitizing the physiology signal. The PC analysis of such data and elimination of those principal components that best correlated with the directly recorded interference (Figure 4.11*c*) resulted in a 'clean' signal (bottom trace of Figure 4.11*b*).

(b) Microelectrode measurements of the neural signal

(i) Imaging the recording site

Figure 4.12*a* shows the electrodes used for the combined imaging and physiology experiments, together with the different types of sensors used to compensate the gradient interference. Figure 4.12*b* is an anatomical scan ($T_E/T_R = 8.9$, $T_R = 2000$ ms, FOV = 96 mm $\times$ 96 mm, and a 512 $\times$ 384 matrix reconstructed to 512 $\times$ 512, slice thickness of 0.5 mm) acquired with the FLASH sequence (Haase *et al.* 1986). Similar scans were typically used for the precise localization of the electrode tip. Here, the electrode tip is located in the middle layers of the primary visual cortex. The image demonstrates the limited susceptibility artefacts caused by the miniature electrode tip. Although of smaller SNR, spin-echo T_2 weighted images are usually even

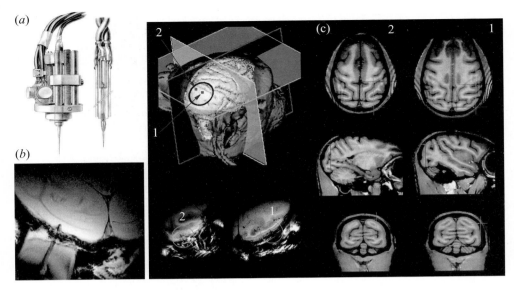

Fig. 4.12. See also Plate 18. (*a*) The microelectrodes and their holder consisting of three concentric, metallic cylinders, the innermost serving as the contact point for the electrode, the middle as the far-interference sensor and the outermost as the ground. The three-coil magnetic-field sensor used to compensate for near interference is also shown. (*b*) FLASH scan (see § 4.5*b*(i)) showing the location of the electrode-tip in the primary visual cortex. (*c*) A reconstruction of the position of the two electrodes from the three-dimensional MDEFT scans (top left) with orthogonal views (right). At the bottom left the inversion-recovery images show the actual electrodes (double electrode recording).

less susceptible to such artefacts. In most scans, a functional signal could be obtained in the immediate vicinity of the microelectrode. Figure 4.12*c* shows a typical three-dimensional reconstruction of the electrode position (here two electrodes) from a multislice anatomical scan (three-dimensional MDEFT; $T_E/T_R = 4/14.9$ ms, four segments).

Figure 4.13*a* demonstrates the neural activity (black trace) recorded in such a combined experiment superimposed on the BOLD fMRI signal (red). The yellow trace shows the effective (root mean square) value of the neural signal obtained for non-overlapping windows of 250 ms (the T_R of imaging). The neural signal shown was digitized, denoised as described in § 4.5*a*, and reduced from 22.3 to 7 kHz. It is a comprehensive signal characterized by time-varying spatial distributions of action potentials (spikes) superimposed on relatively slow varying field potentials. The action potentials can be isolated from the other signals by using template matching or other statistical pattern recognition techniques (Figure 4.13*b*).

The instantaneous or mean rate of such spikes is the neuronal variable most frequently examined with respect to a sensory stimulus or behavioural state, and the one recently used to examine quantitatively the relationship of the BOLD signal to neural activity by comparing human fMRI data with electrophysiological data in monkeys performing the same task (Heeger *et al.* 2000; Rees *et al.* 2000; for a review see Heeger & Ress 2002). At this point it is therefore worth taking a moment to consider what aspects of cortical processing the commonly reported spikes represent. Or, more generally, what kind of cortical activity is actually measured by the microelectrodes?

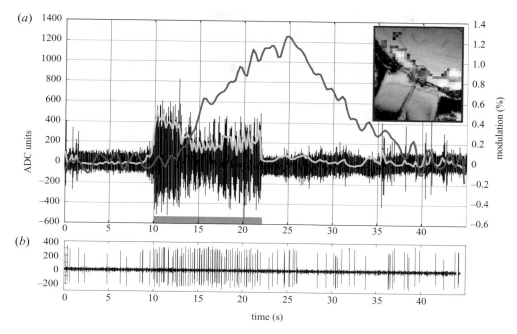

Fig. 4.13. See also Plate 19. The neural signal. (*a*) The comprehensive signal, with its effective values in yellow and the BOLD activation in red. The BOLD response is the average time-series of the voxels within the green circle of the T_2^*-weighted image in the inset. The green horizontal bar shows the stimulus presentation period. Black trace, raw; yellow trace, root mean square. (*b*) A sequence of single action potentials included in the comprehensive signal. The spikes were isolated using statistical methods. Their rate is one of the parameters often compared with the haemodynamic response. In most extracellular recordings, in particular in those conducted with behaving animals, such isolated action potentials commonly reflect the 'output' activity of a studied area (see § 4.5*b*(v)).

(ii) What is measured by the electrodes?

Almost all physiology studies in conscious animals report extracellular recordings. While the principles at work during the recording of transmembrane electrical events with intracellular electrodes are reasonably well understood, the interpretation of such extracellular recordings often proves very difficult. Most variations in such signals are closely related to the architecture of neuronal sites, making a comprehensive quantitative treatment of this subject enormously complicated.

In the classical treatment of the topic, a neuron is considered to be embedded in an extracellular medium that acts as a volume conductor (Lorente de Nó 1947) (for a detailed review on field potentials see Freeman (1975); for background in biophysics see Aidley 1989; Johnston & Wu 1995; Koch 1999). When the membrane potential between two separate regions of such a neuron is different, there is a flow of current in the neuron matched by a return current through the extracellular path. Active regions of the membrane are considered to act as a current *sink* and inactive ones as a *source* for the active regions. Such extracellular field potentials add up linearly and algebraically throughout the volume conductor. Thus, with respect to a remote or indifferent electrode potential, fields generated by, say, two neurons may add to or cancel each other depending upon the relative timing of their action potentials. Synchronous activation of many neurons lying in an array within the brain will result in a large field potential that is very similar to the action potential of a single neuron within that array. At least, that is what would happen if the volume conductor behaved like an ohmic resistor and was isotropic; but in actuality this is not the case. It is actually made up largely of neuronal elements with a comparatively small portion of the total volume occupied by extracellular fluid. The membrane of the neurons 'adds' a great deal of capacitance and makes it unlikely that current will flow uniformly in all directions around the neuron. In fact, the orientation of dendrites and axons dramatically influences the summation of the potentials. In other words, although theoretical calculations are useful, understanding the content of the comprehensive signal acquired by the electrode requires systematic experimentation and good knowledge of the microanatomical cortical architecture.

Figure 4.14*b* is a schematic drawing of neo-cortex (a section of the primary visual cortex of monkeys illustrated in Figure 4.14*a*) with some basic neuron types and their interconnections (for comprehensive reviews see Szentagothai 1978; Martin 1988; Lund *et al.* 1994). The pyramidal cells with their prominent apical dendrites are the principal (projection) neurons, representing the sole cortical output. They project to other brain areas and to the spinal cord, but also have recurrent collaterals projecting locally. They receive input from other pyramidal cells (recurrent input) and from a number of interneurons, including the spiny stellate cells, chandelier cells and the small and large basket cells. Input to the pyramidal cells may also be of thalamic (specific) and cortical (association) origin. The pyramidal cells are highly polarized, and their apical dendrites are always perpendicular to the pial surface of the brain. They are thus an exquisite example of a so-called *open field* geometrical arrangement (Figure 4.14*c*), because the dendrites face in one direction and the soma in another. This produces strong dendrite-to-soma dipoles when they are activated by synchronous synaptic input. Other neurons are oriented horizontally, and may contribute less efficiently or not at all to the sum of potentials.

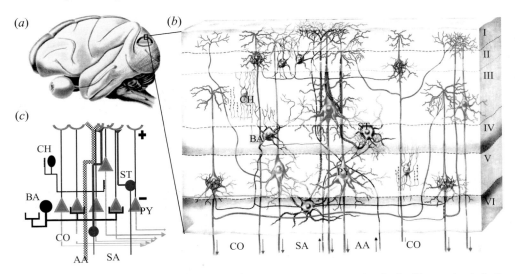

Fig. 4.14. See also Plate 20. Cortical circuitry. (*a*) Lateral view of a monkey brain. The section is in the striate cortex. (*b*) Neuronal types and connections. (*c*) Model of basic cortical circuitry showing the 'open field' arrangement of pyramidal cells. The parallel unidirectional arrangement of apical dendrites facilitates the summation of field potentials by generating strong dipoles (see § 4.5*b*(ii)). Abbreviations: CH, chandelier; BA, basket; PY, pyramidal; ST, stellate cells; SA, specific afferents; AA, association afferents; CO, pyramidal cell axons representing cortical output.

If a microelectrode is inserted into a brain site, say at a point in cerebral cortex, the measured potential with respect to a distant site actually reflects many different action potentials of various sizes, some at high amplitudes and others at amplitudes that are barely discriminable from the thermal noise at the electrode tip. The spikes are superimposed on many other waves of lower frequency. Traditionally, the spikes and the slower voltage variations are separated from one another by high- and low-pass filtering, respectively, and this band separation is thought to reflect different types of activity. A filter cut-off of *ca.* 300–400 Hz is used in most recordings to obtain MUA (above 400 Hz) and (LFPs (below 300 Hz).

(iii) Origin of LFPs and MUA: the logic of frequency-band separation
The rationale behind this frequency-band separation can be understood on the basis of some simple theoretical considerations (unpublished simulations). Spikes are fast events lasting only

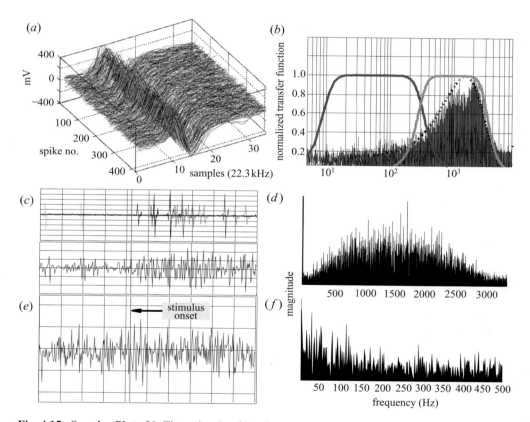

Fig. 4.15. See also Plate 21. The rationale of band separation in extracellular recordings. (*a*) Isolated action potentials. (*b*) The average spectrum of these potentials is shown with the blue surface plot. The red and green traces represent the transfer functions of the chosen filters. They correspond to the LFPs and MUA, respectively. Red trace, LFP transfer function; green trace, MUA transfer function; dotted black trace, average spike-spectrum. (*c*) Top, using the isolated spikes, spike trains were simulated by using the interspike probability distributions measured in the actual experiment. Bottom, the simulated spikes are summed up to obtain artificial MUA. (*d*) The spectrum of such activity. (*e,f*) Simulations for pEPSPs.

0.4–0.5 ms and 0.7–1.0 ms for axons and soma, respectively. EPSPs or IPSPs, on the other hand, may last several milliseconds and range from a couple to 100 ms. In other words, they are slow waves. A spectral analysis of these two types of waveforms shows quantitatively that they fall into two different frequency bands. More specifically, individual action potentials in the comprehensive signal can be detected and isolated using a variety of statistical pattern recognition techniques. Figure 4.15*a* shows 392 isolated action potentials. The power spectrum of each spike is computed and the average of these spectra is plotted in Figure 4.15*b* (dotted black trace). The blue line shows the actual spectrum of the MUA from the same session. Note the similarity between the spectral power distribution of the MUA with that of a single spike waveform. Superimposed on this plot are the frequency responses of the filters used to split the original signal into bands. For our measurements the LFPs (red trace) were extracted by bandpass filtering between 10 and 300 Hz, and the MUA (green trace) by bandpass filtering between 300 and 3000 Hz. It can be seen that the average spectrum of a spike is well within the region thought to represent MUA. The latter is, after all, the result of a summation of many such waveforms (spikes) shifted randomly in time, and it does not substantially change the spectral power distribution, a fact shown by the simulations in Figure 4.15*c,d*.

In the same vein, the average spectrum of simulated population pEPSPs shows substantially higher energy in the low-frequency range (below 150 Hz) than in the MUA range. The summation of such potentials (Figure 4.15*e*), even without any synchronicity constraints, yields the spectrum shown in Figure 4.15*f*. To a large extent, therefore, population EPSPs and MUA are separated in the frequency domain. But the inverse may not be always true, in the sense that a considerable synchronization of spikes exhibiting significant periodicity at different frequencies may yield power in the low-frequency range. However, such intrusion will take the form of single spectral peaks rather than a broad enhancement over the entire LFP range. All in all, MUA most probably represents the average spiking of small neural populations around the electrode, and LFPs represent the weighted averages of dendrosomatic postsynaptic signals reflecting input activity (afferent or local). The synchronization of input activity facilitates the summation of LFPs, although their slow nature, which itself facilitates summation as well, does not impose strict synchronization constraints.

(iv) Origin of LFP and MUA: experimental evidence
The aforementioned simple theoretical considerations are consistent with experimental work. The extracellular current flow does indeed vary from one recording site to another as a direct function of neuronal size (Nelson 1966), and the magnitude of axonal spikes directly correlates with the size of the transmitting axon (Gasser & Grundfest 1939; Hunt 1951). Furthermore, it has been shown that fast activity (i.e. activity in the 'MUA range' mentioned in § 4.5*b*(iii)) is a characteristic property of a given brain site (Buchwald & Grover 1970), varying considerably in amplitude from one brain region to another but remaining relatively constant for any particular site (e.g. neocortex versus hippocampus). In combined physiology–histology experiments. Moreover, it was found that homogeneous populations of large cells occur at sites of large amplitude fast activity and vice versa (Grover & Buchwald 1970). Thus, the specificity of the fast activity reflects the magnitude of variation of extracellular spike potentials rather than artefacts such as variations in the recording system, fibre discharge contamination or differences in local tissue impedances. Thus, the large amplitude of fast activity reflects large-amplitude extracellular potentials and small-amplitude fast activity is correlated with small potentials.

Fast MUA can be measured whenever the impedance of the electrode is sufficiently low, so that spikes from single units do not predominate in the signal. Electrodes with exposed tips of *ca.* 100 μm (impedance from 40 to 120 kΩ), for example, were estimated to record from a sphere of radius equal to 50–350 μm (Grover & Buchwald 1970; Legatt *et al.* 1980; Gray *et al.* 1995), whereby the activity from each point within the sphere is weighted by a factor depending on the distance of the point from the tip of the electrode (Nicholson & Llinas 1971). Recent simultaneous intracellular and extracellular tetrode recordings from single neurons showed that the amplitude of the average extracellular spike decreases rapidly as a function of the distance of the tip from the soma, with the largest amplitudes recorded at distances smaller than 50 μm; at distances greater than 140 mm, no extracellular spike activity could be discerned from the background noise (Henze *et al.* 2000). In conclusion, depending on the recording site and the electrode properties, the MUA most probably represents a weighted sum of the extracellular action potentials of neurons within a sphere of *ca.* 200–300 μm radius, with the electrode at its centre. Spikes produced by the synchronous firings of many cells can, in principle, be enhanced by summation and thus detected at a larger distance (Huang & Buchwald 1977; Arezzo *et al.* 1979).

LFPs, on the other hand, were shown to correlate with synaptic interactions and less often with MUA. Initial evidence for this came from combined EEG and intracortical recordings showing that the slow wave activity in the EEG is largely independent of the neuronal spiking (Fromm & Bond 1964, 1967; Ajmone-Marsan 1965; Buchwald *et al.* 1965). These studies indicated that slow field fluctuations reflect the extent and geometry of dendrites in each recording site and are not correlated with cell size. More recent evidence comes from current-source density analysis and combined field potential and intracellular recordings. The former has indicated that LFPs actually reflect a weighted average of synchronized dendrosomatic components of synaptic signals of a neural population within 0.5–3 mm of the electrode tip (Mitzdorf 1987; Juergens *et al.* 1999). The upper limits of the spatial extent of LFP summation were indirectly calculated by computing the phase coherence of LFPs as a function of inter-electrode distance in experiments with simultaneous multiple- electrode recordings (Juergens *et al.* 1996).

Combined intracellular and field potential recordings also indicate a synaptic–dendritic origin for the LFPs. Experiments comparing membrane and network properties typically investigate the phase locking of membrane potential oscillations (rhythmic discharges) to certain frequency bands. Traditionally, low-frequency signal modulations are classified in a number of specific frequency bands initially introduced in the EEG literature (see Elul 1969, 1971; Pedley & Traub 1990). For one, EEG is classified in three distinct groups: rhythmic, arrhythmic and dysrhythmic. The first two appear in normal subjects and refer to waves of approximately constant frequency and no stable rhythms, respectively. The latter refers to rhythms or patterns of EEG activity that characteristically appear in patient groups and rarely or never in healthy subjects. Rhythmic EEG is further subdivided into frequency bands known as delta (δ, 0–4 Hz), theta (θ, 4–8 Hz), alpha (α, 8–12 Hz), beta (β, 12–24 Hz), and gamma (γ, 24–40/80 Hz) that are typically characterized by different amplitudes (Lindsley & Wicke 1974; Steriade & Hobson 1976; Basar 1980; Steriade 1991). The classification is based on the strong correlation of each band with a distinct behavioural state. In humans, delta and theta, for instance, are generally associated with sleep and have the largest amplitudes in EEG activity; alpha waves are associated with a state of relaxed wakefulness and beta and gamma with intense mental activity. These last two are characterized by very small amplitudes. Such rhythmic patterns are associated with the thalamocortical loops and are modulated by the ascending network system and basal forebrain (Steriade 1991; Steriade *et al.* 1993).

Important insights into the origin of LFPs come from studies examining the relationship of activity in any of the frequency bands described in the previous paragraph to changes in the membrane potential of individual neurons. Recently, for instance, the relationship between membrane and network properties of lateral septum neurons to the theta band was studied in the rat hippocampus (Pedemonte *et al.* 1998). The DB and the MSN are thought to act as θ-rhythm pacemakers, because cells in these nuclei display rhythmic membrane oscillations and bursting discharge patterns (Barrenechea *et al.* 1995), while lesions of these nuclei abolish this rhythm (Gray & Ball 1970; Apostol & Creutzfeldt 1974). Furthermore, the lateral septum is thought to provide feedback input from hippocampus to DB and MSN (see Raisman 1966). Inter-actions within this pathway were investigated by making simultaneous extracellular recordings of LFPs and intracellular recordings of transmembrane potentials from neurons exhibiting rhythmic discharges or phase locking to theta oscillations. The results indicated that the rhythmic discharge patterns of septal neurons are due to synaptic interactions (Pedemonte *et al.* 1998). Membrane oscillations in lateral septal neurons, for instance, are phase locked to hippocampal theta activity, the amplitude of the former being dependent on the amplitude of the field changes. Furthermore, current injections showed that hyperpolarization increases and depolarization decreases the amplitude of oscillations, indicating that EPSPs may make a greater contribution to the generation of periodicity than IPSPs (Pedemonte *et al.* 1998).

Similar conclusions were drawn in combined intra- and extracellular recordings in invertebrates. The antennal lobe of locust has a mixed population of projection and local (inter-) neurons (for a review see Laurent *et al.* 2001). The former are excitatory and project to the MB and lateral protocerebral lobe; the latter are inhibitory. Neither class has intrinsic oscillatory properties, and both show rhythmic activity patterns only during natural (odour) or electrical stimulation. Simultaneous recordings from the antennal lobe and the MB showed that stimulation evokes reproducible, phase locked 20–30 Hz oscillations in the membrane of PNs and the LFPs of MB neurons (Wehr & Laurent 1999). Here, too, paired intracellular recordings and pharmacological manipulations indicate that to a large extent LFP changes originate in the synaptic interactions within the antennal lobe.

But rhythmic activity related to some of the EEG frequency bands has also been reported for the spiking principal neurons. Many pyramidal neurons in layer 5 of the neocortex show prolonged, 5–12 Hz rhythmic firing patterns due to intrinsic membrane properties such as sodium conductance, which is essential for rhythmicity, and calcium-dependent conductance, which strongly modifies it (Silva *et al.* 1991). Although synaptic networks of intrinsically rhythmic neurons may still be the origin of the synchronized cortical oscillations, spiking activity—in this case—will be tightly correlated with the LFPs and will contribute to the modulation of their amplitude. Similar behaviour has been reported for a biophysically distinct class of pyramidal cells (chattering cells) in the superficial cortex layers of cats (Gray & McCormick 1996). Their oscillatory behaviour (20–60 Hz), accompanied by periodic changes in the membrane potential, is induced in response to suprathreshold depolarizing current injection or visual stimulation, and is absent during periods of spontaneous activity. Oscillations were also observed in the peripheral olfactory system of insects (locust, *Schistocerca americana*) (Laurent & Davidowitz 1994), the olfactory cortex of rats and rabbits (Granger & Lynch 1991), and the somatosensory cortex of monkeys (Mountcastle *et al.* 1990; Ahissar & Vaadia 1990; Recanzone *et al.* 1992; Romo & Salinas 1999). New insights into their generation, as well as into intracortical processing in general, came from the study of inhibitory networks in hippocampus (Buzsaki & Chrobak 1995; Kandel & Buzsaki 1997; Kocsis *et al.* 1999).

In conclusion, MUA is obtained by bandpass filtering of the comprehensive neural signal in a frequency range of 400 to a few thousand Hz, and it represents the weighted average of the spiking activity within a sphere of approximately one-third of a millimetre radius with the microelectrode at its centre. It most probably includes dendritic spikes and activity from interneurons. LFPs, on the other hand, predominantly reflect synaptic events, including synchronized afferent or local spiking activity. They are obtained by low-pass filtering the signal to permit frequencies below 300 Hz, or by bandpass filtering it between 10 and 300 Hz, to exclude the sleep-related slow oscillations or changes due to anaesthesia. Spatial summation of LFPs occurs within a couple of millimetres from the electrode tip.

(v) Spike rates of single units in extracellular recordings reflect cortical output activity
Although LFP and MUA activity conveys important information regarding the role of small neuronal populations in sensory processing or behaviour, most neuro-physiological studies, in particular those in behaving animals, concentrate on the activity of isolated single units. It is therefore worth considering the question of which neuronal types are usually reported in such experiments. The frequency with which certain neuronal types appear in extracellular recordings depends on their relative density, the size of their spikes, electrode properties and the stability of the recordings. For equivalent transmembrane action potentials, the discharge of a large neuron generates a substantially greater flow of membrane current and a larger extracellular spike than a small cell, and the resulting extracellular field remains above recording noise levels over a greater distance. Theoretically, one would expect larger neurons (cells with 20–30 μm diameter or greater) to generate a potential of 100 μV or more within a 100 μm diameter sphere with the electrode tip at its centre (Rall 1962). It follows that spikes generated by such large neurons may remain above the noise level over a greater distance from the cell than do spikes from small neurons, and thus microelectrodes are likely to sample their somas or axons preferentially. In addition, recordings from such neurons tend to be less sensitive to small motions, a quality which is critical for the stability of recordings in the alert behaving animal. Smaller neurons require the electrode tip to lie considerably closer to that neuron than to any other active ones of comparable size. If the tip is too close, it will usually injure a small cell, and if it is too far away, it becomes difficult to isolate the cell. Thus, the measured spikes represent very small neural populations of one or just a few isolated large cells, that in the cortex are by and large the principal cells (e.g. pyramidal cells in the cerebral cortex and Purkinje neurons in the cerebellar cortex).

Various investigators have also demonstrated such a microelectrode sampling bias experimentally. In a systematic study, Towe & Harding (1970) stimulated the PTNs of cats at the medullar level with stimulus intensities that would activate all the axons in the pyramidal tract, and computed the distribution of conduction speeds and the expected latencies by simultaneously recording in the peri-cruciate cortex. They then compared these distributions with those expected on the basis of the histological fibre spectrum, namely from the distribution of 'axon sizes'. They found that although the pyramidal tract of cats consists mainly of small axons (low-conduction speed and thus long latencies), the latencies obtained during the experiment (antidromic response latencies) were mostly short (around 1 ms). Due to the fact that all the axons were stimulated, they indicated that a bias towards neurons with large bodies is evident in extracellular recordings. A similar electrode bias was reported in the monkey PTN system (Humphrey & Corrie 1978).

It follows that the vast majority of experiments employing extracellular recordings report on the activity of principal cells, namely on the output of a cortical area related to a given stimulus or task. This is particularly true for experiments in the alert, behaving animal or human (Fried *et al.* 1997; Kreiman *et al.* 2000*a,b*), during which even slight movements make holding smaller neurons for a sufficiently long time an extremely difficult task. Furthermore, recording from interneurons (e.g. inhibitory cells) is often very difficult as well, for their response is often uncorrelated to the stimulus or behaviour state of the animal.

4.6. The neural origin of bold response

(a) Magnitude changes in LFPs and MUA during visual stimulation

The contribution of MUA and LFP signals to the haemodynamic response was examined by applying time-dependent frequency analysis to the raw data. Typically, after stimulus presentation a transient increase in power was observed across all frequencies, followed by a lower level of activation that was maintained for the entire duration of the stimulus presentation. A prominent characteristic in all spectrograms was a marked stimulus-induced increase in the magnitude of the LFP, which was always larger than that observed for MUA. A decrease in neural activity was also observed immediately after the termination of the stimulus.

To confirm these results a spectrogram was computed across all the scans for the first 6 s of the neural response averaged over all the data collected during 6, 12, 12.5, and 24 s-long stimulus presentation (Figure 4.16). The time series at each frequency is expressed in units of standard deviation (s.d.) of the activity in the prestimulus period and therefore represents the SNR of the response at that frequency. The average LFP and MUA responses were computed as the mean vector of the time-series in the frequency regions 40–130 Hz (red dashed lines) and 300–1500 Hz (green dashed lines). Figure 4.16b shows these mean curves together with

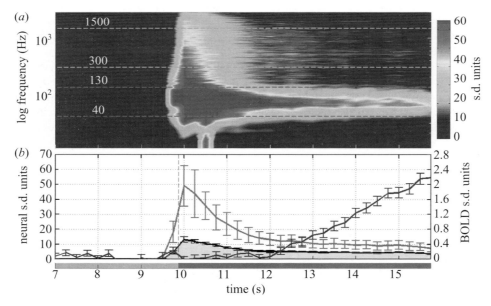

Fig. 4.16. See also Plate 22. Time-dependent frequency analysis for the population data. (a) Spectrogram of the first 6 s of the neural response averaged over all data. Each time-course is expressed in units of the standard deviation of the prestimulus period. Colour coding indicates the reliability of the signal change for each frequency (SNR). Red and green dashed lines show the LFP and MUA frequency bands, respectively. Mean = 72.96; s.d. = 21.04. (b) Mean LFP (red), MUA (black) and total (light green surface) neural response averaged across all frequencies, together with the BOLD signal (blue). Note that the 'activity increase' seemingly occurring before the stimulus presentation is due solely to the windows used to create the spectrograms. The two vertical axes show the difference in the SNR of the neural and BOLD signals. Across all the data a difference of approximately one order of magnitude was found in the reliability of the two signals. From Logothetis *et al.* (2001), with permission.

the total average over all frequencies and the BOLD responses for all data in s.d. units. Note the marked difference in SNR (scale of the vertical axes) between the neural and the BOLD signals. Such a difference can, in principle, result in statistical rejection of the activation of various regions during mapping experiments, despite the fact that the underlying neural activity is highly robust and significant.

(b) Adaptation reveals BOLD response without MUA

A fraction of all multi-unit responses were found to be transient; they showed an initial increase in amplitude and then returned to the baseline within 2–4 s. Figure 4.17 illustrates simultaneous recordings of haemodynamic responses, LFPs and transient single-unit activity and MUA in the striate cortex. As can be seen, both the SDF, representing the instantaneous firing rate of one or a few neurons whose spike waveform could be identified, and the MUA show strong adaptation, returning to the baseline ca. 2.5 s after stimulus onset. By contrast, the activity underlying the LFPs remains elevated for the entire duration of the visual stimulus. There was no single observation period or recording site for which the opposite result was observed, namely a highly correlated MUA signal and an uncorrelated or missing LFP signal. Similarly, we never observed MUA that was larger in magnitude than the measured LFP activity magnitude, or that the MUA–SNR ratio was higher than the LFP–SNR ratio. These findings indicate that BOLD activation may reflect the neural activity related to the input and the local processing in any given area rather than the output spiking activity.

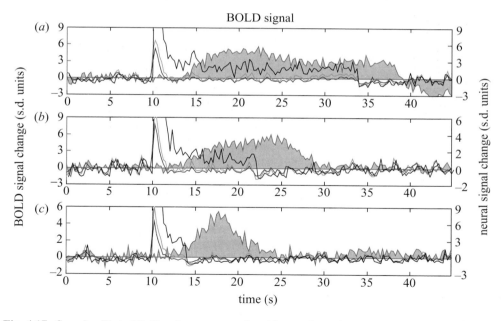

Fig. 4.17. See also Plate 23. Simultaneous neural and haemodynamic recordings from a cortical site showing a transient neural response. (*a*–*c*) Responses to pulse stimuli of 24, 12, and 4 s. Pink tint, BOLD; black trace, LFP; green trace, MUA; blue trace, SDF. Note that both single- and multiple-unit responses adapt a couple of seconds after stimulus onset, with LFP remaining the only signal correlated with the BOLD response. The SDF (see § 4.6*b*) reflects the instantaneous firing rate of a small population of neurons whose action potential could be identified and isolated during the analysis using standard mathematical methods. Note the covariation of the rate of such isolated spikes with the filtered MUA. From Logothetis *et al.* (2001), with permission.

(c) LFP activity predicts the BOLD response better than MUA

In a linear system, the relationship between input and output can be characterized completely by the haemodynamic impulse response function. Although the constraint of linearity may not apply to the haemodynamic system under all stimulation conditions, we initially applied linear systems analysis to examine the relationship of the BOLD fMRI signal to the different types of neural activities. Correlation analysis was applied to both the measurements obtained during visual stimulation and the measurements of spontaneous activity. The impulse response of the system is the cross covariance function of the neural and BOLD responses. The estimated impulse response functions were used to convolve the LFP and MUA responses to various stimuli. Figure 4.18 shows the neural responses as well as the measured and estimated BOLD responses for four different stimulus durations. Residual analysis showed increased errors (in the least-square sense) for longer pulse durations. Simple visual inspection of the data from the 24 s long stimulus presentation (Figure 4.18*d*) shows greatly increased residuals after the initial ramp of the BOLD response, indicating the existence of nonlinearities not captured by the Wiener–Kernel analysis applied here to the data. Deconvolution of the BOLD response (Figure 4.19) showed that estimation of the neural response is relatively accurate for low-temporal frequencies (up to 0.16 Hz). Increasing temporal frequency strongly

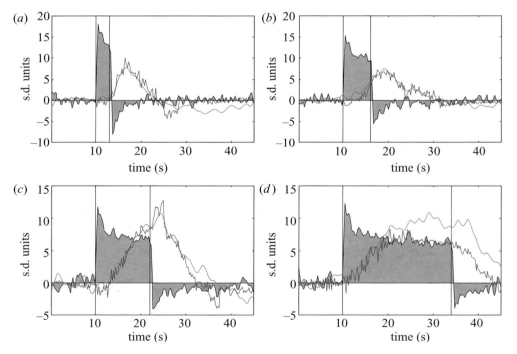

Fig. 4.18. See also Plate 24. The measured LFP response as well as the measured and estimated BOLD response. (*a*) Pulse = 3 s; contrast = 100%; (*b*) pulse = 6 s; contrast = 6 100%; (*c*) pulse = 12 s; contrast = 100%; (*d*) pulse = 24 s; contrast = 100%. The grey trace is the measured LFP signal; the blue trace is the measured BOLD and the red trace is the estimated BOLD. Residual analysis showed an increased error for a longer pulse duration. Visual inspection of the data from a 24 s long stimulus presentation revealed greatly increased residuals after the initial ramp of the BOLD response, suggesting the existence of nonlinearities not captured by the Wiener–Kernel analysis applied here to the data.

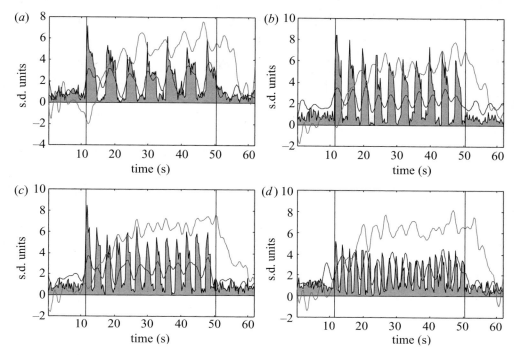

Fig. 4.19. See also Plate 25. Deconvolution of the BOLD response. Estimation of the neural response was relatively accurate for low-temporal frequencies (0.16 Hz). Increasing the temporal frequency strongly increased the residuals; with frequencies higher than 0.21 Hz reconstruction of the neural response no longer being possible. Area plots show measured neural responses. The grey trace is the measured LFP signal, the blue trace is the measured BOLD and the red trace the estimated neural response. (*a*) Flicker rate = 0.16 Hz, contrast = 100%; (*b*) flicker rate = 0.21 Hz, contrast = 100%; (*c*) flicker rate = 0.25 Hz, contrast = 100%; (*d*) flicker rate = 0.4 Hz, contrast = 100%.

increased the residuals. For stimulation frequencies higher than 0.21 Hz, reconstruction of the neural response was not possible (Figure 4.19*c,d*). Moreover, residual analysis similarly showed lower errors (in the least-square sense) overall in LFP-based estimates than in estimates based on MUA responses. Figure 4.20*a* plots the distribution of determination coefficients (normalized residuals) for BOLD estimates from LFP and MUA using impulse functions computed from the LFP–BOLD and MUA–BOLD covariance, respectively. The LFP accounted for *ca.* 7.6% more of the variance in the fMRI responses than the MUA. The difference, although small, was statistically significant. Finally, residuals were found to vary in a similar manner for both LFP and MUA (Figure 20*b*).

(d) BOLD signal and cortical activity: input, local processing and output

Taken together, these results indicate that changes in the LFPs relate better to the evolution of the BOLD signal than those of the spiking activity of single or multiple neurons. I have already discussed the rationale behind LFP–MUA band separation and the reason the former is thought to represent cortical input and local, intracortical processing and the latter the weighted sum of spiking activity. With these arguments in mind, the results of the combined

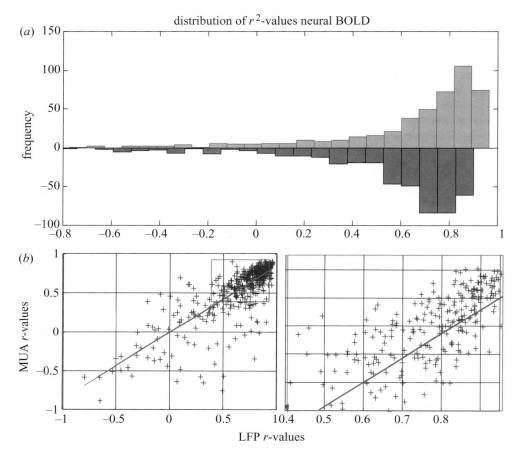

Fig. 4.20. See also Plate 26. (*a*) Distribution of the coefficient of determination (r^2) of LFP (pink) and MUA (grey). The r^2-values for LFP were significantly higher than for MUA. The plot includes data collected with pulse stimuli of 24, 12, 6, and 4 s, with $N = 460$, LFP mean = 0.521, LFP mode = 0.672, MUA mean = 0.410 and MUA mode = 0.457. (*b*) Covariation of the estimation error. The right plot is a magnified section of the left scatter plot.

physiological and fMRI experiments indicate that the BOLD signal mainly reflects the incoming specific or association inputs into an area, and the processing of this input information by the local cortical circuitry (including excitatory and inhibitory interneurons). Naturally, in most cases such activity will be closely related to the output of that area. Incoming signals are processed and usually cause activation of the area's projection neurons. However, in cases in which the incoming signals are modulatory, or the projection neurons are inhibited by local interneurons, spiking activity measured with microelectrodes will be a poor predictor of the BOLD response. A number of experiments demonstrate the plausibility of this argument.

In a recent study, Tolias *et al.* (2001) used an adaptation technique (Grill-Spector *et al.* 1999; Kourtzi & Kanwisher 2001) to study the brain areas processing motion information. They repeatedly imaged a monkey's brain while the animal viewed continuous motion in a single, unchanging direction. Under these conditions, the BOLD response gradually became smaller as the visual neurons adapted to the unchanging stimulation. When the direction of motion was abruptly reversed, the measured brain activity immediately showed a partial recovery or rebound. The extent of this rebound was considered to be an index of the average directional selectivity of neurons in any activated area.

The results confirmed previous electrophysiological studies revealing a distributed network of visual areas in the monkey that process information about the direction of motion of a stimulus. In fact, BOLD signal increases were found in a number of visual areas, including V1, V2, V3, and V5 (MT). The results also confirmed previous fMRI studies providing indirect evidence of interactions between directionally selective neural populations in human area MT by measuring BOLD activity during the motion after-effect (Tootell *et al.* 1995; He *et al.* 1998). What came as a surprise, however, was the strong activation of area V4. Single-unit recordings have repeatedly demonstrated the very weak involvement of this area in motion processing (e.g. Desimone & Schein 1987). BOLD fMRI, alternatively, indicated that the rebound activity, and thus the sensitivity of this area, is as pronounced as that of the area V5 (see Figure 4.21).

An explanation of this result is possible based on the arguments developed earlier. Areas V4 and MT are extensively interconnected (Felleman & Van Essen 1983; Maunsell & Van Essen 1983; Ungerleider & Desimone 1986; Steele *et al.* 1991), yet the properties of MT neurons differ considerably from those of V4. What purpose does the extensive interconnectivity serve? The visual system combines a large number of attributes into unified percepts. Areas related to motion, colour or form will certainly be coactivated and signal the presence of a single moving object under normal viewing conditions. Although they process separate stimulus properties, each area may be influencing the sensitivity of the others by providing some kind of 'modulatory' input, which in and of itself is insufficient to drive the pyramidal cells recorded in a typical electrophysiology experiment. BOLD fMRI in such cases will reveal significant activation and will appear to provide results that do not match those of neurophysiology. In this manner a number of experiments in monkeys appear to be inconsistent with fMRI experiments

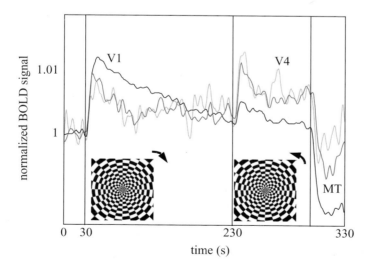

Fig. 4.21. See also Plate 27. A visual adaptation paradigm was used to localize visual areas that process information about the direction of motion (modified from Tolias *et al.* (2001)). The BOLD signal in area V5 (MT) adapted more quickly than in V1, reflecting the difference in motion processing between these areas. Surprisingly, area V4 showed adaptation as strong and as fast as area V5, which is characterized by a much larger number of directional neurons.

employing the same tasks or stimulation conditions (Tong *et al.* 1998; Gandhi *et al.* 1999; Polonsky *et al.* 2000; Kastner & Ungerleider 2000) (see also review by Blake & Logothetis (2002)), as the synaptic activity produced by lateral or feedback input is visible with imaging but not always with single-unit recordings. A good example is the measurement of the effects of spatial attention on neural activation. Attentional effects on the neurons of striate cortex have indeed been very difficult to measure in monkey electrophysiology experiments (Luck *et al.* 1997; McAdams & Maunsell 1999). However, for similar tasks strong attentional effects have been readily measurable with fMRI in human V1 (Tong *et al.* 1998; Gandhi *et al.* 1999; Kastner & Ungerleider 2000). In addition, attentional effects in area V4 were found to be considerably larger in human fMRI than monkey electrophysiology (Kastner *et al.* 1998; Ress *et al.* 2000).

An exquisite example of dissociation between intracortical processing and output of a brain structure was recently offered by Mathiesen *et al.* (1998, 2000), who demonstrated that both LFPs and CBF can increase at the same time that spiking activity ceases. These investigators stimulated the parallel fibres of cerebellum while recording Purkinje cell activity. Purkinje cells are the projection neurons of cerebellum and represent the only output of the structure. They form the Purkinje cell layer that is sandwiched between the molecular and granular layers. The input to the cerebellar cortex consists of the mossy and climbing fibres. The granule cells are at the 'input' side. Their axons ascend to the molecular layer where they bifurcate in a T-shape to give rise to the parallel fibres, that run strictly parallel to the axis of the folium. These axons can be selectively stimulated with a bipolar electrode using small currents. Their stimulation causes monosynaptic excitation of the Purkinje cells and disynaptic inhibition of the same neurons through the basket cells. The net effect is an inhibition of the Purkinje cells' spike activity, although at the same time synaptic activity may be increased. Mathiesen *et al.* (1998) actually demonstrated exactly this by measuring LFPs, single-unit activity and changes in cerebral flow. Both LFPs and CBF were found to increase when the spiking activity ceased.

Interestingly a very early indication that the top–down modulation of activity in a sensory area resulting from its massive feedback inputs may cause greater changes in cerebral circulation than the activity elicited by a simple sensory stimulus came from the clinical study mentioned in § 4.2. After many studies, during which the bruit from the patient's occipital lobe was systematically recorded, the neurosurgeon Fulton (1928) indicated that 'it was *the effort to discern objects that were just at the limit of Walter K.'s acuity* that brought on the increases of the bruit', rather than merely presenting visual stimuli to his eyes. When no attentive behaviour and mental effort were required no increases in the bruit could be observed. The increase of the bruit during tasks requiring attentional efforts may well have been the result of top–down influences on the human visual system, as has been recently demonstrated in imaging studies (Shulman *et al.* 1997; Tong *et al.* 1998; Gandhi *et al.* 1999; Kastner & Ungerleider 2000).

(e) *LFPs and energy budget*

It should be noted that the greater contribution of LFP activity to the fMRI signal is consistent with recent findings regarding the bioenergetics underlying this signal. It has been shown that neural activity and energy metabolism are closely coupled (see Sokoloff 1989). Recent studies show that a quantitative relationship can actually be established between imaging signals and the cycling of certain cerebral neurotransmitters (Shulman & Rothman 1998; Magistretti *et al.* 1999; Rothman *et al.* 1999), as synaptic activity is tightly coupled to glucose uptake (Pellerin & Magistretti 1994; Takahashi *et al.* 1995). More specifically, stoichiometric studies using NMR spectroscopy indicate that the utilization of Glu, the dominant excitatory neurotransmitter of the brain (*ca.* 90% of the synapses in GM are excitatory; Braitenberg & Schuez 1998), is equal to the rate at which this molecule is converted to Gln in the brain (Sibson *et al.* 1998). The Glu to Gln conversion occurs in the astrocytes and the required energy is provided by glycolysis. Astrocytes are specialized glia cells which are massively connected with both neurons and the brain's vasculature, and are enriched in glucose transporters. The transporters are driven by the electrochemical gradient of Na^+; for this reason there is a tight coupling between Glu and Na^+ uptake. Both Glu to Gln conversion and Na^+ restoration require ATP. Gln is subsequently released by astrocytes and taken up by the neuronal terminals to be reconverted to Glu (for review see Magistretti & Pellerin 1999). Calculations based on these findings indicate that the energy demands of glutamatergic neurons account for 80–90% of total cortical glucose usage in rats (Sibson *et al.* 1998) and humans (Pan *et al.* 2000).

In addition, electrical microstimulation experiments have indicated that glucose utilization mainly reflects presynaptic activity. In such experiments the increase in glucose utilization is assessed during orthodromic and antidromic stimulation, with the former activating both pre- and postsynaptic terminals and the latter activating only postsynaptic terminals. Increases were only observed during orthodromic stimulation (Kadekaro *et al.* 1985, 1987; Nudo & Masterton 1986) (for review see Jueptner & Weiller 1995). Taken together, these results indicate that the lion's share of brain energy consumption is due to presynaptic activity (restoration of gradients) and neurotransmitter cycling.

Recent calculations have challenged the notion that presynaptic activity is the major energy consumer in the brain (Attwell & Laughlin 2001). These investigators drew up an energy budget by recalculating the contribution of presynaptic activity, but also computing the energy required to restore all gradients changed by postsynaptic activity and action potentials. In their budget, that is based on computations of the number of vesicles released per action potential, the number of postsynaptic receptors activated per vesicle released, the metabolic consequences of activating a single receptor and changing ion fluxes, and neurotransmitter recycling, the largest portion of energy expenditure is attributed to the postsynaptic effects of Glu (*ca.* 34% of the energy in rodents and 74% in humans is attributed to postsynaptic events, mainly excitatory postsynaptic currents). Both pre- and postsynaptic currents are dominant elements of the LFPs, which—as mentioned in the previous paragraph—were indeed found to correlate best with the haemodynamic changes in the cerebral and cerebellar cortex.

4.7. Conclusion

In conclusion, the results of simultaneous fMRI and electrophysiological recordings presented here clearly show that the BOLD contrast mechanism directly reflects the neural responses elicited by a stimulus. Moreover, to a first approximation, BOLD responses and neural responses are shown to have a linear relationship for stimulus presentation of short duration. Neural signals are characterized by considerably higher SNR than the haemodynamic response, indicating that the extent of activation in human fMRI experiments is very often under-estimated to a significant extent due to the variation in the vascular response. Finally, the haemodynamic response appears to be better correlated with the LFPs, implying that activation in an area is often likely to reflect the incoming input and the local processing in a given area rather than the spiking activity. While it is reasonable to expect that output activity will usually correlate with neurotransmitter release and pre- and postsynaptic currents, when input into a particular area plays what is primarily a modulatory role, fMRI experiments may reveal activation in areas in which no single-unit activity is found in physiological experiments.

The author thanks Dr A. Ghazanfar, Dr C. Koch, Dr D. Leopold, Dr W. Newsome, Dr J. Pfeuffer, Dr G. Rainer, M. Sereno, Dr S. Smirnakis, Dr A. Tolias and Dr B. Wandell for reading the manuscript and for many useful suggestions, D. Blaurock for English correction and editing and K. Lamberty for the drawings. This research was supported by the Max Planck Society. All experiments reviewed here were approved by the local authorities and were in full compliance with the guidelines of the European Community (EUVD 86/609/EEC) for the care and use of laboratory animals.

References

Abragam, A. 1961 *Principles of nuclear magnetism*. Oxford University Press.

Ackerman, J. J., Grove, T. H., Wong, G. G., Gadian, D. G. & Radda, G. K. 1980 Mapping of metabolites in whole animals by ^{31}P NMR using surface coils. *Nature* **283**, 167–170.

Ahissar, E. & Vaadia, E. 1990 Oscillatory activity of single units in a somatosensory cortex of an awake monkey and their possible role in texture analysis. *Proc. Natl Acad. Sci. USA* **87**, 8935–8939.

Aidley, D. J. 1989 *The physiology of excitable cells*. Cambridge University Press.

Ajmone-Marsan, C. 1965 Electrical activity of the brain: slow waves and neuronal activity. *Israel J. Med. Sci.* **1**, 104–117.

Albright, T. D. 1984 Direction and orientation selectivity of neurons in visual area MT of the macaque. *J. Neurophysiol.* **52**, 1106–1130.

Ames, A. 2000 CNS energy metabolism as related to function. *Brain Res.—Brain Res. Rev.* **34**, 42–68.

Ances, B. M., Zarahn, E., Greenberg, J. H. & Detre, J. A. 2000 Coupling of neural activation to blood flow in the somatosensory cortex of rats is time-intensity separable, but not linear. *J. Cerebral Blood Flow Metabolism* **20**, 921–930.

Apostol, G. & Creutzfeldt, O. D. 1974 Crosscorrelation between the activity of septal units and hippocampal EEG during arousal. *Brain Res.* **67**, 65–75.

Arezzo, J., Legatt, A. D. & Vaughan, H. G. J. 1979 Topography and intracranial sources of somatosensory evoked potentials in the monkey. I. Early components. *Electroencephalography Clin. Neurophysiol.* **46**, 155–172.

Attwell, D. & Laughlin, S. B. 2001 An energy budget for signaling in the grey matter of the brain. *J. Cerebral Blood Flow Metabolism* **21**, 1133–1145.

Axel, L. 1984 Blood flow effects in magnetic resonance imaging. *Am. J. Roentgenology* **143**, 1157–1166.

Axel, L. 1986 Blood flow effects in magnetic resonance imaging. *Magn. Resonance A.*, 237–244.

Bandettini, P. A., Wong, E. C., Hinks, R. S., Tikofsky, R. S. &. Hyde, J. S. 1992 Time course E.P.I. of human brain function during task activation. *Magn. Resonance Med.* **25**, 390–397.

Bandettini, P. A., Kwong, K. K., Davis, T. L., Tootell, R. B., Wong, E. C., Fox, P. T., Belliveau, J. W., Weisskoff, R. M. & Rosen, B. R. 1997 Characterization of cerebral blood oxygenation and flow changes during prolonged brain activation. *Hum. Brain Mapping* **5**, 93–109.

Barrenechea, C., Pedemonte, M., Nunez, A. & Garcia-Austt, E. 1995 *In vivo* intracellular recordings of medial septal and diagonal band of Broca neurons: relationships with theta rhythm. *Exp. Brain Res.* **103**, 31–40.

Basar, E. 1980 *EEG-brain dynamics: relation between EEG and brain evoked potentials*. Amsterdam: Elsevier-North Holland Biomedical.

Belle, V., Delon-Martin, C., Massarelli, R., Decety, J., Le, B., Benabid, A. L. & Segebarth, C. 1995 Intracranial gradient-echo and spin-echo functional MR angiography in humans. *Radiology* **195**, 739–746.

Belliveau, J. W., Kennedy, D. N., McKinstry, R. C., Buchbinder, B. R., Weisskoff, R. M., Cohen, M. S., Vevea, J. M., Brady, T. J. & Rosen, B. R. 1991 Functional mapping of the human visual cortex by magnetic resonance imaging. *Science* **254**, 716–719.

Blake, R. & Logothetis, N. K. 2002 Visual competition. *Nature Rev. Neurosci.* **3**, 13–23.

Bloch, F., Hansen, W. W. & Packard, M. 1946 The nuclear induction experiment. *Phys. Rev.* **70**, 474–485.

Bock, C., Schmitz, B., Kerskens, C. M., Gyngell, M. L., Hossmann, K. A. & Hoehn-Berlage, M. 1998 Functional MRI of somatosensory activation in rat: effect of hyper-capnic up-regulation on perfusion- and BOLD-imaging. *Magn. Resonance Med.* **39**, 457–461.

Bonhoeffer, T. & Grinvald, A. 1996 Optical imaging based on intrinsic signals. In *Brain mapping, the methods* (ed. A. W. Toga & J. C. Mazziotta), pp. 55–97. New York: Academic.

Bonmassar, G., Anami, K., Ives, J. & Belliveau, J. W. 1999 Visual evoked potential (VEP) measured by simultaneous 64-channel EEG and 3T fMRI. *NeuroReport* **10**, 1893–1897.

Boxerman, J. L., Bandettini, P. A., Kwong, K. K., Baker, J. R., Davis, T. L., Rosen, B. R. & Weisskoff, R. M. 1995*a* The intravascular contribution to fMRI signal change: Monte Carlo modeling and diffusion-weighted studies *in vivo*. *Magn. Resonance Med.* **34**, 4–10.

Boxerman, J. L., Hamberg, L. M., Rosen, B. R. & Weisskoff, R. M. 1995*b* MR contrast due to intravascular magnetic susceptibility perturbations. *Magn. Resonance Med.* **34**, 555–566.

Braitenberg, V. & Schuez, A. 1998 *Cortex: statistics and geometry of neuronal connectivity*. Berlin: Springer.

Brewer, A. A., Press, W., Logothetis, N. K. & Wandell, B. 2002 Visual areas in macaque cortex measured using functional MRI. *J. Neurosci.* (In the press.)

Brooks, R. A., Battocletti, J. H., Sances, A., Larson, S. J., Bowman, R. L. & Kudravcev, V. 1975 Nuclear magnetic relaxation in blood. *IEEE Trans. Biomed. Engng.* **22**, 12–18.

Buchwald, J. S. & Grover, F. S. 1970 Amplitudes of background fast activity characteristic of specific brain sites. *J. Neurophysiol.* **33**, 148–159.

Buchwald, J. S., Hala, E. S. & Schramm, S. A. 1965 Comparison son of multi-unit activity and EEG activity recorded from the same brain site in chronic cats during behavioral conditioning. *Nature* **205**, 1012–1014.

Burke, M., Schwindt, W., Ludwig, U., Hennig, J. & Hoehn, M. 2000 Facilitation of electric forepaw stimulation-induced somatosensory activation in rats by additional acoustic stimulation: an fMRI investigation. *Magn. Resonance Med.* **44**, 317–321.

Buxton, R. B. 2001 The elusive initial dip. *Neuroimage* **13**, 953–958.

Buxton, R. B. & Frank, L. R. 1997 A model for the coupling between cerebral blood flow and oxygen metabolism during neural stimulation. *J. Cerebral Blood Flow Metabolism* **17**, 64–72.

Buxton, R. B., Wong, E. C. & Frank, L. R. 1998 Dynamics of blood flow and oxygenation changes during brain activation: the balloon model. *Magn. Resonance Med.* **39**, 855–864.

Buzsaki, G. & Chrobak, J. J. 1995 Temporal structure in spatially organized neuronal ensembles: a role for interneuronal networks. *Curr. Opin. Neurobiol.* **5**, 504–510.

Callaghan, P. T. 1991 *Principles of nuclear magnetic resonance microscopy*. Oxford University Press.

Cannestra, A. F., Pouratian, N., Bookheimer, S. Y., Martin, N. A., Becker, D. P. & Toga, A. W. 2001 Temporal spatial differences observed by functional MRI and human intra-operative optical imaging. *Cerebral Cortex* **11**, 773–782.

Chang, C. & Shyu, B. C. 2001 A fMRI study of brain activations during non-noxious and noxious electrical stimulation of the sciatic nerve of rats. *Brain Res.* **897**, 71–81.

Colby, C. L., Duhamel, J.-R. & Goldberg, M. E. 1993 Ventral intraparietal area of the macaque: anatomic location and visual response properties. *J. Neurophysiol.* **69**, 902–914.

Cormack, A. M. 1973 Reconstruction of densities from their projections, with applications in radiological physics. *Phys. Med. Biol.* **18**, 195–207.

Darian-Smith, C. & Gilbert, C. D. 1995 Topographic reorganization in the striate cortex of the adult cat and monkey is cortically mediated. *J. Neurosci.* **15**, 1631–1647.

Das, A. & Gilbert, C. D. 1995 Receptive field expansion in adult visual cortex is linked to dynamic changes in strength of cortical connections. *J. Neurophysiol.* **74**, 779–792.

Davis, T. L., Kwong, K. K., Weisskoff, R. M. & Rosen, B. R. 1998 Calibrated functional M.R.I.: mapping the dynamics of oxidative metabolism. *Proc. Natl Acad. Sci. USA* **95**, 1834–1839.

De Valois, R. L., Yund, E. W. & Hepler, N. 1982 The orientation and direction selectivity of cells in macaque visual cortex. *Vis. Res.* **22**, 531–544.

Desimone, R. & Schein, S. J. 1987 Visual properties of neurons in area V4 of the macaque: sensitivity to stimulus form. *J. Neurophysiol.* **57**, 835–868.

Desimone, R. & Ungerleider, L. G. 1986 Multiple visual areas in the caudal superior temporal sulcus of the macaque. *J. Comp. Neurol.* **248**, 164–189.

Deyoe, E. A., Bandettini, P., Neitz, J., Miller, D. & Winans, P. 1994 Functional magnetic resonance imaging (FMRI) of the human brain. *J. Neurosci. Meth.* **54**, 171–187.

Disbrow, E., Roberts, T. P., Slutsky, D. & Krubitzer, L. 1999 The use of fMRI for determining the topographic organization of cortical fields in human and nonhuman primates. *Brain Res.* **829**, 167–173.

Disbrow, E. A., Slutsky, D. A., Roberts, T. P. & Krubitzer, L. A. 2000 Functional MRI at 1.5 tesla: a comparison of the blood oxygenation level-dependent signal and electrophysiology. *Proc. Natl Acad. Sci. USA* **97**, 9718–9723.

Dow, B. M. 1974 Functional classes of cells and their laminar distribution in monkey visual cortex. *J. Neurophysiol.* **37**, 927–946.

Dubowitz, D. J., Chen, D. Y., Atkinson, D. J., Scadeng, M., Martinez, A., Andersen, M. B., Andersen, R. A. & Bradley, W. G. J. R. 2001 Direct comparison of visual cortex activation in human and nonhuman primates using functional magnetic resonance imaging. *J. Neurosci. Meth.* **107**, 71–80.

Duvernoy, H. M., Delon, S. & Vannson, J. L. 1981 Cortical blood vessels of the human brain. *Brain Res. Bull.* **7**, 519–579.

Ehman, R. L. & Felmlee, J. P. 1989 Adaptive technique for high-definition MR imaging of moving structures. *Radiology* **173**, 255–263.

Elul, R. 1969 The physiological interpretation of amplitude histograms of the EEG. *Electroencephalography Clin. Neurophysiol.* **27**, 703–704.

Elul, R. 1971 The genesis of the EEG. *Int. Rev. Neurobiol.* **15**, 227–272.

Engel, S. A., Rumelhart, D. E., Wandell, B. A., Lee, A. T., Glover, G. H., Chichilnisky, E.-J. & Shadlen, M. N. 1994 fMRI of human visual cortex. *Nature* **369**, 525.

Engel, S. A., Glover, G. H. & Wandell, B. A. 1997 Retinotopic organization in human visual cortex and the spatial precision of functional MRI. *Cerebral Cortex* **7**, 181–192.

Ernst, R. R. & Anderson, W. A. 1966 Application of Fourier transform spectroscopy to magnetic resonance. *Rev. Sci. Instrum.* **37**, 93–102.

Ernst, T. & Hennig, J. 1994 Observation of a fast response in functional MR. *Magn. Resonance Med.* **32**, 146–149.

Farmer, T. H., Cofer, G. P. & Johnson, G. A. 1990 Maximizing contrast to noise with inductively coupled implanted coils. *Investigative Radiology* **25**, 552–558.

Felleman, D. J. & Van Essen, D. C. 1983 The connections of area V4 of macaque extrastriate cortex. *Soc. Neurosci. Abstracts* **9**, 153.

Fox, P. T. & Raichle, M. E. 1986 Focal physiological uncoupling of cerebral blood flow and oxidative metabolism during somatosensory stimulation in human subjects. *Proc. Natl Acad. Sci. USA* **83**, 1140–1144.

Fox, P. T., Mintun, M. A., Raichle, M. E., Miezin, F. M., Allman, J. M. & Van Essen, D. C. 1986 Mapping human visual cortex with positron emission tomography. *Nature* **323**, 806–809.

Fox, P. T., Raichle, M. E., Mintun, M. A. & Dence, C. 1988 Nonoxidative glucose consumption during focal physiologic neural activity. *Science* **241**, 462–464.

Frahm, J., Merboldt, K. D., Hanicke, W., Kleinschmidt, A. & Boecker, H. 1994 Brain or vein—oxygenation or flow? On signal physiology in functional MRI of human brain activation. *Nucl. Magn. Resonance Biomed.* **7**, 45–53.

Frahm, J., Kruger, G., Merboldt, K. D. & Kleinschmidt, A. 1996 Dynamic uncoupling and recoupling of perfusion and oxidative metabolism during focal brain activation in man. *Magn. Resonance Med.* **35**, 143–148.

Freeman, W. J. 1975 *Mass action in the nervous system.* New York: Academic.

Fried, I., MacDonald, K. A. & Wilson, C. L. 1997 Single neuron activity in human hippocampus and amygdala during recognition of faces and objects. *Neuron* **18**, 753–765.

Fromm, G. H. & Bond, H. W. 1964 Slow changes in the electrocorticogram and the activity of cortical neurons. *Electroencephalography Clin. Neurophysiol.* **17**, 520–523.

Fromm, G. H. & Bond, H. W. 1967 The relationship between neuron activity and cortical steady potentials. *Electroencephalography Clin. Neurophysiol.* **22**, 159–166.

Frostig, R. D., Lieke, E. E., Ts'o, D. Y. & Grinvald, A. 1990 Cortical functional architecture and local coupling between neuronal activity and the microcirculation revealed by *in vivo* high-resolution optical imaging of intrinsic signals. *Proc. Natl Acad. Sci. USA* **87**, 6082–6086.

Fukushima, E. 1989 *NMR in biomedicine; the physical basis.* New York: American Institute of Physics.

Fulton, J. F. 1928 Observations upon the vascularity of the human occipital lobe during visual activity. *Brain* **51**, 310–320.

Gandhi, S. P., Heeger, D. J. & Boynton, G. M. 1999 Spatial attention affects brain activity in human primary visual cortex. *Proc. Natl Acad. Sci. USA* **96**, 3314–3319.

Garwood, M., Ugurbil, K., Rath, A. R., Bendall, M. R., Ross, B. D., Mitchell, S. L. & Merkle, H. 1989 Magnetic resonance imaging with adiabatic pulses using a single surface coil for RF transmission and signal detection. *Magn. Resonance Med.* **9**, 25–34.

Gasser, H. S. & Grundfest, H. 1939 Axon diameters in relation to the spike dimensions and the conduction velocity in mammalian A fibers. *Am. J. Physiol.* **127**, 393–414.

Gati, J. S., Menon, R. S. & Rutt, B. K. 2000 Field strength dependence of functional MRI signals. In *Functional MRI* (ed. C. T. Moonen & P. A. Bandettini), pp. 277–282. Berlin: Springer.

Glover, G. H. & Lai, S. 1998 Self-navigated spiral fMRI: interleaved versus single-shot. *Magn. Resonance Med.* **39**, 361–368.

Glover, G. H. & Lee, A. T. 1995 Motion artifacts in fMRI: comparison of 2DFT with PR and spiral scan methods. *Magn. Resonance Med.* **33**, 624–635.

Goldberg, M. E. & Wurtz, R. H. 1972 Activity of superior colliculus in behaving monkey. I. Visual receptive fields of single neurons. *J. Neurophysiol.* **35**, 542–559.

de Graaf, R. A. 1998 *In vivo NMR spectroscopy: principles and techniques.* Chichester: Wiley.

Granger, R. & Lynch, G. 1991 Higher olfactory processes: perceptual learning and memory. *Curr. Opin. Neurobiology* **1**, 209–214.

Gray, C. M. & McCormick, D. A. 1996 Chattering cells—superficial pyramidal neurons contibuting to the generation of synchronous oscillations in the visual cortex. *Science* **274**, 109–113.

Gray, C. M., Maldonado, P. E., Wilson, M. & McNaughton, B. 1995 Tetrodes markedly improve the reliability and yield of multiple single-unit isolation from multi-unit recordings in cat striate cortex. *J. Neurosci. Meth.* **63**, 43–54.

Gray, J. A. & Ball, G. G. 1970 Frequency-specific relation between hippocampal theta rhythm, behavior, and amobarbital action. *Science* **168**, 1246–1248.

Grill-Spector, K., Kushnir, T., Edelman, S., Avidan, G., Itzchak, Y. & Malach, R. 1999 Differential processing of objects under various viewing conditions in the human lateral occipital complex. *Neuron* **24**, 187–203.

Grover, F. S. & Buchwald, J. S. 1970 Correlation of cell size with amplitude of background fast activity in specific brain nuclei. *J. Neurophysiol.* **33**, 160–171.

Gruetter, R., Boesch, C., Martin, E. & Wuthrich, K. 1990 A method for rapid evaluation of saturation factors in *in vivo* surface coil NMR spectroscopy using B1-insensitive pulse cycles. *NMR Biomed.* **3**, 265–271.

Haacke, E. M., Lai, S., Yablonskiy, D. A. & Lin, W. L. 1995 *In vivo* validation of the BOLD mechanism—a review of signal changes in gradient echo functional MRI in the presence of flow. *Int. J. Imaging Systems Technology* **6**, 153–163.

Haacke, E. M., Brown, R. W., Thompson, M. R. & Venkatesan, R. 1999 *Magnetic resonance imaging: principles and sequence design.* New York: Wiley-Liss.

Haase, A., Frahm, J., Matthaei, D., Hanicke, W. & Merboldt, K.-D. 1986 FLASH imaging. Rapid NMR imaging using low flip-angle pulses. *J. Magn. Resonance* **67**, 258–266.

Hahn, E. L. 1950 Spin echoes. *Phys. Rev.* **80**, 580–594.

Hawken, M. J., Parker, A. J. & Lund, J. S. 1988 Laminar organization and contrast sensitivity of direction-selective cells in the striate cortex of the Old World monkey. *J. Neurosci.* **8**, 3541–3548.

He, S., Cohen, E. R. & Hu, X. P. 1998 Close correlation between activity in brain area MT/V5 and the perception of a visual-motion after effect. *Curr. Biol.* **8**, 1215–1218.

Heeger, D. J. & Ress, D. 2002 What does fMRI tell us about neuronal activity? *Nature Rev. Neurosci.* **3**, 142–151.

Heeger, D. J., Huk, A. C., Geisler, W. S. & Albrecht, D. G. 2000 Spikes versus BOLD: what does neuroimaging tell us about neuronal activity? *Nature Neurosci.* **3**, 631–633.

Hendrich, K., Xu, Y., Kim, S. G. & Ugurbil, K. 1994 Surface coil cardiac tagging and ^{31}P spectroscopic localization with B1-insensitive adiabatic pulses. *Magn. Resonance Med.* **31**, 541–545.

Henze, D. A., Borhegyi, Z., Csicsvari, J., Mamiya, A., Harris, K. D. & Buzsaki, G. 2000 Intracellular features predicted by extracellular recordings in the hippocampus *in vivo. J. Neurophysiol.* **84**, 390–400.

Hess, A., Stiller, D., Kaulisch, T., Heil, P. & Scheich, H. 2000 New insights into the hemodynamic blood oxygenation level-dependent response through combination of functional magnetic resonance imaging and optical recording in gerbil barrel cortex. *J. Neurosci.* **20**, 3328–3338.

Hoffmann, E. J., Phelps, M. E., Mullani, N. A., Higgins, C. S. & Ter Pogossian, M. M. 1976 Design and performance characteristics of a whole-body positron transaxial tomograph. *J. Nucl. Med.* **17**, 493–502.

Hoogenraad, F. G., Pouwels, P. J., Hofman, M. B., Reichenbach, J. R., Sprenger, M. & Haacke, E. M. 2001 Quantitative differentiation between BOLD models in fMRI. *Magn. Resonance Med.* **45**, 233–246.

Hsu, E. W., Hedlund, L. F. & MacFall, J. R. 1998 Functional MRI of the rat somatosensory cortex—effects of hyperventilation. *Magn. Resonance Med.* **40**, 421–426.

Hu, X. & Kim, S. G. 1994 Reduction of signal fluctuation in functional MRI using navigator echoes. *Magn. Resonance Med.* **31**, 495–503.

Hu, X., Le, T. H. & Ugurbil, K. 1997 Evaluation of the early response in fMRI in individual subjects using short stimulus duration. *Magn. Resonance Med.* **37**, 877–884.

Huang, C. M. & Buchwald, J. S. 1977 Interpretation of the vertex short-latency acoustic response: a study of single neurons in the brain stem. *Brain Res.* **137**, 291–303.

Humphrey, D. R. & Corrie, W. S. 1978 Properties of pyramidal tract neuron system within a functionally defined subregion of primate motor cortex. *J. Neurophysiol.* **41**, 216–243.

Hunt, C. 1951 The reflex activity of mammalian small-nerve fibres. *J. Physiol. Lond.* **115**, 456–469.

Hyde, J. S., Jesmanowicz, A., Grist, T. M., Froncisz, W. & Kneeland, J. B. 1987 Quadrature detection surface coil. *Magn. Resonance Med.* **4**, 179–184.

Hyde, J. S., Biswal, B. B. & Jesmanowicz, A. 2001 High-resolution fMRI using multislice partial k-space GR-EPI with cubic voxels. *Magn. Resonance Med.* **46**, 114–125.

Hyder, F., Shulman, R. G. & Rothman, D. L. 1998 A model for the regulation of cerebral oxygen delivery. *J. Appl. Physiol.* **85**, 554–564.

Jezzard, P., Rauschecker, J. P. & Malonek, D. 1997 An *in vivo* model for functional MRI in cat visual cortex. *Magn. Resonance Med.* **38**, 699–705.

Johnston, D. & Wu, S. M. 1995 *Foundations of cellular neurophysiology.* Cambridge, MA: MIT Press.

Jones, M., Berwick, J., Johnston, D. & Mayhew, J. 2001 Concurrent optical imaging spectroscopy and laser-Doppler flowmetry: the relationship between blood flow, oxygenation, and volume in rodent barrel cortex. *Neuroimage* **13**, 1002–1015.

Jueptner, M. & Weiller, C. 1995 Review—does measurement of regional cerebral blood flow reflect synaptic activity—implications for PET and fMRI. *Neuroimage* **2**, 148–156.

Juergens, E., Eckhorn, R., Frien, A. & Woelbern, T. 1996 *Brain and evolution,* p. 418. Berlin: Thieme.

Juergens, E., Guettler, A. & Eckhorn, R. 1999 Visual stimulation elicits locked and induced gamma oscillations in monkey intracortical- and EEG-potentials, but not in human EEG. *Exp. Brain Res.* **129**, 247–259.

Kaas, J. H., Krubitzer, L. A., Chino, Y. M., Langston, A. L., Polley, E. H. & Blair, N. 1990 Reorganization of retinotopic cortical maps in adult mammals after lesions of the retina. *Science* **248**, 229.

Kadekaro, M., Crane, A. M. & Sokoloff, L. 1985 Differential effects of electrical stimulation of sciatic nerve on metabolic activity in spinal cord and dorsal root ganglion in the rat. *Proc. Natl Acad. Sci. USA* **82**, 6010–6013.

Kadekaro, M., Vance, W. H., Terrell, M. L., Gary, H. J., Eisenberg, H. M. & Sokoloff, L. 1987 Effects of antidromic stimulation of the ventral root on glucose utilization in the ventral horn of the spinal cord in the rat. *Proc. Natl Acad. Sci. USA* **84**, 5492–5495.

Kamada, K., Pekar, J. J. & Kanwal, J. S. 1999 Anatomical and functional imaging of the auditory cortex in awake mustached bats using magnetic resonance technology. *Brain Res. Brain Res. Protocols* **4**, 351–359.

Kandel, A. & Buzsaki, G. 1997 Cellular-synaptic generation of sleep spindles, spike-and-wave discharges, and evoked thalamocortical responses in the neocortex of the rat. *J. Neurosci.* **17**, 6783–6797.

Kastner, S. & Ungerleider, L. G. 2000 Mechanisms of visual attention in the human cortex. *A. Rev. Neurosci.* **23**, 315–341.

Kastner, S., De Weerd, P., Desimone, R. & Ungerleider, L. G. 1998 Mechanisms of directed attention in the human extra-striate cortex as revealed by functional MRI. *Science* **282**, 108–111.

Kennan, R. P., Zhong, J. & Gore, J. C. 1994 Intravascular susceptibility contrast mechanisms in tissues. *Magn. Resonance Med.* **31**, 9–21.

Kennan, R. P., Scanley, B. E. & Gore, J. C. 1997 Physiologic basis for BOLD MR signal changes due to hypoxia/hyperoxia: separation of blood volume and magnetic susceptibility effects. *Magn. Resonance Med.* **37**, 953–956.

Kennan, R. P., Scanley, B. E., Innis, R. B. & Gore, J. C. 1998 Physiological basis for BOLD MR signal changes due to neuronal stimulation: separation of blood volume and magnetic susceptibility effects. *Magn. Resonance Med.* **40**, 840–846.

Kety, S. S. & Schmidt, C. F. 1948 Nitrous oxide method for the quantitative determination of cerebral blood flow in man: theory, procedure, and normal values. *J. Clin. Investigations* **27**, 475–483.

Kim, D. S., Duong, T. Q. & Kim, S. G. 2000 Reply to: can current fMRI techniques reveal the microarchitecture of cortex? *Nature Neurosci.* **3**, 414.

Kim, S. G., Hendrich, K., Hu, X., Merkle, H. & Ugurbil, K. 1994 Potential pitfalls of functional MRI using conventional gradient-recalled echo techniques. *Nucl. Magn. Resonance Biomed.* **7**, 69–74.

Kim, S. G. & Ugurbil, K. 1997 Comparison of blood oxygenation and cerebral blood flow effects in fMRI: estimation of relative oxygen consumption change. *Magn. Resonance Med.* **38**, 59–65.

Kim, S. G., Hu, X., Adriany, G. & Ugurbil, K. 1996 Fast interleaved echo-planar imaging with navigator: high resolution anatomic and functional images at 5 Tesla. *Magn. Resonance Med.* **35**, 895–902.

Koch, C. 1999 *Biophysics of computation: information processing in single neurons.* New York: Oxford University Press.

Kocsis, B., Bragin, A. & Buzsaki, G. 1999 Interdependence of multiple theta generators in the hippocampus: a partial coherence analysis. *J. Neurosci.* **19**, 6200–6212.

Kourtzi, Z. & Kanwisher, N. 2001 Representation of perceived object shape by the human lateral occipital complex. *Science* **293**, 1506–1509.

Krakow, K., Woermann, F. G., Symms, M. R., Allen, P. J., Lemieux, L., Barker, G. J., Duncan, J. S. & Fish, D. R. 1999 EEG-triggered functional MRI of interictal epileptiform activity in patients with partial seizures. *Brain* **122**, 1679–1688.

Krakow, K., Allen, P. J., Symms, M. R., Lemieux, L., Josephs, O. & Fish, D. R. 2000 EEG recording during fMRI experiments: image quality. *Hum. Brain Mapping* **10**, 10–15.

Kreiman, G., Koch, C. & Fried, I. 2000a Imagery neurons in the human brain. *Nature* **408**, 357–361.

Kreiman, G., Koch, C. & Fried, I. 2000b Category-specific visual responses of single neurons in the human medial temporal lobe. *Nature Neurosci.* **3**, 946–953.

Kruger, G., Kleinschmidt, A. & Frahm, J. 1996 Dynamic MRI sensitized to cerebral blood oxygenation and flow during sustained activation of human visual cortex. *Magn. Resonance Med.* **35**, 797–800.

Kwong, K. K., Belliveau, J. W., Chesler, D. A., Goldberg, I. E., Weisskoff, R. M., Poncelet, B. P., Kennedy, D. N., Hoppel, B. E., Cohen, M. S. & Turner, R. 1992 Dynamic magnetic resonance imaging of human brain activity during primary sensory stimulation. *Proc. Natl Acad. Sci. USA* **89**, 5675–5679.

Lahti, K. M., Ferris, C. F., Li, F. H., Sotak, C. H. & King, J. A. 1998 Imaging brain activity in conscious animals using functional MRI. *J. Neurosci. Meth.* **82**, 75–83.

Laurent, G. & Davidowitz, H. 1994 Encoding of olfactory information with oscillating neural assemblies. *Science* **265**, 1872–1875.

Laurent, G., Stopfer, M., Friedrich, R. W., Rabinovich, M. I., Volkovskii, A. & Abarbanel, H. D. 2001 Odor encoding as an active, dynamical process: experiments, computation, and theory. *A. Rev. Neurosci.* **24**, 263–297.

Lauterbur, P. C. 1973 Image formation by induced local interactions: examples emplying nuclear magnetic resonance. *Nature* **242**, 190–191.

Le, B., Hassler, M., Reutenauer, H., Decorps, M., Camuset, J. P., Crouzet, G. & Benabid, A. L. 1987 MRI of the cervical spine. Creation of a surface coil. Technical and clinical results. *J. Radiologie* **68**, 579–586.

Lee, S. P., Duong, T. Q., Yang, G., Iadecola, C. & Kim, S. G. 2001 Relative changes of cerebral arterial and venous blood volumes during increased cerebral blood flow: implications for BOLD fMRI. *Magn. Resonance Med.* **45**, 791–800.

Legatt, A. D., Arezzo, J. & Vaughan, H. G. J. 1980 Averaged multiple unit activity as an estimate of phasic changes in local neuronal activity: effects of volume-conducted potentials. *J. Neurosci. Meth.* **2**, 203–217.

Lindauer, U., Royl, G., Leithner, C., Kuhl, M., Gold, L., Gethmann, J., Kohl-Bareis, M., Villringer, A. & Dirnagl, U. 2001 No evidence for early decrease in blood oxygenation in rat whisker cortex in response to functional activation. *Neuroimage* **13**, 988–1001.

Lindsley, D. B. & Wicke, J. D. 1974 The electroencephalogram: autonomous electrical activity in man and animals. In *Electroencephalography and human brain potentials* (ed. R. F. Thomson & M. M. Patterson), pp. 3–83. New York: Academic.

Logothetis, N. K. 2000 Can current fMRI techniques reveal the microarchitecture of cortex? *Nature Neurosci.* **3**, 413.

Logothetis, N. K., Guggenberger, H., Peled, S. & Pauls, J. 1999 Functional imaging of the monkey brain. *Nature Neurosci.* **2**, 555–562.

Logothetis, N. K., Peled, S. & Pauls, J. 1998 Development and application of fMRI for visual studies in monkeys. *Soc. Neurosci. Abstracts* **24**, 11.

Logothetis, N. K., Pauls, J., Augath, M., Trinath, T. & Oeltermann, A. 2001 Neurophysiological investigation of the basis of the fMRI signal. *Nature* **412**, 150–157.

Logothetis, N. K., Merkle, H., Augath, M., Trinath, T. & Ugurbil, K. 2002 Ultra-high resolution fMRI in monkeys with implanted RF coils. *Neuron* **35**, 227–242.

Lopez-Villegas, D., Kimura, H., Tunlayadechanont, S. & Lenkinski, R. E. 1996 High spatial resolution MRI and proton MRS of human frontal cortex. *Nucl. Magn. Resonance Biomed.* **9**, 297–304.

Lorente de Nó, R. 1947 Analysis of the distribution of action currents of nerve in volume conductors. *Studies Rockefeller Inst. Med. Res.* **132**, 384–477.

Luck, S. J., Chelazzi, L., Hillyard, S. A. & Desimone, R. 1997 Neural mechanisms of spatial selective attention in areas V1, V2 and V4 of macaque visual cortex. *J. Neurophysiol.* **77**, 24–42.

Lund, J. S., Yoshioka, T. & Levitt, J. B. 1994 Substrates for interlaminar connections in area V1 of macaque monkey cerebral cortex. In *Primary visual cortex in primates* (ed. A. Peters & K. S. Rockland), pp. 37–60. New York: Plenum Press.

Luo, Y., de, G., DelaBarre, L., Tannus, A. & Garwood, M. 2001 BISTRO: an outer-volume suppression method that tolerates RF field inhomogeneity. *Magn. Resonance Med.* **45**, 1095–1102.

McAdams, C. J. & Maunsell, J. H. 1999 Effects of attention on orientation-tuning functions of single neurons in macaque cortical area V4. *J. Neurosci.* **19**, 431–441.

McArdle, C. B., Crofford, M. J., Mirfakhraee, M., Amparo, E. G. & Calhoun, J. S. 1986 Surface coil M.R. of spinal trauma: preliminary experience. *Am. J. Neuroradiology* **7**, 885–893.

Magistretti, P. J. & Pellerin, L. 1999 Cellular mechanisms of brain energy metabolism and their relevance to functional brain imaging. *Phil. Trans R. Soc. Lond.* B **354**, 1155–1163. (DOI 10.1098/rstb.1999.0471.)

Magistretti, P. J., Pellerin, L., Rothman, D. L. & Shulman, R. G. 1999 Neuroscience—energy on demand. *Science* **283**, 496–497.

Malonek, D. & Grinvald, A. 1996 Interactions between electrical activity and cortical microcirculation revealed by imaging spectroscopy: implications for functional brain mapping. *Science* **272**, 551–554.

Malonek, D., Dirnagl, U., Lindauer, U., Yamada, K., Kanno, I. & Grinvald, A. 1997 Vascular imprints of neuronal activity: relationships between the dynamics of cortical blood flow, oxygenation, and volume changes following sensory stimulation. *Proc. Natl Acad. Sci. USA* **94**, 14 826–14 831.

Mandeville, J. B., Marota, J. J., Ayata, C., Zaharchuk, G., Moskowitz, M. A., Rosen, B. R. & Weisskoff, R. M. 1999*a* Evidence of a cerebrovascular postarteriole windkessel with delayed compliance. *J. Cerebral Blood Flow Metabolism* **19**, 679–689.

Mandeville, J. B., Marota, J. J., Ayata, C., Moskowitz, M. A., Weisskoff, R. M. & Rosen, B. R. 1999*b* MRI measurement of the temporal evolution of relative CMRO2 during rat forepaw stimulation. *Magn. Resonance Med.* **42**, 944–951.

Mandeville, J. B., Jenkins, B. G., Kosofsky, B. E., Moskowitz, M. A., Rosen, B. R. & Marota, J. J. 2001 Regional sensitivity and coupling of BOLD and CBV changes during stimulation of rat brain. *Magn. Resonance Med.* **45**, 443–447.

Mansfield, P. 1977 Multi-planar image formation using N.M.R. spin echoes. *J. Phys.* C **10**, L55–L58.

Marota, J. J., Ayata, C., Moskowitz, M. A., Weisskoff, R. M., Rosen, B. R. & Mandeville, J. B. 1999 Investigation of the early response to rat forepaw stimulation. *Magn. Resonance Med.* **41**, 247–252.

Martin, E., Joeri, P., Loenneker, T., Ekatodramis, D., Vitacco, D., Hennig, J. & Marcar, V. L. 1999 Visual processing in infants and children studied using functional MRI. *Pediatric Res.* **46**, 135–140.

Martin, K. A. C. 1988 From single cells to simple circuits in the cerebral cortex. *Q. J. Exp. Psychol.* **73**, 637–702.

Mathiesen, C., Caesar, K., Akgoren, N. & Lauritzen, M. 1998 Modification of activity-dependent increases of cerebral blood flow by excitatory synaptic activity and spikes in rat cerebellar cortex. *J. Physiol.* **512**, 555–566.

Mathiesen, C., Caesar, K. & Lauritzen, M. 2000 Temporal coupling between neuronal activity and blood flow in rat cerebellar cortex as indicated by field potential analysis. *J. Physiol.* **523** (Pt. 1), 235–246.

Matwiyoff, A. M. & Brooks, W. M. 1999 Instrumentation. In *Magnetic resonance imaging* (ed. D. D. Stark & W. Bradley), pp. 15–32. St Louis, MO: Mosby.

Maunsell, J. H. & Van Essen, D. C. 1983 The connections of the middle temporal visual area (MT) and their relationship to a cortical hierarchy in the macaque monkey. *J. Neurosci.* **3**, 2563–2586.

Mayhew, J., Johnston, D., Martindale, J., Jones, M., Berwick, J. & Zheng, Y. 2001 Increased oxygen consumption following activation of brain: theoretical footnotes using spectroscopic data from barrel cortex. *Neuroimage* **13**, 975–987.

Menon, R. S., Ogawa, S., Tank, D. W. & Ugurbil, K. 1993 4 Tesla gradient recalled echo characteristics of photic stimulation-induced signal changes in the human primary visual cortex. *Magn. Resonance Med.* **30**, 380–386.

Menon, R. S., Ogawa, S., Hu, X., Strupp, J. P., Anderson, P. & Ugurbil, K. 1995 BOLD based functional MRI at 4 Tesla includes a capillary bed contribution: echo-planar imaging correlates with previous optical imaging using intrinsic signals. *Magn. Resonance Med.* **33**, 453–459.

Menon, V., Ford, J. M., Lim, K. O., Glover, G. H. & Pfefferbaum, A. 1997 Combined event-related fMRI and EEG evidence for temporal-parietal cortex activation during target detection. *NeuroReport* **8**, 3029–3037.

Merkle, H., Garwood, M., and Ugurbil, K. 1993 Dedicated circularly polarized surface coil assemblies for brain studies at 4 Tesla. In *Proc. SMRM, 12th Annual Meeting, New York*, p. 1358.

Mitzdorf, U. 1987 Properties of the evoked potential generators: current source-density analysis of visually evoked potentials in the cat cortex. *Int. J. Neurosci.* **33**, 33–59.

Mosso, A. 1881 *Ueber den Kreislauf des Blutes im Menschlichen Gehirn.* Leipzig: Verlag von Veit.

Mountcastle, V. B., Steinmetz, M. A. & Romo, R. 1990 Frequency discrimination in the sense of flutter: psychophysical measurements correlated with postcentral events in behaving monkeys. *J. Neurosci.* **10**, 3032–3044.

Nakahara, K., Hayashi, T., Konishi, S. & Miyashita, Y. 2002 Functional MRI of macaque monkeys performing a cognitive set-shifting task. *Science* **295**, 1532–1536.

Nelson, P. G. 1966 Interaction between spinal motoneurons of the cat. *J. Neurophysiol.* **29**, 275–287.

Nicholson, C. & Llinas, R. 1971 Field potentials in the alligator cerebellum and theory of their relationship to Purkinje cell dendritic spikes. *J. Neurophysiol.* **34**, 509–531.

Nudo, R. J. & Masterton, R. B. 1986 Stimulation-induced [14]C2-deoxyglucose labeling of synaptic activity in the central auditory system. *J. Comp. Neurol.* **245**, 553–565.

Obata, S., Obata, J., Das, A. & Gilbert, C. D. 1999 Molecular correlates of topographic reorganization in primary visual cortex following retinal lesions. *Cerebral Cortex* **9**, 238–248.

Ogawa, S. & Lee, T. M. 1990 Magnetic resonance imaging of blood vessels at high fields: *in vivo* and *in vitro* measurements and image simulation. *Magn. Resonance Med.* **16**, 9–18.

Ogawa, S., Lee, T. M., Nayak, A. S. & Glynn, P. 1990*a* Oxygenation-sensitive contrast in magnetic resonance image of rodent brain at high magnetic fields. *Magn. Resonance Med.* **14**, 68–78.

Ogawa, S., Lee, T. M., Kay, A. R. & Tank, D. W. 1999*b* Brain magnetic resonance imaging with contrast dependent on blood oxygenation. *Proc. Natl Acad. Sci. USA* **87**, 9868–9872.

Ogawa, S., Tank, D. W., Menon, R., Ellermann, J. M., Kim, S. G., Merkle, H. & Ugurbil, K. 1992 Intrinsic signal changes accompanying sensory stimulation: functional brain mapping with magnetic resonance imaging. *Proc. Natl Acad. Sci. USA* **89**, 5951–5955.

Ogawa, S., Menon, R. S., Tank, D. W., Kim, S. G., Merkle, H., Ellermann, J. M. & Ugurbil, K. 1993 Functional brain mapping by blood oxygenation level-dependent contrast magnetic resonance imaging. A comparison of signal characteristics with a biophysical model. *Biophys. J.* **64**, 803–812.

Ogawa, S., Menon, R. S., Kim, S. G. & Ugurbil, K. 1998 On the characteristics of functional magnetic resonance imaging of the brain. *A. Rev. Biophys. Biomol. Struct.* **27**, 447–474.

Pan, J. W. (and 10 others) 2000 Spectroscopic imaging of glutamate C4 turnover in human brain. *Magn. Resonance Med.* **44**, 673–679.

Pauling, L. & Coryell, C. 1936 The magnetic properties and structure of hemogblogin. *Proc. Natl Acad. Sci. USA* **22**, 210–216.

Pedemonte, M., Barrenechea, C., Nunez, A., Gambini, J. P. & Garcia-Austt, E. 1998 Membrane and circuit properties of lateral septum neurons: relationships with hippocampal rhythms. *Brain Res.* **800**, 145–153.

Pedley, T. A. & Traub, R. D. 1990 Physiological basis of the EEG. In *Current practice of clinical electroencephalography* (ed. D. D. Daly & T. A. Pedley), pp. 107–137. New York: Raven Press.

Pellerin, L. & Magistretti, P. J. 1994 Glutamate uptake into astrocytes stimulates aerobic glycolysis: a mechanism coupling neuronal activity to glucose utilization. *Proc. Natl Acad. Sci. USA* **91**, 10 625–10 629.

Pfeuffer, J., Van, D., Ugurbil, K., Hu, X. P. & Glover, G. H. 2002*a* Correction of physiologically induced global off resonance effects in dynamic echo-planar and spiral functional imaging. *Magn. Resonance Med.* **47**, 344–353.

Pfeuffer, J., Van de Moortele, Yacoub, E., Shmuel, A., Adriany, G., Andersen, P., Merkle, H., Garwood, M., Hu, X. & Ugurbil, K. 2002*b* Zoomed functional imaging in the human brain at 7 Tesla with simultaneous high spatial and high temporal resolution. *Neuroimage* (In the press.)

Phelps, M. E., Hoffman, E. J., Mullani, N. A. & Ter Pogossian, M. M. 1975 Application of annihilation coincidence detection to transaxial reconstruction tomography. *J. Nucl. Med.* **16**, 210–224.

Polonsky, A., Blake, R., Braun, J. & Heeger, D. J. 2000 Neuronal activity in human primary visual cortex correlates with perception during binocular rivalry. *Nature Neurosci.* **3**, 1153–1159.

Purcell, E. M., Torrey, H. C. & Pound, C. V. 1946 Resonance absorption by nuclear magnetic moments in a solid. *Physiol. Rev.* **64**, 37–38.

Rabi, I. I., Zacharias, J. R., Millman, S. & Kusch, P. 1938 A new method for measuring nuclear magnetic moment. *Phys. Rev.* **55**, 526–535.

Rabi, I. I., Millman, S. & Kusch, P. 1939 The molecular beam resonance method for measuring nuclear magnetic moments. *Phys. Rev.* **55**, 643–674.

Raichle, M. E. 2000 A brief history of human functional brain mapping. In *The systems* (ed. A. W. Toga & J. C. Mazziotta), pp. 33–75. San Diego: Academic.

Raichle, M. E., Grubb, R. L. J., Eichling, J. O. & Ter Pogossian, M. M. 1976 Measurement of brain oxygen utilization with radioactive oxygen-15, experimental verification. *J. Appl. Physiol.* **40**, 638–640.

Rainer, G., Augath, M., Trinath, T. & Logothetis, N. K. 2001 Nonmonotonic noise tuning of BOLD fMRI signal to natural images in the visual cortex of the anesthetized monkey. *Curr. Biol.* **11**, 846–854.

Raisman, G. 1966 The connexions of the septum. *Brain* **89**, 317–348.

Rall, W. 1962 Electrophysiology of a dendritic neuron. *Biophys. J.* **2**, 145–167.

Recanzone, G. H., Merzenich, M. M. & Schreiner, C. E. 1992 Changes in the distributed temporal response properties of SI cortical neurons reflect improvements in performance on a temporally based tactile discrimination task. *J. Neurophysiol.* **67**, 1071–1091.

Rees, G., Friston, K. & Koch, C. 2000 A direct quantitative relationship between the functional properties of human and macaque V5. *Nature Neurosci.* **3**, 716–723.

Ress, D., Backus, B. T. & Heeger, D. J. 2000 Activity in primary visual cortex predicts performance in a visual detection task. *Nature Neurosci.* **3**, 940–945.

Roemer, P. B., Edelstein, W. A., Hayes, C. E., Souza, S. P. & Mueller, O. M. 1990 The NMR phased array. *Magn. Resonance Med.* **16**, 192–225.

Romo, R. & Salinas, E. 1999 Sensing and deciding in the somatosensory system. *Curr. Opin. Neurobiol.* **9**, 487–493.

Rosen, B. R., Belliveau, J. W., Aronen, H. J., Kennedy, D., Buchbinder, B. R., Fischman, A., Gruber, M., Glas, J., Weisskoff, R. M. & Cohen, M. S. 1991 Susceptibility contrast imaging of cerebral blood volume: human experience. *Magn. Resonance Med.* **22**, 293–299.

Rothman, D. L., Sibson, N. R., Hyder, F., Shen, J., Behar, K. L. & Shulman, R. G. 1999 *In vivo* nuclear magnetic resonance spectroscopy studies of the relationship between the glutamate-glutamine neurotransmitter cycle and functional neuroenergetics. *Phil. Trans. R. Soc. Lond.* B **354**, 1165–1177. (DOI 10.1098/rstb.1999.0472.)

Roy, C. S. & Sherrington, C. S. 1890 On the regulation of the blood supply of the brain. *J. Physiol. Lond.* **11**, 85–108.

Rudin, M. 1987 MR microscopy on rats in vivo at 4.7 T using surface coils. *Magn. Resonance Med.* **5**, 443–448.

Schiller, P. H., Finlay, B. L. & Volman, S. F. 1976 Quantitative studies of single-cell properties in monkey striate cortex. I. Spatiotemporal organization of receptive fields. *J. Neurophysiol.* **39**, 1288–1319.

Schmitt, F., Stehling, M. K. & Turner, R. 1998 *Echo-planar imaging: theory, technique and application.* Berlin: Springer.

Segebarth, C., Belle, V., Delon, C., Massarelli, R., Decety, J., Le, B., Decorps, M. & Benabid, A. L. 1994 Functional MRI of the human brain: predominance of signals from extra-cerebral veins. *NeuroReport* **5**, 813–816.

Sereno, M. E., Trinath, T., Augath, M. & Logothetis, N. K. 2002 Three-dimensional shape representation in monkey cortex. *Neuron* **33**, 635–652.

Sereno, M. I., Dale, A. M., Reppas, J. B., Kwong, K. K., Belliveau, J. W., Brady, T. J., Rosen, B. R. & Tootell, R. B. 1995 Borders of multiple visual areas in humans revealed by functional magnetic resonance imaging. *Science* **268**, 889–893.

Shulman, G. L., Corbetta, M., Buckner, R. L., Raichle, M. E., Fiez, J. A., Miezin, F. M. & Petersen, S. E. 1997 Top-down modulation of early sensory cortex. *Cerebral Cortex* **7**, 193–206.

Shulman, R. G. & Rothman, D. L. 1998 Interpreting functional imaging studies in terms of neurotransmitter cycling. *Proc. Natl Acad. Sci. USA* **95**, 11 993–11 998.

Sibson, N. R., Dhankhar, A., Mason, G. F., Rothman, D. L., Behar, K. L. & Shulman, R. G. 1998 Stoichiometric coupling of brain glucose metabolism and glutamatergic neuronal activity. *Proc. Natl Acad. Sci. USA* **95**, 316–321.

Siesjo, B. o. K. 1978 *Brain energy metabolism.* New York: Wiley.

Silva, L. R., Amitai, Y. & Connors, B. W. 1991 Intrinsic oscillations of neocortex generated by layer 5 pyramidal neurons. *Science* **251**, 432–435.

Silver, X., Ni, W. X., Mercer, E. V., Beck, B. L., Bossart, E. L., Inglis, B. & Mareci, T. H. 2001 *In vivo* H-1 magnetic resonance imaging and spectroscopy of the rat spinal cord using an inductively-coupled chronically implanted RF coil. *Magn. Resonance Med.* **46**, 1216–1222.

Sokoloff, L. 1960 The metabolism of the central nervous system *in vivo.* In *Handbook of physiology–neurophysiology* (ed. J. Field, H. W. Magoun & V. E. Hall), pp. 1843–1864. Washington, DC: American Physiological Society.

Sokoloff, L. 1977 Relation between physiological function and energy metabolism in the central nervous system. *J. Neurochem.* **29**, 13–26.

Sokoloff, L. 1981 Relationships among local functional activity, energy metabolism, and blood flow in the central nervous system. *Fed. Proc. Fedn Am. Socs Exp. Biol.* **40**, 2311–2316.

Sokoloff, L. 1989 Circulation and energy metabolism of the brain. In *Basic neurochemistry* (ed. G. Siegel, B. Agranoff, R. W. Albers & P. Molinoff), pp. 565–590. New York: Raven Press.

Sokoloff, L., Reivich, M., Kennedy, C., DesRosiers, M. H., Patlak, C. S., Pettigrew, K. D., Sakurada, O. & Shinohara, M. 1977 The [C14]deoxyglucose method for the measurement of local cerebral glucose utilization: theory, procedure and normal values in the conscious and anesthetized albino rat. *J. Neurochem.* **28**, 897–916.

Stark, D. D. & Bradley, W. 1999 *Magnetic resonance imaging*. St Louis, MO: Mosby.

Steele, G. E., Weller, R. E. & Cusick, C. G. 1991 Cortical connections of the caudal subdivision of the dorsolateral area (V4) in monkeys. *J. Comp. Neurol.* **306**, 495–520.

Steriade M. 1991 Alertness, quiet sleep, dreaming. In *Cerebral cortex*, pp. 279–357. New York: Plenum.

Steriade, M. & Hobson, J. 1976 Neuronal activity during the sleep–waking cycle. *Progr. Neurobiol.* **6**, 155–376.

Steriade, M., McCormick, D. A. & Sejnowski, T. J. 1993 Thalamocortical oscillations in the sleeping and aroused brain. *Science* **262**, 679–685.

Summers, R. M., Hedlund, L. W., Cofer, G. P., Gottsman, M. B., Manibo, J. F. & Johnson, G. A. 1995 MR microscopy of the rat carotid artery after balloon injury by using an implanted imaging coil. *Magn. Resonance Med.* **33**, 785–789.

Szentagothai, J. 1978 The Ferrier Lecture, 1977. The neuron network of the cerebral cortex: a functional interpretation. *Proc. R. Soc. Lond.* B **201**, 219–248.

Takahashi, S., Driscoll, B. F., Law, M. J. & Sokoloff, L. 1995 Role of sodium and potassium ions in regulation of glucose metabolism in cultured astroglia. *Proc. Natl Acad. Sci. USA* **92**, 4616–4620.

Ter Pogossian, M. M., Eichling, J. O., Davis, D. O., Welch, M. J. & Metzger, J. M. 1969 The determination of regional cerebral blood flow by means of water labeled with radioactive oxygen 15. *Radiology* **93**, 31–40.

Ter Pogossian, M. M., Eichling, J. O., Davis, D. O. & Welch, M. J. 1970 The measure *in vivo* of regional cerebral oxygen utilization by means of oxyhemoglobin labeled with radio-active oxygen-15. *J. Clin. Invest.* **49**, 381–391.

Ter Pogossian, M. M., Phelps, M. E., Hoffman, E. J. & Mullani, N. A. 1975 A positron-emission transaxial tomograph for nuclear imaging (PETT). *Radiology* **114**, 89–98.

Tolias, A. S., Smirnakis, S. M., Augath, M. A., Trinath, T. & Logothetis, N. K. 2001 Motion processing in the macaque: revisited with functional magnetic resonance imaging. *J. Neurosci.* **21**, 8594–8601.

Tong, F., Nakayama, K., Vaughan, J. T. & Kanwisher, N. 1998 Binocular-rivalry and visual awareness in human extra-striate cortex. *Neuron* **21**, 753–759.

Tootell, R. B., Reppas, J. B., Dale, A. M., Look, R. B., Sereno, M. I., Malach, R., Brady, T. J. & Rosen, B. R. 1995 Visual motion aftereffect in human cortical area M.T. revealed by functional magnetic resonance imaging. *Nature* **375**, 139–141.

Towe, A. L. & Harding, G. W. 1970 Extracellular microelectrode sampling bias. *Exp. Neurol.* **29**, 366–381.

Tuor, U. I., Malisza, K., Foniok, T., Papadimitropoulos, R., Jarmasz, M., Somorjai, R. & Kozlowski, P. 2000 Functional magnetic resonance imaging in rats subjected to intense electrical and noxious chemical stimulation of the forepaw. *Pain* **87**, 315–324.

Turner, R., Le Bihan, D., Moonen, C. T., DesPres, D. & Frank, J. 1991 Echo-planar time course MRI of cat brain oxygenation changes. *Magn. Resonance Med.* **22**, 159–166.

Ugurbil, K., Garwood, M., Ellermann, J., Hendrich, K., Hinke, R., Hu, X., Kim, S. G., Menon, R., Merkle, H. & Ogawa, S. 1993 Imaging at high magnetic fields: initial experiences at 4 T. *Magn. Resonance Q.* **9**, 259–277.

Ungerleider, L. G. & Desimone, R. 1986 Cortical connections of visual area MT in the macaque. *J. Comp. Neurol.* **248**, 190–222.

Van Zijl, P. C., Eleff, S. M., Ulatowski, J. A., Oja, J. M., Ulug, A. M., Traystman, R. J. & Kauppinen, R. A. 1998 Quantitative assessment of blood flow, blood volume and blood oxygenation effects in functional magnetic resonance imaging. *Nature Med.* **4**, 159–167.

Vanduffel, W., Fize, D., Mandeville, J. B., Nelissen, K., Van, H., Rosen, B. R., Tootell, R. B. H. & Orban, G. A. 2001 Visual motion processing investigated using contrast agent-enhanced fMRI in awake behaving monkeys. *Neuron* **32**, 565–577.

Vanzetta, I. & Grinvald, A. 1999 Increased cortical oxidative metabolism due to sensory stimulation: implications for functional brain imaging. *Science* **286**, 1555–1558.

Vanzetta, I. & Grinvald, A. 2001 Evidence and lack of evidence for the initial dip in the anesthetized rat: implications for human functional brain imaging. *Neuroimage* **13**, 959–967.

Vlaardingerbroek, M. & Den, B. 1996 *Magnetic resonance imaging: theory & practice.* Berlin: Springer.

Walker, P. M., Robin-Lherbier, B., Escanye, J. M. & Robert, J. 1991 Signal-to-noise improvement in mid-field MRI surface coils: a degree in plumbing? *Magn. Resonance Imaging* **9**, 927–931.

Wandell, B. A., Press, W. A., Brewer, A. & Logothetis, N. K. 2000 fMRI measurements of visual areas and retinotopic maps in monkey. *Soc. Neurosci. Abstracts* **26**, 821.

Wehr, M. & Laurent, G. 1999 Relationship between afferent and central temporal patterns in the locust olfactory system. *J. Neurosci.* **19**, 381–390.

Weisskoff, R. M., Zuo, C. S., Boxerman, J. L. & Rosen, B. R. 1994 Microscopic susceptibility variation and transverse relaxation: theory and experiment. *Magn. Resonance Med.* **31**, 601–610.

Wood, M. L. & Wehrli, F. W. 1999 Principles of magnetic resonance imaging. In *Magnetic resonance imaging* (ed. D. D. Stark & W. Bradley), pp. 1–14. St Louis, MO: Mosby.

Wyrwicz, A. M., Chen, N. K., Li, L. M., Weiss, C. & Disterhoft, J. F. 2000 fMRI of visual system activation in the conscious rabbit. *Magn. Resonance Med.* **44**, 474–478.

Yacoub, E. & Hu, X. 1999 Detection of the early negative response in fMRI at 1.5 tesla. *Magn. Resonance Med.* **41**, 1088–1092.

Zhang, Z. M., Andersen, A. H., Avison, M. J., Gerhardt, G. A. & Gash, D. M. 2000 Functional MRI of apomorphine activation of the basal ganglia in awake rhesus monkeys. *Brain Res.* **852**, 290–296.

Zhong, J., Kennan, R. P., Fulbright, R. K. & Gore, J. C. 1998 Quantification of intravascular and extravascular contributions to BOLD effects induced by alteration in oxygenation or intravascular contrast agents. *Magn. Resonance Med.* **40**, 526–536.

Glossary

2DG	$[^{14}C]$deoxyglucose
BOLD	blood-oxygen-level-dependent
CBF	cerebral blood flow
CBV	cerebral blood volume
CMR	cerebral metabolic rate
CNR	contrast-to-noise ratio
DB	diagonal band of Broca
dHb	deoxyhaemoglobin
EEG	electroencephalography
EPSP	excitatory postsynaptic potential
EPI	echo planar imaging
FID	free induction decay
FLASH	fast low-angle shot
fMRI	functional magnetic resonance imaging
FOV	field of view
Gln	glutamine
Glu	glutamate
GM	grey matter
IPSP	inhibitory postsynaptic potential
LGN	lateral geniculate nuclei
LFP	local field potential
MB	mushroom body
MDEF	modified driven equilibrium Fourier transform

MR   magnetic resonance
MRI   magnetic resonance imaging
MRS   magnetic resonance spectroscopy
MSN   medial septum nuclei
MT   middle temporal visual area
MUA   multi-unit activity
NMR   nuclear magnetic resonance
PET   positron emission tomography
PTN   pyramidal tract neuron
RF   radiofrequency
ROI   region of interest
SDF   spike-density function
SNR   signal-to-noise ratio
WM   white matter

5

Exploring the cortical evidence of a sensory-discrimination process

Ranulfo Romo, Adrián Hernández, Antonio Zainos,
Carlos Brody, and Emilio Salinas

Humans and monkeys have similar abilities to discriminate the difference in frequency between two consecutive mechanical vibrations applied to their fingertips. This task can be conceived as a chain of neural operations: encoding the two consecutive stimuli, maintaining the first stimulus in working memory, comparing the second stimulus with the memory trace left by the first stimulus and communicating the result of the comparison to the motor apparatus. We studied this chain of neural operations by recording and manipulating neurons from different areas of the cerebral cortex while monkeys performed the task. The results indicate that neurons of the primary somatosensory cortex (S1) generate a neural representation of vibrotactile stimuli which correlates closely with psychophysical performance. Discrimination based on microstimulation patterns injected into clusters of S1 neurons is indistinguishable from that produced by natural stimuli. Neurons from the secondary somatosensory cortex (S2), prefrontal cortex and medial premotor cortex (MPC) display at different times the trace of the first stimulus during the working-memory component of the task. Neurons from S2 and MPC appear to show the comparison between the two stimuli and correlate with the behavioural decisions. These neural operations may contribute to the sensory-discrimination process studied here.

5.1. Introduction

An important problem in brain physiology is the isolation of the sensory representations that guide behavioural decisions. This problem has been investigated in behavioural tasks where the sensory stimuli are under precise quantitative control and the subject's psychophysical performances are quantitatively measured (Talbot *et al.* 1968; Newsome *et al.* 1989; Mountcastle *et al.* 1990). This strategy has allowed the investigation of which attributes of the neural responses elicited by a sensory stimulus are sensorily meaningful (Romo & Salinas 1999, 2001). Indeed, it has been shown that the sensory areas of the cerebral cortex generate representations of the sensory stimuli that correlate closely with psychophysical performances (Newsome *et al.* 1989; Vogels & Orban 1990; Hernández *et al.* 2000). Alternatively, behavioural decisions are reported through motor actions, but it is not clear where and how a sensory representation is converted into a motor output. To answer this question, neurophysiologists have studied the neuronal responses of motor areas during perceptual tasks, and have found that a fraction of the neurons show a link between the sensory inputs and the behavioural decisions (Romo *et al.* 1997, 1993; Merchant *et al.* 1997; Salinas & Romo 1998; Horwitz & Newsome 1999). However, decision making is more than a simple input–output operation (Shadlen & Newsome 2001). For example, regardless of the perceptual task, subjects reach a behavioural decision after the comparison of the current sensory input against a sensory referent, which can be stored in working memory or in long-term memory. Therefore, to understand how the brain carries a perceptual process, we need to isolate where and in what form the current sensory input

R. Romo *et al.*

interacts with a sensory referent that is stored in the memory (Hernández *et al.* 2002). This neural operation, we believe, is the key to understanding how the neuronal circuits elaborate a perceptual process.

We have addressed some of the issues mentioned here in a behavioural task where monkeys discriminate the difference in frequency between two consecutive mechanical vibrations delivered to their fingertips (Figure 5.1; for details see Hernández *et al.* (1997) and Mountcastle *et al.* (1990)). In this task the stimulus can be finely controlled; the same primary

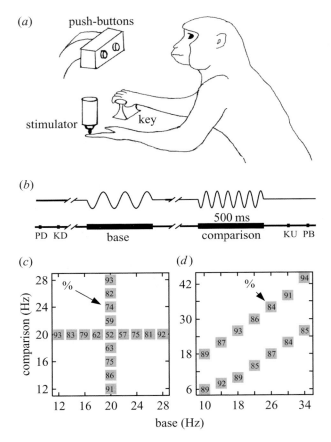

Fig. 5.1. The discrimination task. (*a*) Drawing of a monkey working in the discrimination task. (*b*) The sequence of events during the discrimination trials. The mechanical probe is lowered, indenting the glabrous skin of one digit of the hand (PD); the monkey places his free hand on an immovable key (KD); the probe oscillates vertically, at the base stimulus frequency; after a delay, a second mechanical vibration is delivered at the comparison frequency; the monkey releases the key (KU) and presses either a laterally placed or medially placed push-button (PB) to indicate whether the comparison frequency was higher or lower than the base. (*c,d*) Stimulus sets used during recordings. Each box indicates a base–comparison frequency stimulus pair used; the numbers inside the box indicate the overall percentage of correct trials for the base–comparison pair. The stimulus set illustrated in (*c*) is used to determine the discrimination thresholds; the stimulus set illustrated in (*d*) is used to explore the working-memory component of the task. The combinations of both sets are often used during the recording sessions.

afferents are activated by the two stimuli; there is sensory and motor lateralization; it involves a working-memory mechanism; and decision making is based on the comparison between the current sensory input and the memory trace left by the first stimulus. Thus, the task can be viewed as a chain of neuronal operations. In this paper, we review recent results obtained in this sensory-discrimination task. § 5.2 contains a brief description of the general organization of the somatosensory system and the experiments that paved the way to studying the neuronal processes involved. § 5.3 then describes the neuronal correlates that seem to be associated with the different components of the vibrotactile discrimination.

5.2. The somatosensory system

The somatic and visual systems are useful models for investigating stimulus information processing, and some general principles behind the functional organization of the brain. There are some elements of the organization of the somatosensory system that are relevant in investigating neural coding of sensory stimuli both at the periphery and in the brain. For the sake of simplicity, we restrict this review to the cutaneous information-processing channel.

(a) Cutaneous primary afferents

The human hand contains four types of cutaneous afferent fibres that transmit information of the mechanical stimulus features to the central nervous system (Talbot *et al.* 1968; Darian-Smith 1984; Vallbo & Johansson 1984; Vallbo 1995). Two of these afferent fibres are rapidly adapting: one is anatomically linked to QA and the other to PC. The other two afferent fibres are slowly adapting and are linked to SA-I and SA-II, respectively. The monkey hand possesses these afferent fibres, except SA-II. Although all these afferent fibres respond to a cutaneous stimulus, they become specialized to encoding spatiotemporal features of the stimuli (Talbot *et al.* 1968; Phillips and Johnson 1981). This has been demonstrated in well-designed experiments aimed at exploring their capacities. The degree of sensitivity of these afferent fibres is evidenced by the fact that a psychophysical observer can detect even a single spike evoked in one single primary afferent (Vallbo & Johansson 1984; Vallbo 1995).

(b) Neocortical somatosensory areas

After a relay in the dorsal column nuclei and in the basal complex nuclei of the thalamus, somatosensory information reaches S1. Primate S1 is subdivided into four areas (area 3a, 3b, 1, and 2), each containing a somatotopic representation of the body (Kaas *et al.* 1979; Nelson *et al.* 1980). Tactile information is processed mainly by areas 3b, 1 and 2, which are interconnected (Shanks *et al.* 1985). To a certain extent, neurons in S1 replicate the functional properties of QA, SA-I and PC afferent fibres (Powell & Mountcastle 1959; Mountcastle *et al.* 1969; Sur *et al.* 1984) and are referred to as QA, SA and PC neurons. These subtypes are clustered in columns (Mountcastle 1957; Powell & Mountcastle 1959; Sur *et al.* 1984).

Information flows from S1 to the posterior parietal cortex and to the lateral somatosensory areas. As for the visual system, it appears that there is also a dorsal stream and a ventral stream in the cortical organization of the somatosensory system (Mishkin 1979; Murray & Mishkin 1984). According to this organization, the dorsal stream flows through areas 5 and 7b

(Pearson & Powell 1985; Shanks *et al.* 1985; Cavada & Goldman-Rakic 1989), and the ventral stream flows through the lateral somatosensory areas (Pons *et al.* 1987, 1992; Burton *et al.* 1995; Krubitzer *et al.* 1995). The dorsal stream is more likely to be associated with processing the somatosensory information that reaches the PM cortex (Godshalk *et al.* 1984; Cavada & Goldman-Rakic 1989; Leichnetz 1989; Tokuno & Tanji 1993). The operations through this dorsal stream could be important for self-initiated or stimulus-triggered voluntary movements involving sensory processing. The ventral stream is more likely to be associated with fine discrimination and the recognition of stimulus patterns. This processing reaches also the PM cortex (Godshalk *et al.* 1984; Cavada & Goldman-Rakic 1989; Leichnetz 1989) and the PFC (Preuss & Goldman-Rakic 1989; Carmichael & Price 1995), and might be associated with the fine discrimination of stimulus objects. Interestingly, both streams reach M1 (Leichnetz 1989; Tokuno & Tanji 1993), and both should drive the motor representations during sensory tasks that require an indication of decision making. The functional meaning of these streams, however, needs to be investigated further, especially with regard to what aspects of somatosensory perception they contribute to.

5.3. Forming a sensation via a neural code

Talbot *et al.* (1968) and Werner & Mountcastle (1965) pioneered this enterprise almost four decades ago. The key conceptual advance was to combine psychophysics and neurophysiology, two experimental disciplines that had previously been divorced in sensory research. Talbot *et al.* (1968) and Werner (1980) used mechanical stimuli, applied to the fingertips of humans, that changed in one dimension; they measured the subjective estimates quantitatively. Then they recorded in anaesthetized monkeys the responses of cutaneous afferent fibres using the same stimuli in the psychophysical experiments (Werner & Mountcastle 1965; Talbot *et al.* 1968). Their goal was to determine the relationship between the subjective sensation and the evoked peripheral activity produced by the stimuli. Indeed, they found a close relationship between the psychophysical performance and the neural activity evoked by the stimuli (Werner & Mountcastle 1965; Talbot *et al.* 1968). These pioneering experiments have been adapted since then as a tool for exploring the neural codes that underlie a sensation in the different sensory modalities.

(a) Peripheral coding of vibrotactile stimuli

A sensory neural code is activity produced by a natural stimulus, which correlates with the psychophysical performance. Defining the peripheral coding of a somatosensory stimulus implies that this approach might facilitate exploring the central neural mechanisms of somatosensory perception. Talbot *et al.* (1968) pioneered this research area using the sensory modality of the sense of flutter vibration. They showed that, depending on the range of frequency of the mechanical vibrations applied to the skin on the hand, two sensations can be elicited: the sensation of flutter at low frequencies (range of 5–50 Hz) and the sensation of vibration at high frequency (range of 60–300 Hz). Talbot *et al.* (1968) first quantified amplitude detection thresholds in humans, and then showed that the sensitivities of QA and PC afferents account for performance in the low- and high-frequency regimes, respectively. This correspondence between perceptual and anatomical submodalities was later confirmed and extended by recording and microstimulating afferent fibres in human subjects (Ochoa & Torebjörk 1983; Macefield *et al.* 1990; Vallbo & Johansson 1984; Vallbo 1995).

There were two major observations about the nature of the peripheral neural code underlying flutter–vibration perception (Talbot *et al.* 1968). First, the QA and PC afferents respond periodically to the periodic structure of the stimulus frequency. Second, the QA afferents hardly change in firing rate over a frequency range of 10–50 Hz, while the PC afferents increase their firing rate as a function of increasing stimulus frequency (60–250 Hz). It was thus concluded that high frequencies could be encoded by the total number of PC spikes produced—a rate code (Shadlen & Newsome 1994; Singer & Gray 1995)—but low frequencies could not, because the number of QA spikes seemed to be constant in the flutter range; they had to be encoded in the regular, periodic spikes produced by the flutter stimuli in the QA afferents—a temporal code. However, direct microstimulation of QA afferents produced flutter sensations of frequencies that were perceived to increase with the evoked firing rate (Ochoa & Torebjörk 1983). If the frequency of the microstimulation current increases in the range of 5–100 Hz—presumably producing a proportional increase in QA firing rate—human subjects report gradual increases in the perceived flutter frequency at a constant intensity (Ochoa & Torebjörk 1983).

The experiments established the roles that the different cutaneous afferents play in coding temporal stimuli. Clearly, the QA and PC systems encode the temporal features of the stimuli. Interestingly, it has been shown that the SA-I afferent system transmits information regarding the spatial properties of the stimulus features (Johnson & Hsiao 1992). The neural coding of the physical properties of the stimuli seems to define and limit the capacity of the psychophysical observer to detect, recognize and discriminate the stimuli. These important observations paved the way for further investigation of the cortical processing of somatosensory inputs during perceptual tasks.

5.4. Cortical coding of vibrotactile stimuli and the link to perception

Compared with our knowledge of tactile coding in afferent fibres, the central mechanisms are less understood. This has been due in part to the difficulties in adapting somatosensory tasks in behaving monkeys. Tracing a neural code from the periphery to the cerebral cortex has remained the leading idea in understanding somatosensation. The key here is the use of well-designed psychophysical tasks in behaving monkeys. In § 5.4 we review developments in this research area.

(a) Psychophysics

Mountcastle *et al.* (1972) adapted the vibrotactile task used initially in human subjects to behaving monkeys. They trained monkeys to detect amplitudes and discriminate stimuli frequencies in the flutter range (Mountcastle *et al.* 1972; LaMotte & Mountcastle 1975). With intense training, monkeys developed stimulus-frequency amplitude-detection thresholds that were almost indistinguishable from those quantified in human subjects in identical conditions (Mountcastle *et al.* 1972). In addition, the discrimination of two consecutive stimulus frequencies delivered to the hands (Figure 5.1) was similar to those measured in humans in identical conditions (LaMotte & Mountcastle 1975; Mountcastle *et al.* 1990). These results indicate that monkeys could be an appropriate model for exploring the central neural mechanisms associated with the flutter task. The discrimination flutter task is particularly rich in that comparison of f_2 is made against the memory trace left by f_1. To solve this task the psychophysical observer requires a number of cognitive processes such as detection, working memory, comparison and decision making (Mountcastle *et al.* 1990; Hernández *et al.* 1997; Romo *et al.* 1998). Some other tasks require that monkeys categorize moving tactile stimuli (Romo *et al.* 1993, 1996), detect roughness in surfaces (Sinclair & Burton 1993; Jiang *et al.* 1997) or discriminate tactual stimulus orientation and form (Hsiao *et al.* 1993; Burton *et al.* 1997). All these tasks require attention to be focused on the stimulus with indication of performance given through voluntary movements; that is, from sensation to action. Investigators using these somatosensory tasks want to unravel the central mechanisms associated with the different components of these psychophysical tasks.

(b) Coding of vibrotactile stimuli in S1

If QA afferents reliably encode the periodic structure of the flutter stimulus frequency, the question then is whether QA neurons of S1 do this in a similar fashion, or whether there is another way of encoding the stimuli. Shortly after their work on cutaneous afferent fibres, Mountcastle *et al.* (1969) studied the responses of S1 neurons. Two decades later, S1 neurons were re-recorded, this time in behaving monkeys trained to detect and discriminate flutter-stimuli frequencies (Mountcastle *et al.* 1990). The results support the previous findings. First, it was found that QA neurons of S1, like their afferent fibres, fire periodically in phase with mechanical oscillations. Second, their firing rates seem to change little in the flutter range (this conclusion was based, however, on data from 17 neurons). Third, the psychophysical performance matched the inferred performance based on the discriminability of the periodic inter-spike intervals (Mountcastle *et al.* 1990). It followed that, as proposed before, the stimulus frequency could not be encoded by S1 firing rates; the stimulus frequency had to be encoded temporally, in the serial order of evoked spikes (Talbot *et al.* 1968; Mountcastle *et al.* 1969, 1990).

In support of this proposal, using flutter stimuli, Recanzone *et al.* (1992) compared psychophysical data from monkeys to S1 recordings in separate experiments from the same animals. The comparison was consistent with a temporal coding mechanism, and firing rates were not seen to vary with the stimulus frequency (however, the range of frequencies tested was quite narrow and the animals were anaesthetized). Recanzone *et al.* (1992) made another important observation: that spike timing associated with the sine wave was much more precise in trained animals compared with untrained monkeys. Thus, on the basis of these results, a psychophysical observer should exploit the periodic spike timing evoked in the QA neurons of S1 for sensory discrimination.

Arguments in favour of this proposal could be strengthened if a large number of neurons were studied, and if neurons were studied in awake animals during the flutter-discrimination task (Figure 5.1). Hernández *et al.* (2000) and Salinas *et al.* (2000) trained monkeys to discriminate between flutter stimulus frequencies and recorded many neurons with QA properties in areas 3b and 1 of S1. Each recorded neuron with QA properties was studied during the discrimination task. There were three major results. First, the majority of neurons from S1 were phase-locked to the input stimulus frequency; however, almost one-third of the QA neurons modulated their firing rates as a function of the stimulus frequency (Salinas *et al.* 2000). The second important finding was that QA neurons that modulate their firing rates were affected by the task condition; that is, they increased their transmitted information about the stimulus frequency during task performance (Salinas *et al.* 2000). Third, only those neurons that varied their firing rates as a function of the stimulus frequency were affected in the error trials (Salinas *et al.* 2000).

These findings question the unique role of periodic spike timing in discrimination of flutter stimuli, and indicate that a firing rate code cannot be discarded (Salinas *et al.* 2000). But, apart from this, what do these findings indicate? They indicate the presence of two sub-populations of QA neurons in S1 that behave differently in response to a periodic mechanical stimulus (Hernández *et al.* 2000; Salinas *et al.* 2000). These two subpopulations might be arranged in an hierarchical fashion: QA neurons that respond periodically might be closer to the input stimulus, and those that modulate their firing might integrate the responses of the periodic neurons and transform them into a rate code (Hernández *et al.* 2000). Such last-order neurons of the QA circuit could distribute the neural representation to those structures anatomically linked to S1, in order to solve the sensory-discrimination task. However, further studies are needed to see whether this is so.

(c) Neuronal correlates of vibrotactile discrimination in S1

A more direct test of the role of periodicity in flutter discrimination is measuring the discrimination capabilities of these subtypes of QA neurons associated with psychophysical performance (Figure 5.1). Another test is to prove whether the evoked neural activity during discrimination in S1 is sufficient for sensory performance. Finally, it is necessary to test whether the temporal order of the spikes is important for sensory discrimination. These are incisive tests to validate the meaning of the neural encoding of the flutter stimuli in S1. We now review recent findings on these points.

The vibrotactile-discrimination task requires the comparison of f_2 against f_1 (Hernández *et al.* 1997). As indicated in § 5.4c Hernández *et al.* (2000) and Salinas *et al.* (2000) found two types of responses in QA neurons of S1: one that is periodically entrained by the stimulus frequency, and another that, although not periodically entrained, has average firing rates during the stimulus period that are modulated as a function of the stimulus frequency. To investigate which one of these two representations is associated with psychophysical performance, Hernández *et al.* (2000) determined the probability that an observer (a cortical region central to S1) could distinguish the difference between the two stimuli. This could be based on a comparison of the neuronal response distributions of f_2 made against the neuronal response distributions of f_1. According to this, the observer could use a simple rule: if the number of spikes during the second stimulus is higher than during the first stimulus, then f_2 is higher than f_1. The same rule can be used when considering the periodicity values: if the periodicity (estimated as the frequency with greatest power in a Fourier transform of the spiking responses) during the second stimulus period (f_2) is higher than during the first stimulus (f_1), then f_2 is higher than f_1. The effect of this type of rule is equivalent to determining the area under the curve ROC (Green & Swets 1966) generated by the neuronal response distributions for each pair of stimulus frequencies, using both periodicity and firing rate values (Hernández *et al.* 2000). The area under each of these two ROC curves is an estimate of the proportion of correct trials that an optimal observer would obtain by comparing the numbers of spikes or periodicity. In pairs of stimulus frequencies where the neuronal response distributions of f_2 are much higher than the neuronal distributions of f_1, the ROC values are close to 1; if the neuronal response distributions of f_2 are much lower than the neuronal response distributions of f_1, then the ROC values are close to zero; and for overlapping distributions, intermediate ROC values are found. The ROC values were then used to compute

the neurometric functions. Psychophysical and neuronal discrimination thresholds are calculated as half the difference between the stimulus frequency identified as higher than the standard in 75% of trials and that frequency identified as higher in 25% of the trials. These are read
directly from the logistic functions expressed in hertz. Using this analysis, we are now in the
position to address the question of which of the two representations is meaningful for frequency discrimination.

   Neurometric functions based on the periodicity or firing rate of single S1 neurons were
directly compared with the psychometric thresholds (Hernández *et al.* 2000). The results of this
analysis show that neurometric threshold values based on periodicity are far lower than the
psychometric thresholds (Figure 5.2*a,b*). This is not the case when neurometric thresholds
based on the firing rate are compared with the psychometric thresholds (Figure 5.2*c,d*). They
are very close to the psychometric thresholds. The goal of computing neurometric functions
was not only to reveal the relationship between the neuronal responses of S1 to the mechanical
stimulus, but also to discern whether these neural signals account for the psychometric behaviour. However, this leads to the question: what is the functional meaning of the periodic neural
signal in S1? One possible role is that they simply represent the temporal structure of the stimulus and that monkeys do not use this exquisite representation for frequency discrimination.
This would be the case if, for example, discrimination was based on the mean number of spikes
(or bursts) fired by the population of QA neurons as a function of the stimulus frequency.
Consistent with this idea, Hernández *et al.* (2000) found QA neurons in S1 whose firing rates
are modulated by the stimulus frequencies, and their neurometric thresholds based on firing
rates are similar to the monkey's psychophysical thresholds (Figure 5.2*c,d*). However, these
measurements do not prove they are sufficient for discrimination (Romo *et al.* 1998, 2000).

   One experiment that could give an insight about the functional meaning of the periodic
spike structure of the evoked activity in S1 would be to test whether monkeys could discriminate between the two stimuli when the periodicity is broken. If monkeys failed to discern the
difference in the mean frequency between the two stimuli, this would support the proposal
that the flutter-stimuli discrimination depends on the periodic structure of the spike trains
evoked in S1. However, Romo *et al.* (1998) noted that monkeys were able to extract the mean
frequency from the non-periodic signals and that the psycho-physical measures were almost
identical with the periodic stimuli.

   Hernández *et al.* (2000) then studied QA neurons in one of two conditions: as monkeys
discriminated periodic stimuli; and as monkeys discriminated aperiodic stimuli. Due to the
aperiodic stimulus design, even highly stimulus-entrained neurons do not carry information
about stimulus frequency in their periodicity. Clearly, neurometric thresholds based on the
firing rate were again closely associated with the psychometric thresholds (Figure 5.2*e,f*).
As in the periodic condition, a psychophysical observer could exploit the firing rate for the
frequency discrimination of aperiodic stimuli. These results indicate that an observer could
solve this task with a precision similar to that of a monkey, based only on the firing rate produced during the stimulus periods.

(d) Probing the flutter coding by microstimulation of S1

Unequivocal proof that the activity of a localized cortical neuronal population provides sufficient basis for a specific cognitive function has not been obtained. Neurophysiological studies often reveal close associations between neuronal activity and sensory events, but then does
such activity have an impact on perception and subsequent behaviour? We typically assume

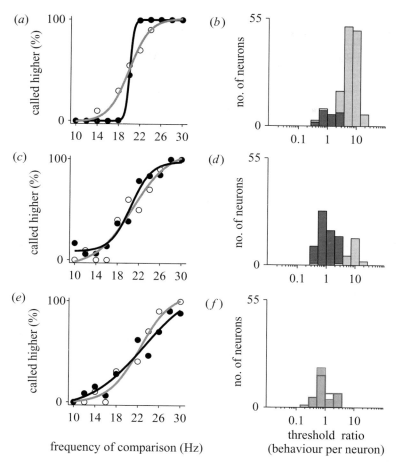

Fig. 5.2. See also Plate 28. Comparison between S1 neurons and the psychophysical responses during vibrotactile discrimination (illustrated in Figure 5.1c). (*a,c,e*) Percentage of trials in which the comparison was higher or lower than the base. The solid lines are sigmoidal fits to the data; for each curve, the threshold is proportional to its maximum steepness. White circles and grey lines indicate the monkey's performance during one discrimination run. The black circles and black curves indicate the performance of an ideal observer that based his decision on the periodicity (*a*) or mean firing rate (*c*) of evoked spike trains of single neurons recorded while the monkey discriminated. (*b*) Numbers of S1 neurons with the indicated threshold ratios. The yellow bars correspond to neurometric thresholds based on the periodicity of evoked spike trains; the red bars correspond to neurometric thresholds based on the evoked firing rate. The data are from all neurons with significant periodic spike entrainment. (*d*) As in (*b*), but data are from all neurons with significant rate modulation. (*e*) As in (*a*) but aperiodic stimuli were applied. (*f*) Threshold ratios from all neurons tested with both periodic and aperiodic stimuli. Neurometric thresholds were computed from firing rates in periodic (red thick lines) and aperiodic (cyan bars) conditions. (Modified from Hernández *et al.* 2000.)

this to be so, but this is hard to verify. Intracortical microstimulation has provided the most compelling evidence to date of a causal link between the activity of localized populations of neurons and specific cognitive functions (Britten & Wezel 1998; Salzman *et al.* 1990; Romo *et al.* 1998, 2000). Electrical microstimulation directly activates small cluster of neurons, and has been shown to bias a monkey's choice during the decision stage of an ongoing perceptual task (Seidemann *et al.* 1998; Gold & Shadlen 2000). A convenient model that can be used to answer this question is the flutter sensation, for which humans and monkeys have similar discrimination thresholds (Hernández *et al.* 1997; Mountcastle *et al.* 1990). During the vibro-tactile-discrimination task, subjects pay attention to the frequency of the first (base) stimulus, store a trace of it during the delay period between the two stimuli and compare the stored trace with the frequency of the second (comparison) stimulus. This task, therefore, contains a number of cognitive processes, such as stimulus detection, working memory, discrimination between the two stimuli and decision making. These cognitive processes should be initiated by the evoked neuronal activity in S1 (Romo & Salinas 1999, 2001). As reviewed in § 5.2b, the QA circuit of S1 distributes the representation of the flutter stimuli to more central structures anatomically linked to it to solve this task. Romo *et al.* (1998) used intracortical microstimulation in S1 to manipulate the neural code for flutter discrimination.

An initial approach was to manipulate the comparison stimulus frequency during the dis-crimination task (Romo *et al.* 1998). In each trial of the task, the monkeys discriminated between the frequency of two successively presented sinusoidal vibrations, termed the base stimulus and the comparison stimulus, that were delivered to the fingertips. After the animals mastered the discrimination of the mechanical stimuli, microstimulation of S1 was substituted for the comparison stimulus in half of the trials (Figure 5.3*a*). The artificial stimuli consisted of periodic current bursts delivered at the same comparison frequencies as the mechanical comparison stimulus. The microstimulation sites in S1 were selected to have QA neurons with receptive fields on the fingertips at the location of the mechanical stimulating probe. Remarkably, the monkeys could discriminate between the mechanical (base) and electrical (comparison) signals with performance profiles indistinguishable from those obtained with natural stimuli only (Figure 5.3*a*). The artificially induced sensation probably closely resembled natural flutter (Romo *et al.* 1998).

To investigate the role of spike periodicity in flutter discrimination, aperiodic microstimu-lation patterns were also applied in the QA neurons of S1 (Romo *et al.* 1998). The same mean frequencies were also used in this condition—20 Hz still corresponded to 10 current bursts delivered in 500 ms—but the current bursts were separated by random time intervals. The monkeys had to compare the base and comparison frequencies just as before, and microstim-ulation and mechanical stimulation trials were again inter-leaved. From the very beginning, the animals were able to discriminate between the aperiodic signals with practically the same performance level as that reached with natural, periodic vibrations (Figure 5.3*b*). Periodic and aperiodic stimuli are, of course, different in the time course of the stimulating pulses, but the neural codes for flutter frequency underlying the discriminations performed by the monkeys might be the same for both. If so, the result might imply that spike periodicity does not play a functional role in our monkey's performance of the frequency discrimination task.

Due to the design of this task, comparison of f_2 is made against the memory trace of the first stimulus. Romo *et al.* (2000) wondered whether, in addition to using artificial stimuli during the decision-making stage of the task, monkeys could store and use a quantitative trace of an electrical stimulus delivered to the QA neurons in S1 in place of the first mechanical stimulus. They also wondered whether monkeys could perform the entire task on the basis of purely artificial stimuli. This would demonstrate that the activation of QA neurons was suffi-cient to initiate the entire cognitive process involved in the task.

Again, the mixed mechanical–microstimulation protocol was used, in which microstimula-tion trials were randomly intermixed with standard, purely mechanical, trials (Romo *et al.* 2000).

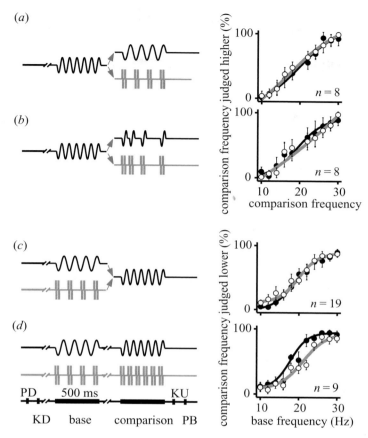

Fig. 5.3. Psychophysical performance in frequency discrimination with natural mechanical stimuli delivered to the fingertips and with artificial electrical stimuli delivered to clusters of neurons of area 3b. Monkeys were trained to compare two vibratory stimuli presented sequentially to the fingertips (illustrated in Figure 5.1). To receive a reward, they had to indicate correctly whether the frequency of the comparison stimulus was higher or lower than the first. Both frequencies changed from trial to trial. The diagrams on the left show two types of trials that were interleaved during the experiments. In half of the trials, the monkeys compared two mechanical vibrations delivered on the skin. In the other half, one or both stimuli could be replaced by electrical frequencies microinjected into clusters of QA neurons of area 3b. The curves on the right-hand side show the animals' performance in the different situations, illustrated on the left-hand side. Black and white circles indicate the mechanical and electrical stimuli, respectively. (*a*) Psychophysical performance using periodic stimuli; the comparison stimulus could be either mechanical or electrical frequencies. (*b*) Psychophysical performance when the comparison stimulus was aperiodic and could be either mechanical or artificial stimulus frequencies. (*c*) Psychophysical performance when the base stimulus was periodic and could be either mechanical or artificial stimulus frequencies. (*d*) Psychophysical performance when both periodic mechanical stimuli could be replaced by periodic artificial stimulus frequencies. In (*a*) vibrotactile stimuli were mechanical sinusoids. In (*b*) vibrotactile stimuli were trains of short mechanical pulses; each of these pulses consisted of a single-cycle sinusoid lasting 20 ms. In (*a*) and (*b*), the *y*-axis corresponds to the percentage of times the monkeys called f_2 (*x*-axis) higher than f_1 (20 Hz). In (*c*) and (*d*), the *y*-axis corresponds to the percentage of times the monkeys called the comparison stimulus (20 Hz) lower than base stimuli at the frequency specified in the *x*-axis. (Modified from Romo *et al.* 1998, 2000.) PD, probe down; KD, key down; KU, key up; PB, push-button.

The frequency pairs and event sequence were the same in both the mechanical and microstimulation trials, except that in the microstimulation trials the first or both mechanical stimuli were replaced by trains of current pulses injected in the S1 and delivered at the frequency of the mechanical stimulus they were replacing. The design of the stimulus set allowed the exploration of the working-memory component of the task and the determination of the discrimination thresholds.

Psychophysical performance with the electrical microstimulation patterns in S1, at the mechanical base stimulus frequencies they were replacing, was similar to those measured with the mechanical stimulus (Figure 5.3c). These results show that monkeys were able to memorize the base artificial stimulus frequency and make quantitative comparisons of f_2 against the trace left by the artificial stimulus. As for replacing the comparison stimulus with electrical patterns, monkeys could not reach the usual level of performance when clusters of SA neurons were microstimulated; nor could they discriminate when microstimulation patterns were made at the border between the QA and SA clusters (Romo *et al.* 2000). These control experiments tell us about the specificity of the QA circuit of S1 in flutter discrimination. Finally, in most sessions in which the two mechanical stimuli were replaced by microstimulated patterns, monkeys were able to reach discrimination levels close to those measured when mechanical stimuli were delivered to their fingertips (Figure 5.3d). This indicates that microstimulation elicits quantitative memorizable and discriminable percepts, and shows that activation of the QA circuit of S1 is sufficient to initiate the entire subsequent neural process associated with flutter discrimination (Romo *et al.* 2000).

In flutter discrimination, the first stimulus has to be detected and memorized. Comparison of the second stimulus is made against the trace left by the first stimulus, and a decision is then projected to the motor apparatus to indicate discrimination. Accurate performance of the task can be consistent only with induction of a sensory percept during both stimulus periods. The reviewed results indicate that the whole sequence of events that leads to discrimination could be initiated by artificial stimulus patterns injected into the QA circuit of S1. Thus, the neural activity produced by either the natural or the artificial stimulus can be used as the basis for sensory discrimination by a psychophysical observer. The results tell us also that periodicity does not play a functional role in our monkey's performance of the frequency discrimination. Psychophysical performance with periodic or aperiodic electrical patterns injected in S1 can be discriminated similarly to when they are delivered to the fingertips.

5.5. Coding of vibrotactile stimuli in cortical areas central to S1

The results reviewed here are the basis for exploring the somatosensory network central to S1. This is an important enterprise, considering that S1 is only one of many brain structures that participate in somatosensory perception. But, in the flutter task, what is the neuronal representation of flutter stimuli in structures that are central to S1? Assuming that it is periodicity, do S2 neurons represent flutter stimuli in the same format? What is the neural correlate for flutter discrimination in structures central to S1? An obvious candidate to explore these questions is S2. S1 is strongly connected with S2 (Burton *et al.* 1995; Krubitzer *et al.* 1995). This central somatosensory region belongs to the ventral stream (Mishkin 1979; Murray & Mishkin 1984).

(a) Coding of flutter stimuli in S2

Unlike the majority of S1 neurons, very few S2 neurons are periodically entrained by the flutter stimuli (Salinas *et al.* 2000). There are basically three groups of neuronal responses during the stimulus periods: the first group increases the firing rate as a function of the stimulus frequency; the second group decreases the firing rate as a function of increasing stimulus frequency; and the third group responds but is not modulated as a function of the stimulus frequency. According to this, there is a dramatic change in the flutter representation from S1 to S2. Clearly, the most interesting responses in S2 are those which modulate their firing rate as a function of the stimulus frequency. These responses are affected by the animal's state (Salinas *et al.* 2000). These responses are more prominent during the discrimination task than when the same stimuli are delivered in non-working conditions. These distinct populations operate simultaneously in S2 and should produce a computation that is useful for frequency discrimination in an analogous manner to that reported in central visual areas such as the middle temporal cortex (Britten *et al.* 1992). Finally, an important result obtained in S2 neurons is that many of them retain information about the base stimulus during the initial part of the delay period between the two stimulus frequencies (Figure 5.4c). This is also the case for the stimulation periods: that is, if the neuron increases its firing rate as a function of the base stimulus frequency, the same representation is maintained during the initial part of the delay. We consider this to be a neural correlate of the working-memory component of the task

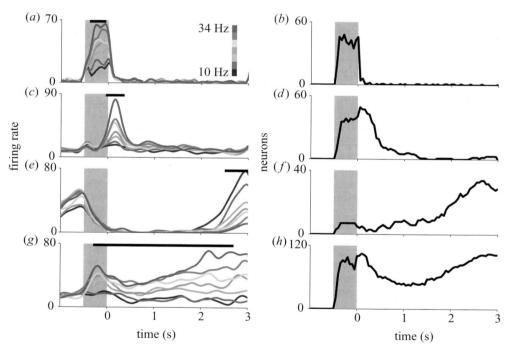

Fig. 5.4. See also Plate 29. Neuronal response types during the delay period. (*a,c,e,g*) Single-neuron spike-density function from four different neurons. The dark bars above each plot indicate the times during which the neuron's firing rate carried a significant (*p* < 0.01) monotonic signal about the base stimulus (Romo *et al.* 1999). (*c,g*) Positive monotonic encoding neurons about the base stimulus. (*e*) Negative monotonic encoding neuron about the base stimulus. (*b,d,f,h*) Total number of recorded neurons (during fixed 3 s delay period runs) carrying a significant signal about the base stimulus, as a function of time relative to the beginning of the delay period. The base stimulus period is shaded grey; colour gradient from 10 to 34 Hz. (*a,b*) S1, (*c,d*) S2, (*e,f*) MPC and (*g,h*) PFC (Modified from Salinas *et al.* 2000; Romo *et al.* 1999; Hernández *et al.* 2002.)

(Salinas *et al*. 2000). This information must be translated to structures central to S2 that contain a network for working memory in this task. An important observation is that S1 neurons do not show any trace of the base stimulus during the delay period (Figure 5.4*a*).

(b) Parametric encoding of flutter stimuli during working memory

As reviewed in § 5.5a, some neurons of S2 retain the base stimulus frequency during the early component of the delay period (Salinas *et al*. 2000). They do so by retaining the base stimulus frequency monotonically during the early memorization component of the task (Salinas *et al*. 2000). Where, then, is this early representation projected and held during the whole delay period between the two flutter stimuli? Is this associated with the stimulus parameters? Romo *et al*. (1999) recorded in the PFC and sought to determine the neuronal correlate for the working-memory component of this task. Although there is no clear direct input from S2 or S1 to the PFC, in a pilot experiment Romo *et al*. (1999) recorded above and below the principal sulcus in the PFC while a monkey performed the flutter-discrimination task. Recordings in the first monkey indicated that the inferior convexity of the PFC contained neurons whose activity varied, during the delay period between the two stimuli, as a monotonic function of the stimulus frequency. This finding was then further investigated in three more animals performing the flutter-discrimination task. Some of the delay responses responded most weakly after stimulation with the lowest base frequency, and increased their firing rates steadily as the frequencies increased (positive monotonic encoding; Figure 5.4*g*). Others had discharge rates that varied inversely (negative encoding; not shown here). Interestingly, this representation is not different from that found in S2 (Salinas *et al*. 2000) and in the MPC (Figure 5.4*e*) during the vibrotactile-discrimination task (Hernández *et al*. 2002). The main difference between these structures is that S2 encoded the base stimulus frequency during the early component of the delay period (Figure 5.4*d*; Salinas *et al*. 2000), PFC neurons show early, persistent and late encoding (Figure 5.4*h*; Romo *et al*. 1999), and MPC neurons show late delay activity (Figure 5.4*f*), just before the beginning of the second, comparison stimulus. Thus, the base stimulus frequency, a scalar analogue value, appeared to be encoded directly in the neuron's firing rate (also a scalar analogue value), most often in a smoothly graded fashion. The smooth monotonic encoding found in S2, the PFC and the MPC is consistent with the existence of a parametric, rather than categorical, representation of the memorized stimulus during the working-memory component of this task. In the same vein, these results could indicate that monotonic encoding might be the basic representation of sensory magnitude continua during working memory, in tasks that require ordinal comparisons between scalar analogue stimuli.

Monotonic encoding of the stimulus frequency in the PFC and MPC may be derived from inputs from S2, and not from S1 (Figure 5.4*a,b*). However, it is not clear to what extent the delay activity in the PFC and MPC depends on S2, or to what extent this delay activity is elaborated in the local circuits of each of these structures. For example, S2 is anatomically connected with the MPC but it is not clear that S2 is connected with the PFC (reviewed in § 5.5a). At this moment, we can only say that these structures display, at different times, the encoding of the sensory stimulus during the working-memory period of this task. Further experiments are required to show the connectivity between these cortical areas and whether these structures are part of a large cortical network (Fuster 1997) that combines past and current sensory information to generate motor actions. These results constitute a neurophysiological demonstration that neurons of the PFC and MPC can retain sensory information induced by non-visual modalities.

5.6. Neuronal correlates of the comparison process

Reaching a decision in the vibrotactile-discrimination task requires comparison between the memory trace of the first stimulus and the current sensory input (Hernández *et al.* 1997). We sought evidence of this process in S1, but as indicated already, the activity of these neurons do not combine past and current sensory information to generate behavioural decisions; they encode the current sensory input. This is not the case in S2 and in the MPC, where we found neuronal activity that seemed to reflect the comparison process that preceded the behavioural decision (Hernández *et al.* 2002; R. Romo, A. Hernández, C. Brody, A. Zainos and L. Lemus, unpublished data). We review in § 5.6 recent results that seem to indicate the dynamics of the comparison process.

(a) Neuronal correlates of the comparison process in S2

As we expected for a somatosensory cortex, S2 neurons encoded the two stimulus frequencies in their firing rate (Salinas *et al.* 2000). But, surprisingly, many S2 neurons first encoded the base (f_1) stimulus, then responded differentially during the comparison (f_2) stimulus (R. Romo, A. Hernández, C. Brody, A. Zainos and L. Lemus, unpublished data). By 'differential' we mean that the activity is selective for the comparison $f_2 > f_1$ or $f_2 < f_1$ trials during correct discriminations. We wondered whether the responses quantified during f_2 depended on f_1, even though f_1 had been applied 3 s earlier, or whether they simply reflected their association with the motor responses. We studied the nature of this differential response. To quantify this, we determined the probability that an observer, measuring only the neuronal response during the f_2 period, could discriminate correctly between $f_2 > f_1$ trials and $f_2 < f_1$ trials for the same f_2 (discrimination indices have been adapted after Green & Swets (1966) by Britten *et al.* (1992), Dodd *et al.* (2001) and Kim & Shadlen (1999)). Indeed, a large number of these neurons reflected this fact. That is, they had discrimination indices that deviated from 0.5. However, a crucial question, as indicated above, is whether these differential responses indicate the comparison between f_1 and f_2, or the differential response that is implemented to indicate discrimination. We ruled out the presence of a simple differential motor activity associated with the push-button presses (Figure 5.1*a*) by testing these S2 neurons in a control task where the same vibrotactile stimuli were used, but animals had to follow a visual cue to produce the motor response. In this condition, all neurons reduced the deviation from 0.5, indicating that the differential activity observed during the comparison period depends on the actual computation between f_1 and f_2 and does not reflect a purely motor response aimed to press one of the two push-buttons.

If the discharges during the comparison period are the product of the interaction between f_1 and f_2, then the trace of f_1 and the current f_2 could be observed during the comparison period before the discharges indicated the motor responses. To further quantify the interaction between f_1 and f_2 during the comparison period and beyond it, we used a multivariate regression analysis (Draper & Smith 1981). We fit the activity of each differential response over the periods before, during and after the comparison period, as a linear function of both f_1 and f_2. The responses, which in principle could be an arbitrary function of both f_1 and f_2, were reasonably well approximated by a general linear fit to both f_1 and f_2 as follows:

firing rate $= a_1 \times f_1 + a_2 \times f_2 +$ constant.

In this formula, the coefficients a_1 and a_2 serve as direct measurements of firing rate dependence on f_1 and f_2, respectively. Three lines are of particular importance in these fits. Points that fall on the $a_1 = 0$ axis represent responses that are a function of f_2 (the sensory evidence of f_2; blue dots in Figure 5.5). Points that fall on the $a_2 = 0$ axis represent responses that are a function of f_1 (the memory trace of f_1; yellow dots in Figure 5.5). And points that fall on the $a_1 = -a_2$ line represent responses that are functions of the difference between f_1 and f_2

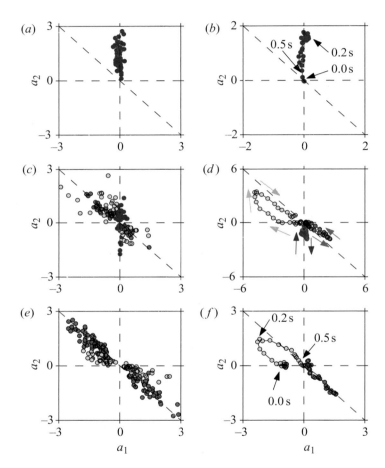

Fig. 5.5. See also Plate 30. Responses during the second stimulus. (*a,c,e*) Coefficients resulting from fitting firing rates from S1, S2, and MPC neurons, during the second stimulus, as linear functions of both f_2 (a_2) and f_1 (a_1). Each dot represents coefficients for one neuron; only neurons with fits significantly different from (0,0) are shown. (*b,d,f*) Dynamics of individual responses for S1, S2, and MPC neurons. Each row shows data from one neuron. In all panels, time = 0 corresponds to the start of the second stimulus. Each symbol in (*b*), (*d*) and (*f*) corresponds to fits of 100 ms, separated from its neighbours in steps of 25 ms. Blue dots represent neurons that responded as a function of f_2 (sensory response); yellow dots represent neurons that carried the first information of f_1 (the memory trace) then f_1 interacted with f_2 (differential response); red dots represent neurons that indicated the difference between f_1 and f_2. (*a,b*) S1, (*c,d*) S2 and (*e,f*) MPC (Hernández *et al.* 2002; R. Romo, A. Hernández, C. Brody, A. Zainos and L. Lemus, unpublished data).

(red dots in Figure 5.5). This last consideration is of particular importance because, in this task, correct behaviour depends on the sign of the difference between f_1 and f_2.

The analysis revealed the contributions of f_1 and f_2 during the comparison period for S2 neurons (Figure 5.5c,d; for a comparison see in Figure 5.5a,b the responses of S1 neurons during the f_2 period). Interestingly, when they are plotted as a function of the evolution of the comparison process, it is clearly observed that some neurons evolve from coding the sensory stimuli (which could be f_1 or f_2; see three examples in Figure 5.5d: blue dots indicate a sensory response; yellow dots indicate that the neurons carry information of f_1 then show the difference between f_1 and f_2; red dots indicate a purely differential response) to a differential response that is consistent with the motor output. Indeed, the analysis of the error trials indicated that the differential response correlated with the behavioural choice; that is, the selection of the push-button.

These results are important because they show that an early sensory area shows not only the representation of the current sensory input (f_2; blue dots in Figure 5.5c,d), but also the representation of the sensory referent (f_1; yellow dots in Figure 5.5c,d) which is stored in the working memory. These two processes are important ingredients for the resulting differential responses between f_1 and f_2 (red dots in Figure 5.5c,d) that correlate with the behavioural decisions. As S2 neurons do not store information about the f_1 stimulus during the later part of the delay period, the comparison process in S2 could be made between the input from S1 that provides information on the current stimulus and an input from the frontal cortical areas that carries information on the base stimulus during the later part of the delay period. However, more experiments are needed to show whether this is so. The comparison process is reported by a voluntary motor action, and anatomical studies have shown that S2 projects to the motor areas of the frontal lobe (reviewed in § 5.6a). We explored the possibility that the motor areas reflect the behavioural decision during the vibrotactile-discrimination task.

(b) Neuronal correlates of the comparison process in the MPC

As indicated in § 5.6a, anatomical studies in monkeys have shown that S1 and S2 are serially connected (Pons *et al.* 1987, 1992; Burton & Fabri 1995; Burton *et al.* 1995; Krubitzer *et al.* 1995), and that one of the major outputs from S2 leads to the motor areas of the frontal lobe (Jones & Powell 1969; Pandya & Kuypers 1969; Jones *et al.* 1978; Jürgens 1984; Luppino *et al.* 1993). If we consider a serial processing model, in principle S2 could process the S1 representation of the vibrotactile stimuli and transmit its output to the motor cortices. As indicated in § 5.6a, S2 neurons show a transformation of the S1 vibrotactile representation (Salinas *et al.* 2000) and appear to reflect activity associated with the comparison of the two stimuli (R. Romo, A. Hernández, C. Brody, A. Zainos and L. Lemus, unpublished data). The question that arises is whether there is a truly clear distinction between those areas presumably dedi-cated to sensory processing and those traditionally viewed as motor areas. There are two possibilities. First, the motor areas could process a fully formed decision signal in order to generate an appropriate set of motor commands. In this case the information and processes used before reaching a decision should be mostly absent from motor cortical activity. Second, the motor areas could participate more actively in the formation of a behavioural decision, in which case they should reflect details about the sensory inputs regardless of the motor outcome. We tested these two possibilities by recording single neurons in the MPC while monkeys performed the vibrotactile-discrimination task (Hernández *et al.* 2002).

The responses of single neurons in the MPC were extremely informative of the sequence of the discrimination process. For example, during the base stimulus, some of the neurons had graded responses as a function of f_1 and displayed a trace of it at the end of the delay period between the two stimuli. Interestingly, during the comparison period these neurons showed information about f_1 or f_2 and then reflected in their activities the difference between the two stimuli (Figure 5.5*e,f*). This differential activity was correlated with the motor response only during the discrimination task; these neurons lost their differential responses when tested in the light-instruction task mentioned above.

As for the S2 neurons, we studied the dynamics of the comparison process, and sought evidence of whether this process is due to an interaction between the past (f_1) information and the current sensory stimulus (f_2). A sub-population of the differential neurons displayed information about f_1 (the memory trace; yellow dots in Figure 5.5*e,f*; in Figure 5.5*e* the dots represent individual neurons; figure 5*f* details the response profiles of a neuron) during the comparison period and their responses evolved to a differential activity that corresponded to an interaction between the f_1 and f_2 stimuli (red dots in Figure 5.5*e,f*; in Figure 5.5*e* the dots represent individual neurons; in figure 5*f* the response profile of a neuron is given). These responses could be confined to the comparison period or be prolonged to the reaction and movement time periods of the behavioural motor responses. Thus, what is typically observed in the MPC during the comparison period is that initially some neurons encode f_1 or f_2, and later these and other units encode the difference between f_1 and f_2.

The results indicate that activity in the MPC reflects many aspects of the vibrotactile-discrimination task, not just the motor component. Distinct subpopulations of MPC neurons are activated during the period where the comparison between stimuli presumably takes place, and their activities during the end of the comparison process are consistent with the behavioural decision. This process appears to precede activity in M1 during the behavioural response associated with this sensory-discrimination task (Mountcastle *et al.* 1992; R. Romo, A. Hernández, C. Brody, A. Zainos and L. Lemus, unpublished data).

5.7. Concluding remarks

The vibrotactile-discrimination task requires perceiving a stimulus, storing it in working memory, combining the stored trace with current sensory input and producing a decision that is communicated to the motor apparatus. This temporal sequence is reflected in the activity of some neuronal populations of different cortical areas of the parietal and frontal lobes. Our results indicate that neurons central to S1 do not simply wait for a signal-encoding decision, but instead participate in almost every step of its generation by integrating working-memory and sensory inputs. Similar processes may occur in other discrimination tasks that require comparison between sensory stimuli. Finally, an important question which needs to be addressed in this and in similar tasks is how the cortical neuronal circuits interact to produce a comparison between the current sensory input and those sensory representations stored in working or in long-term memory. Revealing this neural process must be key to understanding this finest brain operation that leads to behavioural decisions.

The research of R. R. was supported in part by an International Research Scholars Award from the Howard Hughes Medical Institute and from grants from the Millennium Science Initiative, CONACyT and DGAPA-UNAM. The authors thank S. Méndez and L. Lemus for technical assistance.

References

Britten, K. H. & Wezel, R. J. 1998 Electrical microstimulation of cortical MST biases heading perception in monkeys. *Nature Neurosci.* **1**, 59–63.

Britten, K. H., Shadlen, M. N., Newsome, W. T. & Movshon, J. A. 1992 The analysis of visual motion: a comparison of neuronal and psychophysical performance. *J. Neurosci.* **12**, 4745–4765.

Burton, H. & Fabri, M. 1995 Ipsilateral intracortical connections of physiologically defined cutaneous representations in areas 3b and 1 of macaque monkeys. *J. Comp. Neurol.* **355**, 508–538.

Burton, H., Fabri, M. & Alloway, K. 1995 Cortical areas within the lateral sulcus connected to cutaneous representations in areas 3b and 1: a revisited interpretation of the second somatosensory area in macaque monkeys. *J. Comp. Neurol.* **355**, 539–562.

Burton, H., Sinclair, R. J., Hong, S. Y., Pruett, J. R. & Wang, K. C. 1997 Tactile-spatial and cross-modal attention effects in the second somatosensory and 7b cortical areas of rhesus monkeys. *Somatosens. Mot. Res.* **14**, 237–267.

Carmichael, S. T. & Price, J. L. 1995 Sensory and premotor connections of orbital and medial prefrontal cortex of macaque monkeys. *J. Comp. Neurol.* **363**, 642–664.

Cavada, C. & Goldman-Rakic, P. S. 1989 The posterior parietal cortex in rhesus monkeys: I. Parcellation of areas based on distinctive limbic and sensory corticocortical connections. *J. Comp. Neurol.* **287**, 393–421.

Darian-Smith, I. 1984 The sense of touch: performance and peripheral neural processes. In *Handbook of physiology: section I. The nervous system, vol. III. Sensory processes, part 2* (ed. J. M. Brookhart & V. B. Mountcastle), pp. 739–788. Bethesda, MD: American Physiological Society.

Dodd, J. V., Krug, K., Cumming, B. G. & Parker, A. J. 2001 Perceptually bistable three-dimensional figures evoke high choice probabilities in cortical area MT. *J. Neurosci.* **21**, 4809–4821.

Draper, N. & Smith, H. 1981 *Applied regression analysis*. 2nd edn. New York: Wiley.

Fuster, J. M. 1997 Network memory. *Trends Neurosci.* **20**, 451–459.

Godshalk, M., Lemon, R. B., Kuypers, H. G. & Ronday, H. K. 1984 Cortical afferents and efferents of monkey postarcuate area: an anatomical and electrophysiological study. *Exp. Brain Res.* **56**, 410–424.

Gold, J. I. & Shadlen, M. N. 2000 Representation of a perceptual decision in developing oculomotor commands. *Nature* **404**, 390–394.

Green, D. M. & Swets, J. A. 1966 *Signal detection theory and psychophysics*. New York: Wiley.

Hernández, H., Salinas, E., Garcia, R. & Romo, R. 1997 Discrimination in the sense of flutter: new psychophysical measurements in monkeys. *J. Neurosci.* **17**, 6391–6400.

Hernández, A., Zainos, A. & Romo, R. 2000 Neuronal correlates of sensory discrimination in the somatosensory cortex. *Proc. Natl Acad. Sci. USA* **97**, 6091–6096.

Hernández, A., Zainos, A. & Romo, R. 2002 Temporal evolution of a decision-making process in medial premotor cortex. *Neuron* **33**, 959–972.

Horwitz, G. D. & Newsome, W. T. 1999 Separate signals for target selection and movement specification in the superior colliculus. *Science* **284**, 1158–1161.

Hsiao, S. S., Johnson, K. O. & O'Shaughnessy, D. M. 1993 Effects of selective attention of spatial form processing in monkey primary and secondary somatosensory cortex. *J. Neurophysiol.* **70**, 444–447.

Jiang, W., Tremblay, F. & Chapman, C. E. 1997 Neuronal encoding of texture changes in the primary and in the secondary somatosensory cortical areas of monkeys during passive texture discrimination. *J. Neurophysiol.* **77**, 1656–1662.

Johnson, K. O. & Hsiao, S. S. 1992 Neural mechanisms of tactual form and texture perception. *A. Rev. Neurosci.* **15**, 227–250.

Jones, E. G. & Powell, T. P. S. 1969 Connexions of the somatic sensory cortex of the rhesus monkey. I. Ipsilateral cortical connexions. *Brain* **92**, 477–502.

Jones, E. G., Coulter, J. D. & Hendry, S. H. 1978 Intracortical connectivity of architectonic fields in the somatic sensory, motor and parietal cortex of monkeys. *J. Comp. Neurol.* **181**, 291–347.

Jürgens, U. 1984 The efferent and afferent connections of the supplementary motor area. *Brain Res.* **300**, 63–81.

Kaas, J. H., Nelson, R. J., Sur, M., Lin, C. S. & Merzenich, M. M. 1979 Multiple representations of the body within the primary somatosensory cortex of primates. *Science* **204**, 521–523.

Kim, J. N. & Shadlen, M. N. 1999 Neuronal correlates of a decision in the dorsolateral prefrontal cortex of the macaque. *Nature Neurosci.* **2**, 176–185.

Krubitzer, L., Clarey, J., Tweendale, R., Elston, G. & Calford, M. A. 1995 A redefinition of somatosensory areas in the lateral sulcus of macaque monkeys. *J. Neurosci.* **15**, 3821–3839.

LaMotte, R. H. & Mountcastle, V. B. 1975 Capacities of humans and monkeys to discriminate between vibratory stimuli of different frequency and amplitude: correlation between neural events and psychophysical measurements. *J. Neurophysiol.* **38**, 539–559.

Leichnetz, G. R. 1989 Afferent and efferent connections of the dorsolateral precentral gyrus (area 4, hand/arm region) in the macaque monkey, with comparisons to area 8. *J. Comp. Neurol.* **254**, 460–492.

Luppino, G., Matelli, M., Camarda, R. M. & Rizzolatti, G. M. 1993 Cortico-cortical connections of area F3 (SMA-proper) and area F6 (Pre-SMA) in the macaque monkey. *J. Comp. Neurol.* **338**, 114–140.

Macefield, G., Gandevia, S. C. & Burke, D. 1990 Perceptual responses to microstimulation of single afferents innervating joints, muscles and skin of the human hand. *J. Physiol.* **429**, 113–129.

Merchant, H., Zainos, A., Hernández, A., Salinas, E. & Romo, R. 1997 Functional properties of primate putamen neurons during the categorization of tactile stimuli. *J. Neurophysiol.* **77**, 1132–1154.

Mishkin, M. 1979 Analogous neural models for tactual and visual learning. *Neurophychologia* **17**, 139–151.

Mountcastle, V. B. 1957 Modality and topographic properties of single neurons of cat's somatic sensory cortex. *J. Neurophysiol.* **20**, 408–434.

Mountcastle, V. B., Talbot, W. H., Sakata, H. & Hyvärinen, J. 1969 Cortical neuronal mechanisms in flutter-vibration studied in unanesthetized monkeys. Neuronal periodicity and frequency discrimination. *J. Neurophysiol.* **32**, 452–484.

Mountcastle, V. B., LaMotte, R. H. & Carli, G. 1972 Detection thresholds for stimuli in humans and monkeys: comparison with thresholds events in mechanoreceptive afferent nerve fibers innervating the monkey hand. *J. Neurophysiol.* **25**, 122–136.

Mountcastle, V. B., Steinmetz, M. A. & Romo, R. 1990 Frequency discrimination in the sense of flutter: psychophysical measurements correlated with postcentral events in behaving monkeys. *J. Neurosci.* **10**, 3032–3044.

Mountcastle, V. B., Atluri, P. P. & Romo, R. 1992 Selective output-discriminative signals in the motor cortex of waking monkeys. *Cerebr. Cortex* **2**, 277–294.

Murray, E. A. & Mishkin, M. 1984 Relative contributions of SII and area 5 to tactile discrimination in monkeys. *Behav. Brain Res.* **11**, 67–83.

Nelson, R. J., Sur, M., Felleman, D. J. & Kaas, J. H. 1980 Representations of the body surface in the postcentral parietal cortex of *Macaca fascicularis*. *J. Comp. Neurol.* **192**, 611–643.

Newsome, W. T., Britten, K. H. & Movshon, J. A. 1989 Neuronal correlates of a perceptual decision. *Nature* **341**, 52–54.

Ochoa, J. & Torebjörk, E. 1983 Sensations evoked by intraneural microstimulation of single mechanoreceptor units innervating the human hand. *J. Physiol.* **42**, 633–654.

Pandya, D. N. & Kuypers, H. G. 1969 Cortico-cortical connections in the rhesus monkey. *Brain Res.* **13**, 13–36.

Pearson, R. C. & Powell, T. P. S. 1985 The projection of primary somatic sensory cortex upon area 5 in the monkey. *Brain Res.* **356**, 89–107.

Phillips, J. R. & Johnson, K. O. 1981 Tactile spatial resolution. II. Neural representations of bars, edges, and gratings in monkey primary afferents. *J. Neurophysiol.* **46**, 1192–1203.

Pons, T. P., Garraghty, P. E., Friedman, D. P. & Mishkin, M. 1987 Physiological evidence for serial processing in somatosensory cortex. *Science* **237**, 417–420.

Pons, T. P., Garraghty, P. E. & Mishkin, M. 1992 Serial and parallel processing of tactual information in somatosensory cortex of rhesus monkeys. *J. Neurophysiol.* **68**, 518–527.

Powell, T. P. S. & Mountcastle, V. B. 1959 Some aspects of the functional organization of the cortex of the postcentral gyrus of the monkey: a correlation of findings obtained in a single unit analysis with cytoarchitecture. *Bull. Johns Hopkins Hosp.* **105**, 133–162.

Preuss, T. M. & Goldman-Rakic, P. S. 1989 Connections of the ventral granular frontal cortex of macaques with perisylvian premotor and somatosensory areas: anatomical evidence for somatic representation in primate frontal association cortex. *J. Comp. Neurol.* **282**, 293–316.

Recanzone, G. H., Merzenich, M. M. & Schreiner, C. E. 1992 Changes in the distributed temporal response properties of SI cortical neurons reflect improvements in performance on a temporally based tactile discrimination task. *J. Neurophysiol.* **67**, 1071–1091.

Romo, R. & Salinas, E. 1999 Sensing and deciding in the somatosensory system. *Curr. Opin. Neurobiol* **9**, 487–493.

Romo, R. & Salinas, E. 2001 Touch and go: decision-making mechanisms in somatosensation. *A. Rev. Neurosci.* **24**, 107–137.

Romo, R., Ruiz, S., Crespo, P., Zainos, A. & Merchant, H. 1993 Representation of tactile signals in primate supplementary motor area. *J. Neurophysiol.* **70**, 2690–2694.

Romo, R., Merchant, H., Zainos, A. & Hernández, A. 1996 Categorization of somaesthetic stimuli: sensorimotor performance and neuronal activity in primary somatic sensory cortex of awake monkeys. *NeuroReport* **7**, 1273–1279.

Romo, R., Merchant, H., Zainos, A. & Hernandez, A. 1997 Categorical perception of somesthetic stimuli: psychophysical measurements correlated with neuronal events in primate medial premotor cortex. *Cerebr. Cortex* **7**, 317–326.

Romo, R., Hernández, A., Zainos, A. & Salinas, E. 1998 Somatosensory discrimination based on cortical microstimulation. *Nature* **392**, 387–390.

Romo, R., Brody, C. D., Hernández, A. & Lemus, L. 1999 Neuronal correlates of parametric working memory in the prefrontal cortex. *Nature* **339**, 470–473.

Romo, R., Hernández, A., Zainos, A., Brody, C. D. & Lemus, L. 2000 Sensing without touching: psychophysical performance based on cortical microstimulation. *Neuron* **26**, 273–278.

Salinas, E. & Romo, R. 1998 Conversion of sensory signals into motor commands in primary motor cortex. *J. Neurosci.* **18**, 499–511.

Salinas, E., Hernández, A., Zainos, A. & Romo, R. 2000 Periodicity and firing rate as candidate neural codes for the frequency of vibrotactile stimuli. *J. Neurosci.* **20**, 5503–5515.

Salzman, D., Britten, K. H. & Newsome, W. T. 1990 Cortical microstimulation influences perceptual judgements of motion direction. *Nature* **346**, 174–177.

Seidemann, E., Zohary, E. & Newsome, W. T. 1998 Temporal gaiting of neural signals during performance of a visual discrimination task. *Nature* **394**, 72–75.

Shadlen, M. N. & Newsome, W. T. 1994 Noise, neural codes and cortical organization. *Curr. Opin. Neurobiol.* **4**, 569–579.

Shadlen, M. N. & Newsome, W. T. 2001 Neural basis of a perceptual decision in the parietal cortex (area LIP) of the rhesus monkey. *J. Neurophysiol.* **86**, 1916–1936.

Shanks, M. F., Person, R. C. & Powell, T. P. S. 1985 The ipsilateral cortico-cortical connexions between the cytoarchitectonic subdivisions of the primary somatic sensory cortex in the monkey. *Brain Res.* **356**, 67–88.

Sinclair, R. J. & Burton, H. 1993 Neuronal activity in the second somatosensory cortex of monkeys (*Macaca mulatta*) during active touch of gratings. *J. Neurophysiol.* **70**, 331–350.

Singer, W. & Gray, C. M. 1995 Visual feature integration and the temporal correlation hypothesis. *A. Rev. Neurosci.* **18**, 555–586.

Sur, M., Wall, J. T. & Kaas, J. H. 1984 Modular distribution of neurons with slowly adapting and rapidly adapting responses in area 3b of somatosensory cortex in monkeys. *J. Neurophysiol.* **51**, 724–744.

Talbot, W. H., Darian-Smith, I., Kornhuber, H. H. & Mountcastle, V. B. 1968 The sense of flutter-vibration: comparison of the human capacity response patterns of mechanoreceptive afferents from the monkey hand. *J. Neurophysiol.* **31**, 301–334.

Tokuno, H. & Tanji, J. 1993 Input organization of distal and proximal forelimb areas in the monkey primary motor cortex: retrograde double labeling study. *J. Comp. Neurol.* **333**, 199–209.

Vallbo, A. B. 1995 Single-afferent neurons and somatic sensation in humans. In *The cognitive neurosciences* (ed. M. S. Gazzaniga), pp. 237–252. Cambridge, MA: MIT Press.

Vallbo, A. B. & Johansson, R. S. 1984 Properties of cutaneous mechanoreceptors in the human hand related to touch sensations. *Hum. Neurobiol.* **3**, 3–14.

Vogels, R. & Orban, G. A. 1990 How well do response changes of striate neurons signal differences in orientations: a study in the discriminating monkey. *J. Neurosci.* **10**, 3543–3558.

Werner, G. 1980 The study of sensation in physiology. In *Medical physiology*, vol. 1 (ed. V. B. Mountcastle), pp. 605–628. St Louis, MO: Mosby.

Werner, G. & Mountcastle, V. B. 1965 Neural activity in mechanoreceptive cutaneous afferents: stimulus-response relations, Weber functions, and information transmission. *J. Neurophysiol.* **28**, 459–497.

Glossary

M1	primary motor cortex
MPC	medial premotor cortex
PC	Pacinian receptor organ
PFC	prefrontal cortex
PM	premotor
QA	Meissner receptor organ
ROC	receiver operating characteristic
S1	primary somatosensory cortex
S2	secondary somatosensory cortex
SA-I	Merkel organ
SA-II	Ruffini organs

6

Neuronal activity and its links with the perception of multi-stable figures

Andrew J. Parker, Kristine Krug, and Bruce G. Cumming

In order to isolate the neuronal activity that relates to the making of perceptual decisions, we have made use of a perceptually ambiguous motion stimulus. This stimulus lies on the boundary between two perceptual categories that correspond to clockwise and counter-clockwise rotation of a three-dimensional figure. It consists of a two-dimensional pattern of moving dots that are capable of generating these two, distinct, three-dimensional percepts. We have studied the responses of neurons in cortical area V5/MT whilst macaque monkeys report judgements about the perceptual configuration of this stimulus. We extract a quantitative statistic called 'choice probability' that expresses the covariation of neuronal activity and perceptual choice. An analysis of choice probabilities shows that the pool of neurons involved in the perceptual decisions is a tightly constrained subset of the population of sensory neurons relevant to the perceptual task.

6.1. Introduction

Since the 19th century, the search for localization of function within the brain has become steadily more intense. The fundamental significance of many regions of the cortex has been recognized, such that we are now able to identify with certainty, in a given individual, that some cortical regions are always associated with specific aspects of motor function, others with specific topographical maps of visual information, and so on. This understanding has been achieved through a multi-disciplinary approach, involving the integration of information from studies of humans who have suffered accidental brain damage, and studies of animals in which discrete lesions have been placed experimentally.

In parallel, the anatomical study of the cellular structure of the nervous system has identified the single neuron as the elementary building block from which the operations of the nervous system are constructed. Although it is now very clear that single neurons have a fundamental role in the cellular organization and signalling of the cortex, it remains unclear whether analysis at the level of single neurons provides a sufficient basis for understanding the functional operations of the nervous system. Of particular interest are the means by which it supports important cognitive functions, such as perception, attention, learning, memory and the planning and execution of movements.

Barlow (1995) has cogently argued that the signals within single nerve cells are central to understanding the operation of the nervous system. In his view, the firing of individual nerve cells amounts to a form of assertion about the presence of stimulus features in the environment. In his original conception, Barlow (1972) considered perceptual decisions to be governed, not uniquely by a single neuron, but by a small number of highly influential neurons: Barlow specifically used the analogy of a 'College of Cardinals', who 'directly and simply cause the elements of our perception'.

6.2. Neuronal activity and multi-stable figures

From this perspective, experimental investigations of a relationship between the firing of single neurons and perceptual decisions are of great significance. Nonetheless, several serious issues arise, if one simply approaches this question by choosing a set of stimuli and proceeding to explore the firing patterns of sensory neurons. First, unless a psychophysical observer is set a particular task to perform, there is no guarantee that any perceptual decision is formed. Furthermore, in order to ensure the accuracy of these perceptual decisions, it is necessary to monitor the level of performance of the task. Second, when sensory neurons are excited by a range of external stimuli, changes in the firing patterns of those neurons may arise for two distinct reasons. One source of excitation arises from factors that are genuinely related to the perceptual decisions made by the observer. These are the factors that we wish to isolate and study. The other source of excitation is more commonly studied and in many ways better understood: for any neuron that is tuned to a sensory stimulus, much of the change in firing rates will simply reflect the fact that some stimuli are more effective than others in exciting the neuron.

For this reason, an ideal configuration for studying, in isolation, the factors that lead to perceptual decisions is one in which the external stimulus is constant but its perceptual interpretation may change. The classic examples of this type are given by perceptually ambiguous figures, such as the duck–rabbit figure devised by Jastrow (see Figure 6.1). In this case, the figure may be seen either as the drawing of a duck or as the drawing of a rabbit. Another example is the Necker cube, in which a picture of a wire-frame cube can take on one of two interpretations as a perspective representation of the cube.

Clearly, in order to exploit ambiguous figures of this kind in a neurophysiological experiment, it is necessary to make reliable recordings from neurons that respond selectively to one of the unambiguous versions of these figures. Neurons of this type are found mostly at high levels of visual processing within brain areas, such as the inferotemporal cortex. Selectivity for these parameters entails the presence of signals relating to object identity (in the case of the duck–rabbit) or three-dimensional linear perspective (in the case of the Necker cube).

Fig. 6.1. This perceptually reversible figure was devised in 1900 by the psychologist Jastrow and is universally referred to as the 'duck–rabbit' figure.

The diversity of possible selectivity for visual features, and the fact that such neurons are widely dispersed anatomically, makes this experimental approach difficult. Accordingly, simpler paradigms have been sought that rely upon features of visual coding that are more commonly encountered at earlier stages within the visual pathway.

(a) Binocular rivalry

One example is presented by binocular rivalry, in which dissimilar patterns, such as horizontal and vertical stripes, are presented to the left and right eyes of an observer. Under these conditions, the patterns do not fuse into a single binocular object but the visibility of the patterns alternates. This change in appearance has been used as a way of achieving the goal of a constant external stimulus, whose perception is altered by factors intrinsic to the nervous system. Although a great deal has been learnt from this approach (Leopold & Logothetis 1996), a number of questions about the perceptual phenomenon are not completely resolved. First, the identity of the alternating percepts has been questioned (Kovács et al. 1996; Logothetis et al. 1996; Lee & Blake 1999). The classical view is that the picture dominates first in one eye and then in the other eye, with the implication that the switch is from one eye to the other. A more recent view is that the switch is from the picture of one object to the other. This interpretation is supported by the observation that a percept of rivalry may still be obtained when the pictures presented to left and right eyes are fractured images in monocular view but comprise two whole images only after binocular combination (Kovács et al. 1996). In this case, the experience is of rivalry between the two objects, even though neither eye alone ever receives a view of either of the whole objects. Both types of process (eye rivalry and stimulus rivalry) appear to be at work in human vision (Logothetis et al. 1996; Lee & Blake 1999).

A second issue is that the switch from one interpretation to the other in the classic binocular rivalry paradigm is not always complete and instantaneous in all parts of the image at the same time. For example, recent observations suggest a dynamic process that sweeps across the cortical coordinates of an image, changing its appearance over time (Wilson et al. 2001). These issues about the different functional mechanisms underlying the emergence of rivalrous percepts and the temporal dynamics of rivalry make the phenomenon more complex than it initially seemed.

There is an additional issue in using the binocular rivalry paradigm in an experiment that studies the behavioural responses of non-human species. Although it is possible to train an animal to respond differentially to samples of the two percepts in binocular rivalry, it is not so easy to guarantee that these responses consistently transfer to the rivalrous stimulus. Suppose, for example, an animal is trained to respond differently to the monocular presentation of horizontal and vertical bars. The animal may well transfer this performance to a binocular rivalry paradigm and report faithfully whether the horizontal or vertical bars are predominant. Nonetheless, for human observers there is a perceptible difference between the monocular presentation of horizontal bars and the same set of horizontal bars when they emerge as the dominant figure out of a rivalrous percept. It seems very likely that macaque monkeys would also be able to perceive the difference between rivalrous and non-rivalrous patterns. We cannot know in advance exactly how a difference of this kind might be reflected in the firing patterns of neurons that we would plan to study, or whether the monkey might alter its behavioural strategy, if it can perceive the difference. It is therefore logical to seek alternative paradigms that retain the essence of the binocular rivalry approach with fewer of its complexities.

(b) Ambiguity in structure-from-motion

One stimulus that has been exploited is based on the ambiguity of three-dimensional form depicted by motion information (so called 'structure from motion'; Ullman 1979). A transparent cylinder or sphere that is rotating about its axis can be depicted purely by the motion of dots randomly placed on the surface of the object. When the dots are displayed by parallel geometric projection onto a flat surface such as a computer screen, the motion of the individual dots within the plane of the display has a sinusoidal velocity profile (Treue *et al.* 1991). In terms of dot movements on the computer screen, a cylinder rotating around its principal axis has two planes of dots moving in opposite directions, each corresponding to the rear or front surface according to the direction of rotation of the cylinder. Without an additional cue to specify which direction of dot motion on the computer screen belongs to the front or to the rear surface, the direction of rotation of the cylinder is ambiguous, although its speed of rotation and its three-dimensional structure are not. Binocular disparity can provide the necessary cue for disambiguating these stimuli: cylinders in which the front and rear surfaces are clearly separated by binocular depth have a single, unambiguous direction of rotation. Changing the relationship between direction of motion and binocular depth reverses the direction of rotation (see Figure 6.2).

The use of binocular disparity to disambiguate the direction of rotation of these stimuli provides a powerful advantage over binocular rivalry. Small disparities exert a statistical effect, biasing judgements about the direction of rotation, whilst larger disparities can completely fix the direction of rotation. Thus, if a set of different binocular disparities is used, a classical psychometric function for rotation judgements can be built up in which the majority

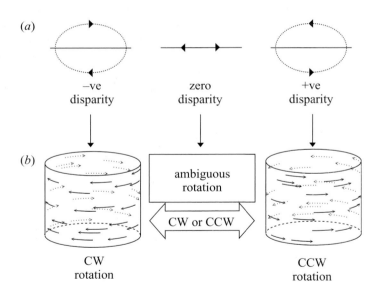

Fig. 6.2. A schematic diagram showing the construction of three-dimensional cylinder stimuli rotating on their axes. The pattern of motion in the dots on the surface specifies the three-dimensional structure of the object. The arrows on the surface indicate the speed and direction of motion of individual dots. When the front and rear surfaces are separated by binocular disparity, the direction of rotation of the cylinder is determined. When the surfaces have the same zero disparity, the direction of rotation is ambiguous but is seen as definitely rotating one way or the other. (*a*) View from above; (*b*) appearance. CW, clockwise; CCW, counter-clockwise.

of stimuli have non-zero disparities that separate the front and rear surfaces. This function changes smoothly from 0% clockwise judgements (as viewed from above) to 100% as the disparity is changed. In this paradigm, the ambiguous stimulus with zero disparity lies in the middle of the curve and these stimuli comprise a minority of those experienced by the observer. Crucially, in a single trial the ambiguous stimulus cannot be distinguished readily from an unambiguous stimulus. This leads to a way of checking the integrity or honesty of the subject's judgements about direction of rotation, through monitoring their performance when small non-zero disparities are added to form unambiguous stimuli. This latter point is particularly relevant when an animal has to be trained to give behavioural responses to report the perceived direction of rotation of the cylinder.

The rotating cylinder stimulus shares one advantage with binocular rivalry: it allows us to probe for evidence of perceptually related signals in areas of the cortex that have already been well characterized in terms of their basic sensory capabilities. In particular, the extra-striate visual cortical area V5/MT contains neurons sensitive to both direction of motion (Dubner & Zeki 1971) and binocular disparity (Maunsell & Van Essen 1983). Since the perceptual resolution of the ambiguous cylinder depends entirely on the specific combination of binocular disparity and motion, there is an obvious case for beginning investigations of this type in cortical area V5/MT. If a neuron is sensitive to the combination of leftwards motion and disparities nearer than the binocular fixation point, then it will respond to an unambiguous vertical cylinder if it is rotating clockwise rather than counter-clockwise. Thus, we are able to generate a tightly controlled experiment on single neurons whose basic sensory properties are relatively straightforward to characterize.

Bradley et al. (1998) showed that neurons in area V5/MT respond in a stimulus-driven way to the disparities in the cylinder, often increasing their response monotonically with the disparity of unambiguous cylinders. Moreover, the firing of these neurons reflects not just the sensory characteristics of the stimulus, but also the monkey's perceptual judgements about the direction of rotation of ambiguous cylinders of zero disparity.

Recent work from our laboratory has revealed that the link between the firing of these neurons and the perceptual judgements is in many respects much tighter than initially appreciated. In the first part of this paper, we summarize these findings and present them in the context of other work that has investigated the neuronal basis of perceptual ambiguity. Specifically, we (i) confirm the basic observations of Bradley et al. (1998); (ii) show how such results can be expressed quantitatively as choice probabilities (Britten et al. 1996; Parker & Newsome 1998); and (iii) demonstrate that the presence of a perceptually related signal is tightly linked to the neuron's sensory capabilities in signalling the direction of rotation of the cylinder. In the second part of the paper, we present the potential links between the presence of perceptually related signals and other modulatory effects upon these neurons, most notably neuronal firing related to changes of attentional state. We also consider the distribution and specificity of these perceptually related neuronal signals across the population of V5/MT neurons. Our aim is to identify the groups of single neurons that are critically involved in perceptual decisions and to study how the formation of perceptual decisions is supported by coordinated activation at the neuronal level.

(c) Quantitative indices of perceptually related changes in firing

The basic phenomenon that we need to describe is an association between the firing of a neuron and the perceptual choices of the subject who is performing a psychophysical decision.

Each decision is made on a single trial, in response to a single presentation of the stimulus. The structure of such a trial is illustrated in Figure 6.3. Initially, the macaque monkey looks at the fixation target. During this time, a stimulus is presented over the receptive field of the neuron that is being recorded; the basic properties of the receptive field, such as its location, size and stimulus preferences, have been characterized previously. At the end of the stimulus presentation, a decision is required from the monkey in order to obtain a reward. Therefore, the paradigm provides for two choice targets, which the monkey has been previously trained to associate with particular stimulus conditions, such as the left choice target with a clockwise rotation of a cylinder stimulus. The decision of the monkey, the stimulus conditions and the neuronal response are all recorded for analysis. During the analysis, the neuronal activity is sorted according to the decision made on that trial. For some neurons, the activity is stronger when one decision is made rather than another, even though the external stimulus is the same.

Our overall concern in this line of work is to search for evidence about the perceptual relevance of neuronal signals. One way of gathering such evidence, whilst at the same time avoiding the issue of a measurement scale for neuronal activity, is to confine the observations to a qualitative classification of whether there was an increase or decrease in neuronal firing associated with making one choice rather than another. Qualitatively, there is a clear hypothesis to be advanced. Suppose that a perceptual decision is made about an ambiguous stimulus, a decision of the form that a cylinder is rotating clockwise or, for a binocularly rivalrous stimulus, that the stimulus presented to the left eye is currently visible. The suggestion is that we expect the firing rates to be increased in those neurons whose basic sensory preference is

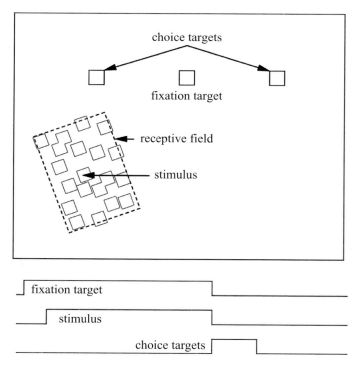

Fig. 6.3. Schematic version of the display viewed by the macaque monkey observer and the sequence of events within a given trial.

for clockwise rotation or for the presentation of stimuli to the left eye. A great deal of valuable analysis can be carried out in this way, purely by inspecting the qualitative corres-pondence between neuronal preference and the direction of the perceptually related change in neuronal firing (Logothetis *et al.* 1996).

However, decision-related activity is useless as a neuronal signal if it remains anatomically locked in one cortical area and unable to influence other neurons within the brain. Notably, in the cases that we are considering, there must be a link from sensory areas of the brain to those involved with oculomotor control. The biophysical properties of neurons mean that, when one neuron synapses with another, the excitation of the post-synaptic neuron depends, to a significant degree, on whether enough action potentials are fired within a sufficiently short time-period by the pre-synaptic neuron. Therefore, we need to consider the magnitude, as well as the sign, of the neuronal response.

In many areas of science, the choice of a measurement scale for the description of observa-tions often has a profound influence on the conclusions that can be reached from the results. Two different measures of the magnitude of the neuronal response have been explored for the description of perceptually related changes. One of these is to record the increase, or decrease, of activity in terms of the number of extra action potentials associated with a particular deci-sion. Closely related to this are measures such as the percentage change in firing rate: these measures have been used to compare the magnitude of decision-related changes in firing across a large sample of neurons from a particular cortical area (Bradley *et al.* 1998). A significant improvement on measures that are linearly related to firing rate or spike counts is to examine the statistical reliability of the perceptually related change in firing. Measures of this type take account not only of the size of the mean change in firing rate averaged across many experi-mental trials, but also the trial-to-trial variability of the perceptually related change in firing.

There are two advantages in using statistical measures to describe perceptually related changes in neuronal activity. First, the perceptual decisions themselves have a statistical character, with different decisions being made about the same stimulus over a sequence of presentations. Expressing neuronal activity in statistical terms gives us a common currency for describing both neuronal activity and behavioural decisions. Second, if we wish to under-stand how groups of single neurons generate psychophysical decisions, then we can use the same common currency to pool the signals from those single neurons in a way that has statistical validity.

(d) Choice probability

Britten *et al.* (1996) introduced the concept of choice probability to measure decision-related changes in firing of V5/MT neurons during a task that measured thresholds for the discrimina-tion of motion direction. Choice probability expresses the statistical confidence with which the experimenter can predict the monkey's psychophysical decision at the end of the trial in which an ambiguous stimulus was presented. In the absence of additional information, the experimenter could only make a random choice at the end of the trial about what the monkey would decide. With a binary choice decision (such as 'leftwards' versus 'rightwards' in a motion discrimination task), the experimenter on average would therefore be 50% correct. By taking account of the firing of the neuron that is being recorded at the time, the experimenter can do better than this chance performance. If, on average, the firing of the neuron is greater when the monkey makes a specific choice (for example, 'leftwards' for the motion task or 'clockwise' for the cylinder task), then the experimenter can improve the prediction rate above

0.5 by analysing the firing of the sensory neuron. At the other extreme, we can conceive of an outcome in which the neuron perfectly predicts the future decision of the animal. In this case, even though there might be some statistical variation in the firing of the neuron, the distributions of firing rates related to the two decisions would be completely non-overlapping. This extreme case of a perfect prediction corresponds to a choice probability of 1.

Previously, we introduced a qualitative classification of the relationship between the sensory preference of the neuron and the perceptually related change in firing. In terms of choice probability, this is expressed by whether the choice probability is below or above 0.5. Choice probabilities above 0.5 indicate that a neuron whose sensory preference is for condition *A* rather than *B* also increases its firing when the perceptual choice is *A* rather than *B*. Conversely, choice probabilities below 0.5 indicate the opposite (somewhat paradoxical) outcome, in which a neuron with a sensory preference for *A* actually increases its firing when the perceptual choice is *B* rather than *A*.

(e) Perceptually ambiguous cylinders give strong choice probabilities

In our work, we have combined the use of these statistical measures of decision-related changes in firing with a task in which the monkey was trained to indicate its perception of the direction of rotation of a cylinder stimulus. This combination allows us to express in a much more precise way just how the signals from single neurons lead to the emergence of a particular perceptual state. It also leads to a rational, statistical basis for examining the conjoint activity of groups of neurons.

The detailed calculation of choice probability is shown in Figure 6.4*a,b* for two neurons. The basic tuning of both neurons is such that their firing rates change monotonically as the binocular disparity between the front and rear surfaces of the cylinder is altered. As shown in Figure 6.2, negative disparities correspond to clockwise rotation of the cylinder and positive disparities to counter-clockwise rotation. The psychophysical responses of the macaque monkeys are also shown. Note that the psychophysical sensitivity to binocular disparity as measured within this paradigm is excellent. Only tiny amounts of separation by disparity, in the neighbourhood of the threshold for the binocular discrimination of depth differences (Prince *et al.* 2000), are required to disambiguate the direction of rotation of the cylinder.

The analysis of choice probability concentrates on the trials in which all the dots in the cylinder had zero disparity. Figure 6.4*a*(ii), *b*(ii) show the neuronal impulse counts for these trials, coded with different symbols to indicate the monkey's psychophysical response in each trial. For the responses of the neuron in the Figure 6.4*a*(ii), impulse counts are generally higher when the animal reported that the ambiguous cylinder was rotating in a clockwise direction. The two groups of impulse counts form two statistical distributions, whose separation can be measured by non-parametric methods from ROC analysis (Green & Swets 1966). Beginning with the highest impulse count and proceeding to the lowest, for each value of spike count (designated 'crit'—criterion level) in Figure 6.4, the probability of achieving that spike count is plotted on the ordinate for the trials in which the monkey's response was clockwise ('pref', thus in concordance with the sensory preference of the neuron) and on the abscissa for the trials where the response was counter-clockwise ('null', in opposition to the sensory preferences of the neuron). Where there is a difference between the firing rates associated with the two choices, the plot shows a consistent deviation away from the positive diagonal towards the top-left corner, as seen for the neuron in Figure 6.4*a*(iii). The area under

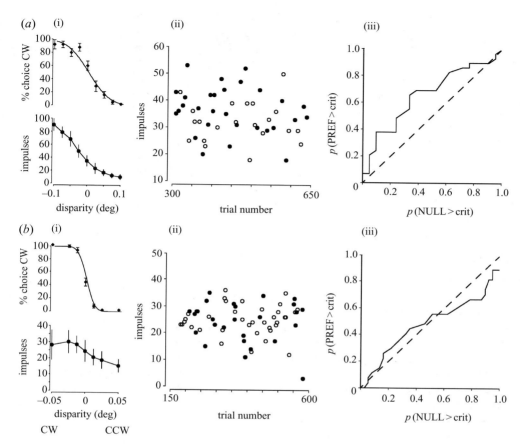

Fig. 6.4. The calculation of choice probability for two individual neurons (see text for explanation). (*a*) Neuron with a choice probability of 0.66, close to the average for the population. (*b*) Neuron with a choice probability of 0.48, close to 0.5 and showing no decision-related firing. (*a*)(i), (*b*)(i) psychophysical performance (% choice CW) and neuronal activity (impulses in a 2 s period) against disparity of cylinder (see Figure 6.2). (*a*) (ii) Fifty trials at zero disparity; 29 CW choice (filled circles) and 21 CCW choice (empty circles.) (*b*) (ii) Sixty-four trials at zero disparity; 27 CW choice (filled circles) and 37 CCW choice (empty circles). (*a*) (iii), (*b*) (iii) For zero disparity trials shown in (ii), ordinate shows probability that a criterion level of neuronal firing is exceeded when the monkey chose CW (pref) and abscissa shows probability that the same criterion is exceeded when the monkey chose CCW (null). For abbreviations, see Figure 6.2.

these solid curves is the choice probability: for the neuron in the Figure 6.4*a*(iii), this has a value of 0.67, close to the average for the population.

Figure 6.5 summarizes the measurement of choice probability in the cylinder task for a sample of 93 neurons from cortical area V5/MT in two macaque monkeys (Dodd *et al.* 2001). The average choice probability is 0.67, considerably greater than a random value of 0.5. This value is also considerably greater than the value of 0.56 reported in the same brain area by Britten *et al.* (1996) for their motion discrimination task. The filled parts of the histogram indicate those neurons for which the measured choice probabilities were individually significant in a bootstrap test (at $p < 0.05$).

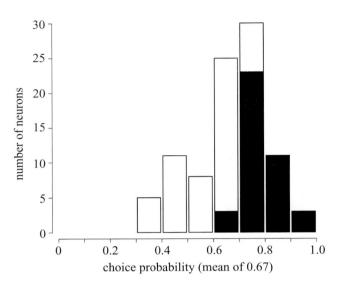

Fig. 6.5. The distribution of choice probabilities for 93 neurons from cortical area V5/MT in two macaque monkeys. Filled histograms: significant $p < 0.05$; open histograms: non-significant. (From Dodd *et al.* (2001)).

Note that Figure 6.5 shows no neurons with statistically significant choice probabilities lower than 0.5. This is in marked contrast to the earlier work of Bradley *et al.* (1998), in which many neurons appeared to show the paradoxical effect of increasing their firing for perceptual choices that are the opposite of their basic sensory preference. The reasons for this discrepancy are discussed in detail in Dodd *et al.* (2001), but the chief differences lie in the statistical treatment of the data and, most significantly, in the fact that in our study the monkeys were working close to the psychophysical limits of performance.

6.3. The composition of the decision pool

For the present discussion, we will refer to the set of neurons that exhibit a decision-related component in their firing as the decision pool, and contrast this set of neurons with those neurons that carry sensory information relevant to the cylinder task, which we will refer to as the sensory pool. The results in Figure 6.5 indicate that the decision pool is defined rather exactly as a subset of the pool of sensory neurons. Only neurons whose receptive fields carry accurate sensory information for judging the direction of rotation of unambiguous cylinders also carry the decision-related component of neuronal activity when ambiguous cylinders are viewed. This is demonstrated by the fact that there are no significant choice probabilities below 0.5 in Figure 6.5. Moreover, for the small number of neurons that had no definite sensory tuning for the direction of rotation of the cylinder, we also found that none of these exhibited a choice probability significantly different from 0.5 (two-tailed test).

This conclusion, that choice probability is highly specific, is in sharp contrast to the previous conclusions with the cylinder stimuli in cortical area V5/MT (Bradley *et al.* 1998). It is also distinct from the pattern of results reported for binocular rivalry (Leopold & Logothetis

1996, 1999; Logothetis *et al.* 1996). In both studies, some neurons showed perceptually related modulations, consistent with their basic sensory response, whereas others showed paradoxical forms of perceptual modulation in opposition to, or apparently unrelated to, their sensory properties. This specificity of choice probability forms the focus of our current work: we aim to define the nature and extent of the neuronal pool within V5/MT that carries signals that relate to perceptual decisions. Our working hypothesis is that perceptual modulation is indeed linked tightly to the underlying sensory properties of the neurons.

(a) Choice probability and pool size

The size of the choice probability in the cylinder task is in itself a valuable indicator of the nature and size of the neuronal decision pool. The remarkable aspect of the size of the measured choice probability is quite simply that, when searching with a microelectrode within V5/MT, it is common to encounter neurons whose firing is strongly predictive of the decisions of the monkey. Consider briefly the proposition that statistical variations in the firing of the neurons are uncorrelated between one neuron and its neighbours, and that these variations determine the fluctuations in the psychophysical reports of the monkey. In this case, if we were to observe a choice probability of 1 when recording from a neuron, then we must have been recording from the only neuron in the V5/MT region of the cortex that shows a significant choice probability. The neuronal pool size involved in the perceptual decision would be 1, and we would have been extraordinarily lucky as experimenters ever to record the activity of just that particular neuron. Let us move away from this extreme by just a small step. Suppose that rather than a pool size of 1, we have a pool size of two neurons, with the proviso that in each particular trial only one of these two neurons (at random) carries a decision-related signal. In those trials, where the neuron does carry the decision-related signal, then the signal is statistically unambiguous; in trials when the neuron does not carry the decision-related signal, we would be forced to guess at random the future decision of the monkey. In this case, the measured choice probability would be 0.75 (comprising 50% of trials when the neuron's signal is wholly accurate and 25% where we succeed due to chance). With three neurons, the predicted choice probability would be 0.66, a value close to the mean of the experimentally observed distribution shown in Figure 6.5.

These hypothetical considerations make two points very clearly. First, the assumption of a zero correlation between the neuronal signals is highly unrealistic. Rather, there is likely to be a strong degree of correlation within the neuronal population. Nearby neurons that share inputs from the source of the decision-related signal will tend to fire simultaneously, either because those neurons all receive the decision-related signal or simply because they have strong local interconnections with each other. Second, owing to the correlation between neuronal signals, the presence of a high choice probability from a particular neuron is unlikely to mean that this individual neuron has a unique or highly specialized role in forming the perceptual decision. In our most recent work, we examine these conclusions in detail.

(b) Interneuronal correlation

It has been recognized for some time that correlated firing within a pool of sensory neurons has significant consequences for the ability of a neuronal population to support the making of perceptual decisions (Johnson *et al.* 1973; Parker & Newsome 1998). Significant gains in sensitivity to weak sensory stimuli could potentially be achieved by averaging the activity of many neurons, but the presence of correlations in neuronal firing means that such gains are limited by the degree of interneuronal correlation. At the extreme, where the statistical variability is completely correlated between all neurons, there are no gains at all from averaging the activity of multiple neurons. Correlated variability between neurons therefore limits the sensitivity of the neuronal pool to weak sensory signals. Equivalently, this means that for a particular level of neuronal sensitivity, larger neuronal pool sizes are required to sustain a particular level of psychophysical performance when there is a modest degree of interneuronal correlation (Shadlen *et al.* 1996).

The model of Shadlen *et al.* (1996) proposes a link between three parameters: the degree of interneuronal correlation, the neuronal pool size and the sensitivity of individual neurons within the pool to the externally presented sensory stimulus. Within the model, these three parameters govern the predicted level of two additional experimental measures: the choice probability and the behavioural, psychophysical sensitivity of the animal to the sensory stimulus. This model was developed to understand the discrimination of the direction of movement of weak motion stimuli. As already noted, in this paradigm, the choice probability measured within V5/MT for random dot motion stimuli is 0.56 (Britten *et al.* 1996), much closer to 0.5 than the value of 0.67 for the cylinder task studied here. For the stimuli used in the direction discrimination task, Zohary *et al.* (1994) measured the interneuronal correlation as 0.19. We also found values very close to this, using similar stimuli within our experimental set-up (Krug *et al.* 2000*b*, 2001).

Consistent with the predictions of the Shadlen model, we find that when the choice probability is higher, the interneuronal correlation with the cylinder stimulus is also higher. When estimated by measuring the correlation between the activity of a single neuron and the activity of its near-neighbours (recorded as multi-unit activity), the interneuronal correlation in the cylinder task is as high as 0.44 for cortical sites where the stimulus preferences of the single-unit and multi-unit responses are closely matched (Krug *et al.* 2000*b*). However, it should be noted that the large values of choice probability and interneuronal correlation found for the cylinder task place our data outside the range of parameters that have been explored thoroughly in the model of Shadlen *et al.* (1996).

(c) Signals entering the decision pool

The nature of the signals that enter the decision pool is a topic of some debate. One view arises out of the development of a theory of the origins of choice probability (Shadlen *et al.* 1996). Here, it is thought that the decision signal arises owing to fluctuations in the firing patterns of sensory neurons within V5/MT, or neurons that project there. The decision on each trial is essentially driven by the exact level of activation of sensory neurons in V5/MT, so the trial-by-trial psychophysical decisions are sensitive to the trial-by-trial fluctuations in neuronal firing. This mechanism is the source of correlation of neuronal activity and psychophysical decision. This view of decision-related effects in neuronal firing is essentially a so-called 'bottom-up' view, in which fluctuations early in the sensory process form the limit on psychophysical performance (Barlow & Tripathy 1997).

However, for extra-striate cortical areas, attentional modulation of cortical signals needs to be taken as a serious possibility in the context of perceptual decisions about ambiguous stimuli. Specifically for cortical area V5/MT, perceptually related modulations of firing have been attributed both to perceptual effects (Britten *et al.* 1996; Bradley *et al.* 1998) and to attentional effects (Treue & Maunsell 1996, 1999; Treue & Trujillo 1999). The attentional effects largely take the form of changes in the gain of the stimulus-induced response. Thus, when the animal is attending to a location covered by the neuron's receptive field or to a stimulus feature normally signalled by the neuron, the response of the neuron is enhanced multiplicatively.

The obvious question is whether the changes of firing rate are brought about by manipulating attention and those that are linked to the eventual decision of the animal are the same phenomenon. Arguably, the decision of the animal in a choice probability paradigm might be formed early in the stimulus presentation. In the case of a completely ambiguous stimulus, which has no correct answer, it might be that the animal's response is dominated by a perceptual bias that is set up even before the stimulus is presented. The bias would persist through the stimulus presentation specifically on ambiguous stimulus trials, because in those trials the stimulus does nothing to alter the initial perceptual bias of the animal. If such a bias were in reality to consist of a shift of attention towards the expected stimulus configuration, then the effect of choice on neurons in V5/MT might be explained entirely in terms of an attentional effect. Note, however, that if attention is involved, the effects of choice on neuronal firing could be accounted for only by feature-based effects of attention, not spatial effects.

Of course, this argument was considered in the earliest choice probability papers (Celebrini & Newsome 1994; Britten *et al.* 1996). Here, the main line of argument for rejecting this possibility was the lack of an effect of choice on firing rates in the pre-stimulus period, before the stimulus was physically present. Since attention has been reported to enhance firing rates for this pre-stimulus period, particularly in cortical areas other than V5/MT, it was argued that attention was unlikely to be the only source of the choice-related effects. However, if the effect of attention is primarily a change in the gain of the stimulus-related response, this line of argument becomes much weaker.

It is reasonable to question whether feature-based attention might be a sufficient account of the choice-related effects observed in V5/MT. At least, it must be accepted that the present designs of experiments in this area allow this as a theoretical possibility. Moreover, the size of some of the attentional effects reported from V5/MT (Treue & Maunsell 1999) would be sufficient to account for the decision-related effects that are being discussed here.

Are there any indications that might guide our thinking? One distinguishing characteristic of an attentional process is that it should reflect, to some degree, the expectations of the observer. An instruction to attend to a target, whether delivered verbally or signalled by a contingency in the experimental paradigm, clearly should have some influence on a process that claims to have some relationship with the neural mechanisms of attention. Of course, it is always possible for attention to be subsequently diverted, but at least the initial direction of attention should be present.

In the course of our experiments on choice-related firing to cylinder stimuli in cortical area V5/MT (Dodd *et al.* 2001), we found that the monkey's choice of direction of rotation in a particular ambiguous trial is sometimes influenced by the response given in the preceding trial. Specifically, for one animal, there was a moderate tendency to stick with a successful (rewarded) response. Thus, in a fully ambiguous trial, in response to which there was no correct answer and rewards were delivered randomly in half the trials, the animal had a tendency to choose the same response that it had made in the immediately preceding, *unambiguous* trial. This is a pattern that has been characterized as 'win, stay', by analogy with the behaviour of some human gamblers.

This pattern of behaviour might add considerable complexity to the analysis of choice probability. Accordingly, we examined the size of the measured choice probability separately for trials with ambiguous stimuli that were preceded by the two possible types of preceding unambiguous trial (Dodd *et al.* 2001). Taken over the dataset as a whole, we found that although the decision in the preceding trial had a moderate effect on the animal's choices in the current trial, it had no consistent effect on the size of the choice-related modulation of neuronal firing. Therefore, at least by this *post hoc* analysis, the effect of prior expectation on the decision-related neural activity is weaker than the effect of the ultimate choice made by the animal. The effect of attention on neuronal firing seems unlikely, by itself, to offer a complete account of decision-related activity.

(d) The decision pool and how it is formed

Until this point in the discussion, we have assumed that the pool of neurons that carries information about the perceptual decision (as assessed by the presence of a choice probability) is the same as the pool of neurons that carries information about the external sensory stimulus. Indeed, several aspects of the design of the experiment have been arranged to ensure that the search for decision-related changes in firing is confined primarily to 'relevant' neurons— where 'relevant' means those neurons that are well tuned to the binocular disparity of the cylinder stimulus. This assumption that the decision pool is the same as the sensory pool is, however, sustained by important aspects of our data. For example, the absence of significant choice probabilities lower than 0.5 cannot be explained by the selection procedure used to choose neurons for testing, since the selection criterion does not depend upon whether a neuron responds more strongly to clockwise or counter-clockwise cylinders.

Nonetheless, when this issue is investigated in more detail, there is evidence that shows that the relevant decision pools must be formed and dissolved dynamically, so that the simple correspondence of sensory and decision pools appears to break down. Britten *et al.* (1996) addressed the question for the motion discrimination task, chiefly by considering cases in which the stimulus was removed away from the receptive field of the neuron and placed elsewhere in the visual field. In these circumstances, the decision-related component of the neuronal firing was absent. With the cylinder stimulus, we are in a much stronger position to assess these effects, simply because the choice probabilities with an optimally arranged stimulus are so much greater.

Rather than examine the spatial specificity of the decision-related activity, we have concentrated on the featural specificity. This is because the influences that generate the decision-related signal are fundamentally involved in differentiating between two stimulus configurations presented in the same spatial location. The direction of rotation of the cylinder is revealed by the binocular disparity that separates its front and rear surfaces. Accordingly, we have examined whether neurons that show strong decision-related activity in the cylinder task are generally implicated in other perceptual decisions about stereoscopic depth. There is already independent evidence for a role of V5/MT in stereoscopic depth perception, based on results with electrical microstimulation (DeAngelis *et al.* 1998) and, very recently, on the observation of measurable choice probabilities in a binocular correlation task (DeAngelis & Uka 2001).

We have applied a test to V5/MT neurons based on their responses to binocularly anti-correlated stimuli (Cumming & Parker 1997). Binocularly anti-correlated random-dot stereograms are created with a random-dot pattern that consists of bright and dark dots on a grey background; the pairing of the dots between the left and right eyes is arranged such that each bright dot in one eye is partnered with a dark dot in the other eye. Under suitable stimulus conditions (Cumming *et al.* 1998), binocular stereoscopic depth perception fails with these stimuli. In both V1 and MST, many binocular neurons respond in a disparity-specific way to binocularly anti-correlated patterns with an inversion of the shape of their disparity

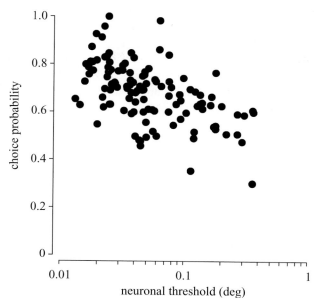

Fig. 6.6. The relationship between choice probability and the neuronal threshold of a sample of 119 neurons from cortical area V5/MT in two macaque monkeys. The neurometric threshold is calculated by applying ROC analysis to the statistical separation of two distributions of neuronal firing, each in response to a different disparity. The neurometric threshold is defined here as the difference in the values of binocular disparity that sustains a separation of the two distributions by one standard deviation. The neurometric threshold is thus high when the neuron is relatively poor at discriminating one disparity configuration from another. The threshold improves if the variability of the neuronal activity is lower and/or a small change in disparity produces on average a large change in response ($r = -0.488, p < 0.001$).

tuning curves in comparison with the response to binocular correlation (Cumming & Parker 1997; Takemura *et al.* 2001). Such disparity-specific responses in the absence of a stereoscopic depth percept indicate that these neurons code for a preliminary stage in stereoscopic depth processing.

We reasoned that, if the presence of choice probabilities in the cylinder task was simply an issue of whether a neuron had a 'general purpose' role in stereoscopic depth perception, then there should be an association between the presence of choice probabilities and the type of response to binocularly anti-correlated stimuli. Neurons that show strong inverted responses under binocular anti-correlation should have weak choice probabilities, and those that do not have strong inverted responses should have strong choice probabilities. We are able to reject the hypothesis of an association between these two measures of neuronal involvement in binocular depth perception (Krug *et al.* 2000*a*).

All neurons that carry a decision-related signal in the cylinder task also carry a specific signal about binocular disparity. However, the presence or absence of a general role in the perception of binocular depth, as assessed by binocular anti-correlated stimuli, is not predictive for the presence of a decision-related signal. This is despite the fact that binocular anti-correlation is highly disruptive of psychophysical performance in the rotating cylinder task (K. Krug, B. G. Cumming and A. J. Parker, unpublished data).

At present, we have one clear indicator of the composition of the decision pool that derives from measurements of the fundamental sensory capabilities of the neurons that we have tested. These results are illustrated in Figure 6.6. The ordinate of the figure plots choice probability, as calculated previously. The abscissa plots the neurometric threshold of the neuron (Tolhurst *et al.* 1983; Newsome *et al.* 1989; Prince *et al.* 2000). The data show a substantial correlation between choice probability and neuronal threshold, indicating that those V5/MT neurons with the greatest sensitivity to the stimulus disparity represent the neurons at the heart of the decision pool (since these neurons show the strongest choice probabilities). A correlation of this type is evident in the results of Britten *et al.* (1996), but the relationship there is weaker than the one shown in Figure 6.6.

Earlier, we observed that all statistically significant choice probabilities are greater than 0.5 and concluded that the decision pool is formed from a set of sensory neurons with quite specific receptive field properties. Here we see that the decision pool has a strong representation only from certain neurons within this set. Neurons with strong choice probabilities for perceptually ambiguous cylinders are those that also have the greatest sensitivity to the disparity signal that is present in the unambiguous cylinder stimuli. Therefore, the decision pool is a tightly constrained subset of the relevant sensory pool.

6.4. Conclusions

We have examined how the activity of single neurons relates to perceptual decisions in a well-defined region of the extra-striate visual cortex (V5/MT). The strategy to isolate decision-related activity is to examine the responses to perceptually ambiguous stimuli according to how the monkey classifies them. We can define a decision pool as the set of neurons that show strong perceptually related signals, as measured by choice probability. In many respects, the decision pool is defined by the stimulus preference of the neurons. Decision-related activity is confined to neurons that also signal the presence of one of the configurations of the unambiguous stimulus, in other words, by means of sensory information alone. Decision-related activity is also significantly linked to the underlying sensory performance of the neurons: neurons with high sensitivity also show high choice probabilities. In our future work, we will examine in more detail the time-course of activity within the decision pool, the temporal relationships between the neuronal activation of members of the decision pool and the important issue of whether the pool of neurons involved in the decision is statically identifiable, as previously assumed, or forms dynamically as the stimulus presentation unfolds. This information will enable us to propose locations for the source of the decision-related signal and understand functionally how and why the signal is generated.

This work was supported by the Wellcome Trust. K. K. holds a Dorothy Hodgkin Fellowship of The Royal Society and B. G. C. was supported by a University research fellowship from The Royal Society.

References

Barlow, H. B. 1972 Single units and sensation: a neuron doctrine for perceptual psychology? *Perception* **1**, 371–394.
Barlow, H. B. 1995 The neuron doctrine in perception. In *The cognitive neurosciences* (ed. M. Gazzaniga), pp. 415–436. Cambridge, MA: Bradford Book, MIT Press.

Barlow, H. B. & Tripathy, S. P. 1997 Correspondence noise and signal pooling in the detection of coherent visual motion. *J. Neurosci.* **17**, 7954–7966.

Bradley, D. C., Chang, G. C. & Andersen, R. A. 1998 Encoding of three-dimensional structure-from-motion by primate area MT neurons. *Nature* **392**, 714–717.

Britten, K. H., Newsome, W. T., Shadlen, M. N., Celebrini, S. & Movshon, J. A. 1996 A relationship between behavioral choice and the visual responses of neurons in macaque MT. *Vis. Neurosci.* **13**, 87–100.

Celebrini, S. & Newsome, W. T. 1994 Neuronal and psychophysical sensitivity to motion signals in extrastriate area MST of the macaque monkey. *J. Neurosci.* **14**, 4109–4124.

Cumming, B. G. & Parker, A. J. 1997 Responses of primary visual cortical neurons to binocular disparity without depth perception. *Nature* **389**, 280–283.

Cumming, B. G., Shapiro, S. E. & Parker, A. J. 1998 Disparity detection in anticorrelated stereograms. *Perception* **27**, 1367–1377.

DeAngelis, G. C. & Uka, T. 2001 Contribution of MT neurons to depth discrimination. II. Correlation of response and behavioral choice. *Soc. Neurosci. Abstr.* **27**, 680.13.

DeAngelis, G. C., Cumming, B. G. & Newsome, W. T. 1998 Cortical area MT and the perception of stereoscopic depth. *Nature* **394**, 677–680.

Dodd, J. V., Krug, K., Cumming, B. G. & Parker, A. J. 2001 Perceptually bistable figures lead to high choice probabilities in cortical area MT. *J. Neurosci.* **21**, 4809–4821.

Dubner, R. & Zeki, S. M. 1971 Response properties and receptive fields of cells in an anatomically-defined region of the superior temporal sulcus in the monkey. *Brain Res.* **35**, 528–532.

Green, D. M. & Swets, J. A. 1966 *Signal detection theory and psychophysics.* New York: Wiley.

Johnson, K. O., Darian-Smith, I. & LaMotte, C. 1973 Peripheral neural determinants of temperature discrimination in man: a correlative study of responses to cooling skin. *J. Neurophysiol.* **36**, 347–370.

Kovács, I., Papathomas, T. V., Yang, M. & Féher, Á. 1996 When the brain changes its mind: interocular grouping during binocular rivalry. *Proc. Natl Acad. Sci. USA* **93**, 15 508–15 511.

Krug, K., Cumming, B. G. & Parker, A. J. 2000*a* The role of single MT(V5) neurons in stereo perception in the awake macaque. *Eur. J. Neurosci.* **12**, 285.

Krug, K., Cumming, B. G. & Parker, A. J. 2000*b* Experimental manipulation of interneuronal correlation in MT(V5) of the awake behaving macaque. *Soc. Neurosci. Abstr.* **26**, 2086.

Krug, K., Cumming, B. G. & Parker, A. J. 2001 High choice probabilities are associated with high interneuronal correlations in MT(V5) of the awake behaving macaque (Abstr.). *J. Vis.* **1**, 399a.

Lee, S. H. & Blake, R. 1999 Rival ideas about binocular rivalry. *Vis. Res.* **39**, 1447–1454.

Leopold, D. A. & Logothetis, N. K. 1996 Activity changes in early visual cortex reflect monkeys' percepts during binocular rivalry. *Nature* **379**, 549–553.

Leopold, D. A. & Logothetis, N. K. 1999 Multistable phenomena: changing views in perception. *Trends Cogn. Sci.* **3**, 254–264.

Logothetis, N. K., Leopold, D. A. & Sheinberg, D. L. 1996 What is rivalling during binocular rivalry? *Nature* **380**, 621–624.

Maunsell, J. H. R. & Van Essen, D. C. 1983 Functional properties of neurons in middle temporal visual area of the macaque monkey. 2. Binocular interactions and sensitivity to binocular disparity. *J. Neurophysiol.* **49**, 1148–1167.

Newsome, W. T., Britten, K. H. & Movshon, J. A. 1989 Neuronal correlates of a perceptual decision. *Nature* **341**, 52–54.

Parker, A. J. & Newsome, W. T. 1998 Sense and the single neuron: probing the physiology of perception. *A. Rev. Neurosci.* **21**, 227–277.

Prince, S. J. D., Pointon, A. D., Cumming, B. G. & Parker, A. J. 2000 The precision of single neuron responses in cortical area V1 during stereoscopic depth judgments. *J. Neurosci.* **20**, 3387–3400.

Shadlen, M. N., Britten, K. H., Newsome, W. T. & Movshon, J. A. 1996 A computational analysis of the relationship between neuronal and behavioral responses to visual motion. *J. Neurosci.* **16**, 1486–1510.

Takemura, A., Inoue, Y., Kawano, K., Quaia, C. & Miles, F. A. 2001 Single-unit activity in cortical area MST associated with disparity-vergence eye movements: evidence for population coding. *J. Neurophysiol.* **85**, 2245–2266.

Tolhurst, D. J., Movshon, J. A. & Dean, A. F. 1983 The statistical reliability of signals in single neurons in cat and monkey visual cortex. *Vis. Res.* **23**, 775–785.

Treue, S. & Maunsell, J. H. R. 1996 Attentional modulation of visual motion processing in cortical areas MT and MST. *Nature* **382**, 539–541.

Treue, S. & Maunsell, J. H. R. 1999 Effects of attention on the processing of motion in macaque middle temporal and medial superior temporal visual cortical areas. *J. Neurosci.* **19**, 7591–7602.

Treue, S. & Trujillo, J. C. M. 1999 Feature-based attention influences motion processing gain in macaque visual cortex. *Nature* **399**, 575–579.

Treue, S., Husain, M. & Andersen, R. A. 1991 Human perception of structure from motion. *Vis. Res.* **31**, 59–75.

Ullman, S. 1979 *The interpretation of visual motion*. Cambridge, MA: MIT Press.

Wilson, H. R., Blake, R. & Lee, S. H. 2001 Dynamics of travelling waves in visual perception. *Nature* **412**, 907–910.

Zohary, E., Shadlen, M. N. & Newsome, W. T. 1994 Correlated neuronal discharge and its implications for psychophysical performance. *Nature* **370**, 140–143.

Glossary

MT   middle temporal visual area
ROC receiver operating characteristic

7

The role of attention in visual processing

John H. R. Maunsell and Erik P. Cook

Attention to a visual stimulus typically increases the responses of cortical neurons to that stimulus. Because many studies have shown a close relationship between the performance of individual neurons and behavioural performance of animal subjects, it is important to consider how attention affects this relationship. Measurements of behavioural and neuronal performance taken from rhesus monkeys while they performed a motion detection task with two attentional states show that attention alters the relationship between behaviour and neuronal response. Notably, attention affects the relationship differently in different cortical visual areas. This indicates that a close relationship between neuronal and behavioural performance on a given task persists over changes in attentional state only within limited regions of visual cortex.

7.1. Introduction

Attention is an important factor in sensory processing. Directing attention to a particular location in the visual field improves detection and discrimination, and shortens reaction times in that location relative to others (see Pashler 1998). When behavioural performance is near threshold, attention can reliably make the difference between success and failure. Attention also affects the responses of sensory neurons. Neurons typically respond more strongly when the stimulus that drives them is the focus of attention (see Braun *et al.* 2001). Behavioural performance depends on the activity of sensory neurons. Little is known, however, about how the behavioural effects of attention are related to the changes that it produces in sensory representations.

This question can be approached experimentally because there appears to be a close relationship between behavioural performance on a particular task and the activity of individual sensory neurons. When the sensitivity of individual neurons is compared with the behavioural capabilities of the organism, the ability of a neuron to report about a stimulus can be about as good as that of the observer, provided the task involves stimuli that are closely matched to the preferences of the neuron in question (reviewed by Parker & Newsome 1998). This close correspondence between neuronal and behavioural performance indicates that behavioural performance depends on, and closely follows, the selectivity of sensory neurons (Barlow 1985).

Given this correspondence between neuronal and behavioural performance, and the observation that attention changes the responses of sensory neurons, it is natural to ask whether effects of attention on behavioural performance might be fully explained by changes that attention causes in the responses of sensory neurons. To address this issue, it is necessary to consider the magnitude and quality of effects that attention has on neuronal responses. In the sections that follow, we consider attentional effects on neuronal responses in the context of visual cortex, for which the most detailed and extensive data are available. We then describe recent experiments from our laboratory that directly examine how attention can affect the relationship between neuronal and behavioural performance.

7.2. The magnitude of modulation of neuronal responses by attention

Spatial attention has been found to affect neuronal responses in every visual cortical area examined. Most neurons respond more strongly when the subject attends to a stimulus within their receptive field, compared with attention to another stimulus far from the receptive field. However, the amount by which attention alters neuronal responses can vary greatly between different visual areas, and between neurons within a given visual area. Task demands can also affect the amount by which attention alters responses.

Within any visual area, neurons differ in the degree to which they are influenced by spatial attention. Figure 7.1 shows a representative distribution of attentional modulations, based on a sample of neurons from area V4 in monkey visual cortex. The average modulation was a 26% increase in response when attention was directed to the receptive field stimulus, but the responses of some neurons were twofold or threefold stronger. The responses of other neurons were not obviously affected by attention, and still others responded more strongly when attention was directed away from the receptive field. A broad range of effects that includes both positive and negative modulations is typical for studies of attention in visual cortex. Why different neurons show different degrees of attentional modulation is not understood, nor has the degree of attentional modulation been shown to correlate with other properties of the neurons.

Attentional modulation also differs between visual areas. Modulation by attention is typically weakest in the earliest stages of visual cortex, and strongest in the latest stages. This increase has not been studied extensively, but it is apparent in comparing results from different reports. The best data come from individual studies that have recorded from different cortical areas in the same animals while they performed a given task. Figure 7.2 shows the average attentional modulation in different cortical areas that were examined in this way in our laboratory. Average attentional modulation is plotted as a function of the level of cortical processing, as defined by the hierarchy of Felleman & Van Essen (1991). In each study, areas at later stages had stronger average attentional modulation. These results were based on extracellular

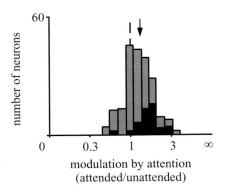

Fig. 7.1. Typical distribution of attentional modulation for visual cortex. Responses were recorded from 197 neurons in area V4 while monkeys performed a task that directed their attention towards or away from a stimulus in the receptive field of the neuron being recorded. Most neurons responded more strongly when the animal paid attention to the stimulus in the receptive field (average increase 26%, indicated by arrow). However, the distribution was broad, and some neurons responded more strongly when the animal directed its attention away from the receptive field. Response changes that were statistically significant are shown in black. (Data from McAdams & Maunsell (1999a).)

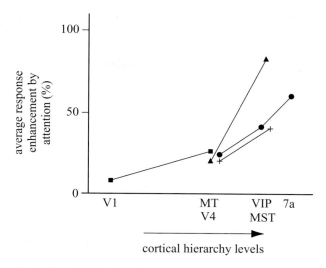

Fig. 7.2. Average attentional modulation in visual cortical areas. The average response enhancement reported from studies that measured the effects of attention in two or more cortical areas in the same subjects while they performed a given task are shown. Positions on the *x*-axis are assigned according to the hierarchical levels defined by Felleman & Van Essen (1991). More attention modulation is found in later stages of cortical processing (squares, McAdams & Maunsell (1999*a*); crosses, Treue & Maunsell (1999); circles, Ferrera *et al.* (1994); triangles, Cook & Maunsell (2002)). (Based on Cook & Maunsell (2002).)

recording of individual action potentials, but stronger modulation at later stages of visual cortex has also been seen by using current source density measurements (Mehta *et al.* 2000).

It is not known why attentional modulations are stronger in later cortical levels. While it is tempting to imagine that neuronal activity related to attention accumulates in successive levels of processing, this seems unlikely given that sensory responses arriving from different sources do not appear to accumulate in this way. Similarly, the notion that neuronal signals related to attention are inserted at the latest stages of processing and diminish as they are fed back to earlier stages seems unlikely. It seems probable that the degree of modulation is optimized for each cortical level. There is little reason to believe that the cerebral cortex would be unable to prevent undesirable accumulation or diminution of signals that altered sensory responses.

In addition to the range of attentional modulation seen within and between visual areas, individual neurons can show different degrees of attentional modulation depending on task demands. Task demand can be affected either by the number of relevant items or by the complexity of the processing to be performed on the relevant items (Lavie & Tsal 1994; Urbach & Spitzer 1995; Sade & Spitzer 1998). Mountcastle *et al.* (1981, 1987) showed that most neurons in area 7a and neighbouring regions were far more responsive when an animal was engaged in a visual task than when the same retinal stimuli were presented during periods of alert wakefulness when no fixation was required. Neuronal responses in inferotemporal cortex have also been found to be progressively stronger as a fixating animal goes from a situation where the stimulus is irrelevant, to monitoring the stimulus to detect its dimming, to discriminating the shape or texture of the stimulus (Spitzer & Richmond 1991). Similarly, the responses of V4 neurons are stronger when an animal performs a more difficult version of an orientation change detection task (Spitzer *et al.* 1988). The effects of task demand may be related to arousal or vigilance, but they can affect spatial attention. In some circumstances, modulation by spatial attention can be more than twice as strong during a difficult task (Boudreau & Maunsell 2001).

The attentional modulation of the responses of individual neurons can vary not only between tasks but also within trials. Motter (1994) provided a clear example of the dynamics of attention. He trained monkeys to do a task in which an instruction redirected their spatial attention in the middle of some trials. Neurons in V4 changed their responses within a few hundred milliseconds of the new instruction. Other studies have shown that attentional modulation can vary systematically during the course of task trials (e.g. McAdams & Maunsell 1999a; Reynolds et al. 2000). These observations indicate that attentional modulation of individual neurons is dynamic, and varies over a time-course of no more than a few hundred milliseconds.

In summary, attentional modulation of neuronal signals varies substantially within and between areas, and the modulation of individual neurons can vary depending on task demands, and probably other factors. This variable aspect of attentional modulations makes comparisons between different experiments problematic. It also means that there is little point in seeking a specific, fundamental value to describe the effect of attention on a neuron or area.

Although attention substantially alters sensory responses (e.g. Figures 7.1 and 7.2), it does not usually eliminate responses to unattended stimuli. Occasional neurons are described that respond only when the animal attends to the stimulus in their receptive field, but no report has described this as typical for neurons in a visual area. While it is likely that more neurons would show this sort of gating by attention in extremely demanding tasks, those tasks are not representative of the effort of most visual tasks. When animals perform tasks that approximate the attentional demands of everyday visual functions, attention substantially emphasizes the cortical representation of behaviourally relevant stimuli relative to others, but does not obliterate most signals about other stimuli.

7.3. The quality of modulations of neuronal responses by attention

In addition to changing the magnitude of neuronal responses, attention might affect the information contained in the neuronal signal. For example, does attention change the preferred orientation or speed, or the sharpness of tuning for different stimulus attributes? The relationship between tuning for stimulus dimensions and the quality of information conveyed by a population of neurons is complex (Zhang & Sejnowski 1999), and it is difficult to argue that attention should have a particular effect on selectivity to produce better behavioural performance. Nevertheless, it is important to examine whether changes in neuronal stimulus selectivity are associated with attention. Only a handful of studies have addressed this question, but they suggest that attention does not systematically alter the selectivity of neurons. Instead, attention appears to act by increasing the responsiveness of neurons without changing the selectivity or reliability of responses.

McAdams & Maunsell (1999a) measured the orientation tuning of V4 neurons when attention was directed towards the orientation of a stimulus in their receptive fields, and when it was directed to the colour of a distant stimulus. Responses were stronger with attention directed to the receptive field, but responses to all orientations were increased by the same proportion. Figure 7.3 shows average orientation tuning curves for the two conditions in that study. Although responses were on average ca. 30% stronger when attention was directed to the receptive field, there was no systematic change in the sharpness of orientation tuning. Treue & Martínez Trujillo (1999) similarly found that attention increased the strength of

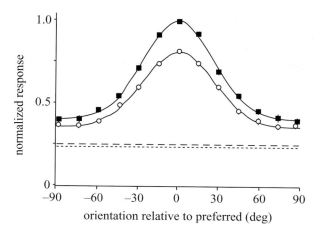

Fig. 7.3. Average normalized tuning curves for 262 V4 neurons tested when the stimulus was attended (filled symbols) or ignored (open symbols). Tuning curves for each cell were normalized to the peak response in the attended condition, and shifted left or right to bring each cell's preferred orientation into alignment. Gaussian functions were then fitted to the averaged data for each behavioural state. Dashed and dotted lines represent the average spontaneous activities in the attended and unattended states respectively. Although the amplitude of the normalized tuning curves changed markedly when the animal attended to the stimulus (amplitude: 0.46–0.60), the width did not ($\sigma = 37.8$–$37.5°$. (Data from McAdams & Maunsell (1999a).)

responses of neurons in MT but did not change the sharpness of their directional tuning. In V4, the spatial profiles of receptive fields appear to scale proportionally when attention is directed at different locations near the receptive field, without changing the shape of the receptive field profile (Connor *et al.* 1996, 1997). Additionally, orientation tuning curves measured in inferotemporal cortex using reward-contingent and non-reward-contingent stimuli differ in response strength but not in the sharpness of tuning (Vogels & Orban 1994).

Similarly, attention does not appear to alter the underlying reliability of cortical responses. When the same stimulus is presented many times, cortical neurons respond with different numbers of spikes for different presentations. This variability is captured by the relationship between the mean strength of a neuron's response and the variance of the response measured over many presentations of the same stimulus. In most cases, the variance of the spike counts is proportional, and generally close to, the mean spike count (e.g. Tolhurst *et al.* 1981; Geisler & Albrecht 1997). Attention does not affect the relationship between the mean and variance of responses for neurons in area V4 (McAdams & Maunsell 1999b). Although attention changes the average responsiveness of neurons, it does not alter the variance associated with a given level of response.

While in many situations attention appears to increase the sensitivity of neurons without obviously affecting their underlying stimulus selectivity, there are cases where attention does alter selectivity. For example, Moran & Desimone (1985) described how attention altered the receptive fields of V4 neurons to emphasize the region around the stimulus to which the subject was attending (see also Luck *et al.* 1997). A shift in a neuron's receptive field profile is not consistent with a simple change in its sensitivity. Nevertheless, a shift in receptive fields can be explained by simple changes in sensitivity that occur at earlier levels in cortical processing (see Maunsell & McAdams 2001), and are consistent with a mechanism that increases responses to attended stimuli relative to others in the scene.

While more stimulus dimensions and more visual areas must be examined before firm conclusions can be drawn, the results described above indicate that attention selectively enhances responses to attended stimuli, without changing the feature selectivity of the responsive neurons. This enhancement is similar to what occurs when neurons are presented with stimuli that are more intense, or better suited to the stimulus preferences of the neuron, such as better matched to a preferred colour or speed of motion. For example, increasing stimulus contrast typically makes a neuron's response stronger without changing its selectivity for orientation, direction, spatial frequency or stimulus position (Dean 1981; Holub & Morton-Gibson 1981; Sclar & Freeman 1982; Albrecht & Hamilton 1982; Skottun *et al.* 1987; Geisler & Albrecht 1997). Similarly, selectivity for one stimulus dimension generally does not differ greatly between measurements made using a stimulus that is optimal or suboptimal for another stimulus dimension (see McAdams & Maunsell 1999*a*); for example, measurements of direction selectivity at an optimal and suboptimal speed, (Rodman & Albright 1987), although there are exceptions (e.g. Roy & Wurtz 1990). Attention also mimics the way that stimulus changes alter responses without affecting the relationship between response strength and response variance (Dean 1981; Tolhurst *et al.* 1983; Snowden *et al.* 1992).

The notion that attention acts in a manner similar to increasing stimulus intensity is supported by the recent results of Reynolds *et al.* (2000). They measured responses of V4 neurons to stimuli of different contrasts, which were or were not attended by the subject. Attention increased neuronal responses in a manner that was similar to the effect of increasing the contrast of each stimulus by a given amount.

7.4. Attention, neuronal responses, and behavioural performance

Attention does not appear to alter the nature or structure of the representations in cortex. Instead it serves to highlight particular stimuli within the existing representational framework. This observation suggests an explanation for the behavioural effects of selective visual attention. Focusing attention on a stimulus influences neuronal responses in a way that is similar to increasing stimulus intensity. Like attention, increased stimulus intensity results in neurons responding more strongly, but does not sharpen their tuning for different stimulus features. If the effect of attention on neurons was functionally equivalent to higher intensity or salience of the attended stimuli, the behavioural advantages associated with selective attention— better detection, discrimination, and reaction time—might be explained by changes in the representations in sensory cerebral cortex. Thus, attention may make attended stimuli appear more intense or salient by enhancing their representations in sensory cortex.

The possibility that changes in neuronal responses in sensory cortex can fully account for the behavioural advantages associated with attention raises an important question about the relationship between neuronal sensitivity and behavioural capabilities. As mentioned in § 7.1, studies that have compared neuronal and behavioural performance have often found that under appropriate conditions, the signals of individual neurons can be as reliable as the subject's behaviour in distinguishing between stimuli (see Parker & Newsome 1998). Does the correspondence between neuronal and behavioural performance remain fixed when attention alters neuronal responses? We examined this question by comparing neuronal and behavioural responses between different attentional states (Cook & Maunsell 2002).

Because many studies of neuronal performance in visual cortex have been done in areas with directionally selective neurons, we trained two monkeys (*Macaca mulatta*) to do a motion detection task that made it possible to measure neuronal and behavioural responses to stimuli in conditions of high and low attention. The animal viewed a screen on which two patches of dynamic random dots appeared. At the start of each trial, there was no net motion in either patch of dots (0% motion coherence), and the animal's task was to rapidly release a lever when dots of either patch began to move coherently in one direction. The motion signal on each trial was randomly selected from preset levels of coherence. One of the patches filled the receptive field of the neuron being recorded, and coherent motion in either patch matched the preferred direction and speed of the neuron.

Motion appeared in only one patch on each trial, and the animal was cued at the start of the trial as to which patch was likely to contain the motion. Critically, the cue was valid on only about 80% of the trials. On the remaining trials motion occurred at an uncued location. These invalidly cued trials made it possible to measure behavioural and neuronal responses to stimuli to which the animal directed relatively little attention (Posner 1980). The behavioural performance of both animals showed that they used the cue on each trial to direct most of their attention to the patch of dots that was likely to contain the motion. Moderate motion coherence was typically detected on more than 80% of trials when it appeared in the cued location, but on fewer than 40% of trials when it appeared in the uncued location. (These behavioural data cannot distinguish whether the animal simultaneously attended to the cued and uncued locations with different amounts of attention allocated to each, or if instead all of its attention was assigned to one patch at any instant, with the proportion of time spent attending to each patch depending on the cue. However, the neurophysiological recordings indicate that the animal allocated different amounts of attention to the two patches, and that these amounts did not vary during the stimulus presentations (see Cook & Maunsell 2002, Figure 7.10).)

We recorded from neurons in MT and VIP. We chose these areas because both contain neurons that respond selectively to motion. Responses from a typical MT neuron are shown in Figure 7.4. The filled symbols in Figure 7.4*a* show the average response of the neuron to different levels of motion coherence in the receptive field when the animal had been cued to attend to that location. The dashed line shows the average level of response to the 0% motion stimulus that preceded the motion. As expected, stronger motion produced stronger responses. The open symbol shows the neuron's average response to the medium motion strength (15% coherence) in the receptive field on trials in which the animal had been instructed to attend to the other location. Although the same motion appeared in the receptive field, the response was weaker. While measurements of responses to unattended stimuli of different motion coherences would have been valuable, it was not practical to collect those data because invalid cues had to be restricted to a small percentage of the trials.

Figure 7.4*b* shows the animal's behavioural performance on the same trials on which the neuronal responses were recorded. The filled symbols plot performance when the animal was attending to the receptive field and the motion occurred there. The open symbol is the behavioural performance for detecting the onset of the medium motion coherence in the receptive field when attention had been directed to the other patch of random dots. Giving the animal an invalid cue caused performance to drop from *ca.* 85% correct to only *ca.* 25% correct.

The question we wanted to address was whether the decreases in neuronal and behavioural performance caused by directing attention were the same as those that might have occurred by keeping attention fixed and reducing the motion strength: is behavioural performance the same for an attended, weak stimulus and an unattended, strong stimulus if they both produce

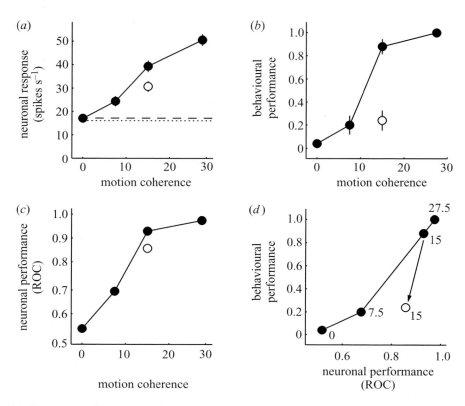

Fig. 7.4. Responses of a representative MT neuron. (*a*) Responses to motion stimuli with different levels of coherence. Motion coherence corresponds to the strength of the motion signal. At 0% coherence, there is no net motion. Each filled circle is the average response during the first 300 ms after the onset of motion with the coherence indicated. The dashed line is the average response to the 0% coherence stimulus that appeared before the onset of coherent motion. The open circle is the response to 15% coherent motion in the receptive field that appeared on trials when the animal's attention had been directed away from the receptive field. The dotted line is the response to 0% coherent motion in those trials. Error bars in all panels are the standard errors of the means, and are sometimes smaller than the symbols. As expected, directing attention away from the receptive field reduced neuronal responses. (*b*) Behavioural performance for the same trials used to collect the neuronal responses. The open circle shows that the animal's ability to detect the 15% coherent stimulus was greatly reduced when its attention was directed away from the location of the motion. (*c*) Neuronal performance. Neuronal responses were converted into performance using ROC based on 300 ms immediately before and after the onset of motion. (*d*) The data from (*b* and *c*) are replotted parameterized by motion coherence. The value by each symbol gives the associated motion coherence. The data from the cases when the animal attended to the location of the motion define a function, but the open symbol, from trials on which the animal's attention was directed away from the stimulus, does not lie on that function. Thus, directing attention away from the stimulus does not have the same effect as reducing motion coherence while keeping attention fixed.

the same neuronal response? To examine this, we converted the neuronal responses into a measure of performance using ROC analysis (Green & Swets 1966). This analysis evaluates how well an ideal observer could detect the presence of motion if the only signal available were the spikes of the neuron. For this analysis, we counted spikes in 300 ms windows immediately before and after the onset of the motion, for each of the conditions. The ROC performance based on the neuronal signal is plotted in Figure 7.4c as a function of motion coherence. ROC values run from 1.0, which corresponds to perfect performance, to 0.5, which corresponds to performance that is no better than guessing. The neuronal response to the medium motion coherence could support good performance when the receptive field location had been cued, and the neuronal performance was only slightly reduced when the same stimulus appeared with attention directed elsewhere (open symbol).

One way to assess whether shifting attention is equivalent to changing stimulus strength is to plot neuronal and behavioural performance against one another, parameterized by the coherence of the motion. In Figure 7.4d, each point represents the behavioural and neuronal performance for a particular motion coherence, as indicated by the numbers beside each point. If the effect of attention were equivalent to changing stimulus strength, then the point for the invalid cue should lie on the function described by the filled symbols. In this case, it does not: it lies substantially to the right of the function. Shifting attention modulated the neuronal response by less than would be needed to account for the modulation of behavioural performance. This result was typical for neurons in MT. The responses of most MT neurons were weakly affected by attention. The average modulation among 93 neurons was about a 15% change in response. Attention had a more pronounced effect on behavioural performance, and for most neurons the attentional modulation of the neuronal response was too small to account for the attentional modulation of the behavioural response.

A different result was found in VIP. VIP receives input from MT (Maunsell & Van Essen 1983; Ungerleider & Desimone 1986), and like MT, most of its neurons are direction selective (Colby et al. 1993; Cook & Maunsell 2002). Most neurons in VIP had strong attentional modulation; too strong to match the behavioural modulation by attention. The responses of a representative VIP neuron are shown in Figure 7.5, which has the same format as Figure 7.4. Figure 7.5a shows that the neuron's responses were profoundly affected by attention. Although the neuron responded strongly to the medium motion coherence when the animal was attending to the receptive field, the same stimulus produced almost no response when the animal was attending elsewhere. The dashed and dotted lines show that attention also affected the response to the 0% motion. The response to unattended moderate motion was less than the response to the 0% coherent motion when it was attended. Although the neuron's responses were devastated when attention was directed elsewhere, in this particular case the animal's behaviour was only slightly reduced (Figure 7.5b). Plotting neuronal performance against behavioural performance showed that attention did not have the same effect as changes in the motion coherence of attended stimuli (Figure 7.5d). Unlike MT, however, the point for the unattended stimulus lies to the left of the function defined by the points for the attended stimuli. This means that the attentional modulation of the neuronal response was stronger than what would be expected based on the modulation of the behavioural response. The responses of most neurons in VIP were strongly modulated by attention, and it was common to find that the neuronal modulation was greater than the associated behavioural modulation.

The responses of all the neurons recorded in MT and VIP are summarized in Figure 7.6. Data from each animal and each area are plotted separately. Each plot shows the average neuronal and behavioural performance associated with high, medium, and low levels of motion coherence, and for the medium motion coherence when it was in the uncued location. For MT data from both animals, the means for the performance on the uncued condition lie to the right of the function defined by the cued condition, although by different amounts for the two animals. For VIP, the means for the performance on the uncued condition lie to the left of the function, although barely so for animal 1. The differences between the two animals arise in part from greater

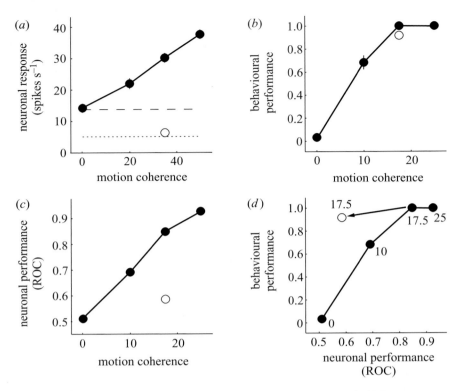

Fig. 7.5. Responses of a representative VIP neuron. Same format as Figure 7.4. (*a*) Responses to motion stimuli with different levels of coherence; (*b*) behavioural performance for the same trials used to collect the neuronal responses; (*c*) neuronal performance; and (*d*) the data from (*b*) and (*c*) replotted parameterized by motion coherence. Attention modulated the neuronal response far more than expected based on its modulation of behavioural performance.

overall attentional modulation for animal 2. The average neuronal modulation for animal 2 was 28% for MT and 94% for VIP, compared with 12% for MT and 68% for VIP in animal 1.

The analyses in Figures 7.4–7.6 compare neuronal performance measured using ROC against behavioural performance measured as a percentage of stimuli correctly detected. Might different measures reveal a better correspondence between neuronal and behavioural, or better correspondence between the animals? For example, neuronal response might be measured as absolute or relative rate of firing, and behavioural response might be measured as reaction time. We have tested these and other measures of neuronal and behavioural performance. Different analyses change the shapes of the functions and shift the unattended points slightly left or right, but none changed the qualitative appearance of the results shown in Figure 7.6 (see Cook & Maunsell 2002). We do not believe that any analysis could bring all the unattended points onto the functions defined by the attended points.

These results show that the relationship between neuronal response and behavioural performance can be changed by attention. Although attention substantially affected behavioural performance, it had relatively little effect on the responsiveness of MT neurons. Thus, similar levels of neuronal performance in MT were associated with different levels of behavioural

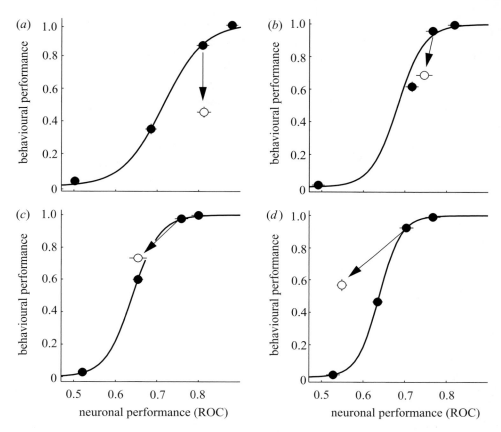

Fig. 7.6. Summary of the effects of attention on neuronal and behavioural performance. (*a*) Animal 1, MT; (*b*) animal 2, MT; (*c*) animal 1, VIP; and (*d*) animal 2, VIP. Each panel is a plot of neuronal versus behavioural performance in the form shown in Figures 7.4*d* and 7.5*d*. The filled circles are the average performance for high, medium, and low motion coherence and solid bars are sigmoidal fits. Averages from individual neurons were combined to produce these plots. Error bars are the standard errors of the means. Open circles are performance for the medium coherence when the subject's attention was directed away from the stimulus. Although the subjects differed somewhat, the unattended points for the MT are both to the right of the functions for the attended stimuli, and the unattended points for the VIP are both to the left of the functions for the attended stimuli. The effects of attention are not readily equated to changes in motion coherence.

performance. In VIP, the relationship between neuronal response and performance was also affected by attention, but in this case the attention affected neuronal performance more than behavioural performance.

While there are several possible reasons for this outcome, differences in the amount of attentional modulation across visual cortex provide a probable explanation. Attentional modulation of neuronal responses is greater in later stages of cortical processing (Figure 7.2). Although the origin of this difference is not known, it should have consequences for the relationship between neuronal and behavioural performance. If stimulus–response functions are similar between areas (as they are for MT and VIP; Figures 7.4*a* and 7.5*a*), then a given change in behavioural performance caused by changes in attention will be matched only by a specific change in neuronal response. Because attentional modulation varies between areas, a match between the change in neuronal response and behaviour can be centred only on a particular level of cortical processing. It is possible that the neurons at some level between MT and VIP had an average attentional modulation that was well matched to the average behavioural modulation. If so, then neurons in this region might have responses that closely matched behavioural performance across manipulations of either stimulus strength or attentional state.

The notion that behavioural performance might be most closely associated with neurons that are intermediate in cortical processing raises the question of why behaviours would not be based on the neurons with the greatest attentional modulation. The answer is probably that the neurons with the greatest attentional modulation do not have response properties that are optimal for the task. Neurons with the greatest attentional modulation typically lie at the highest levels of cortical processing, and have complex response properties. For example, although neurons in both MT and VIP are directionally selective, VIP neurons have more elaborate response properties. VIP neurons respond to several types of visual and extraretinal signals, including optic flow patterns, tactile stimulation of the face, vestibular stimulation, and the position of the eyes in the orbits (Schaafsma & Duysens 1996; Schaafsma *et al.* 1997; Colby & Goldberg 1999). Although these neurons are strongly modulated by attention, their specialization for these more complex response properties is likely to make them less reliable than other neurons for detecting the onset of the motion used in the experiments described here.

An analysis of the responses we collected from MT and VIP indicates that neurons in VIP are not better suited than MT neurons for detecting the motion used in our task. Figure 7.7 shows distributions of neuronal performance for the two areas. A broad range of performance was found in both areas, but in both animals the median performance was slightly better for MT. These distributions are based on responses to the medium motion coherence when it appeared in the cued location, but MT performance was also better for the other levels of motion coherence. Thus, neurons at later levels of cortical processing are not necessarily better suited for all tasks.

We know of no data that strongly suggest that behavioural performance should always depend on neurons in the highest levels of visual cortex. Basing performance on those representations would introduce a substantial restriction, because far fewer neurons would be available if only the highest levels are accessed. Rather than depending on those neurons that are most modulated by attention, behavioural performance is likely to be based on those neurons with response properties that provide the most sensitive signals for the current task. This suggestion is consistent with observations on perceptual learning that indicate that earlier or later cortical levels are involved in learning different types of visual discriminations (Ahissar & Hochstein 1997). In the case of our motion detection task, neurons with the greatest sensitivity might be found at a level intermediate to MT and VIP, and behaviours might be most closely linked to the performance of those neurons. Were that the case, it would be natural for behaviour to be modulated by attention to the same extent that those best-suited neurons were modulated by attention. If, in a different task, behavioural performance was best served by representations in later stages of visual cortex, where attentional modulation is strong, we would expect that behaviour would be more susceptible to attentional modulation.

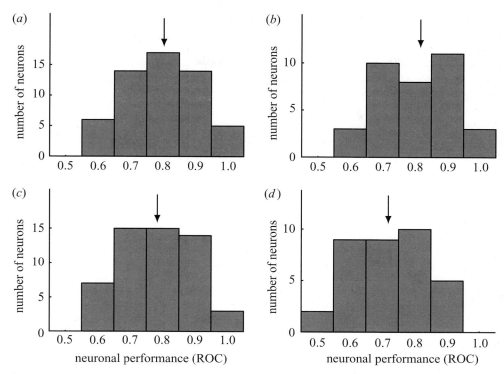

Fig. 7.7. Neuronal performance detecting the onset of stimulus motion. (*a*) Animal 1, MT; (*b*) animal 2, MT; (*c*) animal 1, VIP; and (*d*) animal 2, VIP. ROC analysis was carried out using 300 ms periods immediately before and after the onset of medium motion coherence when it occurred in the cued location. The median values for the MT were 0.80 and 0.82 for animals 1 and 2, and the median values for the VIP were 0.78 and 0.72, respectively. Thus, the performance of MT neurons was slightly superior. The MT performance was also better for low and high motion coherence.

7.5. Conclusion

More data will be needed before we will know whether the relationship between neuronal and behavioural performance persists across attentional states for any region of the visual cortex. Nevertheless, the results described here indicate that a correspondence across attention states will be limited to a restricted level of processing, the location of which will vary depending on the task being performed.

Even if neurons at a given level do preserve a fixed relationship between neuronal and behavioural performance across attentional states for a task, it would not necessarily mean that those neurons were more or less important than others for performing the task. Similarly, it would say nothing about how large a pool of neurons contribute to a decision. A cortical region that had a close match would be a good candidate for being the centre of the relevant neurons, but the pool size might be large or small without appreciably affecting the mean neuronal performance. Additionally, a correspondence between average neuronal performance and average behavioural performance would not reveal which cortical region was most involved, because behavioural performance might be based on the best neurons in a population, rather than the average (see Parker & Newsome 1998).

Much remains to be learned about how the activity of individual neurons is translated into behavioural decisions. Nevertheless, progress in this area is essential for understanding how the brain works. Manipulation of attention may prove to be a valuable approach to exploring how neurons contribute to particular behaviours.

We thank our many colleagues who contributed to the studies reviewed here and provided comments on the manuscript, including W. Bosking, C. E. Boudreau, J. J. DiCarlo, G. M. Ghose, C. Hocker, C. J. McAdams, D. Murray, T. Williford and T. Yang. Supported by NIH R01 EY05911. J. H. R. M. is an investigator with the Howard Hughes Medical Institute.

References

Ahissar, M. & Hochstein, S. 1997 Task difficulty and the specificity of perceptual learning. *Nature* **387**, 401–406.

Albrecht, D. G. & Hamilton, D. B. 1982 Striate cortex of monkey and cat: contrast response function. *J. Neurophysiol.* **48**, 217–237.

Barlow, H. B. 1985 The twelfth Bartlett memorial lecture: the role of single neurons in the psychology of perception. *Q. J. Exp. Psychol.* **37**, 121–145.

Boudreau, C. E. & Maunsell, J. H. R. 2001 Is spatial attention a limited resource for V4 neurons? *Soc. Neurosci. Abstr.* **27**, 574.3.

Braun, J., Koch, C. & Davis, J. L. 2001 *Visual attention and cortical circuits*. Cambridge, MA: MIT.

Colby, C. L. & Goldberg, M. E. 1999 Space and attention in parietal cortex. *A. Rev. Neurosci.* **22**, 319–349.

Colby, C. L., Duhamel, J. R. & Goldberg, M. E. 1993 Ventral intraparietal area of the macaque: anatomic location and visual response properties. *J. Neurophysiol.* **69**, 902–914.

Connor, C. E., Gallant, J. L., Preddie, D. C. & Van Essen, D. C. 1996 Responses in area V4 depend on the spatial relationship between stimulus and attention. *J. Neurophysiol.* **75**, 1306–1308.

Connor, C. E., Preddie, D. C., Gallant, J. L. & Van Essen, D. C. 1997 Spatial attention effects in macaque area V4. *J. Neurosci.* **17**, 3201–3214.

Cook, E. P. & Maunsell, J. H. R. 2002 Attentional modulation of behavioral performance and neuronal responses in middle temporal and ventral intraparietal areas of macaque monkey. *J. Neurosci.* **22**, 1994–2004.

Dean, A. F. 1981 The variability of discharge of simple cells in the cat striate cortex. *Exp. Brain Res.* **44**, 437–440.

Felleman, D. J. & Van Essen, D. C. 1991 Distributed hierarchical processing in the primate cerebral cortex. *Cerebr. Cortex* **1**, 1–47.

Ferrera, V. P., Rudolph, K. K. & Maunsell, J. H. R. 1994 Responses of neurons in the parietal and temporal visual pathways during a motion task. *J. Neurosci.* **14**, 6171–6186.

Geisler, W. S. & Albrecht, D. G. 1997 Visual cortex neurons in monkeys and cats: detection, discrimination and identification. *Visual Neurosci.* **14**, 897–919.

Green, D. M. & Swets, J. A. 1966 *Signal detection theory and psychophysics*. New York: Wiley.

Holub, R. A. & Morton-Gibson, M. 1981 Response of visual cortical neurons of the cat to moving sinusoidal gratings: response–contrast functions and spatiotemporal interactions. *J. Neurophysiol.* **46**, 1244–1259.

Lavie, N. & Tsal, Y. 1994 Perceptual load as a major determinant of the locus of selection in visual attention. *Percept. Psychophys.* **56**, 183–197.

Luck, S. J., Chelazzi, L., Hillyard, S. A. & Desimone, R. 1997 Neural mechanisms of spatial selective attention in areas V1, V2 and V4 of macaque visual cortex. *J. Neurophysiol.* **77**, 24–42.

McAdams, C. J. & Maunsell, J. H. R. 1999*a* Effects of attention on orientation-tuning functions of single neurons in macaque cortical area V4. *J. Neurosci.* **19**, 431–441.

McAdams, C. J. & Maunsell, J. H. R. 1999*b* Effects of attention on the reliability of individual neurons in monkey visual cortex. *Neuron* **23**, 765–773.

Mehta, A. D., Ulbert, I. & Schroeder, C. E. 2000 Intermodal selective attention in monkeys. I. Distribution and timing of effects across visual areas. *Cerebr. Cortex* **10**, 343–358.

Maunsell, J. H. R. & McAdams, C. J. 2001 Effects of attention on the responsiveness and selectivity of individual neurons in visual cerebral cortex. In *Visual attention and cortical circuits* (ed. J. Braun, C. Koch & J. L. Davis), pp. 103–119. Cambridge, MA: MIT.

Maunsell, J. H. R. & Van Essen, D. C. 1983 The connections of the middle temporal visual area (MT) and their relationship to a cortical hierarchy in the macaque monkey. *J. Neurosci.* **3**, 2563–2586.

Moran, J. & Desimone, R. 1985 Selective attention gates visual processing in the extrastriate cortex. *Science* **229**, 782–784.

Motter, B. C. 1994 Neural correlates of feature selective memory and pop-out in extrastriate area V4. *J. Neurosci.* **14**, 2190–2199.

Mountcastle, V. B., Andersen, R. A. & Motter, B. C. 1981 The influence of attentive fixation upon the excitability of the light-sensitive neurons of the posterior parietal cortex. *J. Neurosci.* **1**, 1218–1235.

Mountcastle, V. B., Motter, B. C., Steinmetz, M. A. & Sestokas, A. K. 1987 Common and differential effects of attentive fixation on the excitability of parietal and prestriate (V4) cortical visual neurons in the macaque monkey. *J. Neurosci.* **7**, 2239–2255.

Parker, A. J. & Newsome, W. T. 1998 Sense and the single neuron: probing the physiology of perception. *A. Rev. Neurosci.* **21**, 227–277.

Pashler, H. E. 1998 *The psychology of attention.* Cambridge, MA: MIT.

Posner, M. I. 1980 Orienting of attention. *Q. J. Exp. Psychol.* **32**, 3–25.

Reynolds, J. H., Pasternak, T. & Desimone, R. 2000 Attention increases sensitivity of V4 neurons. *Neuron* **26**, 703–714.

Rodman, H. R. & Albright, T. D. 1987 Coding of visual stimulus velocity in area MT of the macaque. *Vision Res.* **27**, 2035–2048.

Roy, J. P. & Wurtz, R. H. 1990 The role of disparity-sensitive cortical neurons in signalling the direction of self-motion. *Nature* **348**, 160–162.

Sade, A. & Spitzer, H. 1998 The effects of attentional spread and attentional effort on orientation discrimination. *Spat. Vision* **11**, 367–383.

Schaafsma, S. J. & Duysens, J. 1996 Neurons in the ventral intraparietal area of awake monkey closely resemble neurons in the dorsal part of the medial superior temporal area in their response to optic flow. *J. Neurophysiol.* **76**, 4056–4068.

Schaafsma, S. J., Duysens, J. & Gielen, C. C. A. M. 1997 Responses in ventral intraparietal area of awake macaque monkey to optic flow patterns corresponding to rotation of planes in depth can be explained by translation and expansion effects. *Visual Neurosci.* **14**, 633–646.

Sclar, G. & Freeman, R. D. 1982 Orientation selectivity in the cat's striate cortex is invariant with stimulus contrast. *Exp. Brain Res.* **46**, 457–461.

Skottun, B. C., Bradley, A., Sclar, G., Ohzawa, I. & Freeman, R. D. 1987 The effects of contrast on visual orientation and spatial frequency discrimination: a comparison of single cells and behavior. *J. Neurophysiol.* **57**, 773–786.

Snowden, R. J., Treue, S. & Andersen, R. A. 1992 The response of neurons in area V1 and MT of the alert rhesus monkey to moving random dot patterns. *Exp. Brain Res.* **88**, 389–400.

Spitzer, H. & Richmond, B. J. 1991 Task difficulty: ignoring, attending to, and discriminating a visual stimulus yield progressively more activity in inferior temporal neurons. *Exp. Brain Res.* **83**, 340–348.

Spitzer, H., Desimone, R. & Moran, J. 1988 Increased attention enhances both behavioral and neuronal performance. *Science* **240**, 338–340.

Tolhurst, D. J., Movshon, J. A. & Thompson, I. D. 1981 The dependence of response amplitude and variance of cat visual cortical neurons on stimulus contrast. *Exp. Brain Res.* **41**, 414–419.

Tolhurst, D. J., Movshon, J. A. & Dean, A. F. 1983 The statistical reliability of signals in single neurons in cat and monkey visual cortex. *Vision Res.* **23**, 775–785.

Treue, S. & Martínez Trujillo, J. C. 1999 Feature-based attention influences motion processing gain in macaque visual cortex. *Nature* **399**, 575–579.

Treue, S. & Maunsell, J. H. R. 1999 Effects of attention on the processing of motion in macaque middle temporal and medial superior temporal visual cortical areas. *J. Neurosci.* **19**, 7591–7602.

Ungerleider, L. G. & Desimone, R. 1986 Cortical connections of visual area MT in the macaque. *J. Comp. Neurol.* **248**, 190–222.

Urbach, D. & Spitzer, H. 1995 Attentional effort modulated by task difficulty. *Vision Res.* **35**, 2169–2177.

Vogels, R. & Orban, G. A. 1994 Activity of inferior temporal neurons during orientation discrimination with successively presented gratings. *J. Neurophysiol.* **71**, 1428–1451.

Zhang, K. & Sejnowski, T. J. 1999 Neuronal tuning: to sharpen or broaden? *Neural Comput.* **11**, 75–84.

Glossary

MST   medial superior temporal area
MT   middle temporal visual area
ROC   receiver operating characteristic
VIP   ventral intraparietal area

8

The neural selection and control of saccades by the frontal eye field

Jeffrey D. Schall

Recent research has provided new insights into the neural processes that select the target for and control the production of a shift of gaze. Being a key node in the network that subserves visual processing and saccade production, the frontal eye field (FEF) has been an effective area in which to monitor these processes. Certain neurons in the FEF signal the location of conspicuous or meaningful stimuli that may be the targets for saccades. Other neurons control whether and when the gaze shifts. The existence of distinct neural processes for visual selection and saccade production is necessary to explain the flexibility of visually guided behaviour.

8.1. Introduction

Figure 8.1*a* shows the eye movements produced by a monkey inspecting an array of stimuli to locate a specific target. The rapid shifts of gaze that redirect the fovea of the retina, which provides high-acuity vision, onto a new point in the image are called saccades. Saccades tend to direct gaze to conspicuous features in the scene. Or, if a particular strategy or goal is employed, the gaze can then concentrate on appropriate inconspicuous elements in the image (e.g. Yarbus 1967). Natural vision is accomplished through a cycle of fixation and visual analysis interrupted by saccadic eye movements. Figure 8.1*b* illustrates the variability of fixation durations over time. In this short period of just nine saccades between the stimuli, the fixation durations ranged from 85 to 320 ms. Similar fixation durations have been observed in humans performing a scanning visual-search task (e.g. Hooge & Erkelens 1996), with even more variability when viewing more engaging natural scenes (Viviani 1990). These delays must arise from the processes that are carried out upon the fixation of each element and before the saccade to the next. While fixating a point in an image, at least two processes take place. First, perceptual processing analyses the object in the fovea to ascertain its identity and the image in the periphery to locate the target for the next saccade. Second, response preparation precedes the saccade. These processes take some time.

A network of structures in the brain produces and conveys the signals necessary to select a target and produce a saccade. This review focuses on the role of the FEF in the selection of targets for saccades and the control of the initiation of saccades. The kinds of neural activity and modulation observed in the FEF occur in related structures such as the superior colliculus or posterior parietal cortex. Thus, an essential fact is that the processes that will be described occur concurrently in a network of inter-connected structures. This fact precludes the assignment of any particular function exclusively to a given part of the brain.

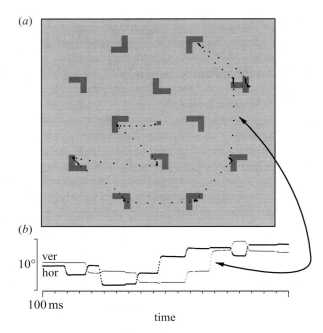

Fig. 8.1. (*a*) Pattern of gaze shifts made by a monkey searching for a randomly orientated T shape among L shapes. The T shape among the L-shape array appeared after the monkey fixated the central square. On this trial, the monkey's first saccade was to the left, followed by a sequence of eye movements around the perimeter of the array. This leads to the question of what neural events selected certain elements but not others in the array? (*b*) Plots of eye position in the horizontal (thick) and vertical (thin) axis as a function of time during the viewing period. The first leftward saccade corresponds to the first downward deflection in the plot of eye position in the horizontal axis. The vertical saccade to the target is highlighted by the arrow. The interval spent fixating each L shape varied from less than 100 ms to *ca*. 300 ms. This leads to the question of what neural processes account for the variable amount of time spent foreating the various effectively identical elements? (Adapted from Schall & Thompson 1999.)

8.2. Frontal eye fields

The FEF, located in prefrontal cortex, is an area that contributes to transforming visual signals into saccade commands (reviewed by Schall 1997; Schall & Thompson 1999). Thus, the FEF has two facets—one motor and the other sensory.

The evidence for the motor function of the FEF is not controversial. Low-intensity electrical stimulation of the FEF elicits saccades (e.g. Bruce *et al.* 1985). This direct influence is mediated by neurons in the FEF that modulate activity specifically before and during saccades (Bruce & Goldberg 1985; Schall 1991; Hanes & Schall 1996; Hanes *et al.* 1995, 1998). The neurons in the FEF that generate movement-related or fixation-related activity are located in layer 5 and innervate the superior colliculus (Segraves & Goldberg 1987; Sommer & Wurtz 1998*a*, 2001) and parts of the neural circuit in the brainstem that generates saccades (Segraves 1992). These neurons, in concert with counterparts in the superior colliculus (Sparks 1978; Munoz & Wurtz 1993, 1995; Dorris *et al.* 1997; Dorris & Munoz 1998), produce signals necessary to produce saccadic eye movements. Experiments probing the control of saccades in monkeys provide evidence for the sufficiency of the activity of presaccadic movement-related neurons in the FEF to specify whether and when saccades will be produced (Hanes & Schall 1996; Hanes *et al.* 1998). Reversible inactivation studies provide evidence for the necessity of the FEF to produce saccades (Dias *et al.* 1995; Sommer & Tehovnik 1997). These findings complement earlier observations that the ablation of the FEF causes an initially severe impairment in saccade production that recovers in some but not all respects over time (e.g. Schiller *et al.* 1987; Schiller & Chou 1998, 2000*a,b*).

The evidence that the FEF is involved in visual function is equally compelling. The FEF is reciprocally connected with a multitude of visual cortical areas in both the dorsal and ventral streams (Huerta *et al.* 1987; Baizer *et al.* 1991; Schall *et al.* 1995*b*; Stanton *et al.* 1995; Barone *et al.* 2000) (Figure 8.2). The more ventrolateral portion of the FEF, which is responsible for generating shorter saccades, is interconnected with the perifoveal representation in retinotopically organized areas, from areas that represent central vision in the inferotemporal cortex and from other areas having no retinotopic order. The more ventrolateral portion of the FEF (which produces shorter saccades) is interconnected with the perifoveal representation in retinotopically organized areas, with areas that represent central vision in inferotemporal cortex and with other areas having no retinotopic order. By contrast, the mediodorsal FEF (which produces longer saccades) is interconnected with the peripheral visual field representation of retinotopically organized areas, with areas that emphasize peripheral vision or have no retinotopic

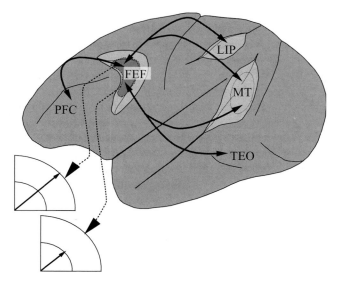

Fig. 8.2. A summary of the connections of the FEF. The FEF contributes to the preparation and initiation of saccades through projections to the superior colliculus and brainstem saccade generator. There is a rough topographic map of saccade amplitude in the FEF; the shorter saccades are represented ventrally and the longer saccades medially. The FEF is reciprocally connected with a multitude of extrastriate visual areas in both the dorsal and ventral streams. The projections are topographically organized; the foveal representation of retinotopic areas projects to the ventrolateral part of the FEF and the peripheral representation projects to the dorsomedial part of the FEF. These diverse visual inputs convey an elaborate representation of the image to the centres that will specify which saccade to produce. The FEF is also connected with areas in the prefrontal cortex. These connections convey the influence of context that can supplement or override the outcome of visual processing. PFC, prefrontal cortex; FEF, frontal eye field; LIP, lateral interparietal area; MT, middle temporal visual area; TEO, tempero-occipital visual area.

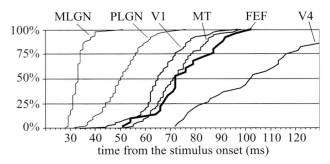

Fig. 8.3. Cumulative distributions of the times of first response to an optimal visual stimulus are plotted for the indicated stages of the visual pathway. (Modified from Schmolesky *et al.* 1998.) MLGN, magnocellular layers of the dorsal lateral geniculate nucleus; PLGN, parvocellular layers of the dorsal lateral geniculate nucleus; V1, primary visual cortex; MT, middle temporal visual area; V4, visual area 4.

order and are multimodal. In fact, the FEF is unique in the extent of its connectivity with the extrastriate visual cortex (Jouve *et al.* 1998). Another source of visual signals to the FEF is the central thalamus; the FEF is innervated mainly by the lateral segment of the mediodorsal nucleus as well as part of neighbouring thalamic nuclei (Huerta *et al.* 1986). Neurons in these nuclei convey visual signals to the FEF (Schlag & Schlag-Rey 1984; Sommer & Wurtz 1998*b*). Due to the extensive convergence of afferents from the thalamus and multiple extrastriate visual areas, individual neurons in the FEF receive signals representing the colour, form, depth, direction of motion and so on of objects in the image. Such convergence seems desirable for a system to select targets for gaze shifts regardless of the visual properties of the target, akin to a salience map.

While the FEF is commonly regarded as being situated rather high in the hierarchy of visual areas (e.g. Felleman & Van Essen 1991), it should not be overlooked that the FEF provides abundant connections to many extrastriate visual areas. In fact, according to a recent analysis of intracortical connectivity, the FEF may be in a feed-forward anatomical relation to prestriate areas such as V4 (Barone *et al.* 2000). Thus, the FEF can influence the activation of neurons in the extrastriate visual cortex. Certainly, the visual response latencies of FEF neurons are early enough to allow this possibility (Schmolesky *et al.* 1998; Figure 8.3).

Finally, in addition to the connections with the visual cortex, the FEF is also connected to specific areas in the prefrontal cortex (e.g. Stanton *et al.* 1993). These pre-frontal connections can endow the FEF with sensitivity to the context of history and goals. In other words, as described in §8.3, neural responses in the FEF to a given stimulus configuration can be modulated subtly or dramatically according to the preceding experience of the monkeys.

8.3. Selection of a target among uniform distractors

The visual-search paradigm has been used extensively to investigate visual selection and attention (reviewed by Egeth & Yantis 1997; Wolfe 1998). The results of many experiments distinguish two modes of visual search. One mode is the efficient visual search for, say, a black spot among several grey spots (Figure 8.4). The second mode is the less efficient, more effortful search for, say, a randomly orientated T shape among randomly orientated L shapes (Figure 8.1).

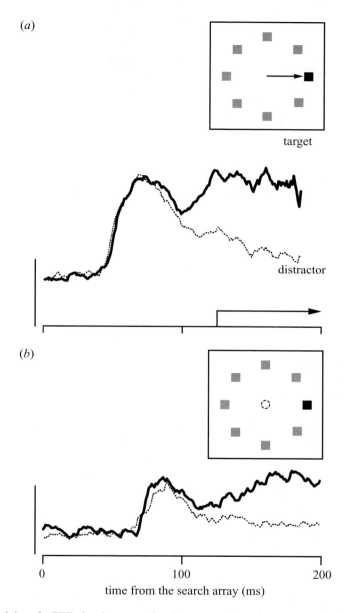

Fig. 8.4. The activity of a FEF visual neuron after the presentation of a pop-out search array when the monkey (*a*) produced or (*b*) withheld a saccade to the oddball. Each plot shows the activation when the oddball stimulus appeared in the receptive field (solid line) and when distractors appeared in the receptive field (dotted line). When a saccade was produced to foveate the target, the initial response to the search array did not discriminate the target from a distractor. However, after *ca.* 100 ms, the activation evolved so that the neural representation of the distractors was suppressed and the activation representing the location of the target was sustained or elevated. When no saccade was produced, the level of activation was attenuated, but the same selection process was observed. Thus, the neural-selection process was not contingent on production of the saccade. The vertical scale represents 100 spikes s^{-1}.
(Modified from Thompson *et al.* 1996, 1997.)

To investigate how the brain selects targets for visually guided saccades, we have recorded the activity of neurons in the FEF of monkeys trained to shift their gaze to the oddball target in two complementary pop-out visual search arrays (Schall & Hanes 1993; Schall *et al.* 1995*a*; Thompson *et al.* 1996; Bichot *et al.* 2001*b*). Most visually responsive cells in the FEF responded initially indiscriminately to the target or the distractor of the search array in their receptive field (Figure 8.4*a*). The absence of a feature-selective response in the FEF during visual search is consistent with earlier work (Mohler *et al.* 1973). However, before the gaze shifted, a selection process transpired by which most visually responsive cells in the FEF ultimately signalled the location of the oddball target stimulus. Notably, in spite of the well-known variability of spiking of cortical neurons, the representation of the location of the target by FEF neurons is very reliable; combining the signals from no more than 10 selective FEF neurons is sufficient to signal the location of the target with as much fidelity as the monkeys' performance (Bichot *et al.* 2001*b*).

A visual target selection process has been observed in the FEF during natural scanning eye movements (Burman & Segraves 1994). Similar results have also been obtained under somewhat different conditions in the superior colliculus (Ottes *et al.* 1987; Basso & Wurtz 1998) and posterior parietal cortex (Gottlieb *et al.* 1998; Contantinidis & Steinmetz 2001). The selection of the target expressed by visuomotor structures such as the FEF is surely related to, if not based on, the selection process observed in the extrastriate visual cortex (e.g. Chelazzi *et al.* 1993, 1998; Motter 1994*a,b*; Luck *et al.* 1997).

The result does not distinguish whether this selection process corresponds to explicit visual selection or to saccade preparation. A series of experiments has been conducted to evaluate these alternative hypotheses. In one study, FEF activity was recorded while monkeys maintained fixation during the presentation of a search array with a single conspicuous oddball (Thompson *et al.* 1997). Although no saccade was made to the oddball, FEF neurons still discriminated the oddball from distractors at the same time and to the same degree as when a gaze shift was produced (Figure 8.4*b*). Thus, the visual selection observed in the FEF does not require saccade execution. This study also concluded that saccade preparation was not happening because the saccade made after the trial was completed was rarely directed to the location where the oddball had been. Another experiment created a condition in which monkeys frequently shifted their gaze to a location different from that occupied by a target. Even when the gaze shifted away from the pop-out oddball of a search array, visual neurons in the FEF represented the current location of the target (Murthy *et al.* 2001). Given the evidence that attention is allocated automatically to the conspicuous oddball in a search array, these findings are consistent with the hypothesis that the activation of visually responsive neurons in the FEF corresponds to or guides the covert orientating of visual attention.

Further evidence for the dissociation between neural selection of the target by FEF neurons and the production of saccades was obtained by analysing the time needed by FEF neurons to locate the target in relation to saccade latency. This work is motivated by the general hypothesis that behavioural response times are occupied by more or less distinct stages of processing (Donders 1868; Sternberg 1969). A series of studies has investigated how the time of visual target selection relates to the total time taken to initiate the saccade. During the search for a single, conspicuous target in a search array the large majority of visually responsive neurons in the FEF discriminated the target from distractors at a constant interval after a search-array presentation (Thompson *et al.* 1996; Sato *et al.* 2001; Figure 8.5). This finding indicates that at least under the conditions of a efficient, pop-out search, a relatively constant period of time is needed to locate potential targets, and the additional variability in saccade latency is introduced by the time to prepare and execute the eye movement. When the

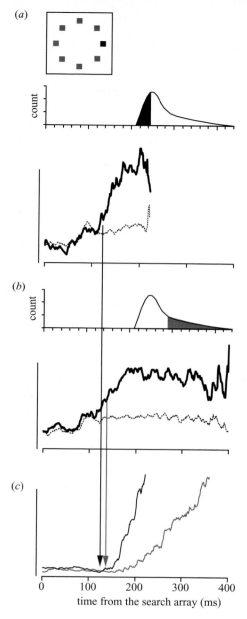

Fig. 8.5. Relation of the time of the neural target selection to the time of the saccade initiation. The activity of a FEF neuron representing the target (thick) or distractors (thin) is shown during trials with saccades of the shortest (*a*) or longest (*b*) latencies. The upper plot in (*a*) and (*b*) indicates the distribution of saccade latencies within the range selected for the analysis of the activity shaded. The thin vertical arrows indicate the time of neural-target selection for each group of trials. The neuron discriminated the target from the distractors after a relatively constant interval after presentation of the search array. The vertical scale represents 100 spikes s^{-1}. (Modified from Sato *et al.* 2001). (*c*) The time of saccade initiation is specified by the activation of another population of neurons. This population may or may not have a visual response, but the neuron saccades are initiated when the activation in a different pool of neurons reaches a threshold. These neurons may or may not have a visual response, but they do discharge in a manner sufficient to control whether and when a saccade will be produced. The variability of saccade latency can be accounted for by randomness in the time taken by the premovement activity to reach the threshold.

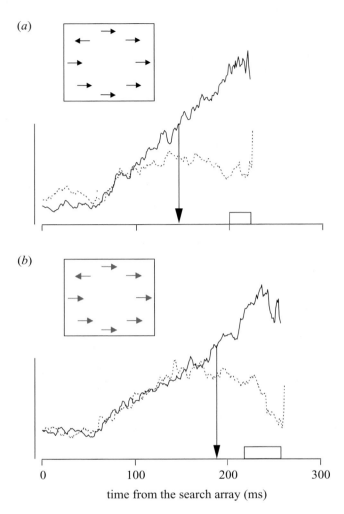

Fig. 8.6. Effect of search difficulty on the time course of target selection. Activity of a FEF neuron during interleaved trials searching for a target that was easy (*a*) or difficult (*b*) to distinguish from the distractors. The neural selection of the target is delayed in the difficult search. (Modified from Sato *et al.* 2001.)

discrimination of the target is more difficult because the target more closely resembles distractors and the search is less efficient (Duncan & Humphreys 1989; Wolfe 1998), the time taken by FEF neurons to locate the target increases and accounts for a larger fraction of the variability in saccade latency (Bichot *et al.* 2001*b*; Sato *et al.* 2001; Figure 8.6).

8.4. Control of saccade initiation

The results just reviewed indicate that certain neurons in the FEF produce a signal that specifies the location of a target for a saccade but does not dictate when or even necessarily where the eyes will move. As described in §8.2, a population of neurons in a network including the FEF and superior colliculus linked through the basal ganglia and thalamus provide the input to the brainstem saccade generator. The activation of these neurons is necessary to produce a saccade; therefore, it is appropriate to identify response preparation with the activation of these presaccadic, movement neurons (also referred to as build-up neurons or prelude neurons). Saccades are initiated when the level of activation in this network reaches a certain level (Sparks 1978; Hanes & Schall 1996; Dorris & Munoz 1998). The timing variability of saccade latency is accounted for by randomness in the time needed for the presaccadic activity to reach the triggering threshold. The variability in the time taken to reach the threshold can originate in the time of onset and in the rate of growth of the activation. The growth of movement activity begins at a fixed interval after the appearance of a visual target for a speeded saccade, but under conditions with less clear targets (e.g. Thompson & Schall 2000) or imposed delays (e.g. Riehle & Requin 1993), the beginning of movement activity can occur at a more variable time. Most of the variability of saccade latency in a direct response to a visual target was accounted for by randomness in the rate of growth of activity to the threshold (Hanes & Schall 1996; Figure 8.5c).

To investigate the neural control of movement initiation, we have implemented a behavioural paradigm with monkeys, referred to as the countermanding paradigm, which was originally designed to investigate human performance (Logan & Cowan 1984). The countermanding paradigm probes a subject's ability to control the production of movements in a reaction-time task that infrequently presents an imperative 'stop signal'. In the oculomotor version, monkeys were trained to make a saccade to a peripheral target unless a stop signal was presented, in which case they must withhold the movement; the stop signal was the reappearance of the fixation spot (Hanes & Schall 1995; Hanes & Carpenter 1999) or another kind of stimulus (Cabel et al. 2000).

Performance on this task can be accounted for by a race between a process that generates the movement and a process that inhibits the movement (Logan & Cowan 1984). This race model provides an estimate of the time needed to cancel the planned movement, the stop-signal reaction time. Oculomotor stop-signal reaction times average ca. 100 ms in monkeys (Hanes & Schall 1995) and are slightly longer in humans (Hanes & Carpenter 1999; Cabel et al. 2000).

The countermanding paradigm provides experimental leverage such that one can determine whether single neurons generate signals that are sufficient to control the production of movements. The logic of the countermanding paradigm establishes two criteria that a neuron must meet to play a direct role in the control of movement. First, the neuron must discharge differently when a saccade is initiated versus when a saccade is withheld. Second, the difference in activity must occur within the time that the movement is cancelled as measured by the stop-signal reaction time. This approach was applied to neural activity recorded in the FEF (Hanes et al. 1998). The first main finding was that movement-related activity in the FEF, which began to grow towards the trigger threshold, failed to reach the threshold activation when movements were cancelled but instead decreased rapidly after the stop signal was presented (Figure 8.7). Likewise, fixation-related activity in the FEF, which began to decrease before the saccade, increased rapidly after the stop signal was presented. Moreover, the modulation of the movement- and fixation-related activity differentiated between execution and inhibition of the movement before the stop-signal reaction time had elapsed. Therefore, according to the logic of the countermanding paradigm, the activity of these neurons was sufficient to specify whether or not the saccade would be produced. The same result has been observed in the superior colliculus (Hanes & Paré 1998).

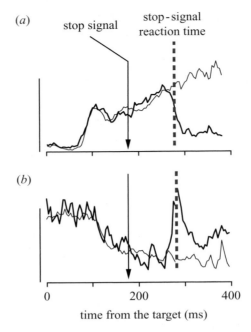

Fig. 8.7. Relationship between the FEF activity and cancelling a movement. (*a*) Activity of a movement neuron in the FEF in trials in which the movement was produced but would have been cancelled if the stop signal had been presented (thin line) is compared with activity on trials when the planned saccade was cancelled because the stop signal appeared (thick line). The time of the stop signal is indicated by the solid vertical arrow. The time needed to cancel the planned movement, the stop-signal reaction time, is indicated by the dashed vertical line. The activity when the movement was cancelled decayed immediately before the stop-signal reaction time. (*b*) Activity of a fixation neuron in the FEF when saccades were initiated (thin line) or cancelled (thick line). The time of the stop signal is indicated by the solid vertical arrow. The time needed to cancel the planned movement, the stop-signal reaction time, is indicated by the dashed vertical line. The activity when the movement was cancelled increased immediately before the stop-signal reaction time. The vertical scale bar marks 100 spikes s^{-1} (modified from Hanes *et al.* 1998).

By contrast, most neurons with visual responses but no saccade-related activity exhibited no modulation associated with cancelling the planned movement and those that did were modulated well after the stop-signal reaction time, too late to make any difference to gaze control. These results indicate that distinct types of neurons can be identified that convey signals related more exclusively to visual processing or to saccade production. The distinction between these different pools of neurons provides the basis for different stages of processing and the according flexibility in mapping responses onto stimuli.

8.5. Selection of a target requiring knowledge

Several lines of evidence demonstrate that gaze can be guided as much by knowledge as by the visual features of stimuli. For example, cognitive strategies can override both covert (e.g. Bacon & Egeth 1994) and overt (e.g. Bichot *et al.* 1996) selection of a single oddball in a search array. Also, target selection is influenced by implicit memory representations arising through short-term priming of location or stimulus features for covert (e.g. Maljkovic & Nakayama 1994, 1996) and overt (Bichot & Schall 1999*b*; McPeek *et al.* 1999) orienting. In addition, experts are more likely than novices to ignore conspicuous but irrelevant parts of a visual image from their field of expertise (e.g. Nodine *et al.* 1996; Chapman & Underwood 1998; Nodine & Krupinski 1998). Finally, the pattern of visual fixation can be influenced by verbal instructions (Yarbus 1967). This means that selection of targets for gaze shifts can be influenced by experience.

To study the effects of training experience on gaze behaviour and associated neural activity in the FEF, monkeys were trained exclusively with search arrays that contained a single item of a constant colour among distractor items of another constant colour (e.g. always a red target among green distractors or always a green target among red distractors; Bichot *et al.* 1996). Control monkeys were trained to shift their gaze to the oddball of both configurations of the search array (i.e. alternating between red among green and green among red). The control monkeys shifted their gaze to the oddball stimulus, regardless of the feature that defined it. By contrast, experimental monkeys persistently directed their gaze to stimuli with the colour of the target even when the configuration of the array was switched for a few trials. In other words, when the experimental monkeys were presented with the search array complementary to that with which they had been trained, they shifted gaze to one of the distractors (that was the colour of the over-learned target) and not to the target (even though it was the oddball). As described, FEF neurons in control monkeys did not exhibit feature selectivity, but their activity evolved to signal the location of the odd-ball stimulus. In monkeys trained exclusively with a search array with constant target and distractor colours, however, about half of the FEF neurons became colour selective. That is, if the over-learned target fell in the receptive field the neurons responded strongly, but if the over-learned distractors fell in the receptive field the neurons' response was significantly weaker or absent. This gives rise to the question of how this initial selective response might arise in the FEF. One possibility is that appropriate bias signals are delivered to the FEF from prefrontal areas. Other studies have demonstrated that the selective properties of prefrontal neurons can change according to rules or strategies (e.g. White & Wise 1999; Wallis *et al.* 2001).

Knowledge gained through experience is necessary when objects of interest cannot be located based only on their visual features. Such cases are exemplified by a visual search for a conjunction of features such as colour and shape in which an explicit memory representation is needed to identify the target (e.g. Treisman & Sato 1990). A recent study investigated how the brain combines knowledge with visual processing to locate targets for eye movements by training monkeys to perform a visual search for a target defined by a unique combination of colour and shape (e.g. red cross). The colour–shape combination that defined the target were rotated randomly between sessions. Two separate, contextual influences were exerted on gaze behaviour and the neural-selection process: visual similarity to the target and the history of target properties (Bichot & Schall 1999*a*,*b*). The evidence for the influence of visual similarity was that monkeys made occasional errant saccades during this conjunction search that tended to direct their gaze to distractors that resembled the current target. Similar observations have been made with human observers during covert (Kim & Cave 1995) and overt orientating (Findlay 1997; Motter & Belky 1998).

When monkeys successfully shifted their gaze to the target, FEF neurons not only discriminated the target from the distractors but also discriminated among the non-selected distractors resulting in more activation for distractors that shared a target feature than for distractors that shared none (Figure 8.8). Thus, the pattern of neural discrimination among

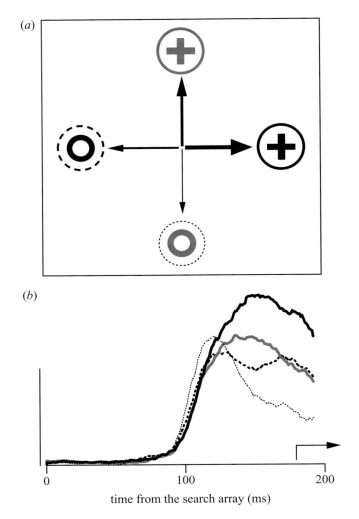

Fig. 8.8. The visual selection of a remembered target during a conjunction search. The assignment of the patterns of neural activation and the incidence of saccades to the alternative stimuli is indicated in the upper diagram of the search array. (*a*) The width of the arrows in the search array represents the incidence of sac-cades to the different stimuli. Most saccades were made to the target (black cross). Occasional errant sac-cades were directed to distractors that were the same shape or colour as the target (black circle, grey cross) more often than to the distractor that shared neither feature with the target (grey circle). In addition, errant saccades exhibited an additional tendency to shift the gaze to the distractor that had been the target in the previous experimental session (grey cross). (*b*) The evolution of activity of a FEF neuron is shown during conjunction search when the target stimulus (black solid line), same-colour distractors (dashed line), same-shape distractors (grey line) and the opposite distractors (dotted line) fell in the receptive field. The range of saccade latencies to the target is indicated on the abscissa. The initial response did not distinguish the target from the various kinds of distractors but the activation for the target rapidly became greater, while the activation for the distractors was reduced. The degree of suppression of the distractor activation varied according to whether the distractors resembled the target or had been the target in the previous session. The vertical scale bar marks 50 spikes s^{-1}. (Modified from Bichot & Schall 1999*a*.)

non-selected distractors corresponded to the pattern of errors that reveal the allocation of attention. Evidently, a template of the target held in memory influenced performance and activity.

During conjunction search, the history of stimulus presentation across sessions also affected the selection process. If an error was made, monkeys showed a significant tendency (in addition to the visual similarity tendency just described) to shift their gaze to the distractors that had been the target in the previous session. Recordings from FEF neurons during trials with correct saccades to the conjunction target revealed a corresponding discrimination among distractors with more activation for distractors that had been the target during the previous session. This effect was evident across sessions that were more than a day apart and persisted throughout the experimental sessions. The longer duration of this influence distinguishes this learning effect from the short-term priming during pop-out searches that lasts for about 10 trials or 30 s in humans (Maljkovic & Nakayama 1994; McPeek et al. 1999) as well as monkeys (Bichot & Schall 1999b).

The source of this contextual modulation observed in the FEF is not known. Recent findings have prompted the suggestion that dorsolateral prefrontal cortex encodes rules for guiding behaviour (e.g. White & Wise 1999; Wallis et al. 2001). The activity of neurons in dorsolateral prefrontal areas rostral to the FEF has been described during visual searching (Rainer et al. 1998; Hasegawa et al. 2000), but the selection was more 'all or none' because the responses began after the selection process was completed. Thus, under these search conditions non-target stimuli did not activate cells in the prefrontal areas 12 and 46. Much more research is needed to understand how arbitrary rules influence saccade target selection.

8.6. Conclusion

The picture that emerges from these experiments is that the visual-selection process occupies a certain amount of time. The activation leading to a saccade-movement activity begins to grow as the selection process is completed and (for reasons that are not clear) the rate of growth of activity leading to the movement varies such that sometimes the gaze shifts sooner and sometimes the gaze shifts later. Due to the delayed and variable growth of the pre-movement activity, the occurrence of a subsequent stimulus can result in adaptive cancellation of the original saccade. Evidence from many studies of event-related potentials also supports the validity of partitioning reaction time into perceptual and response periods (reviewed by Coles et al. 1995).

These two stages—visual selection and response preparation—are distinct and only loosely coupled. The variability of fixation duration described earlier can be explained by variation in the movement preparation process independent of the visual-selection process. In fact, it is possible for the saccade-preparation process to become activated before identification of the currently fixated element and selection of the next target are completed. For example, during visual-search movement neurons with no visual response in the FEF can exhibit partial activation for non-target stimuli that resemble the target (Bichot et al. 2001a). Indeed, the excessive activation of movement neurons can result in premature, erroneous saccades such as those illustrated in Figure 8.1. The independence of visual selection and response preparation is also necessary to explain the production of saccades that are not directed to the location of the selected target. For example, it is possible to withhold a saccade or even to shift the gaze in the direction opposite to a visual target (Hallett & Adams 1980). In monkeys producing antisaccades, visually responsive neurons in the FEF or superior colliculus respond if the target falls in the receptive field and the movement neurons are active for saccades into the movement field if it is a pro- or an anti-saccade (Everling et al. 1999; Everling & Munoz 2000).

To summarize, the evolution of visually evoked activity in the FEF represents the process and outcome of the selection of targets for orientating. This selection process can represent not only the target for an overt gaze shift but also the location of a covert attention shift. Clearly, the visual selection observed in the FEF depends on afferents conveying feature selectivity from the various visual areas. However, recall that the FEF provides extensive feedback connections to the extrastriate visual cortex (Baizer *et al.* 1991; Schall *et al.* 1995*b*; Barone *et al.* 2000) and so we should not overlook the possibility that the state of neural activity in the FEF can influence neural processing in the extrastriate visual cortex. The distinction between visual processing and selection and movement preparation and execution is warranted by neural data and necessary to explain the arbitrary and flexible guidance of movements by vision.

This work was supported by grants R01-EY08890, R01-MH55806, P30-EY08126, the McDonnell-Pew Program in Cognitive Neuroscience and by the McKnight Endowment Fund for Neuroscience.

Macaque monkeys (*Macaca mulatta* and *Macaca radiata*) were used in accordance with NIH guidelines and the policies of the Vanderbilt Animal Care and Use Committee.

References

Bacon, W. F. & Egeth, H. E. 1994 Overriding stimulus-driven attentional capture. *Perception Psychophys.* **55**, 485–496.

Baizer, J. S., Ungerleider, L. G. & Desimone, R. 1991 Organization of visual inputs to the inferior temporal and posterior parietal cortex in macaques. *J. Neurosci.* **11**, 168–190.

Barone, P., Batardiere, A., Knoblauch, K. & Kennedy, H. 2000 Laminar distribution of neurons in extrastriate areas projecting to visual areas V1 and V4 correlates with the hierarchical rank and indicates the operation of a distance rule. *J. Neurosci.* **20**, 3263–3281.

Basso, M. A. & Wurtz, R. H. 1998 Modulation of neuronal activity in superior colliculus by changes in target probability. *J. Neurosci.* **18**, 7519–7534.

Bichot, N. P. & Schall, J. D. 1999*a* Effects of similarity and history on neural mechanisms of visual selection. *Nature Neurosci.* **2**, 549–554.

Bichot, N. P. & Schall, J. D. 1999*b* Saccade target selection in macaque during feature and conjunction visual search. *Vis. Neurosci.* **16**, 81–89.

Bichot, N. P., Schall, J. D. & Thompson, K. G. 1996 Visual feature selectivity in frontal eye fields induced by experience in mature macaques. *Nature* **381**, 697–699.

Bichot, N. P., Chenchal Rao, S. & Schall, J. D. 2001*a* Continuous processing in macaque frontal cortex during visual search. *Neuropsychologia* **39**, 972–982.

Bichot, N. P., Thompson, K. G., Chenchal Rao, S. & Schall, J. D. 2001*b* Reliability of macaque frontal eye field neurons signaling saccade targets during visual search. *J. Neurosci.* **21**, 713–725.

Bruce, C. J. & Goldberg, M. E. 1985 Primate frontal eye fields I: single neurons discharging before saccades. *J. Neurophys.* **53**, 603–635.

Bruce, C. J., Goldberg, M. E., Bushnell, C. & Stanton, G. B. 1985 Primate frontal eye fields II: physiological and anatomical correlates of electrically evoked eye movements. *J. Neurophys.* **54**, 714–734.

Burman, D. D. & Segraves, M. A. 1994 Primate frontal eye field activity during natural scanning eye movements. *J. Neurophys.* **71**, 1266–1271.

Cabel, D. W., Armstrong, I. T., Reingold, E. & Munoz, D. P. 2000 Control of saccade initiation in a countermanding task using visual and auditory stop signals. *Exp. Brain Res.* **133**, 431–441.

Chapman, P. & Underwood, G. 1998 Visual search of driving situations: danger and experience. *Perception* **27**, 951–964.

Chelazzi, L., Duncan, J., Miller, E. K. & Desimone, R. 1998 Responses of neurons in inferior temporal cortex during memory-guided visual search. *J. Neurophys.* **80**, 2918–2940.

Chelazzi, L., Miller, E. K., Duncan, J. & Desimone, R. 1993 A neural basis for visual search in inferior temporal cortex. *Nature* **363**, 345–347.

Coles, M. G. H., Smid, H. G. O. M., Scheffers, M. K. & Otten, L. J. 1995 Mental chronometry and the study of human information processing. In *Electrophysiology of mind: event-related brain potentials and cognition* (ed. M. D. Rugg & M. G. H. Coles), pp. 86–131. Oxford University Press.

Contantinidis, C. & Steinmetz, M. A. 2001 Neuronal responses to area 7a to multiple-stimulus displays. I. Neurons encode the location of the salient stimulus. *Cerebr. Cortex* **11**, 581–591.

Dias, E. C., Kiesau, M. & Segraves, M. A. 1995 Acute activation and inactivation of macaque frontal eye field with GABA-related drugs. *J. Neurophys.* **74**, 2744–2748.

Donders, F. C. 1868 On the speed of mental processes. In *Attention and performance II* (trans. W. G. Koster, 1969), pp. 412–431. Amsterdam, North-Holland.

Dorris, M. C. & Munoz, D. P. 1998 Saccadic probability influences motor preparation signals and time to saccadic initiation. *J. Neurosci.* **18**, 7015–7026.

Dorris, M. C., Pare, M. & Munoz, D. P. 1997 Neuronal activity in monkey superior colliculus related to the initiation of saccadic eye movements. *J. Neurosci.* **17**, 8566–8579.

Duncan, J. & Humphreys, G. W. 1989 Visual search and stimulus similarity. *Psychol. Rev.* **96**, 433–458.

Egeth, H. E. & Yantis, S. 1997 Visual attention: control, representation, and time course. *A. Rev. Psychol.* **48**, 269–297.

Everling, S. & Munoz, D. P. 2000 Neuronal correlates for preparatory set associated with pro-saccades and anti-saccades in the primate frontal eye field. *J. Neurosci.* **20**, 387–400.

Everling, S., Dorris, M. C., Klein, R. M. & Munoz, D. P. 1999 Role of primate superior colliculus in preparation and execution of anti-saccades and pro-saccades. *J. Neurosci.* **19**, 2740–2754.

Felleman, D. J. & Van Essen, D. C. 1991 Distributed hierarchical processing in the primate cerebral cortex. *Cerebral Cortex* **1**, 1–47.

Findlay, J. M. 1997 Saccade target selection during visual search. *Vis. Res.* **37**, 617–631.

Gottlieb, J. P., Kusunoki, M. & Goldberg, M. E. 1998 The representation of visual salience in monkey parietal cortex. *Nature* **391**, 481–484.

Hallett, P. E. & Adams, B. D. 1980 The predictability of saccadic latency in a novel voluntary oculo-motor task. *Vis. Res.* **20**, 329–339.

Hanes, D. P. & Carpenter, R. H. S. 1999 Countermanding saccades in humans: evidence for a race-to-threshold process. *Vis. Res.* **39**, 2777–2791.

Hanes, D. P. & Paré, M. 1998 Neural control of saccade production studied with the countermanding paradigm: superior colliculus. *Soc. Neurosci. Abstr.* **24**, 418.

Hanes, D. P. & Schall, J. D. 1995 Countermanding saccades in macaque. *Vis. Neurosci.* **12**, 929–937.

Hanes, D. P. & Schall, J. D. 1996 Neural control of voluntary movement initiation. *Science* **274**, 427–430.

Hanes, D. P., Thompson, K. G. & Schall, J. D. 1995 Relationship of presaccadic activity in frontal and supplementary eye field to saccade initiation in macaque: Poisson spike train analysis. *Exp. Brain Res.* **103**, 85–96.

Hanes, D. P., Patterson, W. F. & Schall, J. D. 1998 The role of frontal eye field in countermanding saccades: visual, movement and fixation activity. *J. Neurophys.* **79**, 817–834.

Hasegawa, R. P., Matsumoto, M. & Mikami, A. 2000 Search target selection in monkey prefrontal cortex. *J. Neurophysiol.* **84**, 1692–1696.

Hooge, I. T. & Erkelens, C. J. 1996 Control of fixation duration in a simple search task. *Percept. Psychophys.* **58**, 969–976.

Huerta, M. F., Krubitzer, L. A. & Kaas, J. H. 1986 Frontal eye field as defined by intracortical micros-timulation in squirrel monkeys, owl monkeys and macaque monkeys. I. Subcortical connections. *J. Comp. Neurol.* **253**, 415–439.

Huerta, M. F., Krubitzer, L. A. & Kaas, J. H. 1987 Frontal eye field as defined by intracortical micros-timulation in squirrel monkeys, owl monkeys and macaque monkeys. II. Cortical connections. *J. Comp. Neurol.* **265**, 332–361.

Jouve, B., Rosenstiehl, P. & Imbert, M. 1998 A mathematical approach to the connectivity between the cortical visual areas of the macaque monkey. *Cerebral Cortex* **8**, 28–39.

Kim, M. S. & Cave, K. R. 1995 Spatial attention in search for features and feature conjunctions. *Psychol. Sci.* **6**, 376–380.

Logan, G. D. & Cowan, W. B. 1984 On the ability to inhibit thought and action: a theory of an act of control. *Psychol. Rev.* **91**, 295–327.

Luck, S. J., Chelazzi, L., Hillyard, S. A. & Desimone, R. 1997 Neural mechanisms of spatial selective attention in areas V1, V2 and V4 of macaque visual cortex. *J. Neurophys.* **77**, 24–42.

McPeek, R. M., Maljkovic, V. & Nakayama, D. 1999 Saccades require focal attention and are facilitated by a short-term memory system. *Vis. Res.* **39**, 1555–1566.

Maljkovic, V. & Nakayama, K. 1994 Priming of pop-out: I. Role of features. *Memory Cogn* **22**, 657–672.

Maljkovic, V. & Nakayama, K. 1996 Priming of pop-put: II. The role of position. *Perception Psychophys.* **58**, 977–991.

Mohler, C. W., Goldberg, M. E. & Wurtz, R. H. 1973 Visual receptive fields of frontal eye field neurons. *Brain Res.* **61**, 385–389.

Motter, B. C. 1994a Neural correlates of attentive selection for colour or luminance in extrastriate area V4. *J. Neurosci.* **14**, 2178–2189.

Motter, B. C. 1994b Neural correlates of feature selective memory and pop-out in extrastriate area V4. *J. Neurosci.* **14**, 2190–2199.

Motter, B. C. & Belky, E. J. 1998 The guidance of eye movements during active visual search. *Vis. Res.* **38**, 1805–1815.

Munoz, D. P. & Wurtz, R. H. 1993 Fixation cells in monkey superior colliculus. I. Characteristics of cell discharge. *J. Neurophysiol.* **70**, 559–575.

Munoz, D. P. & Wurtz, R. H. 1995 Saccade-related activity in monkey superior colliculus. I. Characteristics of burst and buildup cells. *J. Neurophysiol.* **73**, 2313–2333.

Murthy, A., Thompson, K. G. & Schall, J. D. 2001 Dynamic dissociation of visual selection from saccade programming in frontal eye field. *J. Neurophysiol.* **86**, 2634–2637.

Nodine, C. F. & Krupinski, E. A. 1998 Perceptual skill, radiology expertise, and visual test performance with NINA and WALDO. *Academic Radiol.* **5**, 603–612.

Nodine, C. F., Kundel, H. L., Lauver, S. C. & Toto, L. C. 1996 Nature of expertise in searching mammograms for breast masses. *Academic Radiol.* **3**, 1000–1006.

Ottes, F. P., Van Gisbergen, J. A. M. & Eggermont, J. J. 1987 Collicular involvement in a saccadic colour discrimination task. *Exp. Brain Res.* **66**, 465–478.

Rainer, G., Asaad, W. F. & Miller, E. K. 1998 Selective representation of relevant information by neurons in the primate prefrontal cortex. *Nature* **393**, 577–579.

Riehle, A. & Requin, J. 1993 The predictive value for performance speed of preparatory changes in neuronal activity of the monkey motor and premotor cortex. *Behav. Brain Res.* **53**, 35–49.

Sato, T., Murthy, A., Thompson, K. G. & Schall, J. D. 2001 Search efficiency but not response interference affects visual selection in frontal eye field. *Neuron* **30**, 583–591.

Schall, J. D. 1991 Neuronal activity related to visually guided saccades in the frontal eye fields of rhesus monkeys: comparison with supplementary eye fields. *J. Neurophysiol.* **66**, 559–579.

Schall, J. D. 1997 Visuomotor areas of the frontal lobe. In *Extrastriate cortex of primates.Cerebral cortex*, vol. 12 (ed. K. Rockland, A. Peters & J. H. Kaas), pp. 527–638. New York: Plenum Press.

Schall, J. D. & Hanes, D. P. 1993 Neural basis of saccade target selection in frontal eye field during visual search. *Nature* **366**, 467–469.

Schall, J. D. & Thompson, K. G. 1999 Neural selection and control of visually guided eye movements. *A. Rev. Neurosci.* **22**, 241–259.

Schall, J. D., Hanes, D. P., Thompson, K. G. & King, D. J. 1995a Saccade target selection in frontal eye field of macaque I. Visual and premovement activation. *J. Neurosci.* **15**, 6905–6918.

Schall, J. D., Morel, A., King, D. J. & Bullier, J. 1995b Topography of visual cortical afferents to frontal eye field in macaque: functional convergence and segregation of processing streams. *J. Neurosci.* **15**, 4464–4487.

Schiller, P. H. & Chou, I. H. 1998 The effects of frontal eye, field and dorsomedial frontal cortex lesions on visually guided eye movements. *Nature Neurosci.* **1**, 248–253.

Schiller, P. H. & Chou, I. 2000a The effects of anterior arcuate and dorsomedial frontal cortex lesions on visually guided eye movements in the rhesus monkey: 1. Single and sequential targets. *Vis. Res.* **40**, 1609–1626.

Schiller, P. H. & Chou, I. 2000b The effects of anterior arcuate and dorsomedial frontal cortex lesions on visually guided eye movements: 2. Paired and multiple targets. *Vis. Res.* **40**, 1627–1638.

Schiller, P. H., Sandell, J. H. & Maunsell, J. H. R. 1987 The effect of frontal eye field and superior colliculus lesions on saccadic latencies in the rhesus monkey. *J. Neurophysiol.* **57**, 1033–1049.

Schlag, J. & Schlag-Rey, M. 1984 Visuomotor functions of central thalamus in monkey. II. Unit activity related to visual events, targeting, and fixation. *J. Neurophysiol.* **51**, 1175–1195.

Schmolesky, M. T., Wang, Y., Hanes, D. P., Thompson, K. G., Leutgeb, S., Schall, J. D. & Leventhal, A. G. 1998 Signal timing across the macaque visual system. *J. Neurophysiol.* **79**, 3272–3278.

Segraves, M. A. 1992 Activity of monkey frontal eye field neurons projecting to oculomotor regions of the pons. *J. Neurophysiol.* **68**, 1967–1985.

Segraves, M. A. & Goldberg, M. E. 1987 Functional properties of corticotectal neurons in the monkey's frontal eye fields. *J. Neurophysiol.* **58**, 1387–1419.

Sommer, M. A. & Tehovnik, E. J. 1997 Reversible inactivation of macaque frontal eye field. *Exp. Brain Res.* **116**, 229–249.

Sommer, M. A. & Wurtz, R. H. 1998a Composition and topographic organization of signals sent from the frontal eye field to the superior colliculus. *J. Neurophysiol.* **83**, 1979–2001.

Sommer, M. A. & Wurtz, R. H. 1998b Frontal eye field neurons orthodromically activated from the superior colliculus. *J. Neurophysiol.* **80**, 3331–3335.

Sommer, M. A. & Wurtz, R. H. 2001 Frontal eye field sends delay activity related to movement, memory, and vision to the superior colliculus. *J. Neurophysiol.* **85**, 1673–1685.

Sparks, D. L. 1978 Functional properties of neurons in the monkey superior colliculus: coupling of neuronal activity and saccade onset. *Brain Res.* **156**, 1–16.

Stanton, G. B., Bruce, C. J. & Goldberg, M. E. 1993 Topography of projections to the frontal lobe from the macaque frontal eye fields. *J. Comp. Neurol.* **330**, 286–301.

Stanton, G. B., Bruce, C. J. & Goldberg, M. E. 1995 Topography of projections to posterior cortical areas from the macaque frontal eye fields. *J. Comp. Neurol.* **353**, 291–305.

Sternberg, S. 1969 The discovery of processing stages: extensions of Donders' method. *Acta Psychologica* **30**, 276–315.

Thompson, K. G. & Schall, J. D. 2000 Antecedents and correlates of visual detection and awareness in macaque prefrontal cortex. *Vis. Res.* **40**, 1523–1538.

Thompson, K. G., Hanes, D. P., Bichot, N. P. & Schall, J. D. 1996 Perceptual and motor processing stages identified in the activity of macaque frontal eye field neurons during visual search. *J. Neurophysiol.* **76**, 4040–4055.

Thompson, K. G., Bichot, N. P. & Schall, J. D. 1997 Dissociation of target selection from saccade planning in macaque frontal eye field. *J. Neurophysiol.* **77**, 1046–1050.

Treisman, A. & Sato, S. 1990 Conjunction search revisited. *J. Exp. Psychol. Hum. Perception Performance* **16**, 459–478.

Viviani, P. 1990 Eye movements in visual search: cognitive, perceptual and motor control aspects. In *Eye movements and their role in visual and cognitive processes* (ed. E. Kowler), pp. 353–393. New York: Elsevier.

Wallis, J. D., Anderson, K. C. & Miller, E. K. 2001 Single neurons in prefrontal cortex encode abstract rules. *Nature* **411**, 953–956.

White, I. M. & Wise, S. P. 1999 Rule-dependent neuronal activity in the prefrontal cortex. *Exp. Brain Res.* **126**, 315–335.

Wolfe, J. M. 1998 Visual search. In *Attention* (ed. H. Pashler), pp. 13–74. Hove, UK: Psychological Press.

Yarbus, A. L. 1967 *Eye movements and vision*. New York: Plenum.

Glossary

FEF   frontal eye field

9

Evidence concerning how neurons of the perirhinal, cortex may effect familiarity discrimination

M. W. Brown and Z. I. Bashir

Many studies indicate that recognition memory involves at least two separable processes, familiarity discrimination and recollection. Aspects of what is known of potential neuronal substrates of familiarity discrimination are reviewed. Lesion studies have established that familiarity discrimination for individual visual stimuli is effected by a system centred on the perirhinal cortex of the temporal lobe. The fundamental change that encodes prior occurrence of such stimuli appears to be a reduction in the response of neurons in anterior inferior temporal (including perirhinal) cortex when a stimulus is repeated. The neuronal responses rapidly signal the presence of a novel stimulus, and are evidence of long-lasting learning after a single exposure. Computational modelling indicates that a neuronal network based on such a change in responsiveness is potentially highly efficient in information theoretic terms. Processes that occur in long-term depression within the perirhinal cortex provide candidate synaptic plastic mechanisms for that underlying the change, but such linkage remains to be experimentally established.

9.1. Evidence for the involvement of the perirhinal cortex in recognition memory

Anyone who has known a friend or relative in the early stages of Alzheimer's disease will be aware that one of the distressing manifestations of the condition is the constant repetition of questions and stories by the sufferer. In registering these repetitions the normal observer is using a mechanism that has been impaired in the disease sufferer. In the normal person, the ability to judge what is novel and what is familiar, what has occurred recently and what has never been encountered before, is commonplace and usually effortless. Such judgements of prior occurrence are the central process of recognition memory (Mandler 1980). Recent research has identified what appears to be at least part of the neuronal mechanisms underlying familiarity discrimination (Brown & Xiang 1998; Brown & Aggleton 2001).

This research has indicated a central role in familiarity discrimination for changes in neuronal responses in the perirhinal cortex of the temporal lobe when visual stimuli are seen more than once. The perirhinal cortex (classically, Brodmann's area 35, but more recently redefined to include both areas 35 and 36; Amaral *et al.* 1987; Burwell *et al.* 1995) is a strip of cortex found anteriorly and inferiorly in the medial temporal lobe of primates. It lies lateral to the hippocampal formation to which it provides many inputs (Burwell *et al.* 1995; Suzuki 1996; Burwell & Amaral 1998; Lavenex & Amaral 2000). It also lies medial and anterior to area TE of von Bonin and Bailey (1947), a high-order visual processing area. The perirhinal cortex receives information from widespread areas of the cerebral cortex, including areas involved in visual (notably area TE in monkeys), auditory, somatosensory and olfactory processing, as well as return pathways from the hippocampal formation (Burwell *et al.* 1995; Suzuki 1996; Burwell & Amaral 1998; Lavenex & Amaral 2000). It is similarly placed with broadly equivalent connections in the rodent (Witter *et al.* 1989, 2000; Burwell *et al.* 1995; Shi & Cassell 1997). Thus, it is a multimodal area at the top end of the hierarchy of sensory processing areas (Felleman & Van Essen 1991; Lavenex & Amaral 2000; Witter *et al.* 2000). Indeed, one of its functions has been suggested to be a role in the perception of objects as entities in themselves (Buckley & Gaffan 1998*a*; Murray & Bussey 1999). Such regions, where the sensory processing streams provide information concerning stimulus identity, are well placed for involvement in processes to do with memory for the past history of the stimulus. Indeed, there is evidence that the perirhinal cortex is involved in paired associate learning, and aversive and appetitive conditioning as well as in recognition memory (Murray *et al.* 1993, 1998; Corodimas & LeDoux 1995; Higuchi & Miyashita 1996; Suzuki 1996; Buckley & Gaffan 1998*b*; Murray & Bussey 1999). This review is concerned with the functions of the perirhinal cortex in the familiarity discrimination component of recognition memory. The potential contributions of the hippocampal system to spatial and recollective aspects of recognition memory have been reviewed elsewhere (Aggleton & Brown 1999; Brown & Aggleton 2001).

The crucial role of the perirhinal cortex in visual recognition memory has been established by ablation studies, chiefly in the monkey (Zola-Morgan *et al.* 1989; Gaffan & Murray 1992; Meunier *et al.* 1993, 1996; Suzuki *et al.* 1993), but also in the rat (Otto & Eichenbaum 1992; Mumby & Pinel 1994; Ennaceur *et al.* 1996). Thus, there is gross impairment of tasks, particularly visual delayed matching or non-matching to sample tasks, that depend for their successful performance upon judgement of the prior occurrence of infrequently repeated individual items (Murray 1996; Murray & Bussey 1999; Brown & Aggleton 2001). Although the degree of impairment following hippocampal lesions is still in dispute, all groups agree that the impairment following perirhinal lesions is far greater than that following either hippocampal, amygdalar or prefrontal lesions (Aggleton *et al.* 1986; Mumby *et al.* 1992, 1995; Zola-Morgan & Squire 1993; Zola-Morgan *et al.* 1994; Alvarez *et al.* 1995; Murray 1996; Meunier *et al.* 1997; Murray & Mishkin 1998; Aggleton & Brown 1999; Beason-Held *et al.* 1999; Murray & Bussey 1999; Zola *et al.* 2000; Baxter & Murray 2001; Brown & Aggleton 2001). By contrast, if task complexity is increased, particularly if a judgement dependent on spatial memory is required, then hippocampal lesions produce major impairments (O'Keefe & Nadel 1978; Morris *et al.* 1982; Aggleton *et al.* 1986; Eichenbaum *et al.* 1994, 1996; Gaffan 1994; Liu & Bilkey 1998; Murray *et al.* 1998; Aggleton & Brown 1999; Brown & Aggleton 2001). In summary, there is strong evidence from primate and rat ablation studies that the perirhinal cortex is a nodal point of a system that is concerned with judgements concerning the prior occurrence of individual visual items.

9.2. Evidence concerning candidate neuronal mechanisms of familiarity discrimination

Given the crucial involvement of the perirhinal cortex in familiarity discrimination, are there candidate neuronal mechanisms that could explain the behavioural results? Any mechanism must be capable of explaining learning that occurs in a single exposure, must be long-lasting, and must have high capacity, in particular the ability to remember the prior occurrence of potentially large numbers of complex stimuli at the same time. The mechanism should be manifest in both trained and untrained situations because familiarity discrimination itself (and correspondingly its counterpart process, novelty detection) should not need to be learned.

It must also occur for stimuli encountered by the subject for the first and second times, and not merely for stimuli that are being frequently encountered and hence are highly familiar. Evidence for potential mechanisms comes from studies of the response characteristics of perirhinal neurons. Indeed, more than one potential substrate (correlate of relative familiarity) has been discovered by recording the responses of neurons during the performance of recognition memory tasks by monkeys (Gross *et al.* 1979; Fuster & Jervey 1981; Brown *et al.* 1987; Miller & Desimone 1994; Xiang & Brown 1997; Brown & Xiang 1998). These putative candidate substrates are response differences between match and mismatch trials, delay activity, response reductions or response increments on stimulus repetition, and synchronized neuronal firing; see Figure 9.1. However, of these mechanisms, only one, response reductions on stimulus repetition, has so far been demonstrated to have the necessary properties and to occur in a variety of behavioural situations (Brown & Xiang 1998; Brown & Aggleton 2001).

The first discovered difference in responsiveness of inferior temporal neurons in a recognition memory task was that between responses on match and mismatch trials while monkeys performed a delayed matching task (Gross *et al.* 1979). Such differences have been commonly reported in tasks where a match/mismatch judgement must be made to a single target stimulus on each trial and the target stimuli are selected from a small number of frequently repeating items (e.g. Gross *et al.* 1979; Mikami & Kubota 1980; Brown 1982; Riches *et al.* 1991; Nakamura & Kubota 1995; Young *et al.* 1997). However, such differences do not signal whether

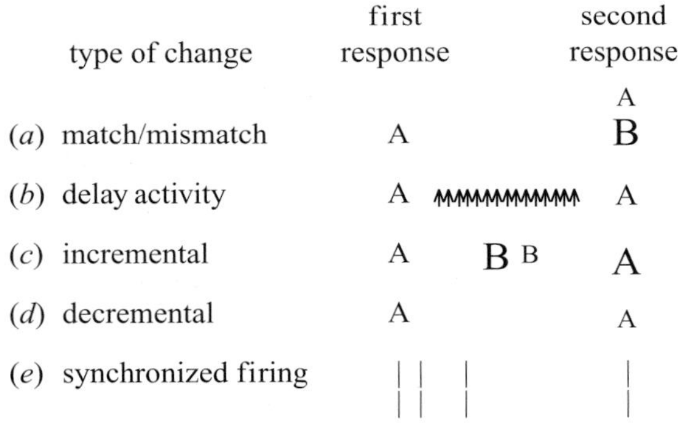

Fig. 9.1. Schematic representation of types of neuronal activity change found in perirhinal cortex during performance of familiarity discrimination tasks. The size of letter represents the magnitude of response to an individual stimulus. A change in size denotes a change in response on repetition. (*a*) Match/mismatch response differences. Neuronal responses may be larger or smaller on match compared with non-match trials in tasks where the repetition of one target stimulus must be judged on each trial and small stimulus sets are used. (*b*) Delay activity. The sustained activity between the initial presentation of a stimulus and its repetition is represented by the arrows. (*c*) Response enhancement. When an animal is taught that responding to the repetition of a target stimulus leads to reward whereas other repeated stimuli do not, responses to the repetition of the target stimulus may be enhanced. (*d*) Response reductions. The response when a stimulus has been encountered before is reduced compared with its first presentation. In fact, there is more than one type of such response reductions, with there being three different, commonly found patterns of neuronal response on stimulus repetition (Xiang & Brown 1998*b*). These different patterns of response imply that there is more than one underlying type of synaptic plasticity responsible for the response changes (Fahy *et al.* 1993; Brown & Xiang 1998; Xiang & Brown 1998*b*). (*e*) Simultaneous firing. The approximate coincidence of the spikes of two individual neurons could carry information concerning the familiarity of a stimulus, for example if such coincidences varied between the first and second presentations of the stimulus.

a particular stimulus is novel or familiar, merely that the trial type is match or non-match (Riches *et al.* 1991). Accordingly, such differences cannot provide a substrate of general familiarity discrimination (Riches *et al.* 1991; Brown & Xiang 1998; Brown & Aggleton 2001).

The next discovered potential mechanism, delay activity, is a persistent change in neuronal firing that occurs in the delay interval after the presentation of a stimulus in the acquisition phase of a memory task, and lasts until the occurrence of the same or a different stimulus in the subsequent behavioural choice/decision phase (Fuster & Jervey 1981; Riches *et al.* 1991; Miller *et al.* 1993; Colombo & Gross 1994; Miller & Desimone 1994; Desimone 1996). Delay activity has not been demonstrated under conditions that require long-term rather than short-term memory—that is, where more than one stimulus must be remembered at a time—or when the eventual occurrence of the choice phase of a task is unpredictable: i.e. may not occur until after a delay of many minutes filled with other activities (Desimone 1996; Brown & Xiang 1998; Brown & Aggleton 2001). Thus, delay activity has not been shown to persist over long periods of time, nor has it been shown that such a system has a high information storage capacity. It may rather represent a substrate of an attentive or short-term memory mechanism that could contribute to short-term recognition memory (Desimone 1996; Brown & Xiang 1998).

Similarly, responses that increment on repetition, that is, they are larger to a repeated stimulus than to one occurring for the first time, have only been observed when an animal has been trained to discriminate between a specific stimulus that, when repeated, signals the availability of reward and other stimuli that, when repeated, do not signal the availability of reward (Miller & Desimone 1994). Again, these response increments have only been demonstrated under conditions where only one stimulus need be held in the mind at a time. In such situations, as already indicated above, short-term memory and attentive mechanisms provide alternative means of solving the task (Brown & Xiang 1998; Brown & Aggleton 2001). Furthermore, response increments have not been shown to occur when time delays are long.

By contrast, response reductions on stimulus repetition have been found under a variety of conditions (Brown *et al.* 1987; Riches *et al.* 1991; Eskandar *et al.* 1992; Fahy *et al.* 1993; Li *et al.* 1993; Miller *et al.* 1993; Sobotka & Ringo 1993; Miller & Desimone 1994; Zhu *et al.* 1995; Xiang & Brown 1998*b*). An example is shown in Figure 9.2. The detailed properties of such neuronal response reductions on stimulus repetition have been extensively reviewed elsewhere (Brown 1996; Desimone 1996; Eichenbaum *et al.* 1996; Ringo 1996; Brown & Xiang 1998; Suzuki & Eichenbaum 2000; Brown & Aggleton 2001) and so will be only briefly presented here. In monkeys they have been shown to occur under closely controlled conditions and are not explicable by changes in alertness, attention, motivation, eye movements or other behavioural changes (Brown & Xiang 1998). Such response reductions occur after a single exposure to an initially novel stimulus even if the ensuing delay before the recurrence of the stimulus is 24 h or more (Fahy *et al.* 1993; Xiang & Brown 1998*b*; e.g. Figure 9.3). Critically, these reductions are found even when many stimuli must be remembered simultaneously and when intervals between repetitions are filled with presentations of other stimuli to which attention is being paid, so that long-term memory mechanisms are essential to task performance (Xiang & Brown 1998*b*). No other type of response change capable of signalling information adequate to explain recognition memory processes has been reported in perirhinal cortex under conditions that necessitate the use of long-term memory. The high capacity of the system is demonstrated by the finding of such reductions for repetitions of new stimuli even when an animal has already seen many hundreds of such items (Xiang & Brown 1998*b*). Moreover, neuronal response reductions are found whether or not an animal is using the stimulus repetitions to obtain reward, and in rats as well as monkeys

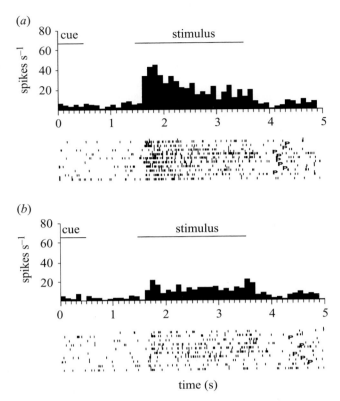

Fig. 9.2. Example response reduction on stimulus repetition. Illustrated are the cumulated peristimulus-time histograms and rasters showing the times of occurrence of individual action potentials for trials on each of which one of 10 different unfamiliar pictures was presented for either the first (*a*) or the second (*b*) time. Note the response reduction with stimulus repetition. The neuron's activity was recorded from perirhinal cortex while pictures were presented to a monkey performing a serial recognition memory task in which juice rewards were obtained for left-sided presses for first presentations and right-sided presses for repeat presentations. One picture appeared on each trial and the types of trial were pseudorandomly ordered so that the occurrence of first and repeat presentations were not predictable by the monkey. Control trials (see Fahy *et al.* 1993) established that the response reduction was not explicable either by the animal's behavioural responses or by changes in eye movements; all correct trials were rewarded. (Reproduced with permission from Fahy *et al.* (1993).)

(Riches *et al.* 1991; Fahy *et al.* 1993; Zhu *et al.* 1995; Brown & Xiang 1998). As response reductions occur even in situations where an animal has received no specific training on a recognition memory task, they must be endogenous rather than induced by training. Personal experience indicates that any general familiarity discrimination mechanism needs to be able operate automatically and without direct or immediate feedback from reward systems.

Far less is known concerning the potential involvement of synchronized neuronal firing in familiarity discrimination. It has been hypothesized that such coincident or near coincident firing may carry important information in other systems (Abeles 1982; Singer & Gray 1995). Significant interactions have been revealed by cross-correlating the simultaneously recorded activity of pairs of neurons in monkeys (Gawne & Richmond 1993; Xiang & Brown 1997;

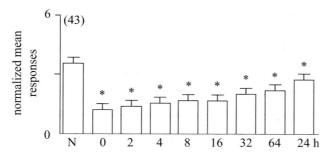

Fig. 9.3. Population memory span. Illustrated are the population mean (+s.e.m.) responses of 43 neurons recorded in anterior inferior temporal and entorhinal cortex to the first presentations of novel stimuli (N) and their repetition after varying numbers of intervening trials on which other stimuli were shown. The final bar (24 h) represents the response to stimuli not seen since the previous day. An asterisk implies a significant reduction in response compared to N. Ordinate: mean firing rate in 0.5 s after stimulus onset normalized relative to prestimulus activity (= 1). The data were obtained while monkeys performed a serial recognition memory task; for details see Xiang & Brown (1998*b*).

Brown & Xiang 1998; Erickson *et al.* 2001). These interactions suggest that information of potential importance to recognition memory is being carried by relationships between the activities of perirhinal neurons. However, the incidence of simultaneous (within 6 ms) action potentials produced by simultaneously recorded pairs of neurons is very low. Moreover, more crucially, the timing of the occurrence of such simultaneous firing is typically late rather than early after stimulus onset, and is usually more closely related to the occurrence of an animal's behavioural response than to the stimulus onset itself (Brown 2000; J.-Z. Xiang and M. W. Brown, unpublished observations). Accordingly, the information carried by such firing provides a much slower signal than is provided by the change in firing rate of the individual neurons.

9.3. Evidence for synaptic changes occurring in perirhinal cortex

Although the ablation studies establish the importance of perirhinal cortex for familiarity discrimination, and the recording studies establish that there are neurons within this cortex whose response reductions on stimulus repetition signal the type of information that is required to judge prior occurrence for individual stimuli, none of the evidence reviewed so far establishes where the synaptic changes that underlie the neuronal response changes may first be generated. However, important evidence is provided by the speed and incidence of response reductions that survive over long delays between the first and subsequent occurrence of a stimulus. Although in monkeys neuronal response reductions are found more posteriorly, in earlier stages of the visual processing stream, these reductions do not survive more than some seconds or when more than a very few other stimuli are shown before a particular stimulus is repeated (Baylis & Rolls 1987; Maunsell *et al.* 1991; Miller *et al.* 1991; Vogels *et al.* 1995). Correspondingly, such response reductions cannot explain those found in anterior area TE and perirhinal cortex, that survive many intervening stimulus presentations and delay intervals of many hours (Xiang & Brown 1998*b*). Responses are reduced with stimulus repetition for *ca.* 25% of all recorded neurons in anterior TE, perirhinal cortex, and entorhinal cortex (Miller *et al.* 1993; Xiang & Brown 1998*b*). For over 50% of the neurons whose responses change on stimulus repetition, such reductions are found even after a 24 h delay, the incidence of such long memory spans being highest in perirhinal cortex (Xiang & Brown 1998*b*). Ablation of entorhinal cortex in monkeys produces only a transient impairment of delayed non-matching to sample (Meunier *et al.* 1993; Leonard *et al.* 1995), so that the critical change cannot be dependent on entorhinal cortex. Thus, the critical response changes must be first generated in anterior TE and perirhinal cortex, or be fed back to these areas from further on in the processing stream.

A remarkable property of the response reductions is the speed with which they signal prior occurrence. Latency measures across all the neurons displaying response reductions in anterior area TE in the monkey have established that within 90 ms of stimulus onset there is a significant difference in the population's activity, dependent on whether the stimulus is novel or previously seen (Xiang & Brown 1998*b*). In many neurons the latency of the response change is the same (to within the experimental error of 10–20 ms) as the latency of the neuron's visual response (Fahy *et al.* 1993; Miller *et al.* 1993; Xiang & Brown 1998*b*; e.g. Figure 9.4). The speed of this change means that the initial change in response cannot be being generated as a result of feedback from areas such as the hippocampus or prefrontal cortex. Recordings in the monkey hippocampus and prefrontal cortex support this view. Thus, the incidence of response changes on the repetition of infrequently encountered individual stimuli in the hippocampus is less than 1% (Rolls *et al.* 1989, 1993; Riches *et al.* 1991; Xiang & Brown 1998*b*). As for inferior temporal cortex, it is important to note that other hippocampal changes have been shown in rats as well as monkeys for highly familiar, frequently repeated stimuli

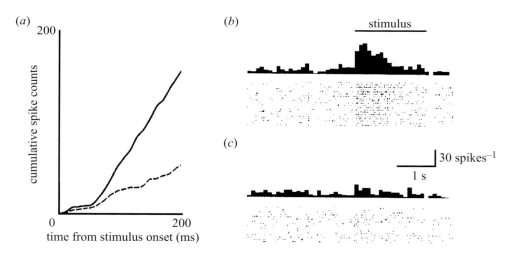

Fig. 9.4. Speed of processing. (*a*) The cumulated action potential counts after stimulus onset (time = 0) for 20 novel (continuous line) and 20 familiar (dashed line) pictures for a neuron recorded in area TE. Note that the divergence of the counts occurs early (*ca.* 75 ms) and at approximately the same latency as the neuron starts to respond (shown by the increase in slope of the line for the novel trials). Peristimulus-time histograms and rasters for 20 novel (*b*) and 20 familiar (*c*) pictures for a neuron recorded in area TE. The data were obtained while a monkey performed a serial recognition memory task; for details see Xiang & Brown (1998*b*). Such cumulative counts were normalized for each neuron and then subjected to an analysis of variance across all the neurons whose responses changed on stimulus repetition to establish the population differential latency in response to novel and familiar stimuli.

where the occurrence of only one stimulus need be remembered at a time (Riches *et al.* 1991; Colombo & Gross 1994; Eichenbaum *et al.* 1996; Hampson *et al.* 1999; Wiebe & Staubli 1999). However, it has been shown in monkeys that these responses do not reliably signal information about the familiarity or novelty of infrequently encountered individual stimuli (Riches *et al.* 1991), and so cannot form a basis for general familiarity discrimination. Moreover, the latencies of the changes in monkey hippocampal neuronal responses to infrequently repeated stimuli are long compared with those in anterior TE and perirhinal cortex (Rolls *et al.* 1993; Xiang & Brown 1998*b*). The incidence of response changes on stimulus repetition is much higher in certain parts of monkey prefrontal cortex, but again the latencies of these changes are much longer than in temporal cortex (Miller *et al.* 1996; Xiang & Brown 1998*a*; Miller 1999). Again, although changes in neuronal responses on stimulus repetition have been described in subcortical regions, such as the monkey basal forebrain nucleus (Rolls *et al.* 1982; Wilson & Rolls 1990), these changes occur with a longer latency than those in anterior inferior temporal and perirhinal cortex (Brown & Xiang 1998). Additionally, it seems implausible that the relatively small number of neurons involved in such subcortical areas could have the information-processing capacity to themselves first discriminate amongst hundreds of complex visual stimuli: such capacity is a prerequisite for the judgement of the prior occurrence of such stimuli. (Indeed, it is important to note that there is evidence of such capacity for area TE and perirhinal cortex.) Thus, there is no evidence that the initial response reductions on stimulus repetition are fed back to anterior TE and perirhinal cortex from other brain regions.

Because, as indicated above, there is no evidence that the response reductions can arise as a result of feed-forward signals from more posterior visual areas, at least the initial reductions in response must be being generated in anterior TE and/or perirhinal cortex. For visual processing, ablation experiments cannot easily decide between anterior TE and perirhinal cortex as ablating TE de-afferents perirhinal cortex. The response changes occur at shorter latency in anterior TE than in perirhinal cortex, but the memory spans of the response changes tend to be longer in perirhinal cortex than anterior TE. Thus, there is good evidence from the monkey that response changes are generated within the region encompassing anterior TE and perirhinal cortex. Moreover, the recording data provide some evidence in favour of changes being generated in both anterior TE and perirhinal cortex. Alongside this, the available evidence from lesion studies provides the best evidence for the critical region being the perirhinal cortex, but without excluding the involvement of area TE.

9.4. Evidence from computational modelling for the feasibility of using neuronal response reductions as a basis for familiarity discrimination

Assuming that neuronal response reductions in perirhinal cortex provide the substrate for familiarity discrimination, could such a system explain human capabilities? Human abilities are very impressive in the laboratory as well as in everyday life, and include speed, accuracy and huge capacity (Standing 1973; Seeck *et al.* 1997; Hintzman *et al.* 1998). Recent computational modelling based on the observed properties of perirhinal response reductions has established the plausibility of such changes as a substrate (Bogacz *et al.* 1999, 2001). The basic premise of the modelling is that individual synapses undergo a plastic, use-dependent change upon their initial activation by a stimulus. This synaptic change stores the prior occurrence of the individual stimulus. In the models, the necessary synaptic changes could be effected by processes determined at individual synapses, such as those that are utilized by long-term potentiation or LTD (Ito 1989; Bliss & Collingridge 1993; Linden 1994; Bear & Abraham 1996; Kemp & Bashir 2001; Figure 9.5). On this basis, such models can be made to operate using biologically plausible learning rules and connectivity.

Theoretical calculations and simulations indicate that under optimal conditions the capacity of such models to discriminate the familiarity of stimuli is potentially very large: the number of stimuli whose familiarity can be judged is proportional to the number of modifiable synapses (Bogacz 2001; Bogacz et al. 2001). Thus, if it is assumed, based on data from Insausti et al. (1998) and Xiang & Brown (1998b), that in the human perirhinal cortex there are ca. 10^7 neurons that judge familiarity and each has ca. 10^4 synapses, the Bogacz et al. (2001) model can be calculated as being able to discriminate the familiarity of ca. 10^9 stimuli with an error rate of 1%. This capacity corresponds to that required to register and remember with high accuracy the occurrence of a new picture every ca. 3 s over a lifetime of 100 years. It is possible to achieve such a high capacity because the network is required to supply as its output only the relative familiarity of a stimulus. Correspondingly, the number of neurons required is less than 0.1% of those in the whole cerebral cortex. As the output required is not complex, such a network can potentially arrive at a decision within milliseconds. Thus, for a relatively small outlay, the brain can possess a system that signals the novelty or familiarity of a stimulus with high speed and accuracy.

In fact, several different network architectures can potentially enable familiarity discrimination to be performed rapidly and accurately with the capacity to make familiarity

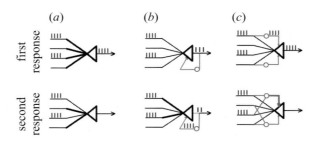

Fig. 9.5. Computational models for familiarity discrimination. The fundamental synaptic changes for three possible models are illustrated schematically: (a) based on anti-Hebbian learning (in which the primary change is a weakening of synaptic strength, for example as in LTD), (b) based on Hebbian learning (in which the primary change is an increase of synaptic strength, for example as in long-term potentiation), and (c) based on Hebbian learning between inhibitory interneurons and excitatory neurons. Triangles represent excitatory neurons and circles inhibitory interneurons. Horizontal lines on the left side of each diagram denote inputs to the network, that is, axons of neurons whose activity encodes visual stimuli, that on the right of the output. Vertical lines representing spikes indicate that the corresponding neuron is active, a lack of spikes that it is inactive. The thickness of an input line indicates the strength of the synaptic connection. The upper row of diagrams illustrates the synaptic strengths and neuronal responses for a novel stimulus, and the lower row of diagrams those values after modification and when the stimulus is presented again (i.e. is familiar). In order to maintain the overall level of excitability of a network and to maximize its efficiency, in all cases compensatory changes are made in the strengths of unstimulated synapses (not illustrated). The Hebbian model (b) uses increased inhibition to prevent there being increased responses for repeated stimuli. Precise details of an implementation of the Hebbian model are given in Bogacz et al. (2001).

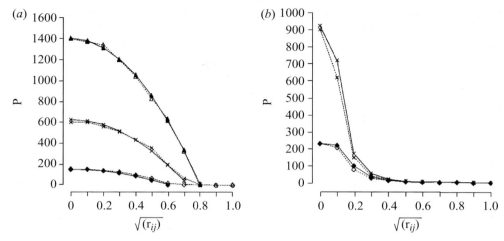

Fig. 9.6. The influence of correlation on capacity. Illustrated are the results of simulations and theoretical predictions of the number of stimuli (patterns: P) that can be stored by networks employing anti-Hebbian (*a*) or Hebbian (*b*) learning rules for different values (r_{ij}) of the mean coefficient of correlation between their responses. (In (*a*) open diamonds, $n = 100$; crosses with dashed line, $n = 200$; open triangles, $n = 300$; filled diamonds, $n = 100$ (predicted); crosses with solid line, $n = 200$ (predicted); filled triangles, $n = 300$ (predicted). In (*b*) open diamonds, $n = 100$ simulation; filled diamonds, $n = 100$ prediction; crosses with dashed line, $n = 200$ simulation; crosses with solid line, $n = 200$ prediction.) Note that the storage capacity of the computational models is markedly reduced if the responses of the neurons are correlated with each other. For the Bogacz *et al.* (2001) model, and for other models using increases in synaptic efficacy (Hebbian learning) as the fundamental storage mechanism, both theoretical calculations and simulations indicate that capacity falls off rapidly even for very small values of r_{ij}. By contrast, if synaptic efficacy is reduced for active synapses (anti-Hebbian learning), then capacity is relatively little affected even at moderate values of the correlation coefficient. Note that the square root of r_{ij} is plotted on the abscissa.

judgements for large numbers of stimuli. However, the particular architectures and learning rules have major influences both on the maximum capacity of the model and on whether the types of responses simulated in the model mirror those observed in the real brain (Bogacz 2001; Bogacz *et al.* 2001). Simulations of different models have recently revealed that the capacity of a model depends crucially on the degree of correlation between the responses of the individual neurons to the incoming stimuli; see Figure 9.6. Clearly, if all the neurons responded in the same way to each different stimulus, the capacity of the whole model could be no more than the capacity of one of the individual component neurons, and would be correspondingly very low. It is therefore essential that the mechanisms within the network act to de-correlate responses so that individual neurons can make independent calculations of the familiarity of a stimulus. All previously published computational networks for discriminating familiarity have used synaptic enhancement as the fundamental synaptic change (Bogacz *et al.* 1999, 2001; Sohal & Hasselmo 2000; Bogacz 2001; Norman & O'Reilly 2001). (The models also employ some form of synaptic weakening of relatively unstimulated synapses to maintain a constant overall level of network excitability.) In fact, within perirhinal cortex, response increments on stimulus repetition are unusual and unimpressive in magnitude (Li *et al.* 1993; Xiang & Brown 1998*b*). Such response increments are an essential feature of models that combine feature detection (learning a representation) with familiarity discrimination, as the increased responses are designed to signal (represent) the presence of a particular stimulus (Sohal & Hasselmo 2000; Norman & O'Reilly 2001). However, if the representation has not yet been learnt and hence feature extraction is incomplete, the responses of the network's neurons are necessarily not independent (and hence are correlated). For this reason, simulations indicate that these models have a capacity that is greatly reduced compared with that theoretically possible when responses are uncorrelated (Bogacz 2001).

In the published Bogacz *et al.* (2001) model, the fundamental synaptic change was one of enhancement on stimulus repetition, with response increments being prevented by network connections that increased inhibition for repeated stimuli. This architecture was chosen as it used learning rules based on those that have been widely established in the real brain and resulted in neuronal responses that mimicked those observed in the real perirhinal cortex. Nevertheless, it remains necessary for correlations between responses to be very low ($r_{ij} < 0.05$) for a high capacity to be achieved by this model (Bogacz 2001; see Figure 9.6). However, if the primary synaptic change is decremental rather than incremental, the neuronal responses tend to become less rather than more correlated as a result of the synaptic change that stores the occurrence. Correspondingly, the capacity of the network is far less affected by initial correlations between the responses of its neurons (Bogacz 2001; see Figure 9.6). The reason for this difference may be understood in principle from the following considerations. Fundamentally, if an incremental change is used the network moves in the direction of feature extraction, that is, neurons responsive to a particular stimulus feature tend to become more responsive to it when it recurs in the future, while (through compensatory mechanisms) originally less responsive neurons become even less responsive. Such an outcome is favourable to building a representation by feature extraction. However, as shown by simulations, a familiarity discrimination network is far more efficient if feature extraction has already been completed and the responses of its component neurons are de-correlated, that is, essentially, the neurons of the network act to emphasize what is particular rather than what is commonplace in a stimulus (Bogacz 2001). Thus, modelling provides an explanation for the observed direction of response change (reductions rather than increments) on stimulus repetition in perirhinal cortex. The counterpart of this direction of change is that for a novel stimulus the system generates a large signal which can potentially be used to allow further processing of the novel stimulus elsewhere (possibly including the setting up of a new representation outside the familiarity discrimination network).

Thus, computational modelling demonstrates that neuronal response reductions in perirhinal cortex could potentially be used as a basis for familiarity discrimination: the necessary speed, accuracy and capacity are theoretically achievable. The models rely on activity-dependent, synapse-specific plasticity. Plastic mechanisms that do not produce changes that are localized to specific synapses would result in a catastrophic loss of capacity. Moreover, as measurements in perirhinal cortex indicate that there are many more excitatory than inhibitory synapses (Thompson *et al.* 2001), a high capacity can only be achieved by having modifiable excitatory synapses. Both long-term potentiation and LTD rely on activity-dependent, synapse-specific plastic mechanisms. The above-presented arguments based on computational modelling indicate that employing as the primary plastic mechanism one that reduces synaptic efficacy is likely to prove more efficient than employing one that enhances efficacy. This raises the question as to whether there is evidence for appropriate decremental candidate plastic mechanisms in perirhinal cortex.

9.5. Evidence for decremental synaptic plastic changes in rat perirhinal cortical slices

Activity-dependent LTD of synaptic transmission has been shown to occur in many different regions of the central nervous system (Linden 1994; Bear & Abraham 1996; Kemp & Bashir 2001), and to utilize a variety of different mechanisms of induction and expression. In this section mechanisms of LTD that have recently been identified in adult rat perirhinal cortex *in vitro* will be reviewed.

(a) Glutamate receptor-dependent LTD

Most fast synaptic communication within the central nervous system occurs via the release of the neurotransmitter glutamate acting on a variety of different receptors. Thus, the modulation of glutamatergic transmission is an appropriate starting point in addressing the mechanisms that may underlie the changes in signalling that occur during learning and memory. Glutamate receptors consist of ionotropic (AMPA, NMDA, and kainate, named after their pharmacological agonists) and mGlu subgroups. Synaptic plasticity induced by various means and in different regions of the central nervous system is often dependent on the synaptic activation of NMDA receptors. Consistent with this, NMDA receptor activation in rat perirhinal cortical slices leads to the induction of synaptic plastic changes, either long-term potentiation or LTD according to the pattern of stimulation given (Bilkey 1996; Ziakopoulos *et al.* 1999). Interestingly, however, mGlu receptors play a vital role in perirhinal LTD and it is findings relating to the role of these receptors that will now be discussed. These receptors are G-protein coupled and consist of three classes: mGlu groups I, II, and III based on their pharmacological profile, sequence homology and signalling cascades. Group I receptors are coupled to inositol phospholipid hydrolysis, while group II and group III receptors are negatively coupled to adenylyl cyclase (Conn & Pin 1997; De Blasi *et al.* 2001).

Activation of mGlu receptors by bath application of appropriate pharmacological agonists has been examined *in vitro* to test whether these receptors have a potential role in the induction of lasting synaptic depression (McCaffery *et al.* 1999). Agonists of group I (3,5-dihydroxyphenyl-glycine) and group II mGlu receptors ((2S,2'R,3'R)-2-(2',3'-dicarboxycyclopropyl)glycine) each produced LTD of excitatory synaptic transmission in perirhinal cortex (McCaffery *et al.* 1999). The application of mGlu receptor agonists has also been shown to result in LTD in other regions of the central nervous system, including subfield CA1 of the hippocampus (Fitzjohn *et al.* 1999; Overstreet *et al.* 1997; Palmer *et al.* 1997; Schnabel *et al.* 1999; Huber *et al.* 2000), dentate gyrus (O'Mara *et al.* 1995; Huang *et al.* 1999) and prefrontal cortex (Otani *et al.* 1999). In CA1 it is most probable that this form of LTD relies on activation of the mGlu5 subtype receptor, because LTD is also induced by the selective mGlu5 agonist CHPG (Palmer *et al.* 1997). At present, however, it is not known which of the group I subtypes (mGlu1/5) or which of the group II subtypes (mGlu2/3) are involved in mGlu receptor-induced LTD in perirhinal cortex.

(b) Activity-dependent LTD

As pharmacological activation of mGlu receptors produced LTD, it was probable that synapse-specific, activity-dependent LTD would also involve activation of these receptors. Indeed, in perirhinal cortex *in vitro*, group I and group II mGlu receptor activation as well as

NMDA receptor activation was found to be necessary for the production of LTD when this was induced by LFS (1 Hz stimulation; 200 stimuli) in neurons voltage clamped at −70 mV (Cho *et al.* 2000). By contrast, group II mGlu receptor activation was not required for LTD when this was induced by LFS paired with depolarization to −40 mV. One explanation for the voltage dependence of the involvement of group II mGlu receptors in LTD is that a synergy exists between group I and group II mGlu receptors (Schoepp *et al.* 1996; Mistry *et al.* 1998). This synergy can enhance the calcium release from intracellular stores that normally results from activation of group I mGlu receptors (Cho *et al.* 2000). Thus, when calcium influx resulting from NMDA receptor activation is limited, for example, at resting membrane potentials (−70 mV), the mGlu receptor synergy may provide the extra calcium required for LTD. However, the mGlu receptor synergy may be unnecessary for LTD when calcium influx from NMDA receptor activation is enhanced, as it is at depolarized membrane potentials (−40 mV) (see Figure 9.7).

Thus, the mechanisms of induction of LTD discovered in perirhinal cortical slices are interesting for a number of reasons. First, there is only one other report of activity-dependent LTD

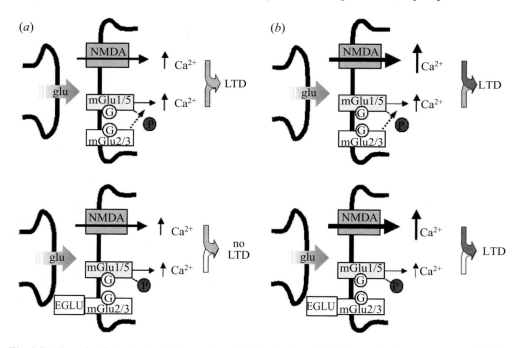

Fig. 9.7. The role of glutamate (glu) receptors in the induction of LTD (based on data from rat perirhinal slices). (*a*) At −70 mV calcium ion influx through NMDA receptor channels is minimized by a voltage-dependent magnesium block. Group II mGlu receptors (mGlu2/3) enhance the calcium mobilization due to group I mGlu receptor (mGlu1/5) activation by a mechanism that may rely on mGlu1/5 dephosphorylation. The combination of NMDA and mGlu receptor-mediated calcium mobilization results in the induction of LTD. Blocking group II mGlu receptors prevents the synergy between mGlu receptors and reduces the calcium signal. This prevents the induction of LTD. (*b*) At −40 mV calcium ion influx through NMDA receptor channels is increased due to the removal of the voltage-dependent magnesium block. Under these conditions, whilst blocking group II mGlu receptor activation with EGLU ((S)-alpha-ethylglutamate) reduces the mGlu-dependent calcium signal, it does not block the induction of LTD because there is still a sufficient rise in calcium ion concentration to induce LTD. The G in a circle represents 'G protein'.

that requires activation of both NMDA and mGlu receptors; in the great majority of forms of LTD so far investigated, induction of LTD is dependent either on NMDA receptors alone or on mGlu receptors alone (Kemp & Bashir 2001). This may mean that the mechanisms of LTD that pertain in perirhinal cortex may be restricted to a specialized subset of brain regions. Second, differences in experimental conditions in perirhinal cortex can dramatically alter the mechanisms underlying the induction of LTD. Whilst this has not yet been tested in other brain regions, such a property may provide explanation for some of the discrepancies between the reported involvement or lack of involvement of different mGlu receptors in LTD both *in vitro* and *in vivo* (Kemp & Bashir 2001). Given the dependency on a neuron's membrane potential of mGlu receptor involvement, it will be interesting to investigate *in vitro* whether fluctuations in membrane potential that occur under physiological conditions *in vivo*—such as during theta or gamma oscillations—will have similar determining effects on the involvement of group II mGlu receptors in LTD. Studies to date *in vitro* have utilized relatively prolonged stimulation (lasting minutes) in order to induce experimental LTD. However, the decrement that occurs *in vivo* in monkeys with stimulus repetition is observable even when a stimulus is repeated within *ca.* 1 s (Miller *et al.* 1993). Thus, it will be important to test whether neuronal activity of the type that occurs *in vivo* can also induce LTD *in vitro*, and whether such differences in induction protocols alter the underlying mechanisms employed. Additionally, if the involvement of mGlu receptor-dependent LTD mechanisms in recognition memory is to be established, it will be crucial to test the role of mGlu receptors in tasks requiring such memory and in the neuronal response decrements that occur in these tasks.

(c) Acetylcholine receptor-dependent LTD

Although the majority of studies in a variety of regions of the central nervous system show that LTD can be blocked by either NMDA or mGlu receptor antagonists, there are some studies which show a requirement for activation of other, or additional, receptors (De Mendonça *et al.* 1997; Katsuki *et al.* 1997; Kemp & Bashir 1997; Berretta & Cherubini 1998; Kirkwood *et al.* 1999; Otani *et al.* 1999). Given the evidence suggesting that acetylcholine may play a crucial role in learning and memory (e.g. Drachman & Leavitt 1974; Everitt & Robbins 1997; Tang *et al.* 1997; Easton *et al.* 2001), the effects of acetylcholine receptor activation have been sought in perirhinal cortex *in vitro*. Application of the cholinergic agonist CCh resulted in a depression of evoked synaptic transmission that persisted long after agonist washout (Massey *et al.* 2001). The induction of this form of LTD was prevented by the selective M1 receptor antagonist pirenzepine. Furthermore, CCh–LTD required neither coactivation of NMDA receptors nor evoked synaptic transmission for its induction (see Figure 9.8). These results indicate that appropriate activation of acetylcholine receptors can result in the induction of LTD (Massey *et al.* 2001). Preliminary *in vitro* data (K. Cho, M. W. Brown and Z. I. Bashir, unpublished observations) also indicate that synapsespecific, activity-dependent LTD is prevented by pharmacological blockade of muscarinic receptors by scopolamine. Scopolamine has been shown previously to impair object recognition memory in rats, monkeys and humans (Drachman & Leavitt 1974; Huston & Aggleton 1987; Aggleton *et al.* 1988; Tang *et al.* 1997).

9.6. Evidence still required: future directions

In summary, there is good evidence from ablation studies that the perirhinal cortex is essential for familiarity discrimination for infrequently encountered individual visual stimuli.

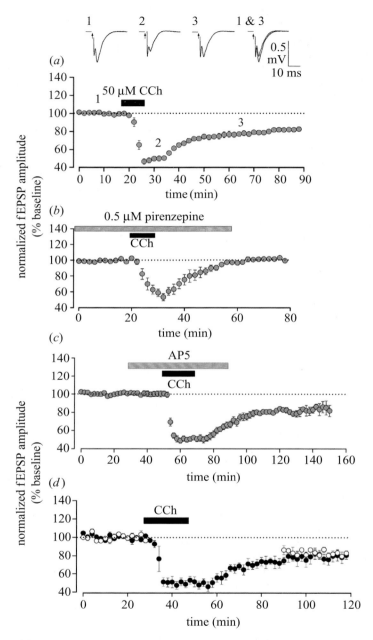

Fig. 9.8. Muscarinic receptor-mediated LTD in rat perirhinal cortical slices. (*a*) The application of CCh results in long-lasting depression (CCh–LTD) of synaptic transmission that is (*b*) blocked by the M1 muscarinic receptor antagonist pirenzepine. The transient depression is, however, unaffected by M1 antagonism. (*c*) The NMDA receptor antagonist AP5 does not prevent CCh–LTD. (*d*) The induction of CCh–LTD does not require synaptic stimulation. Stimulation through one electrode (on the temporal side) was discontinued during and for 40 min after application of CCh; however, LTD still occurred in this input.

Black circles, temporal; white circles, entorhinal; fEPSP, field excitatory post-synaptic potential.

There is also strong evidence that the neural substrate of this process is the reduction in neuronal responses on stimulus repetition. Computational modelling has established the plausibility of such a neuronal substrate because it is possible to construct networks using biologically realistic parameters that will perform familiarity discrimination with the required high speed and high capacity. Moreover, candidate mechanisms have been identified, such as that resulting in LTD, which could produce synapse-specific reductions in neuronal responsiveness in perirhinal cortex.

Nevertheless, the presence of LTD in rat perirhinal slices studied *in vitro* does not establish that allied mechanisms are used to effect familiarity discrimination *in vivo*. It is a necessary, though not a sufficient, condition that pharmacological or molecular genetic manipulations have effects that are consistent upon perirhinal LTD mechanisms, perirhinal neuronal response reductions on stimulus repetition, and familiarity discrimination as measured behaviourally, if the hypotheses presented are valid. Studies are now needed to test the consistency of the effects of such manipulations across the different levels of analysis, thereby seeking to establish some commonality of mechanisms, if the neural substrates of familiarity discrimination are to be further elucidated.

The authors' work is funded by the MRC, BBSRC and the Wellcome Trust. The authors are grateful to Kei Cho, Andy Doherty, Brad Fry and Peter Massey for help in preparation of the manuscript.

References

Abeles, M. 1982 Role of cortical neuron: integrator or coincidence detector? *Isr. J. Med. Sci.* **18**, 83–92.

Aggleton, J. P. & Brown, M. W. 1999 Episodic memory, amnesia and the hippocampal–anterior thalamic axis. *Behav. Brain Sci.* **22**, 425–489.

Aggleton, J. P., Hunt, P. R. & Rawlins, J. N. P. 1986 The effects of hippocampal lesions upon spatial and non-spatial tests of working memory. *Behav. Brain Res.* **19**, 133–146.

Aggleton, J. P., Nicol, R. M., Huston, A. E. & Fairbairn, A. F. 1988 The performance of amnesic subjects on tests of experimental amnesia in animals: delayed matching-to-sample and concurrent learning. *Neuropsychologia* **26**, 265–272.

Alvarez, P., Zola-Morgan, S. & Squire, L. R. 1995 Damage limited to the hippocampal region produces long-lasting memory impairment in monkeys. *J. Neurosci.* **15**, 3796–3807.

Amaral, D. G., Insausti, R. & Cowan, W. M. 1987 The entorhinal cortex of the monkey. I. Cytoarchitectonic organization. *J. Comp. Neurol.* **264**, 326–355.

Baxter, M. G. & Murray, E. A. 2001 Opposite relationship of hippocampal and rhinal cortex damage to delayed non-matching-to-sample deficits in monkeys. *Hippocampus* **11**, 61–71.

Baylis, G. C. & Rolls, E. T. 1987 Responses of neurons in the inferior temporal cortex in short term and serial recognition memory tasks. *Exp. Brain Res.* **65**, 614–622.

Bear, M. F. & Abraham, W. C. 1996 Long-term depression in hippocampus. *A. Rev. Neurosci.* **19**, 437–462.

Beason-Held, L. L., Rosene, D. L., Killiany, R. J. & Moss, M. B. 1999 Hippocampal formation lesions produce memory impairment in the rhesus monkey. *Hippocampus* **9**, 562–574.

Berretta, N. & Cherubini, E. 1998 A novel form of long-term depression in the CA1 area of the adult rat hippocampus independent of glutamate receptors activation. *Eur. J. Neurosci.* **10**, 2957–2963.

Bilkey, D. K. 1996 Long-term potentiation in the *in vitro* perirhinal cortex displays associative properties. *Brain Res.* **733**, 297–300.

Bliss, T. V. P. & Collingridge, G. L. 1993 A synaptic model of memory: long-term potentiation in the hippocampus. *Nature* **361**, 31–39.

Bogacz, R. 2001 Computational models of familiarity discrimination in the perirhinal cortex. PhD thesis, University of Bristol, UK.

Bogacz, R., Brown, M. W. & Giraud-Carrier, C. 1999 High capacity neural networks for familiarity discrimination. In *Proc. Ninth Int. Conf. Artificial Neural Networks*, pp. 773–776. IEE.

Bogacz, R., Brown, M. W. & Giraud-Carrier, C. 2001 Model of familiarity discrimination in the peri-rhinal cortex. *J. Comput. Neurosci.* **10**, 5–23.

Brown, M. W. 1982 Effect of context on the responses of single units recorded from the hippocampal region of behaviourally trained monkeys. In *Neuronal plasticity and memory formation. IBRO mono-graph series*, vol. 9 (ed. C. Ajmone-Marsan & H. Matthies), pp. 557–573. New York: Raven Press.

Brown, M. W. 1996 Neuronal responses and recognition memory. *Semin. Neurosci.* **8**, 23–32.

Brown, M. W. 2000 Temporally structured neuronal activity and recognition memory processes. *Eur. J. Neurosci.* **12**(Suppl. 11), 449.

Brown, M. W. & Aggleton, J. P. 2001 Recognition memory: what are the roles of the perirhinal cortex and hippocampus? *Nature Rev. Neurosci.* **2**, 51–61.

Brown, M. W. & Xiang, J. Z. 1998 Recognition memory: neuronal substrates of the judgement of prior occurrence. *Prog. Neurobiol.* **55**, 149–189.

Brown, M. W., Wilson, F. A. W. & Riches, I. P. 1987 Neuronal evidence that inferomedial temporal cor-tex is more important than hippocampus in certain processes underlying recognition memory. *Brain. Res.* **409**, 158–162.

Buckley, M. J. & Gaffan, D. 1998*a* Perirhinal cortex ablation impairs visual object identification. *J. Neurosci.* **18**, 2268–2275.

Buckley, M. J. & Gaffan, D. 1998*a* Perirhinal cortex ablation impairs configural learning and paired-associate learning equally. *Neuropsychologia* **36**, 535–546.

Burwell, R. D. & Amaral, D. G. 1998 Cortical afferents of the perirhinal, postrhinal, and entorhinal cortices of the rat. *J. Comp. Neurol.* **398**, 179–205.

Burwell, R. D., Witter, M. P. & Amaral, D. G. 1995 Perirhinal and postrhinal cortices of the rat: a review of the neuroanatomical literature and comparison with findings from the monkey brain. *Hippocampus* **5**, 390–408.

Cho, K., Kemp, N., Noel, J., Aggleton, J. P., Brown, M. W. & Bashir, Z. I. 2000 A new form of long-term depression in the perirhinal cortex. *Nature Neurosci.* **3**, 150–156.

Colombo, M. & Gross, C. G. 1994 Responses of inferior temporal cortex and hippocampal neurons dur-ing delayed matching to sample in monkeys (*Macaca fascicularis*). *Behav. Neurosci.* **108**, 443–455.

Conn, P. J. & Pin, J.-P. 1997 Pharmacology and functions of metabotropic glutamate receptors. *A. Rev. Pharmacol. Toxicol.* **37**, 205–237.

Corodimas, K. P. & LeDoux, J. E. 1995 Disruptive effects of post-training perirhinal cortex lesions on conditioned fear: contributions of contextual cues. *Behav. Neurosci.* **109**, 613–619.

De Blasi, A., Conn, P. J., Pin, J.-P. & Nicoletti, F. 2001 Molecular determinants of metabotropic glutam-ate receptor signalling. *Trends Pharmacol. Sci.* **22**, 114–120.

De Mendonça, A., Almeida, T., Bashir, Z. I. & Ribeiro, J. A. 1997 Endogenous adenosine attenuates long-term depression and depotentiation in the CA1 region of the rat hippocampus. *Neuropharmacology* **36**, 161–167.

Desimone, R. 1996 Neural mechanisms for visual memory and their role in attention. *Proc. Natl Acad. Sci. USA* **93**, 13 494–13 499.

Drachman, D. A. & Leavitt, J. 1974 Human memory and the cholinergic system. *Arch. Neurol.* **30**, 113–121.

Easton, A., Parker, A. & Gaffan, D. 2001 Crossed unilateral lesions of medial forebrain bundle and either inferior temporal or frontal cortex impair object recognition memory in rhesus monkeys. *Behav. Brain Res.* **121**, 1–10.

Eichenbaum, H., Otto, T. & Cohen, N. J. 1994 Two functional components of the hippocampal memory system. *Behav. Brain Sci.* **17**, 449–518.

Eichenbaum, H., Schoenbaum, G., Young, B. & Bunsey, M. 1996 Functional organization of the hip-pocampal memory system. *Proc. Natl Acad. Sci. USA* **93**, 13 500–13 507.

Ennaceur, A., Neave, N. & Aggleton, J. P. 1996 Neurotoxic lesions of the perirhinal cortex do not mimic the behavioural effects of fornix transection in the rat. *Behav. Brain Res.* **80**, 9–25.

Erickson, C. A., Jagadeesh, B. & Desimone, R. 2001 Clustering of perirhinal neurons with similar prop-erties following visual experience in the adult monkey. *Nat. Neurosci.* **3**, 1143–1148.

Eskandar, E. N., Richmond, B. J. & Optican, L. M. 1992 Role of inferior temporal neurons in visual memory. I. Temporal encoding of information about visual images, recalled images, and behavioral context. *J. Neurophysiol.* **68**, 1277–1295.

Everitt, B. J. & Robbins, T. W. 1997 Central cholinergic systems and cognition. *A. Rev. Psychol.* **48**, 649–684.

Fahy, F. L., Riches, I. P. & Brown, M. W. 1993 Neuronal activity related to visual recognition memory: long-term memory and the encoding of recency and familiarity information in the primate anterior and medial inferior temporal and rhinal cortex. *Exp. Brain Res.* **96**, 457–472.

Felleman, D. J. & Van Essen, D. C. 1991 Distributed hierarchical processing in the primate cerebral cortex. *Cerebr. Cortex* **1**, 1–47.

Fitzjohn, S. M., Kingston, A. E., Lodge, D. & Collingridge, G. L. 1999 DHPG-induced LTD in area CA1 of juvenile rat hippocampus: characterisation and sensitivity to novel mGlu receptor antagonists. *Neuropharmacology* **38**, 1577–1583.

Fuster, J. M. & Jervey, J. P. 1981 Inferotemporal neurons distinguish and retain behaviorally relevant features of visual stimuli. *Science* **212**, 952–955.

Gaffan, D. 1994 Scene-specific memory for objects: a model of episodic memory impairment in monkeys with fornix transection. *J. Cogn. Neurosci.* **6**, 305–320.

Gaffan, D. & Murray, E. A. 1992 Monkeys (*Macaca fascicularis*) with rhinal cortex ablations succeed in object discrimination learning despite 24 h intertrial intervals and fail at matching to sample despite double sample presentations. *Behav. Neurosci.* **106**, 30–38.

Gawne, T. J. & Richmond, B. J. 1993 How independent are the messages carried by adjacent inferior temporal cortical-neurons? *J. Neurosci.* **13**, 2758–2771.

Gross, C. G., Bender, D. B. & Gerstein, G. L. 1979 Activity of inferior temporal neurons in behaving monkeys. *Neuropsychologia* **17**, 215–229.

Hampson, R. E., Simeral, J. D. & Deadwyler, S. A. 1999 Distribution of spatial and nonspatial information in dorsal hippocampus. *Nature* **402**, 610–614.

Higuchi, S. I. & Miyashita, Y. 1996 Formation of mnemonic neuronal responses to visual paired associates in inferotemporal cortex is impaired by perirhinal and entorhinal lesions. *Proc. Natl Acad. Sci. USA* **93**, 739–743.

Hintzman, D. L., Caulton, D. A. & Levitin, D. J. 1998 Retrieval dynamics in recognition and list discrimination: further evidence of separate processes of familiarity and recall. *Memory Cogn.* **26**, 449–462.

Huang, L., Killbride, J., Rowan, M. J. & Anwyl, R. 1999 Activation of mGluRII induces LTD via activation of protein kinase A and protein kinase C in the dentate gyrus of the hippocampus *in vitro*. *Neuropharmacology* **38**, 73–83.

Huber, K. M., Kayser, M. S. & Bear, M. F. 2000 Role for rapid dendritic protein synthesis in hippocampal mGluR-dependent long-term depression. *Science* **288**, 1254–1257.

Huston, A. E. & Aggleton, J. P. 1987 The effects of cholinergic drugs upon recognition memory in rats. *Q. J. Exp. Psychol.* B **39**, 297–314.

Insausti, R., Juottonen, K., Soininen, H., Insausti, A. M., Partanen, K., Vainio, P. & Laakso, M. P. 1998 MR volumetric analysis of the human entorhinal, perirhinal and temporopolar cortices. *Am. J. Neuroradiol.* **19**, 659–671.

Ito, M. 1989 Long-term depression. *A. Rev. Neurosci.* **12**, 85–102.

Katsuki, H., Izumi, Y. & Zorumski, C. F. 1997 Noradrenergic regulation of synaptic plasticity in the hippocampal CA1 region. *J. Neurophysiol.* **77**, 3013–3020.

Kemp, N. & Bashir, Z. I. 1997 A role for adenosine in the regulation of long-term depression in the adult rat hippocampus *in vitro*. *Neurosci. Lett.* **225**, 189–192.

Kemp, N. & Bashir, Z. I. 2001 Long-term depression: a cascade of induction and expression mechanisms. *Prog. Neurobiol.* **65**, 339–365.

Kirkwood, A., Rozas, G., Kirkwood, J., Perez, F. & Bear, M. F. 1999 Modulation of long-term synaptic depression in visual cortex by acetylcholine and norepinephrine. *J. Neurosci.* **19**, 1599–1609.

Lavenex, P. & Amaral, D. G. 2000 Hippocampal–neocortical interactions: a hierarchy of associativity. *Hippocampus* **10**, 420–430.

Leonard, B. W., Amaral, D. G., Squire, L. R. & Zola-Morgan, S. 1995 Transient memory impairment in monkeys with bilateral lesions of the entorhinal cortex. *J. Neurosci.* **15**, 5637–5659.

Li, L., Miller, E. K. & Desimone, R. 1993 The representation of stimulus familiarity in anterior inferior temporal cortex. *J. Neurophysiol.* **69**, 1918–1929.

Linden, D. J. 1994 Long-term synaptic depression in the mammalian brain. *Neurone* **12**, 457–472.

Liu, P. & Bilkey, D. K. 1998 Perirhinal cortex contributions to performance in the Morris water maze. *Behav. Neurosci.* **112**, 304–315.

McCaffery, B., Cho, K., Bortolotto, Z. A., Aggleton, J., Brown, M. W., Conquet, F., Collingridge, G. L. & Bashir, Z. I. 1999 Synaptic depression induced by pharmacological activation of metabotropic glutamate receptors in the perirhinal cortex *in vitro*. *Neuroscience* **93**, 977–984.

Mandler, G. 1980 Recognizing: the judgment of previous occurrence. *Psychol. Rev.* **87**, 252–271.

Massey, P. V., Bhabra, G., Cho, K., Brown, M. W. & Bashir, Z. I. 2001 Activation of muscarinic receptors induces protein synthesis-dependent long-lasting depression in the perirhinal cortex. *Eur. J. Neurosci.* **14**, 145–152.

Maunsell, J. H. R., Sclar, G., Nealey, T. A. & DePriest, D. D. 1991 Extraretinal representations in area V4 in the macaque monkey. *Vis. Neurosci.* **7**, 561–573.

Meunier, M., Bachevalier, J., Mishkin, M. & Murray, E. A. 1993 Effects on visual recognition of combined and separate ablations of the entorhinal and perirhinal cortex in rhesus monkeys. *J. Neurosci.* **13**, 5418–5432.

Meunier, M., Hadfield, W., Bachevalier, J. & Murray, E. A. 1996 Effects of rhinal cortex lesions combined with hippocampectomy on visual recognition memory in rhesus monkeys. *J. Neurophysiol.* **75**, 1190–1205.

Meunier, M., Bachevalier, J. & Mishkin, M. 1997 Effects of orbital frontal and anterior cingulate lesions on object and spatial memory in rhesus monkeys. *Neuropsychologia* **35**, 999–1015.

Mikami, A. & Kubota, B. 1980 Inferotemporal neuron activities and color discrimination with delay. *Brain Res.* **182**, 65–78.

Miller, E. K. 1999 The prefrontal cortex: complex neural properties for complex behavior. *Neurone* **22**, 15–17.

Miller, E. K. & Desimone, R. 1994 Parallel neuronal mechanisms for short-term memory. *Science* **263**, 520–522.

Miller, E. K., Gochin, P. M. & Gross, C. G. 1991 Habituation-like decrease in the responses of neurons in inferior temporal cortex of the macaque. *Vis. Neurosci.* **7**, 357–362.

Miller, E. K., Li, L. & Desimone, R. 1993 Activity of neurons in anterior inferior temporal cortex during a short-term memory task. *J. Neurosci.* **13**, 1460–1478.

Miller, E. K., Erickson, C. A. & Desimone, R. 1996 Neural mechanisms of visual working memory in prefrontal cortex of the macaque. *J. Neurosci.* **16**, 5154–5167.

Mistry, R., Golding, N. & Challiss, R. A. J. 1998 Regulation of phosphoinositide turnover in neonatal rat cerebral cortex by group I and II selecetive metabotropic glutamate receptor agonists. *Br. J. Pharmacol.* **123**, 581–589.

Morris, R. G. M., Garrud, P., Rawlins, J. N. P. & O'Keefe, J. 1982 Place navigation impaired in rats with hippocampal lesions. *Nature* **297**, 681–683.

Mumby, D. G. & Pinel, J. P. J. 1994 Rhinal cortex lesions and object recognition in rats. *Behav. Neurosci.* **108**, 11–18.

Mumby, D. G., Wood, E. R. & Pinel, J. P. J. 1992 Object recognition memory in rats is only mildly impaired by lesions of the hippocampus and amygdala. *Psychobiology* **20**, 18–27.

Mumby, D. G., Pinel, J. P. J., Kornecook, T. J., Shen, M. J. & Redila, V. A. 1995 Memory deficits following lesions of hippocampus or amygdala in the rat: assessment by an object-memory test battery. *Psychobiology* **23**, 26–36.

Murray, E. A. 1996 What have ablation studies told us about the neural substrates of stimulus memory? *Semin. Neurosci.* **8**, 13–22.

Murray, E. A. & Bussey, T. J. 1999 Perceptual-mnemonic functions of the perirhinal cortex. *Trends Cogn. Neurosci.* **3**, 142–151.

Murray, E. A. & Mishkin, M. 1998 Object recognition and location memory in monkeys with excitotoxic lesions of the amygdala and hippocampus. *J. Neurosci.* **18**, 6568–6582.

Murray, E. A., Gaffan, D. & Mishkin, M. 1993 Neural substrates of visual stimulus–stimulus association in rhesus monkeys. *J. Neurosci.* **13**, 4549–4561.

Murray, E. A., Baxter, M. G. & Gaffan, D. 1998 Monkeys with rhinal cortex damage or neurotoxic hippocampal lesions are impaired on spatial scene learning and object reversals. *Behav. Neurosci.* **112**, 1291–1303.

Nakamura, K. & Kubota, K. 1995 Mnemonic firing of neurons in the monkey temporal pole during a visual recognition memory task. *J. Neurophysiol.* **74**, 162–178.

Norman, K. A. & O'Reilly, R. C. 2001 Modelling hippocampal and neocortical contributions to recognition memory: a complementary learning systems approach. Technical report 01–02, University of Colorado, Boulder CO, USA.

O'Keefe, J. & Nadel, L. 1978 *The hippocampus as a cognitive map.* Oxford University Press.

O'Mara, S. M., Rowan, M. J. & Anwyl, R. 1995 Metabotropic glutamate receptor-induced homosynaptic long-term depression and depotentiation in the dentate gyrus of the rat hippocampus *in vitro*. *Neuropharmacology* **34**, 983–989.

Otani, S., Auclair, N., Desce, J. M., Roisin, M. P. & Crepel, F. 1999 Dopamine receptors and groups I and II mGluRs cooperate for long-term depression induction in rat prefrontal cortex through converging postsynaptic activation of MAP kinases. *J. Neurosci.* **19**, 9788–9802.

Otto, T. & Eichenbaum, H. 1992 Complementary roles of the orbital prefrontal cortex and the perirhinal–entorhinal cortices in an odorguided delayed-nonmatching-to-sample task. *Behav. Neurosci.* **106**, 762–775.

Overstreet, L. S., Pasternak, J. F., Colley, P. A., Slater, N. T. & Trommer, B. L. 1997 Metabotropic glutamate receptor mediated long-term depression in developing hippocampus. *Neuropharmacology* **36**, 831–844.

Palmer, M. J., Irving, A. J., Seabrook, G. R., Jane, D. E. & Collingridge, G. L. 1997 The group I mGlu receptor agonist DHPG induces a novel form of LTD in the CA1 region of the hippocampus. *Neuropharmacology* **36**, 1517–1532.

Riches, I. P., Wilson, F. A. W. & Brown, M. W. 1991 The effects of visual stimulation and memory on neurons of the hippocampal formation and the neighboring parahippocampal gyrus and inferior temporal cortex of the primate. *J. Neurosci.* **11**, 1763–1779.

Ringo, J. L. 1996 Stimulus specific adaptation in inferior temporal and medial temporal cortex of the monkey. *Behav. Brain Res.* **76**, 191–197.

Rolls, E. T., Perrett, D. I., Caan, A. W. & Wilson, F. A. W. 1982 Neuronal responses related to visual recognition. *Brain* **105**, 611–646.

Rolls, E. T., Miyashita, Y., Cahusac, P. M. B., Kesner, R. P., Niki, H., Feigenbaum, J. D. & Bach, L. 1989 Hippocampal neurons in the monkey with activity related to the place in which a stimulus is shown. *J. Neurosci.* **9**, 1835–1845.

Rolls, E. T., Cahusac, P. M. B., Feigenbaum, J. D. & Miya-shita, Y. 1993 Responses of single neurons in the hippocampus of the macaque related to recognition memory. *Exp. Brain Res.* **93**, 299–306.

Schnabel, R., Kilpatrick, I. C. & Collingridge, G. L. 1999 An investigation into signal transduction mechanisms involved in DHPG-induced LTD in the CA1 region of the hippocampus. *Neuropharmacology* **38**, 1585–1596.

Schoepp, D. D., Salhoff, C. R., Wright, R. A., Johnson, B. G., Burnett, J. P., Mayne, N. G., Belagage, R., Wu, S. & Monn, J. A. 1996 The novel metabotropic glutamate receptor agonist 2R,4R-APDC potentiates stimulation of phosphoinositide hydrolysis in the rat hippocampus by 3,5-dihy-droxyphenylglycine: evidence for a synergistic interaction between group I and group II receptors. *Neuropharmacology* **35**, 1661–1672.

Seeck, M., Michel, C. M., Mainwaring, N., Cosgrove, R., Blume, H., Ives, J., Landis, T. & Schomer, D. L. 1997 Evidence for rapid face recognition from human scalp and intracranial electrodes. *NeuroReport* **8**, 2749–2754.

Shi, C. J. & Cassell, M. D. 1997 Cortical, thalamic, and amygdaloid projections of rat temporal cortex. *J. Comp. Neurol.* **382**, 153–175.

Singer, W. & Gray, C. M. 1995 Visual feature integration and the temporal correlation hypothesis. *A. Rev. Neurosci.* **18**, 555–586.

Sobotka, S. & Ringo, J. L. 1993 Investigations of long-term. *Neural substrates of familiarity discrimination* M. W. Brown and Z. I. Bashir 1095 recognition and association memory in unit responses from inferotemporal cortex. *Exp. Brain Res.* **96**, 28–38.

Sohal, V. S. & Hasselmo, M. E. 2000 A model for experience-dependent changes in the responses of infero-temporal neurons. *Comput. Neural Systems* **11**, 169–190.

Standing, L. 1973 Learning 10 000 pictures. *Q. J. Exp. Psychol.* **25**, 207–222.

Suzuki, W. A. 1996 The anatomy, physiology and functions of the perirhinal cortex. *Curr. Opin. Neurobiol.* **6**, 179–186.

Suzuki, W. A. & Eichenbaum, H. 2000 The neurophysiology of memory. *Ann. NY Acad. Sci.* **911**, 175–191.

Suzuki, W. A., Zola-Morgan, S., Squire, L. R. & Amaral, D. G. 1993 Lesions of the perirhinal and parahippocampal cortices in the monkey produce long-lasting memory impairment in the visual and tactual modalities. *J. Neurosci.* **13**, 2430–2451.

Tang, Y., Mishkin, M. & Aigner, T. G. 1997 Effects of muscarinic blockade in perirhinal cortex during visual recognition. *Proc. Natl Acad. Sci. USA* **94**, 12 667–12 669.

Thompson, J., Brown, M. W. & Stewart, M. G. 2001 Measures of synaptic density in the perirhinal cortex of rats exposed to novel or familiar stimuli. *Soc. Neurosci. Abstr.* **27**, 537.28.

Vogels, R., Sary, G. & Orban, G. A. 1995 How task-related are the responses of inferior temporal meurons? *Vis. Neurosci.* **12**, 207–214.

von Bonin, G. & Bailey, P. 1947 *The neocortex of* Macaca mulatta. Urbana: University of Illinois Press.

Wiebe, S. P. & Staubli, U. V. 1999 Dynamic filtering of recognition memory codes in the hippocampus. *J. Neurosci.* **19**, 10 562–10 574.

Wilson, F. A. W. & Rolls, E. T. 1990 Neuronal responses related to the novelty and familiarity of visual stimuli in the substantia innominata, diagonal band of Broca and the periventricular region of the primate basal forebrain. *Exp. Brain Res.* **80**, 104–120.

Witter, M. P., Groenewegen, H. J., Lopes da Silva, F. H. & Lohman, A. H. M. 1989 Functional organization of the extrinsic and intrinsic circuitry of the parahippocampal region. *Progr. Neurobiol.* **33**, 161–253.

Witter, M. P., Naber, P. A., Van Haeften, T., Machielsen, W. C. M., Rombouts, S. A. R. B., Barkhof, F., Scheltens, P. & Lopes da Silva, F. H. 2000 Cortico-hippocampal communication by way of parallel parahippocampal–subicular pathways. *Hippocampus* **10**, 398–410.

Xiang, J. Z. & Brown, M. W. 1997 Processing visual familiarity and recency information: neuronal interactions in area TE and rhinal cortex. *Brain Res. Abstr.* **14**, 69.

Xiang, J.-Z. & Brown, M. W. 1998*a* Encoding of relative familiarity and recency information in orbital, ventromedial and dorsolateral prefrontal cortices and anterior cingulate gyrus. *Soc. Neurosci. Abstr.* **28**, 561.20.

Xiang, J. Z. & Brown, M. W. 1998*b* Differential neuronal encoding of novelty, familiarity and recency in regions of the anterior temporal lobe. *Neuropharmacology* **37**, 657–676.

Young, B. J., Otto, T., Fox, G. D. & Eichenbaum, H. 1997 Memory representation within the parahippocampal region. *J. Neurosci.* **17**, 5183–5195.

Zhu, X. O., Brown, M. W. & Aggleton, J. P. 1995 Neuronal signalling of information important to visual recognition memory in rat rhinal and neighbouring cortices. *Eur. J. Neurosci.* **7**, 753–765.

Ziakopoulos, Z., Tillett, C. W., Brown, M. W. & Bashir, Z. I. 1999 Input- and layer-dependent synaptic plasticity in the rat perirhinal cortex *in vitro*. *Neuroscience* **92**, 459–472.

Zola, S. M., Squire, L. R., Teng, E., Stefanacci, L., Buffalo, E. A. & Clark, R. E. 2000 Impaired recognition memory in monkeys after damage limited to the hippocampal region. *J. Neurosci.* **20**, 451–463.

Zola-Morgan, S. & Squire, L. R. 1993 Neuroanatomy of memory. *A. Rev. Neurosci.* **16**, 547–563.

Zola-Morgan, S., Squire, L. R., Amaral, D. G. & Suzuki, W. A. 1989 Lesions of perirhinal and parahippocampal cortex that spare the amygdala and hippocampal formation produce severe memory impairment. *J. Neurosci.* **9**, 4355–4370.

Zola-Morgan, S., Squire, L. R. & Ramus, S. J. 1994 Severity of memory impairment in monkeys as a function of locus and extent of damage within the medial temporal lobe memory system. *Hippocampus* **4**, 483–495.

Glossary

AMPA   alpha-amino-3-hydroxy-5-methyl-4-isoalone propionic acid
CCh   carbachol
LFS   low-frequency stimulation
LTD   long-term depression
mGlu   metabotropic glutamate
NMDA   *N*-methyl-D-aspartate

10

The neural basis of episodic memory: evidence from functional neuroimaging

Michael D. Rugg, Leun J. Otten and Richard N. A. Henson

We review some of our recent research using functional neuroimaging to investigate neural activity supporting the encoding and retrieval of episodic memories, that is, memories for unique events. Findings from studies of encoding indicate that, at the cortical level, the regions responsible for the effective encoding of a stimulus event as an episodic memory include some of the regions that are also engaged to process the event 'online'. Thus, it appears that there is no single cortical site or circuit responsible for episodic encoding. The results of retrieval studies indicate that successful recollection of episodic information is associated with activation of lateral parietal cortex, along with more variable patterns of activity in dorsolateral and anterior prefrontal cortex. Whereas parietal regions may play a part in the representation of retrieved information, prefrontal areas appear to support processes that act on the products of retrieval to align behaviour with the demands of the retrieval task.

10.1. Episodic memory

We use the term 'episodic memory' to refer to the set of cognitive processes that support the ability consciously to recollect unique events and the context in which they occurred (for a recent review, see Baddeley *et al.* (2001)). The processes include ones that are engaged when an event is experienced and that lead to the formation of a new memory representation (encoding processes), and others that support the recollection of the event at some later time (retrieval processes). In the experiments reported here, the events are discrete experimental stimuli, usually words. These items were presented to volunteers in a 'study phase', usually in the context of a specific task that constrains the nature of the processing engaged by each item. Memory for the items was tested in a subsequent 'test phase' with a 'direct' memory test, such as yes–no recognition.

In the following sections, we describe findings from some of our recent studies in which brain activity was non-invasively measured in healthy volunteers as they performed tasks that engage episodic encoding and retrieval. It is important to note that while such studies in principle permit a distinction to be made between neural systems supporting encoding and retrieval—a distinction that is hard to draw on the basis of lesion data alone (Fletcher *et al.* 1997)—this does not mean that these two 'stages' of memory should be regarded as being independent of one another. As was pointed out by Tulving *et al.* (1994), among others, in as much as an event is interpreted in terms of its meaning, its encoding is intimately associated with retrieval of information, albeit from 'semantic' rather than episodic memory. The retrieval of episodic information or, indeed, the mere presentation of a stimulus that triggers a retrieval attempt (a 'retrieval cue'), are events that may themselves be subject to episodic encoding (cf. Moscovitch & Nadel 1998). It should also be kept in mind that episodic memories can be elicited by a variety of tests that employ a range of different kinds of retrieval cue (e.g. 'copy' cues in tests of recognition memory, 'partial' cues in cued recall). There are no grounds for assuming *a priori* that the neural correlates of either encoding or retrieval are independent of how memory is tested. Thus, it is an empirical question which of the findings obtained with one kind of memory test generalize to other kinds.

10.2. Functional neuroimaging methods

A description and comparison of methods for the noninvasive measurement of human brain activity can be found in Rugg (1999). The methods can broadly be divided into those based on haemodynamic measures, notably PET and fMRI, and those that detect neural activity through the measurement of time-varying scalp electrical (EEG) or magnetic (MEG) fields. The signals detected by both classes of method appear predominantly to reflect—directly in the case of electrophysiological measures, indirectly in the case of haemodynamic methods— the aggregated post-synaptic activity of relatively large populations of neurons (Wood 1987; Logothetis *et al.* 2001; see also Logothetis § 4). Whereas the resulting measures of stimulus- and task-related neural activity are considerably coarser than those yielded by single-neuron studies, they can be obtained concurrently from the entire brain. Thus, neuroimaging methods can identify the set of functionally specialized neuronal populations that are active during a given cognitive task, allowing a 'systems-level' analysis of the neural correlates of task engagement. On the negative side, however, the methods provide little information about the precise form of the neural activity, and hence the local neural computations, that take place within these populations to give rise to the detected signal. Such information remains the province of invasive studies and can be obtained only very rarely in humans (see Heit *et al.* (1990) and Cameron *et al.* (2001) for examples relevant to memory).

In the studies described in §§ 10.3 and 10.4, neural correlates of memory processing were obtained using both electrophysiological (EEG) and haemodynamic measures (fMRI). In each case, activity was obtained using an 'event-related' approach, which permits characterization of the neural activity elicited in response to the presentation of individual experimental stimuli. Whereas event-related methods have been employed with EEG recordings for more than 30 years (Donchin & Lindsley (1969); so-called ERPs), only within the last five years have analogous methods been developed for fMRI (Dale & Buckner 1997; Josephs *et al.* 1997; Zarahn *et al.* 1997). Using the event-related approach, it is possible to measure and contrast the time-locked modulations of neural activity elicited by different classes of experimental items, even when these classes are defined *post hoc* on the basis of the subject's behavioural responses. This makes it possible to investigate, at the level of the single item, differences in brain activity associated with successful versus unsuccessful memory performance (e.g. 'hits' versus 'misses' in a recognition memory task). Whereas fMRI has far better spatial resolution than the ERP method, the sluggishness of the haemodynamic response means that the temporal resolution of event-related fMRI signals is typically of the order of hundreds of milliseconds. This compares unfavourably with the millisecond-level resolution that can be attained with ERPs. Thus, the two methods provide complementary perspectives on event-related brain activity.

10.3. Studies of encoding

In a series of recent studies, we have investigated the neural correlates of episodic encoding by studying what have become known as 'subsequent memory effects' (see Rugg (1995) and

Wagner *et al.* (1999) for reviews of early work). In the subsequent memory procedure (see Figure 10.1), event-related activity elicited by a series of study items is contrasted according to whether the items were remembered or forgotten on a subsequent memory test, the assumption being that differences in activity that 'predict' successful versus unsuccessful memory reflect the differential engagement of processes supporting effective encoding. Clearly, there are circumstances when this assumption is likely to be invalid, or when any such differences would convey only trivial information about memory encoding. For example, if subjects attended to only some study items while ignoring others, there would be a strong correlation between the engagement of attentional processes and subsequent memory performance. Thus, the resulting subsequent memory effects would largely reflect differences in neural activity related to differential allocation of attention rather than to differences connected more directly to memory encoding. To anticipate, such confounds are unlikely to exist in the experiments described in § 10.3*a*. In each case, 'online' measures of performance were obtained during the study tasks. Trials on which errors were committed were eliminated from the analysis and, across the experiments, we observed no consistent differences in reaction time for study items that were subsequently remembered as opposed to those that were forgotten. Thus, the subsequent memory effects that we observed in brain activity were unlikely to have been confounded by factors contributing to the general efficiency with which study items were processed.

(a) Semantic versus non-semantic encoding

Our first fMRI study (Otten *et al.* 2001) took as its starting point previous findings indicating that the left inferior prefrontal cortex plays a key part in the episodic encoding of verbal material. These findings came from 'blocked' PET and fMRI studies in which activity was obtained

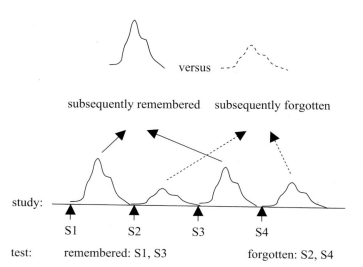

Fig. 10.1. The subsequent memory paradigm. The experiment is split into a 'study' and a 'test' phase. During the study phase, neural activity is recorded while volunteers are presented with a series of items. Later, their memory for the items is tested. The neural activity elicited by each item at study is then sorted according to whether the item was remembered or forgotten on the subsequent memory test. The differences between the neural activity elicited by subsequently remembered and subsequently forgotten items are taken as putative neural correlates of memory encoding.

while subjects engaged in tasks that were known *a priori* to produce differences in subsequent memory (e.g. semantic versus non-semantic processing (Kapur *et al.* 1994; Demb *et al.* 1995; Wagner *et al.* 1998); full versus divided attention (Shallice *et al.* 1994); intentional memorizing versus passive reading (Kapur *et al.* 1996; Kelley *et al.* 1998)), as well as from previous event-related fMRI studies using the subsequent memory procedure (Wagner *et al.* 1998). Together with other results pointing to a role for the left prefrontal cortex in semantic processing (Poldrack *et al.* 1999), these findings were taken as evidence that activation of the left prefrontal cortex during successful encoding reflects its role in meaning-based processing; the greater the engagement of this region, the greater the semantic processing accorded a study item and hence the greater the probability of successful subsequent retrieval (Tulving *et al.* 1994; Gabrieli *et al.* 1998; Wagner *et al.* 1998, 1999; Buckner *et al.* 1999).

The first aim of our experiment was to investigate the relationship between the regions exhibiting a subsequent memory effect for semantically studied words, and regions where activity was greater for study items subjected to semantic rather than non-semantic processing. If the subsequent memory effects exclusively reflect modulation of semantic processing, they should be found only in regions also sensitive to the semantic versus non-semantic contrast.

The second aim of the experiment was to investigate whether the pattern of subsequent memory effects found for semantically encoded items extends to effects elicited by items encoded non-semantically. For example, is the left prefrontal region generically involved in the episodic encoding of verbal material, as was suggested following early neuroimaging results (Tulving *et al.* 1994), or does the participation of this region in encoding depend upon the explicit engagement of semantic processing?

We addressed these issues by scanning volunteers while they performed two randomly interleaved study tasks, only one of which necessitated semantic processing. Items comprised visually presented words. These were preceded by one of two possible cues that signalled whether the upcoming word required an animacy (does the word refer to a living or nonliving entity?) or an alphabetical (are the first and last letters in alphabetical order?) judgement. About 15 min later, recognition memory for all of the study items, now intermixed with a set of unstudied words, was tested with a four-choice procedure (confident old, non-confident old, confident new, non-confident new). Study items were defined as 'remembered' if they were confidently judged to be old and 'forgotten' if they were either incorrectly judged to be new or judged old with low confidence (non-confident old judgements were about as likely for unstudied words as they were for studied words, indicating that these judgements mainly reflected guessing).

Figure 10.2*a* illustrates where subsequent memory effects were found for items subjected to animacy judgements. The regions include both ventral (BA 47) and dorsal (BA 9/44 and 45) regions of the inferior frontal gyrus bilaterally, albeit more strongly on the left, a medial superior prefrontal region (not illustrated) and left anterior and posterior hippocampal formation. Figure 10.2*b* shows which of these effects remained after 'masking' with the outcome of the between-task contrast so as to leave only those voxels in which task (animacy > alphabetic) and subsequent memory effects coexisted. It can be seen that only in the left ventral prefrontal cortex and left anterior hippocampal formation did task and subsequent memory effects overlap. Figure 10.2*c* shows that subsequent memory effects for the alphabetical task were found in two regions, left ventral prefrontal cortex and left anterior hippocampal formation, both of which also exhibited subsequent memory effects in the semantic task.

These findings have two principal implications. First, whereas some of the regions exhibiting subsequent memory effects in the animacy task overlapped with those sensitive to the

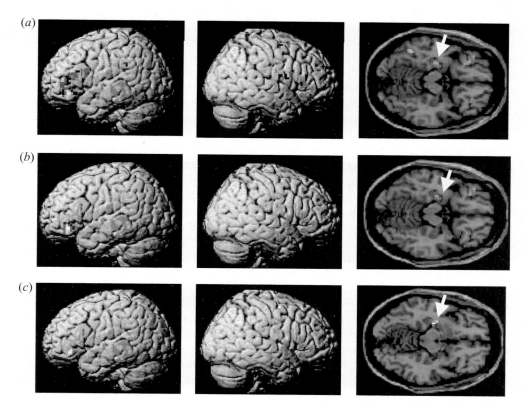

Fig. 10.2. See also Plate 31. Data from Otten *et al.* (2001). (*a*) Regions showing significant ($p < 0.001$) fMRI signal increases for subsequently remembered versus subsequently forgotten words from the animacy task. Subsequent memory effects can be seen in the prefrontal cortex bilaterally and in two regions of the left hippocampal formation. (*b*) Subsequent memory effects in the animacy task, masked by the regions that showed significant signal increases for the animacy versus alphabetical contrast (both contrasts thresholded at $p < 0.001$). Overlap between subsequent memory and task effects was found in the left ventral prefrontal cortex and the left anterior hippocampus. (*c*) Regions showing subsequent memory effects for words studied in the alphabetical task. The effects are evident in the left ventral prefrontal cortex and the left anterior hippocampus. All results in this and subsequent figures are rendered onto the Montreal Neurological Institute reference brain. The arrows denote the left anterior hippocampus. The colour of activated voxels (red→yellow) indicates the level of statistical significance beyond the threshold.

semantic versus non-semantic contrast, several other regions did not. Activity in these latter regions may, therefore, support processes unrelated to semantic processing that nonetheless facilitate subsequent memory. Second, the findings offer no support for the idea that the neural circuitry supporting effective episodic encoding is task sensitive: subsequent memory effects in the alphabetical task were found exclusively in a subset of the regions exhibiting these effects in the animacy task (cf. Baker *et al.* 2001).

We discuss the functional significance of these findings in § 10.3d, after describing the results of three further experiments that took this initial study as their starting point. The first of these (Otten & Rugg 2001*a*) was motivated by concerns that the failure to find evidence of qualitatively different subsequent memory effects in the two study tasks might have been a consequence of the non-semantic task that we elected to employ. As would be expected for such a 'shallow' task (Craik & Lockhart 1972), relatively few items were subsequently recognized (see Table 10.1). The low level of recognition performance for the alphabetical task ($p_{Hit} - p_{FalseAlarm}$ for confident recognition responses was 0.19, compared with 0.48 for the animacy task) raises the possibility that the subsequent memory contrast lacked power because of the relatively small number of items contributing to the 'Remembered' category. Another possibility is that the processing needed to perform the alphabetical task may have led to the formation of episodic memory representations that were so weak as to be unable to support subsequent recognition memory judgements. By this possibility, the only alphabetically encoded words to be given a correct recognition judgement were those that also received incidental semantic processing. As a consequence, the neural correlates of episodic encoding in the alphabetical task were a weak reflection of those seen for the animacy task.

In light of these possibilities, we repeated our original experiment (with some minor procedural modifications) using a different non-semantic task: syllable judgement. This task, which required subjects to judge whether the number of syllables in a word was odd or even, places heavy demands on phonological processing and yielded somewhat better subsequent memory performance than did the alphabetical task employed previously (see Table 10.1). $p_{Hit} - p_{FalseAlarm}$ for confident responses was 0.29 as opposed to 0.19 in the previous study. By contrast, scores for the animacy task were very similar across the two experiments (0.51 versus 0.48 for the present and previous experiments, respectively).

The subsequent memory effects for the animacy judgement task are shown in Figure 10.3a. At our standard statistical threshold ($p < 0.001$), these effects were more limited in their spatial extent than was the case in our first experiment and were observed solely in the medial prefrontal cortex and in the dorsal part of the left inferior frontal gyrus. With the employment of a more liberal threshold (Figure 10.4a), the effects more closely approximated those observed previously, although there remained no sign of any effects in the vicinity of the hippocampus. Figures 10.3b and 10.4b illustrate the findings for the syllable judgement task. In striking contrast to the animacy task, subsequent memory effects failed to achieve statistical significance in any part of the left prefrontal cortex, even at the relatively liberal threshold of $p < 0.01$. Robust effects were found, however, in bilateral parietal and fusiform regions and in the left occipital cortex. The same parietal regions were also revealed in an inter-task

Table 10.1. Proportions of trials[*] given a 'sure old' judgement in the recognition memory tests of Otten *et al.* (2001) and Otten & Rugg (2001a).

	experiment	
word type	Otten *et al.* (2001)	Otten & Rugg (2001a)
old		
semantic study task	0.58 (0.19)	0.59 (0.15)
non-semantic study task	0.29 (0.15)	0.37 (0.14)
new	0.10 (0.07)	0.07 (0.06)

Values are across-volunteer means (s.d.). The semantic decision task consisted of animacy judgements in both experiments. The non-semantic decision task consisted of alphabetical judgements in Otten *et al.* (2001) and syllable judgements in Otten & Rugg (2001a).

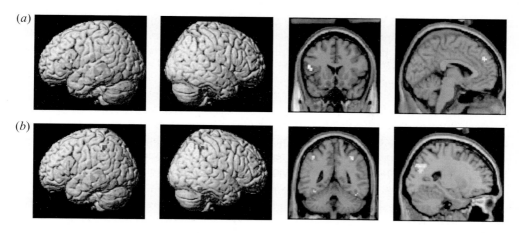

Fig. 10.3. See also Plate 32. Regions showing significant ($p < 0.001$) subsequent memory effects in Otten & Rugg (2001*a*). (*a*) Subsequent memory effects in the animacy task were found in the left inferior and medial frontal regions. (*b*) Subsequent memory effects in the syllable task were found in the bilateral intraparietal sulcus, the bilateral fusiform gyrus and the left superior occipital gyrus.

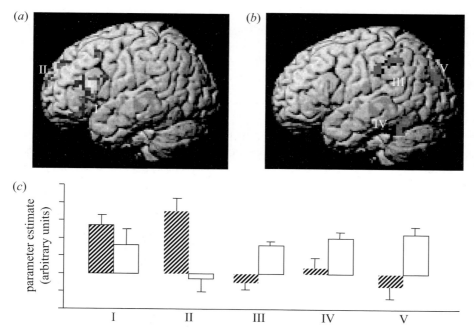

Fig. 10.4. See also Plate 33. Comparison of the subsequent memory effects in the (*a*) animacy and (*b*) syllable study tasks of Otten & Rugg (2001*a*). The effects are illustrated at a significance threshold of $p < 0.01$. (*c*) The parameter estimates for subsequent memory effects in the animacy and alphabetical tasks are depicted for the voxels showing the peak effect in (I) the left inferior frontal gyrus, (II) the medial frontal gyrus, (III) the intraparietal sulcus, (IV) the fusiform gyrus, and (V) the left superior occipital gyrus. For regions III and IV, the parameter estimates were averaged across homotopic voxels in each hemisphere. The bars show the standard error of the mean. Significant region by task interactions were found for the subsequent memory effects in all but the left frontal region. Hatched bars, animacy task; open bars, syllable task.

contrast that identified where activity was greater for items subjected to syllable rather than animacy judgements, indicating that these regions support processes engaged selectively by the syllable task. The most important implication of these findings, however, is that they indicate that subsequent memory effects can differ in their localization according to the nature of the processing engaged during study.

(b) Electrophysiological subsequent memory effects

A second follow-up to our original experiment employed ERPs rather than fMRI as a measure of item-related brain activity (Otten & Rugg 2001*b*). As in the original experiment, subsequent memory effects were contrasted according to whether study words had been subjected to animacy or alphabetical judgements. The study was motivated by two considerations. First, whereas subsequent memory effects in ERPs have been described since the late 1970s (Chapman *et al.* 1978; Sanquist *et al.* 1980; see Rugg 1995 and Wagner *et al.* 1999 for reviews), little data existed regarding the sensitivity of these effects to the manipulations of the study task along the lines described above (e.g. Paller *et al.* 1987). Second, the fMRI findings give little insight into the time course of encoding-related brain activity, a question for which the ERP method is well suited.

Some of the findings from this experiment are shown in Figure 10.5. As shown in Figure 10.5*a*, the ERP subsequent memory effect for semantically studied items took the form of a sustained increase in positivity for remembered words, consistent with numerous previous findings (Rugg 1995; Wagner *et al.* 1999). The scalp distribution of this effect (Figure 10.5*b*) showed a tendency to evolve with time, from an initial quite focal maximum over the left frontal scalp to a more posterior distribution later on. Figure 10.5*c* shows the subsequent

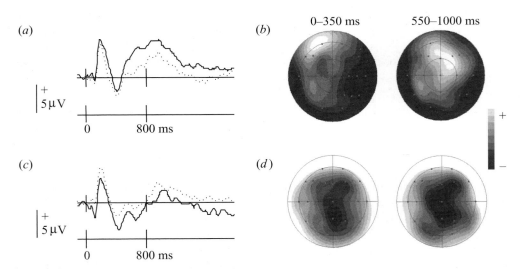

Fig. 10.5. Data from Otten & Rugg (2001*b*). (*a*) Group-averaged ERP waveforms from a midfrontal electrode site demonstrating the subsequent memory effect for words studied in the animacy task. (*b*) Scalp distribution of the subsequent memory effect in the animacy task in the 0–350 and 550–1000 ms time ranges. (*c*,*d*) As for (*a*,*b*), but for the alphabetical study task. Note the differing polarity of the subsequent memory effects in each task and their early onset in both tasks. Solid lines, subsequently remembered; dotted lines, subsequently forgotten.

memory effect for the alphabetical task. In marked contrast to that for animacy judgements, the effect takes the form of greater *negativity* for subsequently remembered items, the distribution of which remained fairly stable over time (Figure 10.5*d*).

Two main conclusions emerge from these results. First, and most starkly, the conclusion drawn on the basis of our fMRI findings about the qualitative similarity of the subsequent memory effects obtained in the animacy and alphabetical encoding tasks is called into question. In the present case, the effects associated with the two tasks were qualitatively different. These findings indicate that encoding-related neural activity in the two tasks differed in location (such that the generators of the activity in the animacy and alphabetical tasks were orientated sufficiently differently to give rise respectively to scalp-positive and scalp-negative effects), in their neurophysiological characteristics, or both. Whatever the reason, the findings indicate that encoding-related neural activity is task-dependent, a conclusion more in line with the second of our fMRI studies than the original one. The reasons for the disparity between our fMRI and ERP results are unclear, although it is important to note that there are several reasons why data from the two methods may not always be convergent (Rugg 1999).

The second conclusion to emerge from the ERP results, equally evident for both tasks, is in respect of the timing of the subsequent memory effects. As is evident in Figure 10.5*a,c*, the effects emerged extremely early, seemingly at the time of stimulus onset. Due to the fact that the waveforms were aligned on the pre-stimulus baseline, these observations indicate that the effects probably began before the onset of the stimulus, possibly in response to the task cue, which was presented some 2.7 s earlier. Thus, the effects observed here (and, possibly, in the two fMRI studies described in § 10.3*a*) seem likely to reflect a combination of stimulus-elicited and pre-stimulus activity.

(c) Item- versus state-related activity

The last of our fMRI encoding studies to be described here (Otten *et al.* 2002) was in part motivated by an important implication of the ERP findings. The finding that subsequent memory effects can be elicited by a pre-stimulus cue raises the possibility that encoding is affected not only by the processing received by a study item, but also by differences in general 'state', as reflected by neural activity unrelated to the processing of specific items (see Figure 10.6). The distinction between item- and state-related processes has long been a subject of debate in the interpretation of findings from studies of episodic retrieval (Rugg & Wilding 2000), but has received less attention with respect to the neural correlates of encoding (although see Fernández *et al.* 1999). The experiment described here constitutes our first effort to determine whether the distinction is relevant to the understanding of the determinants of successful encoding.

To separate item- and state-related activity, it is necessary to use a design that ensures that the two classes of activity are as uncorrelated as possible (cf. Chawla *et al.* 1999; Donaldson *et al.* 2001). We achieved this by employing a series of task blocks, during each of which individual study items were presented at highly variable inter-stimulus intervals (Figure 10.7). The blocks were separated by short rest periods, at the end of which a cue was presented to signal whether the items in the upcoming block required an animacy or a syllable judgement (these tasks were identical to those employed in the second of the experiments described in § 10.3*a*). The principal question was whether state-related neural activity associated with engagement in the study tasks (i.e. task-related activity remaining after the removal of transient activity elicited by the study items) reflected efficacy of encoding. We addressed this

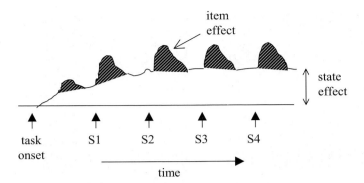

Fig. 10.6. Schematic illustration of state- and item-related brain activity. State-related activity is elicited by engagement in the experimental task and is tonically maintained throughout the task epoch. Item-related activity (hatched areas) is elicited in response to the presentation of specific experimental stimuli.

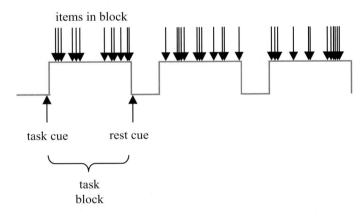

Fig. 10.7. Design for investigation of state- and item-related effects using fMRI. Cues were continuously present during entire task and rest blocks. During the task blocks, items are presented at irregular intervals. By judicious selection of these intervals, the correlation between the regressors employed to model the state- and item-related signal changes can be kept acceptably low (Chawla *et al.* 1999).

question by performing, separately for each encoding task, a block-wise analysis that identified regions where state-related activity covaried with the number of items that were subsequently confidently recognized.

We focus here on the animacy task, as this yielded the clearest and most robust findings. Figure 10.8 illustrates the results of both the aforementioned state-related analysis and also our 'standard' analysis of item-related subsequent memory effects. Turning to these latter results first (Figure 10.8*a*), the most notable finding was that subsequent memory effects were once again observed in the left inferior prefrontal cortex. It is also noteworthy that whereas effects were also observed in ventral anterior temporal cortex, there was no sign of an effect in the vicinity of the hippocampus. As shown in Figure 10.8*b*, the analysis of state-related effects revealed two regions in which activity predicted the number of items from a block that would later be remembered: a medial parietal area in which greater activity was

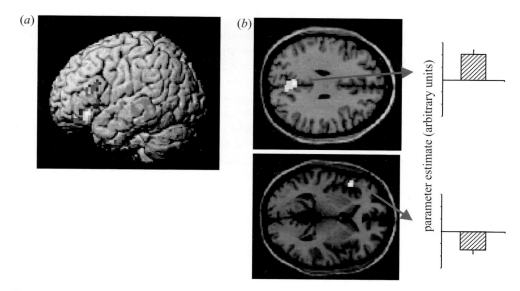

Fig. 10.8. See also Plate 34. (*a*) Subsequent memory effects for items studied in the animacy task of Otten *et al.* (2002). Effects can be seen in the ventral and dorsal inferior frontal gyrus, and anterior ventral temporal cortex. Results are illustrated at a threshold of $p < 0.001$. (*b*) Regions where state-related activity during the animacy task blocks covaried ($p < 0.001$) with the number of subsequently recognized items. Greater activity was associated with better memory performance in the medial parietal cortex, and with worse performance in the left inferior prefrontal cortex. The bars show the mean parameter estimates and standard errors for the voxels showing the peak effect in each region.

associated with better performance and a left inferior frontal region where the reverse relationship was obtained. The latter region was part of the same left frontal area that showed a subsequent memory effect at the item level.

Two main conclusions can be derived from these findings. First, subsequent memory performance is indeed associated with variations in state-related activity, indicating a role for factors such as 'set' in the modulation of efficacy of encoding (cf. the notion of 'retrieval mode'; Wheeler *et al.* 1997; Düzel *et al.* 1999; Rugg & Wilding 2000). Second, the same region can demonstrate both item- and state-related subsequent memory effects. Intriguingly, the relationship between these 'shared' effects in the present experiment was reciprocal, inviting speculation about a trade-off in this left frontal region between the resources allocated to item- and state-related processing. Further research is required both to replicate these findings and to begin to elucidate their functional significance.

(d) Concluding comments

Before further discussion of the implications of these findings, mention should be made of an important caveat related to the use of recognition memory to assess subsequent memory performance. It has been proposed that recognition judgements are supported by two kinds of memory (Mandler 1980; Jacoby & Kelley 1992). Recognition can occur when a test item elicits retrieval of a specific past episode involving the item ('recollection')—the focus of interest in the current studies. It is argued, however, that a test item can also be recognized on the basis of its 'familiarity'—an acontextual form of memory held to be dissociable from recollection on phenomenal (Gardiner & Java 1993), functional (Yonelinas *et al.* 1998) and neurological (Aggleton & Brown 1999) grounds. The question thus arises whether the subsequent memory effects described in § 10.3*a–c* are associated with the encoding of 'true' episodic memories rather than memory representations supporting subsequent familiarity judgements.

A full answer to this question will have to await the more extensive use of retrieval tasks where familiarity plays less of a role than it appears to do in yes–no recognition. There are, however, grounds for thinking that at least some of the findings described here are relevant specifically to episodic memory. First, by focusing on confident recognition judgements, we biased our definition of 'remembered' items in favour of those recognized on the basis of recollection (Yonelinas *et al.* 1996). Second, findings similar to some of those described here have been reported in studies employing retrieval tasks designed explicitly to distinguish between recollection- and familiarity-based recognition. For example, Henson *et al.* (1999*a*) reported that left prefrontal (BAs 9 and 47) activity at study was greater for subsequently recognized words that were assigned 'Remember' rather than 'Know' judgements (introspective judgements held to distinguish between recognition based on recollection as opposed to familiarity (Tulving 1985; Gardiner & Java 1993)). Similar findings, albeit for the right prefrontal cortex, were reported by Brewer *et al.* (1998) in a study employing pictures. An alternative means of separating recognition based on episodic retrieval and familiarity is to employ a retrieval task that requires both a recognition judgement and a judgement as to the context in which the test item was originally encoded (a 'source' judgement). The assumption underlying this procedure is that recognition accompanied by successful contextual retrieval is more likely to have involved recollection than when contextual retrieval is unsuccessful. Using such a procedure with pictures of common objects, Cansino *et al.* (2002) observed subsequent memory effects in, among other regions, an area of the left inferior frontal gyrus (BA 44/6) that overlapped part of the left frontal region found by Otten *et al.* (2001) to exhibit subsequent memory effects for confidently recognized words.

On the assumption that our findings do indeed reflect the neural correlates of episodic encoding, the question arises as to the light they shed on the encoding process and its neural bases. As already mentioned, one key conclusion is that, at the cortical level, there does not seem to be a single region or circuit that supports episodic encoding regardless of the nature of the processing engaged at the time an event is experienced (Otten & Rugg 2001*a*; see also Davachi *et al.* 2001). Rather, it appears that effective encoding is associated with the enhancement of activity in regions supporting the 'online' processing of an event; regions that will differ depending on the specific cognitive operations that are engaged. Whether the different regions demonstrating such effects (e.g. Figure 10.4) act cooperatively to form a durable memory representation, or whether instead they operate independently, is an important and unresolved question.

A related issue concerns the functional significance of the subsequent memory effects revealed in these and other studies. (Note that we are confining ourselves here to effects taking the form of greater activity for subsequently remembered relative to forgotten items, and do not consider the reverse pattern (Otten & Rugg 2001*c*; Wagner & Davachi 2001)). Why should enhanced activity in certain brain regions be associated with better subsequent memory? For the reasons outlined in § 10.1, it is unlikely that the effects merely reflect such factors as differential allocation of attention, or 'time on task'. An alternative possibility is that the effects reflect the benefits to memory of processing an item beyond what is required for immediate purposes. This notion is a generalization of a proposal originally formulated to account for subsequent memory effects in the left inferior prefrontal cortex in relation to its role in semantic processing (Gabrieli *et al.* 1998). It raises the intriguing question of exactly what causes some items to receive 'additional' processing? Presumably this is determined by a combination of subject and item variables that are likely to prove difficult to disentangle.

The final issue to be mentioned relates to the role of the medial temporal lobe and, in particular, the hippocampus, in episodic encoding. Evidence from human and animal lesion studies indicates that the hippocampal formation plays a fundamental role in episodic memory and several theoretical accounts propose that it is crucial for successful encoding (e.g. Alvarez & Squire 1994; O'Reilly & McClelland 1994). The finding of hippocampal subsequent memory effects in the study of Otten *et al.* (2001) is consistent with these accounts and, arguably, unsurprising. One might argue, for example, that the effects reflect the relatively greater hippocampal activity required to process the 'additional' information that helps make an item memorable (see above and Otten *et al.* 2001). More surprising, perhaps, is that most published studies employing the subsequent memory procedure have not reported hippocampal subsequent memory effects (for other exceptions see Kirchhoff *et al.* 2000; Davachi *et al.* 2001), a pattern reflected on a smaller scale across the three fMRI studies described in § 10.3*a–c*. While we are confident that the finding of a hippocampal effect in our first study was not a false positive (the finding has been replicated both in currently unpublished studies in our own laboratory and elsewhere; Fletcher *et al.* 2002), we have no explanation for why subsequent memory effects in this structure are found so inconsistently.

10.4. Episodic retrieval

Episodic retrieval—recollection—occurs when an interaction between a 'retrieval cue' and a memory representation leads to the consciously accessible reconstruction of a past episode (Tulving 1983). The theoretical framework that we currently employ for the interpretation of ERP and haemodynamic studies of episodic retrieval is outlined in Rugg & Wilding (2000). There it was argued that it is useful to distinguish between processes that operate on a retrieval cue in the course of an attempt to retrieve information from memory (pre-retrieval processes) and processes that operate on the products of a retrieval attempt (post-retrieval processes).

We confine ourselves here to a discussion of these latter processes, focusing on the neural correlates of the retrieval and subsequent processing of recently acquired episodic information (so-called 'retrieval success' effects). To identify these correlates, certain methodological requirements must be met. First, it is necessary to characterize separately the activity elicited by test cues giving rise to successful versus unsuccessful retrieval. Early PET and fMRI studies of episodic retrieval, in which 'blocked' designs were employed, do not meet this requirement (for reviews, see Fletcher *et al.* 1997; Desgranges *et al.* 1998). The confounding of state- and item-related effects (Figure 10.6) that occurs with such designs makes it difficult to distinguish between the phasic activity elicited by specific cues (e.g. recognition memory test items) and tonic activity associated with mere engagement in the retrieval task. Furthermore, blocked designs do not permit separate assessment of activity associated with different classes of response (e.g. recognition hits versus misses). For these reasons, the neural correlates of successful retrieval are better studied with event-related methods.

A second desirable feature of studies of episodic retrieval is the use of retrieval tests that allow the neural correlates of recollection to be separated from those associated with other forms of memory. As was discussed in § 10.3*d*, simple 'yes–no' recognition does not suffice in this respect because recognition judgements can be based not only on episodic retrieval, but also a seemingly qualitatively different form of memory—familiarity (see also Brown & Bashir 2002). Again, as already noted, this difficulty can be overcome by the employment of procedures— such as 'Remember–Know' and source memory tasks—that allow identification of items whose recognition was accompanied by recollection of details of the study episode.

Most studies in which the above two methodological requirements were met have employed the ERP method and have led to the identification of what appears to constitute an electro-physiological 'signature' of recollection-based recognition memory (§ 10.4*b*). By contrast, most event-related fMRI studies of successful retrieval have employed yes–no recognition memory (for a review, see Rugg & Henson 2002). In these studies, the regions reported most consistently as showing greater activity for old than for new items are the left anterior prefrontal cortex (BA 9/10) and the lateral and medial parietal cortex (BA 7/39/40).

Findings from two event-related fMRI experiments (Henson *et al.* 1999*a*; Eldridge *et al.* 2000) that employed the Remember–Know procedure indicate that activity in some of these regions may be selectively associated with recollection. As illustrated in Figure 10.9, Henson *et al.* (1999*a*) observed greater activity in the left anterior prefrontal and lateral parietal regions (as well as in the posterior cingulate) for recognized items judged as 'Remembered' rather than 'Known'. Similar findings were described by Eldridge *et al.* (2000). Unlike Henson *et al.* (1999*a*), these authors also found that items judged as remembered elicited greater activity in the hippocampal formation.

(a) Event-related fMRI study of the exclusion task

We investigated the neural correlates of recognition memory using a procedure—based on the 'exclusion' task devised by Jacoby (1991)—more closely related to source memory than to introspective report. Study items were words presented in one of two contexts, defined by the combination of font colour and spatial position (e.g. green–left versus red–right). At test, the studied words, intermixed with unstudied ones, were presented in central vision in a white

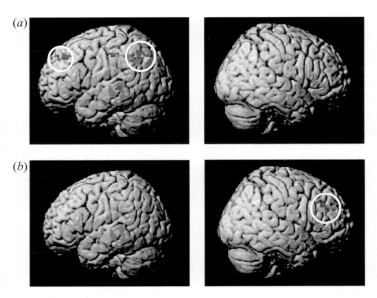

Fig. 10.9. See also Plate 35. Data from Henson *et al.* (1999*a*). (*a*) Regions demonstrating greater activity for recognized items receiving Remember rather than Know judgements. These regions include the left anterior prefrontal and left lateral parietal cortex (indicated with white circles). (*b*) Right dorsolateral prefrontal region where the activity was greater for items receiving Know rather than Remember judgements. Images thresholded at $p < 0.01$.

font. Words that had been studied in one of the contexts were designated as 'targets' and required a 'yes' response. Words studied in the other context—'non-targets'—had to be classified along with the unstudied words as 'new'. Following Jacoby (1991), we assume that whereas target items can be classified correctly on the basis of either recollection or familiarity, this is not so for non-targets. For these items, a correct response requires that familiarity be 'opposed' by the recollection that the item belongs to the non-target context. Thus, only recollection can serve as the basis for the correct classification of non-target items.

We looked for regions associated with the retrieval and subsequent processing of episodic information by contrasting the activity elicited by correctly classified non-targets and unstudied words. Unlike the contrasts employed in most previous studies of recognition memory, this comparison permits the neural correlates of successful retrieval to be assessed while holding constant factors linked to response choice—the same 'no' response is given to both classes of item. At issue is whether any of the regions identified by this contrast correspond to those identified as associated with recollection in the aforementioned Remember–Know experiments. As can be seen in Figure 10.10, two regions—the left anterior prefrontal (BA 10) and the lateral parietal cortex (BA 7/39/40)—are in the general vicinity of regions revealed in Henson et al. (1999a; see Figure 10.9) (although it should be noted that the anterior prefrontal area identified in that study is dorsal to the one illustrated in Figure 10.10). Enhanced activity for non-targets was also found in regions not identified in the Remember minus Know subtraction; these regions included the right anterior and dorsolateral prefrontal cortex.

The results for the lateral parietal and left anterior prefrontal regions converge with previous findings to indicate that their engagement is a neural correlate of recollection and can be found across a range of different task and response requirements. This conclusion contrasts with that for the right prefrontal cortex and, in particular, for the right dorsolateral region illustrated in Figure 10.10. As shown in Figure 10.9, in the experiment of Henson et al. (1999a) the same region exhibited greater activity for items attracting Know than Remember judgements, that is, for items judged old in the *absence* of recollection. Henson et al. (1999a) found that, even when compared with the activity elicited by unstudied items, words attracting Remember judgements failed to activate the right dorsolateral region.

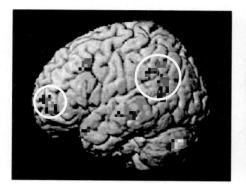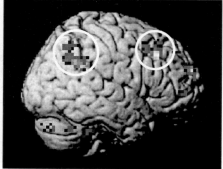

Fig. 10.10. See also Plate 36. Data from Rugg *et al.* (2002) illustrating regions where activity was greater for correctly classified non-target items than for correctly classified new words in their recognition exclusion task. The regions include left anterior prefrontal, bilateral parietal and right dorsolateral prefrontal cortex (indicated by circles). Images thresholded at $p < 0.01$.

How can these seemingly disparate results be reconciled? An important clue comes from an experiment where recognition memory judgements were accompanied by confidence ratings rather than Remember–Know judgements (Henson *et al.* 2000). Henson *et al.* (2000) found that right dorsolateral activity was greater for items attracting low rather than high confidence judgements, regardless of the items' study history. They proposed that this region supports processes contributing to the 'monitoring' or 'evaluation' of the products of a retrieval attempt. They argued that when information supporting a recognition judgement was relatively impoverished, monitoring operations would be engaged to a greater extent than when the information was less ambiguous. This account sits well with the findings from the experiment described here: a correct response to a non-target item required not merely information that an item was 'old', but identification of the source of that information. Presumably, it was the 'post-retrieval' monitoring and evaluation operations necessitated by this latter requirement that engaged the right dorsolateral prefrontal region (see also Henson *et al.* 1999*b*). By contrast, a correct 'new' judgement could be based on the mere detection of novelty, without the need for further evaluation. The latencies of the responses to the two classes of word support this account, in that it took, on average, more than 200 ms longer to respond to non-targets (1392 ms) than to unstudied words (1165 ms).

The general picture to emerge from the foregoing discussion is one in which recognition accompanied by episodic retrieval is associated with engagement of both lateral parietal cortex and a variety of prefrontal areas. Whereas parietal and left anterior prefrontal activity seem to be relatively invariant across variations in task requirements, other prefrontal activity, especially in the right dorsolateral region, appears to be task sensitive. Right dorsolateral activity showed up as 'recollection related' in one study (Figure 10.10) and 'familiarity related' in another (Figure 10.9; Henson *et al.* 1999*a*), depending apparently upon which experimental conditions make the greater demands on post-retrieval monitoring operations.

(b) Relationship between fMRI and ERP correlates of recollection

The picture detailed in § 10.4*a* is broadly in line with that emerging from studies using ERPs to investigate episodic retrieval (see Rugg & Allan (2000) and Friedman & Johnson (2000) for reviews). Many of these studies have described the so-called 'left parietal old–new effect'. This is a positive shift in ERPs elicited by correctly classified old items relative to waveforms elicited by new items. The effect (see Figure 10.11) begins *ca.* 400–500 ms post-stimulus, is maximal over the left parietal scalp and, on the basis of its sensitivity to a variety of experimental variables, has been interpreted as a neural correlate of recollection (Rugg & Allan 2000). Notably, as is the case for the lateral parietal activity reported in fMRI studies, the left parietal ERP effect is larger for items accorded as Remember rather than Know judgements (Smith 1993; Düzel *et al.* 1997) and can be elicited in exclusion tasks by correctly classified non-targets (Wilding & Rugg 1997; Cycowicz *et al.* 2001). It has been proposed that the left parietal effect reflects cortical activity supporting the hippocampally mediated 'reactivation' or 'reinstatement' of retrieved information (Rugg *et al.* 1998*b*). An alternative possibility, arguably more compatible with the role posited for the parietal cortex in attention (Kastner & Ungerleider 2000), is that the effect reflects an attentional shift or orientating triggered by successful episodic retrieval. On the basis of current evidence, it seems reasonable to suppose that the parietal activity identified in event-related fMRI studies of recognition memory, which is frequently more prominent on the left (Rugg & Henson 2002), is the haemodynamic correlate of the left parietal ERP effect.

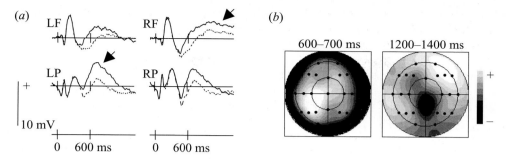

Fig. 10.11. An example of left parietal and right frontal ERP effects, taken from Mark & Rugg (1998). (*a*) Group-averaged waveforms elicited by recognized items receiving correct source judgements ('recollected') and correctly classified new items ('correct rejections') from left and right frontal and parietal electrode sites. Left parietal and right frontal old–new effects are indicated by the arrows. Solid line, recollection; dotted line, correct rejection. (*b*) Scalp distributions of the two effects, obtained by subtracting waveforms elicited by correct rejections from those elicited by recollected items. The distributions show the characteristic scalp maxima of the two effects and their differing time courses.

A second ERP effect to have been associated with recollection-based recognition is the 'right frontal old–new effect'. This effect begins later than the left parietal effect and takes the form of a sustained positive shift with an amplitude maximum over the right frontal scalp (see Figure 10.11). The effect is most evident in tasks, such as source memory, where recollected information must be evaluated before an appropriate response can be selected. It has been interpreted as a correlate of 'post-retrieval' operations engaged when retrieved information must be represented, maintained and monitored with respect to its relevance to current behavioural goals (Rugg & Allan 2000; Rugg & Wilding 2000). It is possible that the right frontal ERP effect reflects, at least in part, the right dorsolateral activity illustrated in Figures 10.9 and 10.10 and reported in other fMRI experiments. In support of this idea is the finding that, as is the case for right dorsolateral activity, the right frontal ERP effect is not associated invariably with successful episodic retrieval. In one study of old–new recognition memory, the effect was elicited by items that, by virtue of their impoverished encoding, could be judged old only on the basis of weak familiarity information (Rugg *et al.* 2000). Such judgements would presumably place heavy demands on the monitoring operations held to be supported by the right dorsolateral prefrontal cortex (Henson *et al.* 1999*a,b*; 2000).

Whereas left parietal and right frontal ERP effects appear to map quite well onto analogous fMRI effects, it should be borne in mind that there is currently no direct evidence to support the proposed mapping. Moreover, it is difficult to find ERP parallels for other fMRI findings. In particular, we noted that the left anterior prefrontal cortex was among the regions identified in fMRI studies as likely to be associated with recognition based upon recollection. It has been suggested that activity in this region supports the switching between cognitive operations (Fletcher & Henson 2001), perhaps as a result of the need to engage post-retrieval processing. We are unaware, however, of an ERP effect that might be an analogue of this fMRI finding. Whereas frontally distributed ERP effects additional to (and earlier than) the right frontal effect have been reported in several studies of recognition memory, these have been interpreted as correlates of priming or familiarity rather than recollection (e.g. Rugg *et al.* 1998*a*; Curran 2000; Tsivilis *et al.* 2001). The development of formal methods for the integration of ERP and fMRI data is likely to make a major contribution to the resolution of this and other apparent anomalies. It is important to bear in mind, however, that the correspondence between the neural correlates of memory processing revealed by electrophysiological and haemodynamic data is likely to be less than perfect (Rugg 1999).

(c) Role of the hippocampus in retrieval

Whereas Eldridge *et al.* (2000) reported greater activity in the hippocampal formation for 'recollected' than 'non-recollected' items, we failed to find evidence of such an effect in either our earlier study (Henson *et al.* 1999*a*) or in the one described here. These negative results are typical of event-related fMRI studies of recognition memory (Rugg & Henson 2002). The finding of Eldridge *et al.* (2000) seems unlikely to represent an anomaly, however, as elevated hippocampal activity for items likely to have elicited strong recollection has also been reported in other studies (Cabeza *et al.* 2001; Cansino *et al.* 2002). In the study of source memory by Cansino *et al.* (2002), for example, greater activity was elicited in the hippocampal formation by recognized items given correctly rather than incorrect source judgements. These positive findings are consistent with the proposal that retrieval-related hippocampal activity is associated specifically with recollection (Schacter *et al.* 1996; Rugg *et al.* 1997) and, more generally, with the view that the hippocampal formation forms part of a circuit serving episodic retrieval rather than the recovery of non-episodic information such as item familiarity (e.g. Aggleton & Brown 1999). The exact circumstances that lead to a detectable increase in hippocampal activity during episodic retrieval nonetheless remain unclear (for further discussion, see Schacter & Wagner (1999) and Rugg & Henson (2002)). One possibility, consistent with the findings from our first encoding experiment (Otten *et al.* 2001), is that contrasts between studied and unstudied items often fail to reveal retrieval-related effects because they are 'cancelled' by the encoding-related activity elicited by unstudied items (Fletcher *et al.* 1995; Rugg *et al.* 1997). We know of no direct evidence in support of this possibility, however. In short, as is also true for encoding (§ 10.3*d*), positive findings obtained for the hippocampal formation are consistent with evidence from other methodologies, but shed little new light on the role of this structure in episodic retrieval.

10.5. Outstanding issues

We have focused on the loci and temporal properties of neural activity engaged during the encoding and retrieval of episodic memories. In addition, we have tried to describe our experiments in a way that allows the reader to appreciate some of the methodological issues involved in using non-invasive, event-related measures of brain activity to address such questions. Among the numerous issues raised by our and others' results, two stand out. First, the importance of developing methods for the integration of electrophysiological and haemodynamic data, permitting the derivation of a measure of neural activity with good spatial *and* good temporal resolution. Second, the need to use such a measure to investigate how the different brain regions identified in the above experiments interact during memory tasks. It will then be possible to gain an understanding of how these regions interact to form the functional networks that support the formation and retrieval of episodic memories.

The approach outlined in the present paper has identified several brain regions that had not previously been linked strongly with episodic memory (e.g. parietal and anterior prefrontal cortex). As such, it has brought a fresh perspective to the question of the neural bases of this fundamental cognitive function. It is important to acknowledge, however, that by themselves functional imaging data do not permit strong conclusions as to the regions that are *necessary* for the formation and retrieval of episodic memories (this is a specific case of the more general problem of drawing causal inferences from 'correlational' data, a problem that extends beyond functional neuroimaging to include other methodologies, such as single-neuron recordings). To draw such conclusions, convergent evidence is required from studies investigating memory performance after different brain regions have been rendered dysfunctional, as a result of either a lesion or, perhaps, the use of a reversible method such as transcranial magnetic stimulation (Rossi *et al.* 2001). The present findings identify some of the regions that should be targeted in such studies, and provide clues to their possible functional roles.

The authors and their research are supported by the Wellcome Trust. Additional research support is provided by a cooperative award from the UK Medical Research Council.

References

Aggleton, J. P. & Brown, M. W. 1999 Episodic memory, amnesia, and the hippocampal–anterior thalamic axis. *Behav. Brain Sci.* **22**, 425–444.

Alvarez, P. & Squire, L. R. 1994 Memory consolidation and the medial temporal lobe: a simple network model. *Proc. Natl Acad. Sci. USA* **91**, 7041–7045.

Baddeley, A., Conway, M. & Aggleton, J. (eds) 2001 Episodic memory. *Phil. Trans. R. Soc. Lond.* B **356**, 1341–1515.

Baker, J. T., Sanders, A. L., Maccotta, L. & Buckner, R. L. 2001 Neural correlates of verbal memory encoding during semantic and structural processing tasks. *Neuroreport* **12**, 1251–1256.

Brewer, J. B., Zhao, Z., Desmond, J. E., Glover, G. H. & Gabrieli, J. D. E. 1998 Making memories: brain activity that predicts how well visual experience will be remembered. *Science* **281**, 1185–1187.

Brown, M. W. & Bashir, Z. I. 2002 Evidence concerning how neurons of the perirhinal cortex may affect familiarity discrimination. *Phil. Trans. R. Soc. Lond.* B **357**, 1083–1095. (DOI 10.1098/ rstb.2002.1097.)

Buckner, R. L., Kelley, W. M. & Petersen, S. E. 1999 Frontal cortex contributes to human memory formation. *Nat. Neurosci.* **2**, 311–314.

Cabeza, R., Rao, S. M., Wagner, A. D., Mayer, A. R. & Schacter, D. L. 2001 Can medial temporal lobe regions distinguish true from false? An event-related functional MRI study of veridical and illusory recognition memory. *Proc. Natl Acad. Sci. USA* **98**, 4805–4810.

Cameron, K. A., Yashar, S., Wilson, C. L. & Fried, I. 2001 Human hippocampal neurons predict how well word pairs will be remembered. *Neuron* **30**, 289–298.

Cansino, S., Maquet, P., Dolan, R. J. & Rugg, M. D. 2002 *Brain activity underlying encoding and retrieval of source memory. Cerebr. Cortex.* (In the press.)

Chapman, R. M., McCrary, J. W. & Chapman, J. A. 1978 Short-term memory: the 'storage' component of human brain responses predicts recall. *Science* **202**, 1211–1214.

Chawla, D., Rees, G. & Friston, K. J. 1999 The physiological basis of attentional modulation in extrastriate visual areas. *Nat. Neurosci.* **2**, 671–676.

Craik, F. I. M. & Lockhart, R. S. 1972 Levels of processing: a framework for memory research. *J. Verbal Learning Verbal Behav.* **11**, 671–684.

Curran, T. 2000 Brain potentials of recollection and familiarity. *Mem. Cogn.* **28**, 923–938.

Cycowicz, Y. M., Friedman, D. & Snodgrass, J. G. 2001 Remembering the color of objects: an ERP investigation of source memory. *Cerebr. Cortex* **11**, 322–334.

Dale, A. & Buckner, R. 1997 Selective averaging of rapidly presented individual trials using fMRI. *Hum. Brain Mapping* **5**, 329–340.

Davachi, L., Maril, A. & Wagner, A. D. 2001 When keeping in mind supports later bringing to mind: neural markers of phonological rehearsal predict subsequent remembering. *J. Cogn. Neurosci.* **13**, 1059–1070.

Demb, J. B., Desmond, J. E., Wagner, A. D., Vaidya, C. J., Glouer, G. H. & Gabrieli, J. D. E. 1995 Semantic encoding and retrieval in the left inferior prefrontal cortex: a functional MRI study of task difficulty and process specificity. *J. Neurosci.* **15**, 5870–5878.

Desgranges, B., Baron, J.-C. & Eustache, F. 1998 The functional neuroanatomy of episodic memory: the role of the frontal lobes, the hippocampal formation, and other areas. *Neuroimage* **8**, 198–213.

Donaldson, D. I., Petersen, S. E., Ollinger, J. M. & Buckner, R. L. 2001 Dissociating state and item components of recognition memory using fMRI. *Neuroimage* **13**, 129–142.

Donchin, E. & Lindsley, D. B. (eds) 1969 *Average evoked potentials:methods,results,and evaluations.* Washington, DC: US Government Printing Office.

Düzel, E., Yonelinas, A. P., Mangun, G. R., Heinze, H. J. & Tulving, E. 1997 Event-related brain potential correlates of two states of conscious awareness in memory. *Proc. Natl Acad. Sci. USA* **94**, 5973–5978.

Düzel, E., Cabeza, R., Picton, T. W., Yonelinas, A. P., Scheich, H., Heinze, H. J. & Tulving, E. 1999 Task-related and item-related brain processes of memory retrieval. *Proc. Natl Acad. Sci. USA* **16**, 1794–1799.

Eldridge, L. L., Knowlton, B. J., Furmanski, C. S., Bookheimer, S. Y. & Engel, S. A. 2000 Remembering episodes: a selective role for the hippocampus during retrieval. *Nature Neurosci.* **3**, 1149–1152.

Fernández, G., Brewer, J. B., Zhao, Z., Glover, G. H. & Gabrieli, J. D. E. 1999 Level of sustained entorhinal activity at study correlates with subsequent cued-recall performance: a functional magnetic resonance imaging study with high acquisition rate. *Hippocampus* **9**, 35–44.

Fletcher, P. C. & Henson, R. N. A. 2001 Prefrontal cortex and human memory—insights from functional neuroimaging. *Brain* **124**, 849–881.

Fletcher, P. C., Frith, C. D., Grasby, P. M., Shallice, T., Frackowiak, R. S. & Dolan, R. J. 1995 Brain systems for encoding and retrieval of auditory–verbal memory: an *in vivo* study in humans. *Brain* **118**, 401–416.

Fletcher, P. C., Frith, C. D. & Rugg, M. D. 1997 The functional neuroanatomy of episodic memory. *Trends Neurosci.* **20**, 213–218.

Fletcher, P. C., Stephenson, C. M. E., Carpenter, T. A., Donovan, T. & Bullmore, E. T. 2002 Hippocampal and prefrontal activity during encoding tasks is predictive of subsequent memory: an event-related fMRI study. *Cortex.* (In the press.)

Friedman, D. & Johnson Jr, R. 2000 Event-related potential (ERP) studies of memory encoding and retrieval: a selective review. *Microsci. Res. Technology* **51**, 6–28.

Gabrieli, J. D. E., Poldrack, R. A. & Desmond, J. E. 1998 The role of left prefrontal cortex in language and memory. *Proc. Natl Acad. Sci. USA* **95**, 906–913.

Gardiner, J. M. & Java, R. I. 1993 Recognising and remembering. In *Theories of memory* (ed. A. Collins, M. A. Conway, S. E. Gathercole & P. E. Morris), pp. 163–188. Hillsdale, NJ: Erlbaum.

Heit, G., Smith, M. E. & Halgren, E. 1990 Neuronal activity in the human medial temporal lobe during recognition memory. *Brain* **113**, 1093–1112.

Henson, R. N. A., Rugg, M. D., Shallice, T., Josephs, O. & Dolan, R. J. 1999*a* Recollection and familiarity in recognition memory: an event-related functional magnetic resonance imaging study. *J. Neurosci.* **19**, 3962–3972.

Henson, R. N. A., Shallice, T. & Dolan, R. J. 1999*b* Right prefrontal cortex and episodic memory retrieval: a functional MRI test of the monitoring hypothesis. *Brain* **122**, 1367–1381.

Henson, R. N. A., Rugg, M. D., Shallice, T. & Dolan, R. J. 2000 Confidence in recognition memory for words: dissociating right prefrontal roles in episodic retrieval. *J. Cogn. Neurosci.* **12**, 913–923.

Jacoby, L. 1991 A process dissociation framework: separating automatic from intentional uses of memory. *J. Memory and Language* **30**, 513–541.

Jacoby, L. L. & Kelley, C. 1992 Unconscious influences of memory: dissociations and automaticity. In *The neuropsychology of consciousness* (ed. A. D. Milner & M. D. Rugg), pp. 201–233. London: Academic.

Josephs, O., Turner, R. & Friston, K. J. 1997 Event-related fMRI. *Hum. Brain Mapping* **5**, 243–248.

Kapur, S., Craik, F. I. M., Tulving, E., Wilson, A. A., Houle, S. & Brown, G. M. 1994 Neuroanatomical correlates of encoding in episodic memory: levels of processing effect. *Proc. Natl Acad. Sci. USA* **91**, 2008–2011.

Kapur, S., Tulving, E., Cabeza, R., McIntosh, R., Houle, S. & Craik, F. I. M. 1996 Neural correlates of intentional learning of verbal materials: a PET study in humans. *Cogn. Brain Res.* **4**, 243–249.

Kastner, S. & Ungerleider, L. G. 2000 Mechanisms of visual attention in the human cortex. *A. Rev. Neurosci.* **23**, 315–341.

Kelley, W. M. (and 10 others) 1998 Hemispheric specialization in human dorsal frontal cortex and medial temporal lobe for verbal and nonverbal memory encoding. *Neuron* **20**, 927–936.

Kirchhoff, B. A., Wagner, A. D., Maril, A. & Stern, C. E. 2000 Prefrontal-temporal circuitry for episodic encoding and subsequent memory. *J. Neurosci.* **20**, 6173–6180.

Logothetis, N. K., Pauls, J., Augath, M., Trinath, T. & Oeltermann, A. 2001 Neurophysiological investigation of the basis of the fMRI signal. *Nature* **412**, 150–157.

Mandler, G. 1980 Recognizing: the judgement of previous occurrence. *Psychol. Rev.* **87**, 252–271.

Mark, R. E. & Rugg, M. D. 1998 Age effects on brain activity associated with episodic memory retrieval: an electrophysiological study. *Brain* **121**, 861–873.

Moscovitch, M. & Nadel, L. 1998 Consolidation and the hippocampal complex revisited: in defense of the multiple-trace model. *Curr. Opin. Neurobiol.* **8**, 297–300.

O'Reilly, R. C. & McClelland, J. L. 1994 Hippocampal conjunctive encoding, storage, and recall: avoiding a trade-off. *Hippocampus* **4**, 661–682.

Otten, L. J. & Rugg, M. D. 2001*a* Task-dependency of the neural correlates of episodic encoding as measured by fMRI. *Cerebr. Cortex* **11**, 1150–1160.

Otten, L. J. & Rugg, M. D. 2001*b* Electrophysiological correlates of memory encoding are task-dependent. *Cogn. Brain Res.* **12**, 11–18.

Otten, L. J. & Rugg, M. D. 2001*c* When more means less: neural activity related to unsuccessful memory encoding. *Curr. Biol.* **11**, 1528–1530.

Otten, L. J., Henson, R. N. A. & Rugg, M. D. 2001 Depth of processing effects on neural correlates of memory encoding: relationship between findings from across- and within-task comparisons. *Brain* **124**, 399–412.

Otten, L. J., Henson, R. N. A. & Rugg, M. D. 2002 State- and item-related neural correlates of successful memory encoding. *Nature Neurosci.* (Submitted.)

Paller, K. A., Kutas, M. & Mayes, A. R. 1987 Neural correlates of encoding in an incidental learning paradigm. *Electroencephalographical Clin. Neurophysiol.* **67**, 360–371.

Poldrack, R. A., Wagner, A. D., Prull, M. W., Desmond, J. E., Glover, G. H. & Gabrieli, J. D. E. 1999 Functional specialization for semantic and phonological processing in the left inferior prefrontal cortex. *Neuroimage* **10**, 15–35.

Rossi, S., Cappa, S. F., Babiloni, C., Pasqualetti, P., Miniussi, C., Carducci, F., Babiloni, F. & Rossini, P. M. 2001 Prefontal cortex in long-term memory: an 'interference' approach using magnetic stimulation. *Nat. Neurosci.* **4**, 948–952.

Rugg, M. D. 1995 Event-related potential studies of memory. In *Electrophysiology of mind* (ed. M. D. Rugg & M. G. H. Coles), pp. 132–170. New York: Oxford University Press.

Rugg, M. D. 1999 Functional neuroimaging in cognitive neuroscience. In *Neurocognition of language* (ed. P. Hagoort & C. Brown), pp. 15–36. Oxford University Press.

Rugg, M. D. & Allan, K. 2000 Memory retrieval: an electrophysiological perspective. In *The new cognitive neurosciences* (ed. M. S. Gazzaniga), pp. 805–816. Cambridge, MA: MIT Press.

Rugg, M. D. & Wilding, E. L. 2000 Retrieval processing and episodic memory. *Trends Cogn. Sci.* **4**, 108–115.

Rugg, M. D. & Henson, R. N. A. 2002 Episodic memory retrieval: an (event-related) functional neuroimaging perspective. In *The cognitive neuroscience of memory encoding and retrieval* (ed. A. E. Parker, E. L. Wilding & T. Bussey). Hove: Psychology Press. (In the press.)

Rugg, M. D., Fletcher, P. C., Frith, C. D., Frackowiak, R. S. J. & Dolan, R. J. 1997 Brain regions supporting intentional and incidental memory: a PET study. *Neuroreport* **8**, 1283–1287.

Rugg, M. D., Mark, R. E., Walla, P., Schloerscheidt, A. M., Birch, C. S. & Allan, K. 1998*a* Dissociation of the neural correlates of implicit and explicit memory. *Nature* **392**, 595–598.

Rugg, M. D., Walla, P., Schloerscheidt, A. M., Fletcher, P. C., Frith, C. D. & Dolan, R. J. 1998*b* Neural correlates of depth of processing effects on recollection: evidence from brain potentials and positron emission tomography. *Exp. Brain Res.* **123**, 18–23.

Rugg, M. D., Allan, K. & Birch, C. S. 2000 Electrophysiological evidence for the modulation of retrieval orientation by depth of study processing. *J. Cogn. Neurosci.* **12**, 664–678.

Rugg, M. D., Henson, R. N. A. & Robb, W. G. K. 2002 Neural correlates of retrieval processing in the prefrontal cortex during recognition and exclusion tasks. *Neuropsychologia.* (Submitted.)

Sanquist, T. F., Rohrbaugh, J. W., Syndulko, K. & Lindsley, D. B. 1980 Electrocortical signs of levels of processing: perceptual analysis and recognition memory. *Psychophysiology* **17**, 568–576.

Schacter, D. L. & Wagner, A. D. 1999 Medial temporal lobe activations in fMRI and PET studies of episodic encoding and retrieval. *Hippocampus* **9**, 7–24.

Schacter, D. L., Alpert, N. M., Savage, C. R., Rauch, S. L. & Albert, M. S. 1996 Conscious recollection and the human hippocampal formation: evidence from positron emission tomography. *Proc. Natl Acad. Sci. USA* **93**, 321–325.

Shallice, T., Fletcher, P., Frith, C. D., Grasby, P., Frackowiak, R. S. J. & Dolan, R. J. 1994 Brain regions associated with acquisition and retrieval of verbal episodic memory. *Nature* **368**, 633–635.

Smith, M. E. 1993 Neurophysiological manifestations of recollective experience during recognition memory judgments. *J. Cogn. Neurosci.* **5**, 1–13.

Tsivilis, D., Otten, L. J. & Rugg, M. D. 2001 Context effects on the neural correlates of recognition memory: an electrophysiological study. *Neuron* **31**, 497–505.

Tulving, E. 1983 *Elements of episodic memory*. Oxford University Press.

Tulving, E. 1985 Memory and consciousness. *Can. Psychol.* **26**, 1–12.

Tulving, E., Kapur, S., Craik, F. I. M., Moscovitch, M. & Houle, S. 1994 Hemispheric encoding/retrieval asymmetry in episodic memory: positron emission tomography findings. *Proc. Natl Acad. Sci. USA* **91**, 2016–2020.

Wagner, A. D. & Davachi, L. 2001 Cognitive neuroscience: forgetting of things past. *Curr. Biol.* **23**, 964–967.

Wagner, A. D., Schacter, D. L., Rotte, M., Koutstaal, W., Maril, A., Dale, A. M., Rosen, B. R. & Buckner, R. L. 1998 Building memories: remembering and forgetting of verbal experiences as predicted by brain activity. *Science* **281**, 1188–1191.

Wagner, A. D., Koutstaal, W. & Schacter, D. L. 1999 When encoding yields remembering: insights from event-related neuroimaging. *Phil. Trans. R. Soc. Lond.* B **354**, 1307–1324. (DOI 10.1098/rstb.1999.0481.)

Wheeler, M. A., Stuss, D. T. & Tulving, E. 1997 Toward a theory of episodic memory: the frontal lobes and autonoetic consciousness. *Psychol. Bull.* **121**, 331–354.

Wilding, E. L. & Rugg, M. D. 1997 Event-related potentials and the recognition memory exclusion task. *Neuropsychologia* **35**, 119–128.

Wood, C. C. 1987 Generators of event-related potentials. In *A textbook of clinical neurophysiology* (ed. A. M. Halliday, S. R. Butler & R. Paul), pp. 535–567. New York: Wiley.

Yonelinas, A. P., Dobbins, I., Szymanski, M. D., Dhaliwal, H. S. & King, L. 1996 Signal-detection, threshold, and dual-process models of recognition memory: ROCs and conscious recollection. *Conscious Cogn.* **5**, 418–441.

Yonelinas, A. P., Kroll, N. E., Dobbins, I., Lazzara, M. & Knight, R. T. 1998 Recollection and familiarity deficits in amnesia: convergence of remember–know, process dissociation, and receiver operating characteristic data. *Neuropsychology* **12**, 323–339.

Zarahn, E., Aguirre, G. K. & D'Esposito, M. 1997 A trial-based experimental design for fMRI. *Neuroimage* **5**, 179–197.

Glossary

BA	Brodmann area
EEG	electroencephalogram
ERP	event-related potential
fMRI	functional magnetic resonance imaging
MEG	magnetoencephalogram
PET	positron emission tomography

11

Against memory systems

David Gaffan

The medial temporal lobe is indispensable for normal memory processing in both human and non-human primates, as is shown by the fact that large lesions in it produce a severe impairment in the acquisition of new memories. The widely accepted inference from this observation is that the medial temporal cortex, including the hippocampal, entorhinal, and perirhinal cortex, contains a memory system or multiple memory systems, which are specialized for the acquisition and storage of memories. Nevertheless, there are some strong arguments against this idea: medial temporal lesions produce amnesia by disconnecting the entire temporal cortex from neuromodulatory afferents arising in the brainstem and basal forebrain, not by removing cortex; the temporal cortex is essential for perception as well as for memory; and response properties of temporal cortical neurons make it impossible that some kinds of memory trace could be stored in the temporal lobe. All cortex is plastic, and it is possible that the same rules of plasticity apply to all cortical areas; therefore, memory traces are stored in widespread cortical areas rather than in a specialized memory system restricted to the temporal lobe. Among these areas, the prefrontal cortex has an important role in learning and memory, but is best understood as an area with no specialization of function.

11.1. Introduction

Large medial temporal lesions in the human brain produce an amnesic syndrome in which the acquisition of new memories is impaired in a devastating fashion (Scoville & Milner 1957; Corkin *et al.* 1997). Equally, medial temporal lesions in macaque monkeys (rhesus monkeys, *Macaca mulatta*, and cynomolgus monkeys, *Macaca fascicularis*) produce severe impairments in many memory tasks (Mishkin 1982; Gaffan *et al.* 2001). The inference has frequently been drawn that the cortex of the primate medial temporal lobe, including the hippocampal cortex and the rhinal cortex, can be characterized as a memory system (Mishkin 1982; Squire & Zola-Morgan 1991). A modification of this view is that the temporal lobe contains multiple memory systems, since smaller lesions within the temporal lobe produce dissociable impairments in different memory tasks (Gaffan 1994*a*). This idea, of multiple memory systems within the temporal lobe, is now widely accepted (Aggleton & Brown 1999; Kim & Baxter 2001).

Objections to the inference of a memory system or systems in the brain, from the existence of the amnesic syndrome, have been expressed forcefully, but only rarely (Horel 1978; Vanderwolf & Cain 1994). The arguments against that inference are now more powerful than ever. My purpose in reviewing them here is not just to point out the weaknesses in the hypothesis of memory systems. I also explore ideas about memory processing and cortical plasticity, and ideas about cortical localization of function, that might replace the idea that some cortical areas are functionally specialized as memory systems.

Section 11.2 presents evidence that the functions of temporal cortical areas are not just in memory, but also in perception and in the control of locomotion. Section 11.3 summarizes recent findings which show that dense amnesia after medial temporal lobe lesions is not due to the removal of specific cortical areas, but to the widespread disruption of temporal cortical function that is produced by disconnection of temporal cortex from the projections ascending to it from the basal forebrain and midbrain. Section 11.4 shows from the properties of normal human memory that the nature of some memories makes it impossible that they could be acquired in the temporal lobe, in the light of what is known about the response properties of temporal lobe neurons. In § 11.5 I argue that the plasticity of frontal cortex makes this cortex a plausible site for memory storage; however, all cortex is plastic. In § 11.6 I propose that cortical localization of function is not arbitrary, but hierarchical, and in § 11.7 I propose that the prefrontal cortex is not just the apex of a hierarchy of specialized cortical areas, but also the level at which the principle of hierarchically organized localized specialization of function is discarded. Section 11.8 discusses the rules of cortical and subcortical plasticity: the simplest hypothesis of a rule for cortical plasticity, consistent with the observations discussed here, is that the activity of cortical neurons comes to perform whatever function maximizes the probability of cortical arousal subsequent to that activity. In the concluding § 11.9, I argue that the concept of memory systems is harmful.

11.2. The functions of temporal cortical areas are not just in memory

Two of the most prominent temporal cortical areas that have been assigned a memory function are the hippocampal and perirhinal cortices. In rodents the memory function of the hippocampus is specifically in spatial memory, and this role in memory function can be seen as just a part of a hippocampal specialization for processing certain kinds of spatial information and for controlling locomotion (Horel 1978; Whishaw & Maaswinkel 1998). In addition, in macaques hippocampal lesions lead to severe impairments in spatial tasks (Murray *et al.* 1998), as do lesions of the main output pathway of the hippocampus, the fornix (Gaffan & Harrison 1989*b*). However, in this species, and also in humans, the picture is complicated by the fact that some of the impairments following lesions either to the hippocampus or to the fornix are in tasks which are not overtly spatial, such as scene learning and story recall. These, however, can be attributed to the important part played by spatial information in contextual retrieval (Gaffan 1992, 1994*c*). Moreover, discrete hippocampal lesions in monkeys can leave many powerful forms of non-spatial memory intact (Murray *et al.* 1993; Murray & Mishkin 1998), or only very mildly impaired (Baxter & Murray 2001*a,b*; Zola & Squire 2002), and discrete fornix lesions do not reliably impair some demanding memory tasks, either in humans (Aggleton *et al.* 2000) or in monkeys (Gaffan *et al.* 1984). Further complications arise from the uncertain specificity of hippocampal lesions in humans (Gaffan & Hornak 1997) and in monkeys (Baxter & Murray 2001*a,b*; Zola & Squire 2002). The controversial history of hippocampal involvement in memory function has recently been reviewed in detail elsewhere (Gaffan 2001). In brief, many non-spatial aspects of memory function are substantially independent of the hippocampus and fornix, and the main role of the hippocampus in primates as well as in rodents is in spatial information processing rather than in memory *per se*.

It should be noted, however, that denial of the status of memory system to the hippocampus does not depend specifically on accepting its spatial role. The data clearly show that hippocampal or fornix lesions do not lead to global severe memory impairments; if, in addition, they do lead to impairments in some specific kind of information processing, then the function of the hippocampus is less appropriately described as memory than as processing that specific kind of information, whether or not it happens to be spatial information (Ridley & Baker 1991; Brasted *et al.* 2002).

For the perirhinal cortex a similar argument leads to the conclusion that this area cannot be characterized as having only a memory function. Experiments on object-recognition memory in monkeys, in the tasks of delayed matching or non-matching to sample, appeared to indicate a role in memory function for the perirhinal cortex, either alone or in combination with the entorhinal cortex (Meunier *et al.* 1993; Eacott *et al.* 1994). In these experiments the monkeys with the cortical ablations appeared to simply forget the sample object faster than the controls: they performed the task at almost normal levels when there was a short retention interval between the sample presentation and the test trial, but their impairment became more severe as the retention interval lengthened. However, an alternative interpretation of this result is possible. A series of subsequent experiments has shown visual perceptual impairments in monkeys with lesions limited to the perirhinal cortex (Buckley *et al.* 1997, 2001; Buckley & Gaffan 1997, 1998*a–c*).

One aspect of these perceptual impairments that is particularly important is that they interact with task difficulty. For example, Buckley *et al.* (2001) investigated effects of perirhinal cortex lesions in an oddity judgement task. The monkeys were shown an array of six objects on each trial, and were required to choose the odd object in each array. The five non-odd objects were five different views of a single object, but the odd object was a different object; the objects which played the role of odd and non-odd objects in each array changed randomly from trial to trial, ensuring that the monkeys had to proceed by oddity judgements rather than by learning about individual objects as predictors of reward. However, some objects are quite easy to recognize as the same object in different views, while other objects appear very different in different views. It was thus possible to classify the different objects used in the experiment, on the basis of the monkeys' pre-operative performance in the oddity task, into six levels of difficulty. The impairment produced by perirhinal cortex ablations in this task was not noticeable with the objects that were easy to recognize, but increased markedly as the level of difficulty increased.

Formally this interaction of the lesion effect with task difficulty is similar to the results from object-recognition memory (Meunier *et al.* 1993; Eacott *et al.* 1994). In both cases, the impairment increases as the difficulty of the task increases. Forgetting, as the retention interval increases, is just one way of increasing task difficulty. But the oddity impairment is not a memory impairment, as the task requires no memory from trial to trial except memory for the oddity principle, and the results from the easy levels of task difficulty showed that the monkeys with rhinal cortex lesions had not forgotten the principle of oddity judgement. Thus, the simplest summary of these results is that rhinal or perirhinal cortex lesions impair a monkey's ability to identify individual objects. The impairment emerges most clearly when this ability is taxed, either by requiring object-recognition memory function across an interval, in delayed matching to sample, or by making object identity difficult to judge perceptually, in oddity judgements with different views of the same object.

11.3. Dense amnesia after medial temporal lobe lesions is not due to the removal of specific cortical areas, but to the widespread disruption of temporal cortical function by subcortical disconnection

Since the early unsuccessful attempts by Orbach *et al.* (1960) and by Correll & Scoville (1965) to replicate in the monkey the severe and global amnesia seen in the patient H. M. (Scoville & Milner 1957), it has repeatedly been shown that temporal cortical ablations in monkeys do not produce dense global amnesia. Although medial temporal ablations that are intended to remove the hippocampus and amygdala bilaterally do produce in the monkey severe impairment in object-recognition memory (Mishkin 1982), these lesions leave memory function in reward-association tasks unimpaired (Malamut *et al.* 1984) or only very mildly impaired (Correll & Scoville 1965: see also Gaffan & Lim 1991). This pattern of results is quite different from what is seen in human amnesia, because reward-association memory is severely impaired in human amnesia (Oscar-Berman & Zola-Morgan 1980; Hood *et al.* 1999). Although the emphasis in recent years has switched to the entorhinal and perirhinal cortex for an explanation of the impairments produced by these lesions in the early experiments with monkeys, the same problem arises: ablations of these rhinal cortical areas in the monkey similarly leave reward-association memory unimpaired (Gaffan & Murray 1992) or impaired only in special circumstances (Buckley & Gaffan 1997). A frequently proposed solution to this problem, to the effect that reward-association memory is truly memory in the human brain but not truly memory in the monkey brain (Mishkin & Petri 1984; Fernandez-Ruiz *et al.* 2001), is merely circular reasoning (Horel 1978; Gaffan 2001). Of course, if a bilateral temporal cortical ablation in the monkey is made extensive enough to include the cortex in the lateral temporal lobe, lateral to the perirhinal and parahippocampal cortex, then a more severe impairment in visual reward-association tasks appears; but in this case the perceptual effects are even more severe than those of perirhinal cortex lesions, and the effect as a whole is more appropriately described as being perceptual rather than a memory impairment (Heywood *et al.* 1995).

We have recently found, however, that a much more global and severe memory impairment can be produced in the monkey by surgically interrupting the axons in the white matter of the medial temporal lobe, rather than removing the medial temporal cortex. These axons include projections that rise from the basal forebrain and midbrain to innervate widespread areas of lateral as well as medial temporal cortex. The ascending axons reach the temporal cortex through three routes (Selden *et al.* 1998): in the fornix–fimbria; in fibres of passage through the amygdala; and in the anterior temporal stem (the white matter surrounding the amygdala dorsally and laterally). All three of these routes are interrupted by surgical excisions in patient H. M. (for the anterior temporal stem damage, see panels H–J of figure 2 in the report by Corkin *et al.* (1997)). When all three routes (but not any subset of only two routes) are interrupted in the monkey, a severe memory impairment results (Gaffan *et al.* 2001; Maclean *et al.* 2001) and this includes not only impairment in object-recognition memory but also, crucially, impairment in reward-association memory, that was absent from the earlier attempts to replicate in the monkey the global amnesia seen in the patient H. M.

The effect of these disconnections in macaque monkeys is shown in Figure 11.1*a*, TS + AM + FX. The plot shows the percentage of errors on successive trials in a reward-association task that tests a very powerful form of memory in the monkey, which we have called object-in-place memory, and which is similar in some respects to human memory for events (Gaffan 1994*c*). Notice that the effect of the three-part interruption (TS + AM + FX) is devastating, producing performance almost at chance even at levels of task difficulty which allowed almost perfect performance pre-operatively. Notice also that fornix transection alone in this task (FX in Figure 11.1) produces a relatively mild impairment, just as it does in the human brain (Aggleton *et al.* 2000; Figure 11.1*b*) and that the effect of the three-part disconnection is much more severe than that. Furthermore, the monkeys with this disconnection were able to retrieve at least some information that had been acquired pre-operatively (Gaffan *et al.* 2001). In all these three respects, the impairment produced by the three-part disconnection in

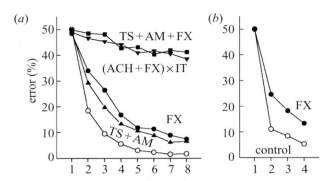

Fig. 11.1. Data redrawn from experiments by Aggleton *et al.* (2000); Easton *et al.* (2002) and Gaffan *et al.* (2001). Both panels show learning in lists of 'object-in-place' scenes. (*a*) Results from macaque monkeys pre-operatively (pre, white circles) and following bilateral lesions to the anterior temporal stem and amygdala (TS + AM, black triangles), fornix (FX, black circles), and the combination of those three lesions (TS + AM + FX, black squares); also following the combination of a unilateral inferior temporal cortical ablation in one hemisphere with a unilateral fornix transection and cholinergic lesion in the other hemisphere ((ACH + FX) × IT, black inverted triangles). (*b*) Results from humans performing the same task after removal of colloid cysts from the third ventricle, divided into patients with bilateral fornix section (FX, black circles) and patients with fornix intact (control, white circles).

the monkey resembles human dense amnesia. The effect can be attributed to axonal interruption rather than to the small amount of cortical damage that was produced by the section of anterior temporal stem and amygdala, because the powerful effect emerged only when fornix transection, which was carried out without any cortical damage at all, was added to the other two transections (TS + AM).

The same functional effect can be produced when the same structures are disconnected by a very different surgical manipulation in the monkey, namely disconnection by crossed unilateral lesions. In these experiments the inferior temporal cortex, through which visual information arrives in the temporal lobe, is ablated in only one hemisphere. In the other hemisphere either the cell bodies (Easton *et al.* 2002) or the axons (Easton & Gaffan 2000*b*, 2001; Easton *et al.* 2001) of the basal forebrain are ablated. Each of these unilateral lesions alone has little effect on memory, but when the two are present in opposite hemispheres the result is that the pathway from the basal forebrain to the temporal cortex is no longer available for visual information in either hemisphere, as the projections are almost exclusively ipsilateral. The effect of a unilateral subcortical lesion aimed at the cholinergic cells of the basal forebrain and at the fornix in one hemisphere, and crossed with a unilateral inferior temporal cortex ablation in the other hemisphere (Easton *et al.* 2002), is also shown in Figure 11.1*a*, (ACH + FX) × IT. The effect is indistinguishable from that of the combined transection of the pathways TS + AM + FX. The similar effects of these two very different surgical manipulations in the monkey, and the similarity of each of them to the effect of a yet different surgical procedure in the human brain (Corkin *et al.* 1997), support the idea that their common feature, namely the subcortical disconnection of temporal cortex, explains dense amnesia after temporal-lobe lesions, in both humans and monkeys.

A defining feature of human anterograde amnesia is that the acquisition of new memories is much more profoundly impaired than other, apparently equally demanding, tasks that demand the exercise of skills learned before the onset of amnesia, such as vocabulary knowledge and intelligence tests (Lezak 1983). Similar observations can be made in monkeys with experimentally induced temporal-lobe amnesia; these animals do not forget the general rules of the experimental tasks that they learned pre-operatively, such as how to operate the touchscreen, and they can remember many object–reward associations that they learned pre-operatively (Easton & Gaffan 2000*b*; Gaffan *et al.* 2001). This leads to the question of why the disconnection of the ascending pathway from the basal forebrain and midbrain to the temporal cortex has this marked impact on the acquisition of new memories. One possible answer is that some or all of the ascending influences are specifically required for the process of cortical plasticity, and are not as important for cortical information processing that does not require plasticity, such as the retrieval of old memories or the exercise of skills that were acquired pre-operatively. Another possible answer is simply that the acquisition of new memories is fundamentally a more fragile process than these other processes, as purely behavioural interventions, such as the requirement to perform a distracting concurrent task, affect acquisition more than retrieval (Naveh-Benjamin *et al.* 1998). These two answers are not mutually exclusive, however, and it is not necessary to decide between them in order to accept that the loss of these ascending influences impairs the acquisition of new memories more than the retrieval of old memories.

This new hypothesis of the origin of dense amnesia after temporal-lobe lesions has important implications for understanding human amnesia, particularly for the relationship between amnesia after discrete temporal-lobe lesions, amnesia in early stages of Alzheimer's disease, and amnesia in multi-infarct dementia (Mesulam 1995). However, my present focus is on its implications for localized memory systems. If temporal-lobe amnesia is ascribed to the interruption of ascending axons from the basal forebrain and midbrain, it is quite implausible to think that those axons constitute a memory system. A memory system must receive and store complex information, but the ascending axons from the basal forebrain and midbrain convey an arousal signal rather than complex information (Semba 1991; Easton & Gaffan 2000*a*).

To summarize the argument so far, we have seen that the effects of lesions in the cortical temporal areas that are thought to be the constituents of a putative temporal-lobe memory system, namely the hippocampal and the rhinal cortices, reveal two features that are difficult to reconcile with the idea that they constitute a memory system. The first difficulty is that in the monkey selective lesions in these cortical areas do not produce memory impairments as severe as those that are seen in human temporal-lobe amnesia, which were the original impetus for the hypothesis of memory systems itself. The second difficulty is that the effects of these lesions show that the cortical areas should be characterized as processing a certain kind of information, spatial information or object-identity information, rather than as being specialized for memory; and, in the case of object-identity information, it can clearly be seen that the impairment of this processing ability, after perirhinal lesions, is manifest in perceptual tasks that do not require new memory formation. Further, it is not possible to save the memory-systems hypothesis by extending the putative cortical memory system beyond the hippocampal and rhinal cortices into the lateral temporal-lobe cortex, lateral to the perirhinal and parahippocampal cortices, because the perceptual effects of a lesion in this area are even more obvious and severe than the perceptual effects of perirhinal cortex lesions.

The rival hypothesis is that memory function and perception are not separately localized in specific cortical areas. In medial temporal-lobe amnesia a widespread disruption of temporal cortical function, including the lateral temporal cortex as well as the rhinal and hippocampal cortex, is produced by the disconnection of the temporal cortex from the basal forebrain and midbrain. This disconnection produces dense anterograde amnesia because the acquisition of new memories is more vulnerable to the effects of the disconnection than are the other processes that the same cortical areas are involved in, such as perception, locomotion, and memory retrieval.

11.4. Some memories cannot be acquired in the temporal lobe

A further difficulty for the hypothesis of temporal-lobe memory storage can be seen in some properties of normal memory. The problem arises from the fact that the representation of complex visual scenes in the temporal lobes is divided at the vertical meridian of the visual field between the two hemispheres. When a monkey sees a single object that is presented against a large blank background, many neurons in the temporal lobe in both hemispheres respond to the object and signal its identity, even when the object is confined to one visual hemifield (Chelazzi *et al.* 1998). However, a single object presented against a large blank background is not a natural condition of object vision and memory. In an only slightly more naturalistic condition, when two objects are presented, with one object in each visual hemifield, the responses of the temporal cortex neurons are quite different. Now, neurons in the temporal lobe of each hemisphere respond only to the object that is in the visual hemifield contralateral to the hemisphere; their activity is not significantly affected by the object in the ipsilateral hemifield, even when the monkey is attending only to the object in the ipsilateral hemifield (Chelazzi *et al.* 1998). This poses a problem for understanding the memory of objects that are presented in this fashion, that is, in scenes having at least one object in each visual hemifield. Consider the case where an object, a constituent of a visual scene that contains other objects, is presented for learning in one visual hemifield but is subsequently presented for a recognition-memory test in the opposite hemifield. In the learning trial, neurons in only one temporal lobe respond to the object, and in the retention-test trial, neurons in only the other temporal lobe respond to the object. All proposals as to the neural basis of object memory assume that the memory of an object is stored as a modification in neurons that respond to the presentation of the object (Sakai & Miyashita 1991; Sakai *et al.* 1994; Bogasz *et al.* 2001), and indeed it is difficult to see how neurons that do not respond to the presentation of an object could either lay down or retrieve a memory of it. It thus follows, from the electrophysiological data, that in the case we are considering, where the target object in a scene is presented in opposite hemifields at learning and at the retention test, neurons in neither of the two temporal lobes have both the opportunity to lay down and also the opportunity to retrieve a memory of the target object. Therefore, if object memories are stored either exclusively or mainly as modifications of neurons within the temporal lobe, the memory of the object should either fail or suffer a substantial decrement in this case.

Hornak *et al.* (2002) performed an experiment to test this counter-intuitive prediction in normal human subjects. The subjects were asked to remember a set of objects that were always presented for learning in pairs with one object in each hemifield. At the subsequent retention test, each object that had been presented for learning was now presented again, together with a novel foil object in the opposite visual hemifield, and the subject indicated which of the two objects was the one that had been presented for learning. Between the acquisition presentation and the retention test, some of the objects changed their retinal position. The shift could be from one hemifield to the other ('horizontal shift') or a change of the same distance within a hemifield ('vertical shift'). Control objects were presented in the same retinal location at both acquisition and retention ('no change'). Further, these changes in retinal location, between the acquisition and the retention test, were produced in different ways in two different tasks: by keeping a single constant fixation point for the subject's eyes, and changing the position of the object on the display screen ('constant fixation') or by keeping the position of the object on the display screen the same, but changing the position of the subject's fixation point ('changing fixation'). The results with constant fixation confirmed the effect that one should expect if temporal-lobe neurons contribute to the storage of object memories: retention accuracy after horizontal shifts was less accurate (68.6% correct) than retention accuracy after vertical shifts (74.7% correct). The size of the effect, which was much less than a total failure of memory in the horizontal shift condition, suggests that temporal-lobe neurons store only part of the memory trace of the objects; nevertheless, the effect was highly reliable statistically, and to this extent confirms the prediction derived from the electrophysiological data. However, the results with changing fixation did not show that effect: retention accuracy after horizontal shifts was the same (73.1% correct) as after vertical shifts (71.0% correct). Though identical in terms of the retinal positions of objects in the various conditions, these two tasks are quite different from each other in the natural memory performances they resemble. In the task with constant fixation the subject repeatedly sees the same view of the apparatus from exactly the same fixation point, and memory in this task thus resembles the natural task of reconstructing in memory a complex scene in which one fixated only one object. The task with changing fixation requires the subject to fixate different positions in successive views, and memory in this task thus resembles the natural task of reconstructing in memory a complex scene that was inspected with successive saccades to different fixation points. The results from the task with changing fixation show that we do indeed possess the ability to store a memory of the scene that is not hemifield specific, a memory that cannot be stored in the temporal lobes.

These results imply that neuronal activity in the temporal lobe not only contributes to memory storage in the temporal lobe but also contributes to memory storage in extra-temporal cortical areas, in which a visual representation that is not hemifield specific must be stored. Thus, the severe visual memory impairment that is produced by medial temporal lesions is not to be explained by assuming that all visual memories are normally stored within the temporal lobe.

As originally pointed out by Horel (1978), a lesion in the white matter of the anterior medial temporal lobe, which can be either bilateral (Scoville & Milner 1957) or unilateral (Hornak *et al.* 1997), interrupts the uncinate fascicle, in which cortico-cortical axons transmit information between the temporal and prefrontal cortices. If the prefrontal cortex is an important site for the storage of extra-temporal memories, as § 11.5 suggests, then the interruption of this pathway could explain the impairment of extra-temporal as well as temporal memory storage in patients with these lesions.

11.5. Frontal and other cortical plasticity

Where could memories be stored outside the temporal lobe? One obvious candidate area is the prefrontal cortex. Ample evidence in non-human primates indicates that the prefrontal cortex is essential to normal memory function, not just in working memory but in a wide range of memory and learning functions (Gaffan & Harrison 1980*a*; Parker & Gaffan 1998*a*,*b*). Extensive but selective and bilaterally symmetrical prefrontal lesions, of the kind that are studied in these experiments with monkeys, are rarely if ever seen clinically. However, closely related evidence comes from bilaterally symmetrical lesions of one of the main thalamic nuclei related to the prefrontal cortex, MD. Lesions in MD produce memory impairment in both humans (Hodges & McCarthy 1993) and monkeys (Gaffan & Parker 2000), and it is likely that this results from disrupting the dense reciprocal connections between MD and the prefrontal cortex, rather than the very light projection that MD receives from the temporal lobe (Gaffan & Parker 2000). However, MD lesions in humans also produce impairments in a reasoning and fluency test that are also sensitive to frontal cortex damage (Hodges & McCarthy 1993), and in this respect the effects of MD lesions are different from temporal-lobe amnesia. Given this prefrontal involvement in the memory function, one might expect that a syndrome resembling temporal-lobe amnesia would follow if the prefrontal cortex were deprived of the ascending influences that the prefrontal cortex, like the temporal cortex, receives from the basal forebrain and midbrain. In the monkey this disconnection can be produced by crossed unilateral lesions of the frontal cortex and the axons of the basal forebrain, and severe memory impairments are seen after this disconnection (Easton & Gaffan 2001; Easton *et al.* 2001). It is possible that basal forebrain axons ascending to the prefrontal cortex in the human brain pass through a bottleneck in the posterior ventromedial part of the frontal white matter, and that damage at this bottleneck is the explanation of the dense amnesia that can be produced by rupture of aneurysms of the anterior communicating artery in this region (Diamond *et al.* 1997).

There is ample evidence in monkeys to indicate that neurons in the prefrontal cortex adapt their activity in response to the demands of whatever task the animal is trained in (Duncan 2001). In the light of this evidence it may seem attractive to propose that this adaptive plasticity is the special defining feature of prefrontal cortex function. However, it is difficult to reconcile that proposal with the fact that other cortical areas adapt their activity in response to task demands in a similar way. This plasticity is seen not only in the temporal (Sakai & Miyashita 1991) and somatosensory cortex (Pascual Leone & Torres 1993) but even in the occipital cortex (Fiorentini *et al.* 1972; Schoups *et al.* 2001). For these reasons, frontal plasticity should not be thought of as being qualitatively different from other cortical plasticity. How, then, should the involvement of the prefrontal cortex in learning and memory be characterized? Many authors have commented on the difficulty of characterizing prefrontal cortex function in cognitive terms in any satisfactory manner (Wise *et al.* 1996; Duncan 2001; Gaffan 1994*b*). Temporal and frontal specialization of function, whether in memory or in any other cognitive domain, needs to considered within the broader context of the nature of the cortical localization of function, as discussed in § 11.6.

11.6. Cortical localization of function is not arbitrary but hierarchical

The hypothesis we began from, namely that the function of the medial temporal cortex is memory, is an example of the products of a widespread style of hypothesis formation in cognitive neuroscience. In this style, the function of a cortical area can be anything that the theoretician's ingenuity can reconcile with a dataset. It can be an everyday mental function such as memory or emotion (Rolls 1999), or an invented function such as behavioural inhibition (Gray & McNaughton 2000), or an operationally defined process like recognition memory (Gaffan 1976). An alternative to this undisciplined theorization is the idea that cortical specialization of a function is hierarchically organized in a principled fashion.

The contrast between these two approaches can be illustrated in the prestriate visual cortex. Until recently, it was widely believed that the prestriate cortex contained a 'plethora of visual areas in each of which a relatively simple attribute of the visual image is analysed by the cells' (Cowey 1982, p. 7). According to this view, the attributes to which each area is devoted—colour, movement, depth, texture, and so on—can only be discovered empirically and separately, since the different areas function in parallel with each other. An alternative to this view has been developed by Lennie (1998). He proposes that, with the exception of movement information in optical flow analysis, information about these different attributes of a visual stimulus is kept together in all the visual areas—as seems to be required by the similar selectivities of neurons in the different areas to all of these attributes (Lennie 1998, figure 4). He explains the specialization of the different areas as serial stages in a hierarchical processing system. Each stage performs all the analysis that can be performed at that stage, given the information that is available in the input to that stage, and then passes the results on to higher stages for further processing.

The account of Lennie (1998) of visual function in the prestriate cortex is similar in many ways to an analysis of visual function in the temporal cortex that has been put forward by Murray & Bussey (1999) and Buckley & Gaffan (2000). This again relies on the idea of hierarchical processing. According to Murray & Bussey (1999) and Buckley & Gaffan (2000), simple object features such as colour are analysed in the modality-specific visual association cortex of the inferior temporal lobe lateral and posterior to the perirhinal cortex (area TE of von Bonin & Bailey (1947)); these features are then passed on to the perirhinal cortex, which analyses the conjunctions of object features, that is, the configuration of features that defines a unique object. Some of the evidence for this account, for example, is that colour-threshold tests and object-memory tests doubly dissociate the effects of lesions in area TE and in the perirhinal cortex (Buckley *et al.* 1997), and that colour-oddity judgements and simple-shape oddity judgements are not impaired by perirhinal lesions in the same way as oddity judgements based on object identity are, even when the colour- or shape-oddity judgements are made very difficult by choosing similar colours or shapes (Buckley *et al.* 2001). This hierarchical model of the perirhinal and inferior temporal cortex can be seen as an extension of the scheme of Lennie (1998) for the prestriate cortex. Similarly, the monkey's memory for objects presented in complex scenes depends on an interaction between the spatial information derived from the hippocampus and the object-identity information derived from the perirhinal cortex (Gaffan & Parker 1996), and this is again an extension of the hierarchical principle: object-in-place information in complex scenes must necessarily depend on prior extraction of information about places and object identities.

Another aspect of cortical localization brought out in the review of Lennie (1998) is the idea that cortical localization allows interactions between neurons within a specialized area to take place without needing long axons, which are expensive in terms of requiring space within the head. Thus, if evolution can 'know' in advance of an individual animal's experience that a group of neurons will need to interact with each other, it makes sense to put them into a specialized local area.

In these ways, the multiple double dissociations that ablation experiments have revealed in the temporal lobe, between the functions of area TE and the perirhinal cortex and the hippocampus-fornix (Gaffan 1994*a*; Buckley *et al.* 1997), should not be interpreted as evidence for a series of unrelated functional specializations, each of which has to be studied independently in its own right and with its own set of hypotheses and theories; rather, the functional specializations are derived from, and are fully explained by, the necessity of hierarchical organization, and of local grouping of neurons that need to interact with each other.

11.7. Prefrontal cortical function in a hierarchical scheme

This hierarchical approach can be naturally extended to the prefrontal cortex, which appears to be the apex of the hierarchy, in the sense that this cortical area is the furthest removed from the periphery (Jones & Powell 1970). However, this is not all there is to say about the position of the prefrontal cortex within a scheme of hierarchically organized cortical areas.

One of the most surprising aspects of prefrontal function is the absence of clear functional subdivisions within such a large area of cortex. Cytoarchitectonic subdivision of areas within the prefrontal cortex is contentious; unlike the divisions of the frontal cortex outside the prefrontal cortex, where the divisions are clear and widely agreed, within the prefrontal cortex the cytoarchitectonic areas are unclear, and the areas delineated by different investigators bear almost no similarity to each other (Akert 1964). Due to the fact that these areas are not universally agreed anatomical entities such as the striate cortex or the hippocampus, one should not have a strong expectation based on simply cytoarchitectural grounds that they must really be functionally different from each other. Differences between the electrophysiological properties or the haemodynamic responses of different areas would suggest such functional subdivisions, and some such differences have been observed, but they are neither consistent from study to study nor strong (Duncan 2001).

The absolute proof of such functional subdivisions could come only from double dissociations between the effects of different lesions within the prefrontal cortex. In spite of many ablation experiments in the macaque monkey designed to look for such double dissociations, I know of only one possible success, that of Butter (1969). However, Butter himself in this paper did not interpret his data as being strong evidence for specialization within the prefrontal cortex but quite the reverse. His experiment, with three different cognitive tasks and six different lesions within the prefrontal cortex, tested for a total of 45 different possible double dissociations, one for each pair of tasks and pair of lesions; however, he discovered only one. In assessing double dissociations it is important to distinguish between the prefrontal cortex and other cortical areas that are in the frontal lobe but are not prefrontal, and are not removed from the periphery but close to inputs and outputs; these include motor areas such as the frontal eye fields, the premotor and supplementary motor cortex, and several cingulate motor areas, and also the anterior olfactory nucleus on the posterior-medial part of the orbital surface—which was one of the lesions in the only double dissociation of Butter (1969). Thus, studies in macaques reporting double dissociations within the frontal cortex, but not within the prefrontal cortex, are not relevant to the issue of specialization within prefrontal cortex function, however valuable in themselves they are (Petrides 1987, figures 11,12). In the marmoset, however, the extent of the prefrontal, as opposed to the other frontal, cortex is not completely clear (Peden & von Bonin 1947; Garey 1994; Preuss 1995; Wallis *et al.* 2001). Finally, while the evidence for subdivided function is weak, the evidence for parallel function within macaque prefrontal cortex is strong. Parker & Gaffan (1998*b*) found that complete removal of the prefrontal cortex in the monkey produced a devastating impairment in even the simplest possible learning task, the acquisition of a single object–reward association, but that even the acquisition of multiple concurrent object–reward associations was not significantly impaired by removal of the ventral half of the prefrontal cortex. This result shows that the dorsal half of the prefrontal cortex is able to substitute fully for the ventral half in this task, even though objects and rewards are thought to be preferentially processed in the ventral half. In this way, it seems that the commonality of function between different parts of the prefrontal cortex is more important than minor differences between areas.

One response to this whole state of affairs is to hope that if only the cytoarchitectural divisions were drawn just right, and the lesions and experimental tasks were designed just right, then ablation experiments in macaque monkeys would reveal many double dissociations within the prefrontal cortex; this is the approach taken by Passingham (1993). I think it is more realistic to conclude that the apparent lack of strong heterogeneity of function within the very large area of prefrontal cortex is telling us something important about the function of this cortex. What it may indicate is that, after a certain level of processing has been achieved, the hierarchical system of localized function is no longer appropriate. The two advantages of this scheme that were identified in § 11.6 were that: information can be analysed in a certain hierarchical order that can be predicted in advance; and interactions within a subset of neurons that can be predicted in advance to require such interactions can take place locally without requiring long axons. However, some types of information analysis that an individual may benefit from are not predictable in advance. To support unpredictable processing demands it is necessary to abandon local grouping after a certain stage and allow neurons to interact at random. It is unsurprising in this context that it is the animals of highly intelligent and adaptable species—humans, apes and Old World monkeys—that alone possess a large area of prefrontal cortex (Preuss 1995). Certainly this would also explain why conditional discrimination tasks, in which animals learn quite arbitrary rules, are so sensitive to the effects of prefrontal cortex lesions in macaques. According to this view the prefrontal cortex is not just the apex of a hierarchy of specialized cortical areas, but also the level at which the principle of hierarchically organized localized specialization of function is discarded. This explains why the prefrontal cortex occupies such a large area without strongly differentiated functional subdivisions.

11.8. Rules of cortical and subcortical plasticity

As noted in § 11.5, electrophysiological studies of the prefrontal cortex show that neurons in the prefrontal cortex adapt their activity flexibly to task demands. More specifically, Chen *et al.* (2001) have suggested that prefrontal neurons change in response to instrumental training, that is, their activity is shaped by rewards and punishments. Before considering this proposal further, note that it applies equally to cortical plasticity outside the prefrontal cortex, as well as to the prefrontal cortex. A recent experiment by Schoups *et al.* (2001) in the striate cortex shows this very clearly. These authors trained monkeys to discriminate between lines of two orientations that were near to 45° (*ca.* 44–46°). The effect of training was to change the orientation tuning curves in those striate-cortex neurons in which the peak sensitivity was 12–20° removed from 45°;, either clockwise or anticlockwise. These neurons had the steepest slope of their orientation tuning curve at 45°and were therefore best able to make fine discriminations among orientations near to 45°, as the task demanded; and the effect of training was that the slope of the tuning curve of these neurons at this steepest point became steeper, thus improving the monkey's discriminative ability in the trained task. Many other examples of perceptual learning in the cortex can be explained by the simple assumption that trained stimuli expand their representation in the cortex; this could explain, for example, the expanded finger representation in the cortex in Braille readers (Pascual Leone & Torres 1993), and several other kinds of perceptual learning (reviewed by Gaffan 1996). However, such an explanation cannot apply to the experiment by Schoups *et al.* (2001), as these authors emphasize; the trained stimuli did not expand their cortical representation, and the cortical change resulting from training was not an expanded representation but an alteration in tuning curves. Rather, it appears necessary to explain their results as showing instrumental training effects, similar to those in the prefrontal cortex that Chen *et al.* (2001) discuss; the striate neurons changed in such a way as to maximize rewards.

This idea of instrumental training of cortical neurons is unfamiliar, but it is not difficult in principle to see how such training effects could occur. The idea of instrumental reinforcement is that an association is strengthened when reinforcement follows, even though reinforcement is not itself a term in the strengthened association—reinforcement is neither the retrieval cue for the association, nor the information recalled by the association (Sutton & Barto 1998). Translating this into neural terms to apply instrumental learning to cortical neurons, the necessary assumption is that reward delivery sends a neuromodulatory signal to cortical neurons, that is, a signal that does not directly elicit action potentials. Then the synapses that have been active before reward delivery, corresponding to the associations in psychological terms, need to be strengthened. The result is not that the neurons come to signal reward but that their activity comes to perform whatever function maximizes the probability of reward delivery subsequent to that activity.

Of course, the range of functions available to striate-cortex neurons is far narrower than the range of functions available to prefrontal cortex neurons, because of the restricted kind of information that is available presynaptically to striate neurons. Further, the changes observed by Schoups *et al.* (2001) were not necessarily only the direct effects of changes within the neurons that showed the changed tuning curves, but could possibly reflect a secondary effect of changes in other neurons; however, the same qualification applies to changes in the responses of the prefrontal neurons. Subject to these qualifications, the basic idea of synaptic weights being strengthened by instrumental reinforcement is necessary to explain the results from the striate cortex by Schoups *et al.* (2001) just as much as to explain the examples from the frontal cortex discussed by Duncan (2001) and Chen *et al.* (2001). The rules of cortical plasticity could be much more complicated than any of the possibilities I have discussed, but it is hard to see that a simpler idea could explain these results.

A modification of this proposal needs to be made, however, in order to accommodate the memory of aversive events. If instrumental learning were the only principle of memory formation, punishment would have to induce forgetting. To avoid this implausible consequence, it is preferable to assume that the neuromodulatory signal is not generated only by reward but by any event of significance to the animal, whether rewarding or aversive. This signal could correspond to the cortical arousal signal that is carried by the ascending influences from the basal forebrain and midbrain, discussed in § 11.3. Thus, the simplest hypothesis of a rule for cortical plasticity consistent with the observations I have discussed is that the activity of cortical neurons comes to perform whatever function maximizes the probability of cortical arousal subsequent to that activity.

Memory performance, such as the ability to recognize an object that has been seen before, could be a by-product of the synaptic changes that are generated by such a mechanism when an object is encountered and elicits some cortical arousal. If that is the only mechanism of cortical plasticity, however, it will not account for instrumental learning in the traditional sense, that is, the fact that animals learn to produce rewards and do not learn to produce punishments. Thus, a different kind of plasticity will be required subcortically to instantiate instrumental learning itself. Waelti *et al.* (2001) suggest that dopaminergic neurons, many of which project into the basal ganglia, provide teaching signals for associative learning: this could support a mechanism for reward-guided instrumental learning in the basal ganglia. This putative subcortical mechanism of instrumental learning receives the output of the cortex, however, so the memory functions provided by the cortex will be available to guide instrumental action. On the basis of monkeys' memory performance in a win–shift, lose–stay task, I proposed (Gaffan 1985) that rewards have two effects on plasticity in the brain: they lay down memories and also, independently, shape instrumental action. The present hypothesis extends this earlier hypothesis by supposing that memories are in the cortex and instrumental habits are in the basal ganglia. This is reminiscent of the proposal by Mishkin & Petri (1984) that habit learning is in the basal ganglia. However, unlike Mishkin & Petri (1984), I do not think that when a monkey learns some new object discrimination for food reward, a new habit is laid down in the basal ganglia. Rather, I propose that neurons in the basal ganglia acquire, in many such experiences with different objects, the habit of approaching those objects that evoke the memory of food reward, and the new discrimination is acquired by a cortical change as the new object becomes associated in memory with food.

11.9. Conclusion

I have drawn attention to some implications of the concept of memory systems that are not supported by the evidence. These include the idea that memories are stored exclusively in the putative memory systems, and the idea that the function of the putative memory systems is best characterized as memory. However, the concept of memory systems is in many ways attractive and useful. It enables electrophysiological, neuroanatomical, and cognitive studies to proclaim their clear relevance, which I do not doubt, to those problems of memory disorder that are such a prominent part of many brain diseases; and, for similar reasons, it allows the general drift of a research program to be conveyed instantly to a lay audience. In view of these advantages of the concept it might be thought churlish to insist on the falsity of its implications; after all, if medial temporal lesions produce amnesia, as they certainly do, then is this not sufficient in itself to justify the concept of a medial temporal memory system or systems in some sense, even if in detail some of the apparent implications of that idea have to be subsequently modified? Against this tolerant view it is necessary to show not simply that some implications of the concept are in conflict with the evidence but that the concept itself is harmful. This review has identified two ways in which the concept of memory systems impedes progress. In the study of cortical localization of function, it is a prominent instantiation of the idea that the functions of cortical areas can be characterized intuitively and in a haphazard and piecemeal fashion, and it thus stands in the way of a systematic hierarchical explanation of functional localization and its breakdown in the prefrontal cortex. Additionally, in the study of cortical plasticity, it stands in the way of the simple hypothesis that all cortical areas have the same rules of plasticity.

References

Aggleton, J. P. & Brown, M. W. 1999 Episodic memory, amnesia, and the hippocampal anterior thalamic axis. *Behav. Brain Sci.* **22**, 425–489.

Aggleton, J. P. (and 10 others) 2000 Differential cognitive effects of colloid cysts in the third ventricle that spare or compromise the fornix. *Brain* **123**, 800–815.

Akert, K. 1964 Comparative anatomy of frontal cortex and thalamocortical connections. In *The frontal granular cortex and behavior* (ed. J. M. Warren & K. Akert), pp. 372–396. New York: McGraw-Hill.

Baxter, M. G. & Murray, E. A. 2001*a* Effects of hippocampal lesions on delayed nonmatching-to-sample in monkeys: a reply to Zola and Squire. *Hippocampus* **11**, 201–203.

Baxter, M. G. & Murray, E. A. 2001*b* Opposite relationship of hippocampal and rhinal cortex damage to delayed non-matching-to-sample deficits in monkeys. *Hippocampus* **11**, 61–71.

Bogasz, R., Brown, M. W. & Giraud-Carrier, C. 2001 Model of familiarity discrimination in the perirhinal cortex. *J. Comput. Neurosci.* **10**, 5–23.

Brasted, P. J., Bussey, T. J., Murray, E. A. & Wise, J. S. P. 2002 Fornix transection impairs conditional visuomotor learning in tasks involving nonspatially differentiated responses. *J. Neurophysiol.* **87**, 631–633.

Buckley, M. J. & Gaffan, D. 1997 Impairment of visual object-discrimination learning after perirhinal cortex ablation. *Behav. Neurosci.* **111**, 467–475.

Buckley, M. J. & Gaffan, D. 1998*a* Learning and transfer of object–reward associations and the role of the perirhinal cortex. *Behav. Neurosci.* **112**, 15–23.

Buckley, M. J. & Gaffan, D. 1998*b* Perirhinal cortex ablation impairs configural learning and paired-associate learning equally. *Neuropsychologia* **36**, 535–546.

Buckley, M. J. & Gaffan, D. 1998*c* Perirhinal cortex ablation impairs visual object identification. *J. Neurosci.* **18**, 2268–2275.

Buckley, M. J. & Gaffan, D. 2000 The hippocampus, perirhinal cortex and memory in the monkey. In *Brain, perception, memory: advances in cognitive neuroscience* (ed. J. J. Bolhuis), pp. 279–298. Oxford University Press.

Buckley, M. J., Gaffan, D. & Murray, E. A. 1997 Functional double-dissociation between two inferior temporal cortical areas: perirhinal cortex vs middle temporal gyrus. *J. Neurophysiol.* **97**, 587–598.

Buckley, M. J., Booth, M. C. A., Rolls, E. T. & Gaffan, D. 2001 Selective perceptual impairments following perirhinal cortex ablation. *J. Neurosci.* (In the press.)

Butter, C. M. 1969 Perseveration in extinction and in discrimination reversal tasks following selective frontal ablations in *Macaca mulatta. Physiol. Behav.* **4**, 163–171.

Chelazzi, L., Duncan, J., Miller, E. K. & Desimone, R. 1998 Responses of neurons in inferior temporal cortex during memory-guided visual search. *J. Neurophysiol.* **80**, 2918–2940.

Chen, N.-H., White, I. M. & Wise, S. P. 2001 Neuronal activity in dorsomedial frontal cortex and prefrontal cortex reflecting irrelevant stimulus dimensions. *Exp. Brain Res.* **139**, 116–119.

Corkin, S., Amaral, D. G., Gonzalez, R. G., Johnson, K. A. & Hyman, B. T. 1997 H.M.'s medial temporal lobe lesion: findings from magnetic resonance imaging. *J. Neurosci.* **17**, 3964–3979.

Correll, R. E. & Scoville, W. B. 1965 Effects of medial temporal lobe lesions on visual discrimination performance. *J. Comp. Physiol. Psychol.* **60**, 175–181.

Cowey, A. 1982 Sensory and non-sensory visual disorders in man and monkey. *Phil. Trans. R. Soc. Lond.* B **298**, 3–13.

Diamond, B. J., Deluca, J. & Kelley, S. M. 1997 Memory and executive function in amnesic and non-amnesic patients with aneurysms of the anterior communicating artery. *Brain* **120**, 1015–1025.

Duncan, J. 2001 An adaptive coding model of neural function in prefrontal cortex. *Nature Rev. Neurosci.* **2**, 820–829.

Eacott, M. J., Gaffan, D. & Murray, E. A. 1994 Preserved recognition memory for small sets, and impaired stimulus identification for large sets, following rhinal cortex ablation in monkeys. *Eur. J. Neurosci.* **6**, 1466–1478.

Easton, A. & Gaffan, D. 2000*a* Amygdala and the memory of reward: the importance of fibres of passage from the basal forebrain. In *The amygdala: a functional analysis*, 2nd edn (ed. J. P. Aggleton), pp. 569–586. Oxford University Press.

Easton, A. & Gaffan, D. 2000*b* Comparison of perirhinal cortex ablation and crossed unilateral lesions of the medial forebrain bundle from the inferior temporal cortex in the rhesus monkey: effects on learning and retrieval. *Behav. Neurosci.* **114**, 1041–1057.

Easton, A. & Gaffan, D. 2001 Crossed unilateral lesions of the medial forebrain bundle and either inferior temporal or frontal cortex impair object–reward association learning in rhesus monkeys. *Neuropsychologia* **39**, 71–82.

Easton, A., Parker, A. & Gaffan, D. 2001 Crossed unilateral lesions of medial forebrain bundle and either inferior temporal or frontal cortex impair object recognition memory in Rhesus monkeys. *Behav. Brain Res.* **121**, 1–10.

Easton, A., Ridley, R. M., Baker, H. F. & Gaffan, D. 2002 Unilateral lesions of the cholinergic basal fore-brain and fornix in one hemisphere and inferior temporal cortex in the opposite hemisphere produce severe learning impairments in rhesus monkeys. *Cerebr. Cortex* **12**, 729–736.

Fernandez-Ruiz, J., Wang, J., Aigner, T. G. & Mishkin, M. 2001 Visual habit formation in monkeys with neurotoxic lesions of the ventrocaudal neostriatum. *Proc. Natl Acad. Sci. USA* **98**, 4196–4201.

Fiorentini, A., Ghez, C. & Maffei, L. 1972 Physiological correlates of adaptation to a rotated visual field. *J. Physiol.* **227**, 313–322.

Gaffan, D. 1976 Recognition memory in animals. In *Recall and recognition* (ed. J. Brown), pp. 229–242. London: Wiley.

Gaffan, D. 1985 Hippocampus: memory, habit and voluntary movement. In *Animal intelligence* (ed. L. Weiskrantz), pp. 87–99. Oxford: Clarendon.

Gaffan, D. 1992 Amnesia for complex naturalistic scenes and for objects following fornix transection in the Rhesus monkey. *Eur. J. Neurosci.* **4**, 381–388.

Gaffan, D. 1994a Dissociated effects of perirhinal cortex ablation, fornix transection and amygdalectomy: evidence for multiple memory systems in the primate temporal lobe. *Exp. Brain Res.* **99**, 411–422.

Gaffan, D. 1994b Interaction of temporal lobe and frontal lobe in memory. In *Motor and cognitive functions of the prefrontal cortex* (ed. A. M. Thierry, J. Glowinski, P. S. Goldman-Rakic & Y. Christen), pp. 129–138. Berlin: Springer.

Gaffan, D. 1994c Scene-specific memory for objects: a model of episodic memory impairment in monkeys with fornix transection. *J. Cogn. Neurosci.* **6**, 305–320.

Gaffan, D. 1996 Associative and perceptual learning and the concept of memory systems. *Cogn. Brain Res.* **5**, 69–80. [Reprinted in 1997 *Brain and mind* (ed. M. Ito), pp. 129–151. Amsterdam: Elsevier.]

Gaffan, D. 2001 What is a memory system? Horel's critique revisited. *Behav. Brain Res.* **127**, 5–11.

Gaffan, D. & Harrison, S. 1989a A comparison of the effects of fornix transection and sulcus principalis ablation upon spatial learning by monkeys. *Behav. Brain Res.* **31**, 207–220.

Gaffan, D. & Harrison, S. 1989b Place memory and scene memory: effects of fornix transection in the monkey. *Exp. Brain Res.* **74**, 202–212.

Gaffan, D. & Hornak, J. 1997 Amnesia and neglect: beyond the Delay–Brion system and the Hebb synapse. *Phil. Trans. R. Soc. Lond.* B **352**, 1481–1488. (DOI 10.1098/rstb.1997.0135.)

Gaffan, D. & Lim, C. 1991 Hippocampus and the blood supply to TE: parahippocampal pial section impairs visual discrimination learning in monkeys. *Exp. Brain Res.* **87**, 227–231.

Gaffan, D. & Murray, E. A. 1992 Monkeys (*Macaca fascicularis*) with rhinal cortex ablations succeed in object discrimination learning despite 24-hr intertrial intervals and fail at matching to sample despite double sample presentations. *Behav. Neurosci.* **106**, 30–38.

Gaffan, D. & Parker, A. 1996 Interaction of perirhinal cortex with the fornix-fimbria: memory for objects and object-in-place memory. *J. Neurosci.* **16**, 5864–5869.

Gaffan, D. & Parker, A. 2000 Mediodorsal thalamic function in scene memory in rhesus monkeys. *Brain* **123**, 816–827.

Gaffan, D., Saunders, R. C., Gaffan, E. A., Harrison, S., Shields, C. & Owen, M. J. 1984 Effects of fornix transection upon associative memory in monkeys: role of the hippocampus in learned action. *Q. J. Exp. Psychol.* **36B**, 173–221.

Gaffan, D., Parker, A. & Easton, A. 2001 Dense amnesia in the monkey after transection of fornix, amygdala and anterior temporal stem. *Neuropsychologia* **39**, 51–70.

Garey, L. J. 1994 *Brodmann's 'Localization in the cerebral cortex' translated with editorial notes and an introduction*. London: Smith-Gordon.

Gray, J. A. & McNaughton, N. 2000 *The neuropsychology of anxiety: an enquiry into the functions of the septo-hippocampal system*, 2nd edn. Oxford University Press.

Heywood, C. A., Gaffan, D. & Cowey, A. 1995 Cerebral achromatopsia in monkeys. *Eur. J. Neurosci.* **7**, 1064–1073.

Hodges, J. R. & McCarthy, R. A. 1993 Autobiographical amnesia resulting from bilateral paramedian thalamic infarction: a case study in cognitive neurobiology. *Brain* **116**, 921–940.

Hood, K. L., Postle, B. R. & Corkin, S. 1999 An evaluation of the concurrent discrimination task as a measure of habit learning: performance of amnesic subjects. *Neuropsychologia* **37**, 1375–1386.

Horel, J. A. 1978 The neuroanatomy of amnesia: a critique of the hippocampal memory hypothesis. *Brain* **101**, 403–445.

Hornak, J., Oxbury, S., Oxbury, J., Iversen, S. D. & Gaffan, D. 1997 Hemifield-specific visual recognition memory impairments in patients with unilateral temporal lobe removals. *Neuropsychologia* **35**, 1311–1315.

Hornak, J., Duncan, J. & Gaffan, D. 2002 The role of vertical meridian in visual memory for objects. *Neuropsychologia*. (In the press.)

Jones, E. G. & Powell, T. P. S. 1970 An anatomical study of converging sensory pathways within the cerebral cortex of the monkey. *Brain* **93**, 793–820.

Kim, J. J. & Baxter, M. G. 2001 Multiple brain-memory systems: the whole does not equal the sum of its parts. *Trends Neurosci.* **24**, 324–330.

Lennie, P. 1998 Single units and visual cortical organization. *Perception* **27**, 889–935.

Lezak, M. D. 1983 *Neuropsychological assessment*, 2nd edn. New York: Oxford University Press.

Maclean, C. J., Gaffan, D., Baker, H. F. & Ridley, R. M. 2001 Visual discrimination learning impairments produced by combined transections of the anterior temporal stem, amygdala and fornix in marmoset monkeys. *Brain Res.* **888**, 34–50.

Malamut, B. L., Saunders, R. C. & Mishkin, M. 1984 Monkeys with combined amygdalo-hippocampal lesions succeed in object discrimination learning despite 24-hour intertrial intervals. *Behav. Neurosci.* **98**, 759–769.

Mesulam, M. M. 1995 Cholinergic pathways and the ascending reticular activating system of the human brain. *Ann. NY Acad. Sci.* **757**, 169–179.

Meunier, M., Bachevalier, J., Mishkin, M. & Murray, E. A. 1993 Effects on visual recognition of combined and separate ablations of the entorhinal and perirhinal cortex in rhesus monkeys. *J. Neurosci.* **13**, 5418–5432.

Mishkin, M. 1982 A memory system in the monkey. *Phil. Trans. R. Soc. Lond.* B **298**, 85–95.

Mishkin, M. & Petri, H. L. 1984 Memories and habits: some implications for the analysis of learning and retention. In *Neuropsychology of memory*, 1st edn (ed. L. R. Squire & N. Butters), pp. 287–296. New York: Guilford Press.

Murray, E. A. & Bussey, T. J. 1999 Perceptual mnemonic function of the perirhinal cortex. *Trends Cogn. Sci.* **3**, 142–151.

Murray, E. A. & Mishkin, M. 1998 Object recognition and location memory in monkeys with excitotoxic lesions of the amygdala and hippocampus. *J. Neurosci.* **18**, 6568–6582.

Murray, E. A., Gaffan, D. & Mishkin, M. 1993 Neural substrates of visual stimulus–stimulus association in rhesus monkeys. *J. Neurosci.* **13**, 4549–4561.

Murray, E. A., Baxter, M. G. & Gaffan, D. 1998 Monkeys with rhinal cortex damage or neurotoxic hippocampal lesions are impaired on spatial scene learning and object reversals. *Behav. Neurosci.* **112**, 1291–1303.

Naveh-Benjamin, M., Craik, F. I. M., Guez, J. & Dori, H. 1998 Effects of divided attention on encoding and retrieval processes in human memory: further support for an asymmetry. *J. Exp. Psychol.: Learning Memory Cogn.* **24**, 1091–1104.

Orbach, J., Milner, B. & Rasmussen, T. 1960 Learning and retention in monkeys after amygdala–hippocampus resection. *Arch. Neurol.* **3**, 230–251.

Oscar-Berman, M. & Zola-Morgan, S. 1980 Comparative neuropsychology and Korsakoff's syndrome. II. Two-choice visual discrimination learning. *Neuropsychologia* **18**, 513–525.

Parker, A. & Gaffan, D. 1998a Interaction of frontal and perirhinal cortices in visual object recognition memory in monkeys. *Eur. J. Neurosci.* **10**, 3044–3057.

Parker, A. & Gaffan, D. 1998b Memory after frontal temporal disconnection in monkeys: conditional and nonconditional tasks, unilateral and bilateral frontal lesions. *Neuropsychologia* **36**, 259–271.

Pascual Leone, A. & Torres, F. 1993 Plasticity of the sensorimotor cortex representation of the reading finger in Braille readers. *Brain* **116**, 39–52.

Passingham, R. E. 1993 *The frontal lobes and voluntary action*. Oxford University Press.

Peden, J. K. & von Bonin, G. 1947 The neocortex of Hapale. *J. Comp. Neurol.* **86**, 37–68.

Petrides, M. 1987 Conditional learning and the primate frontal cortex. In *The frontal lobes revisited* (ed. E. Perecman), pp. 91–108. New York: IRBN Press.

Preuss, T. M. 1995 Do rats have prefrontal cortex? The Rose–Woolsey–Akert program reconsidered. *J. Cogn. Neurosci.* **7**, 1–24.

Ridley, R. M. & Baker, H. F. 1991 A critical evaluation of monkey models of amnesia and dementia. *Brain Res. Rev.* **16**, 15–17.

Rolls, E. T. 1999 *The brain and emotion.* Oxford University Press.

Sakai, K. & Miyashita, Y. 1991 Neural organization for the long-term memory of paired associates. *Nature* **354**, 152–155.

Sakai, K., Naya, Y. & Miyashita, Y. 1994 Neuronal tuning and associative mechanisms in form representation. *Learning Memory* **1**, 83–105.

Schoups, A., Vogels, R., Qian, N. & Orban, G. 2001 Practising orientation identification improves orientation coding in V1 neurons. *Nature* **412**, 549–553.

Scoville, W. B. & Milner, B. 1957 Loss of recent memory after bilateral hippocampal lesions. *J. Neurol. Neurosurg. Psychiat.* **20**, 11–21.

Selden, N. R., Gitelman, D. R., Salamon-Murayama, N., Parrish, T. B. & Mesulam, M. M. 1998 Trajectories of cholinergic pathways within the cerebral hemispheres of the human brain. *Brain* **121**, 2249–2257.

Semba, K. 1991 The cholinergic basal forebrain: a critical role in cortical arousal. In *The basal forebrain: anatomy to function* (ed. T. C. Napier, P. W. Kalivas & I. Hanin), pp. 197–217. New York: Plenum.

Squire, L. R. & Zola-Morgan, S. 1991 The medial temporal lobe memory system. *Science* **253**, 1380–1386.

Sutton, R. S. & Barto, A. G. 1998 *Reinforcement learning: an introduction.* Cambridge, MA: MIT Press.

Vanderwolf, C. H. & Cain, D. P. 1994 The behavioral neurobiology of learning and memory: a conceptual reorientation. *Brain Res. Rev.* **19**, 264–297.

von Bonin, G. & Bailey, P. 1947 *The neocortex of* Macaca mulatta. Urbana: University of Illinois Press.

Waelti, P., Dickinson, A. & Schultz, W. 2001 Dopamine responses comply with basic assumptions of formal learning theory. *Nature* **412**, 43–48.

Wallis, J. D., Dias, R., Robbins, T. W. & Roberts, A. C. 2001 Dissociable contributions of the orbitofrontal and lateral prefrontal cortex of the marmoset to performance on a detour reaching task. *Eur. J. Neurosci.* **13**, 1797–1808.

Whishaw, I. Q. & Maaswinkel, H. 1998 Rats with fimbria–fornix lesions are impaired in path integration: a role for the hippocampus in 'sense of direction'. *J. Neurosci.* **18**, 3050–3058.

Wise, S. P., Murray, E. A. & Gerfen, C. R. 1996 The frontal cortex–basal ganglia system in primates. *Crit. Rev. Neurobiol.* **10**, 317–356.

Zola, S. M. & Squire, L. R. 2002 Relationship between magnitude of damage to the hippocampus and impaired recognition memory in monkeys. *Hippocampus* **11**, 92–98.

Glossary

ACH   acetylcholine
AM   amygdala
FX   fornix
MD   mediodorsal thalamic nucleus
TS   temporal stem

12

The prefrontal cortex: categories, concepts and cognition

Earl K. Miller, David J. Freedman, and Jonathan D. Wallis

The ability to generalize behaviour-guiding principles and concepts from experience is key to intelligent, goal-directed behaviour. It allows us to deal efficiently with a complex world and to adapt readily to novel situations. We review evidence that the prefrontal cortex—the cortical area that reaches its greatest elaboration in primates—plays a central part in acquiring and representing this information. The prefrontal cortex receives highly processed information from all major forebrain systems, and neurophysiological studies suggest that it synthesizes this into representations of learned task contingencies, concepts and task rules. In short, the prefrontal cortex seems to underlie our internal representations of the 'rules of the game'. This may provide the necessary foundation for the complex behaviour of primates, in whom this structure is most elaborate.

12.1. Introduction

Although our brains have developed exquisite mechanisms for recording specific experiences, it is not always advantageous for us to take the world too literally. A brain limited to storing an independent record of each experience would require a prodigious amount of storage and burden us with unnecessary details. Instead, we have evolved the ability to detect the commonalities among experiences and store them as abstract concepts, general principles and rules. This is an efficient way to deal with a complex world and allows the navigation of many different situations with a minimal amount of storage. It also allows us to deal with novelty. By extracting the essential elements from our experiences, we can generalize to future situations that share some elements but may, on the surface, appear very different.

For example, consider the concept 'camera'. We do not have to learn anew about every camera that we may encounter. Just knowing that the item is a camera communicates a great deal of knowledge about its parts, functions and operations. Or consider the set of rules invoked when we dine in a restaurant, such as 'wait to be seated', 'order' and 'pay the bill'. These rules are long divorced from the specific circumstances in which they were learned and thus give us an idea about what to expect (and what is expected of us) when we try out a new restaurant. Hearing that a '*coup d'etat*' has occurred communicates the 'gist' of what happened without having to hear the details.

While much is known about the encoding of physical attributes and specific experiences, relatively little is known about how abstract information is encoded in the brain. This may be because this is relatively more difficult to study than the neural correlates of physical attributes, such as shape. By definition, these categories and concepts are labels that transcend physical appearance. Think of all the wildly different-looking objects that are considered to be chairs. However, it is not always easy to disentangle encoding of categories from similarity. Let us say that we discover some neurons somewhere in a monkey's brain that become activated whenever it views a tree. Are these neurons really encoding the category 'tree'? They might be encoding the fact that trees happen to look more like one another than many other objects. Further, development of abstract representations requires a considerable amount of experience; learning a general principle requires a wide range of experiences so that underlying rules can be extracted.

Our laboratory has conducted experiments to establish how abstract information is represented in the brain. We trained monkeys on tasks that allowed them to group different stimuli and experiences into categories or behaviour-guiding rules. We summarize some of that work and discuss its implications for an understanding of a neural basis of high-level cognitive function. We have focused on a brain region that is central to high-level cognitive function, the PFC.

12.2. The prefrontal cortex

The PFC is an ideal place to look for neural correlates of abstract information. It occupies a far greater proportion of the human cerebral cortex than in other animals, suggesting that it might contribute to those cognitive capacities that distinguish humans from animals (Fuster 1995; Figure 12.1). On initial examination, PFC damage has remarkably little overt effect; patients can perceive and move, there is little impairment in their memory and they can appear remarkably normal in casual conversation. However, despite the superficial appearance of normality, PFC damage seems to devastate a person's life. They have difficulty in sustaining attention, in keeping 'on task', and seem to act on whims and impulses without regard to future consequences. This pattern of high-level deficits coupled with a sparing of lower-level basic functions has been called a 'dysexecutive syndrome' (Baddeley & Della Sala 1996) and 'goal neglect' (Duncan et al. 1996).

Indeed, the anatomy of the PFC suggests that it is well-suited for a role as the brain's 'executive'. It can synthesize information from a wide range of brain systems and exert control over behaviour (Nauta 1971). The collection of cortical areas that comprise the PFC have interconnections with brain areas processing external information (with all sensory systems and with cortical and subcortical motor system structures), as well as internal information (limbic and midbrain structures involved in affect, memory and reward) (see Figure 12.2). Correspondingly, its neurons are highly multimodal and encode many different types of information from all stages of the perception–action cycle (Fuster 1995). They are activated by stimuli from all sensory modalities, before and during a variety of actions, during memory for past events, in anticipation of expected events and behavioural consequences, and are modulated by internal factors such as motivational and attentional state (see the review in Miller & Cohen 2001). Because of its highly multimodal nature and its apparent role in higher mental life, the PFC seemed like an ideal place to begin our search for neural correlates of the abstract information needed for intelligent behaviour.

12.3. The prefrontal cortex and perceptual categories

Because perceptual categories often group together very different looking things, their representation must involve something beyond the sort of neural tuning that underlies the encoding of physical attributes, that is, gradual changes in neural activity as certain attributes gradually change (e.g. shape, orientation, direction). Instead, categories have sharp boundaries (not gradual transitions) and members of the same category are treated as equivalent even though their physical appearance may vary widely.

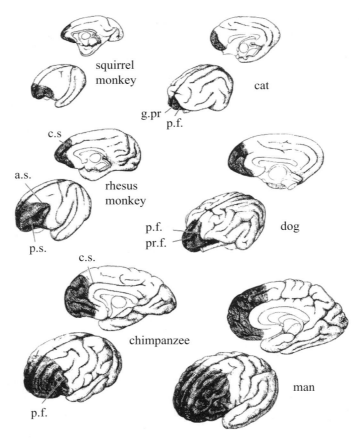

Fig. 12.1. The relative size of the PFC in different animals. Abbreviations: a.s., arcuate sulcus; c.s., cingulate sulcus; g.pr., gyrus proreus; p.f., presylvian fissure; p.s., principal sulcus; pr.f., proreal fissure. From Fuster (1995).

Consider a simple example of a perceptual category: crickets sharply divide a certain range of pure tones into 'mate' versus 'bat' (a predator) (Wyttenbach *et al.* 1996). Even though the input varies along a continuum, behaviour is binary. Across a wide range of lower frequencies, crickets will turn towards the sound source because it may be a potential mate. However, at a certain point (16 kHz), the behaviour suddenly flips: crickets begin to turn away from the sound source because it could be a bat. Crickets make virtually no distinction between frequencies over a wide range on either side of the boundary; they approach or avoid with equal reliability. This type of representation is illustrated schematically in Figure 12.3. Presumably, the ability to transform the raw sensory inputs into distinct categories evolved because it is advantageous; in this case, it optimizes reproductive behaviour while minimizing fatal mistakes. Similar effects are evident in humans' perception of 'b' versus 'p' (Lisker & Abramson 1970).

The elaborate behavioural repertoire of advanced animals naturally depends on more elaborate categorization abilities. The mental lexicon of primates, for example, includes abstract categories that are characterized along multiple dimensions that are often difficult to define precisely, such as 'tool'. In addition, advanced animals have an enormous capacity to learn

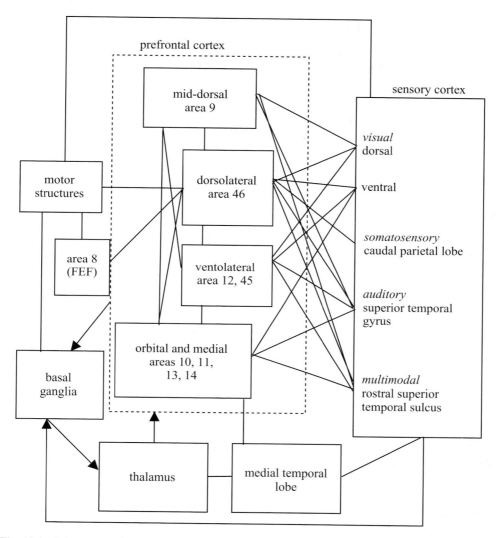

Fig. 12.2. Schematic diagram of extrinsic and intrinsic connections of the PFC. Most connections are reciprocal; the exceptions are noted by arrows. From Miller & Cohen (2001).

and adapt. Most of our categories are acquired through experience (we learn what a 'chair' is) and we can continually modify and update our categories as we learn more about them. The ability of monkeys to learn complex perceptual categories has been catalogued in studies that have taught them categories such as animal versus non-animal (Roberts & Mazmanian 1988), food versus non-food (Fabre-Thorpe *et al.* 1998), tree versus non-tree, fishes versus non-fishes (Vogels 1999*a*) and ordinal numbers (Orlov *et al.* 2000). Pigeons also have a remarkable ability to learn such distinctions (Bhatt *et al.* 1988; Young & Wasserman 1997).

   Where such categories are encoded in the brain is unclear. In primates, they could be represented and stored in the same areas of the visual cortex that analyse form and are critical for remembering individual objects, such as the ITC. They might also be evident in the

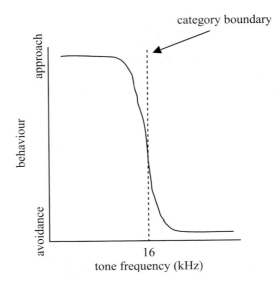

Fig. 12.3. Schematic representation of categorical perception using crickets' responses to a continuum of pure tones as an example. Based on Wyttenbach *et al.* (1996).

brain regions that receive the results of visual processing from the ITC and are critical for planning and guiding behaviour, such as the PFC. Both the ITC and PFC contain neurons selective for complex stimuli such as trees, fishes, faces, brushes, etc. (Desimone *et al.* 1984; Tanaka *et al.* 1991; Vogels 1999*b*). But whether or not this selectivity reflects category information *per se* has not been determined. With a large, amorphous category (e.g. food, human, etc.), the category boundaries are unknown. Thus, characteristics diagnostic of category representations (sharp transitions and little within-category distinction) cannot be tested. This is not to say that ITC neural selectivity would not make important contributions to category representation, it is just not clear whether it represents category membership *per se*.

To test for neural correlates of perceptual categories, we trained monkeys to categorize computer-generated stimuli into two categories, 'cats' and 'dogs' (Freedman *et al.* 2001; Figure 12.4). A novel three-dimensional morphing system was used to create a large set of parametric blends of six prototype images (three species of cats and three breeds of dogs) (Beymer & Poggio 1996; Shelton 2000). By blending different amounts of cat and dog, we could smoothly vary shape and precisely define the boundary between the categories (greater than 50% of a given type). As a result, stimuli that were close to, but on opposite sides of, the boundary were similar, whereas stimuli that belong to the same category could be dissimilar (e.g. the 'cheetah' and 'house cat').

Two monkeys performed a DMC task (Figure 12.5) that required judgement of whether successively presented sample and test stimuli were from the same category or not. For training, samples were chosen from throughout the cat and dog morph space. After training, classification performance was high (*ca.* 90% correct), even when the samples were close to the category boundary. The monkeys classified dog-like cats (60% cat, 40% dog) correctly *ca.* 90% of the time, and misclassified them as dogs only 10% of the time, and vice versa. Thus, the monkeys' behaviour indicated the sharp boundary that is diagnostic of a category representation.

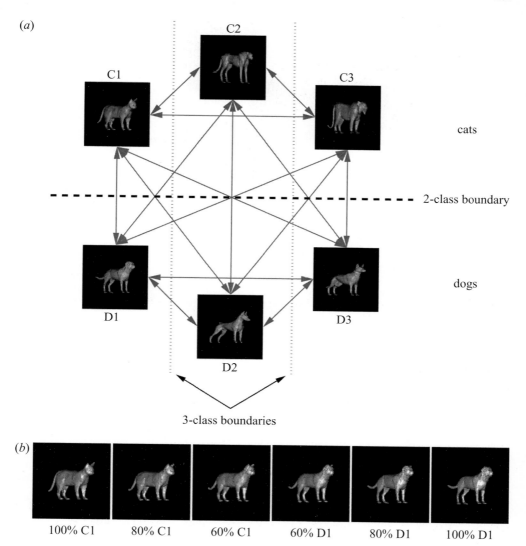

(a)

C2

C1

C3

cats

- - - - 2-class boundary

dogs

D1

D3

D2

3-class boundaries

(b)

| 100% C1 | 80% C1 | 60% C1 | 60% D1 | 80% D1 | 100% D1 |

Fig. 12.4. (*a*) Monkeys learned to categorize randomly generated 'morphs' from the vast number of possible blends of six prototypes. For neurophysiological recording, 54 sample stimuli were constructed along the 15 morph lines illustrated here. (*b*) Morphs along the C1–D1 line. From Freedman *et al.* (2001).

The dog-like cats were treated as cats, even though they were more similar in appearance to the cat-like dogs just across the category boundary than they were to the prototype cats.

We recorded in the lateral PFC, the PFC region directly interconnected with the ITC, and found many examples of neurons that seemed to encode category membership. Two examples are shown in Figure 12.6. Note that their activity was different from dog-like (60%) cats and cat-like (60%) dogs, yet similar between these stimuli and their respective prototypes. In other words, PFC neurons seemed to make the same sharp distinctions that were evident in the monkeys' behaviour and are indicative of categorical representations, and collected different

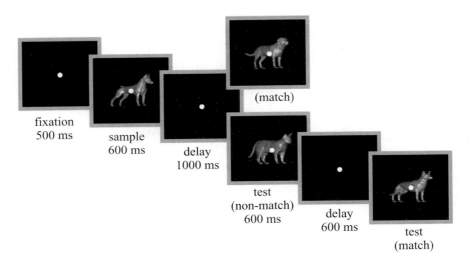

Fig. 12.5. The delayed match-to-category task. A sample was followed by a delay and a test stimulus. If the sample and test stimulus were the same category (a match), monkeys were required to release a lever before the test disappeared. If they were not, there was another delay followed by a match. Equal numbers of match and non-match trials were randomly interleaved. From Freedman *et al.* (2001).

stimuli together irrespective of their exact physical experience. Category information seemed to predominate in the PFC; across the neural population, tuning was significantly shifted towards representing category rather than individual stimuli (Freedman *et al.* 2001).

As our monkeys had no experience with cats or dogs prior to training, it seemed likely that these effects resulted from training. To test for learning effects, we retrained one monkey on the DMC task after defining two new category boundaries that were orthogonal to the original boundary (Figure 12.4). This created three new classes; each contained morphs centred around one cat prototype and one dog prototype (e.g. the cheetah and the 'doberman'). After training, we found that PFC neural activity shifted to reflect the new, but not the old, categories. An example of a single neuron is shown in Figure 12.7. It showed a significant effect of category during the delay period when data were sorted according to the (currently relevant) three-category scheme; it distinguished one of the categories from the other two (Figure 12.7*a*). By contrast, when the data were sorted using the old category scheme, there was no differentiation between the now-irrelevant cat and dog categories (Figure 12.7*b*).

Our results illustrate that, with experience, category information can become incorporated at the single-neuron level, much as physical attributes of stimuli are. This did not have to be the case: in principle, categories might have been encoded in another fashion. For example, categories might have been encoded at the ensemble level, as an emergent property of neurons that represent their defining features. This ability to carve category membership into the tuning of single neurons may allow for the quick and effortless classification of familiar items.

Our results might reflect a relative specialization of the PFC in encoding category membership. Categories, after all, are typically defined by their behavioural relevance, and the PFC plays a central part in planning voluntary behaviours. Conversely, the traditional roles of the PFC and ITC are in cognitive functions versus object vision and recognition, respectively. PFC damage causes deficits in attention, working memory and response inhibition, but usually spares object recognition, long-term memory and 'high-level' visual analysis (Fuster 1989;

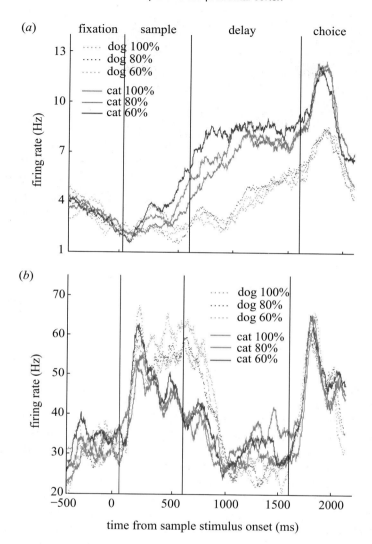

Fig. 12.6. See also Plate 37. The average activity of two single neurons to stimuli at the six morph blends. The vertical lines correspond (from left to right) to sample onset, offset and test stimulus onset. Activity is pooled over match and non-match trials.

Miller & Cohen 2001). By contrast, ITC damage causes deficits in visual discrimination and learning (Gross 1973; Mishkin 1982) and category-specific agnosias (e.g. for faces) in humans (Gainotti 2000). It might be that the category information in the PFC was retrieved from long-term storage in the ITC for its immediate use in the task. Interactions between the PFC and ITC underlie the storage and/or recall of visual memories and associations (Rainer *et al.* 1999; Tomita *et al.* 1999). Tomita *et al.* (1999) demonstrated that top-down signals from the PFC were needed to activate long-term visual memories stored in the ITC. A similar relationship may exist for the recall of visual categories. In either case, it seems that category information is strongly represented in the PFC, a finding consistent with its role in high-level cognitive functions and in guiding behaviour. The relative contribution of the ITC remains to be determined.

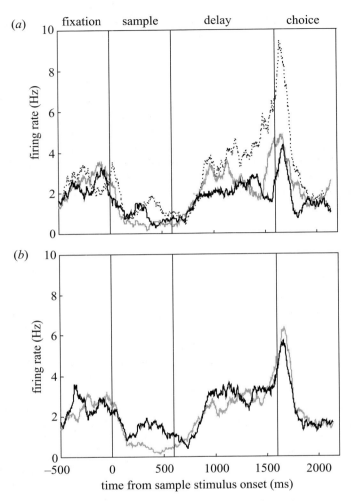

Fig. 12.7. Activity of a single PFC neuron after the monkey was trained on the three-category scheme (see Figure 12.4). (*a*) The neuron's activity when the data were sorted based on the three-category scheme (category A, black line; category B, grey line; category C, dotted line). (*b*) The same neuron's activity was data-sorted by the now-irrelevant two-category scheme (black line, cats; grey line, dogs).

12.4. The prefrontal cortex and rules

It is not only useful to group different sensory stimuli into meaningful categories, it is also useful to group specific experiences of our interactions with the environment along common themes, that is, as behaviour-guiding principles or rules. To this end, our brains have evolved mechanisms for detecting and storing often-complex relationships between situations, actions and consequences. By gleaning this knowledge from past experiences, we can develop a 'game plan' that allows us to extrapolate and infer which goals are available in similar situations in the future and what actions are likely to bring us closer to them.

A standard behavioural test of rule learning in monkeys is conditional associative learning (Passingham 1993). This refers to a class of tasks that require learning associative relationships that are arbitrary and extend beyond the simple one-to-one, stimulus–response mappings that underlie reflexive reactions to the environment. In conditional learning tasks, a given input does not invariably lead to a given output. Whether or not a given response is successful depends on additional, contextual, information. For example, reaching for popcorn can be rewarding, but only if one takes other information into account; if the popcorn belongs to another person, the result could be disastrous. Taking into account complex relationships in order to decide between alternative actions is, presumably, why volition evolved.

To make predictions about which actions are likely to achieve a given goal in a given situation, we need to form a pattern of associations between their internal representations that describes their logical relationship (Dickinson 1980). Decades of behavioural research have illustrated that the brain has learning mechanisms that are exquisitely sensitive to behaviourally informative associations (and insensitive to, or even discount, associations that are not informative). The underlying neural ensemble of a goal-directed task, then, might be comprised of neurons whose activity reflects task contingencies. Many studies have shown that prefrontal neurons do have this property. This work has focused on the lateral PFC because it seems to be a site of convergence of the information needed to solve conditional sensori–motor tasks. It is directly interconnected with the higher-order sensory and motor cortex and indirectly connected (via the ventromedial PFC) with limbic structures that process 'internal' information, such as memory and reward (Goldman-Rakic 1987; Pandya & Barnes 1987; Fuster 1989; Barbas & Pandya 1991). The neural activity in the lateral PFC reflects this; many of its neurons exhibit multimodal responses (Vaadia *et al.* 1986; Watanabe 1992; Rao *et al.* 1997; Rainer *et al.* 1998*a,b*; White & Wise 1999). Further, the lateral PFC is critical for normal learning of conditional associations between sensory cues and voluntary actions (Petrides 1985*a*, 1990; Gaffan & Harrison 1988; Eacott & Gaffan 1992; Parker & Gaffan 1998*b*). Indeed, following training on conditional learning tasks, as many as 50% of the neurons in the lateral PFC show conjunctive tuning for learned associations between cues, voluntary actions and rewards.

For example, Watanabe (1990, 1992) trained monkeys to perform tasks in which visual and auditory cues signalled, in different trials, whether a reward would or would not be delivered. The majority of lateral PFC neurons were found to reflect the association between a cue and a reward. A given neuron might be activated by a cue, but only when it signalled a reward. By contrast, another neuron might be activated only by a cue that signalled 'no reward'. In our own experiments, we have trained monkeys to associate, in different blocks of trials, each of two cue objects with an eye saccade to the right or to the left (Asaad *et al.* 1998). We found that the activity of 44% of randomly selected lateral PFC neurons reflected associations between objects and the saccades that they instructed (Figure 12.8). Other neurons had activity that reflected the cues or the saccades alone, but they were fewer in number. Fuster *et al.* (2000) have recently shown that PFC neurons can also reflect learned associations between visual and auditory stimuli.

Importantly, these changes do not require a prodigious amount of experience. Changes in PFC neural properties are evident after one day's experience and can be detected after just a few minutes of training. For example, Bichot *et al.* (1996) studied the FEFs, part of Brodmann's area 8 that is important for voluntary eye movements. Normally, neurons in this area fire selectively to saccade targets appearing in certain visual field locations. However, when monkeys were trained to search for a target defined by a particular visual attribute (e.g. red), the neurons in the FEFs acquire sensitivity to that attribute (Bichot *et al.* 1996).

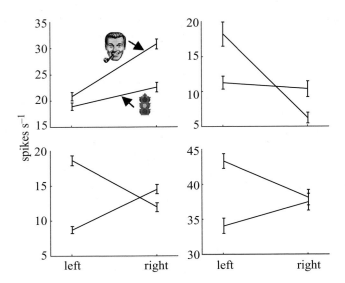

Fig. 12.8. The activity of four single prefrontal neurons when each of two objects, on different trials, instructed either a saccade to the right or a saccade to the left. The lines connect the average values obtained when a given object cued one or the other saccade. The error bars show the standard error of the mean. Note that, in each case, the neuron's activity depends on both the cue object and the saccade direction and that the tuning is nonlinear or conjunctive. That is, the level of activity to a given combination of object and saccade cannot be predicted from the neuron's response to the other combinations. Adapted from Asaad *et al.* (1998).

When monkeys were trained to search for a different target every day, neurons not only discriminated the current target but also distracting stimuli that had been a target on the previous day relative to stimuli that had been targets even earlier (Bichot & Schall 1999). Monkeys were also more likely to make errors in choosing that distracting stimulus. It was as though the previous day's experience left an impression in the brain that influenced neural activity and the monkey's behaviour.

We also observed evidence for rapid plasticity in our study of learning of conditional object–saccade associations in the PFC (Asaad *et al.* 1998). Initially, the monkeys chose their responses at random, but learned the correct cue–response pairing over a few (5–15) trials. As they learned the association, neural activity representing the forthcoming saccadic response appeared progressively earlier in successive trials. In other words, the initiation of response-related delay activity gradually shifted with learning—from a point in time just before the execution of the response and reward delivery to an earlier point in time, nearly coincident with the presentation of the cue.

Further support for a role for PFC neurons in representing task demands comes from training monkeys to alternate between different task rules. This adds another level of complexity beyond the conditional tasks described above. Now, there is more than one rule assigned to each cue and another cue tells the monkey which rule to use in a given trial. For example, following a given cue, monkeys can learn to direct a response to either the cue's location (spatial matching rule) or an alternative location associated with the cue (associative rule), depending on which rule is currently in effect. When tested in this fashion, many PFC neurons show rule-specific activity. For example, a PFC neuron might respond to a given visual cue when the monkey is using an associative rule, but exhibit weak or no activity under identical sensory and attentional conditions that differed only in that the monkey was using a spatial rule instead (White & Wise 1999; Asaad *et al.* 2000). Also, when monkeys switch between different tasks, many PFC neurons show shifts in baseline activity that communicates which task is currently being performed (Asaad *et al.* 2000; Figure 12.9). Such effects have been found in the PFC for associative versus spatial rules, for object matching versus spatial matching versus associative rules, and for shape matching versus object matching rules (Hoshi *et al.* 1998; White & Wise 1999; Asaad *et al.* 2000).

In all of these cases, however, the rules are relatively literal or concrete. A certain cue, or set of cues, always signals a specific response. As noted, knowledge from our past experiences can be applied to a wider range of future circumstances if we abstract general principles or

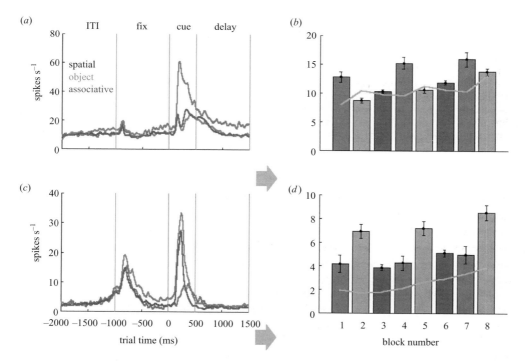

Fig. 12.9. See also Plate 38. Spike rate versus time histograms for two neurons, each sorted by task. The final second of the three-second ITI is represented by the first 1000 ms (−2000 to −1000 ms). Fixation occurs soon after (*ca.* −1000 to −800 ms). Cue presentation occurs at the time-point marked 0 ms. Task-related differences in baseline firing rate were generally observed to begin in the fixation period. While the activity of some neurons diverged almost coincident with initial fixation (c), the activity of others diverged progressively as the appearance of the cue became more imminent (a). The bar graphs (b,d) demonstrate the reproducibility of these small task-specific changes in activity across multiple repetitions of the same task. The mean fixation-period firing rate (with standard errors) for each block of trials is shown for the two neurons in (a) and (c). The bars are colour-coded to reflect the task being performed in each block, and the colours match those in the histograms to the left. The light grey line superimposed over these bars shows the activity of these neurons during the second immediately preceding the ITI.

rules rather than specific cue–response contingencies. The ability of the PFC to represent abstract rules, those not tied to specific stimuli or actions, was recently addressed in our laboratory (Wallis *et al.* 2001).

Monkeys were trained to use two abstract rules: 'match' versus 'non-match'. They faced a computer screen and viewed two successively presented pictures. If the match rule was in effect, the monkeys released the lever if the pictures were the same and continued to hold the lever if the pictures were different. If the non-match rule was in effect, the reverse was true; monkeys released if the pictures were different and held if they were the same. The rule was randomly instructed in each trial by the presentation of a cue at the same time as the first picture was presented. To disambiguate neuronal responses to the physical properties of the cue from responses to the rule that the cues instructed, cues signifying the same rule were taken from different modalities, while cues signifying different rules were taken from the same modality (Figure 12.10). The monkeys could perform this task well above chance levels even when they were seeing a stimulus for the very first time. This indicates that they had abstracted two overarching principles of the task that could then be applied to novel stimuli— the minimal definition of an abstract rule.

The most prevalent activity across the PFC was the encoding of the current rule. Figure 12.11 shows a good example of a rule-selective neuron that exhibited greater activity when the match rule was in effect than when the non-match rule had been indicated. This activity cannot be explained by the physical properties of the cue or the picture, since activity was the same regardless of which cue was used to instruct the monkey, and regardless of which picture the monkey was remembering. It cannot be related to the upcoming response since the monkey did not know whether the second-presented picture would require a response. Nor could it be related to differences in reward expectation, since the expectation of reward was the same regardless of which rule was in effect. Furthermore, the performance of the monkeys was virtually identical for the two types of rules (error rates differed by less than 0.1% and reaction times by less than 7 ms). Thus, the most parsimonious explanation is that the differences in activity reflected the abstract rule that the monkey was currently using to guide its behaviour.

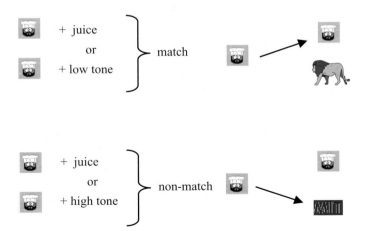

Fig. 12.10. Schematic diagram of the abstract rules task. Monkeys switched between choosing a test stimulus that did or did not match the sample depending on whether the match or non-match rule was in effect. The cues that signalled these rules are shown on the left.

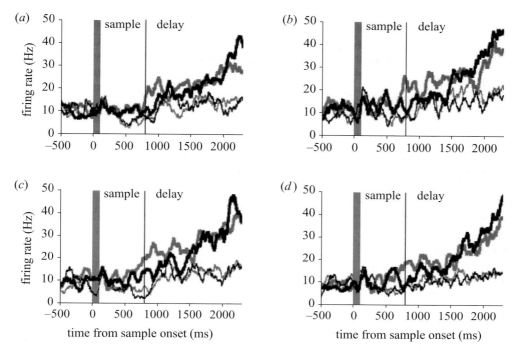

Fig. 12.11. A neuron exhibiting rule selectivity. The neuron shows greater activity during *match* trials, regardless of which cue signified the rule or which object was remembered. (*a*) Sample object 1; (*b*) sample object 2; (*c*) sample object 3; (*c*) sample object 4. The vertical grey bar marks the cue epoch. Match (juice) and match (low tone) are represented by thick black and grey bars, respectively. Non-match (juice) and non-match (high tone) are represented by thin black and grey bars, respectively.

What function does the ability to abstract a rule serve? It is a form of generalization that permits a shortcut in learning, thereby allowing the animal to maximize the amount of reward available from a particular situation. To illustrate this, consider the above task. The monkey could potentially solve the task as a series of paired associates (in fact, 16 associations, consisting of four different pictures each paired with four different stimuli). For example, the monkey might learn that whenever the chef is presented with a drop of juice, then at the test phase the correct response is to choose the chef. But notice that this type of learning tells the monkey nothing about which response is appropriate to a lion appearing with a drop of juice. In other words, unless the monkey abstracts the rule that juice indicates that the monkey should match, then each time new pictures are used the monkey would have to learn an entirely new set of 16 associations by trial and error. The problem with this trial-and-error learning is that errors are lost opportunities for reward. Given that the monkeys performed well above chance when they encountered novel pictures, it is clear that they are not engaging in trial-and-error learning, but rather have abstracted two rules that they can then apply as required.

This shortcut that abstraction of the rule permits is also reflected in the neuronal encoding. It would be entirely possible for the monkey to solve the task without single cells encoding the rule. For example, there might be two populations of cells, one encoding the match and non-match rule when the cues are presented in the auditory modality, and one encoding this information in the taste modality. But such a solution is computationally expensive, since if a third modality was introduced a third population of cells would be required. It is more efficient to abstract a rule that cues presented in different modalities commonly instruct, and indeed this is the solution that the brain uses. The prevalence of neurons encoding such rules in the PFC is consistent with the loss of flexibility that is observed after prefrontal damage in both monkeys and humans. It is not inconsistent with studies emphasizing the role of the PFC in working memory or planning, but indicates that an important component of these processes might be the use of behaviour-guiding rules.

12.5. Prefrontal cortex and cognitive control

The results presented above suggest that PFC activity reflects categories and rules. This seems consistent with conjectures that a cardinal PFC function may be the acquisition and representation of the formal demands of tasks, the guiding concepts and principles that provide a foundation for complex, intelligent behaviour. In order to understand this, we must turn to theories of cognitive control—the ability of the brain to coordinate processing among its millions of neurons in order to direct them toward future goals.

(a) Controlled versus automatic behaviours

In order to understand what we mean by 'cognitive control', it is important to understand the distinction between controlled and automatic behaviours. Much of our behaviour is automatic, that is, direct reactions to our immediate environment that do not tax our attention. For example, if someone suddenly throws a baseball at your face, you might reflexively duck. You may not have willed this behaviour; it just seems to happen. Many such reflexive, automatic processes are 'wired' into our nervous systems by evolution. However, others can be acquired through a great deal of experience, as learning mechanisms gradually imprint highly familiar behaviour. If you are walking a highly familiar route and traffic is light, you may traverse a great distance (and even negotiate turns) with little awareness of having done so. In these cases, your behaviour is driven in a 'bottom-up' fashion: largely determined by stimuli in the immediate environment and their ability to trigger behaviours with which they are strongly associated. In neural terms, they are dependent on well-established neural pathways waiting to be fired off by the correct input.

However, if something unexpected happens on your walk, you need to 'take charge' of your actions. You pay attention to your surroundings and try to anticipate and accommodate the action of others; you may even decide to take an alternative route. In this case, your behaviour is not governed by simple input–output, stimulus–response relationships. You use your knowledge of the world: the current objective (arriving at work intact) and results from previous experiences to weigh the alternatives and consequences. Because these behaviours tax your attention and seem to be driven by 'internal' information (knowledge about unseen goals and how to achieve them) and thus are initiated by us and not by the environment, they are referred to as 'controlled'. The same basic sensory, memory and motor processes that mediated automatic behaviour can be engaged. However, now they are not simply triggered by the environment, they are shaped and controlled in a top-down fashion, by our knowledge of how the world works. The observations that PFC neurons encode acquired information about task contingencies, categories and rules suggest it as a source of top-down signals.

The observation that humans with PFC damage seem impulsive makes sense in light of this distinction between controlled and automatic behaviours. Without the PFC to provide top-down signals about expectations of goals and required behaviours, the patient simply reacts to their environment with whatever behaviours are strongly associated with the cues that are immediately present. Shallice & Burgess (1991) examined this by using a 'shopping test'. They described frontal lobe-damaged patients who are able to execute simple routines in which clear sensory cues could elicit a familiar action (e.g. buy a loaf of bread). However, they were unable to carry out an errand that involved organizing a series of such routines because they kept going 'off task'. They would, for example, enter shops that were irrelevant to the errand, just because they happened to be passing them. Another example is utilization behaviour. A patient with PFC damage will impulsively use items placed in front of them such as a comb or, in (hopefully) one case, a urinal. It seems that the basic elements of behaviour are intact, but that the patients override prepotent, reflexive, responses to coordinate behaviour in accord with an unseen goal.

A classic test of the ability to learn and follow goal-orientated rules is the Wisconsin Card Sorting Test (Milner 1963). Subjects are instructed to sort cards according to the shape, colour or number of symbols appearing on them. They start with one rule (e.g. colour) and, once that is acquired, the rule changes until all of the cards have been sorted using all possible rules. Normal humans have little difficulty with this task. By contrast, humans with prefrontal damage can learn the first sorting criterion (a relatively simple mapping between a stimulus attribute and a response) but then are unable to escape it; they cannot override the previous behaviour and do not realize that when the rule changes and they must learn a new one (Milner 1963). Monkeys with PFC lesions are impaired in similar tasks (Dias *et al.* 1996). PFC damage in humans or monkeys, or disconnecting the PFC from its sensory inputs in monkeys, also produces deficits in a standard test of rule learning, the aforementioned conditional learning tasks (Petrides 1985*a*,*b*; Gaffan & Harrison 1988, 1991; Murray & Wise 1997; Parker & Gaffan 1998*a*; Murray *et al.* 2000).

(b) A theory of the prefrontal cortex and cognitive control

In summary, we have seen that PFC damage seems to disrupt cognitive control, the ability of animals to direct action toward unseen goals, and leaves them at the mercy of the environment. We discussed neurophysiological studies that indicate that the PFC represents task-relevant knowledge such as categories and rules. How these properties are acquired, and how they are used for cognitive control, have been addressed in a model of PFC by Miller and Cohen (Miller & Cohen 2001).

In this view, the ability to form representations of the formal demands of behaviour stems from the position of the PFC at the top of the cortical hierarchy (Fuster 1995). The PFC is a network of neural circuits that is interconnected with cortical regions that analyse virtually all types of sensory inputs, and with regions involved in generating motor outputs. It is also in direct contact with a wide array of subcortical structures that process, among other things, 'internal' information such as motivational state. The PFC thus provides a venue in which information from distant brain systems can interact through relatively local circuitry. During learning, reward-related signals could act on the PFC to strengthen pathways—the associative links—between the neurons that processed the information that led to a reward. As a result, the PFC rapidly constructs a pattern of activity that represents goals and the means to achieve them. This, in essence, is a representation of the logic of the task, a task model that reflects the constellation of relevant information and their inter-relations. In neural terms, this could amount to a 'map' of the neural pathways in the brain that is needed to solve the task. Cognitive control results from the PFC sending excitatory signals from this representation back to the brain structures that provide the PFC with input. These signals arise from the ability of many PFC neurons to sustain their activity. These chronic signals reflecting the task demands can enhance the activity of neurons that process task-relevant information (that match the model) in other brain systems and thereby select the forebrain neural path-ways that are needed to solve the task at hand.

To understand how this selection takes place, consider visual attention. In the visual system, neurons processing different aspects of the visual scene compete with each other for activation, by mutually inhibiting one another. This is thought to be important for enhancing contrast and separating a figure from its background. The neurons that 'win' the competition and remain active are those that incur a higher level of activity. The biased competition model posits that visual attention exploits this circuitry (Desimone & Duncan 1995). In voluntary shifts of attention, a competitive advantage comes from excitatory signals (thought to originate from the PFC) that represent the expected stimulus. These excitatory signals enhance the activity of neurons in the visual cortex that process that stimulus and, by virtue of the mutual inhibition, suppress activity of neurons processing other stimuli. This notion of excitatory bias signals that resolve local competition can be extended from visual attention to cognitive control in general (Miller 1999, 2000). By enhancing the activity of neurons representing task-relevant information, those representing irrelevant information are simultaneously suppressed and neural activity is steered down the pathways needed to solve the task at hand.

For an illustrative example of how this might work, consider the cartoon shown in Figure 12.12. Processing units are shown that correspond to cues (C1, C2, C3). They can be thought of as neural representations of sensory events, internal states, stored memories, etc. in corresponding neural systems. Also shown are processing units that correspond to the motor circuits mediating two responses (R1 and R2). We have set up the sort of flexible situation for which the PFC is thought to be important. Namely, one cue (C1) can lead to one of two responses (R1 or R2), depending on the situation (C2 or C3). Imagine that you suddenly decide that you want a beer (and let us consider that to be cue C1). If you are at home (C2), then you get up and get one (R1). But if you are in a pub (C3), you ask for one instead (R2). These conditional associations form the 'if–then' rules that are fundamental building blocks of voluntary behaviour (Passingham 1993). How does the PFC construct these representations?

In an unfamiliar situation, information flows into the PFC relatively unchecked. But then reward-related signals from successful (rewarded) experiences foster the formation of associations between the PFC neurons that had processed the information immediately preceding reward. This signal may be an influx of dopamine from the mid-brain VTA neurons that are sensitive to reward and, through the basal ganglia, influence the PFC (Passingham 1993; Schultz & Dickinson 2000). As this neural ensemble becomes established, it becomes self-reinforcing. It sends signals back to other brain systems, biasing their processing towards matching information and thus refining the inputs to the PFC. As learning proceeds, reward-related signals from VTA neurons appear progressively earlier as they become evoked by the events that first predict reward (Schultz & Montague 1997). Through repeated iterations of this process, more and more task-relevant information is linked into the PFC representation; it 'bootstraps' from direct associations with reward to a multivariate network of associations that can describe a complex, goal-directed task.

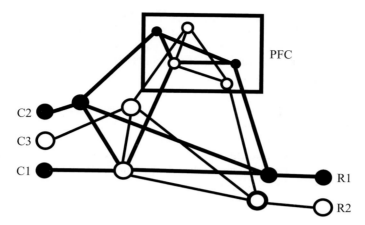

Fig. 12.12. Schematic diagram of a posited role for the PFC in cognitive control. Information on sensory inputs, current motivational state, memories, etc. (e.g. 'cues' such as C1, C2, and C3) as well as information about behaviour (e.g. 'responses' such as R1 and R2) is indicated. Reward signals foster the formation of a task model, a neural representation that reflects the learned associations between task-relevant information. A subset of the information (e.g. C1 and C2) can then evoke the entire model, including information about the appropriate response (e.g. R1). Excitatory signals from the PFC feed back to other brain systems to enable task-relevant neural pathways. Thick lines indicate activated pathways, thin lines indicate inactive pathways.

Once the PFC representation is established, a subset of the information (such as the cues) can activate the remaining elements (such as the correct response). So, if we want a beer (C1) and we are at home (C2), the corresponding PFC representation containing the correct response (R1) is activated and sustained until the response is executed. The resulting excitatory bias signals from the PFC then feed back to other brain regions, selecting the appropriate pathway needed for the task (e.g. C1–R1). A different pattern of cues (e.g. cues 1 and 3 in Figure 12.12) evokes a different PFC model and a different pattern of bias signals selects other neural pathways (C1–R2). With repeated selection of these pathways, they can become established independently of the PFC. As this happens, the PFC becomes less involved and the behaviour becomes habitual or automatic.

This particular view of PFC function is not without peer or precedent. Fuster first proposed that PFC neurons encode task-relevant contingencies between stimuli and/or responses, particularly when they are separated by gaps in time (as so often happens with extended, goal-directed behaviours) (Fuster 1985). Neurons that explicitly encode task contingencies and rules are used in neural network models of cognitive control by Changeux and Dehaene (Changeux & Dehaene 1993; Dehaene *et al.* 1998). The models of Cohen and colleagues use a layer (thought to correspond to the PFC) that represents task demands or 'context' (Cohen & Servan-Schreiber 1992). Wise *et al.* (1996) proposed that a cardinal PFC function is the acquisition of behaviour-guiding rules. Shimamura independently proposed a role for the PFC directly analogous to the Miller and Cohen model (Shimamura 2000).

Central to our model, and indeed all physiologically inspired models of PFC function, is the ability of PFC neurons to sustain their activity for several seconds in the absence of further stimulation. This is crucial for several reasons. As previously mentioned, gaps in time are an inevitable consequence of extended goal-directed behaviours. Thus, sustained activity allows PFC neurons to learn relationships (associations) between stimuli and/or responses that are separated in time (Fuster 1985). It also allows task rules to be maintained until the task is completed. But conveying information by sustained activation affords more than the ability to bridge temporal gaps. O'Reilly and Munakata have pointed out that it is an ideal format for transmitting the knowledge needed for cognitive control to other brain systems (O'Reilly & Munakata 2000).

A tenet of modern neuroscience is that long-term storage in the brain depends on strengthening some neural connections and weakening others, that is, by changing synaptic weights. Encoding information in structural changes has obvious advantages for information storage; it allows for very long-term memories. But the resulting memories are relatively inflexible; once a neural circuit is established, it will tend to fire in the same way every time it is triggered. Also, changing the strength of a synapse only affects the neurons that share the synapse. Thus, the information encoded in a pattern of synaptic weights only affects the firing of the neurons that form that particular circuit and is only expressed when that circuit is fired. Cognitive control, however, requires that a given pattern of information (the task demands) affect many brain circuits; it is used to orchestrate processing in many different brain systems. It is apparent, therefore, that the information needs to be encoded in a different format. Sustained activity is such a format. Because information is encoded in a pattern of sustained activity (rather than only in a pattern of synaptic weights), it can be propagated across the brain. Thus, the ability of sustained activity to tonically influence other brain systems is probably important for coordinating diverse processing around a specific goal. It also affords flexibility; if cognitive control stems from a pattern of information maintained in the PFC, changing behaviour is as easy as changing the pattern (O'Reilly & Munakata 2000; Miller & Cohen 2001).

Finally, the central role of sustained activity might explain the severely limited capacity of controlled processes. While we can carry out a number of automatic processes simultaneously, our ability to carry out controlled processes is limited by the low capacity of our attention. If the information for cognitive control is expressed in a unique pattern of ongoing activity distributed across many simultaneously active neurons—a population code—then there will be a natural capacity limitation. Trying to represent more than just a few items at the same time would degrade information because the unique patterns impinging on a given set of neurons would overwrite and interfere with one another.

12.6. Summary and conclusions

The ability to take charge of one's actions and direct them towards future, unseen goals is called cognitive control. Virtually all theories of cognition posit that cognition depends on functions specialized for the acquisition of information about goals and the means to achieve them. These functions exert a top-down influence on the lower-level automatic processes that mediate sensory analysis, memory storage and motor outputs, orchestrating and directing them toward a given goal.

The PFC, a brain structure that reaches its greatest complexity in the primate brain, seems to have a central role in cognitive control. It has access to, and the means to influence processing in, all major forebrain systems and can provide a means to synthesize the diverse information related to a given goal. As we have established, PFC neurons seem to have a crucial ability for cognitive control; they convey the knowledge that animals acquire about a given goal-directed task. Their ability to develop abstracted representations frees the organism from specific associations and endows it with the ability to generalize and develop overarching concepts and principles. This ability is consistent with observations of a loss of flexibility after PFC damage and may form a foundation for the complex, intelligent behaviour that is often seen in primates.

This work has been supported by the National Institutes of Health, the RIKEN-MIT Neuroscience Research Center, the Pew Foundation, The McKnight Foundation, The Sloan Foundation and the Whitehall Foundation. The authors thank Marlene Wicherski for her valuable comments on the manuscript.

References

Asaad, W. F., Rainer, G. & Miller, E. K. 1998 Neural activity in the primate prefrontal cortex during associative learning. *Neuron* **21**, 1399–1407.

Asaad, W. F., Rainer, G. & Miller, E. K. 2000 Task-specific activity in the primate prefrontal cortex. *J. Neurophysiol.* **84**, 451–459.

Baddeley, A. & Della Sala, S. 1996 Working memory and executive control. *Phil. Trans. R. Soc. Lond.* B **351**, 1397–1403.

Barbas, H. & Pandya, D. 1991 Patterns of connections of the prefrontal cortex in the rhesus monkey associated with cortical architecture. In *Frontal lobe function and dysfunction* (ed. H. S. Levin, H. M. Eisenberg & A. L. Benton), pp. 35–58. New York: Oxford University Press.

Beymer, D. & Poggio, T. 1996 Image representations for visual learning. *Science* **272**, 1905–1909.

Bhatt, R. S., Wasserman, E. A., Reynolds, W. F. & Knauss, K. S. 1988 Conceptual behavior in pigeons: categorization of both familiar and novel examples from four classes of natural categories. *J. Exp. Psych: Anim. Behav. Process.* **14**, 219–234.

Bichot, N. P. & Schall, J. D. 1999 Effects of similarity and history on neural mechanisms of visual selection. *Nat. Neurosci.* **2**, 549–554.

Bichot, N. P., Schall, J. D. & Thompson, K. G. 1996 Visual feature selectivity in frontal eye fields induced by experience in mature macaques. *Nature* **381**, 697–699.

Changeux, J. P. & Dehaene, S. 1993 Formal models for cognitive functions associated with the prefrontal cortex. In *Exploring brain functions: models in neuroscience* (ed. T. A. Poggio & D. A. Glaser). Chichester: Wiley.

Cohen, J. D. & Servan-Schreiber, D. 1992 Context, cortex, and dopamine: a connectionist approach to behavior and biology in schizophrenia. *Psychol. Rev.* **99**, 45–77.

Dehaene, S., Kerszeberg, M. & Changeux, J. P. 1998 A neuronal model of a global workspace in effortful cognitive tasks. *Proc. Natl Acad. Sci. USA* **95**, 14 529–14 534.

Desimone, R. & Duncan, J. 1995 Neural mechanisms of selective visual attention. *A. Rev. Neurosci.* **18**, 193–222.

Desimone, R., Albright, T. D., Gross, C. G. & Bruce, C. 1984 Stimulus-selective properties of inferior temporal neurons in the macaque. *J. Neurosci.* **4**, 2051–2062.

Dias, R., Robbins, T. W. & Roberts, A. C. 1996 Primate analogue of the Wisconsin Card Sorting Test: effects of excito-toxic lesions of the prefrontal cortex in the marmoset. *Behav. Neurosci.* **110**, 872–886.

Dickinson, A. 1980 *Contemporary animal learning theory.* Cambridge University Press.

Duncan, J., Emslie, H., Williams, P., Johnson, R. & Freer, C. 1996 Intelligence and the frontal lobe: the organization of goal-directed behavior. *Cogn. Psychol.* **30**, 257–303.

Eacott, M. J. & Gaffan, D. 1992 Inferotemporal–frontal disconnection–the uncinate fascicle and visual associative learning in monkeys. *Eur. J. Neurosci.* **4**, 1320–1332.

Fabre-Thorpe, M., Richard, G. & Thorpe, S. J. 1998 Rapid categorization of natural images by rhesus monkeys. *NeuroReport* **9**, 303–308.

Freedman, D. J., Riesenhuber, M., Poggio, T. & Miller, E. K. 2001 Categorical representation of visual stimuli in the primate prefrontal cortex. *Science* **291**, 312–316.

Fuster, J. M. 1985 The prefrontal cortex, mediator of cross-temporal contingencies. *Hum. Neurobiol.* **4**, 169–179.

Fuster, J. M. 1989 *The prefrontal cortex.* New York: Raven.

Fuster, J. M. 1995 *Memory in the cerebr. cortex.* Cambridge, MA: MIT Press.

Fuster, J. M., Bodner, M. & Kroger, J. K. 2000 Cross-modal and cross-temporal association in neurons of frontal cortex. *Nature* **405**, 347–351.

Gaffan, D. & Harrison, S. 1988 Inferotemporal–frontal disconnection and fornix transection in visuo-motor conditional learning by monkeys. *Behav. Brain Res.* **31**, 149–163.

Gaffan, D. & Harrison, S. 1991 Auditory–visual associations, hemispheric specialization and temporal–frontal interaction in the rhesus monkey. *Brain* **114**, 2133–2144.

Gainotti, G. 2000 What the locus of brain lesion tells us about the nature of the cognitive defect under-lying category-specific disorders: a review. *Cortex* **36**, 539–559.

Goldman-Rakic, P. S. 1987 Circuitry of primate prefrontal cortex and regulation of behavior by repre-sentational memory. In *Handbook of physiology: the nervous system* (ed. F. Plum), pp. 373–417. Bethesda, MD: American Physiology Society.

Gross, C. G. 1973 Visual functions of inferotemporal cortex. In *Handbook of sensory physiology* (ed. R. Jung). Berlin: Springer.

Hoshi, E., Shima, K. & Tanji, J. 1998 Task-dependent selectivity of movement-related neuronal activity in the primate prefrontal cortex. *J. Neurophysiol.* **80**, 3392–3397.

Lisker, L. & Abramson, A. 1970 *The voicing dimension: some experiments in comparing phonetics.* Prague: Academia.

Miller, E. K. 1999 The prefrontal cortex: complex neural properties for complex behavior. *Neuron* **22**, 15–17.

Miller, E. K. 2000 The neural basis of top-down control of visual attention in the prefrontal cortex. In *Attention and performance 18* (ed. S. Monsell & J. Driver). Cambridge, MA: MIT Press.

Miller, E. K. & Cohen, J. D. 2001 An integrative theory of prefrontal function. *A. Rev. Neurosci.* **24**, 167–202.

Milner, B. 1963 Effects of different brain lesions on card sorting. *Arch. Neurol.* **9**, 100–110.

Mishkin, M. 1982 A memory system in the monkey. *Phil. Trans. R. Soc. Lond.* B **298**, 83–95.

Murray, E. A., Bussey, T. J. & Wise, S. P. 2000 Role of prefrontal cortex in a network for arbitrary visuo-motor mapping. *Exp. Brain Res.* **133**, 114–129.

Murray, E. A. & Wise, S. P. 1997 Role of the orbitoventral prefrontal cortex in conditional motor learn-ing. *Soc. Neurosci. Abstr.* **27**, 12.

Nauta, W. J. H. 1971 The problem of the frontal lobe: a re–interpretation. *J. Psychiatr. Res.* **8**, 167–187.

O'Reilly, R. C. & Munakata, Y. 2000 *Computational explorations in cognitive neuroscience: under-standing the mind.* Cambridge, MA: MIT Press.

Orlov, T., Yakovlev, V., Hochstein, S. & Zohary, E. 2000 Macaque monkeys categorize images by their ordinal number. *Nature* **404**, 77–80.

Pandya, D. N. & Barnes, C. L. 1987 Architecture and connections of the frontal lobe. In *The frontal lobes revisited* (ed. E. Perecman), pp. 41–72. New York: The IRBN Press.

Parker, A. & Gaffan, D. 1998a Memory after frontal/temporal disconnection in monkeys: conditional and non-conditional tasks, unilateral and bilateral frontal lesions. *Neuropsychologia* **36**, 259–271.

Parker, A. & Gaffan, D. 1998b Memory after frontal/temporal disconnection in monkeys: conditional and non-conditional tasks, unilateral and bilateral frontal lesions. *Neuropsychologia* **36**, 259–271.

Passingham, R. 1993 *The frontal lobes and voluntary action.* Oxford University Press.

Petrides, M. 1985a Deficits in non-spatial conditional associative learning after periarcuate lesions in the monkey. *Behav. Brain Res.* **16**, 95–101.

Petrides, M. 1985b Deficits on conditional associative-learning tasks after frontal- and temporal-lobe lesions in man. *Neuropsychologia* **23**, 601–614.

Petrides, M. 1990 Nonspatial conditional learning impaired in patients with unilateral frontal but not unilateral temporal lobe excisions. *Neuropsychologia* **28**, 137–149.

Rainer, G., Asaad, W. F. & Miller, E. K. 1998a Memory fields of neurons in the primate prefrontal cor-tex. *Proc. Natl Acad. Sci. USA* **95** (15), 15 008–15 013.

Rainer, G., Asaad, W. F. & Miller, E. K. 1998*b* Selective representation of relevant information by neurons in the primate prefrontal cortex. *Nature* **393**, 577–579.

Rainer, G., Rao, S. C. & Miller, E. K. 1999 Prospective coding for objects in the primate prefrontal cortex. *J. Neurosci.* **19**, 5493–5505.

Rao, S. C., Rainer, G. & Miller, E. K. 1997 Integration of what and where in the primate prefrontal cortex. *Science* **276**, 821–824.

Roberts, W. A. & Mazmanian, D. S. 1988 Concept learning at different levels of abstraction by pigeons, monkeys, and people. *J. Exp. Psychol. Anim. Behav. Proc.* **14**, 247–260.

Schultz, W. & Dickinson, A. 2000 Neuronal coding of prediction errors. *A. Rev. Neurosci.* **23**, 473–500.

Schultz, W. & Montague, P. R. 1997 A neural substrate of prediction and reward. *Science* **275**, 1593–1599.

Shallice, T. & Burgess, P. W. 1991 Deficits in strategy application following frontal lobe damage in man. *Brain* **114**, 727–741.

Shelton, C. 2000 Morphable surface models. *Int. J. Comp. Vis.* **38**, 75–91.

Shimamura, A. P. 2000 The role of the prefrontal cortex in dynamic filtering. *Psychobiology* **28**, 207–218.

Tanaka, K., Saito, H., Fukada, Y. & Moriya, M. 1991 Coding visual images of objects in the inferotemporal cortex of the macaque monkey. *J. Neurophysiol.* **66**, 170–189.

Tomita, H., Ohbayashi, M., Nakahara, K., Hasegawa, I. & Miyashita, Y. 1999 Top-down signal from prefrontal cortex in executive control of memory retrieval (see comments). *Nature* **401**, 699–703.

Vaadia, E., Benson, D. A., Hienz, R. D. & Goldstein Jr, M. H. 1986 Unit study of monkey frontal cortex: active localization of auditory and of visual stimuli. *J. Neurophysiol.* **56**, 934–952.

Vogels, R. 1999*a* Categorization of complex visual images by rhesus monkeys. Part 1: behavioural study. *Eur. J. Neurosci.* **11**, 1223–1238.

Vogels, R. 1999*b* Categorization of complex visual images by rhesus monkeys. Part 2: single-cell study. *Eur. J. Neurosci.* **11**, 1239–1255.

Wallis, J. D., Anderson, K. C. & Miller, E. K. 2001 Single neurons in the prefrontal cortex encode abstract rules. *Nature* **411**, 953–956.

Watanabe, M. 1990 Prefrontal unit activity during associative learning in the monkey. *Exp. Brain Res.* **80**, 296–309.

Watanabe, M. 1992 Frontal units of the monkey coding the associative significance of visual and auditory stimuli. *Exp. Brain Res.* **89**, 233–247.

White, I. M. & Wise, S. P. 1999 Rule-dependent neuronal activity in the prefrontal cortex. *Exp. Brain Res.* **126**, 315–335.

Wise, S. P., Murray, E. A. & Gerfen, C. R. 1996 The frontal–basal ganglia system in primates. *Crit. Rev. Neurobiol.* **10**, 317–356.

Wyttenbach, R. A., May, M. L. & Hoy, R. R. 1996 Categorical perception of sound frequency by crickets. *Science* **273**, 1542–1544.

Young, M. E. & Wasserman, E. A. 1997 Entropy detection by pigeons: response to mixed visual displays after same-different discrimination training. *J. Exp. Psychol. Anim. Behav. Process.* **23**, 157–170.

Glossary

DMC   delayed match-to-category
FEF   frontal eye field
ITC   inferior temporal cortex
ITI   inter-trial interval
PFC   prefrontal cortex
VTA   ventral tegmental area

13

Role of uncertainty in sensorimotor control

Robert J. van Beers, Pierre Baraduc, and Daniel M. Wolpert

Neural signals are corrupted by noise and this places limits on information processing. We review the processes involved in goal-directed movements and how neural noise and uncertainty determine aspects of our behaviour. First, noise in sensory signals limits perception. We show that, when localizing our hand, the central nervous system (CNS) integrates visual and proprioceptive information, each with different noise properties, in a way that minimizes the uncertainty in the overall estimate. Second, noise in motor commands leads to inaccurate movements. We review an optimal-control framework, known as 'task optimization in the presence of signal-dependent noise', which assumes that movements are planned so as to minimize the deleterious consequences of noise and thereby minimize inaccuracy. Third, during movement, sensory and motor signals have to be integrated to allow estimation of the body's state. Models are presented that show how these signals are optimally combined. Finally, we review how the CNS deals with noise at the neural and network levels. In all of these processes, the CNS carries out the tasks in such a way that the detrimental effects of noise are minimized. This shows that it is important to consider effects at the neural level in order to understand performance at the behavioural level.

13.1. Introduction

Neural signals are noisy and this limits the amount of information that a signal can contain. The noise at the single neuronal level translates into uncertainty and variability at the higher, cognitive level. For instance, noise in sensory information about an object's location leads to uncertainty in the position at which the object is perceived, and noise in motor commands results in movement inaccuracy and variability. Noise at the neural level therefore has direct effects at the cognitive level. In this paper, we explore these effects. We mainly use goal-directed arm movements as an example to illustrate the effects.

Goal-directed movements require several different processing steps. First, the target and the hand have to be localized. Second, motor commands have to be determined that can bring the hand to the target position. Finally, the motor commands have to be sent to the arm muscles, resulting in a movement. Neural noise is present at all of these stages and a main theme of this review is that the strategy used to achieve these processes is the one that minimizes the detrimental effects of neural noise. The emerging view therefore is that the neural control of movements, but possibly of other tasks as well, has evolved to maximize fitness. Through natural selection, movement control may have been 'improved' until performance was limited by biophysical constraints, thereby reaching a global or local optimum. Clearly, neural noise is one of the important constraints. Therefore, some of the CNS's functioning at the higher, cognitive level can be understood from the properties of the underlying activity at the lower, neural level.

In this review, we first describe how noise in sensory signals limits spatial perception and how information from different sensory modalities is combined so as to minimize the perceptual uncertainty. We then describe a control framework called TOPS, which formulates how goal-directed movements are planned on the basis of the expected effect of noise in motor commands. We show how the nervous system combines noisy sensory signals and noisy motor output signals during a movement to allow the state of the body to be estimated, and show how these mechanisms can be used to reduce the uncertainty about whether sensory information is due to changes induced by one's own action or by events in the outside world. Finally, we explain how uncertainty can be encoded and decoded by neural networks.

13.2. Sensory noise

If we want to make a goal-directed reaching movement, the nervous system first has to have spatial information about the target and the hand. Their positions are important, as are their orientation, size, shape, etc. Sensory information is used to estimate these quantities.

The amount of information that sensory signals convey about the outside world and about the state of one's body is limited. At the neural level, this is reflected by noise in the neural signals. Neural noise can lead to two kinds of imperfections that can be quantified at the higher level: accuracy, which refers to constant errors, and precision, which refers to variable errors and uncertainty. Here, we mainly address limitations on the precision because these are a direct consequence of neural noise.

Precision is limited by the properties of the sensory receptors. For instance, the size of photoreceptors in the retina sets a limit to visual acuity. Because continuous signals in the outside world must be coded by discrete spikes, noise may be added at later processing stages, which further reduces the precision. Spatial and geometric factors can also play an important role in shaping the characteristics of the precision at the perceptual level. This will be illustrated for visual and proprioceptive information about the position of one's hand.

Visual and proprioceptive localization have been studied in the horizontal plane at waist level (van Beers *et al.* 1998). It was found that, for both modalities, precision depends on the position and, for a given position, the precision also depends on the direction considered. For visual localization, precision decreases with increasing distance from the observer and localization is less precise in depth than in azimuth. This reflects that it is more difficult for the visual system to judge distance than direction (Foley & Held 1972), which is also partly due to the geometry of the setting in which subjects look slantwise down on the table. It is different for proprioceptive localization. Precision decreases with increasing distance from the shoulder, but here, localization is more precise in depth than in azimuth. This is mainly a geometric effect (van Beers *et al.* 1998). Assuming that proprioceptive signals reflect joint angles, the observed pattern can be understood by transforming these signals from joint angles to hand positions (known as the kinematic transformation). Consider, for instance, an almost extended arm (see Figure 13.1). Uncertainty in both the shoulder and elbow angles translates into uncertainty in hand position mainly in azimuth, with less uncertainty in the distance from the shoulder. According to such principles, the 2D precision should vary with arm posture, and this has been observed experimentally (van Beers *et al.* 1998). The precision of both visual and proprioceptive localization thus simply reflects noise in the sensory signals that is translated into the perceptual domain. This is, in essence, also true for auditory localization, which is most precise directly in front of and behind the observer and decreases monotonically towards the periphery (Fedderson *et al.* 1957). This follows from how properties of wave sounds moving around the head vary with direction, but the situation here is more complicated because it also depends on the frequency and, especially for estimating elevation, on the spectral shape of the sound (Middlebrooks & Green 1991).

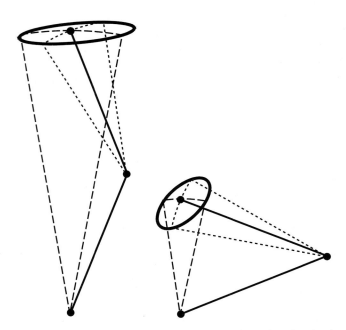

Fig. 13.1. Illustration of the relationship between noise in proprioceptive signals about shoulder and elbow angles and the resulting uncertainty in finger localization. Ellipses represent the precision of proprioceptive localization. The narrower an ellipse in a certain direction, the more precise is the localization. For the almost extended right arm shown on the left, noise in information about the shoulder (dashed lines) and elbow angles (dotted lines) results in uncertainty in approximately the same direction. This results in a relatively high precision in depth, and low precision in azimuth. For the more flexed right arm shown on the right, noise in information about shoulder and elbow angles has effects in different directions. In addition, the effect of shoulder noise is much less than for the extended arm because the distance between the hand and the shoulder is smaller. Consequently, the precision ellipse is smaller and has a different orientation.

When localizing the hand on the basis of simultaneous visual and proprioceptive information, the question arises as to how the CNS integrates the information from different sources. This issue of multisensory integration is of fundamental importance because in everyday life there is an abundance of information from various senses, and combining this into a single percept is one of the complex tasks that our CNS accomplishes continuously. The mechanism can be understood from the non-uniform precision of visual and proprioceptive localization, as explained above. When the right hand is in front of and to the left of the body, the visual and proprioceptive precision ellipses are approximately orthogonal to one another (Figure 13.2*a*). In general, visual and proprioceptive localization have different constant errors (Warren & Schmitt 1980); therefore the visual and proprioceptive ellipses have been plotted at different locations in Figure 13.2*b*. One can now ask where, and with what precision, is the hand localized if both senses provide information simultaneously? There are several possibilities. First, one modality could completely dominate, and the information from the other modality may not be used at all. Second, the CNS could calculate the arithmetic mean of the positions sensed by each modality. Finally, the CNS could calculate a more complicated average.

Absolute dominance of one modality would imply that the hand is localized exactly the same as if the other modality were not present. Simple averaging, irrespective of the

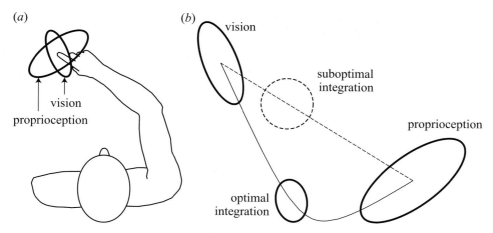

Fig. 13.2. Optimal integration of visual and proprioceptive information about the position of the right hand. (*a*) Top view of a subject. For this hand position, the ellipses representing the precision of visual and proprioceptive localization (not to scale) are approximately orthogonal. (*b*) The visual and proprioceptive ellipses have been plotted at different locations to reflect that vision and proprioception generally have different biases. If integration of visual and proprioceptive information would amount to weighted averaging, irrespective of the direction-dependent precision, the seen hand would be localized on the straight (dashed) line. The circle labelled 'suboptimal integration' represents the best (i.e. producing the smallest variance) way in which this can be done. However, optimal integration does take the direction-dependent precision into account, and this predicts that localization of the seen hand will be as indicated by the ellipse labelled 'optimal integration'. This is the smallest ellipse that can be obtained, indicating that this method minimizes the uncertainty in the overall estimate.

direction-dependent precision, would mean that it is localized on the straight line between the centres of the visual and proprioceptive ellipses. In the case of an arithmetic mean, the percept would be exactly halfway between the two centres, whereas it could be at other places on the straight line were a weighted mean calculated (the larger a modality's weight, the closer it will be localized to the centre of that ellipse). The optimal weighted mean (i.e. the one producing the smallest variance) is illustrated by the dashed circle in Figure 13.2*b*. This seems a reasonable way to fuse the information, but in 2D space there is a better way. The maximum-likelihood estimate (Ghahramani *et al.* 1997), based on the 2D precision of visual and proprioceptive localization, is illustrated by the smallest ellipse in Figure 13.2*b* (van Beers *et al.* 1999). Surprisingly, the centre of this ellipse is not on the straight line between the centres of the visual and proprioceptive ellipses. This can be understood from the orientation of these ellipses. The fusion can be considered as a more complicated weighted averaging in which the weights vary with direction. For instance, in the direction of the major axis of the proprioceptive ellipse, vision is more precise than proprioception and therefore the visual weight is larger than the proprioceptive weight. In the direction orthogonal to that, however, the proprioceptive weight is larger. This explains why the ellipse lies off the straight line.

There is strong experimental support for this model. The predictions for both the constant errors (the mean lying off the straight line) and the variable errors (the variance being smaller than can be expected from any direction-independent weighted mean) have been confirmed experimentally (van Beers *et al.* 1996, 1999). Recently, it has also been tested directly whether the weighting varies with direction (van Beers *et al.* 2002). The visual and proprioceptive weights have been estimated many times using a classical method. In the paradigm of prism adaptation (Welch 1978), subjects view their hand through optical prisms that displace the visual field, inducing a conflict between vision and proprioception. This leads to adaptation of the visual and proprioceptive mappings in order to resolve or reduce the conflict. The magnitudes of the adaptation in the two modalities are a measure for their weights. With normal vision, proprioceptive adaptation has usually been found to be larger than visual adaptation (Welch & Warren 1986). Because the dominant modality will adapt least, this finding has led to the belief that, for spatial localization, vision dominates proprioception. This finding is in accord with the model, because traditional prism adaptation creates a conflict between vision and proprioception in azimuth, which is in a direction in which localization is 'best' for vision and 'worst' for proprioception. The model predicts that the relative weighting and thus the relative adaptation varies with direction. In line with this prediction, it was found that the relative visual adaptation in depth was larger than in azimuth. More than that, proprioception was found to be weighted more heavily than vision in depth.

There is evidence that the CNS uses similar mechanisms to integrate other types of information. For instance, visual and auditory localization (Ghahramani *et al.* 1997) and visual texture and motion cues to depth (Jacobs 1999) are combined according to the 1D equivalent of the mechanism explained above. Therefore, in integration, all of the available information is used and the CNS fuses it in a way that minimizes the uncertainty in the overall estimate. This indicates that the way in which the CNS integrates information from different sources can only be understood from the effects of uncertainty, and therefore of noise at the neural level.

13.3. Motor noise

We now return to goal-directed arm movements. When the hand and the target have been localized, the movement can be planned. Movement planning involves determining the motor commands that will produce the intended movement. A movement is usually specified at a high, symbolic level, such as: 'pick up that glass and drink from it'. However, the motor system works at a low, much more detailed level; it specifies temporal profiles of muscle activations. There is a large gap between these high- and low-level specifications, and the question is how the nervous system bridges this gap. We present a control framework called TOPS, which formulates how goal-directed movements specified at the high level are planned on the basis of properties of the motor system at the low level (Harris & Wolpert 1998).

Given a task, the motor system usually has an infinite number of ways in which to achieve it, due to redundancy in the motor system. This can be illustrated if we consider the simple task of moving the hand from one point in space to another. Such a movement can be made with a range of durations and an infinite number of paths between the start and final hand locations. Given the path, the hand could move along it with infinitely many speed profiles and, for each point on the path, the hand can be placed there with a infinite set of different arm configurations. Similarly, the arm can be held in a given posture stiffly, with opposing muscles co-contracting, or with low co-contraction levels. Finally, the same muscle tension can be generated by different patterns of neural firing. Motor planning can be considered as the problem of selecting one solution from the infinity of possibilities.

Despite the redundancy, humans produce very stereo-typed movements. Hand trajectories are, in general, very smooth, with approximately straight paths (compared with the corresponding trajectories in joint space) and bell-shaped velocity profiles (Morasso 1981;

see also Figure 13.3). Certain movements, however, have a consistent but small amount of curvature (Atkeson & Hollerbach 1985). The faster a movement is executed, the worse is its precision; this relation is characterized by Fitts' law (Fitts 1954). For curved movements, such as in writing and drawing, there is a relation between the curvature and the movement speed, known as the two-thirds power law (Lacquaniti *et al.* 1983). It is interesting to note that saccadic eye movements are also stereotyped, but in a different way. Saccades have approximately symmetrical velocity profiles, although for longer saccades velocity profiles are skewed towards the end of the movement (Collewijn *et al.* 1988). In addition, there is a relationship between the duration and peak velocity of a saccade and its amplitude, known as the main sequence (Bahill *et al.* 1975). Finally, the ocular system has three degrees of freedom but effectively uses them as if there were only two, because the eye position defines the torsion, which is known as Donders' law (Donders 1848) and Listing's law (von Helmholtz 1867).

   Stereotypical patterns of movement are, therefore, the end result of motor learning or evolution, indicating that movements may have been optimized to maximize fitness (Harris 1998). Movements are 'improved' until the performance is limited by biophysical constraints, thereby reaching an optimum. The question then is in what way are arm and eye movements optimal? The idea taken from optimal-control engineering is to define a cost function. The cost can be determined for every possible movement and the optimal movement is the one with the lowest cost. Movement planning then amounts to selecting the movement with the lowest cost. For eye movements, it has been proposed (Enderle & Wolfe 1987) that the cost is movement time. The rationale was that vision is very degraded during a saccade; keeping

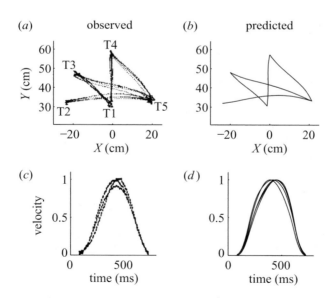

Fig. 13.3. Comparison of observed and predicted trajectories for goal-directed arm movements in the horizontal plane. (*a*) Observed hand paths for five different point-to-point movements (from Uno *et al.* 1989). The origin of the coordinate system is on the shoulder. *X* and *Y* directions represent the transverse and sagittal axes, respectively. (*b*) The optimal hand paths as predicted by the TOPS framework for the same movements as in (*a*). (*c*) Observed velocity profiles for movements from T1 to T3 in (*a*). The other movements had similar bell-shaped velocity profiles. (*d*) Velocity profiles of all the predicted movements shown in (*b*), normalized to have a maximum velocity of 1.

movement time to a minimum would minimize the time for which we are deprived of vision. For arm movements, the observed smoothness has led to the idea that the cost function is the mean-squared jerk (the temporal derivative of the acceleration) of the hand (Hogan 1984; Flash & Hogan 1985), or the mean-squared rate of change of the joint torques (Uno *et al.* 1989). Although these cost functions predicted the observed movements quite well, there were some problems associated with them. First, they seem arbitrary quantities; it is not clear why it would be advantageous to minimize jerk. Second, these quantities are difficult to calculate for the CNS. Third, why would the costs be different for the eye and the arm? The ideal cost would be similar for all systems, simple to compute and have some evolutionary advantage.

In TOPS, the cost is the variability in movement end-points, or, in other words, the expected movement error. This seems to be a sensible quantity because the goal of a movement is to reach the target and this cost directly represents how well this is achieved. In addition, it can be applied to all systems and is easy to compute, because the nervous system usually gets direct feedback about movement errors.

The other assumption in the TOPS framework is that the endpoint variability is due to noise in the motor commands. It assumes signal-dependent noise, which is the standard deviation in the motor command signal is proportional to its magnitude (constant coefficient of variation). This is an important assumption. Constant noise, for instance, would not work because that would predict that the faster a movement is executed, the more precise it will be. This is the converse of the empirical Fitts' law. Signal-dependent noise, however, predicts Fitts' law because a faster movement requires larger motor commands and larger commands are noisier. A smaller endpoint variability can thus be obtained by using smaller motor commands, which results in a longer movement time. The assumption of signal-dependent noise is supported by the empirical finding that the standard deviation in isometric force production is proportional to the mean force (Schmidt *et al.* 1979; Meyer *et al.* 1988). It has been shown (Jones *et al.* 2002) that the basic physiological organization of the motor-unit pool, such as the range of twitch amplitudes and the range of recruitment thresholds, is responsible for this relationship.

The idea behind TOPS is that the CNS aims to minimize the consequences of noise in the motor system. Movement planning uses the redundancy of the motor system to reduce the endpoint variability. Movements predicted by this principle correspond to actual movements. For example, it predicts approximately straight finger trajectories and bell-shaped velocity profiles that match very well with observed trajectories (see Figure 13.3). Optimal trajectories are inherently smooth, because abrupt changes in the trajectory would require large motor commands that would carry more noise than motor commands for smoother trajectories. In addition, Fitts' law and the two-thirds power law are also predicted by TOPS. This framework also works very well for rapid eye movements; for instance, it reproduces saccadic velocity profiles and the main sequence. Moreover, it was recently shown that it also reproduced observed trajectories for the more complicated situation in which both the eye and the head move simultaneously in order to fixate a peripheral target (Wolpert & Harris 2001).

All of these findings strongly support the TOPS framework. TOPS has more predictive power than the various other cost functions proposed for arm and eye movements because it can easily be generalized to other types of movements. The framework is a biologically plausible theoretical underpinning for both eye and arm movements with no need to construct highly derived signals such as jerk to estimate the cost of a movement. Instead, in the TOPS framework, variance of the final position is the cost and this cost is almost directly available to the nervous system via feedback of movement inaccuracy or its consequences, such as time spent in making corrective movements (Meyer *et al.* 1988; Harris 1995). There is no need explicitly to calculate the cost of different movements because the optimal trajectory could be learned from the experience of repeated movements. In addition, the TOPS framework highlights the important effects of noise and uncertainty, and the methods that the CNS has developed to minimize their effects. This stresses the need to take into account the properties at the low, neural level to understand human behaviour at the high, cognitive level.

13.4. Sensorimotor noise

Information about hand position is necessary to plan a goal-directed arm movement. However, due to motor noise, actual movements generally differ from the intended ones, yet we usually reach the target. This is because feedback is used during the movement to make the necessary corrections. This indicates that, during the movement itself, it is also important to have an estimate of the hand's position. It has been described above how visual and proprioceptive information is combined to estimate the position of a static hand. During the course of a movement, however, another source of information can be used as well: a copy of the motor commands sent to the muscles. This efference copy (Sperry 1950; von Holst & Mittelstaedt 1950; Festinger & Canon 1965) can be used to predict the consequence of the motor commands. This prediction is made by an internal forward model (Wolpert *et al.* 1995; Miall & Wolpert 1996); a system that mimics the causal flow of a process by predicting its next state given the current state and the motor command. Due to noise and possible inaccur-acies in the forward model, the predicted new state will, in general, have a finite precision and accuracy.

In estimating the state of the hand, the CNS faces another integration problem: how does it combine sensory inflow about hand position with a prediction of the position based on motor outflow, when the information from both sources is imperfect? This is a problem that has been solved in the engineering field of optimal state estimation. For linear systems, the solution is known as the Kalman filter (Kalman & Bucy 1961; Figure 13.4). This is a linear dynamical system that integrates the motor outflow and the sensory inflow in a way that minimizes the uncertainty in the overall estimate. This optimal integration is achieved at any moment throughout the movement. In the feed-forward path, a forward model predicts the next state on the basis of the efference copy of the motor command, thereby simulating the dynamics of the arm. In the feedback path, the sensory feedback is compared with the sensory feedback predicted by a second forward model, one that mimics the behaviour of the sensory system. The difference between predicted and actual sensory feedback is used to correct the state estimate of the (first) forward model. Because the reliability of the estimate will vary during the movement, the optimal weighting varies over time. This is determined by the time-varying Kalman gain, which determines the optimal weighting to minimize the uncertainty in the overall estimate.

The Kalman filter has been used to model the estimation of hand position immediately after a movement based on motor outflow and proprioceptive feedback (Wolpert *et al.* 1995). Experimental data showed that both the constant and variable errors initially increased monotonically with movement duration. After about 1 s, both remained constant or decreased slightly. The Kalman filter reproduced this pattern. During the early part of the movement, when the current state estimate was accurate, the position predicted by the forward model was weighted heavily. Later, however, the estimate became less reliable, and the weighting shifted smoothly towards the feedback process. Models based purely on sensory feedback or on

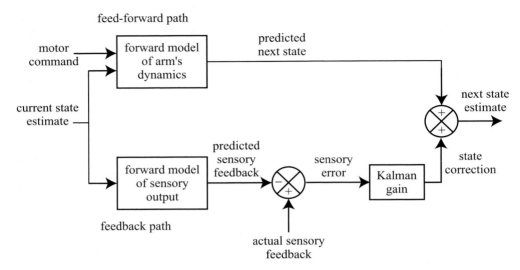

Fig. 13.4. Schematic representation of the Kalman filter that estimates the next state given the motor command and the current state estimate. The model consists of two paths. In the (upper) feed-forward path, a forward model predicts the next state on the basis of the current state estimate and an efference copy of the motor command. In the (lower) feedback path, the actual sensory feedback is compared with the feedback predicted by a forward model of the sensory output (based on the current estimate). The difference between actual and predicted sensory feedback is the sensory error and is used to correct the forward model's state estimate. The Kalman gain determines how the outcome of both paths is weighted.

motor outflow could not reproduce these patterns, thereby providing evidence that information from both sources was used to estimate hand position, in order to reduce the combined effect of sensory and motor noise.

One problem in the estimation of state is that, due to feedback delays, the sensory signals about the state (position and velocity) of the arm will inevitably lag behind the actual state. It takes about 200 ms for visual feedback to influence an ongoing movement (Keele & Posner 1968; Georgopoulos *et al.* 1981; van Sonderen *et al.* 1988), mainly because the photoreceptors in the retina are slow. The corresponding delay for proprioception is somewhat shorter, around 120 ms (Jeannerod 1988). These delays are long compared with the duration of a typical goal-directed movement, which is a serious problem for feedback control. One model developed to deal with time delays is the Smith predictor (Miall *et al.* 1993). This model also uses a forward model of the dynamics of the motor system, but in addition to that it also models the delays present in the system.

It is difficult to prove that the nervous system follows strategies identical to models such as the Kalman filter and the Smith predictor. However, the key ingredient in these architectures is the forward model, and there is strong evidence that the nervous system uses forward models to predict the consequences of motor actions. This has been demonstrated convincingly for the situation in which one could be uncertain about whether sensory information is due to changes induced by one's own action or by a change in the outside world. It is often impossible to distinguish between these two possibilities on the basis of the sensory information only, because similar sensory information can arise for external events or self-generated movements. However, it is possible to distinguish between them when the consequences of one's own actions as predicted by a forward model are taken into account.

This has been studied extensively for tickling sensation. It is well known that healthy humans cannot tickle themselves and that self-administered tactile stimuli feel less ticklish than externally administered tactile stimuli (Weiskrantz *et al.* 1971). This could be explained by the use of forward models (Blakemore *et al.* 1999; Figure 13.5). When motor commands have been sent, the forward model predicts the resulting sensory feedback, which, in the case of tickling movements, would include tactile signals. The predicted feedback is compared with the actual sensory feedback and when these correspond to each other they cancel each other, resulting in the absence of a tickle sensation. However, when one is tickled by some-one else, the forward model does not predict any tactile feedback. The comparison with the actual feedback therefore results in a large sensory discrepancy, giving rise to a strong tickle sensation.

To test this hypothesis, Blakemore *et al.* (1999) asked subjects to move their left hand and to rate the tickle sensation of stimuli that a robot applied to their right hand. The movement of the robot could be coupled to the movement of the subject's left hand. When the robot's movement corresponded exactly to the movement of the left hand, as if the left hand held an object that tickled the right hand, tickle sensation was lower than when the robot tickled the subject when the subject made no movement. Next, movements were tested in which the motion of the left hand determined the robot movement, but now the relationship between action and its consequences were varied parametrically. The ticklishness rating increased sys-tematically with the discrepancy between the action and its predicted consequence, either due to introducing a time delay or a spatial rotation between the motion of the left hand and the displacement of the robot that tickled the right hand. This directly supports the forward model hypothesis because it shows that the tickle sensation increases with the discrepancy between the sensory feedback predicted by a forward model and the actual sensory feedback.

A functional magnetic resonance imaging study (Blakemore *et al.* 1998) showed that more activity was found in bilateral secondary somatosensory cortex and the anterior lobe of the

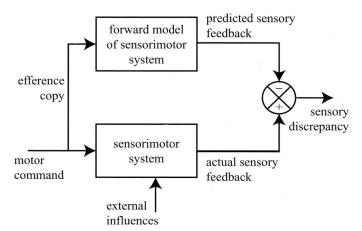

Fig. 13.5. Model used to determine whether sensory information arises from external influences or from a self-produced movement. A forward model predicts the sensory feedback based on an efference copy of the motor command. This prediction is then compared with the actual sensory feedback to pro-duce the sensory discrepancy signal. If there is little or no sensory discrepancy, the sensory information is likely to be the result of a self-generated movement. If a large discrepancy is detected, the sensory information is more likely to be the result of external events.

right cerebellum for externally produced compared with self-produced stimuli. The increase in somatosensory cortex activity probably reflects the increased ticklishness sensation. The observed effect for the cerebellum could reflect the discrepancy between predicted and actual sensory feedback, indicating that the forward model that predicts the sensory consequences of motor commands resides in the cerebellum. This is also suggested by the finding that the cerebellar activity correlates with the delay between hand movement and tactile stimulation (Blakemore *et al.* 2001).

This work has important consequences at the cognitive level. It could be argued that a defect in the central self-monitoring, as described above, might underlie delusions of control experienced by people with schizophrenia (Frith 1992). These patients move their limbs but claim that they are being moved by external agents. To examine whether this symptom may be due to lack of prediction of the consequences of action, Blakemore *et al.* (2000) used a similar paradigm to the previous studies. The results showed that patients with such symptoms did not rate self-produced stimuli as less ticklish than externally produced stimuli, whereas control subjects did rate the self-produced stimuli as less ticklish. This indicates that an impairment in the 'self-monitoring' mechanism, as implemented as a forward model, could cause thoughts or actions to become isolated from the sense of will normally associated with them, leading to symptoms associated with schizophrenia. This highlights the importance of the mechanisms that the nervous system has developed to reduce the uncertainties about whether sensory information is due to self-induced changes or to changes in the outside world.

13.5. Neural noise and network models

In this section, we review noise at the neural and network level. In general, the neural mechanisms by which the CNS copes with uncertainty are still poorly understood. However, recent experimental and computational studies have begun to shed light on both the sources of neural noise and its control. Combined electrophysiological recordings and theoretical analyses have delineated important sources of neuronal noise, while neural network modelling has indicated the existence of links between neural tuning and connectivity and noise control.

Noise is present at every level of the sensorimotor chain. In sensors, errors can arise through an incorrect estimation of sensor characteristics (e.g. temperature, metabolic state, sensor position or activation). Noise is also present in effectors: an incorrect estimate of limb position or muscle fatigue will translate into a motor error. In both proprioceptors and muscles, unavoidable instantaneous noise is added by the transduction between a continuous mechanical signal and a discrete sequence of spikes, through nonlinear dynamical systems (Read & Siegel 1996). The operation of neural networks also generates variability in the signals that are propagated. Synaptic variability (Allen & Stevens 1994; Tsodyks & Markram 1997), local firing synchronization (Stevens & Zador 1998) and chaotic network dynamics (van Vreeswijk & Sompolinsky 1996) have been shown to increase the variance of spike trains, although the isolated neuron is itself extremely reliable (Mainen & Sejnowski 1995). In general, this neural noise can be described by a Poisson distribution (with the notable exception of motor neurons where noise is close to Gaussian (Gomez *et al.* 1986)).

The increase in noise due to the complex architecture of neural networks is compensated by the redundancy of information representation. Indeed, sensory or motor signals are often coded by assemblies of neurons, each of which is tuned to (i.e. discharges maximally for) a given set of signal parameters. This distribution makes the system immune to synaptic failure or to the death of individual neurons. When tuning distribution is uniform (e.g. in primary visual cortex), population activity allows robust information representation if noise is not too correlated between neurons (Abbott & Dayan 1999). Moreover, it has been suggested that a population can encode more than one stimulus or response, thus enabling an internal representation of uncertainty (Zemel *et al.* 1998).

A common problem for neurophysiologists is to decode the information embedded in population activity. Information theory shows how the precision of information retrieval is bounded by the noise. The variance of the best unbiased estimator will necessarily exceed a minimal value called the 'Cramér-Rao bound' (Cox & Hinckley 1974). Pouget and collaborators have described a neural network of broadly tuned neurons that can at the same time recover the information encoded in another population with near-optimal precision (Pouget *et al.* 1998; Deneve *et al.* 1999) and re-encode it in a noise-reduced pattern. Thus, this type of neuronal architecture can clean up the noise before further processing.

The optimal estimation of the information embedded in the collective firing of neurons is also the solution to multisensory integration when sensory inputs from different modalities must be integrated in a common representation. We have seen in the preceding section that humans seem optimally to estimate the position of their hand when they can use both vision and proprioception. That is, they compute the most likely place according to the probability distributions associated with proprioceptive and visual inputs in isolation. This is precisely how an optimal estimator of the corresponding collective neural activity would behave. Thus, principles close to those exposed by Pouget *et al.* (1998) are possibly in operation. However, neurons involved in the localization task are not tuned to a specific value of gaze or arm position, but respond monotonically with gaze or hand position (Hepp & Henn 1985; Helms Tillery *et al.* 1996). In that case, it has been shown that a very simple network can compute an estimate whose variance is close to the Cramér-Rao bound (Guigon & Baraduc 2002). Moreover, this type of network has the capability of learning a new sensory–sensory congruence, e.g. during prism adaptation.

This last point reminds us that neural networks do not only process sensory information to get the best estimate of a raw input, but in general process it to produce an adapted motor response, be it scratching your nose or making a saccade to the right of these words. Sensorimotor transformation schemes that make use of redundancy and broad tuning (Salinas & Abbott 1995; Baraduc *et al.* 2001) are a good solution to minimize the detrimental effects of noise and seem ubiquitous in the CNS (Georgopoulos *et al.* 1982; Kalaska *et al.* 1983; Crutcher & DeLong 1984; Fortier *et al.* 1989). Recently, Todorov (2002) has shown that cosine tuning is an optimal way to minimize motor errors in the presence of signal-dependent noise.

Although these studies have provided clues, how neuronal noise influences the computational schemes in the CNS is a question that has just begun to be investigated.

13.6. Conclusions

We have reviewed a number of activities that the CNS has to perform in order to execute a goal-directed arm movement. We described spatial localization, integration of information from multiple sensory modalities, movement planning and integration of sensory and motor information during movement. The way in which the CNS carries out each of these activities can be understood from the idea that there is noise and uncertainty in the sensory and motor systems, and that the CNS tries to minimize the detrimental effects of this noise. The noise is present at the low, neural level, whereas the way in which tasks are carried out is usually visible at the high, behavioural level, for instance as hand trajectories. This indicates that it is often important to consider effects at the neural level in order to understand performance at the behavioural level. This is true for execution of goal-directed arm movements, but in a more general way, this idea could hold for a much wider class of cognitive tasks.

R.v.B. is supported by the Wellcome Trust. P.B. is supported by an EU Marie Curie training fellowship. This work was supported by the Wellcome Trust, the Human Frontiers Science Programme, McDonnell Foundation and the BBSRC.

References

Abbott, L. F. & Dayan, P. 1999 The effect of correlated variability on the accuracy of a population code. *Neural Comput.* **11**, 91–101.

Allen, C. & Stevens, C. F. 1994 An evaluation of causes for unreliability of synaptic transmission. *Proc. Natl Acad. Sci. USA* **91**, 10 380–10 383.

Atkeson, C. G. & Hollerbach, J. M. 1985 Kinematic features of unrestrained vertical arm movements. *J. Neurosci.* **5**, 2318–2330.

Bahill, A. T., Clark, M. R. & Stark, L. 1975 The main sequence, a tool for studying human eye movements. *Math. Biosci.* **24**, 191–204.

Baraduc, P., Guigon, E. & Burnod, Y. 2001 Recoding arm position to learn visuomotor transformations. *Cerebr. Cortex* **11**, 906–917.

Blakemore, S. J., Wolpert, D. M. & Frith, C. D. 1998 Central cancellation of self-produced tickle sensation. *Nat. Neurosci.* **1**, 635–640.

Blakemore, S. J., Frith, C. D. & Wolpert, D. M. 1999 Spatio-temporal prediction modulates the perception of self-produced stimuli. *J. Cogn. Neurosci.* **11**, 551–559.

Blakemore, S. J., Smith, J., Steel, R., Johnstone, E. C. & Frith, C. D. 2000 The perception of self-produced stimuli in patients with auditory hallucinations and passivity experiences: evidence for a breakdown in self-monitoring. *Psychol. Med.* **30**, 1131–1139.

Blakemore, S. J., Frith, C. D. & Wolpert, D. M. 2001 The cerebellum is involved in predicting the sensory consequences of action. *NeuroReport* **12**, 1879–1884.

Collewijn, H., Erkelens, C. J. & Steinman, R. M. 1988 Binocular coordination of human horizontal saccadic eye-movements. *J. Physiol.* **404**, 157–182.

Cox, D. R. & Hinckley, D. V. 1974 *Theoretical statistics*. London: Chapman & Hall.

Crutcher, M. D. & DeLong, M. R. 1984 Single cell studies of the primate putamen. II. Relations to direction of movement and pattern of muscular activity. *Exp. Brain Res.* **53**, 244–258.

Deneve, S., Latham, P. E. & Pouget, A. 1999 Reading population codes: a neural implementation of ideal observers. *Nat. Neurosci.* **2**, 740–745.

Donders, F. C. 1848 Beitrag zur Lehre von den Bewegungen des menslichen Auges. *Anat. Physiol. Wiss.* **1**, 105–145.

Enderle, J. D. & Wolfe, J. W. 1987 Time-optimal control of saccadic eye-movements. *IEEE Trans. Biomed. Engng.* **34**, 43–55.

Fedderson, W. E., Sandel, T. T., Teas, D. C. & Jeffress, L. A. 1957 Localization of high-frequency tones. *J. Acoust. Soc. Am.* **29**, 988–991.

Festinger, M. L. & Canon, L. K. 1965 Information about spatial location based on knowledge about efference. *Psychol. Rev.* **72**, 373–384.

Fitts, P. M. 1954 The information capacity of the human motor system in controlling the amplitude of movements. *J. Exp. Psychol.* **47**, 381–391.

Flash, T. & Hogan, N. 1985 The coordination of arm movements: an experimentally confirmed model. *J. Neurosci.* **5**, 1688–1703.

Foley, J. M. & Held, R. 1972 Visually directed pointing as a function of target distance, direction, and available cues. *Percept. Psychophys.* **12**, 263–268.

Fortier, P. A., Kalaska, J. F. & Smith, A. M. 1989 Cerebellar neuronal activity related to whole arm-reaching movements in the monkey. *J. Neurophysiol.* **62**, 198–211.

Frith, C. D. 1992 *The cognitive neuropsychology of schizophrenia*. London: Lawrence Erlbaum Associates.

Georgopoulos, A. P., Kalaska, J. F. & Massey, J. T. 1981 Spatial trajectories and reaction times of aimed movements: effects of practice, uncertainty and change in target location. *J. Neurophysiol.* **46**, 725–743.

Georgopoulos, A. P., Kalaska, J. F., Caminiti, R. & Massey, J. T. 1982 On the relations between the direction of two-dimensional arm movements and cell discharge in primate motor cortex. *J. Neurosci.* **2**, 1527–1537.

Ghahramani, Z., Wolpert, D. M. & Jordan, M. I. 1997 Computational models of sensorimotor integration. In *Self-organization, computational maps, and motor control* (ed. P. Morasso & V. Sanguineti), pp. 117–147. Amsterdam, The Netherlands: Elsevier.

Gomez, C., Canals, J., Torres, B. & Delgado-Garcia, J. M. 1986 Analysis of the fluctuations in the interspike intervals of abducens nucleus neurons during ocular fixation in the alert cat. *Brain Res.* **381**, 401–404.

Guigon, E. & Baraduc, P. 2002 A neural model of perceptual-motor alignment. *J. Cogn. Neurosci.* **14**, 538–549.

Harris, C. M. 1995 Does saccade undershoot minimize saccadic flight-time? A Monte-Carlo study. *Vis. Res.* **35**, 691–701.

Harris, C. M. 1998 On the optimal control of behaviour: a stochastic perspective. *J. Neurosci. Meth.* **83**, 73–88.

Harris, C. M. & Wolpert, D. M. 1998 Signal-dependent noise determines motor planning. *Nature* **394**, 780–784.

Helms Tillery, S. I., Soechting, J. F. & Ebner, T. J. 1996 Somatosensory cortical activity in relation to arm posture: non-uniform spatial tuning. *J. Neurophysiol.* **76**, 2423–2438.

Hepp, K. & Henn, V. 1985 Iso-frequency curves of oculomotor neurons in the rhesus monkey. *Vis. Res.* **25**, 493–499.

Hogan, N. 1984 An organizing principle for a class of voluntary movements. *J. Neurosci.* **4**, 2745–2754.

Jacobs, R. A. 1999 Optimal integration of texture and motion cues to depth. *Vis. Res.* **39**, 3621–3629.

Jeannerod, M. 1988 *The neural and behavioural organization of goal-directed movements*. Oxford: Clarendon.

Jones, K. E., Hamilton, A. & Wolpert, D. M. 2002 The sources of signal dependent noise during isometric force production. *J. Neurophysiol.* (In the press.)

Kalaska, J. F., Caminiti, R. & Georgopoulos, A. P. 1983 Cortical mechanisms related to the direction of two dimensional arm movements: relations in parietal area 5 and comparison with motor cortex. *Exp. Brain Res.* **51**, 247–260.

Kalman, R. E. & Bucy, R. S. 1961 New results in linear filtering and prediction. *J. Basic Engng (ASME)* **83D**, 95–108.

Keele, S. W. & Posner, M. I. 1968 Processing of visual feedback in rapid movements. *J. Exp. Psychol.* **77**, 155–158.

Lacquaniti, F., Terzuolo, C. A. & Viviani, P. 1983 The law relating kinematic and figural aspects of drawing movements. *Acta Psychologica* **54**, 115–130.

Mainen, Z. F. & Sejnowski, T. J. 1995 Reliability of spike timing in neocortical neurons. *Science* **268**, 1503–1506.

Meyer, D. E., Abrams, R. A., Kornblum, S., Wright, C. E. & Smith, J. E. K. 1988 Optimality in human motor performance: ideal control of rapid aimed movements. *Psychol. Rev.* **98**, 340–370.

Miall, R. C. & Wolpert, D. M. 1996 Forward models for physiological motor control. *Neural Netw.* **9**, 1265–1279.

Miall, R. C., Weir, D. J., Wolpert, D. M. & Stein, J. F. 1993 Is the cerebellum a Smith predictor? *J. Mot. Behav.* **25**, 203–216.

Middlebrooks, J. C. & Green, D. M. 1991 Sound localization by human listeners. *A. Rev. Psychol.* **42**, 135–159.

Morasso, P. 1981 Spatial control of arm movements. *Exp. Brain Res.* **42**, 223–227.

Pouget, A., Zhang, K. C., Deneve, S. & Latham, P. E. 1998 Statistically efficient estimation using population coding. *Neural Comput.* **10**, 373–401.

Read, H. L. & Siegel, R. M. 1996 The origins of aperiodicities in sensory neuron entrainment. *Neuroscience* **75**, 301–314.

Salinas, E. & Abbott, L. F. 1995 Transfer of coded information from sensory to motor networks. *J. Neurosci.* **15**, 6461–6474.

Schmidt, R. A., Zelaznik, H., Hawkin, B., Frank, J. S. & Quinn, J. T. 1979 Motor-output variability: a theory for the accuracy of rapid motor acts. *Psychol. Rev.* **86**, 415–451.

Sperry, R. W. 1950 Neural basis of the spontaneous optokinetic response produced by visual inversion. *J. Comp. Physiol. Psychol.* **43**, 482–489.

Stevens, C. F. & Zador, A. M. 1998 Input synchrony and the irregular firing of cortical neurons. *Nat. Neurosci.* **1**, 210–217.

Todorov, E. 2002 Cosine tuning minimizes motor errors. *Neural Comput.* **14**, 1233–1260.

Tsodyks, M. V. & Markram, H. 1997 The neural code between neocortical pyramidal neurons depends on neurotransmitter release probability. *Proc. Natl Acad. Sci. USA* **94**, 719–723.

Uno, Y., Kawato, M. & Suzuki, R. 1989 Formation and control of optimal trajectories in human multi-joint arm movements: minimum torque-change model. *Biol. Cybern.* **61**, 89–101.

van Beers, R. J., Sittig, A. C. & Denier van der Gon, J. J. 1996 How humans combine simultaneous proprioceptive and visual position information. *Exp. Brain Res.* **111**, 253–261.

van Beers, R. J., Sittig, A. C. & Denier van der Gon, J. J. 1998 The precision of proprioceptive position sense. *Exp. Brain Res.* **122**, 367–377.

van Beers, R. J., Sittig, A. C. & Denier van der Gon, J. J. 1999 Integration of proprioceptive and visual position-information: an experimentally supported model. *J. Neurophysiol.* **81**, 1355–1364.

van Beers, R. J., Wolpert, D. M. & Haggard, P. 2002 When feeling is more important than seeing in sensorimotor adaptation. *Curr. Biol.* **12**, 834–837.

van Sonderen, J. F., Denier van der Gon, J. J. & Gielen, C. C. A. M. 1988 Conditions determining early modification of motor programmes in response to changes in target location. *Exp. Brain Res.* **71**, 320–328.

Van Vreeswijk, C. & Sompolinsky, H. 1996 Chaos in neuronal networks with balanced excitatory and inhibitory activity. *Science* **274**, 1724–1726.

von Helmholtz, H. 1867 *Handbuch der physiologischen optik, band 3*. Leipzig, Germany: Voss.

von Holst, E. & Mittelstaedt, H. 1950 Das Reafferenzprinzip Wechselwirkungen zwischen Zentralnervensystem und Peripherie. *Naturwissenschaften* **37**, 464–476.

Warren, D. H. & Schmitt, T. L. 1980 Intermodal organization: a methodological localization study. *Percept. Motor Skills* **50**, 1111–1118.

Weiskrantz, L., Elliot, J. & Darlington, C. 1971 Preliminary observations of tickling oneself. *Nature* **230**, 598–599.

Welch, R. B. 1978 *Perceptual modification*. New York: Academic.

Welch, R. B. & Warren, D. H. 1986 Intersensory interactions. In *Handbook of perception and human performance vol. 1: sensory processes and perception* (ed. K. R. Boff, L. Kaufman & J. P. Thomas), pp. 25-1–25-36. New York: Wiley.

Wolpert, D. M. & Harris, C. M. 2001 Optimal saccadic control with motor noise predicts head fixed and head free saccadic trajectories and main sequence. *Soc. Neurosci. Abstr.* 27, 71.36.

Wolpert, D. M., Ghahramani, Z. & Jordan, M. I. 1995 An internal model for sensorimotor integration. *Science* **269**, 1880–1882.

Zemel, R. S., Dayan, P. & Pouget, A. 1998 Probabilistic interpretation of population codes. *Neural Comput.* **10**, 403–430.

Glossary

CNS   central nervous system

TOPS   task optimization in the presence of signal-dependent noise

Index